I0132315

# American Dreams

# AMERICAN DREAMS

Ancestors and Descendants
of
John Zimmermann and Eva Katherine Kellenbenz
Who Were Married in Philadelphia in 1885

By

George J. Hill, M.D., M.A., D.Litt.

HERITAGE BOOKS
2016

# HERITAGE BOOKS
*AN IMPRINT OF HERITAGE BOOKS, INC.*

**Books, CDs, and more—Worldwide**

For our listing of thousands of titles see our website
at
www.HeritageBooks.com

Published 2016 by
HERITAGE BOOKS, INC.
Publishing Division
5810 Ruatan Street
Berwyn Heights, Md. 20740

Copyright © 2016 George J. Hill, M.D., M.A., D.Litt.

Heritage Books by the author:

*American Dreams: Ancestors and Descendants of John Zimmermann and
Eva Katherine Kellenbenz Who Were Married in Philadelphia in 1885*

*Fundy to Chesapeake; The Thompson, Rundall and Allied Families: Ancestors and Descendants of
William Henry Thompson and Sarah D. Rundall, Who Were Married in Linn County, Iowa, in 1889*

*Hill: The Ferry Keeper's Family, Luke Hill and Mary Hout, Who were Married in Windsor, Connecticut,
in 1651 and Fourteen Generations of Their Known and Possible Descendants*

*John Saxe, Loyalist (1732–1808) and His Descendants for Five Generations*

*Quakers and Puritans: The Shoemaker, Warren and Allied Families; Ancestors and Descendants of
William Toy Shoemaker and Mabel Warren, Who Were Married in Philadelphia in 1895*

*Western Pilgrims: The Hill, Stockwell and Allied Families; Ancestors and Descendants of George J. Hill
and Jessie Fidelia Stockwell, Who Were Married in Wright County, Iowa, in 1882*

*The cover and title page photographs of John Zimmermann and
Eva Katherine Kellenbenz are undated, photographer unknown.*

*Images of Albert Walter Zimmermann and his family, Zimmermann and his wife, and photo of
the cover of* Peshawar *are courtesy of the Naval Institute Press, U.S. Naval Institute.*

*Cover designed by Debbie Riley*

All rights reserved. No part of this book may be reproduced or transmitted in any form or by any means,
electronic or mechanical, including photocopying, recording or by any information storage and retrieval system
without written permission from the author, except for the inclusion of brief quotations in a review.

International Standard Book Numbers
Paperbound: 978-0-7884-5736-4
Clothbound: 978-0-7884-5952-8

# American Dreams

**This family portrait shows the American Dream, achieved by John and Eva Zimmermann**

**1905**

**The Family of John Zimmermann (b1855) and Eva Katherine Kellenbenz (b1855)**
**Anna (b1886), Lillian (b1897), William (b1894), John (b1892), Albert (b1902), Clara (b1887)**

Emigrants from Württemberg, Germany, in 1874, who had little to start with in America
He was a teen-aged weaver, and she was a domestic servant

John and Eva are comfortably seated in 1905, surrounded by six calm, handsome children
Their home in Philadelphia, Pennsylvania, is spacious, and they have servants of their own

His inventions were successful, and he became a wealthy man
In 1905, he was consecrated as a bishop in the Reorganized Church of Latter Day Saints
In 1906, he was a partner in Artloom, one of the nation's largest textile corporations

*Dedicated to*
John and Eva Katherine
For their courage and determination

*and to their children*
Who helped them to achieve their dreams

If ever there was an immigrant who came with nothing and experience the thrill of fulfilling his hopes and expectations by coming to America it was John Zimmerman.  With honesty, integrity, hard work and all the other values we hold dear he certainly lived the American dream to the fullest.[*]

----------------------

The German emigrant comes into a country free from the despotism, privileged orders and monopolies, intolerable taxes, and constraints in matters of belief and conscience.  Everyone can travel and settle wherever he pleases.  No passport is demanded, no police mingles in his affairs or hinders his movements. . . Fidelity and merit are the only sources of honor here.  The rich stand on the same footing as the poor; the scholar is not a mug above the most humble mechanics; no German ought to be ashamed to pursue any occupation . . . [In America] wealth and possession of real estate confer not the least political right on its owner above what the poorest citizen has.  Nor are there nobility, privileged orders, or standing armies to weaken the physical and moral power of the people, nor are there swarms of public functionaries to devour in idleness credit for.  Above all, there are no princes and corrupt courts representing the so-called divine 'right of birth.'  In such a country the *talents, energy and perseverance* of a person ... have far greater opportunity to display than in monarchies.[1]

------------------------

But there has been also the *American dream*, that dream of a land in which life should be better and richer and fuller for every man, with opportunity for each according to his ability or achievement.  It is a difficult dream for the European upper classes to interpret adequately, and too many of us ourselves have grown weary and mistrustful of it.  It is not a dream of motor cars and high wages merely, but a dream of social order in which each man and each woman shall be able to attain to the fullest stature of which they are innately capable, and be recognized by others for what they are, regardless of the fortuitous circumstances of birth or position.[2]

---

[*] James Alma[3] Fligg, Jr., grandson of John[1] Zimmermann, letter to George J. Hill, 20 February 2003.

# Foreword

Every family has a history – but few families have an historian with the talents of George Hill. And what rich material he had at his disposal as he wrote this book – one of a tetralogy on the history and genealogy of the families of George J. Hill and his wife Helene Zimmermann. These volumes include *Western Pilgrims, Quakers and Puritans, Fundy to Chesapeake*, and the present work, *American Dreams*.

In his earlier book, *Proceed to Peshawar*[1]*,* Dr. Hill examined an episode in the life of his father-in-law Albert Zimmermann, a U.S. Navy lieutenant whose orders sent him on a little-known intelligence mission to the northwestern frontier of India during World War II. *American Dreams* covers a much more extensive period in describing the genealogy and history of the Zimmermann family.

However, just as *Proceed to Peshawar* has a central figure, Albert Zimmermann, so *American Dreams* has one in his father, John. This extraordinary man, born in 1855 in a small village east of Stuttgart, and trained as a weaver, immigrated to the United States at the age of 19. By dint of ingenuity and enterprise he built a highly successful carpet and tapestry business, brought up a large family with his wife Eva Katherine (née Kellenbenz), and became a bishop in the Reorganized Church of Jesus Christ of Latter Day Saints. The oft-used phrase "the American Dream" characterizes his achievements in life, and provides an appropriate title for this book.

*American Dreams* traces the genealogy of the Zimmermann and Kellenbenz families, both back to the sixteenth century, and forward to their most recent descendants. Most American genealogical researchers making trans-Atlantic connections have followed relatively well-known paths through British and sometimes French sources. Here, Dr. Hill has tackled the less familiar and more difficult task of dealing with German records, and especially with the Swabian dialect. The well-organized Ahnentafels in *American Dreams* will be of primary importance to those interested in the Zimmermann, Kellenbenz, and kindred families. The biographical detail supplied, not only for John Zimmermann but also for many of his descendants, sheds an informative light on American social and economic history, and will engage even those who have no connection with their families.

At a time when issues surrounding immigration are prominent in the public dialogue, *American Dreams* usefully reminds us of the contributions that immigrants have made to American society. An immigrant is like a seed that falls on soil far from the place of its origin. What will grow from it depends upon the nature of the seed, but also on the fertility of the soil, and the salubriousness of the climate. John and Eva Katherine Zimmermann were good transplants; the soil of nineteenth-century America was fertile, and the socio-economic climate, though occasionally harsh, lent itself to their flourishing. They and their many descendants exemplify the American Dream. As we contemplate today's immigrants, let us hope that the American Dream remains comparably vivid and inspiring.

Michael Scott Swisher
Honorary Governor General
National Society, Sons of Colonial New England
Stillwater, Minnesota

---

[1] George J. Hill, *Proceed to Peshawar: The Story of a U.S. Navy Intelligence Mission on the Afghan Border, 1943* (Annapolis, Maryland: Naval Institute Press, 2013).

# Abbreviations

abt or abt. = about
aka or a k a = also known as
B. or b or b. = birth
b.d. = birth date
bp or bp. = baptism
b.p. = birth place
br or b.r. = birth record
c. or ca. = about
ch. = child or children, or church
*cv* or *cf* = which see
D. or d or d. = death
dau or dau. = daughter
d.d. = death date
div = divorce(d)
dsp or d.s.p. = died without progeny
d.p. = death place
f = father
h = husband
Ibid. = the same
*infra* = below
m or m. or md = married
m.r. = marriage record
MS = manuscript
op. cit. = the same work cited
rem. = removed
s or s. = son
sic or *sic* = note; perhaps observe a contradiction at this point
svp or s.v.p. = no issue; without survivors
*supra* = above
unm = unmarried
v.r. or VR or V.R. = vital records
w = wife
wid = widow
wp or w.p. = without progeny; without issue

# The Zimmermann, Kellenbenz and Allied Families

## Ancestral and Collateral Families Discussed (with variable spellings)

**Bollinger • Jäger • Jelin • Kellenbenz • Klement
• Nördlinger • Walter • Zimmermann**

## Some Ancestors of Their Descendants

### Families and Individuals

Adams • Allyn • Alsop • Archibald • Atherton • Avery • Bishop • Boulter • Bourne
Brown • Budd • Cadwalader • Carnwath • Carpenter • Chapin • Chichester • Chubb
Clapp • Comly • Corning • Derehaugh • Dickinson • Eager • Eyre • Feake • Fligg
Fogelman • Fowler • Fuller • Giddings • Gillett • Hale • Halsey • Herrick • Hill
Halsey • Hobby • Holbrook • Holmes • Howell • Hout • Hoyt • Hoxie • Hyde • Iredell
Jackson • Jeanes • Johnson • Jones • Kelley • Kingman • Kinkead • Kinnaman • Knapp
Lee • Leech • Lloyd • Long • Lukens • Lum • Lyon • Manly • McVaugh • Morton
Munroe • Nurse • Ober • Ogden • Op den Graeff • Palgrave • Palmer • Pearson • Pellet
Pennington • Penrose • Phelps • Phippen • Pierce/Pearce/Peirce • Potter • Prince
Poteat • Potts • Prescott • Putnam • Richardson • Rundall/Rundle • Sanghurst • Saxe
Sharpless • Shoemaker • Singletary • Smith • Spalding • Stewart • Stockwell • Stratton
Swaine • Thompson • Thorndike • Tillinghast • Tompkins • Townsend • Trowbridge
Tyson • Underwood • Wall • Walter • Ward • Warren • Weaver • Wheeler • Willard
Brigham Young

### and also

Charlemagne, who was buried in Aachen in A.D. 813
Richard "Strongbow" de Clare, son-in-law of King MacMurrough of Dublin
Governor Roger Conant of the Beverly Colony
Lord George Nathaniel Curzon, 1st Marquess of Kedleston
Edward Fuller, of the *Mayflower*
Lady Godiva
King John "Lackland," who signed the Magna Carta
King Malcolm Canmore III, who killed Macbeth, avenging his father's death
St. Margaret, Queen of Scotland
Sureties of the Magna Carta
Rebecca "Goody" Nurse, hanged as a witch at Salem in 1692
Theodore Roosevelt, Sr., father of President Theodore Roosevelt
Archibald Thompson, who brought the first foot-spinning wheel to America
King William I, "the Conqueror"
William de Warrenne, 1st Earl of Surrey

This Artloom Couch Cover $5.00

# Here is something new —the first time a Gobelin

pattern has been reproduced in this country in a tapestry that is perfectly reversible.

It is a cover of remarkable beauty and we want Journal readers to have the first chance at it. It is a good example of Artloom value. It is our desire to have an Artloom curtain, a couch cover or a table cover, or some bit of Artloom service and beauty in every Journal home. Ask your dealer to show you Artloom couch covers the very next time you go shopping *identify by label Artloom on every piece*.

We have the largest tapestry works in America, and every home maker should have our Style Book H of Artloom curtains, couch covers and table covers. We'll send it when you write.

Philadelphia Tapestry Mills, Philadelphia

# Contents

"American Dreams"                                                          v
Dedication                                                                vi
Foreword                                                                  vii
Abbreviations                                                             viii
Ancestral and Collateral Families, and Ancestors of Descendants          ix
Contents                                                                  xi
Acknowledgements                                                         xiii
Preface                                                                   xv
Introduction                                                             xvii
Ahnentafels
    John Zimmermann's Ancestors                      xxv
    Eva Katherine Kellenbenz's Ancestors             xxvii

Part I       Ancestors of John Zimmermann and Eva Katherine Kellenbenz    1

Their Homeland (*Heimat*) – Swabia – Württemberg    2
The German-speaking *Heimat* was that part of Continental Europe which was located between the French-speaking Gauls, west of the Rhine; the Italian-speakers, south of the Alps; those who spoke the Slavic languages, east of the Elbe and Oder; and the Nordic people, across the North Sea. The German language included many dialects, including those spoken in the lowlands of the Rhine Valley, now known as Dutch; the "proper" German dialects of Prussia, Saxony, and Hannover; and *Schwaben Deutch*, sometimes called "High German," spoken in the foothills, forest land, and Alps of the south. Ancient Swabia included Württemberg, its capital, Stuttgart, and Bavaria.

1.01   Zimmermann Family, and Jäger, Walter, Nördlinger, Bollinger, and Jelin  19
The Zimmermann family of the *kreis* (district) of Heidenheim in Württemberg has been traced back to Mattis Zimmermann, born 1550. His descendants include tradesmen (saddlers, bakers, butchers, and artists), a mayor (*Bürgermeister*), a distinguished citizen (called by the honorific, *Herr*), and three generations of weavers in the village of Gussenstadt.

1.02   Kellenbenz Family, with a Note on the Klement Family  49
The Kellenbenz family has a distinguished history in Württemberg, dating from 1517. The earliest known was Johannes Kellenbenz, who was *Shultheiss* (mayor) of Süssen, near Eislingen, from whence Eva Katherine Kellenbenz came to America. This family also includes a *Bürgermeister* (mayor), hotel-keepers, several generations of physicians, and a famous economic historian of the 20th century, Professor Hermann Kellenbenz.

Part II     John Zimmermann and Eva Katherine Kellenbenz    73

2.03   The Parents – John and Eva
John Zimmermann, his brother, and uncle came to America in the 1870s, where they joined others who were related to them by marriage. The Zimmermanns lived initially in German-speaking areas, but they soon were assimilated into the larger community. Eva Kellenbenz and her sister came as domestic workers. John successfully employed his skills as a weaver, inventor, and businessman, and he became a wealthy textile manufacturer in Philadelphia. He was a partner in several fabric mill companies, including Artloom, and John Zimmermann and Sons. He was ordained as a bishop in the Reorganized Church of Jesus Christ of Latter Day Saints (R.L.D.S.), and he was a generous philanthropist. He and his wife Eva achieved the American Dream, for themselves and their children.

Part III John and Eva (Kellenbenz) Zimmermann's Children, and Their Descendants 149

3.04 Clara 155

She went to the University of Pennsylvania and then studied at the Julliard School; a talented musician; married Albert Hoxie, Jr., founder and director of the famous Philadelphia Harmonica Band, which played for three presidents at the White House and toured widely in America; 3 children, 10 grandchildren.

3.05 Anna 159

Graduated from the University of Pennsylvania, where she was in the Kappa Kappa Gamma sorority; and Philadelphia Academy of Fine Arts, where she studied oil painting; she was a teacher, editor, and artist; married Richard Carlyle Kelley, son of an R.L.D.S. bishop; B.A., University of Iowa; M.A., Columbia University Teachers College; was a teacher, and then joined the Zimmermann family textile businesses; 7 children, 23 grandchildren.

3.06 Emily 169

Died at age 11 from diphtheria.

3.07 John, Jr. 170

Graduate of the University of Pennsylvania; invented and patented new designs for industrial looms; following in his father's footsteps, became a partner and later an officer in the Zimmermann family's textile businesses; married Ethyl Kinnaman; 4 children, 18 grandchildren.

3.08 William 178

Graduate of the University of Pennsylvania; a chemical engineer; entered the family textile business, where he worked closely with his brother John on industrial designs; married Margaret Lukens, a descendant of Quaker families who founded Germantown, Philadelphia, Pa.; 3 children, 8 grandchildren.

3.09 Lillian 183

Graduate of the University of Pennsylvania in 1921; was assistant to the dean of the engineering school at the University of Kansas, where she met James Fligg, son of an R.L.D.S. missionary, then a student; after they were married, he joined the Zimmermann family textile businesses, but retired after a heart attack in 1938; 2 children, 1 grandchild.

3.10 Albert Walter 189

Graduate of the University of Pennsylvania in 1923 with a degree in electrical engineering; joined the Zimmermann textile businesses; was the last member of the family to serve as an officer at Artloom; his journals as a Naval Intelligence officer in India in World War II were later featured in a book, *Proceed to Peshawar*; married Barbara Shoemaker, a descendant of early Quakers of Pennsylvania and New England Puritans; 4 children, 12 grandchildren.

Bibliography 247

Index 255

Appendices 273

A – Zimmermann Family Charts (bef 1642-2009), by Jean Hoxie Naples 273

B – John Zimmermann Family Timeline (1855-1978), by Jean Naples 283

C – Barbara S. Zimmermann, *Mutterings* (1969), excerpts 311

About the Author 315

# Acknowledgments

My wife, Helene (Zimmermann) Hill, granddaughter of John[1] Zimmermann and Eva Katherine Kellenbenz, has been incredibly patient and helpful to me. I could not have undertaken this project without her help. We have enjoyed traveling together for more than fifty-six years. We have retraced the steps taken by our ancestors, and together we have visited and photographed the homes and burial sites of many of the people in this book.

I thank the late Jean (Hoxie) Naples (JHN), great-granddaughter of John[1] Zimmermann and his wife Eva. Jean assembled the unpublished manuscript that provides the timeline for Part II. She added the notes and maps and photos that bring to life the history of John Zimmermann in America. This book would have been impossible to write, except for her careful work. It was completed shortly before she died. JHN wrote in a letter to me in 2009: "John Zimmermann is a very interesting person to me and his story (birth to death) has been truly an adventure in places and time. By studying what he did, and with whom, one can see the influence and impact it had on those around him. His actions do talk louder than his unknown words. He had an opportunity to absorb the grit and the grandness of Philadelphia during a remarkable era. And I am soooo looking forward to finishing 'this of which may be gathered'."[3]

JHN mentions the problem of depression in the Zimmermann family, now called bi-polar disorder, which John[1] Zimmermann's children and grandchildren referred to as "the family disease." She quotes her aunt, Lucille[3] "Cil" (Hoxie) Fleet, who wrote to her in the 1990s, when she began work on the family genealogy: "'Depression: Sad part of it. There is help (through medication and doctors care) – use to be hush-hush. Uncle John Zimmermann [John[2] Zimmermann, Jr.], mother's brother, had it, had to have shock treatments and in hospital for awhile. Cousin Dick Kelley [Richard Carlyle[3] Kelley, Jr.] still bad and in nursing home. Would never admit he was depressed and drank while taking medication, a real no-no. So be aware of signs for it is in the family. Not my folks.' I asked my sisters (who made annual summer trips to see my parents on Cape Cod) if they ever saw any signs in my father [John Zimmermann[3] Hoxie] in his latter years (died in 1984) and they said no. He too died of an aneurysm, at age 66." John Zimmermann's youngest son, Albert Walter[2] Zimmermann, who achieved much success in his lifetime, also suffered from episodes of depression, drank too much, and died of a cerebral aneurysm at age 59. His son, Ambassador Warren[3] Zimmermann, was careful with alcohol and was a wonderful husband and father to his children. He achieved great success as a diplomat, author, and speaker; but he also had episodic depression and was treated with lithium.

I also thank the late Sue (Kelley) Carnwath, who provided much of the genealogy and history of the family of her parents and of their large family, for Part III; and for the charts of the Zimmermann family in Europe, which are the basis for much of Part I, Chapter 1.

I thank Anne Mitchell, a Kellenbenz, who discovered much about the Kellenbenz family in Germany and informed me about their descendants in America. She is the 3d cousin of Helene (Zimmermann) Hill. Both of them are great-great-grandchildren of Johann[B] and Anna Maria (Klement) Kellenbenz. Anne Mitchell's great-grandfather, Gottlieb Kellenbenz, came to Philadelphia and is probably the ancestor of all of those in America who bear the name of Kellenbenz. Gottlieb's older brother Johann Michael[A] Kellenbenz remained in Germany, but three of Johann Michael's children came to Philadelphia; one of them was Eva Katherine[1] Kellenbenz, who married John[1] Zimmermann.

Michael Bowman wrote a valuable, and I believe still unpublished, history of the Reorganized Church of Jesus Christ of Latter Day Saints (R.L.D.S.) in Philadelphia, of which

John Zimmermann was bishop. Bowman also produced two videos which illustrate the story of this church and tell about John Zimmermann's son-in-law – the personally flawed, but ambitious and musically talented Al Hoxie. Michael Bowman also is the source for much information about the other children of John Zimmermann, in their connections to the R.L.D.S. church. I could not have done the work on the church's history in Chapter 3 without his work, his photos, and his correspondence.

Kathryn "Katchie" (Fligg) Lee, a granddaughter of John Zimmermann, gave many of the family photos used in this book to Jean (Hoxie) Naples, who passed them to me. Katchie's recollections became an important part of the history of her parents and of other members of the Zimmermann family.

The late James Fligg, Jr., brother of Katchie, sent me a thoughtful letter in which he recalled his grandfather's life and dream. This letter was the inspiration for the title of this book, and is its epigraph.

John Hower Zimmermann, a great-grandson of John[1] Zimmermann, gave me much information about his grandfather, John[2] Zimmermann, Jr., and other descendants of his grandfather. He also provided a copy of "Mom's Stories," written by his aunt, the late Mary Jane[3] (Zimmermann) Clark, which Mary Jane wrote shortly before her death. Quotations from "Mom's Stories" appear throughout Parts II and III.

Joseph Wallace Carnwath, Jr., another great-grandson, was very helpful. He shows that the traditions of scholarship, research, and the arts have been passed down the line from John and Eva in his branch of the family. I have been enlightened by our correspondence, and by his recollections.

Barbara (Zimmermann) Johnson, daughter of Albert W. and Barbara (Shoemaker) Zimmermann, carefully preserved and labeled many of the iconic family images that appear in this book, including the frontispiece portrait of her grandparents – John and Eva – and their children.

I also thank the following descendants of John and Eva for completing Family Group Record and Biographical Information forms, in the order in which they appear in the Notes: Anita (Kelley) Pearson, Susan (Kelley) Carnwath, Joan (Kelley) Fowler, Carol Ann (Pearson) Ralph, Donald Kelley, Sr., and William Zimmermann, Jr.

I greatly appreciate the continuing support from Heritage Books, Inc., especially Leslie Wolfinger and Debbie Riley.

# Preface

American dreams.  This book is about the dreams of John Zimmermann and Eva Katherine Kellenbenz.  The reader of this book should imagine John and Eva Katherine when they were young people in Württemberg, Germany, and thinking of coming to America.

What were their dreams?

They didn't know each other then.  John Zimmermann would come to America as a nineteen year old man, with a high school education, speaking only German.  He had learned the craft and skill of a textile weaver from his father, and he would expect to carry on that trade in the United States.  Like John, Eva Katherine Kellenbenz was a Lutheran, and she probably had at least an elementary education, but she also spoke only German and had no other skills.

John believed, correctly, that his future in America would begin with his uncle – his father's brother Johann Georg, known as George Zimmermann in America.  Uncle George, a weaver in Germany, had recently come to America and would welcome him into the German community of Elmira, New York.  John may, in fact, have come on the same ship with his uncle, his wife, Margareta, and their six young children.  His uncle George gave up weaving and became a farmer, near Elmira.  But John's dream was to become a successful weaver in America, and he must have imagined that he would find a German woman who shared his dream.  If not in Elmira, it would be in some other German community in America.  And Eva believed, correctly, that if she and her sister came to Philadelphia with a Lutheran pastor as their sponsor, they would be welcomed by the Germans who were already there.  Eva believed that in America, she, too, could find work as a housemaid, marry a German man with good prospects, and have children of her own.

This book tells the story of these young people – John and Eva Katherine – and of how they succeeded in their dreams in America.  The story begins in the state of Württemberg, in southern Germany, where their ancestors had lived in small towns for more than 400 years.  Both towns were a few miles east of Stuttgart, although the Kellenbenz and Zimmermann families did not know each other in Germany.

Part I of this book traces the history of the Zimmermann and Kellenbenz families from the 1400s to the late 1800s, when John and Eva each decided, independently, to come to America.  Part II tells of John and Eva's marriage, of their seven children, and of Eva's death in 1920.  Part II of the book also documents John Zimmermann's amazing success in Philadelphia as an inventor of textile machinery, manager of fabric mills, and businessman; and of his unusual additional life as a philanthropist and bishop of the Reorganized Church of Jesus Christ of Latter Day Saints – the R.L.D.S. church – now called the Community of Christ.  Part II ends with his death in 1936.  Part III of the book follows the lives and careers of the descendants of John and Eva to the present time, including 190 of their descendants, and 80 of those who are known to be their spouses.  John and Eva Zimmermann would be proud to know of their legacy – of the achievements of their descendants and their spouses, including their 7 children, 23 grandchildren, 73 great-grandchildren, 70 great (x2) grandchildren, and 17 known great (x3) grandchildren.

Photograph by Rhoads, Philadelphia

**John Zimmermann and Eva Katherine Kellenbenz**
Wedding photograph, 1885

# Introduction

*American Dreams* is divided into three parts.  Part I, with two chapters, is about the European origin of the families of John Zimmermann and Eva Katherine Kellenbenz.  It begins with the background of the Germanic people, and it then focuses on the homeland of these two families in the Swabian Alb, now the state of Baden-Württemberg in Germany.  Part II continues with the story of John and Eva Katherine, who came separately to America, where they met and were married in Philadelphia.  Part II also tells of the early lives of the seven children.  It also tells of John Zimmermann's remarkable success as an inventor of weaving and dyeing machines, as a businessman in the textile industry, and as a philanthropist and Mormon bishop.  Part III is divided into seven chapters, each of which is devoted to one of John and Eva Katherine's seven children, and of their descendants.

## Part I
## The Ancestors

The part of Central Europe where *Deutsch* (German) has long been spoken was located between Gaul on the west, where French is spoken; Italy on the south; the North Sea to the north; and the Slavic-speaking countries on the east.  Variations of the German language appear in what is now Germany and Austria, in part of Switzerland, and in the Netherlands, and part of Belgium.  Those who speak the Germanic languages have a cultural similarity.  In contrast to their neighbors on each side, they are generally fastidious, even to a fault; they rarely exhibit the "I don't care" shrug of the French, or the "I don't care" gesture of upward palms by the Italian.  The German farmer (*Bauer*), and his Swiss, Dutch, and Nordic counterparts, keeps his house and land tidy, in contrast to the sometimes slovenly peasant or serf, seen elsewhere in Europe, France, Italy, or the British Isles.   John Zimmermann and Eva Katherine Kellenbenz were accustomed to German ways, and they continued them when they came to America.

European history has been greatly affected by differences in religion.  It is remarkable that after the religious wars which followed the Reformation, the area that is now Germany, in contrast to the rest of Europe, became tolerant of both Protestant and Catholic faiths.  In some states, such as Württemberg, many towns had both Lutheran and Catholic churches.  No other country in Europe had such religious diversity.  This tolerance was not perfect:  Quakers and Mennonites were harassed and expelled, and many of them came to Philadelphia in the seventeenth century.  Freedom of religion played a large role in the success of two great American cities – Philadelphia and New York.  The families of John Zimmermann and Eva Kellenbenz had no recent experience with religious intolerance, but the acceptance of alternate religions played an important role in John and Eva's life after they came to America.[4]

Part I, Chapter 1 (Zimmermann Family), is based on charts of this family which were prepared by an official in Gussenstadt, Württemberg.  I saw these charts in the home of John and Eva's granddaughter, Susan (Kelley) Carnwath, where I obtained copies that I used for this book.  Chapter 1 also includes the report of a trip to Europe in 1937 by John Zimmermann's youngest son Albert and his wife, in which they visited the last known relative of Albert Zimmermann in Württemberg: his aged spinster aunt Anna Zimmermann.  She was at that time enjoying the recent recovery of the economy, which she attributed to policies of the new Chancellor, Adolph Hitler.  Albert Zimmermann also visited his Kellenbenz relatives in Stuttgart.  In contrast to Anna Zimmermann, they shared, quietly and in secret, their concerns about Hitler.  Chapter 2

(Kellenbenz Family) is based on records discovered by Anne Mitchell, a great-great-niece of Johann Kellenbenz, father of Eva Katherine Kellenbenz, which she kindly offered to me. The earlier probable line of our Kellenbenz family is shown in Chapter 2 as it appears in a translation of a newspaper article, *Sippe von Kellenbenz*. This piece was published in about 1960 in Stuttgart, the capital city of Baden-Württemberg.

A short profile is also given in Chapter 2 of Professor Hermann Kellenbenz (1913-1990), who was born in Süssen, adjacent to the town of Eislingen, where Eva Katherine Kellenbenz was born in 1855. He is the most notable of all of the Kellenbenz family. By the 1970s, the professor had become recognized as one of the world's leading experts in economic history. Chapter 2 presents documents, translated here from German for the first time, which show that Hermann Kellenbenz, soon after receiving his doctorate, worked in Berlin during World War II on the economic history of the *Judenfrage* (Jewish Question).

Modern travelers to Baden-Württemberg and the adjacent state of Bavaria rarely visit the sites of the concentration and death camps of the Third Reich. The towns and cities in these states, such as Stuttgart and Munich, which were devastated by war, have been rebuilt. The last pages of Part I show the terrible history in Germany in the last half of the 20th century, which needs to be remembered so it will never be repeated.

The history of pre-industrial hand weaving and fabric dyeing is presented next as a background to Part II, which shows John Zimmermann's important contributions to the textile industry in America.

## Part II
## John Zimmermann and Eva Katherine Kellenbenz

Part II, which has but one chapter (no. 3), tells of John Zimmermann's arrival in the New World in 1874, at age 19; of his introduction to America as part of the German community in Elmira, N.Y., where he was welcomed by his recently-arrived uncle and many in-laws; of his relocation to Philadelphia in 1876, for the grand Bi-Centennial exhibition. It tells of the arrival of Eva Katherine Kellenbenz in Philadelphia, and of the marriage of John and Eva in 1885; and of her life until 1920, when she died. It tells of the births of their seven children, one of whom died early of diphtheria; and of the childhood and early lives of the others – their education, careers, marriages and children – up to the time of John Zimmermann's death in 1936. Part II also tells of John's career as a philanthropist and bishop of the Reorganized Church of Jesus Christ of Latter Day Saints (R.L.D.S. church); and of his second marriage, to an older, wealthy widowed woman from Iowa, with children and step-children of her own, within that church. His second wife survived him. Upon his death, she promptly emptied his house in Philadelphia and returned to Iowa, an action which embittered many of John's children, and which resulted in the loss of his letters and other personal papers.

John Zimmermann's beliefs as a Mormon and his leadership in the R.L.D.S. church were coincidental with his work as a rising leader in the textile industry. He actively recruited employees from the German Mormon community, and he was at the same time generous to the Mormon Church. We know, however, nothing about his personal faith or his knowledge of the *Book of Mormon*, and his children never spoke of this to their children. The effects of religion and capitalism in America were eloquently discussed by Max Weber in 1905, in *The Protestant Ethic and the Spirit of Capitalism*, and by many others since then. In 2016, Chris Lehman considered this subject in *The Money Cult: Capitalism, Christianity, and the Unmaking of the*

*American Dream.* Lehman studied American Protestants from the Puritans to the Mormons, and although Lehmann disagreed with some of Weber's conclusions, for both authors, "religious history is the mainstream of American history."[†] In contrast, however, to the argument in Lehman's *Money Cult*, this book will show that John Zimmermann's American Dream was achieved by both the Protestant Ethic, as a Mormon, and the spirit of Capitalism.

Part II also tells of John's activities in the textile industry, including his inventions and his many businesses, beginning as a worker in an established textile mill, and then with a small factory of his own; then a plant in partnership with his older brother George, and then in partnership with another man, named Cameron. After Cameron died, the firm of Cameron and Zimmermann was merged with a firm owned by three Wasserman brothers. The new company formed in 1895 by Zimmermann and the Wassermans was called Philadelphia Tapestry Mills. This company used various brand names and with success, it expanded both vertically and horizontally. At its height, it occupied two square blocks in the Kensington area of north Philadelphia. It was a brick building, six stories or more in height. By 1904, the mill was using the name "Artloom" for its rugs. This company was later renamed as Artloom, and it proclaimed the belief that it was the largest, or at least one of the largest, rug manufacturers in the United States. The success of the Philadelphia Tapestry Mills and Artloom depended on the Wasserman brothers' capital, marketing ability, and savvy business sense; and of John Zimmermann's unique skills – as a recruiter and manager of good workers, and as a self-taught genius in textile engineering. His crucial patents for inventions in manufacturing of textiles included a very wide loom, using a powered shuttle; a method to weave two carpets face to face, and cut them apart, making two carpets in only a little more time and cost than it took to make one; and a new system of dyeing carpets, in which the weft was dyed in advance and woven into the rug, instead of adding a pattern to the rug. These inventions were similar to others in Europe and America that were being developed at about this time, but they were employed to great success by Zimmermann and the Wassermans.

John Zimmermann was, of course, fluent in German, and he was able to identify men in the Protestant German community who would have the same no-nonsense approach to life and work that he did. He was also a stern man, whose unsmiling visage in many photographs correctly portrayed him. He was probably a difficult man to deal with, uncompromising and unyielding. The history of the spelling of his name illustrates this point. Ten years after he arrived in the United States, at about the time of his marriage, for some unknown reason, he changed the spelling from Zimmermann to Zimmerman; and he used the one "n" spelling consistently thereafter until he died. It appears with one "n" in his obituaries. His family name was occasionally misspelled by others, using "nn," but this was not by his choice. At the time his children went to college, each of them began to use the "nn" form of the name, and this has now become the family name: Zimmermann. In fact, over the past fifty-six years, I have never met or corresponded with any of his descendants who were aware that the one "n" spelling was the spelling that the Patriarch of the family preferred and used consistently. The one "n" choice of the Patriarch has been completely forgotten. I will occasionally use the one "n" spelling when

---

[†] Max Weber, *The Protestant Ethic and the Spirit of Capitalism.* [1905] Boston: Unwin Hyman, 1930; Chris Lehmann, *The Money Cult: Capitalism, Christianity, and the Unmaking of the American Dream.* New York: Melville House, 2016; review of Lehman, with comments on Weber, by James Livingston, "The Gospel of Wealth," *New York Times Book Review* (19 June 2016), 19.

it appears in a document or a photograph. However, to avoid confusion, I have decided to use the original German "nn" form of the family name throughout most of this book.

John Zimmermann's first two sons were promptly employed by the Philadelphia Tapestry Mills after they graduated from college. This soon caused strife with his partners, the Wasserman brothers, whose sons also sought employment with the company. John Zimmermann's sons, John Jr. and Bill, had skills in chemistry and engineering, and his oldest son was also a patented inventor, but the Wassermans' sons could offer only business skills, ambitions, and doting fathers. To complicate matters, John and Eva's first two daughters, Clara and Anna, married men who were incompatible with the business operations of the elder Zimmermann and the Wasserman brothers. These sons-in-law did not get along well with John's sons. The eldest daughter's husband, Al Hoxie, soon left the textile business to work as a music teacher, and then was a choir and band director before he wandered off. There was a great spread in age in the generation of the children, and that surely played a role in the family dynamics. The second daughter's husband, Dick Kelley, was the oldest man in that generation of the family. He was five years older than his wife, and very domineering. He was twenty years older than the youngest son, Al. The third son-in-law, Jim Fligg, was also an inventor, with a patent for textile weaving, but he retired early from the family business. And John Zimmermann's sons also had problems of their own. They were brilliant, but they all had periods of serious depression.

The movie *Avalon* presents a fictionalized but somewhat similar situation of a toxic mix of personalities, skills, and problems in a family of recent immigrants who became successful businessmen. *Avalon* is set in Baltimore, and the family is Jewish, whereas the saga of the Zimmermann and Wasserman families is set in Philadelphia, and the conflict in their business involves both a Christian and a Jewish family. Both of the Philadelphia families, however, recently came to America from the same area in Europe – Württemberg – and there can be little doubt that anti-Semitism played a role in the tension. The Zimmermann brothers eventually formed, with their father, two companies of their own – Zimmermann Mills, and John Zimmermann & Sons. They then left the combined company that was formed by their father and the Wasserman brothers, although the youngest son, Albert, also remained as an officer of Artloom.

In spite of all of this strife with the Wassermans, and with the Zimmermann sons' brothers-in-law, John and Eva's three surviving daughters and their three surviving sons continued to have a warm, supportive, friendship with each other. However, in the next generation, in the generation of the grandchildren, the family began to split apart. The three son's wives were very different from each other. John Jr. married a vocalist with a career of her own; Bill married a down-to-earth girl from a prominent old Philadelphia family, and Al married an uppity high-society lady. In the end, the separations that developed in the generations of the children and grandchildren were largely caused by the age differences in John and Eva's children, and differences between the spouses who were chosen by them.

## Part III
### The Descendants of John and Eva Katherine (Kellenbenz) Zimmermann

The lives of about 270 men, women, and children are presented in Part III in either outline form or in biographies, in seven chapters, each of which is devoted to one of the children of John and Eva Katherine (Kellenbenz) Zimmermann. One of them, Emily, died of diphtheria as a child, but the other six married and had descendants. The multi-generational family of John and Eva Katherine is large, and it has been unusually successful. It begs the old question of whether success is genetic or environmental. John Zimmermann was arguably a genius as an inventor, businessman, and leader. He stands apart from the many others who came before him in his ancestry, and those who were his contemporaries in his own family. He was truly unusual. Was his success due to a genetic mutation? Did it pass to his children, and to later generations in the family? Or was the success of his children and their descendants the result of the environment that he created and the things that his wealth provided, such as exceptional educational opportunities, disposable income, time to travel, and the chance to think? There is no simple answer to these questions. The issue was first raised by Charles Darwin's cousin, Sir Francis Galton, in *Hereditary Genius*, and it remains a conundrum to this day.[‡]

Of the six surviving children, all completed high school, and all had additional education. Five graduated from the University of Pennsylvania – two of the daughters, and all three sons. The two daughters were both members of the exclusive sorority, Kappa Kappa Gamma. The three sons were all talented engineering students, and at least one spent an additional year in graduate school. In this generation, the family – the children and their spouses – also showed considerable talent in music and art, and some had a touch of greatness. They were also significant contributors to the activities of their churches and in their communities. And their children also had happy and productive lives, with each other, and with their friends. Eva, before she died in 1920, and John, who died in 1936, saw some of those successes. They had reason to be proud, for they had achieved their American Dreams.

Of the 23 men and women in the second generation – the cousins – who were grandchildren of John and Eva, 22 lived to adulthood, and 21 of them married and had children. The large kindred of 45 men and women and their spouses in this generation include many who were college graduates, and several with advanced degrees. Their institutions included Swarthmore (5); Harvard (5); University of Pennsylvania (3); Smith (3); Oberlin (3); Yale (2); Amherst (1); Brown (1); Duke (1); Lehigh (1); Carleton (1); University of Washington (1); Johns Hopkins (1); Cal Tech (1); and M.I.T. (1). At least two of the spouses were recipients of honorary degrees. One of the spouses was a lawyer; another was an Episcopal bishop. One of the cousins and three of the spouses had the degree of M.D.; two of the cousins and two spouses had the Ph.D. degree. Several were Eagle Scouts and some were parents of Eagle Scouts. One was an ambassador, and one worked for the CIA. At least three were U.S. Army captains and one of the spouses was a U.S. Navy captain. Their skills and hobbies include flying airplanes, playing and singing music; art; ornithology; laboratory and field biology; and engineering. They have been authors of hundreds of scholarly articles, scientific papers, and many books; one

---

[‡] Francis Galton, *Hereditary Genius: An Inquiry into its Laws and Consequences* (London: Macmillan and Co., 1869). Galton argued that heredity was the cause of success in the families that he discussed. His book led to the concept known as "Social Darwinism," which became the intellectual basis for the "eugenics" movement in the early 20th century. Sad to say, the belief in the value of "eugenics" led to such evils as the involuntary sterilization of so-called "defective" men and women in the United States, and then to the killing of the "defectives" during the period of the Third Reich. One of the largest extermination camps of the "defectives" was in Württemberg, just south of Stuttgart. It was a slippery slope from Galton to Hitler. We do know that income is related to academic success. The *New York Times* reported in April 2016 that sixth graders with the highest family income, on average, read a level that is four grades higher than those with the lowest family income. It would therefore not be surprising to find that John Zimmermann's children did well in school. See: Motoko Rich, Amanda Cox, and Matthew Bloch, "Money, Race and Success: How Your School District Compares," *New York Times* (29 April 2016), at http://www.nytimes.com/interactive/2016/04/29/upshot/money-race-and-success-how-your-school-district-compares.html?_r=0.

received a crucial patent which was used by NASA; and they have taught in elementary school, colleges, and graduate schools.  They have been faculty members or did postgraduate study at Harvard, the Mayo Clinic; Duke; U.C.L.A.; U. California (Berkeley); University of Minnesota; University of Massachusetts; Rutgers University; U. of Colorado; and Washington University.

At the time of this writing, nearly a quarter of them are still alive:  five of the cousins – four women and one man – and at least four of their spouses – two men and two women.   A brief summary of the generation of the cousins and their spouses includes:

• A multi-talented musician and private pilot.

• A graduate of Swarthmore; post-graduate work in education; an avid ornithologist; her husband, also a graduate of Swarthmore, M.D., Harvard; pulmonologist and dean at the Mayo Clinic and its medical school.

• Graduate of Lehigh, in Delta Upsilon; Eagle Scout; captain, U.S. Army.

• Graduate of Oberlin with 3 years postgraduate at Oberlin Conservatory of Music; her husband, a graduate of Penn, the Wharton School, and Penn law school; U.S. Army captain; admiralty lawyer and CEO of a large packing company.

• Another graduate of Oberlin; her husband, Oberlin graduate, Duke Ph.D.; was a noted professor of philosophy there.

• A Swarthmore graduate with postgraduate courses at Radcliffe; a career field biologist; her husband, also a Swarthmore graduate; Ph.D. Harvard; award-winning mammalogist at  U. California at Berkeley; recipient of honorary doctorate from Chile.

• Another Swarthmore graduate; post-grad engineering courses at Drexel; with Philco; his wife, also a Swarthmore graduate, is a math teacher at Abington Friends School.

• A graduate of Amherst; Ph.D., Cal Tech; professor of physics, U. Minn.; flute player; his wife, a graduate of Carleton College; plays Baroque music on violin with husband.

• An occupational therapist and mother of four; her three boys are Eagle Scouts; her husband, University of Washington (Seattle) graduate, and athlete; M.D. Hopkins; one of the founders of the specialty of pediatric surgery; many honors and publications.

• A notable professor of biology at U. Mass. (Amherst), with a Ph.D. from M.I.T.; postgraduate study at Harvard Medical School; many publications and teaching awards; his wife is a teacher of French literature.

• A graduate of the University of Pennsylvania, B.F.A.; additional study at Pennsylvania of Fine Arts; career as a painter, illustrator of books and building murals; exhibits; her husband, Episcopal bishop; B.A., Brown; B.D., Gen. Theological Sem.; D.D. (*h.c.*).

• A graduate of Smith College; career, under cover, with C.I.A.; her husband, a U.S.A.I.D. employee, was honored by Greek government for work in WWII.

• Her sister, another graduate of Smith College; Ph.D., Brandeis; notable career in radiation biology; her husband, Yale, B.A.; Harvard Medical School, M.D.; surgeon and captain, USNR.

• Her brother, a graduate of Yale, B.A.; M.A. Cambridge U. (Eng.); career foreign service officer; ambassador; lecturer; author of scholarly articles and two highly praised books; his wife, who attended Smith for nearly four years; supported her husband in his many assignments.

• His brother, a graduate of Harvard College; M.D., University of Pennsylvania; an ophthalmologist; his wife, a laboratory technician, and then mother of three successful daughters.

Less is known about John and Eva's great-grandchildren.  To protect their personal privacy, many of their parents abbreviated their biographies.  I have been able to add to some of them from information available to the public on the internet, as follows:

• One great-grandson is a molecular biologist; he graduated from Yale (1966), and Cambridge University (Ph.D); two of his children are professional musicians, playing for a German audience; another has a Ph.D. from Northwestern and is a consultant in funding of theatre arts.

• Another has two children: one graduated from National Outdoor Leadership School and works in health system management; the other has a Ph.D. in forestry from the University of Montana.

• One is a theoretical chemist whose wife is a molecular biologist.

• The husband of a great-granddaughter, who graduated from Bucknell and Penn State (J.D.), is a judge in Pennsylvania. He was honored as "Child Advocate of the Year" for his landmark ruling, stating that lifetime registration of juvenile sex offenders is unconstitutional.

• A great-granddaughter, a writer and musician, is married to the CEO of Earth Vision Industries, a world-wide marketer of unique resins.

• Her sister is married to the CEO of European Dolphin Safe Monitoring Organisation, a U.K. company, at Earth Island Institute, San Francisco.

• A great-grandson graduated *summa cum laude* from Yale (1970), and from Stanford Law School. He clerked for W. O. Douglas and is a prominent lawyer in San Francisco.

• Another great-grandson is a purchasing agent, whose son is the principal clarinetist for the Nashville Symphony Orchestra; he married an opera *diva* who was a descendant of Brigham Young; they are the parents of two children.

• A great-granddaughter is a graduate of Smith College, whose husband had a law degree and worked in the White House during the administration of President George W. Bush. They have five children.

• Her sister graduated from Colby College and works in advancement/development for a private school; her husband is a free-lance writer. They have two children.

• A great-grandson is a lawyer, who graduated from Rutgers University and Rutgers Law School; he is a public defender. His companion, with a Ph.D. from Rutgers, is the Mellon Professor of Philosophy at Vassar.

• His brother was a composer and poet; his wife, B.A., M.Ed., was a school principal; their daughter, who graduated from the University of West Virginia-Parkersburg, has three children.

• A great-granddaughter is an associate professor of anthropology at Western Michigan University; graduated from Kenyon College; Ph.D., Johns Hopkins University; married to a graduate of Antioch and law school, with honors, at Michigan State University; two children by the same sperm donor.

• Her sister is an accomplished leader of outdoor activities and is an executive trainer. She is a graduate of Sterling College, who worked for the British Embassy in Washington, D.C.

• Another great-granddaughter is a graduate of Duke University and is a curator of art history in Boston.

• Her sister graduated from Yale and married a Yale man who was there at that time.

• Their brother, who also graduated from Yale, is a free lance writer; author of a prize-winning book and co-producer of the movie, *Blackfish*.

• Another great-granddaughter is a graduate of Colgate College; she was a paralegal before she married a lawyer in Massachusetts; they have two children.

• Her sister is a graduate of Colby College; Ph.D. in sociology from Brown; and the mother of two children. Her husband has the M.D. and Ph.D. degrees and is a pulmonologist.

• Another sister has the B.A. degree from Bowdoin College and a master's degree in education from the University of Pennsylvania; two children; her husband is admissions director at Choate.

# AHNENTAFELS

## JOHN ZIMMERMANN

**1. John ZIMMERMANN Sr.,** a weaver, learned to use a handloom in his father's house; an inventor, patented new machinery for making large rugs on a 9-foot wide loom; another patent for weaving face-to-face carpets, making two for the price of one; and a revolutionary warp dyeing machine, enabling patterns to be woven into rugs with colored yarns; co-owner, with three Wasserman brothers, of Philadelphia Tapestry Mills, which later became Artloom, one of the largest rug manufacturers in America; founder and co-owner of Zimmermann Mills and John Zimmermann & Sons, textile mills in Philadelphia; a philanthropist; and bishop for Pennsylvania and New York of the Reorganized Church of Latter Day Saints (R.L.D.S. Church).

He was b. 28 Nov 1855, Gussenstadt, kingdom of Württemberg, now state of Baden-Württemberg, Federal Republic of Germany; d. Philadelphia, Pa., 23 May 1936; buried Philadelphia, Greenmount Cemetery; baptized as a Lutheran, 30 Nov 1855, at Gussenstadt; and baptized again as a member of the R.L.D.S. Church, Philadelphia, 30 Jan 1884; m. 15 Oct 1885, in Philadelphia, **Eva Katherine KELLENBENZ.**

### Second Generation

**2. John ZIMMERMANN,** weaver; made textiles on a handloom in a workshop in his house, assisted by other members of his family; a Lutheran; b. 24 Sep 1821, Gussenstadt, Württemberg; d. Gussenstadt, 25 Jul 1899; m., say 1850, given the date his 1st child was b. (5 Jun 1851), at Gussenstadt.

**3. Anna Ursula JÄGER,** b. 12 Sep 1820; a Lutheran; d. Gussenstadt, 11 Jan 1901.

### Third Generation

**4. Jacob ZIMMERMANN,** weaver; the 1st of 3 generations of Zimmermanns to use a handloom in the family house in Gussenstadt; a Lutheran; b. 9 Jan 1801, probably at Gussenstadt, duchy of Württemberg; d. 16 Jun 1864, Gussenstadt, kingdom of Württemberg; m. Gussenstadt, say 1820, based on b.d. of 1st child (24 Sep 1821).

**5-7.---**

### Fourth Generation

**8. Johann Georg ZIMMERMANN,** day laborer, b. 11 Dec 1768; d. 9 May 1835; m. to a woman whose name is unknown, in say 1800, given the date his 1st child was b. (9 Jan 1801).

**9-15.---**

### Fifth Generation

**16. Sigmund Christoph (aka Sigmund Friedrich) ZIMMERMANN,** butcher, of Gussenstadt, a Lutheran, b. Gussenstadt, Württemberg, 22 Dec 1744; d. Württemberg, probably at Gussenstadt, 30 Oct 1797; m. (1) Württemberg, say 1768, based on b.d. of 1st child (11 Dec 1768), to; m. (2) Anna Catherine Siebold; and (3) Barbara Rehm. He had 13 children, all but two or three of whom d. young; four ch. were by his 1st wife.

**17. Apollonia BÜHNER,** b. 25 May 1745; d. 29 Mar 1776; m., as his 1st wife, to.

**18-31.---**

### Sixth Generation

**32. Georg Christoph (aka F___ Christoph) ZIMMERMANN,** a butcher, b. 1 Mar 1714, Lauterburg, Jagstkreis (Jagst district), Württemberg; d. Gussenstadt, Württemberg, 4 Mar 1779; m. Gussenstadt, 25 Jan 1735.

**33. Margareta (aka Margarethe) SATTLER,** b. 4 Jul 1701, Gussenstadt; d. Gussenstadt, 22 Feb 1768.

**34-63.**

### Seventh Generation

**64. Johann Michael ZIMMERMANN,** a baker in Lauterburg; b. 22 Jun 1679 at Heidenheim, Württemberg; d. 18 Dec 1726, probably at Lauterburg, Württemberg; m. say 1713, given the b. date (1 Mar 1714) of his 1st child.[5]

**65. Maria BARTH,** b. about 1684; d. at Lauterberg, Württemberg, 26 Sep 1714.

**66-127.---**

### Eighth Generation

**128.** *Bürgurmeister* **Johann (aka Albert) Jakob ZIMMERMANN,** a saddler, like his father; served as mayor of Heubach; b. 7 Sep 1642, Heidenheim, Württemberg, 27 Nov 1729; m. 30 Jul 1677, in Heubach, Ostalbkreis (Ostalb district), Württemberg. [6]

**129. Anna WALTER,** b. 8 Sep 1659 in Heubach, Württemberg; d. 31 Mar 1749.

**130-255.---**

### Ninth Generation

**256. Herr Jakob ZIMMERMANN**, a saddler (maker of saddles and tack for horses), b. 16 Jul 1614 in Heidenheim, Württemberg; m. say 1641, given the b. date (7 Sep 1642) of his 1st child.[7]

**257. Apollonia _____**, b. abt 1620.

**258. Hans WALTER**, b. abt 1630 in Württemberg; d. Heubach, Ostalbkreis, Württemberg, 21 Jan 1683; m. 5 Jul 1657, in Heubach.

**259. Barbara NÖRDLINGER**, b. abt 1635 in Langenau, Württemberg; d. Heubach, Württemberg, 23 Oct 1687.

**260-511.**---

### Tenth Generation

**512. Adam ZIMMERMANN**, b. 1578 in Steinheim am Albuch, Heidenheim, Württemberg; d. Heidenheim, Württemberg, 20 Mar 1662; m. 16 Feb 1608, at Heidenheim.[8]

**513. Catharina BOLLINGER**, b. Dec 1587, Heidenheim, Württemberg; d. Heidenheim, 16 Nov 1668.

**514-515.**---

**516. Georg WALTER**, b. abt 1603, Württemberg.

**517. Barbara _____**, b. abt 1603, Württemberg; d. Heubach, Ostalbkreis, Württemberg, 19 Jan 1680.

**518. Hans NÖRDLINGER,** b. abt 1605.

**519-1023.**---

### Eleventh Generation

**1024. Matthis ZIMMERMANN**, b. abt 1550 in Steinheim am Albuch, Heidenheim, Württemberg.

**1025.**---

**1026. Hans BOLLINGER,** b. 5 Mar 1564, Heidenheim; d. Heidenheim, 30 Apr 1633; m. Oct 1584, Heidenheim.

**1027. Walburga JELIN**, b. abt 1565, Heidenheim, Württemberg; d. Heidenheim, 13 Jul 1625.

**1028-2047.**---

### Twelfth Generation

**2048-2051.**---

**2052. Hannss BOLLINGER**, b. abt 1530, Heidenheim, Württemberg.

**2053. Afra _____**, b. abt 1535.

**2054. Peter JELIN,** b. 1535, Heidenheim; m. abt 1560.

**2055. Anna _____**, b. abt 1530.

**2056-4095.**---

### Thirteenth Generation

**4096-4107.**---

**4108. Paulin JELIN**, b. abt 1495, Württemberg; d. aft 1548.

**4109-8191.**---

# AHNENTAFELS

## EVA KATHERINE KELLENBENZ

**1. Eva Katherine (aka Eva Catherine, Catherine, Evakaterina, or Eva Kathryn) KELLENBENZ**, was b. 29 Sep 1855 in Kleineislingen, Donaukreis (Donau district), kingdom of Württemberg (now Eislingen, state of Baden-Württemberg, Germany); she was baptized 2 Oct 1855 as a Lutheran, and never left that denomination; died at Philadelphia, Penna., 12 Oct 1920; buried at Greenmount Cemetery, Front St. near Hunting Park Ave., Philadelphia, beside her daughter Emily; married, 15 October 1855, in Philadelphia, **John ZIMMERMANN**.[9]

### Second Generation

**2. Johann Michael KELLENBENZ**, b. Kleineislingen, Donaukreis, Württemberg; d. Göppingen, Donaukreis, Württemberg, 31 Jul 1888; m. 16 May 1853.

**3. Clara GRÖZINGER**, b. 29 Jul 1828, Ottenbach, Donaukreis, Württemberg; d. Kleineislingen, 9 Nov 1899.

### Third Generation

**4. Johann Georg (known as Georg) KELLENBENZ**, b. 26 Oct 1794, Kleineislingen, Württemberg; d. Kleineislingen, 27 Jan 1870; m. 27 Sep 1820.[10]

**5. Anna Maria CLEMENT (or KLEMENT)**, b. 22 Mar 1797, Kleineislingen; d. Donaukreis, 8 Aug 1871.

**6-7.**---

### Fourth Generation

**8. Johann Jacob (known as Jakob) KELLENBENZ**, b. abt 1766, Kleineislingen; m. abt 1789, Württemberg, perhaps at Württemberger Hof, Schwabisch Hall.

**9. Christina SILLER (or SIHLER)**, b. abt 1766.

**10. Johannes KLEMENT.**

**11. Agnesa Maria SCHUSTER.**

**12-15.**---

### Fifth Generation

**16. Dr. Gottlieb I KELLENBENZ,** surgeon, obstetrician; b. abt 1726.[11]

**17-31.**---

### Sixth Generation

**32.** *Schultheiss* **Johann Jakob KELLENBENZ** (*Schultheiss* = mayor), b. abt 1702.

**33-63.**---

### Seventh Generation

**64. Sebastian KELLENBENZ,** b. abt 1677 in Kleineislingen, Württemberg.

**65-127.**---

### Eighth Generation

**128. George KELLENBENZ.** Born in 1644 in Kleineislingen, Württemberg.

**129-255.**---

### Ninth Generation

**256.** *Schultheiss* **Johannes KELLENBENZ,** called "the Eislinger."[12]

**257-511.**---

## Notes

[1] F. W. Bogen, *The German in America* (Boston, 1851), quoted in Stephen Ozment, *A Mighty Fortress: A New History of the German People* (2004), 170–71. Emphasis in original.

[2] James Truslow Adams, *Epic of America* (1931). Emphasis in original.

[3] JHN (1947-2011) was a great-granddaughter of John[1] Zimmermann (Jean[4]=John R. Naples; John Zimmermann[3] Hoxie; Clara[2]=Albert Hoxie, Jr.; John[1] Zimmermann). This quotation is from her letter to GJH, 8 October 2009. On 23 September 2009 she wrote, "I really enjoyed talking with you . . . It's so nice to connect with someone who understands "THE QUEST" of working on family histories. I'm sending you some of the notes and charts that I have been working on for the last 6 months. As promised, I'll send you the 'story' hopefully by Christmas." JHN didn't say so at that time, but she must have known that she would die of cancer before this book would be published. Her research, notes, photographs, and copied documents made it possible for me to write much of Part II and the first two generations of Part III of this book. Indeed, this book could never have been written without her work. Her quotation may be taken from Herman Melville, *The Confidence-Man: His Masquerade*, Chapter 12, "Story of the Unfortunate Man, From Which May Be Gathered Whether or Not He Has Been Justly So Entitled."

[4] The subject of religion and its impact on the development of the United States has been discussed by many authors. I would mention especially the rigidity of the Puritan Anglicans in New England, who would not accept traditional Anglicans because they used ceremonies which were considered to be Papist, and who were famously harsh toward dissent – they fought with, expelled, and even killed those whom they considered to be Dissenters, including the Pilgrims of Plymouth, Quakers, Anabaptists, and Presbyterians. Roman Catholics and Jews were also unwelcome in colonial New England. In contrast, there was a reasonable accommodation by the Lutheran Dutch leaders of New Amsterdam to other religions, although Quakers, abjuring authority, had problems there, too. Presbyterians were forced to the periphery of the settled lands in New England, and many therefore went to Nova Scotia or settled in the Appalachian Mountains. See David Hackett Fisher, *Albion's Seed*, which describes the four groups of English immigrants who came to America; and a discussion of New Amsterdam in Russell Shorto, *The Island at the Center of the World*. I have previously discussed the subject of religion in colonial America, and how it affected our families. My book, *Western Pilgrims*, speaks of the western movement of those who sought for opportunities, including freedom of religion, that New England did not offer; *Quakers and Puritans* shows the contrast between two groups of immigrants (to Pennsylvania and New England), which confirmed in our families the generalities of *Albion's Seed*; and *Fundy to Chesapeake*, which extended the conclusions of *Albion's Seed*. (Full titles cited in this note are in the Bibliography)

[5] 64. Johann Michael Zimmermann is from the German charts obtained by Sue (Kelley) Carnwath, and transcribed by Jean (Hoxie) Naples; and Kathy Brant Bonnell, "Zimmermann Genealogy," on Rootsweb (details in text).

[6] 128. Johann Jakob Zimmermann is from the charts obtained by Carnwath, and transcribed Naples, supplemented with information from Ancestry.com, besswanger Family Tree.

[7] 256. Herr Jacob Zimmermann is named in the charts by Carnwath, transcribed by Naples (see details in text); additional information about 256. is from various Ancestry.com family trees, and has not been verified from original documents.

[8] 512. Adam Zimmermann and his father 1024. Matthis, and about the Bollinger, Walter, Nördlinger, and Jelin families, are from Ancestry.com family trees, without other documentation.

[9] 1., 2., and 3., from Anne Mitchell, "Kellenbenz Family," with notes and copies of records (see text).

[10] 4. Johann Georg Kellenbenz, and his wife, 5. Anna Maria Clement, are given here as a composite of research by Anne Mitchell (see text), and the Curry and Keegan Family Trees, on Ancestry.com.

[11] The five generations of descent shown here from 256. Johannes Kellenbenz, to 16. Dr. Gottlieb I Kellenbenz, are based on the document *Etwas von der Sippe Kellenbenz* (see text and notes). I cannot be sure that my translation is entirely correct. The original article is in Swabian German, and the precise genealogical definitions are difficult to interpret.

[12] The Kellenbenz family is said to have been in Württemberg since the 14th century, but the line traced in this chapter begins with 256. Johannes Kellenbenz, "the Eislinger," whose father is unknown.

www.tripmondo.com

**Eislingen, Baden-Württemberg**

www.Süssen.de

**Evangelical Church, Süssen**

# PART I

# ANCESTORS OF
# JOHN ZIMMERMANN
# AND
# EVA KATHERINE KELLENBENZ

Swabian Circle (1572), from Wikipédia

## Swabia

# Homeland of the Zimmermann and Kellenbenz Families

## Europe – Germany – Swabia – Württemberg

John Zimmermann and Eva Katherine Kellenbenz came to America from villages in Southern Germany. John came from Gussenstadt and Eva Katherine came from Kleineislingen. These villages still exist, with small populations, although Kleineislingen is now known as Eislingen; it is a suburb of Süssen, formerly called Gross Süssen. The prefix *Klein* ("little") is considered to be redundant for the suburb of the larger town of Süssen. These towns are east of Stuttgart, the capital city of the state of Baden-Württemberg, in the Federal Republic of Germany (*Bundesrepublik Deutschland*). Eislingen is about 16 miles east of Stuttgart, and Gussenstadt is another 8 miles further to the east – i.e., it is 24 miles east of Stuttgart. The road is poor, and the traveling time from Stuttgart to Gussenstadt is estimated by Google maps at 1 hr. 24 min.

### *Heimat*

When John and Eva left Germany to travel to the New World, they left behind more than their relatives and friends and their places of birth; they left their *Heimat*. This word, which has no exact counterpart in English, is sometimes translated as "homeland." The full meaning of *Heimat* includes a sense of place, or nostalgia: in English we would call this "homesickness." Some Europeans have a stronger attachment to their homeland than others, and the spectrum of bonding to a homeland ranges from the Germans (strong) to the international migrants known as Roma (weak).

    An intermediate sense of "homeland" exists in other countries. For instance, most of the immigrants to America from the British Isles left Britain with some reluctance but very few longed to return. The Puritans believed that it was in New England that they would achieve their destiny: to create a "city on the hill" that would be an example for the world. And the Spanish came to the New World believing that nothing could be worse than the area known as *Extremadura* in Spain that they left behind. The French and Dutch came to America planning to stay, and few looked back. In contrast to these peoples, who looked to the New World as a home, many Germans longed for their old homeland after they arrived in America; they were *Heimwehkrank* (home+place+sick).

    The sense of a home place or homeland varies from one part of the United States to another. It is especially strong in the south and west, and weakest in New England. It is seen in the titles of songs such as "My Old Kentucky Home," "Back Home in Indiana," and "Home on the Range." The concept of a regional home place is also present in countless other American songs, such as "Carry Me Back to Old Virginny," "Maryland, My Maryland," and "Georgia on My Mind." And it is there, unstated in other songs, such as "Dixie," "Red River Valley," and "The Yellow Rose of Texas"; in the haunting melody of "Shenandoah"; and in the regionally-oriented music of the "Tennessee Waltz" and "Missouri Waltz." The City of the Big Apple is recalled in "New York, New York," but those words have a message more of conquest than of reunion. And it is a self-inflicted joke in "I'm from Ioway." Of course, the heartache for a homeland is not limited to America. It is most poignantly associated with "Goin' Home," the song composed by William Arms Fisher in 1922 to accompany the Largo theme of Symphony No. 9 by Anton Dvorak; Fisher was a student of Dvorak's. The thought of a homeland also appears in many national anthems and nationally revered songs, such as Verdi's "Va pensiera," Sibelius's "Finlandia," "the Marseilles," "Danny Boy," "O Canada," and Tchaikovsky's "1812 Overture." Germany's "Deutchland Über Alles" has been unwelcome in many places since World War II, and only one verse is still official; perhaps "Lily Marlene" is a better song to remember. The United States has songs which honor a universal home place in the U.S.A., such as "America," "America the Beautiful," and "God Bless America." America also has the martial "Star Spangled Banner," a counterpart to Britain's "God Save the Queen," and the still-divisive "Battle Hymn of the Republic."

## Europe

In order to understand the *Heimat* of the Zimmermann and Kellenbenz families, we need to begin with the geography of Europe, and specifically that of Continental Europe. The continent of Europe is well-defined only on its north, west, and southern extremities; the eastern border is not as well defined. Europe extends from the Arctic Ocean to the Mediterranean Sea and it thus includes the British Isles, Scandinavia, the western portion of Russia, and many off-shore islands such as Malta and Sicily. The east border of the continent is generally defined as a line drawn through Russia from the Urals to the Caucasus Mountains, and thence to the Black Sea. But some say Europe is west of the Ural-Caucasus line, and instead it extends across Russia from the White Sea to the Black Sea. With either definition, the line which defines the south-eastern corner of Europe continues to Istanbul and out through the Bosphorus to the Mediterranean Sea.

## Continental Europe

The part of Europe which is known as Continental Europe is bordered on the west by the Atlantic; on the north by the English Channel, the North Sea and the Baltic Sea; and on the south by the Mediterranean Sea. On the east, Continental Europe extends into Russia, to the ill-defined border mentioned above. Many languages are spoken in Europe, including those derived from Latin (such as Italian, French, Spanish, and Portuguese); Germanic (including Germany, Austria, part of Switzerland, Holland, and part of Belgium); various forms of Slavic (from Poland to the Balkans); the Nordic tongues; Celtic; Hungarian-Estonian-Finnish; Basque; Greek and Macedonian; Turkish; and Arabic. There are stateless peoples, too: the Roma, whose territory extends from the Balkans to France; the so-called Travelers in Ireland and England; and recent immigrants from Africa and Asia. The Jewish people are a special case in Europe, as their diaspora continues. Ashkenazi Jews (originally Yiddish-speaking, from eastern and central Europe) and Sephardic Jews (from Spain, North Africa and the Middle East) were for generations assimilated into local populations. They were sometimes observant as Hebrews in their religious practices, although not always. Over the centuries many Jews, usually observant, were isolated into ghettos or were forcibly displaced – as in Spain in 1492, when Spain also expelled Muslims; or in the pogroms of Imperial Russia; and then by the Nazis and Fascists, and other countries such as Austria and Czechoslovakia that fell under Axis rule in World War II.

This list of European peoples and their languages is not complete, but it is intended to show the complexity of the origins of the people of this continent. Different lists of the European languages and language sub-groups are given by various authorities.

## Central Europe – Germany – the German language

Europe has many parts, and it has many countries. Caesar spoke in his *Commentaries* of the three parts of Gaul, the land of the Franks, as the Belgians, the Celts, and Aquitaine. There was also then the part of France known as Provence, which Caesar called (in Latin) "the Province," but this was at that time technically part of Rome itself. For Caesar, the people east of the Rhine, the Germans, were mysterious. Caesar wrote that the Germans were warlike, migratory hunters. He said that they had no use for agriculture and did not acquire land on which to build houses, although he did express a somewhat grudging admiration for them. Sometime after Caesar's time, German-speaking people gradually began to settle on the land on which they had roamed, east of the Rhine. They were first united as a people by Charlemagne in the 9th century.

German-speaking people have long occupied the part of Continental Europe which is known as Central Europe. They call their language *Deutsch*; in English, it is German. The part of Europe which they inhabit, their land, is thus known as *Deutschland* (Germany), although German is also the language of the adjacent country of Austria and part of Switzerland. The Germans are not of one ethnic group, although they all speak variations, dialects, of the same language. The present nation of Germany is bordered on the north by the North Sea and Baltic Sea; on the south by the Alps; and less precisely by rivers on the east and west. On the west, the major boundary is the Rhine River, although German dialects are also spoken for some distance on the west side of the Rhine. On the east, the Oder River is now the north-eastern border of Germany. Some three million German-speaking people lived east of the Oder River in the hilly country of the Sudeten Mountains (*Ost Sudentenland*) until after World War II. The country of Czechoslovakia was created east of the Oder after World War I from the Austro-Hungarian Empire; it is now the Czech Republic. The south-eastern border of Germany is now constituted by tributaries of the Danube River. The Danube flows from Germany into Austria, Hungary, and on through the Balkans into the Black Sea. The countries of Poland and the Czech Republic are to the east of Germany, each with their own language, and the German-speaking country of Austria, is to the south and east of the Federal Republic of Germany.

The German language has many dialects, including Dutch, which is spoken in lower Rhine valley; and Swabian, a language of the upper Rhine. The dialects in the lower Rhine valley are sometimes called "Low German." However, this term can be taken to mean either lowland or inferior, or both. The pejorative nature of the term is best avoided by simply calling it *Plattdeutsch*. The dialects known collectively as Swabian German, spoken in the highlands of Central Europe, are sometimes called *Hochdeutsch*. Many variations of Swabian German can be heard in the Swabian Alps of Germany (now Baden-Württemberg and Bavaria), and in the adjacent Alpine countries of Switzerland, and Austria. The accents, words, and idioms of residents of the Alps of Germany, Austria, and Switzerland are different from those who live in the northern parts of Germany. Furthermore, many of the words and idioms used in the Alps are not included in dictionaries of the German language. Standard dictionaries are not always helpful anyway, because German is not an easy language to learn and use. German has also been difficult to read, because well into the twentieth century the handwritten script was beautiful, but to an American, it seemed odd; and the fractur font in printed works in German added another layer of incomprehension. Even now, diacritical marks are jarring to the non-German reader; e.g., umlaut, to indicate how the letter should be pronounced, and a superscript line, such as ň, to indicate a doubled letter. The symbol ß (for "ss") is puzzling. German words are often compounded, and a single sentence can be a full paragraph in length. The typical terminal placement of the verb keeps the reader in suspense until the very end.[1]

The appellation *Hochdeutsch* should mean "high" (as in altitude). However, *Hochdeutsch* is also the term used to refer to "proper" (i.e., good) German, as in "Parisian" French or "Castillian" Spanish. Although some references still state that the Swabian dialect is *Hochdeutsch* because it is both "high" (in altitude) and "proper," most German speakers use the term *Hochdeutsch* only to mean the urban lingua franca of cities such as Berlin, Hamburg, and Freiburg; and also generally in northern Germany – in the states of Saxony, Hesse, and Prussia. There is yet one more twist to this confusing term: It is generally agreed that the written language known as *Hochdeutsch* (High German), in contrast to conversational "High German," is derived from the unifying influence of Luther's translation of the Bible. This would be the German equivalent of the King James Version of the Bible, which established the standard of speech in English for several centuries.

## German Culture

Although it is impossible to characterize perfectly all of the members of a family, much less that of an entire country, there seems to be a general agreement that Germans – that is to say, German-speakers and their descendants – are different in many ways from those who speak other languages. Perhaps it is because the Germans have long lived in what was once a densely forested land, between the Rhine and the Oder, and between the mountains of the Alps and the cold waters of the North Sea and the Baltic Sea. They are still conditioned by the Black Forest that still exists on the right bank of the upper Rhine.

Caesar attempted to characterize the Germans, and so will I, although it must be an oversimplification. But I will make the attempt, recalling that Garrison Keillor has found resonance when he tells us, with good humor, that people from Scandinavia and Germany came to [fictional] Lake Wobegon, Minnesota, where "all the women are strong, all the men are good looking, and all the children are above average."

At the time John Zimmermann and Eva Kellenbenz were children, the culture of Germany included, in varying degrees, the notions of strength, work, discipline, and duty. And also, the typical German would show determination and loyalty, unquestioning obedience, patience, and thrift. He was clean and neat, reticent and circumspect. All of his affairs would be in order. He would complete every task, on time, as assigned. The German would be close-mouthed; not a gossiper. The idea of hierarchy was accepted as normal, both in the home and in government. A man would be brave, calm in the face of danger, and stoic. He would be helpful, and sometimes even a bit friendly (but not often), never showing a "kind" face. No sense of humor or irony. Pain would be borne without emotion or a show of discomfort. He would be tidy, efficient, and inventive, but not "clever." His gaze would be unemotional, which might appear to be uncaring or cruel. And perhaps he was cruel at times, and no one would know it.

To rush or run about would imply a lack of preparation. Motion without purpose was frowned upon. Piety, honesty, and respect were common place; charity, too, albeit with some caution. Strangers were welcomed warily, but superstition abounded. And generosity knew its limits. Ostentation in dress or spending was deplored, and modesty was the rule for men and women, in all respects. A man might borrow something or ask to use a piece of land, but he would always offer something fair in exchange. It was unusual to try to borrow money in a village, because debt with interest (usury) would rarely be available. Criminal activity, such as theft, robbery, and assault, were rare. Crimes of passion were also rare, because Germans tend to be "cold-blooded" and thus free of passion. Drinking, especially of beer, was common; but drinking to excess was not. It was understood that these things happen occasionally to men, especially on Octoberfest and on the Tuesday night before Ash Wednesday, but drunken behavior was not acceptable for women. Sexual activity was only for procreation and not for pleasure, at least in public; and what we would call deviant sex was not tolerated. Men and women were faithful to their vows, even if their marriage was an unhappy one. Most first marriages were between young people, of the same social status, in the same village, and who went to the same church. A man and woman would never marry without permission of both families. If a husband or wife died, a second marriage was arranged, and it took place at the time ordained by church and custom.

--------------------

I have said nothing here about the intellectual culture of Germany and its historical development, because there is nothing to indicate that John and Eva were familiar with, much less conversant, such things. There is nothing in their later life that suggests that they had any knowledge or interest in the literature of Germany, or of the philosophy, science, medicine, music, fine art, and performance art of the country. John and Eva were young people in villages, where almost all the men were farmers, and the wives bore children and took care of their house. Their farmland was within walking distance of their homes – even though many of them also had an occupation or craft in the town. John and Eva probably had some elementary schooling, but neither of them had a higher education, at a *Gymnasium*, and they were still young when they left Germany.

I will therefore say nothing more about such matters, except to acknowledge the invaluable contributions that Germans have made to intellectual history. The intellectual, scientific, and artistic work of Germans and Austrians in the 18th and 19th centuries had an enormous positive impact on the rest of the world in those times, and it still resonates with us today. And at the same time, I will not offer here any foretelling of the future, because the future was unknown to John and Eva. However, I must acknowledge the prominent role that Germany took in two World Wars; of the sad state of Germany during the Weimar Republic; of the horror of Hitler's Third Reich and the Holocaust; of the forty-five years when Germany was divided into East and West; and of the Fall of the Berlin Wall in 1990 and re-union as the Federal Republic of Germany.

----------------------

In 1972, I saw an example of German behavior which was about the same as it would have been in 1874, when John Zimmermann left Gussenstadt to come to America. I was with a group of about a dozen men and women from the U.S. and Switzerland in the French Alps, with a Swiss guide. We were traveling the Haute Route on skis from Chamonix, at the foot of Mont Blanc in France, to Zermatt, at the base of the Matterhorn in Switzerland. It is 70km on a direct line from Chamonix to Zermatt, but the 6-day ski route, which passes in and out of Italy, is much longer than this. The route varies with snow conditions and the movement of crevasses, and there are overnight rest stops in high cabins every 10-15 miles. One morning, my group got off to a late start, so we had to wait for other parties to climb, single file, up the glacier to the first pass, on cross-country skis. Each group would usually wind back and forth across the width of the slope to avoid the crevasses. One group was from Switzerland, one from France, another perhaps from Italy, and one – which our guide suggested we watch closely – was from Germany. As he predicted, the Germans took special care to lace up their boots, wax their skis, and adjust their backpacks. They weren't hurrying, and they left later than the others. But they marched, on skis, straight up the glacier, crossing the crevasses by a method that was not obvious to us, and they were at the high pass before any of the other groups arrived. The Germans were efficient and oblivious to danger, and they won a race that no one else had thought to enter, in a way that should have been impossible.

## Swabia

Swabia (*Schwaben*) is the historical name of a large region in southwestern Germany which is now composed of the states (*Lands*) of Baden-Württemberg and Bavaria, east of the Rhine. The name Swabia is derived from a Germanic people, the Suebi, who lived in this area in the 3rd century. The name Swabia for the region first appeared in the 11th century. Swabia was one of the five duchies of the German kingdom (*Reich*), along with Saxony, Franconia, Bavaria, and Lorraine. Swabia was ruled by a succession of dukes until the last duke died in 1313. Swabia's borders varied over the centuries, as various rulers expanded the territory or lost control of parts of it. At one time or another Swabia also included parts of what are now Switzerland and Austria, and, west of the Rhine, the Palatinate and Alsace. In 1331, a league was formed by 22 Swabian free towns or imperial cities, including Ulm, to support the emperor Louis IV. The dukes of Württemberg became the leaders of the Swabian League in the 15th century. The Swabian League reached its height of power in 1488, when its territorial reach included Tirol, Mainz, Trier, Baden, Hesse, Bavaria, and Franconia. The League expired in 1534, as a result of political and religious differences in the Reformation. The legacy of Swabia is still evident in references to the mountainous country – the Swabian Alps (*Alb* or *Jura*) – and by the Swabian dialect of German, which is spoken in the high country of Central Europe. The heart of Swabia was the *Land* of Württemberg, from which John Zimmermann and Eva Kellenbenz immigrated to America.

## Württemberg

Württemberg is now part of the German state of Baden-Württemberg, which is bordered on the west by the Rhine River and France, on the south-west by the German state of Rhineland Palitanate, on the south by Lake Constance and Switzerland, on the east and north-east by Bavaria, and a small portion on the north by the state of Hessen. It is the third largest of the 16 states of the Federal Republic. Baden-Württemberg is known for the *Schwartzwald*, Black Forest, in the land of the Swabian *Alb*. Its highest point is at the mountain of Lemberg, on the divide between two great rivers of Europe, the Rhine and the Danube. The principal river of Baden-Württemberg, the Necktar, passes through the capital city of Stuttgart into the Rhine, and also from Baden-Württemberg, the Danube receives the tributary of the Iller River at Ulm. The economy of Baden-Württemberg is principally agricultural, with most of its area being cultivated. It is famous for its wines. The climate is good, rainfall is abundant, and the land is productive. There are also many forms of industry in the major cities, including the manufacture of fine instruments, chemicals, iron and steel; the automotive plants of Gottlieb Daimler and Hermann Benz were in Stuttgart. And there is still weaving: of linen, wool, and cotton in the towns east of Stuttgart, as it was in the early nineteenth century when the Zimmermann family began weaving in Gussenstadt.

Württemberg takes its name from the Count of Württemberg (also spelled Wirtemberg), who appeared near Stuttgart in about 1081.  His descendants increased the territorial reach of the House of Württemberg westward to the Rhine; and then by marriage, across the Rhine to a territory known as Montbéliard on the border of Alsace.  In 1495, Württemberg was recognized as a duchy, ruled by Eberhard the Bearded (1445-1496).  His successor, Ulrich I (1487-1550), who ruled as duke from 1503, expanded the duchy to the north-west, into the Palatinate.  Ulrich's extravagant spending led to heavy debts and the expulsion of Württemberg from the Swabian League.  The League sold Württemberg to the emperor Charles V in 1520.  Two years later, Charles transferred Württemberg to his brother, who later became the next emperor, Ferdinand I.  However, the imperial plan soon failed.  The onset of the Reformation in 1517 and a rebellion of the peasants in 1525 led to the extinction of the Swabian League in 1534.  In the same year, Ulrich returned in triumph to Württemberg.  He dissolved the monasteries, confiscated church lands, and invited Lutheran leaders to reform the church with Protestant doctrine.  Ulrich temporarily lost control of Württemberg during Charles V's war against the League of Schmalkalden, but he regained it again in 1547.  Ulrich's son Christopher (1515-1568), a Protestant, became duke in 1550.  This was the year in which Mattis Zimmermann, the first known in our family, is said to have been born in Heidenheim, Württemberg.

In 1806, when Frederick II (1754-1816) was ruler of Württemberg, the duchy of Württemberg became a kingdom, and his title became King Frederick I.  The kingdom of Württemberg became a state (*Land*) in the German Empire in 1871.  Württemberg thrived under Hermann von Mittnach, chief minister (1876-1900).  Württemberg obtained special rights in its obligations to the armed forces and it achieved a dramatic increase in its industries.  The new prosperity and opportunities for employment in the cities led to a decline in the previously high rate of emigration.

Württemberg became a parliamentary democracy in 1895.  The kingdom was dissolved after World War I and the Revolution of 1918, and the last king, William II (1848-1921) abdicated.  A republican constitution was enacted in 1919, and Württemberg became a member state in the Weimar Republic.  It suffered less than other parts of Germany from the economic disasters that followed, and which led to the rise of Hitler.  A *Reichsstatthalter* (lieutenant governor) was appointed in 1933 and the state became subordinate to the central government.  The *Landtag* (State Diet) was abolished in the following year.  The Third Reich was soon in total control.  When John Zimmermann's youngest son Albert visited Stuttgart in 1937, he found his relatives to be very cautious, even in their own home, when they spoke of the government.  On 9 August 1937, he furtively filmed Nazi troops from a second floor window of his cousin's home as they marched through Stuttgart with rifles on their shoulders.  Stuttgart was not unusual; the police were also vigilant in other cities, such as Wurtzburg, in Bavaria, where Zimmermann also took surreptitious movies of their activities.[2]

During the Nazi years, the entire Jewish population of Württemberg was deported, and few ever returned.[3]  It has been estimated that there were approximately 30,500 Jews in Baden-Württemberg before the war.  Approximately 8,500 were killed, and only 701 returned after the war.  Unfortunately, the records of concentration camps of Germany are not shown, listed by state, in the table of the U.S. Holocaust Museum.  However, in the alphabetical list of the concentration camps, I see no record of any large camp in Württemberg, although several small holding facilities were apparently established in Württemberg, and Ulm is shown as a feeder camp for Dachau.[4]  Concentration camps were, however, located elsewhere in Swabia: in Baden (now a part of the state of Baden-Württemberg) and in Bavaria (where the infamous Flossenberg concentration camp was located).  And there was also in Gomadingen, 60 miles south of Stuttgart, Grafeneck Castle, one of the largest of the facilities in Germany which the Nazis used for incarceration, sterilization, and killing of psychiatric patients and the mentally retarded.  It is believed that at least 10,500 mentally and physically disabled people, mainly from Bavaria and Baden-Württemberg, were killed, at Grafeneck Castle in 1940.  Most of them were asphyxiated with carbon monoxide.[5]

During the war, the major cities of Württemberg were heavily bombed, and their major buildings were destroyed.  Heavy fighting took place in some parts of the state, especially in Heilbronn-Crailsheim region.  A few cities were spared from destruction, such as Heidelberg, which was, ironically, a hotbed of Nazi activity.  Frieburg suffered from both an accidental bombing by the Germans and carpet bombing by the Allies.  The old city in the center of Stuttgart was destroyed, initially by bombs, and then as it was being taken by the French army in April 1945.  At the end of the war, Northern Württemberg was in the occupation zone of the United States, and the southern part of Württemberg and also the state of Baden were in the French Zone.  Many atrocities were attributed at the end of the war to the troops of France, who were notoriously poorly controlled.[6]  In 1952, the partition was ended and one state was created, known as Baden-Württemberg.  The cities were slowly rebuilt and the wartime destruction is now nearly invisible, although memorials remain.

In the 20th century, enormous economic and social problems were encountered by the members of the Zimmermann and Kellenbenz families who remained in Württemberg.  No close relatives in the Zimmermann family are known to have survived World War II.  Some of the Kellenbenz family did survive and were successful after the war.

## Central Württemberg
### Homeland of John Zimmermann and Eva Katherine Kellenbenz

**Stuttgart, the capital of Baden-Württemberg**

**Eislingen, home of the Kellenbenz family**

**Gussenstadt, home of the Zimmermann family**

Map data ©2016 GeoBasis-DE/BKG (©2009), Google    5 mi

# Great Seal of Baden-Württemberg

Lauchert_Flussterrassen_Schwäbische_Alb fm Wikipedia commons 1-22-16

**View of the Swabish Alps Countryside**

Lemberg-1899, from Wiki-images
**Lemberg, Highest Mountain the Swabish Alps**

Swabische Alb, fm Wikipedia
**Distant view of the Swabish Alps**

# Nektar River

Necktar_near_Heidelberg frm Wikipedia, no credit cited

**Nektar River, near Heidelberg a principal tributary of the Rhine**

Albert Zimmermann, from movie taken 9 August 1937

**Nektar River, near Stuttgart**

# Main River, Wurtzburg, Bavaria

Still shot from movie taken by Albert Zimmermann, August 1937

**The Old Bridge and Marienberg Fortress before World War II**

Wikipedia, Wurtzburg (accessed 6-17-16)

**The Old Bridge and Marienberg Fortress, Rebuilt After World War II**

**Ninety percent of Wurtzburg was destroyed by Allied bombs on 16 March 1945.
The battle for Wurtzburg continued until V-E day, 5 April 1945.
The Main River is the largest eastern tributary of the Rhine River**

# Albert Zimmermann's Photos
# Germany – August 1937

## Scenes Taken With a Hidden Movie Camera

**Nazi Troops Marching Through Stuttgart**
**Photographed from Kellenbenz Family's Second Floor Window**

**An Army Officer, in Black Uniform – Wurtzburg**
**A Policeman, Suddenly Aware That He is Being Photographed – Austria**

# Reminders of World War II, the Nazis, and the Third Reich – 1945

## In Bavaria and Czechoslovakia

**Top to Bottom:** *Ost Sudetenland* (Hitler Youth in the East), Epaulettes of 511st Regiment, Non-Commissioned Officer's Collar Tab, Hitler Youth's Silver Proficiency Badge

------------------

Items were brought back from Bavaria in June 1945 by Gerald L. Hill, American Red Cross Field Director, 97th Infantry Division, 303rd Regimental Combat Team

## Notes

[1] Mark Twain, "The Awful German Language" (*Donaudampschiffahrtsgesellschaftkapitan*) in *A Tramp Abroad* (1880). The full text of this amusing essay can be seen by searching for Twain German on the web. See: https://www.cs.utah.edu/~gback/awfgrmlg.html (accessed 2/11/16).

The German language is especially problematic in countries that were occupied in World War II. For example, it is a common expression for many of us to say *Gesundheit* (God bless you) to someone after a sneeze, but I have found that this is not a good thing to say to a person in the Netherlands who survived World War II. And I learned in 1982 in northern Norway, near Narvik, where the German occupation had been very harsh, the German language was still unacceptable to older people.

[2] Barbara S. Zimmermann, *Mutterings* (Wynnewood, Pa.: Livingston Publishing Co., 1969), 134-5. Her husband, Albert Zimmermann, took movies as they traveled from Great Britain to Holland, Germany, Austria, Switzerland, Italy, and France. In contrast to Germany and Austria, where the movies were brief and were obviously taken cautiously, the movies in the other countries of Europe were longer and taken openly. Six stills made from DVDs of the movies appear in the photo section of this chapter. Albert Zimmermann was probably already working undercover as an intelligence agent. In 1932, he photographed for the FBI some of the participants in a wedding in Philadelphia in German Bund uniforms, saluting, with swastikas on their armbands. From 1942-1945, he was a Naval Intelligence Officer in the U.S. and India. He reached the rank of lieutenant commander at the time he resigned his commission. See George J. Hill, *Proceed to Peshawar: The Story of a U.S. Navy Intelligence Mission on the Afghan Border, 1943* (Annapolis: Naval Institute Press, 2013).

[3] "STUTTGART, Germany (May 17 [1960]) A total of 8,500 of the 30,491 Jews living in this south-German Province of Baden-Württemberg, at the time of Hitler's ascent to power, were exterminated by the Nazis, figures compiled here by the Evangelical Aid Society revealed today. About 21,500 of the Baden- Württemberg Jews succeeded in escaping from Hitlerite Germany, the survey showed. After the collapse of the Nazi regime, in 1945, 701 Jews returned to the province from concentration camps." From http://www.jta.org/1960/05/18/archive/8500-jews-of-baden-wurttemberg-annihilated-by-nazis-survey-shows (accessed 2/1/16).

[4] The ten main concentration camps are shown, each with its list of sub-camps, at: https://www.jewishvirtuallibrary.org/jsource/Holocaust/cclist.html (accessed 2/11/16). None of the 10 major camps are in Baden-Württemberg. One of the camps, Thierenstadt, is actually now in the Czech Republic. The other main camps are Dachau and Flossenberg (Bavaria), Bergen-Belsen (Lower Saxony), Buchenwald and Dora-Millenbau (Thuringia), Orienburg and Ravensbruck (Brandenburg), Neuengamme (Hamburg), and Sachenshausen (Hessen).

[5] "The Grafeneck Euthanasia Centre (German: *NS-Tötungsanstalt Grafeneck*) housed in Grafeneck Castle was one of Nazi Germany's killing centres as part of their forced euthanasia programme. Today, it is a memorial site dedicated to the victims of the state-authorised programme also referred to since as Action T4. At least 10,500 mentally and physically disabled people, predominantly from Bavaria and Baden-Württemberg, were systematically killed during 1940. It was one of the first places in Nazi Germany where people were killed in large numbers in a gas chamber using carbon monoxide. This was actually the beginning of the Euthanasia Programme. Grafeneck is a castle-like property in Grafeneck, a part of the city of Gomadingen in Baden-Württemberg. Built around 1560, the Grafeneck Castle served as a hunting lodge to the dukes of Württemberg. In the 19th Century, it was used as the Forest Service and in 1928 the Samaritan Foundation acquired it, setting up a handicapped home. In 1929, the charitable non-profit organisation *Samariterstiftung* established an asylum for disabled people. At the beginning of World War II in 1939, the building was confiscated by the Nazis. The killings with gas were performed between January and December 1940. Afterwards, it was used to house children and mothers with babies who had fled from the bombing of the cities. Grafeneck Castle served as a killing center - the Nazi *Euthansasieaktion* (later Action T4) killed 10,654 disabled and sick people through lethal injections and gas. They were transported mainly from southern Germany and burned on site in a crematorium. The French occupying forces returned the site in 1946/47 to the Samaritan Foundation or *Samariterstiftung*, who re-established it as a centre for disabled and mentally ill people which still operates to this day. In the fifties, the development of the cemetery began as a memorial. In 2005, the documentation center Grafeneck Memorial was finally built. https://www.google.com/search?newwindow=1&espv=2&rlz=1C1ARAB_enUS454US552&q=grafeneck+killing+center&oq=Grafeneck+c&gs_l=serp.1.2.0j0i22i30l9.19392.21227.0.26111.5.5.0.0.0.0.128.483.3j2.5.0....0...1c.1.64.serp..0.5.481.P4L6WAvUs9M (accessed 2/1/16).

[6] From http://www.tracesofevil.com/ [anonymous] and go to: http://www.tracesofevil.com/2007/04/various-sites-in-germany-contd.html (accessed 2/1/16):

"The Allied ground advance into Germany reached Stuttgart in April 1945. Although the attack on the city was to be conducted by the US Seventh Army's 100th Infantry Division, General DeGaulle found this to be unacceptable, as he felt the capture of the region by Free French forces would increase French influence in post-war decisions. He **treacherously** directed General de Lattre to order the French 5th Armoured Division, 2nd Moroccan Infantry Division, and 3rd Algerian Infantry Division to begin their drive on Stuttgart on 18 April 1945. Two days later, the French forces coordinated with the US Seventh Army for the employment of US VI Corps heavy artillery to barrage the city. The French 5th Armoured Division then captured Stuttgart on 21 April 1945, encountering little resistance. The circumstances of what became known as the 'Stuttgart Crisis' provoked political repercussions up to the White House. **President Truman** was unable to get **DeGaulle** to withdraw troops from Stuttgart . . . The French army occupied Stuttgart until the city was transferred to the American military occupation zone in 1946." [my emphasis]

"When French troops occupied Stuttgart – which was meant to form part of the American Zone as the capital of Württemberg – the Americans ordered them to leave. DeGaulle refused, saying he would stay put until the zones were finalized. . . . The American solution was to offer them some bits of Baden and Württemberg . . . French soldiers' behaviour in Stuttgart, where perhaps 3,000 women and eight men were raped, was thought to have added to American fury at their overstepping their lines. [R. F. Keeling (*Gruesome Harvest*, Chicago, 1947, 56-7) gives the official figure as 1,298, but the Germans thought it more like 5,000.]. MacDonogh, *After the Reich: The Brutal History of the Allied Occupation*."

"The French took a terrible toll in their zone, by forced seizure of food and housing, and by physical violence including mass rapes, in Stuttgart and elsewhere. . . . The official ration in the French zone in January 1947 was 450 calories per day, half the ration of the Belsen concentration camp. James Bacque (94), *Crimes and Mercies*."

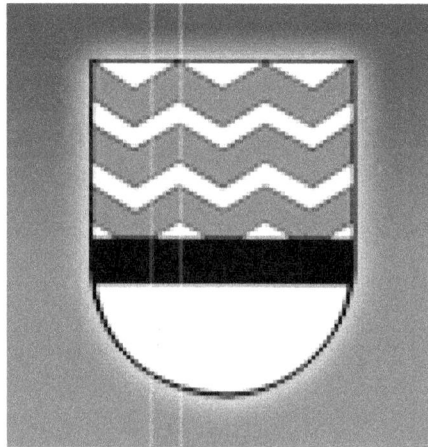

www.wappen-suessen

**Crest of the City
Süssen, Baden-Württemberg**

# 1

## The Zimmermann Family

Zimmermann is one of the more common family names in Germany. The surname Zimmermann is derived from the occupation of carpenter, or wood-worker, although the literal translation of the word *Zimmer* is room, and the word *Zimmermann* in German might therefore appear to be "room-man." Our Zimmermann Family first appeared in the seventeenth century, or perhaps in the late sixteenth century, in the district (*kreis*) of Heidenheim, in the Duchy of Württemberg, now in the German state of Baden-Württemberg.[1] Our branch of this Zimmermann family later moved to Gussenstadt, a village in the district of Heidenheim, Württemberg, and from there to America. This Zimmermann family has been traced by an anonymous German genealogist in Gussenstadt to one Herr Jakob Zimmermann, a saddler, of Heidenheim. Two additional earlier generations can be seen in several other genealogies, and for the sake of completeness, they will be included here.[2]

I believe there are more discoveries yet to be made about the Zimmermanns and their collateral relatives in Germany. The Zimmermann Family Chart, summarized in the Notes to this chapter, shows the line from Jakob Zimmermann down to the immigrants to America, but it does not include anything about the families of the women who married into this Zimmermann family. Ancestry.com shows several generations of the ancestors of Anna Walter, who married Herr Jacob Zimmermann's son. There are no proofs cited for the families on Ancestry.com, but it does suggest that there is something else that can be investigated and possibly proved. I believe there must be records in Heidenheim and Gussenstadt that would show the ancestry of some of the other women who married Zimmermanns. For instance, Anna Ursula Jäger (1820-1901), who married John Zimmermann, is one of them; the family name of Jäger has continued in Gussenstadt into the 21st century. And we can look for the ancestors of Appolonia Bühner (1745-1776), who married Sigmund Christoph Zimmermann, because Ancestry.com shows that there are other contemporaneous Bühner surnames in Gussenstandt. We also may find the Sattler family, ancestors of Margarete Sattler (1701-1768), who married Georg Christopher Zimmermann on 25 January 1735, because others named Sattler were in Gussenstadt at that time. And perhaps also Maria Barth, of Lauterberg (~1684-1714), who married John Michael Zimmermann. There is nothing in the Zimmermann records about the Barth family, and nothing about her family in Ancestry.com, but it is unlikely that her family is from any place except Lauterberg, where she married John Michael Zimmermann.

**1. MATTIS**[J] **ZIMMERMANN**,[3] first of the Zimmermann family in Württemberg, is said to have been born at Steinheim am Albuch, in the district (*Kreis*) of Heidenheim, Württemberg, in 1550. The small town of Steinheim am Albuch now has a population of about 9,000 people and is located 11 km. west of the district capital of Heidenheim. It is notable for a meteorite crater.

In 1550, the year that Mattis Zimmermann was born, was also the year in which the powerful Ulrich I, duke of Württemberg, died. He was succeeded by his son, Christopher (1515-68), a Protestant. This was a time of great unrest in Württemberg. It was stimulated by the Reformation, which began with Martin Luther's posting of Ninety-Five Theses on the door of the Castle Church in Wittenberg [not a cognate of Württemberg], Saxony, on 31 October 1517. The so-called Peasant Rebellion followed in 1524-5. And only five years after Duke Ulrich died and Mattis Zimmermann was born in 1550, the Council of Trent (1545-1563) was convened, and thus began the Counter Reformation. Under Duke Christopher, Württemberg, however, remained staunchly Protestant.

By a wife, whose name is unknown, Matthias Zimmermann had a son:

    **2**    i.      ADAM[I] (1578-1662) +

**2. ADAM[I] ZIMMERMANN,**[4] son of Mattis Zimmermann, is said to have been born at Steinheim am Albuch, Heidenheim, Württemberg, in 1578; died at Heidenheim, 20 March 1662. He married at Heidenheim, 16 February 1608, **Catharina BOLLINGER**, daughter of Hans Bollinger and Walburga Jelin; born at Heidenheim, December 1587; died there, 16 November 1668. They were doubtless Protestants, as have been their descendants. The ruler of Württemberg during his lifetime was the "insignificant" Louis, died 1593, succeeded as duke by "the gifted" Frederick, who died in 1608, and Eberhard III, duke from 1628 to 1674. Frederick obtained the release of Württemberg from subordination to Austria by the Treaty of Prague in 1599, and allied Württemberg with the Lutheran princes in the Evangelical Union of 1608. Self-government reached the local districts, towns, and villages during his reign. The disastrous Thirty-Years war (1618-1648) occurred during Adam Zimmermann's lifetime, and it is somewhat of a miracle that he survived. It is estimated that the population of Württemberg was reduced to one-third of what it had been at the beginning of the war.[1] Eberhard III fled temporarily to Strassbourg, but returned with the Peace of Westphalia, which ended the war.

        Adam and Catharina (Bollinger) Zimmermann had the following children, born at Heidenheim, surname Zimmermann:

           i.      MATTHAEUS[H], b. 4 Dec 1608.
          ii.     WALBURGA, b. 29 Dec 1609.
         iii.    SARA, b. 19 Jan 1611.
  **3**    iv.    Herr JAKOB (1614-) +
          v.     ANNA CATHARINA, b. 5 Feb 1617.
         vi.    MARTHA, b. 24 Feb 1619; d. 4 Mar 1620.
        vii.   MARTHA, b. 27 Nov 1621.
      viii.   ADAM, b. 15 Aug 1622; d. 20 Mar 1662.

**3. Herr JAKOB[H] ZIMMERMANN,**[5] a saddler, son of Adam and Catharina (Bollinger) Zimmermann, was born at Heidenheim, Württemberg, 16 July 1614. Jakob's family must have been relatively prosperous, for he had a good occupation and was known by the honorific of "Herr." The Thirty-Years War (1618-1648), the longest war in European history, had a terrible effect on the Duchy of Württemberg during his lifetime. It undoubtedly had a serious impact on the Zimmermann family, though the record fails to show what that might have been. Recovery was said to be slow. The Zimmermanns were a Protestant family at that time, and the Zimmermanns in Europe continued to be Lutherans thereafter.

He married **Appolonia _____**, born in 1620, whose ancestry is unknown.

        Jakob and Appolonia Zimmermann had the following children, born at Heidenheim, Württemberg, surname Zimmermann:

           i.      ANNA CATHARINA[G], b. 27 Nov 1640.
  **4**    ii.     JOHANN (aka Albert) JAKOB (1642-1729) +
         iii.    ANNA MARIA, b. 1 Dec 1643.
         iv.    HANS JACOB, b. 7 Aug 1646; prob. d. bef 1647.

---

[1] *Encyclopedia Brittanica, Macropedia*, 20:177, says the population of Württemberg was 450,000 in 1618 and 166,000 in 1648.

v.    HANS JACOB, b. 5 Sep 1647.
vi.   WALBURGA, b. 5 Nov 1652; prob. d. bef. 1657.
vii.  WALBURGA, b. 21 Dec 1657.

**4. Bürgurmeister JOHANN JAKOB^G ZIMMERMANN,**[6] saddler, son of Herr Jakob Zimmerman and his wife Appolina, was born at Heidenheim, Württemberg, 7 September 1642; died there, 27 November 1729. He became *Bürgurmeister* (mayor) of Heubach, district of Ostalbkreis, Württemberg, about 15 miles from Heidenheim. The Thirty-Years War was not yet ended when he was born, and in his lifetime, after the end of the war in 1648, Württemberg underwent a slow recovery. From 1688 to 1693, during the War of the Grand Alliance, the country was invaded by the French and had to pay heavily for this. Under Duke Eberhard Louis, who came of age to rule in Württemberg in 1693, the country's defenses and schools were modernized. Johann Jakob Zimmermann surely had an education in a primary school, for this had been made compulsory in 1649. Eberhard Louis granted asylum to the Waldesians in 1699 when they were expelled from France. They brought new industries to Württemberg, including the weaving of textiles from wool and flax, which would later become the occupation for several generations of the Zimmermann family.

He married, 30 July 1677, at Heubach, **Anna WALTER,**[7] daughter of Hans and Barbara (Nördlinger) Walter, of Heubach; born at Heubach, 8 September 1659; died 31 March 1749. Johann Jakob and Anna (Walter) Zimmermann had the following children, born at Heidenheim or Heubach, surname Zimmermann:

5     i.    JOHANN MICHAEL^F (1679-1726) +
      ii.   AGNES, b. 1680.
6     iii.  JOHANN JACOB,[8] b. 30 Mar 1684, Heubach; d. 1 Feb 1754; lived in Heubach; m. 14 Feb 1708, **Anna Maria WIDRUSSEN**; b. 28 Mar 1687; d. 1758; 15 ch.[9]
      iv.   MARIA BARBARA, b. 29 Dec 1688.
      v.    JOHANN GEORG, b. 29 Feb 1696.
      vi.   AGNES, b. 1680.

**5. JOHANN MICHAEL^F ZIMMERMANN,**[10] a baker, son of Johann Jakob Zimmermann and Anna Walter, was born at Heidenheim, Württemberg, Germany, 22 June 1679; died 18 December 1726, probably at Lauterburg, near Heidenheim. He was a baker in Lauterburg.

During his lifetime, Württemberg was ruled by Eberhard Louis as duke until 1733, and then, briefly, by his son Charles Alexander (died 1737). The latter was a Catholic, although he promised to allow his subjects to be Protestant. His efforts to promote Catholicism were opposed by the people, and failed.

Johann Michael Zimmermann married **Maria BARTH**[11]; born in say 1684; died 26 September 1714.

Johann Michael and Maria (Barth) Zimmermann had a child:
7     i.    GEORG CHRISTOPH^E (1714-1779) +

**7. GEORG CHRISTOPH^E ZIMMERMANN,**[12] a butcher, son of Johann Michael Zimmermann and Maria Barth, was born at Lauterburg, Württemberg, Germany, 1 May 1714; died 4 March 1779 at Gussenstadt, Württemberg, Germany. He was a butcher in Gussenstadt, the first of the Zimmermann family to be recorded in that town, which was near Lauterburg and Heidenheim. He came of age during the rule of Eberhard Louis and his son Charles Alexander. After the latter died in 1737, when George Christoph Zimmermann was 23, Württemberg was ruled by Charles Alexander's son Charles Eugene (1728-93), who was proclaimed of age to rule in 1744. The early years of his reign were troubled, for he led Württemberg into the Seven Years' War on the side of the French, and lost to Prussia. After 1770, however, his rule was "tranquil."

Georg Christoph Zimmermann married, 25 January 1735, at Gussenstadt, **Margareta SATTLER**[13]; born at Gussenstadt, 4 July 1701; died there, 22 February 1768.

Georg Christoph and Margareta (Sattler) Zimmermann had the following children, born at Gussenstadt, Württemberg, surname Zimmermann:

|   |      |                                                                                                     |
|---|------|-----------------------------------------------------------------------------------------------------|
|   | i.   | CHRISTOPH[D], b. 10 Oct 1735; d. 5 Jan 1736.                                                         |
| 9 | ii.  | ANNA MARIA, b. 10 Nov 1736; d. 10 Jul 1794; m. (1) **Joseph KRÖNER**, b. ca. 1734; m. (2) **Marx STÖCKLE**; m. (3) **Johann Michael GIEGNER**; b. 8 Nov 1732; d. 16 Mar 1800; 1 ch.[14] |
|   | iii. | CHRISTOPH, b. 18 Jun 1738; d. 3 Jul 1738.                                                            |
| 10 | iv. | JOHANN GEORG, b. 30 Aug 1739; d. 7 Nov 1796; a butcher; m. 14 Sep 1763, **Ursula KÖPF**, b. 1 Jul 1736; d. 25 Jun 1817; perhaps 10 ch.[15] |
|   | v.   | CHRISTOPH, b. 19 Mar 1741.                                                                           |
| 11 | vi. | SIGMUND CHRISTOPH[16] (1744-1797) +                                                                  |

**11. SIGMUND CHRISTOPH[D] ZIMMERMANN**,[17] a butcher, son of Georg Christoph and Margareta (Sattler) Zimmermann, butcher of Gussenstadt, Wurttemberg, was born, probably at Gussenstadt, 22 December 1744; died 30 October 1797, probably at Gussenstadt.

He lived during the period when Württemberg was ruled by a succession of dukes. Charles Eugene (1728-1793) brought the Enlightenment to Württemberg, encouraging manufacturing and the arts and science. He founded the *Hohe Karlsscchule*, the "most modern university of his time." This university was abandoned by his brother and successor Louis Eugene, who died only two years later, in 1795. He and his successor, Frederick Eugene, took the Austrian side in the French Revolutionary War, but the latter was forced to make peace with the French in 1796, and died the next year – as did Sigmund Christoph Zimmermann.

Sigmund Christoph Zimmermann married three times and had 13 children, all but two or three of whom died young. He married (1) **Appolonia BÜHNER**, perhaps daughter of Christoph Bühner; born 25 May 1745; died 29 March 1776. He married (2) **Anna Catherine SEIBOLD**; born 12 March 1749; died 25 January 1790. He married (3) **Barbara REHM**; born 3 March 1757; died 13 September 1797.

Sigmund Christoph and Appolonia (Bühner) Zimmermann had the following children, surname Zimmermann, only two of whom lived to adulthood:

|    |      |                                                                                                   |
|----|------|---------------------------------------------------------------------------------------------------|
| 17 | i.   | JOHANN GEORG[C] (1768-1835) +                                                                      |
|    | ii.  | CHRISTOPH,[18] b. 17 May 1770; d. 1845; day laborer in Heuchstetten; m. 31 Jul 1793 **Appolonia BÜHNER**,[19] daughter of Christop Bühner, b. 1771; d. 1829.[20] |
|    | iii. | ELISABETHA MARGARETHE, b. 1 Nov 1772; d. 12 May 1773.                                              |
|    | iv.  | MELCHIOR, b. 23 Jul 1774; d. 18 Dec 1777.                                                          |

Sigmund Christoph and Anna Catherina (Siebold) Zimmermann had the following children, surname Zimmermann, only one of who may have lived to adulthood:

|      |                                              |
|------|----------------------------------------------|
| i.   | LUDWIG, b. 9 Dec 1777; d. 20 Feb 1778.       |
| ii.  | ANNA MARGARETHE, b. 17 Jan 1779.             |
| iii. | ANNA REGINA, b. 27 Jun 1784; d. 20 Feb 1834. |
| iv.  | JAKOB, b. 18 Sep 1786; d. 14 Jan 1790.       |
| v.   | LUDWIG, b. 10 Jan 1790; d. 15 Feb 1790.      |

Sigmund Christoph and Barbara (Rehm) Zimmermann had the following children, surname Zimmermann, all of whom died within less than two months of age:

    i.       SIGMUND FRIEDRICH, b. 4 Jul 1791; d. 27 Aug 1791.
    ii.      JAKOB, b. 24 Aug 1792; d. 7 Sep 1792.
    iii.    ANNA MARIA, b. 5 Aug 1793; d. 20 Sep 1793.
    iv.   SIGMUND FRIEDRICH, b. 17 Sep 1794; d. 28 Oct 1794.

**17. JOHANN GEORG**[C] **ZIMMERMANN**, a day laborer, son of Sigmund Christoph and Appolonia (Bühner) Zimmermann, was born 11 December 1768; died 9 May 1835. His father was a butcher, whose father was also a butcher in Gussenstadt, and his son was a textile-weaver in Gussenstadt, so it is very likely that he was born and died in Gussenstadt. Why he was not more successful is unknown, but the Zimmermann family was prominent enough to enable his descendants to enjoy some success in Gussenstadt, and later even more success in America.

It was noted previously that he was born during the reign of Charles Eugene, duke of Württemberg (1728-93), and during his lifetime Württemberg was also ruled briefly by two of Charles Eugene's successors. Frederick II (1754-1816) ruled as duke, then elector, and finally as Frederick I, the first king of Württemberg, from 1806. As a laborer, it is unlikely that these changes of rulers made much of a difference in Johann Georg Zimmermann's life. However, Württemberg thrived as Frederick I moved up in the hierarchy of Europe. The kingdom was enlarged to twice the size that it had been as a duchy. Frederick was succeeded in 1816 by his son William I (1781-1864), who ruled during the last twenty years of Johann Georg Zimmermann's life. Württemberg was at peace for all of this time, although William I had problems with the German Confederation and with the two Chambers of the parliament of Württemberg. In 1822, the parliament and King William I granted significant authority to the communes, which may have had a positive impact on the ordinary people in villages. Johann Georg Zimmermann had a son, surname Zimmermann:

  **22**      i.      JACOB[B] (1801-1864) +

**22. JACOB**[B] **(or JAKOB) ZIMMERMANN**,[21] weaver, son of Johann Georg Zimmermann, was born 9 January 1801, probably at Gussenstadt, Duchy of Württemberg; died, probably at Gussenstadt, Kingdom of Württemberg, 16 June 1864. The Duchy of Württemberg became a Kingdom in 1806, and Frederick II, the duke, became King Frederick I. In 1813, after Napoleon was defeated in the Battle of Leipzig, Frederick joined the Allies against him. The Treaty of Fulda guaranteed his kingdom. But Frederick had problems with his foreign allies and his parliament, and the peace in Württemberg was disturbed. Conflict continued with Frederick's son William I (1781-1864), who ascended the throne in 1816. The conflict was resolved, at least in part, when William agreed to an edict in 1822 which granted more authority to the communes. In mid-century, Europe erupted into rebellion. During the revolution of 1848, William allowed a liberal ministry to take office in Württemberg, although he did not personally endorse a political reorganization of Germany. The revolution failed, although Württemberg continued to advance as a nation-state. In 1845, the first railway entered Württemberg. The king died in the same year that his subject, Jacob Zimmermann, died.

Jacob Zimmermann had a weaving shop in one room, adjacent to his house in the small village of Gussenstadt, near Heidenheim, in the *Kreis* (district) of Heidenheim. His family was recorded for six generations in this part of Württemberg, and they had probably lived there for much longer than that. He established the family business of textile weaving. This profession was followed by his descendants for three additional generations in Germany and Pennsylvania.

Jacob Zimmermann had, with a wife whose name is unknown, at least two sons, born in Gussenstadt, surname Zimmermann:

**24** i. JOHN[A] (Johannes) (1821-1899) +

**25** ii. JOHANN GEORG,[22] b. 3 Nov 1842; d., prob in Elmira, N.Y.; weaver, then a farmer in Elmira; came to America in 1874 or 1875, with his family; m. at Gussenstadt, 14 Aug 1864, **Margareta BANTZHAFF**, b. 26 Jun 1841; sister of Michael Bantzhaff (b. 1845), who m. Maria Schwartz (b.1852), sister of Jacob Schwartz (b. 1854), a law student in Elmira, NY, in 1872; it was through the Bantzhaff-Schwartz connection that 25. Johann Georg Zimmermann's nephew, **John Zimmermann**, b.1855 (See #28 below, and Part II of this book), came to Elmira from Germany in 1874; Johann Georg and Margareta (Bantzhaff) Zimmermann had 9 ch.[23]

## 24. JOHN[A] (aka JOHANNES) ZIMMERMANN,[24] weaver, son of Jacob Zimmermann, was born at Gussenstadt, district (*Kreis*) of Heidenheim, state (*Land*) of Württemberg, 24 September 1821; died there, 25 July 1899. He and his brother Johann Georg wove textiles in a one-room shop adjacent to the family house in Gussenstadt which he inherited from his father.

During his long life – nearly 78 years – enormous changes occurred in Württemberg, although many of these events probably had little impact on those living in small towns such as Gussenstadt. There was ferment during the abortive revolution of 1848, when the people clamored for more power. This revolution was relatively bloodless, in contrast to previous periods of strife in Central Europe. The rise of Germany, led by Prussia, in the last half of the century was more of a problem. King William I died in 1864 and was succeeded by his son Charles (1823-1891), who was almost the same age as John Zimmermann. In 1866, Charles, with the support of the people, sided with Württemberg's neighbor, Austria, in its battle with Prussia in the Seven Weeks' War. The swift victory by Prussia was costly to Württemberg, which was forced to pay an indemnity of 8,000,000 gulden. Württemberg then joined Prussia in its successful war against France, and it became a member of the new German Empire in 1871. In the decade of the 1870s, after seeing two wars in less than a decade, many people wondered what the future would hold. Perhaps more wars. Young men have often been drawn or forced into the military, and to battle.

By 1871, Johannes Zimmermann was fifty, and too old to be a soldier. War would not affect him personally unless it came to Gussenstadt. His sons, however, were of an age to be called to service, and they could be to be sent to war at the behest of authorities in Berlin. Each would make his own decision about the future, and they chose to come to America.

John (aka Johannes) Zimmermann married, in say 1850, **Anna Ursula JÄGER**; born 12 September 1820; died at Gussenstadt, 11 January 1901.

Johannes and Anna Ursula (Yäger) Zimmermann had the following children, born at Gussenstadt, surname Zimmermann:

**27** i. JOHANN GEORG[1] (see below).

**28** ii. JOHN[1] (Johannes) (1855-1936) + (See Part II)

  iii. ANNA,[25] b. 2 Jun 1860; died, unmarried, in Uhingen, district of Göppingen, Württemberg, Germany, after 1937; came to the U.S. for a visit; on 1 Jul 1926, she departed from Bremen on SS *Columbus* to Philadelphia, where she lived at 529 Rockland St.; bef 1937, she returned to Uhingen on the Fils River, 37 km W of Gussenstadt.

# John (Johannes) Zimmermann (1821-1899) and His Wife, Anna Ursula Jäger (1820-1901)

Photos are undated, original source unknown, to GJH from Jean Hoxie Naples, courtesy of Katharine (Fligg) Lee

Anna Zimmermann's nephew, Albert Walter[2] Zimmermann, and his wife Barbara (née Shoemaker), visited Anna in 1937 at her home in Uhingen, about 35km east of Stuttgart. Uhingen was about half way, on the same road, that led from Stuttgart to her birthplace in Gussenstadt. Barbara (Shoemaker) Zimmermann wrote about seeing Anna and also their visit to Gussenstadt, in her memoir, *Mutterings*, published in 1969[26]:

> Monday [9 August 1937] – Stuttgart – . . . We had dinner with Al's cousin[2] who speaks very little English. I have accused Al, who claims to speak German, of talking baby talk as he learned it as a baby. No one seemed to understand him at first but he's improving and even I can understand a good deal, a relic of the Illg regime in our household. This [Kellenbenz] cousin is very much opposed to Hitler although she wouldn't talk until we took her up to our room and then in decided undertones.
>
> Tuesday we hired a car and . . . started out for the birthplaces of Al's parents. We found the town but not the house. It was a sweet little town. From there we went up into the Swabian Alps, very beautiful country and after going up for miles we found ourselves on a broad plateau, above all the surrounding mountains, so that not even a peak was visible, a very odd sensation after driving up steep mountains for two or three hours. Here is Gussenstadt where Mr. Zimmermann was born eighty years before and where he started a factory, more than sixty years ago. The original factory is still there and being used, a tiny house with one large factory room attached. This little town has not changed, I'm sure, in those sixty years. It cannot be reached by train and has very little connection or communication with the rest of the world. It is very picturesque, and so sweet and peaceful, I wondered how Mr. Z. had the breadth of vision to leave it, altho' in technical schools (our engineering school) I guess he heard that there were other places. We were a curiosity as a great many people remembered the family even tho' there are none there now. We visited the little cemetery and saw the graves of Al's grandparents[3], date 1820 and 1821! We did stop on the way back to see an aunt, Mr. Z's sister, a nice little old lady (nearly eighty) who lives very happily with a companion maid of many years, in quite a cunning little cottage. Aunt Anna[4] is a great Hitlerite, having lost everything during inflation, and now sitting pretty due to the Nazi regime.

**27. JOHANN GEORG[1] ZIMMERMANN**,[27] "designer" and weaver, eldest of the three children of Johannes and Anna Ursula (Yäger) Zimmermann, was born at Gussenstadt, Württemberg, 5 June 1851; christened 6 June 1851; died, probably in Philadelphia, Penna., between 1920 and 1926. He was the older brother of **28. John Zimmermann**, who married Eva Katherine Kellenbenz; they are the principal subjects of this book. (See Part II)

Johann Georg Zimmermann arrived in the U.S. at age 30, in 1881, recorded in the 1910 census. In the 1881 Philadelphia City Directory, his residence is shown at 2259 Amber, and in 1889 he is shown at 316 Huntington. He married, probably in Philadelphia, in 1882, **Maria ___**, born in Pennsylvania, June 1856, to parents who were born in Germany and immigrated to America before she was born (according to the 1900 census); died in Philadelphia, Pa., probably between 1900 (in the census) and 1910, when her husband was shown as a "widower."

He was initially in business with his younger brother, but returned to Germany with his wife and two children (Anna, age 3, and John, age 2) and was in Germany in June 1888, where

---

[2] She is probably Eugenia (Kellenbenz) Bollacher (see Kellenbenz Family).
[3] John[A] (Johannes) Zimmermann (1821-1899) and Anna Ursula Jäger (1820-1901).
[4] Anna Zimmermann (b. 2 June 1860, Gussenstadt) was the sister of AWZ's father, John[1] Zimmermann (b. 1855).

his third child, George, was born. He must have returned by 1889. His younger brother, John, was in business in 1890 with Archibald Cameron, as Cameron & Zimmerman (one "n" was usually used by the younger brother from time onward). In 1893, John Georg Zimmermann was in Arkansas, where his last child, Walter, was born in August 1893. Johann Georg Zimmermann had returned to Philadelphia by 1900, where he rented a house at 2817 Lawrence St. He lived there with his wife, and his children Anna (15, milliner), John, George, Walter.

On 5 November 1904, he filed a patent for improvements in "Loom for Weaving, Double-Pile Fabric." In 1905, he began manufacturing at Fairhill & Rockland St (5th-6th W. Rockland), to make upholstery goods; and in November and December he filed patents for "Woven Pile Fabric" and a "Loom for Weaving Double-Pile Fabrics." His name was always spelled with two "n's", although in 1905, his brother John's patents spelled his name Zimmerman, with one "n", and that is also how John signed his name. Johann Georg Zimmermann was granted patents in 1907 and 1908 (for "Woven Pile Fabric"). He is shown in the 1910 census as a widower, living at 529 Rockland St., with children Anna; John, designer, textile work; George, foreman, textile mill; and Walter. He was the "brother George," who was mentioned in the obituary of John Zimmerman, who died in 1936.

In 1882 when Johann Georg Zimmermann and his wife Maria _____ had the following children:

     i.       ANNA, b. Oct 1884, Philadelphia, Pa.
     ii.      JOHN, b. Dec 1885, Philadelphia, Pa.; d. 1965.
     iii.     GEORGE, b. Jun 1888, Germany; married and had a family in the U.S.[28]
     iv.     WALTER, b. Aug 1893; gardener for his cousin, William[2] Zimmermann, Sr., son of 28. John[1] Zimmermann; lived near Wyncote, Pa.; had a son, Norman, who m.[29]

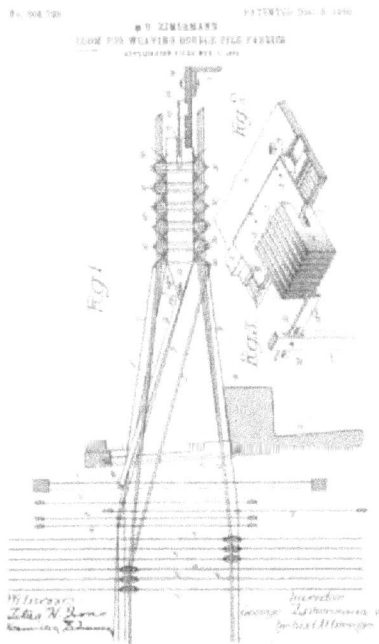

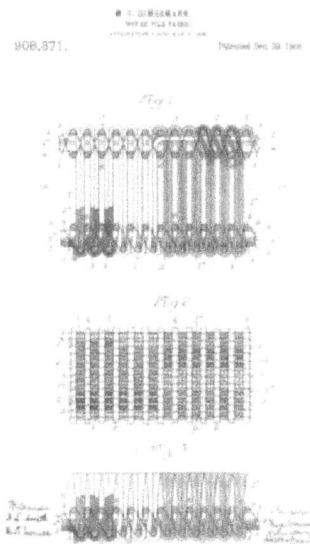

**Johann Georg Zimmermann's Patent Applications (illustrations)**
**G. Zimmermann "Loom for Weaving Double Pile Fabric" (1905) (L)**
**G. Zimmermann "Woven Pile Fabric" (1908) (R)**

# Images for Zimmermann Family
## Baden-Württemberg State, Germany

## Migration of the Zimmermann Family from 1550 to 1875

**Route from Steinheim am Albuch, Heidenheim, Lauterberg, Heuberg, and Gussenstadt**

**Heidenheim, Capital of Heidenheim District (*Kreis*)**

## Heubach, Ostalbkreis District, Baden-Württemberg

Heubach-rosenstein, fm commons.wikimedia

## Gussenstadt, Heidenheim District, Baden-Württemberg

Google Images: Upper L and R by Andreas Marx; lower R by Attila Gimesi; lower L by Jakobsweg

**Village of Gussenstadt in the 20th Century – Views:  Clockwise from Upper L
Entrance to the town; Overview; One of many hiking trails; RR Station (*Bahnhof*)**

29

# Gussenstadt Hotel "Deer"
## *Landgasthof & Hotel Hirsch*

The *Hotel Hirsch* is shown at top in 1900 and above in an undated photo, showing the height of the building before it was remodeled.

The 12 men at the hotel bar were sketched in 1911 by Hans Müller, a young art student. Melchior Jäger, *Schneider* (tailor) probably a relative of Anna Ursula Jäger (1820-1901), who married John[A] Zimmermann (1821-1899), is at lower L in the illustration.

The hotel's present appearance is seen below.

From http://www.hirsch-gussenstadt.de/Familientradition.html

## The Zimmermann Family Charts

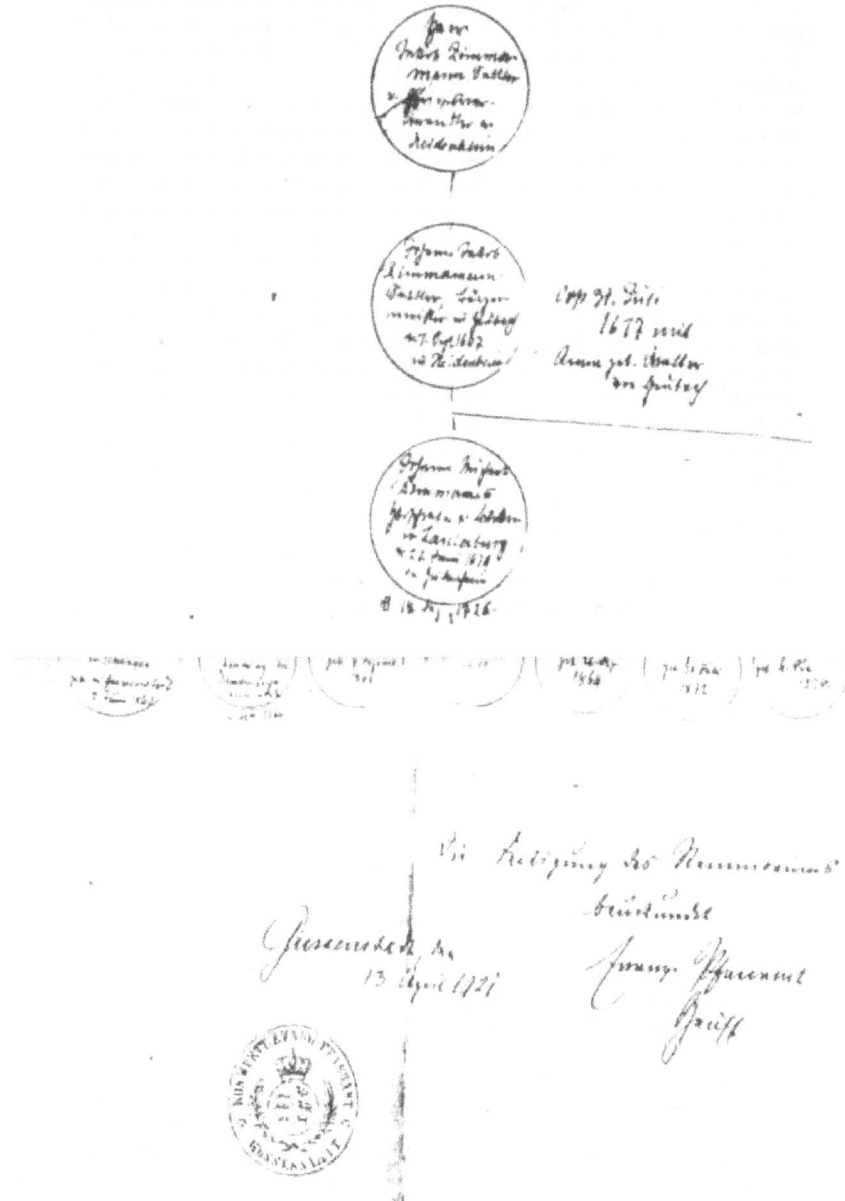

**Detail of Chart 1, showing Herr Jakob Zimmermann (b. 1614) his son Johann (1740-1729) and grandson Johann Michael (1679-1726), and endorsement of chart with seal (bottom)**

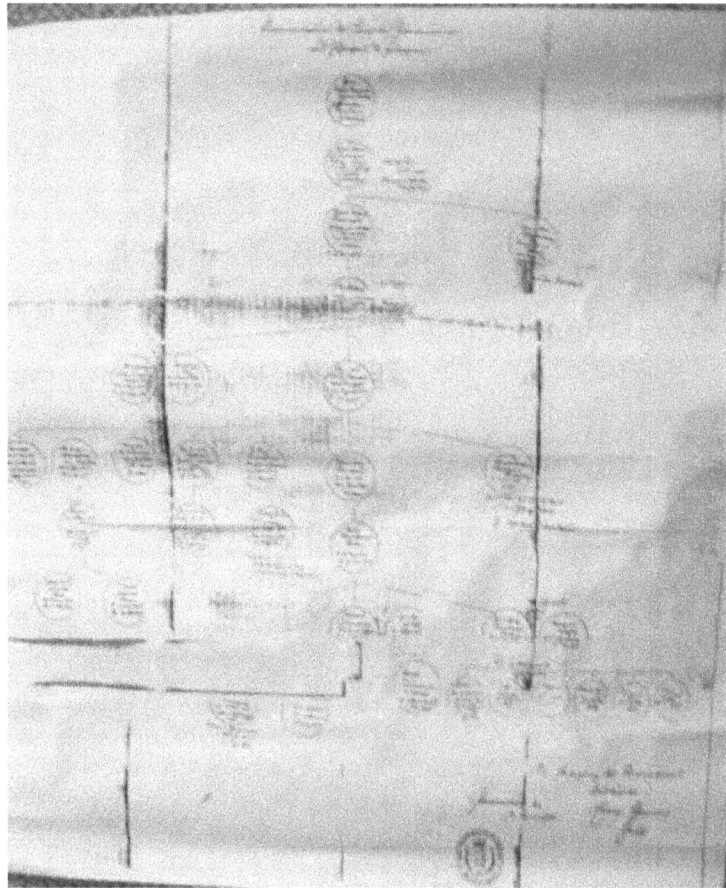

**Chart 1:  9 generations of the family of Herr Jakob Zimmermann (b. 1614)**

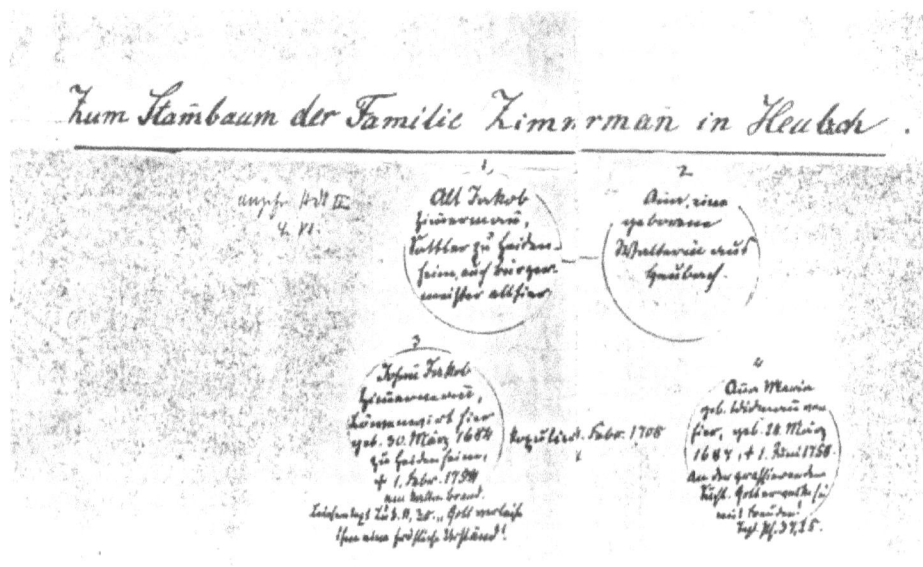

**Chart 3: Detail of *Stambaum der Familie Zimmermann im Heubach*
(Pedigree of Zimmermann Family in Heubach)**

# Notes

---

[1] The **Duchy of Württemberg** became a **kingdom on 1 January 1806**, when Duke Frederick II (d. 1816) who became duke in 1767, assumed the title of King Frederick I. He was succeeded by his son William I, who reigned from 1816-1864, and then by his son Charles I (1823-1891), who reigned from 1864-91. He was succeeded in 1891 by his cousin William II (1848-1921), who reigned until 1918. The **Kingdom of Württemberg became part of the German Empire in 1871**. However, it remained a kingdom until William II abdicated on 30 November 1918, after a **Republic was declared on 14 November 1918.** Baden-Württemberg was formed after World War II from the former states of Baden, Württemberg, and Hohenzollern. **The present state (*Land*) of Baden-Württemberg was established on 25 April 1952**. It is now one of 16 states in the Federal Republic of Germany.

The emigration of the Zimmermanns to America in the 1870's occurred during the reign of Charles I as king of Württemberg.

Five towns are associated with this Zimmermann family in Württemberg. They are encompassed within a circle with a radius of only 5 miles. The towns are: Stenheim am Albuch (a municipality in the district of Heidenheim), Heidenheim (capital city of the district), Heubach (a town in the Ostalbkreis district), Lauterberg (a very small village near Heubach, seen on Google map), and Gussenstadt.

The origin of the name of Gussenstadt is unknown, and the origin is not mentioned anywhere that I can find, either in German or in English. *Gussenstadt* is a compound word that is derived from *Stadt* (town) and the plural of *Guss,* which has many meanings, most of which relate to water (stream, cloudburst, shower) or glaze, or icing. Perhaps the town was named for many cloudbursts. Or it may be named for streams that flow through the town into the Fils River, a tributary of the Nektar River, and then on to the Rhine.

Gussenstadt is now one of seven villages in the municipality of Gerstetten, Heidenheim district. In 2004 Gussenstadt had a population of 1,533. It does not have its own website in English, but much can be learned about Gussenstadt and the surrounding area from the English-language website of the Landgasthof & Hotel Hirsch (aka Guesthouse "Deer" [*Hirsh*, GE = Deer, Eng]). See http://www.hirsch-gussenstadt.de/index_en.html (accessed 1/27/16). This website shows a drawing by a young artist named Hans Müller, of 12 guests who were present in the bar on a day in 1911, including one Melchior Jäger, tailor (04.09.1874 - 20.06.1924). The 37-year old man named Melchoir Jäger (1874-1924) would have been one or two generations younger than Anna Jäger (1820-1901), who married John[A] Zimmermann, father of the emigrant, John[1] Zimmermann. He may, therefore, have been Anna's nephew or great-nephew, and thus a cousin or 2d cousin of John[1] Zimmermann. The drawing was said to be in "'Found' Vol.1, 2001. Kindly supported by Willi Martin Jäger," suggesting that the family of Jäger has persisted in this small village into the 21st century. There may still be some named Jäger there now.

[2] Zimmermann and Kellenbenz Family Charts, prepared from the original German (see below for the origin of the charts). My transcriptions modernize and anglicize some aspects of the script on the charts, and of the original translation of 1921. For example, a double letter (e.g., nn), as in Zimmermann, is rendered when the chart shows a letter with overline (e.g., ň), as in Zimmermaň. Birth is indicated by b. rather than * or *geb.*, and death by d or d. rather than ý. The occupations are shown below as they appear on the chart, with lowercased initial letters, although by tradition, German nouns are normally capitalized.

Chart 1

This is the definitive chart that links Herr Jakob Zimmermann, Founder of the Zimmermann family of Heidenenheim and later of Gussenstadt, to Johannes (John) Zimmerman (1855-1936) in Generation 9, who was born in Gussenstadt and appeared in Philadelphia, Pa., in about 1876. This chart shows that two other Zimmermann men in Generations 8 and 9 came to North America. Johann Georg Zimmermann in Generation 8, who was the uncle of Johannes Zimmermann1855, came in 1884; Johann Georg had six children, some or all of whom must have accompanied him to America. His nephew, Johann George Zimmermann, a first cousin of Johannes1855, was married in Philadelphia in 1882 and had four children.

Chart 1 is in German Script. This magnificent hand-drawn chart is about 20 by 20 inches in size. Portions of this chart were translated and appear as Chart 2, although as will be seen, the translator interpolated some items that do not appear in the German text of Chart 1; e.g., the translator added Generation 10, which does not appear in Chart 1, showing four children of Johann Georg and Maria Zimmermann and six children of Johannes and Eva (Kellenbenz) Zimmermann.

The translation shown in Chart 2 was used in the transcription of Chart 1, insofar as possible. In Chart 1, each person and his or her spouse appears in a circle that is about 1 inch in diameter. In a few instances, as indicated, some text extends outside of the circle; this is generally not legible enough to be translated. Numbers are assigned in a traditional genealogical format, although there are no numbers shown for individuals on the original chart.

Family Tree of the Zimmermann Family of Gussenstadt and/or Heidenheim
(*Stammbaum der Familin Zimmermann uns Gussenstadt o/a Heidenheim*)

Generation 1
1. Herr Jakob Zimmermann, Saddler and _____ in Heidenheim

Generation 2
1.1. Johann Jakob Zimmermann, Saddler, Bürgermeister in Heubach. b. 7 Sept 1642 in Heidenheim. m. 30 July 1677 to Anna Walter of Heubach

Generation 3
1.1.1. Johann Michael Zimmermann, _____ and baker in Lauterburg b. 22 June 1679 in Heidenheim. d. 18 Dec 1726
1.1.2. Johann Jakob Zimmermann, _____ in Heubach b. 30 March 1684. d. 1 Feb 1754  Separate Stammbaum [see Chart 3]

Generation 4
1.1.1.1. F____ Christoph Zimmermann, butcher in Gussenstadt b. 1 May 1714. m. 25 Jan 1735 to Margereta [additional text, about 6 words, illegible]

Generation 5
1.1.1.1.1. Johann Georg Zimmermann, butcher b. 30 Aug 1739. m. 14 Sept 1763 to Ursula Köpf ( 1736-1817) d. 7 Nov 1796
1.1.1.1.2. Sigmund Christoph Zimmermann, butcher b. 22 December 1744. d. 30 Oct 1797

Generation 6
1.1.1.1.1.1. Ingrifon b. 14 ___ 1764  m. 25 ___ 1792 to _____
1.1.1.1.1.2. Johannn Georg Zimmermann, _____ b. 4 Jul 1765. d. 17 Feb 1832
1.1.1.1.1.3. Margarete b. 17 Feb 1767 m. _____ 1783 ____
1.1.1.1.1.4. Johann F_____, _____ _____ b. 21 ___ 1776 d. 1831
1.1.1.1.1.5. Frikopf? Zimmermann, _____ b. 4 Mar 1778 d. 8 May 1851
1.1.1.1.2.1. Johann Georg Zimmermann, day laborer b. 11 Dec 1768 d. 9 May 1835
1.1.1.1.2.2.  Christoph Zimmermann, day laborer in Heuchstetten b. 17 May 1770 m. 31 July 1793 to Appolonia, daughter of Christoph Böhner d. 1845
Separate Family Tree (*Stammbaum*) [see Chart 4]

Generation 7
1.1.1.1.2.1. Anna b. _____ 1796 d. 23 Nov 1876 m. 12 Nov 1834 to Joh. G. Amginter?
1.1.1.1.4.1. F_____ ___ Maria Zimmermann, _____ b. 20 Mar 1818 d. 9 Jan 1873
1.1.1.1.5.1. Frikopf? F___ Zimmermann b. 9 Apr 1805 d. 7 Nov 1843

_____ _____ _____ _____
1.1.1.1.2.1.1 Jakob Zimmermann, weaver b. 9 Jan 1801 d. 16 Jun 1864

Generation 8
1.1.1.1.2.1.1. Johannes Georg Amginter?, weaver b. 21 Jan 1834 d. 20 ___ 1897
1.1.1.1.2.1.2. Jamessa Amginter?, weaver b. 6 Aug 1835 d. 28 ___ 1885
1.1.1.2.1.1.1. Johannes Zimmermann b. 24 Sept 1821 d. 25 Jul 1899 m. Anna Ursula Jäger (1820-1901)
1.1.1.2.1.1.2. Johann Georg Zimmermann, weaver b. 3 Nov 1842 m. in Gussenstadt 14 Aug 1864 to Margereta

(1884 *nach Nordamerika mit familie* [to North America 1884 with family])

Generation 9
1.1.1.1.2.1.1.1.1. Johann Georg Zimmermann _____ in Philadelphia. b. 5 June 1851  m. in Phila. to Maria from Heuchstetten in 1882
1.1.1.1.2.1.1.1.2. Johannes Zimmermann b. 28 Nov 1855 in Gussenstadt m. Eva Katherina Kellenbenz (1855-1920)
1.1.1.1.2.1.1.1.3. Anna Zimmermann  b. in Gussenstadt 2 June 1860 lived in Uhingen - unmarried
1.1.1.1.2.1.1.2.1. Anna b. 8 June 1865
1.1.1.1.2.1.1.2.2. Jakob b. 8 Dec 1866
1.1.1.1.2.1.1.2.3. Katerina b. 10 Aug 1868
1.1.1.1.2.1.1.2.4. Johann Georg b. 26 Dec 1869
1.1.1.1.2.1.1.2.5. Margareta b. 30 Jul 1872
1.1.1.1.2.1.1.2.6. Johannes  b. 11 July 1874

The preparation of the Genealogy (*Tannenbaum*) was witnessed by Evangelical parish office [2 illegible words, perhaps a name]  Hanff /Gussenstadt 13 April 1921 [stamp/seal] showing bisected arms (illegible on left, 3 leopards on right) on an oval shield, surmounted by a crown, and resting on crossed laurels and surrounded by the legend: *KON WURTT.EVANG.FFARRAMT - GUSSENSTADT*

Chart 2 is a translation of part of Chart 1, with additions made as recently as 1974.  Chart 2 focuses on the line from the Founder, Herr Jakob Zimmermann, in the 17th century, to the children of Johannes Zimmermann (b. 1855) and Eva Katherina (Kellenbenz) Zimmermann in Generation 10.  This chart is about 11 inches wide and 17 inches high.  It has been copied onto two pages of 8½ by 11 inches.

The original transcriber / translator of Chart 2 is unknown.  It seems that the transcriber was not fluent in German, for some items are not translated correctly.  It is also likely that someone who knew about the Zimmermann family in both Germany and America added details to the chart at the time it was translated and transcribed, which was probably in the 1970s.  The latest additions are in the lines of Johann Georg Zimmermann's son John ("d. 1965") and Johannes Zimmermann's daughter Anna ("d. 1974").  These items, and all of the other information in Generation 10, do not appear in Chart 1, which was prepared in 1921.

There are no numbers for individuals in Generations 1 through 9, but numbers were shown in Chart 2 for the individuals in Generation 10 (except for Emily Zimmermann, who died young).

Genealogy of the Zimmermann Family from Gussenstadt and/or Heidenheim
(translation of Gussenstadt information)
Generation 1
Herr Jakob Zimmermann, saddler and _____ in Heidenheim

Generation 2
Johann Jakob Zimmermann, saddler, *Bürgermeister* in Heubach.
b. 7 Sept 1642 in Heidenheim.  m. 30 July 1677 to Anna Walter of Heubach

Generation 3
Jakob Zimmermann _____ in Heubach. b. 30 March 1604 d. 1 Feb 1754  Separate Genealogy [see Chart 3]
Johann Michael Zimmermann, _____ and baker in Lauterburg b. 22 June 1679 in Heidenheim d. 18 Dec 1726

Generation 4
Son of Johann Michael 1679:
F_____ Christoph Zimmermann, butcher in Gussenstadt b. 1 May 1714  m. 25 Jan 1735 to Margereta

Generation 5
Johann Georg Zimmermann, butcher  b. 30 Aug 1739  d. 7 Nov 1796  m. 14 Sept 1763 to Ursula Köpf (1736-1817)
Separate Genealogy [A separate chart is not known to exist; Chart 1 shows the descendants of Johann Georg Zimmermann and his wife Ursula Köpf for three generations; they had 5 children, 3 grandchildren, and 2 great-

grandchildren.]
Sigmund Christoph Zimmermann, butcher b. 22 December 1744  d. 30 Oct 1797

Generation 6
Sons of Sigmund Christoph1744:
Johann Georg Zimmermann, day laborer   b. 11 Dec 1768   d. 9 May 1835
Christoph Zimmermann, day laborer in Heuchstetten [although Chart 4 appears to say *Tagelöhner* in Guicfstetten [sic]; i.e., not Heuchstetten] b. 17 May 1770 d. 1845 Separate Genealogy [see Chart 4] m. 31 July 1793 to Appolonia, daughter of Christoph Böhner

Generation 7
Son of Johann Georg1768:
Jacob Zimmermann, weaver b. 9 Jan 1801  d. 16 June 1864

Generation 8
Johannes Zimmermann b. 24 Sept 1821 d. 25 July 1899 m. Anna Ursula Jäger 1820-1901)
Johann Georg Zimmermann, weaver  b. 3 Nov 1842 m. in Gussenstadt 14 Aug 1864 Margereta (to North America 1884 with family)

Generation 9
Children of Johannes1821:
Johann Georg Zimmermann _____ in Philadelphia b. 5 June 1851 m. in Phila to Maria from Heuchstetten in 1882.
Johannes Zimmermann b. 28 Nov 1855 in Gussenstadt m. Eva Katherina Kellenbenz (1855-1920) (came to America in 1873 to avoid conscription Franco-Prussian War).
Anna Zimmermann b. in Gussenstadt 2 June 1860  Lived in Vkingen (?) [or Uhingen?] – unmarried.

Generation 10
Children of Johann Georg1851:
1. Anna
2. John b. 25 Dec 1885 d. 1965
3. George
4. Walter
Children of Johannes1855:
1. Clara b. 1886
2. Anna 1887-1974
  Emily  d.
3. John
4. William 1894
5. Lillian
6. Albert
The preparation of the Genealogy witnessed by Evangelical parish office / Hanff / Gussenstadt / 13 April 1921

Chart 3 shows six generations in a family that is headed by "*Alb* [or *Alt*] *Jakob*" Zimmermann and Anna Zimmermann.  This chart is the Separate Genealogy referred to in Generation 3 of Chart 1, on which the given name of the Zimmermann in this generation is name Johann Jakob, not "*Alb/Alt Jakob*," as it appears on Chart 3.

    This chart is about 12 by 16 inches in size.  The chart shows each descendant in a circle, about one inch in diameter.  The birth date of "*Alb/Alt Jakob*" (i.e., Johann Jakob) is not given, but we know from chart 1 that he was b. in 1642 and married Anna Walter in 1677.  Each person on this chart is given a number, which will be stated here in brackets, viz [1].

    Except in Generations 1 and 2, numbers on this chart are assigned only to descendants, not to spouses.  In generation 2, only a son (#3 Johhann Jakob Zimmermann, 1684-1754) and his wife #4 Anna Maria Widrussenn? 1687-1758 are listed.  They had 15 children, who appear in Generation 3 as #5-19.  Generation 4 represents the 8 children of #18 Johann George Zimmermann and his wife Anna Barbara Strössner?. From this generation, only one child (#27, Johann Jakob Zimmermann, who m. Katharine Margarete _____) is followed in Generation 5: #28 (Joseph Andras? Zimmermann, who m. Maria Katherine Goth?). Generation 6 is a list of eight children of Joseph Andras? and Maria Katherine (Goth?) Zimmermann (#29-36). Some text is added for the individuals and a paragraph is interposed between Generations 3 and 4: *zur 18*. It appears that this handwritten paragraph discusses Johann Georg Zimmermann (#18), father of #20-#27. The bottom of the chart provides its provenance and legitimacy by 4 short lines of text and official seal. Line 2 shows that it was prepared in Heubach? 21? Mai 1912.

[Chart 3] Family Tree of the Zimmermanns of Heubach
*Zum Stammbaum der Familin Zimmermann in Heubach*

Generation 1
1. *Alb [Alt?]* Jakob _____ *Bürgomeister* _____
2. Anna _____ [wife of 1.]

[notations on this line appear to cite a volume and page, and provide a short narrative about *Alb/Alt* Jakob Zimmermann and his wife, Anna _____.]

Generation 2
3. Johann Jakob b. 30 March 1684 d. 1 Feb 1754
4. Anna Maria geb. Widrussenn? [wife of 3.] b. 28 Mar 1687 d. 1 ____ 1758 married 14 Febr. 1708

Generation 3
5. Anna Katharina b. 15 Apr 1709 d. *funf?*
6. Anna Barbara b. 6 Apr 1710 *narfurwebl.*
7. Katharina b. 24 Apr 1711 d. *funf?*
8. Johann Georg b. 14 Aug 1712 d. *funf?*
9. Maria Augusta b. 2 Nov 1713 d. *funf?*
10. Augusta Maria b. 12 Feb 1715 d. *funf?*
11. Augusta Maria b. 2 April 1716 d. *funf?*
12. Maria b. 14 ____ 1718 d.
13. Maria b. 22 Jan 1720 *narfurwebl.*
14. Margarethe? b. 31 Nov 1722 *narfurwebl.*
15. Elizabeta Magdalena? b. 17 Feb 1723 *narfurwebl.*
16. Katharina b. 6 Apr 1725
17. Johann Jakob b. 29 May 1727 __ ___ _____?
18. Johann Georg b. 6 Dec 1728 d. 10 Jan 1792 m. 18 Feb 1760 Anna Barbara Strössner? from Margalstrahnen?
[four lines of text, containing about 30 words, are written below #18]
19. Wolfgang Ulrich b. 20 ____ 1730 d.

Generation 4 (all are descendants of #18)
20. Barbara b. 6 ___ 1752
21. Pfilippina? b. 16 Apr 1754
22. Johann Malifion? b. 26 ___ 1756
23. Andrass b. 3 Feb 1757 d. 1760
24. Johann Georg b. _ Mar 1759 __ _____ __ _____ __
25. Georg Malifion? b. 24 Feb 1761 d. 1761
26. Maria Katharina b. 22 Feb 1772 d. 20 Oct 1772
27. Johann Jakob b. 20 Feb 1774 d. 21 Ap 1815 m. 26 May 1794 Kath. Marg. b. Yousert? d. 24 May 1831.

Generation 5 (Child of #27)
28. Jos. Andrass? b. 14 July 1795 d. 6 Feb 1848 in Gottingen m. 2 Nov 1830 Maria Kath. Gott? b. 9 Oct 1798 d. 1

Jan 1882

Generation 6 (Children of #28)
29. Josaumt?  b. 10 Feb 1828 d. 19 June 1829
30. Jos. ___  b. 26 Dec  1830 d. 4 ___ 1831
31. Kath. Margaret. b. 26 Dec 1830 _____ _____ __ _____ __ _____ [a twin]
32. Johann b. 28 Oct 1832 d. 19 Oct 1833
33. Anna Ursula b. 14 Jan 1834  m. 14 Oct 1867  Jos. Wolf. Miska Zimmermann?
34. Eliabeta   b. 28 Oct 1838 at Geistlingen? __ __ _____ _ _____
35. Jos. Gottlieb b. 8 Feb 1837  d. in Geistlingen?
36. Jos. Andras b. 21 Nov 1839 d. 21 Ap 1841 in Geistlingen?

[seal / stamp with illegible printing]
*Dis U_____ mit ___ _____ _____ _____*
*Grunnbach 31 May 1912 / Anangalififat Nachgfandransti /Frugan*

Chart 4
This diagrammatic family tree shows five (5) generations of the family of Christoph Zimmermann (1770-1845) and Appolonia Böhner (1771-1829).  This chart is about 14 inches high and 48 inches wide.  This is the Separate Genealogy referred to in Generation 6 of Chart 1.
Christoph Zimmermann (b. 1770), who is the head of this branch of the family shown on Chart 4, is the great-great uncle of Johannnes1855, who came to America in about 1873-6 and married Eva Kellenbenz.  Christoph1770 was the younger brother of Johannes1855's great-grandfather, Johann Georg1768.  Both Christoph1770 and Johann Georg1768 were sons of Sigmund Christoph Zimmermann1744.  Christoph1770 is shown in the transcription of Chart 1 as person # 1.1.1.1.2.2.  We will continue with that notation in this chart, adding his descendants, viz.:

Generation 1
1.1.1.1.2.2. Christoph Zimmermann, *Tagelöhner in Guicfstetten* [although Chart 2 says day laborer in Heuchstetten]
b. 1770 d. 1845 *cop.* 1793 *mit* Apollonia *geb.* Böhner b. 1771 d. 1829

Generation 2
1.1.1.1.2.2.1. Johann Michael Zimmermann, *weber* (weaver)
b. 1793  d. 1859 *cop* 1824 *mit* Christine *g.* Banzhaf b. 1794  d. 1874
1.1.1.1.2.2.2. Apollonia Zimmermann b. 1794  d. 1865  *cop* 1837 *mit* Matth. Steger, [occupation] b. 1771 d. 1846
1.1.1.1.2.2.3. Christoph Zimmermann, [occupation] in Granstten b. 1797  d. 1861  *cop* 1825 *mit* Ursula *g.* Hagstotz
1.1.1.1.2.2.4. Johann Georg Zimmermann, *weber* in Gunestten b. 1812  d. 1880  *cop* 1841 *mit* Ursula *g.* Kienle b. 1809  d. 1897

Generation 3
1.1.1.1.2.2.1.1. Thomas Zimmermann, *weber* b. 1824  d. 1869 *cop* 1852 *mit* Apollonia *geb* Zimmermann [sic] b. 1824  d. 1900
1.1.1.1.2.2.1.2. Christoph Zimmermann, *weber* b. 1826  d. 1880 *cop* 1855 *mit* Christine *geb.*Banzhaf [n.b., his mother's name]
1.1.1.1.2.2.1.3. Johanna Zimmermann  b. 1828  d. 1897 [m. (1) Braun; m. (2) Banzaf]
1.1.1.1.2.2.1.4. Johann Georg Zimmermann, *weber* b. 1829 d. 1906 *cop* 1856 *mit* Friedrike *g.* Eberhard b. 1830 d. 1909
1.1.1.1.2.2.1.5. Matthäus Zimmermann, *weber in Ganstetten* b. 1831  d. 1909  *cop* 1857 *mit* Anna Katharina *geb* Banzhaf  b. 1830  d. 1908
1.1.1.1.2.2.1.6. Apollonia Zimmermann  b. 1833  *cop* 1862 *mit* Jakob Rau, *maurer* (journeyman bricklayer) b. 1830 d. 1903
1.1.1.1.2.2.1.7. Anna Maria Zimmermann  b. 1836  d. 1906 *cop* 1862 *mit* Jakob Eckard, *weber u. maurer* (weaver & bricklayer) 1838 - 1898

1.1.1.1.2.2.3.1. Johannes Zimmermann, *weber* in Gastetten  b. 1823  d. 1897  *cop* 1851 *mit* Maria Ursula *g*. Burr  b. 1824  d. 1899

1.1.1.1.2.2.3.2. Apollonia Zimmermann  b. 1826  d. 1892  *cop* 186_  *mit* Jakob Miser?, *zimmermann u.* __ (carpenter & ?)  1815-84

1.1.1.1.2.2.3.3. Christoph Zimmermann b. 1828  cop 1861 mit  Angelika g. Maurer  b. 1831

1.1.1.1.2.2.3.4. Georg Zimmermann, *weber* b. 1830  d. 1870 *cop*  1862 *mit* Christine Barbara g. Wiedenhöfer  b. 1830  d. 1882

1.1.1.1.2.2.4.1. Kunigunde Zimmermann  b. 1844  d. 1901 *cop* 1870 *mit* Michael Strobel Maurer  b. 1840  d. 1908

Generation 4

Henceforth, the letters b. and d. will be omitted when both birth and death years are shown on the chart, and *cop mit* will be rendered as m.  The abbreviation *geb* or *g* will be rendered as "born" or omitted.  Occupations will be rendered in English when they can be translated; otherwise they will be transcribed in approximate German or shown simply as "[occupation]".  The following occupations have been identified on Charts 3 and 4:

*Bäker* = baker

*Fabrikarbeiter* = textile worker

*Mattinenarbeiter* = finish worker

*Maurer* = bricklayer, or journeyman bricklayer

*Tagelöhner* = day laborer

*Weber* = weaver

*Zimmermann* = carpenter (literally, "room-man")

1.1.1.1.2.2.1.1.1. Jakob Zimmermann, weaver 1848-1891 m. Katharine Strobel 1847-1904

1.1.1.1.2.2.1.1.2. Christine Zimmermann  b. 1862  m. 1889 Georg Böhler, [occupation]

1.1.1.1.2.2.1.2.1. Anna Zimmermann  b. 1861 m. Joseph Aierle [occupation] *in Gruslingen kalf.*

1.1.1.1.2.2.1.3.1. Anna Maria Braun b. 1853 m. 1879 Martin Ammann [occupation of *Böhler*]

1.1.1.1.2.2.1.3.2. Christine Banzhaf  1855-1895 m. 1884  Adolf Lautten? B. 1852

1.1.1.1.2.2.1.4.1. Anna Maria Zimmermann  b. 1852 m. Matth. Eckard, weaver  1849-1908

1.1.1.1.2.2.1.4.2. Georg Zimmermann, weaver  1856-1891 m. Margarete Banzhaf  b. 1858

1.1.1.1.2.2.1.4.3. Joh. Michael Zimmermann, day laborer  b. 1857 m. 1884 Maria Kienle  b. 1859

1.1.1.1.2.2.1.5.1. Barbara Zimmermann  b. 1851 in Rams____

1.1.1.1.2.2.1.5.2. Christine Zimmermann  b. 1857 m. Andreas Henlie [occupation] in Heidenheim  b. 1842

1.1.1.1.2.2.1.5.3. Joh. Michael Zimmermann  b. 1859 m. 1889 Christine Schlumberger  b. 1860

1.1.1.1.2.2.1.5.4. Johannes Zimmermann, [occupation]  b. 1862 m. 1891 Barbara Besler

1.1.1.1.2.2.1.5.5. Angelika Zimmermann  b. 1864  m. 1888 Rudolf Jäger [occup.] b. 1863

1.1.1.1.2.2.1.7.1. Johanna Eckard  b. 1860 m. Aug. Heinzmann in _____ *katf*

1.1.1.1.2.2.1.7.2. Joh.Georg Eckard, *fabrikarbeiter* in Gaislingen  b. 1863 m. 1887 Marie Nuding  b. 1867

1.1.1.1.2.2.1.7.3. Christine Eckard  b. 1864  m. 1894 Aug. Ploc_ , *fabrikarbeiter* in Gaislingen  b. 1864

1.1.1.1.2.2.1.7.4. Matthäus Eckard, [occupation] b. 1865 m. 1891 Apollonia Abansfand?

1.1.1.1.2.2.1.7.5. Barbara Eckard  b. 1867

1.1.1.1.2.2.1.7.6. Apollonia Eckard  b. 1872 m. 1905 Johannes Nussen?  (Geislingen) b. 1870

1.1.1.1.2.2.1.7.7. Anna Maria Eckard  b. 1874 m. Johann Leonard Tunnenevoin, laborer in Göggingen  b. 1868

1.1.1.1.2.2.3.1.1. Ursula Zimmermann  1851-1908 m. 1884 Jak. Mayer [occupation] in Grustetten

1.1.1.1.2.2.3.1.2. Barbara Zimmermann  1854-1905 m. Joh. Georg Strobel, weaver in Grustetten b. 1850

1.1.1.1.2.2.3.1.3. Anna Zimmermann  b. 1856 m. 1886 Heinrich Breitinger  [occupation] in Altenkapf

1.1.1.1.2.2.3.1.4. Katharine Zimmermann  b. 1858  m. 1889 Fils Köpf, weaver in Ganstetten (1840-1908)

1.1.1.1.2.2.3.1.5. Christof Zimmermann, [occupation] b. 1860 m. 1890 Magdalene Rau  b. 1863

1.1.1.1.2.2.3.1.6. Georg Zimmermann, [occupation] in Altenkapf  b. 1863 m. Anna Barbara Krauss  b. 1862

1.1.1.1.2.2.3.2.1. Joh. Michael Miser, [occupation] in Heidenheim  b. 1864 m. 1889 Christine Schnäble

1.1.1.1.2.2.3.2.2. Jakob Miser, [occupation] in Zaug  b. 1866 m. 1890 Anna Margarete Schnäble  b. 1867

1.1.1.1.2.2.3.3.1. Christine Zimmermann  b. 1857

1.1.1.1.2.2.3.3.2. Sebastian Zimmermann  b. 1862

1.1.1.1.2.2.3.3.3. Ursula Zimmermann b. 1868 m. 1894 Jakob Weber, bricklayer in Ulm
1.1.1.1.2.2.3.4.1. Christine Zimmermann b. 1865 m. Andr. Bierer, day laborer in Hlingau
1.1.1.1.2.2.4.1.1. Ursula Strobel b. 1873 m. 1902 Georg Gröner, bricklayer b. 1875
1.1.1.1.2.2.4.1.2. Georg Strobel b. 1886 m. 1911 Anna Barbara Banzhaf

Generation 5
1.1.1.1.2.2.1.1.1.1. Georg Zimmermann b. 1886
1.1.1.1.2.2.1.1.2.1. Georg Böhler b. 1890
1.1.1.1.2.2.1.1.2.2. Nikolaus Böhler b. 1891
1.1.1.1.2.2.1.1.2.3. Christine Böhler b. 1893
1.1.1.1.2.2.1.3.1.1. Christian Ammann b. 1880 m. 1904 Maria Kiener b. 1877
1.1.1.1.2.2.1.3.1.2. Johanna Ammann b. 1882 m. Jakob Frei, bricklayer in Genstetten
1.1.1.1.2.2.1.3.1.3. Martin Ammann b. 1886
1.1.1.1.2.2.1.3.1.4. Angelika Ammann b. 1888
1.1.1.1.2.2.1.3.2.1. Julie Lautten b. 1885
1.1.1.1.2.2.1.3.2.2. Heinrich Lautten b. 1887
1.1.1.1.2.2.1.3.2.3. Friedrich Lautten b. 1890
1.1.1.1.2.2.1.4.1.1. Anna Maria Eckard b. 1873
1.1.1.1.2.2.1.4.1.2. Christine Eckard b. 1876 m. 1905 Johannes Dürner, *fabrikarbeiter* (fabric [textile] worker)
1.1.1.1.2.2.1.4.1.3. Margarete Eckard b. 1879 m. 1902 Joh. Christian Maier, *mattinenarbeiter* (finish worker [?polisher])
1.1.1.1.2.2.1.4.2.1. Dorothea Zimmermann b. 1884
1.1.1.1.2.2.1.4.2.2. Maria Zimmermann b. 1888
1.1.1.1.2.2.1.4.3.1. Margarete Hienle b. 1880 m. 1907 Johann Jakob Rüsch, *Lauer in Tsalkstetten*
1.1.1.1.2.2.1.4.3.2. Friedrike Hienle b. 1882 m. 1910 Karl Griun Hobswarth, [occupation] (*grasf.*)
1.1.1.1.2.2.1.4.3.3. Maria Hienle b. 1884 m. 1910 Kargan Rau, day laborer (*grasf.*)
1.1.1.1.2.2.1.4.3.4. Barbara Hienle b. 1886 m. 1909 Michael Dauner, baker (*grasf.*)
1.1.1.1.2.2.1.4.3.5. Christine Hienle b. 1888
1.1.1.1.2.2.1.4.3.6. Luise Hienle b. 1892
1.1.1.1.2.2.1.4.3.7. Jakob Hienle b. 1894
1.1.1.1.2.2.1.4.3.7. Georg Hienle b. 18__
1.1.1.1.2.2.1.4.3.8. Johannes Hienle b. 1898
1.1.1.1.2.2.1.5.2.1. Johannes Henlie b. 1889
1.1.1.1.2.2.1.5.2.2. Christine Henlie b. 1897
1.1.1.1.2.2.1.5.3.1. Johannes Zimmermann b. 1890
1.1.1.1.2.2.1.5.3.2. Georg Zimmermann b. 1892
1.1.1.1.2.2.1.5.5.1. Katharine Jäger b. 1886 m. 1906 Karl Gottfried Idler, [occupation] in Ulfbacs
1.1.1.1.2.2.1.5.5.2. Anna Jäger b. 1892
1.1.1.1.2.2.1.5.5.3. Rudolf Jäger b. 1895
1.1.1.1.2.2.1.7.2.1. Georg Zimmermann b. 1890
1.1.1.1.2.2.1.7.2.2. Heinrich Zimmermann b. 1892
1.1.1.1.2.2.1.7.2.3. Emilie Zimmermann b. 1896
1.1.1.1.2.2.1.7.3.1. Wilhelm Friedrich Plock b. 1900
1.1.1.1.2.2.1.7.4.1. Ludwig Zimmermann b. 1891
1.1.1.1.2.2.1.7.4.2. Maria Zimmermann b. 1895
1.1.1.1.2.2.1.7.4.3. Jakob Zimmermann b. 1900
1.1.1.1.2.2.1.7.4.5. Barbara Zimmermann b. 1902
1.1.1.1.2.2.1.7.4.6. Johannes Zimmermann b. 1906
1.1.1.1.2.2.1.7.6.1. Johannes Nussen b. 1907
1.1.1.1.2.2.1.7.7.1. Johann August Tennenevein b. 1898
1.1.1.1.2.2.1.7.7.2. Klara Maria Tennenevein b. 1902
1.1.1.1.2.2.1.7.7.3. Lydia Tennenevein b. 1909

1.1.1.1.2.2.3.1.1.1. Marie Ursula Mayer  b. 1892
1.1.1.1.2.2.3.1.2.1. Katharine Strobel  b. 1878 m. 1907 Joh. Georg Heydler, bricklayer in Ussingen
1.1.1.1.2.2.3.1.2.2. Ursula Strobel  b. 1880 m. 1907 Joh. Georg Lude, textile worker in Ussingen
1.1.1.1.2.2.3.1.2.3. Anna Strobel  b. 1885  m. Joh. Georg Friz, [occupation] in Ussingen
1.1.1.1.2.2.3.1.2.4. Christine Strobel  b. 1886 m. Johannes Eckard, [occupation] in Grostetten
1.1.1.1.2.2.3.1.4.1. Johann Georg Köpf  b. 1884
1.1.1.1.2.2.3.1.5.1. Anna Maria Zimmermann  b. 1887 m. 1910  Wilh. Frey [occupation]
1.1.1.1.2.2.3.1.6.1. Emma Zimmermann  b. 1891
1.1.1.1.2.2.3.2.1.1. Anna Miser  b. 1891
1.1.1.1.2.2.3.2.1.2. Maria Miser  b. 1893
1.1.1.1.2.2.3.2.1.3. Katharine Miser  b. 1901
1.1.1.1.2.2.3.2.1.4. Adolf Miser  b. 1902
1.1.1.1.2.2.3.2.2.1. Jakob Miser  b. 1891
1.1.1.1.2.2.3.2.2.2. Katharine Miser  b. 1893
1.1.1.1.2.2.3.2.2.3. Johann Georg Miser  b. 1898
1.1.1.1.2.2.3.2.2.4. Anna Christine Miser  b. 1900
1.1.1.1.2.2.3.2.2.5. Karl Michael Miser  b. 1903
1.1.1.1.2.2.4.1.1.1. Karl Gröner  b. 1903

Chart 5
Charts 5 and 6 were signed by Bill Zimmermann of Minneapolis, Minnesota, in 1985.  William "Bill"[3] Zimmermann, Jr., Ph.D. (b. 1930) is a son of William[2] Zimmermann, Sr., son of Johannes[1] (John) Zimmermann (1885-1936), who founded this branch of the Zimmermann Family in America.  Both charts are about the family of Evakaterina Kellenbenz, who married Johannes Zimmermann1885.  Charts 5 and 6 are drawn on 8 by 11 inch paper, in the form of a family tree that is headed by an unnamed Founder, _____ Kellenbenz.  The family tree is converted to a generational outline format, numbering the individuals as was done for Chart 1.

Generation 1
1. _____ Kellenbenz

Generation 2
1.1. Clara Kellenbenz
1.2. Katherina Kellenbenz m. John Zimmermann
1.3. Wilhelm Kellenbenz m. Fanny Lauser

Generation 3
Children of John and Katherine (Kellenbenz) Zimmermann:
[n.b., this list is incomplete and the order is incorrect; there were seven children of John Zimmermann and Evakaterina Kellenbenz, not six - Clara, Anna, Emily (who died young), John, William, Lillian, and Albert]
1.2.1. John Zimmermann
1.2.2. Lillian Zimmermann
1.2.3. Clara Zimmermann
1.2.4. Bill Zimmermann m. Margaret Lukins [sic:  should be Lukens]
1.2.5. Anna Zimmermann
1.2.6. Albert Zimmermann

Children of Wilhelm and Fanny (Lauzer) Kellenbenz:
1.3.1. Fanny m. Wilhelm Kramer
1.3.2. Eugenie m. Siegfried Bollacher

Generation 4

Children of Bill Zimmermann [William Zimmermann, Sr.] and Margaret Lukens
1.2.4.1. Bill m. Betsy (they have three children)
1.2.4.2. Peggy m. Eric Fonkalsrud (they have four children)
1.2.4.3. Bob m. Athlene (they have one child)

Child of Fanny and Wilhelm Kramer:
1.3.1.1. Hans-Joachim Kramer

Children of Eugenie and Siegfried Bollacher:
1.3.3.1. Wolfgang Bollacher  m. Isle _____ (they had three children)
1.3.3.2. Dieter Bollacher m. Isolda _____ (they had three children)
1.3.3.3. Martin Bollacher m. Yvonne _____ (they had two children)

Generation 5
Children of Bill and Betsy Zimmermann:
1.2.4.1.1. Michael Zimmermann
1.2.4.1.2. Sara Zimmermann
1.2.4.1.3. Chris Zimmermann

Children of Peggy and Eric Fonkulsrud:
1.2.4.2.1. Eric Fonkulsrud
1.2.4.2.2. Lynn Fonkulsrud
1.2.4.2.3. David Fonkulsrud
1.2.4.2.4. Robert Fonkulsrud

Child of Bob and Athlene Zimmermann:
1.2.4.3.1. Hannah Zimmermann

Children of Wolfgang and Isle Bollacher:
1.3.3.1.1. Tillman Bollacher (64)
1.3.3.1.2. Sebastian Bollacher (66)
1.3.3.1.3. Christian Bollacher (72)

Children of Dieter and Isolda Bollacher:
1.3.3.2.1. Florian (74)
1.3.3.2.2. Felix (76)
1.3.3.2.3. Philip (77)

Children of Martin and Yvonne Bollacher
1.3.3.3.1. Olivier Bollacher (69)
1.3.3.3.2. Maria Spha? (73)

[s] Bill Zimmermann / 1985

Chart 6

Generation 1
_____ Kellenbenz

Generation 2
1. Clara m. Weigle.  They had Fred [Weigle] and William [Weigle] "Came to USA" [the implication on the chart is that both Fred and William Weigle came to the U.S.]
2. Evakaterina m. Zimmermann . . .

3. Wilhelm m. Fanny Lauser    They had three children

3.a. Eugenia m. Siegfried Bollacher (lawyer in Ludwigsburg; d. 1983 or 1984)

They had three children:

3.a.1. Wolfgang [Bollacher] Lawyer in Ludwigsburg

3.a.2. Dietrich [Bollacher] In finance ministry in Stuttgart

3.a.3. Martin [Bollacher] m.  Professor of German literature in Tübingen

3.b. Anna

3.c. Fanny m. Wilhelm Krämer  Professor of music in high school; founded Ludwigsburg music festival

They had one child:

3.c.1. Hans J. Krämer (b. 1929) Professor of philosophy in Tübingen

--------------------------

Drawn by Bill Zimmermann / March 1985 / Minneapolis

[3] The information about Matthis Zimmermann and his son, Adam, is taken from Ancestry.com family trees, accessed 1/24/2016, as "Matthis Zimmermann" (b. 1550) and "Adam Zimmermann" (b.1578).  The town of Steinheim am Albuch, Heidenheim, Württemberg, is known locally for its meteorite crater.  It had a population of 8,690 in 1980.

[4] The information about Adam Zimmermann is taken from Ancestry.com family trees, showing "Matthis Zimmermann," "Adam Zimmermann" (Ibid.) and "Jacob Zimmermann" b. 1614 and "Catharina Bollinger" b. 1587.

[5] For Herr Jakob Zimmermann and his descendants, see Zimmermann and Kellenbenz Family Charts (Note 1, above), copies made in November 1993 from originals or previous copies in the possession of Sue (Kelley) Carnwath, transcriptions made by George J. Hill [hereafter GJH] 28 February 2003ff.  Sue Carnwath's charts passed to her heirs after her death.  And "John Zimmermann (1855-1936)," letters with enclosures of 20 Nov 2009 and 15 Dec 2009, from Jean Hoxie Naples [hereafter JHN] to GJH, 16 Dec 2009. JHN was at 115 Fir Ridge Lane, Beaufort, NC  29516.

  The information about Jacob (Jakob) Zimmermann is also taken from Ancestry.com family trees: "Jacob Zimmermann" b. 1614 and "Catharina Bollinger" b. 1587 (Ibid.); and "Johann Jakob Zimmermann" b. 1648, accessed 1/24/16, Ancestry.com.

[6] References for JOHANN JAKOB ZIMMERMANN, sometimes also called Johann Albert Jakob Zimmermann: Zimmermann and Kellenbenz Family Charts (Ibid.); "John Zimmermann (1855-1936)" from JHN to GJH (Ibid.); "Johann Jakob Zimmermann" b. 1648 [sic], Ancestry.com.; "Anna Walter" b. 1659, Ancestry.com.  He is in Chart 2, Generation 2.  See also: http://awtc.ancestry.com/cgi-bin/igm.cgi?op=GET&db=*v05t1769&id=I316 (accessed 1/24/16).

[7] For Anna Walter (or Walther), see: SophieDahl2015.03 (accessed on Ancestry.com, 1/24/16; could not access the file "temporarily unavailable"); summary: PUBLIC MEMBER TREE 2 sources / NAME:  Anna (Walther) Walter / BIRTH:  08 Sep 1659 (8 Sep 1659) / DEATH:  31 Mar 1742 – Heubach / MARRIAGE:  31 Jul 1677 / PARENTS: Hans (Walther) Walter, Barbara Nördlinger / SPOUSE:  Johann Jacob Zimmermann.

[8] Johann Jakob Zimmermann is in Zimmermann and Kellenbenz Family Charts (Ibid.), Chart 1, Generation 3; and in Chart 3; and Ancestry.com besswanger Family Tree / PUBLIC MEMBER TREE1 attached record, 1 source / NAME: / Johann Jakob Zimmermann / BIRTH:  30 Mar 1684 - Ostalbkreis, Germany / DEATH:  1 Feb 1754 - Heubach, Ostalbkreis, Baden-Württemberg, Germany / MARRIAGE:  14 Feb 1708 - Heubach, Ostalbkreis, Baden-Württemberg, Germany / PARENTS:  Johann Jakob Zimmermann, Anna Walter / SPOUSE:  Anna Maria Wiedmann.

[9] **6. Johann Jacob [112] (3) ZIMMERMANN** is in Chart 1, Generation 3; and in Chart 3.  Also, from Ancestry.com: besswanger Family Tree / PUBLIC MEMBER TREE1 attached record, 1 source [not available] / NAME: Johann Jakob Zimmermann / BIRTH:  30 Mar 1684 - Ostalbkreis, Germany / DEATH:  1 Feb 1754 - Heubach, Ostalbkreis, Baden-Württemberg, Germany / MARRIAGE:  14 Feb 1708 - Heubach, Ostalbkreis, Baden-Württemberg, Germany / PARENTS:  Johann Jakob Zimmermann, Anna Walter / SPOUSE:  Anna Maria Wiedmann

Johann Jacob and Anna Maria (Wiedmann) Zimmermann had the following children:

      i.      Anna Katarina (5). Born on 15 Apr 1709.

      ii.      Anna Barbara (6). Born on 6 Apr 1710.

      iii.      Katharina (7). Born on 24 Apr 1711.

| | iv. | Johann Georg (8). Born on 14 Aug 1712. |
|---|---|---|
| | v. | Maria Augusta (9). Born on 2 Nov 1713. |
| | vi. | Augusta Maria (10). Born on 12 Feb 1715. |
| | vii. | Augusta Maria (11). Born on 2 Apr 1716. |
| | viii. | Maria (12). Born in 1718. |
| | ix. | Maria (13). Born on 22 Jan 1720. |
| | x. | Margarethe (14). Born on 30 Nov 1722. |
| | xi. | Elizabeta Magdalena (15). Born on 17 Feb 1723. |
| | xii. | Katharina (16). Born on 6 Apr 1725. |
| | xiii. | Johann Jakob (17). Born on 29 May 1727. |
| **8** | xiv. | Johann Georg (18) (1728-1792) |

------------

**8. Johann Georg (18) ZIMMERMANN.** Born on 6 Dec 1728. Johann Georg (18) died on 10 Jan 1792, he was 63. / On 18 Feb 1760 when Johann Georg (18) was 31, he married Anna Barbara STROESSNER / She was from Margalstrahenen. They had the following children:

| | a. | Barbara (20). Born in 1752. |
|---|---|---|
| | b. | Pfilippina (21). Born on 16 Apr 1754. |
| | c. | Johann Malifion (22). Born in 1756. |
| | c. | Andrass (23). Born on 3 Feb 1757. Andrass (23) died in 1760, he was 2. |
| | e. | Johann Georg (24). Born in Mar 1759. |
| | f. | Georg Malifion (25). Born on 24 Feb 1761. Georg Malifion (25) died in 1761. |
| | g. | Maria Katharina (26). Born on 22 Feb 1772. Maria Katharina (26) died on 20 Oct 1772. |
| **12** | h. | Johann Jakob (27) (1774-1815) Born on 20 Feb 1774. Johann Jakob (27) died on 21 Apr 1815, he was 41. On 26 May 1794 when Johann Jakob (27) was 20, he married Katarine Margarete YOUSERT. Katarine Margarete died on 24 May 1831. |
| | | They had one child: |
| | **18** (i). | Josef Andrass (28) (1795-1848) |

**18. Josef Andrass (28) ZIMMERMANN.** Born on 14 Jul 1795. Josef Andrass (28) died in Gottingen, GERMANY on 6 Feb 1848, he was 52. On 2 Nov 1830 when Josef Andrass (28) was 35, he married Maria Katherine GOTT. Born on 9 Oct 1798. Maria Katherine died on 1 Jan 1882, she was 83. They had the following children:

| | 1. | Josaumt (29). Born on 10 Feb 1828. Josaumt (29) died on 19 Jun 1829, he was 1. |
|---|---|---|
| | 2. | Jos. (30) (Twin). Born on 26 Dec 1830. Jos. (30) died in 1831. |
| | 3. | Katherine Margarete (31) (Twin). Born on 26 Dec 1830. |
| | 4. | Johann (32). Born on 28 Oct 1832. Johann (32) died on 19 Oct 1833. |
| | 5. | Anna Ursula (33). Born on 14 Jan 1834. On 14 Oct 1867 when Anna Ursula (33) was 33, she married Jos. Wolf. Miska ZIMMERMANN[5]. |
| | 6. | Elisabeta (34). Born on 28 Oct 1838. |
| | 7. | Jos. Gottlieb (35). Born on 8 Feb 1837. Jos. Gottlieb (35) died in in Geistlingen. |
| | 8. | Jos. Andras (36). Born on 21 Nov 1839. Jos. Andras (36) died in in Geistlingen on 21 Apr 1841, he was 1. |

-------------

| | xv. | Wolfgang Ulrich (19). Born in Apr 1730. |
|---|---|---|

[10] Johann Michael Zimmermann is in Zimmermann and Kellenbenz Family Charts (Ibid.), Chart 1, Generation 3; and Kathy Brant Bonnell, 14 Nov 2009, "Zimmermann Genealogy," in "Goppingen, Württemberg, Germany and Surrounding Villages," on Rootsweb, updated 2009-11-14 (kbonnell@byu.net), sent by JHN to GJH, 20 Nov 2009. Bonnell says b. est 1682, and gives no b.p.; and does not give a date or place of d.

[11] Her name is given only by Bonnell. Ancestry.com is no help in locating her or other members of her family.

[12] Zimmermann and Kellenbenz Family Charts (Ibid.), Chart 1, Generation 4, called F. Christoph Zimmermann. Bonnell calls him Georg Christoph. I will accept this, and the children named by Bonnell, including the two named and numbered by the Zimmermann chart. His wife's name has also been spelled Margarete.

[13] No proof of the relationship, but another contemporary Sattler from Gussenstadt is, on several Ancestry.com trees: / NAME: / Anna Margaretha Sattler / BIRTH: 24 Nov 1706 – Germany / DEATH: Deckenpfronn, Württemberg

(Baden-Württemberg), Germany / MARRIAGE: 1 Nov 1729 - Deckenpfronn, Württemberg (Baden-Württemberg), Germany / PARENTS: Johannes Sattler, Barbara Aichele/ SPOUSE: Johann Georg Aichele.

[14] Anna Regina Geigner, b. 11 May 1781; d. 14 Jun 1783, aet. 2.

[15] **JOHANN GEORG ZIMMERMANN** is in Chart 1, Generation 5, showing 5 children [1111111-1111115].

9 children are given by Kathy Bonnell. One ch. appears on both lists. I will re-order the list and accept the b. & d. dates of Bonnell. On 14 Sep 1763 when Johann Georg [11111] was 24, he married **Anna Ursula KÖPF**. Born on 1 Jul 1736. Anna Ursula died on 25 Jun 1817, she was 80.

They had the following children and descendants:

|   |      |                                                                                                                                                                                                                                                         |
|---|------|----------------------------------------------------------------------------------------------------------------------------------------------------------------------------------------------------------------------------------------------------------|
|   | i.   | Johann Georg. Born on 12 Sep 1762. Johann Georg died in 1763.                                                                                                                                                                                           |
|   | ii.  | Ingrifon [111111]. Born in 1764. In 1792 when Ingrifon [111111] was 28, he married _____ ? (ZIMMERMANN).                                                                                                                                                |

**13**    iii.    Friederike Dorothea (1764-1840) **13. Friederike Dorothea ZIMMERMANN.** Born on 14 Jan 1764. Friederike Dorothea died on 28 Dec 1840, she was 76. Friederike Dorothea married Johann Jakob MERZ, b 25 Jul 1765. Johann Jakob d 5 Nov 1812, he was 47. They had the following children:

     a.    Jakob. Born on 17 Apr 1792. Jakob died on 26 Mar 1797, he was 4.

     b.    Johann Georg. Born on 9 Jan 1794. Johann Georg died on 5 Apr 1797, he was 3.

**19**    c.    Johann Jakob (1798-1887) **19. Johann Jakob MERZ.** Born on 3 May 1798. Johann Jakob died on 27 Apr 1887, he was 88. Johann Jakob married (1) **Anna Catharina HOLDER**. Born on 31 Dec 1795. Anna Catharina d 20 Nov 1846, she was 50. They had the following children:

**23**    (i).    Anna Maria (1830-1904) **23. Anna Maria MERZ.** Born on 2 Feb 1830. Anna Maria died on 22 Apr 1904, she was 74., had 9 ch., 7 of whom died in childhood; only 2 survived; one apparently had 2 children out of wedlock, and the other prob did not marry. Anna Maria married **Johann Michael HUMMEL**. Born on 5 May 1819. Johann Michael d 19 Jun 1895, he was 76. They had the following children:

     1.    Anna Maria. Born on 14 Feb 1860. Anna Maria died on 17 Jan 1863, she was 2.

     2.    Catharina. Born on 12 Nov 1861. Catharina died on 12 Sep 1937, she was 75.

     3.    Christian Friedrich. Born on 22 Sep 1862. Christian Friedrich d 12 Dec 1865, he was 3.

     4.    Karl. Born on 8 Dec 1864. Karl died on 2 Nov 1865.

     5.    Anna Maria. Born on 3 Dec 1865. Anna Maria died on 11 Dec 1865.

     6.    [unknown]. Born on 19 Apr 1865. [unknown] died on 19 Apr 1867, he was 2.

     7.    Karl Friedrich. Born on 17 Feb 1870. Karl Friedrich died in Mar 1870.

     8.    Karl Friedrich. Born on 13 Jul 1871. Karl Friedrich died on 4 Aug 1871.

**26**    9.    Anna Maria (1876-) **26. Anna Maria HUMMEL.** Born in 1876. Children: (a). Albert Friedrich Christian (1895-) (b). Karl Friedrich Otto (1899-)

     (ii).    Jakob Johann. Born on 2 Dec 1831.

     (iii).    Dorothea. Born on 6 Apr 1834. Dorothea died on 22 Apr 1834.

     (iv).    Johann Friedrich. Born on 24 Sep 1835. Johann Friedrich married A. M. SCHMID. Born in est 1837.

     (v).    Dorothea. Born on 30 Dec 1838. Dorothea died on 1 Jun 1839.

**19. Johann Jakob MERZ** married (2) **Maria Catharina FRASCH**. Born on 20 Feb 1811. Maria Catharina died on 12 Mai 1875, she was 64. They had the following children:

     (i).    Gottfried. Born on 4 May 1850. Gottfried died on 10 Sep 1866, he was 16.

     (ii).    Wilhelm. Born on 3 Apr 1852. Wilhelm died in May 1852.

-----------

     d.    Johann Georg. Born on 13 Aug 1799. Johann Georg died on 1 Nov 1800, he was 1.

     e.    Elisabetha. Born on 19 Mar 1801. Elisabetha died on 23 Mar 1807, she was 6.

     f.    Margarethe. Born on 28 Sep 1802. Margarethe died on 30 Jun 1803.

**20**    g.    Johann Friedrich (1807-1866) **20. Johann Friedrich MERZ.** Born on 14 Aug 1807.

Johann Friedrich died on 15 Jul 1866, he was 58; a sad family; Johann and Anna were probably m. in abt 1830; their 1st ch. was born when she was 25 years old; they had 15 children, of whom only 3 survived childhood; and she d. 8 mos after the b. of her last ch. Especially sad to see that two d. on the day they were born; and they had six sons named Johann Friedrich Mertz, for the father, all of whom died. In say 1830 when Johann Friedrich was 22, he married **Anna Maria FRASCH**. Born on 24 Oct 1806. Anna Maria died on 14 Dec 1851, she was 45.

They had the following children:

| | |
|---|---|
| (i). | Johann Jakob. Born on 1 Jun 1831.Johann Jakob married Angelika UHL. |
| (ii). | Anna Catharina. Born on 24 Nov 1833. Anna Catharina died on 12 Feb 1834. |
| (iii). | Johannes. Born on 23 Nov 1834. Johannes died on 19 Jun 1907, he was 72. |
| (iv). | [unnamed]. Born on 13 Jul 1836. [unnamed] died on 13 Jul 1836. |
| (v.) | Johann Friedrich. Born on 3 Sep 1837. Johann Friedrich died on 1 Oct 1837. |
| (vi). | Georg Adam. Born on 4 Nov 1838. Georg Adam died on 21 Nov 1838. |
| (vii). | Sophia Margarethe. Born on 8 Jan 1839. Sophia Margarethe died on 7 Feb 1839., doubtful, because of an insufficient interval after the birth of Georg Adam (4 Nov 1838). |
| (viii). | Johann Friedrich. Born on 2 Nov 1839. Johann Friedrich died on 14 Nov 1839. |
| (ix). | Johann Friedrich. Born on 16 Nov 1840. Johann Friedrich died on 26 Jan 1841. |
| (x). | Georg Adam. Born on 8 Apr 1842. |
| (xi). | Johann Heinrich. Born on 21 May 1843. Johann Heinrich died on 12 Aug 1843. |
| (xii). | Johann Friedrich. Born on 7 Oct 1845. Johann Friedrich died on 27 Oct 1845. |
| (xiii). | Johann Friedrich. Born on 25 Nov 1846. Johann Friedrich died on 5 Feb 1847. |
| (xiv). | Anna Mararethe. Born on 11 Jul 1849. Anna Mararethe died on 4 Oct 1849. |
| (xv). | Sophie Margarethe. Born on 2 Mar 1851. Sophie Margarethe died on 2 Mar 1851. |

-----------

**14**    iv.    Johann Georg [111112] (1765-1832) **14. Johann Georg [111112] ZIMMERMANN.** Born on 4 Jul (or Oct) 1765. Johann Georg [111112] died on 17 Feb 1832 (or 17 Feb 1837), he was 66. In 1790 when Johann Georg [111112] was 24, he married **Anna Ursula STAUDENMAIER**. Born on 12 Feb 1761 in Gussenstadt, Baden-Württemberg. Anna Ursula died in Sohnstetten on 18 Feb 1822, she was 61. She m. (1) 1785, Johann Jakob Jager, b. 1759; she m. (2) Johann Georg Zimmermann, with whom she had a daughter, Anna. They were probably divorced, for before he died, she m. (3) 17 Feb 1795, Leonard Bosch. They had one child:

    **21**    a.    Anna [1111121] (1796-1876) **21. Anna [1111121] ZIMMERMANN.** Born in 1796. Anna [1111121] died on 23 Nov 1876, she was 80. On 12 Nov 1834 when Anna [1111121] was 38, she married Johann G. AMGINTER. They had the following children:

        (i).    Johannes Georg [11111211]. Born on 21 Jan 1834. Johannes Georg [11111211] died in 1897, he was 62. Occupation: Weaver.

        (ii).    Jamessa [11111212]. Born on 6 Aug 1835. Jamessa [11111212] died in 1885, she was 49. Occupation: Weaver.

    v.    Margarethe [111113]. Born on 17 Feb 1767. In 1783 when Margarethe [111113] was 15, she married Georg ZELLER. Born on 25 Jul 1768.

    vi.    Catharina. Born on 10 Mar 1769. Catharina died on 13 Jun 1770, she was 1.

    vii.    Christoph. Born on 7 Aug 1771. Christoph died on 26 Dec 1777, he was 6.

**15**    viii.    Johann Friedrich [111114] (1776-1831) **15. Johann Friedrich [111114] ZIMMERMANN** b 21 Jul 1776. Johann Friedrich [111114] d 5 May 1831, he was 54.

    Child:    a.    F_____ Maria [1111141]. Born on 20 Mar 1818. F_____ Maria [1111141] died on 9 Jan 1873, she was 54.

    ix.    Christoph. Born on 9 May 1778. Christoph died on 5 May 1851, he was 72.

**16**    x.    Frikopf [111115] **16. Frikopf [111115] ZIMMERMANN.** Child:

    a.    Frikopf F. Born on 9 Apr 1805. Frikopf F. died on 7 Nov 1843, he was 38.

[16] [11112] (or Sigmund Friedrich).

[17] Sigmund Christoph Zimmermann is aka Sigmund Friedrich Zimmermann. He is in Chart 1, Generation 5. Sigmund Christoph [11112] (or Sigmund Friedrich) first married **Apollonia BÜHNER**. Born on 25 May 1745. Apollonia died on 29 Mar 1776, she was 30., daughter of Christop Bühne. The chart in JHN says she m. _____ Zimmermann (b. 17 May 1770; d. 1845), but the older chart in Sue Kelley Carnwath's notes shows Sigmund

Christoph [11112] (1744-1797) was the father of Johann George Zimmermann (1768-1835), father of Jacob Zimmermann (1801-1864), father of Johannes Zimmermann (1821-1899), father of John Zimmermann (1855-1936). Sue Carnwath's chart was prepared in Germany, and the dates are all more consistent than in the chart of JHN, so I will accept Carnwath's presentation of the Zimmermann line.

- - - - - - - - - - -

There are others with the surname of Bühner in Gussenstadt in Ancestry.com at that time, but she is not shown.

[18] Christoph Zimmermann is in Chart 1, Generation 6; and Chart 4.

[19] Appolonia BÜHNER is in Chart 4.

[20] His mother's name and his wife's name are the same, as is the name of his maternal grandfather and his father-in-law, but the ages show that they are 2 different generations.

[21] Jakob Zimmermann is in Chart 1, Generation 7. He "wove textiles in a one-room shop adjacent to their house in the tiny village of Gussenstadt, Germany" (JHN).

[22] (says JHN, 20 Nov 2009, p.2), with his family. In Chart 1, Generation 8.

[23] The last child of Johann and Margareta (Bantzhaff) Zimmermann , Michael, was b. in Elmira 30 May 1876. They may have immigrated with Maria & Michael Bantzhaff, whose son was b. in Elmira 9 Sep 1875. Johan Zimmermann and Michael Bantzhaff were neighbors, farmer, in the census of 1800 in Elmira (JHN 20 Nov 2009).

- - - - - - - - - -

On 14 Aug 1864 when Johann Georg [11112112] was 21, he married **Margareta BANTZHAFF**, daughter of ? **BANTZHAFF**, in Gussenstadt, Germany. Born on 26 Jun 1841 in Gustetten (or Sohnstetten), Germany. Margareta died in prob Elmira, N.Y., to which she emigrated in 1875 or 1876.

- - - - - - - - - - -

Margareta, daughter of ____ Bantzhaff, and sister of Michael Bantzhaff, who was b. 1845 in Sohstetten, Germany, 2 1/4 mi N of Gussenstadt. He m. Maria Schwartz, sister of Jakob Schwartz, b. 1854, who was in 1872 a law student in Elmira, NY, age 18. He was of almost the same age as Johann Georg Zimmermann's brother John (b. 1855). He probably welcomed John Zimmermann to Elmiria, which was his first residence in America.

- - - - - - - - - - -

They had the following children:

|      |                                                                                                                                     |
|------|-------------------------------------------------------------------------------------------------------------------------------------|
| i.   | Anna [111121121] Born on 8 Jun 1865 in Germany. Anna [111121121] died in Germany on 6 Aug 1866, she was 1.                          |
| ii.  | Jakob [111121122]. Born on 8 Dec 1866.                                                                                              |
| iii. | Katherine [111121123]. Born on 10 Aug 1868 in Germany.                                                                              |
| iv.  | Johann Georg [111121124]. Born on 26 Dec 1869 in Germany.                                                                           |
| v.   | Margarete (or Margareta) [111121125]. Born on 30 Jul 1872 in Germany.                                                               |
| vi.  | Johannes [111121126]. Born on 11 Jul 1874 in Germany. Johannes [111121126] died in Elmira, N.Y. on 18 Aug 1880, he was 6.          |
| vii. | Martin Albert. Born on 30 May 1876 in Elmira, N.Y.                                                                                  |
| viii.| Arlena. Born in 1878 in Elmira, N.Y.                                                                                                |
| ix.  | Mary. Born in 1879 in Elmira, N.Y.                                                                                                  |

[24] Johannes Zimmermann is sometimes called Johan, although that is an unusual German spelling of an alternate name for Johannes; he may, therefore, have also been known as Johan.

[25] JHN, p.23.

[26] Barbara S. Zimmermann, *Mutterings* (Wynnewood, Pa.: Livingston Publishing Co., 1969), 134-5. Text is lightly edited here.

[27] Johann Georg Zimmermann's birth 5 Jun 1851 and baptism 6 Jun 1851 as a child of Johannes Zimmermann and Anna Ursula Yäger in Gussenstadt, Württemberg, Germany is shown on Ancestry.com on Film 1340159. Nothing more about him in Ancestry.com -- not his m., emigration to America (if it happened), or his d.

The obituary for John Zimmerman (d. 23 May 1936): "JOHN ZIMMERMAN / John Zimmerman, retired textile manufacturer, who died Saturday, will be buried this afternoon following services from his home, 1512 W. Allegheny Ave. He was 81. / Born in Gussenstadt, Germany, Mr. Zimmerman came to Philadelphia in 1876, being attracted by the Centennial Exposition. A few years later he formed a partnership with his brother George, and both entered the textile manufacturing business." [Complete obituary in Part II]

[28] Recollections of his 1C1R, William Zimmermann, Jr.

[29] Recollections of his 1C1R, William Zimmermann, Jr.; also JHN, "John Zimmermann (1855-1936)" to GJH.

# 2

## The Kellenbenz Family

The Kellenbenz Family came to the United States from Württemberg, once a duchy, then a kingdom, and later a *Land* (state) in Germany. It is now one of the sixteen states in the Federal Republic of Germany. The Kellenbenz family has probably lived there for hundreds of years.[1]

The origin and meaning of the surname Kellenbenz is unknown. Kellenbenz is an unusual family name in America, and it is also uncommon in Germany. It is not one of the family names in the index of the standard reference book by George F. Jones, *German-American Names*. There are 14,000 names in the index, and many of the names in the index also have variations, so the total of the names mentioned is perhaps 20,000 or so. The name of Kellenbenz or any other obvious variation of the name does not appear in Jones' book.[2]

Jones tells us that German words are often compounded, so we might look for the origin of Kellenbenz by searching for a combination of Kell or Kellen + Benz. The index of Jones' book shows "Kell, Kelle (ladle, trowel, mason); "Kelle (swamp); and Kellenberger (fr Kellenberg, swamp mountain); surnames derived from *berg*, "the commonest name for mountain," which does not pertain to our family; "name-roots referring to marshes, bogs, and swamps," although it does not mention specifically the names Kell or Kelle; "wares they sold," which suggests that Kelle or Kelle may refer to the maker, seller, or user of the tool of a mason – i.e., a ladle or a trowel. The author says that "People often bore the name of the city of their origin," such as Frankfurter, who "could have come from the large city on the Main," or "the smaller Frankfurt on the Oder or from any of many places where the Franks forded a stream." This reference implies that the surname Kell or Kellen might refer to a city or place. I know of no such place in Württemberg, although there is a Kell, Germany, about 150 km north of Stuttgart, and a Kellen, Germany, on the border of the Netherlands.

The index also shows "Bentsen, son of Bentz," and variations "Bentz, Benz, Benze, Benzel, Bentzel < Bernhard or Benedict," and "Bentzen, son of Bentz"; in Scandanavia, "a man was often designated as the son of his father," and this "system of patronymics was once common in Germany." The implication is that Benz is a patronymic, presumably relating to the son of Bernhard or Benedict. The surname Benz is most famous for the marque of the motor car, "Mercedes-Benz," which is named for the daughter of Hermann Benz. This is certainly a Wurttemberg family name, for Hermann Benz and Gottlieb Daimler were early manufacturers of motor cars in Stuttgart. Indeed, some say that Gottlieb Daimler invented the motor car, and Benz was one of the earliest to follow Damlier into production of the horseless carriage.

If we suppose that Kellenbenz is a conjunction of Kell or Kelle + Benz, it might originally have meant "a mason (or a man of the swamp), son of Bernhard" or "a man from Kellen, son of Benedict." In Germany, as elsewhere in Europe, the origin of the name soon became unimportant. Within a generation or two, the surname name was used to identify a person and his descendants and it no longer related to the origin of the word.

I will discuss the Kellenbenz family in America at a later point in this chapter, but I will give an example here to show how rare the name is in America: the U.S. Federal Census for 1920 shows only 78 individuals – men, women, and children – named Kellenbenz; and the Kellenbenz family name appears in only 6 states. In the entire United States there were only about 14-18 families named Kellenbenz. The computer estimate of the name on Ancestry.com shows that 4-5 families named Kellenbenz were located in the state of Pennsylvania and 4-5 were in Wisconsin; 2-3 families were in Colorado and 2-3 in Michigan; and only one Kellenbenz family was shown to be living in Maryland and one in New Jersey.[3]

## The Kellenbenz Family in Württemberg

The Kellenbenz Family came to the United States from Württemberg, in the Swabian Alps of Central Europe, now the state of Baden-Württemberg in the Federal Republic of Germany. The history of Central Europe, Swabia, and Württemberg is discussed in the introduction to Part I of this book. The genealogy of the Kellenbenz family (*der Sippe Kellenbenz*) of Gross Süßen (Great Süssen) and Klein-Eislingen (now known as Süssen and Eislingen), Württemberg, since 1530, is derived from a newspaper article that was written in German and was published in about 1967. The location of the publication is unknown, and the article does not appear on a Google search in the original German. It was presumably published in Baden-Württemberg. It was written by someone whose initials were shown as "E. T.," but whose full name is unknown.[4]

### Etwas von der Sippe Kellenbenz

Schon um die erste Zeit der Reformation, also vor beinahe 450 Jahren, war einer des Namens Kellenbenz im Filstal ansässig, und zwar in dem daimals zum Gebiet der Reichstadt Ulm gehörenden Pfarrdorf Groß-Süßen. Heute noch blühen verschiendene Zweige dieses Geschlects in Orden des Filstals. Jahrhunderted lang waren immer wieder einige dieser Kellenbenz als Gastwirte tätig, so in Ebersbach, Groß-Süßen, Klein-Eislingen, Stammheim, Waiblingen und Wiesensteig. Aber auch weibliche Gmeder dieser Sippe Kellenbenz waren vielfach mit Vertretern des Gastwirtsgewerbes verheiratet, und es ist zu vermuten, daß dabei meist der Bräutigam auf die schwiegerväterliche, kellenbenzische Gastwirtschaft „eingeheiratet" hat.

Der prominenteste Namensträger der bebesprochenen Sippe war aber der in Tübingen tätige Doctor juris Bartholomäus Kellenbenz, der durch das von ihm im September 1624 mit 4000 Gulden Kapital gestiftete Familien-Stipendium fur Studierende und Handwerkslehrinlinge, damals schon weiten Kreisen bekannt geworden 1st. Dieser Barthomomaus Kellenbenz (geb. 31. August 1562) war der Enkel des eingangs erwahnten Süßener Kellenbenz und das fünfte Kind (unter den sieben Söhnen und fünf Töchtern) von Lorenz Kellenbenz (geb. ca. 1530; gest. 1595), des Gastgebers zum „Adler" in Groß-Süßen. Höcst wahrscheinlicht dürfen wir als Stammhaus der noch feststelibar gewesenen ältesten Kellenbenz das frühere Wirtshaus zum „Adler" in Groß-Süßen annehmen, das dann die Ortsherrschaft, also die Reichsstadt Ulm, im Jahr 1592 dem Lorenz Kellenbenz (geb. 1572), dem Bruder des Stipendien-Stifters, abgekauft hat. Dieses Gebäude wurde später, im Jahre 1826, von der Gemeinde erworben, um zum Schul- und Rathaus umgebaut zu werden.

Der bald zu Ansehen, aber auch Vermögen gekommene Dr. jr. Barthomomäus Kellenbenz heirabete in erster Ehe in Tübingen im Jahr 1588 die schon zweimal verwitwete Margareta, geb. Königsbach (1545 bis 1617, welche zuerst den Professor der Rechte Chilian Vogler (1516 bis 1585) und dann den Professor der Medizin Johann Vischer (1524 bis 1587) zum Gemahl hatte. Im Jahr nach dem Tod seiner ersten Ehefrau verheirabate sich Bartholomaus Kellenbenz 1618 in Tübingen mit einer Catharina, der Witwe des Andreas Walch (Schorndorf).

Die nach damaligem Brauch in umständlichen und langen Sätzen aufgestelle Stiflungsurkunde für das Kellenbenz'sche Stipendium ist auf Seiben 100 ff. des zehnten Heftes (von 1854) in dem von Finanzrat Ferd. Fr. Faber herausgegebenen Sammelwerk „Württ. Familien-Stiftungen" abgedruckt. Die Stifftung, deren Zinsen mit rd. 300 Gulden jährlich zur Verteilung kamen, wurde vom Akadem. Senat der Universität Tübingen verwaltet, bis das Stiftungskapital, wie in andern gleichartigen Fällen, ums Jahr 1922/23 der Inflation verfiel und damit die Stiftungsbestianmungen ihre Grundlage verloren hatten.

Ein Oheim des Stifters, der Hans Kellenbenz, bewirtschaftete schon um 1540/60 die Herberge in Klein-Eislingen. Dann wissen wir, daß ein Vetter des Barthomomäus Kellenbenz, der dreimal verheirabete Lorenz Kellenbenz (gest. 1649) aus Wiensteig, gute zwanzig Jaahre lang die Herberge in Ebersbach innehatte; ein Nikolaus Braun (geb. 1641) hat im Jahr 1664 dort eingeheiratet und die Catharina Kellenbenz (geb. 1644) heimgeführt.

In den letzten Jahrzehnten des 17. Jahrhunderts amtete der Georg Kellenbenz, ein 1644 geborener Sohn des Eislinger Johannes Kellenbenz, als Schultheiß in Klein-Eislingen. Sein ältester Sohn Johannes Kellenbenz (geb. 1670) wurde Gastwirt zur „Traube" in Waiblingen, während dessen nächstfolgender Bruder, der Johann Georg Kellenbenz (1763 bis 1703) sich dem Pfarrersband widmete, zuletzt in Boll. Die Tochter des vorgenannten Schultheißen, die Maria Margareta Kellenbenz (geb. 1681), heiratete den Gastwirt zum „Rad" Andreas Höfelin in Göppingen.—Der drittälteste Schultheißen-Enkel, ein Sohn von Sebastian Kellenbenz (geb. Klein-Eislingen 1677, nämlich der Johann Jakob Kellenbenz (geb. 1702), war auch längere Zeit als Schultheiß der Ortsvorsteher von Klein-Eislingen.

Dann finden wir noch einmal einen Kellenbenz als württembergischen Pfarrer, den in Waiblingen im „Trauben" – Gasthaus geborenen Johannes Kellenbenz (1722 bis 1803), der von 1754 bis 1780 in Rieth und zuletzt in Nußdorf als evangelischer Seelsorger ämtierte.

Schließlich mögen hier noch fünf Namensträger Kellenbenz (Großvater, Vater und dessen drei Söhne) aufgezählt werden, die alle die niedere Arzneikunst erlernt hatten und – mit Ausnahme des Jüngsten – als „Chirurgii" in Klein-Eislingen praktizierten. Der älteste von den vier Söhnen des (zweiten ) Schultheißen Joh. Jakob Kellenbenz, der 1726 geborene Chirurgus Gottlieb I Kellenbenz, schröpfte in Klein-Eislingen, ließ zur Ader und betätigte sich auch als Geburtshelfer. Des Letzteren Sohn, der Chirurgus Gottlieb II Kellenbenz (geb. 1751), welcher im Jahr 1779 eine Jakobine, geb. Schrag, geehelicht hatte, führte die väterliche Praxis weiter. Seine drei in Klein-Eislingen geborenen Söhne haben – als III. Genereation – ebenfalls die niedere Chirurgie erlernt und ausgeübt, so Gottlieb III Kellenbenz (geb. 1784) und Johann Michael Kellenbenz (geb. um 1790) je wiederum in Klein-Eislingen. Der jüngste Bruder, Chirurgus Johann Leonhard Kellenbenz (geb. 1794) ließ sich in Ansbach (Bayern) nieder.

## The Kellenbenz Family[5]
### (*Etwas von der Sippe Kellenbenz*)

For about 450 years since the Reformation began[6], the surname of Kellenbenz has been known in Filstal, in the parish of Greater-Süssen, in the region of the imperial city of Ulm. Different branches of this family are still flourishing there. For many centuries, some of the Kellenbenzs worked as restaurant operators and barkeepers. Some are still active today in Ebersbach, Klein-Eislingen, Stammheim, Waiblingen and Wiesensteig. In addition, female members of the Kellenbenz family have been married to other representatives of the restaurant operator / barkeeper trade, and other Kellenbenz women have often worked for their fathers-in-law in the hotel industry.

The most prominent person in the history of the Kellenbenz family is Bartholomäus Kellenbenz, Doctor Juris (born 31 August 1562), who was active in the city of Tübingen. In September 1624, in the capitol city, he established a family scholarship for the study of handwork with a grant of 4000 gold pieces. Bartholomäus Kellenbenz was the grandchild of Süssener Kellenbenz. He was the fifth child (of seven sons and five daughters) of Lorenz Kellenbenz (born abt. 1530; died 1595). Lorenz Kellenbenz was the host of the "Alder" in Greater-Süssen, which was the oldest tavern in the royal city of Ulm. In 1592 it was owned by Lorenz Kellenbenz [II] (born 1572), who purchased it from the brother of the scholarship founder. This building was acquired in 1826 by Ulm, to be converted into the city hall.

Soon reputation, in addition to fortune, came to Dr. Jur. Bartholomaus Kellenbenz. He married (1) the twice widowed Margarete (born Königsbach, in Tubingen, in the year 1588). Margarete Königsbach's first husband was Professor der Recte [Rector] Chilian Vogler (1516-1585). Her second husband was Johann Vischer, Professor of Medicine (1524-1587). Margarethe (Königsbach) (Vogler) Vischer died in 1618, and Bartholomaus Kellenbenz married (2) Catharina (Schorndort) Walch, in Tübingen, widow of Andreas Walch.

The charter of the foundation for the Kellenbenz scholarship is in the Financial Report of Ferd. Fr. Faber (Würtemberg, 10th booklet, 1854), pp. 100ff. The reports of family foundations which had an interest of 300 gold pieces, to be distributed annually, were printed by the Academic Senate of the University of Tübingen until 1922/23. At that time, the trustees, along with many others, lost the capital of their foundations.

The uncle of the founder, Hans Kellenbenz, was living in Klein-Eislingen around 1540/60. A cousin of the noted Bartholomäus Kellenbenz, Lorenz Kellenbenz (died 1649), from Wiensteig, lived for twenty years in the country of Hergerge in Ebersbach. At about the same time, in 1664, a Nicholas Braun (born 1641) married one Catharina Kellenbenz (born 1644).

In the tenth decade of the 17th century, George Kellenbenz, was born in 1644, son of Johannes Kellenbenz, "the Eislinger," Schultheiss [mayor] in Klein-Eislingen. George Kellenbenz' oldest son, Johannes Kellenbenz (born 1670), became a restaurant operator/ barkeeper in Traube in Waiblingen. His brother Johann George Kellenbenz (1673 to 1703) became a minister in Boll. The daughter of the aforementioned Schultheissen, Maria Margareta Kellenbenz (born 1681), married Andreas Hofelin, a restaurant operator/barkeeper in Göppingen. The third oldest Schutheissen grandchild, a son of Sebastian Kellenbenz (born Klein-Eislingen in 1677), was Johann Jakob Kellenbenz (born 1702). He was also a Schultheiss and was for many years the local chief in Klein-Eislingen.

In Württemberg, in the town of Waiblingen, at the Trauben hotel, was Johannes Kellenbenz (1722 to 1803), also an Protestant pastor from 1745 to 1780 in the village of Rieth.

Finally, I would like to mention three of the name Kellenbenz (grandfather, father and three sons) who have learned the art of medicine, and who (with the exception of Joh. Jakob Kellenbenz, the second, oldest of the four sons), are all doctors practicing in Klein-Eislingen. Doctor Gottlieb Kellenbenz (the first) born in 1726 a surgeon in Klein-Eislingen, applied to deliver babies. In the year 1779, Jakobine (born Schrag), joined her relative, the younger son of Doctor Gottlieb Kellenbenz II (born 1751), in his medical practice. Three generations of the Kellenbenz family in Klein-Eislingen have thus learned to practice medicine: Gottlieb Kellenbenz, III (born 1784) and Johann Michael Kellenbenz (born in 1790) in Klein-Eislingen, while the younger brother, Doctor Johann Leonhard Kellenbenz (born 1794), settled in Ansbach (Bayern). E.F.

**Towns and Cities in Württemberg Associated with the Kellenbenz Family**
**Eislingen and Süssen (formerly Klein-Eislingen and Gross Süssen),**
**Ebersbach, Tübingen, Stammheim, Waiblingen, Wiesensteig, Göppingen,**
**Stuttgart, and Ulm**

**1. JOHANNES[H] KELLENBENZ**,[7] "the Eislinger," was *Shultheiss* (mayor) of Klein-Eislingen, a small town near Gross Süssen, in the duchy of Württemberg. These places are now known as Eislingen and Süssen, in the state (*Land*) of Baden-Württemberg, Germany.

The Kellenbenz family is said to have lived in the area near Süssen since about 1517, or perhaps much earlier. It thus appears that three or four generations of men named Kellenbenz lived near Süssen and who were Johannes Kellenbenz's ancestors, although their names are unknown. They had probably been leading citizens, for Johannes and his sons were mayors of the town. This Johannes Kellenbenz is the first Kellenbenz whose ancestry may be traced with some probability to the emigrant, Eva Katherine Kellenbenz, who married John Zimmermann. Johannes Kellenbenz had, with a wife whose name is unknown, a son:

> 2    i.    GEORG[G] (1644-) +

**2. GEORG[G] KELLENBENZ**, son of Johannes Kellenbenz, "the Eislinger," *Schultheiss* in Klein-Eislingen, Württemberg, was born in 1644. He had, by a wife whose name is unknown:

> 3    i.    JOHANNES, b. 1670; became a restaurant operator/barkeeper in Traube, in Waiblingen; 1 child.[8]
>
>      ii.    JOHANN GEORG, b. 1673; d. 1703; minister in Boll, near Süssen.
>
> 4    iii.    SEBASTIAN[F] (1677-) +
>
>      iv.    MARIA MARGARETA, b. 1681; m. **Andreas HÖFELIN**, restaurant operator/barkeeper in Göppingen.

**4. SEBASTIAN[F] KELLENBENZ**, son of Georg Kellenbenz, was born in Klein-Eislingen, Duchy of Württemberg, in 1677.
Sebastian Kellenbenz had, with a wife whose name is unknown, a son:

> 5    i.    JOHANN JAKOB[E] (1702-) +

**5. JOHANN JACOB[E] KELLENBENZ**,[9] *Schultheiss* (mayor) in Klein-Eislingen, son of Sebastian Kellenbenz, was born in Klein-Eislingen in 1702. Also at about that time, in Württemberg, in the town of Waiblingen, at the Trauben Hotel, there was a man named Johannes Kellenbenz (1722 to 1803). He was also the Protestant pastor from 1745 to 1780 in the village of Rieth. He was presumably related in some way to the Kellenbenz family of Klein-Eislingen; by his age and his name, he could have been the first-born son of Johann Jacob Kellenbenz. Johann Jacob Kellenbenz had, by a wife whose name is unknown, at least one child, and perhaps others:

> 6    i.    Dr. GOTTLIEB[D] I (1726-) +

**6. Dr. GOTTLIEB[D] KELLENBENZ**, known as "the first," a physician, son of Johann Jakob Kellenbenz, was born at Klein-Eislingen, Donaukreis [district of Donau], Kingdom of Württemberg, in 1726. He was the first of three or more generations of men named Gottlieb Kellenbenz. Gottlieb I Kellenbenz was a surgeon in Eislingen, when he applied for a license to deliver babies there. He had, by a wife whose name is unknown, at least one child, and perhaps two. His son and namesake, founded a line of physicians, whereas another possible son was the great-grandfather of Eva Katherine Kellenbenz, the emigrant to America. He had:

> 7    i.    Dr. GOTTLIEB II, b. 1751; a physician; m. a relative, **Dr. Jakobine SCHRAG**, who joined him in medical practice in Klein-Eislingen in 1779; 4 ch., 3 of whom were also physicians.[10]
>
> 8    ii.    ? JOHANN JACOB[C] [aka Jakob] (~1766-) +

**7. Dr. GOTTLIEB II KELLENBENZ,** son of Dr. Gottlieb I Kellenbenz, was born in Klein-Eisligen, Wurttenberg, in 1751. He practiced medicine in Klein-Eislingen. He married a relative, Dr. Jakobine SCHRAG, who joined him in practice in 1779. They had three sons who were also physicians, and one more: Children of Gottlieb II and Jakobine (Schrag) Kellenbenz:

> 9     i.     Dr. GOTTLIEB III, b. 1784; perhaps had a son, Gottlieb, who has descendants in the United States. **11** i. ? GOTTLIEB IV

**11. Gottlieb IV KELLENBENZ,** perhaps the Gottlieb Kellenbenz who m. **Anna Maria STAUDENMAIER**, Kleineislingen; and had a son, Joseph, who m. **Elisabethe Margarete KLEMENT** and had 8 ch., all b. in Kleineislingen, Donaukreis, Werttemberg.

Gottlieb IV Kellenbenz and his wife, Anna Maria Staudenmaier, had one child, and perhaps more:

> 15     i.     Joseph (1836-1880)
>       ii.     JOH. JAKOB II.
>       iii.     Dr. JOHANN MICHAEL, b. 1790.
>       iv.     Dr. JOHANN LEONHARD, b. 1794, physician; settled in Ansbach (Bayern).

**8. JOHANN JACOB<sup>C</sup> [aka Jakob] KELLENBENZ,**[11] born about 1766, in Klein-Eislingen, District of Donau, Kingdom of Württemberg, perhaps the oldest son or perhaps a grandson of Dr. Gottlieb I Kellenbenz, of Klein-Eislingen, near Süssen, now in the state of Baden-Württemberg, Germany. He is not mentioned in the text of *Etwas von der Sippe Kellenbenz* as one of the children of either Dr. Gottlieb I or Dr. Gottlieb II Kellenbenz, so his parentage must be assumed.

He married in about 1789, perhaps at Würtemberger Hof, Schwabisch Hall,[12] now in Baden-Württemberg, **Christina SILLER** (or **SIHLER**), born in 1766. They had a son[13]:

> 10     i.     JOHANN GEORG<sup>B</sup> (known as Georg) (1794-1870) +

**10. JOHANN GEORG<sup>B</sup> (known as Georg) KELLENBENZ,**[14] son of Johann Jacob Kellenbenz and his wife Christina Siller, was born in Kleineislingen, Donaukreis (district of Donau), Württemberg, Germany, 26 October 1794; died there, 27 January 1870. He married, 27 September 1820, perhaps at Württemberg Hof, Swabisch Hall, **Anna Maria CLEMENT** (or **KLEMENT**), daughter of Johannes and Agnesa (Mitchell) Klement; born in 1797; died at Württemberg, 8 August 1871. They had 13 children, two of whose names are known, as follows:

> 12     i.     JOHANN MICHAEL<sup>A</sup> (1825-1888) +
> 13     ii.     [11 more children]; one of these children was a son; he had a son, GEORGE.
> 14     iii.     GOTTLIEB<sup>1</sup> (1839-1907) (see below)

**12. JOHANN MICHAEL<sup>A</sup> KELLENBENZ,** son of Johann Georg Kellenbenz and his wife Anna Maria Clement, was born at Kleineislingen, Donaukreis, Württemberg, Germany, 26 February 1825; died at Göppingen, Donaukreis, Württemberg, 31 July 1888. He married, 18 May 1853, **Clara GRÖZINGER,**[15] born at Ottenbach, Donaukreis, 29 July 1828; died at Kleineislingen, 9 November 1899. Johann Michel Kellenbenz and his wife Clara Grözinger had 16 children. Two of daughters came to America with or following their uncle Gottlieb Kellenbenz, who was married in Philadelphia in 1867 or 1868.

Their children, born at Kleineislingen, surname Kellenbenz, were[16]:

>       i.     CHRISTINA, b. 18 Sep 1855; d. 29 Jan 1858.
>       ii.     EVA KATHARINA, b. 7 Sep 1854; d. 16 Sep 1854.
> 16     iii.     EVA KATHERINE<sup>1</sup> (aka Eva Catherine, Evakaterina, Eva Kathryn or Catherine) (1855-1920) +
>       iv.     ANNA MARIA, b. 27 Mar 1857; d. 26 Nov 1861.
>       v.     CHRISTINA, b. 3 Sep 1858; d. 14 Nov 1858.
> 17     vi.     CLARA KATHARINA ROSINA (1860-~1925)
>       vii.     GOTTLIEB, b. 23 Dec 1861; d. 2 Jun 1862.

|       |       |                                                      |
|-------|-------|------------------------------------------------------|
|       | viii. | ROSINA FRIEDERIKE, b. 13 Dec 1862; d. 2 Dec 1865.    |
|       | ix.   | [son], b. and d., 19 Jan 1864.                       |
| **18**| x.    | KARL WILHELM (1864-)                                 |
|       | xi.   | JOHANN GOTTLIEB, b. 7 Jan 1866.                      |
|       | xii.  | MARIA FRIEDERIKE, b. 18 May 1867; d. 2 Jun 1867.     |
|       | xiii. | AUGUST, b. 21 Aug 1868; d. 10 Sep 1868.              |
|       | xiv.  | ANNA MARIA, b. 6 Sep 1869; d. 23 Oct 1869.           |
|       | xv.   | KARL, b. 27 Jun 1871; d. 18 Jul 1871.                |
|       | xvi.  | RUDOLF, b. 17 Apr 1873; d. 30 Apr 1873.              |

**14. GOTTLIEB**[1] **KELLENBENZ,**[17] son one of the 13 children of Johann Georg and Anna Maria (Clement) Kellenbez, was born at Kleineislingen, Württemberg, 9 May 1839; died at Philadelphia, Pa., 1 Nov 1907; buried there, in Greenmount Cemetery. He married, in 1867 or 1868, **Katharine FRECH,**[18] born 4 July 1847 in Germany, perhaps at Württemberger Hof, Swabish Hall, Württemberg; died at Philadelphia, Pa., 28 September 1924. Gottlieb and Katharine (Frech) Kellenbenz had the following children, born in Philadelphia:

|       |       |                                                                                                                                         |
|-------|-------|-----------------------------------------------------------------------------------------------------------------------------------------|
|       | i.    | GEORGE, b. 5 Aug 1868; d. 1915; worked at Angola Dyeing Co., Hope & Clearfield, Philadelphia, where he was in photo with his brother William, c. 1900-05. |
|       | ii.   | WILLIAM, b. 21 Jul 1870; d. 1949; worked at Angola Dyeing Co., Hope & Clearfield, was in photo with his brother George. |
|       | iii.  | FRED, b. Aug 1872.                                                                                                        |
| **19**| iv.   | HENRY (1873-1951)                                                                                                         |
|       | v.    | CHARLES, b. Jul 1877; d. 1947.                                                                                            |
|       | vi.   | JOHN, b. Jan 1880.                                                                                                        |
|       | vii.  | GOTTLIEB DAVID, b. 24 Sep 1882; d. 1 Jul 1884.                                                                            |
|       | viii. | ALBERT, b. 2 Nov 1882.                                                                                                    |
|       | ix.   | KATIE, b. Dec 1883.                                                                                                       |
|       | x.    | DAVID, b. 4 Jun 1886; d. 5 Aug 1887.                                                                                      |
|       | xi.   | ANDREW, b. Sep 1887.                                                                                                      |
|       | xii.  | GUSTAV, b. 23 Dec 1889; d. 1943.                                                                                          |
| **20**| xiii. | ANNE                                                                                                                      |

**Katharine (Frech) Kellenbenz and her sons, George and William**

**15. JOSEPH KELLENBENZ,** son of Gottlieb and Anna Maria (Staudenmaier) Kellenbenz, was born at Kleineislingen, Wurttemberg, 23 February 1836; christened there, 25 February 1836; died there, 23 February 1880. His father was perhaps the son and namesake of Dr. Gottlieb III Kellenbenz. He married, at Kleineislingen, 3 May 1863, **Elisabeth Margarete KLEMENT**, daughter of Johann Andreas and Elisabeth Margarete (Mönner) Klement; born at Kleineislingen, 24 July 1835; died at Norristown, Montgomery Co., Pa. on 22 December 1910.
Joseph and Elisabeth Margarete (Klement) Kellenbenz had the following children, born at Kleineislingen, surname Kellenbenz:

        i.        LOUIS, b. 20 April 1861; bp. 24 April 1861; d. 13 May 1861.

        ii.       ANNA MARIA, b. 30 June 1863; bp. 5 July 1863; d. 18 July 1863.

        iii.      JOHANN CHRISTIAN, b. 10 November 1864; bp. 13 November 1864; d. 10 May 1956, in Penna.; bur. 14 May 1956 in Huntington Valley, Montgomery Co., Pa., Forest Hills Cem., Prospect Sec., Lot 19, Grave 2; arr. 24 August 1892, Phila., from Switzerland, via Antwerp; m. (1) 4 November 1889, Kleineislingen, **Marie Christiana ZUBER**; b. 1866; d. Springfield, Bucks, Pa., 18 March 1906; m. (2) 12 July 1906, Philadelphia, **Auguste KRAUSE**; b. 1860; d. Haycock, Bucks, Pa., 26 June 1915; m. (3) **Elizabeth SEP**P, b. 1871.

        iv.      GOTTLIEB, b. 16 March 1868; d. 3 May 1868.

        v.       ANNA MARIA, b. 4 April 1869; d. Montgomery Co., Pa., 1 November 1947; arrived in New York, 7 April 1893; m. **Alexander GEHRING**, b. 9 March 1868, Burhburg, Canton, Schaffhausen, Switzerland; d. Montgomery Co., Pa., 15 July 1959. Their great-grandson, Richard Clark, translated the obituary for Hermann Kellenbenz (see below).

        vi.      KATHERINA BARBARA, b. 23 Nov 1872; d. Haycock, Bucks Co., Pa., 11 Apr 1946; m. **William HOOT**, b. Penna., 12 Sep 1864; d. 10 May 1947.

        vii.     ELIZABETH MARGARETE, b. 28 Jun 1875; d. 1922; m. **Georg KESTEL**, b. Kreichheim Bu Landau.

        viii.    JOHANN GOTTLIEB, b. 24 Nov 1877; bp. 2 Dec 1877; d. 1950; arr. New York, 12 Nov 1923; was in Phila. census of 1930; m. **Anna Katharina HILDEBRAND**, b. 1879 in Germany; d. Philadelphia, Pa., May 1971.

**16. EVA KATHERINE (Evakaterina) KELLENBENZ,** third daughter and third of the sixteen children of Johann Michael and Clara (Grözinger) Kellenbenz, was born 28 September 1855 at Kleineislingen, in the kingdom of Württemberg, now simply called Eislingen, in the present state of Baden-Württemberg, near Stuttgart, Germany; died at Philadelphia, Pennsylvania, 12 October 1920. She was buried in Greenmount Cemetery, at Front St. near Hunting Park Ave., beside her daughter Emily. She and two younger sisters were the only survivors of the sixteen children of her parents who lived to become adults. One of the sisters also came to America, probably with their uncle Gottlieb Zimmermann.

    She married, as his first wife, at Philadelphia, 15 October 1885, **John (Johannes) ZIMMERMANN**, son of Johannes and Anna (Yaeger) Zimmermann; born at Gussenstadt, Germany, 28 November 1855; died at Philadelphia, 23 May 1936 (Part II, Chapter 3). They had seven children, of whom six lived to adulthood. (Part III, Chapters 4-10).

**17. CLARA KATHARINA ROSINA KELLENBENZ,**[19] sixth child and sixth of the sixteen children of Johann Michael and Clara (Grözinger) Kellenbenz, was born 15 February 1860 in Kleineislingen, Württemberg, Germany; died between 1925-1930. She came to America with her sister Eva from Stuttgart under the sponsorship of a German Lutheran pastor; they worked as domestics in a Philadelphia home. She married, in 1887, in Philadelphia, **Frederick WEIGLE**. Frederick and Clara (Kellenbenz) Weigle had the following children, surname Weigle:

        i.        FREDERICK, b. Philadelphia.

**21**    ii.       WILLIAM, b. Philadelphia.

**18. KARL WILHELM KELLENBENZ,**[20] third son and tenth of the sixteen children of Johann Michael and Clara (Grozinger) Kellenbenz, was born at Kleineislingen, Wurttemberg, 29 December 1864. He married **Fanny LAUSER**, born after 1855. Their daughters, Anna and Eugenie, both born in Stuttgart, came to the U.S. in 1922 and stayed with the Zimmermanns: Karl Wilhelm and Fanny (Lauser) Kellenbenz had the following children, born in Württemberg, probably in Stuttgart:

> 22    i.      EUGENIA
>        ii.     ANNA.
> 23    iii.    FANNY (-1968)

----------

Albert Walter[2] Zimmermann, son of John[1] Zimmermann, and his wife Barbara (née Shoemaker) visited members of the Kellenbenz family in Stuttgart in the summer of 1937, when they took a trip to Europe. We do not know the names of those who he visited, other than that one was a "cousin" of Al. She was probably Eugenia, who married Siegfried Bollacher (1904- ); she and Al were almost the same age. Movies taken by Al and excerpts from Barbara's diary provide a glimpse of life as it was then in Germany in the period of the Third Reich. It was two years before Hitler invaded Poland and World War II began. The center of Stuttgart and most of the surrounding parts of the city were completely destroyed by Allied bombs in 1944.

> Barbara (Shoemaker) Zimmermann wrote[21]:
> Monday [9 August 1937] – Stuttgart – . . . We had dinner with Al's cousin[1] who speaks very little English. I have accused Al, who claims to speak German, of talking baby talk as he learned it as a baby. No one seemed to understand him at first but he's improving and even I can understand a good deal, a relic of the Illg regime in our household. This cousin is very much opposed to Hitler although she wouldn't talk until we took her up to our room and then in decided undertones.

Still shots from Albert Zimmermann's movies show pleasant scenes of a family of five walking along a path beside a river. Two of the people in the movie are probably Al's cousin Eugenie and her husband, Siegfried Bollacher. The others are possibly Siegfried's brother and perhaps her mother-in-law, and a young woman and a child about two years old, perhaps a sister-in-law and a niece. They are probably walking along the bank of the Nektar River. The upstairs room of the cousin, Eugenie Bolacher, in Stuttgart is likely the place where Al crouched and surreptitiously took a few seconds of movie film. It shows the chilling images of uniformed marching troops, bearing rifles. Still shots from that film appear below. Very few other American tourists ever took movies such as this; I have never seen another one. Al also filmed two other scenes of uniformed police or officers in German-speaking countries; one was in Wurtzburg, Bavaria, and the other was probably in a city in Austria, which by then was incorporated into the Third Reich. In the latter location, there were three policemen standing in the background, near some sort of tower. One of them suddenly realized that he was being photographed. He turned toward Al, who immediately stopped filming.

Al and Barbara also visited England and Scotland on this trip. It was about six months after the abdication of King Edward VIII, and Al's films of Buckingham Palace recorded the changing of the guard for Edward's brother, King George VI. From London, they went to Holland, and then to Germany, Italy, and France before returning to America.

---

[1] She is probably Eugenia (Kellenbenz) Bollacher (see Kellenbenz Family).

# Images of Württemberg – Stuttgart and Surrounding Area
## August 1937

**Still images from movies taken in August 1937 by Albert Zimmermann**

**Ox cart and river (upper R), probably the Nektar River in Stuttgart (upper L)**

**The family is probably that of Al's cousin Eugenia (Kellenbenz) Bollacher and her husband, Siegfried Bollacher, on the R; his brother (name unknown), wife, and daughter (L to center)**

## Police and Military Activities in the Third Reich

**Still images from movies taken in August 1937 by Albert Zimmermann**

**Upper L shows a glimpse of a Nazi officer at the lower R corner, in uniform**
**Upper R shows a policeman, one of a group of three, as he turned to the camera**
**The lower photo shows a platoon of soldiers with rifles, marching in Stuttgart**

**These images were each filmed by Zimmermann for less than three seconds**

**19. HENRY KELLENBENZ,**[22] fourth son and fourth child of Gottlieb and Katharine (Frech) Kellenbenz, was born at Philadelphia, Penna., 8 October 1873; died there, 11 May 1951. He married **Mary Jane CORR**; born at Philadelphia, 8 May 1876; died there, 1 March 1943. Henry and Mary Jane (Corr) Kellenbenz had the following children, born at Philadelphia, Pa.:

|    |      |                                                                            |
|----|------|----------------------------------------------------------------------------|
|    | i.   | CATHERINE, b. 23 Apr 1902; d. 1977.                                        |
|    | ii.  | JOHN J., b. 13 May 1904; d. Philadelphia, Pa. 6 Apr 1940.                 |
|    | iii. | HARRY, b. 30 May 1906; d. Sadsburyville, Chester Co., Pa., May 1981.      |
|    | iv.  | LEONARD, b. 5 Nov 1908; d. Philadelphia, Pa., 31 Jan 1991.               |
|    | v.   | ELLEN F., b. 10 Oct 1910; d. 1981.                                        |
| 24 | vi.  | ANNA (1917-1974)                                                          |
|    | vii. | CHARLES JOSEPH, b. 18 Oct 1918; d. Dade Co., Fla., 14 Dec 1981.          |

**20. ANNE KELLENBENZ**[23] married _____ **MITCHELL**. They had a child:

|    |    |      |
|----|----|------|
| 25 | i. | _____ |

**21. WILLIAM WEIGLE,**[24] second son and second child of Frederick and Clara Katharina Rosina (Kellenbenz) Weigle, married **Anna L. ____**. William and Anna L. Weigle had the following children, born in Philadelphia, Pa.:

|    |      |                                                                                                                      |
|----|------|----------------------------------------------------------------------------------------------------------------------|
|    | i.   | LOUISE, m. _____ **MacCURDY**; relocated to Spring Hill, Fl.                                                         |
|    | ii.  | WILLIAM,[25] b. about 1924; died at Brooksville, Fl., 13 Dec 2000; married **Betty ____**; children: i. Linda. ii. Debra; 5 grandchildren. |
| 26 | iii. | FREDERICK relocated to Spring Hill, Fl.; d. bef 2000; not mention in brother's obit.                                |
|    | iv.  | RUTH, m. _____ **MORNINGRED**; relocated to Spring Hill, Fl.                                                         |

**22. EUGENIA KELLENBENZ,**[26] eldest daughter and first child of Karl Wilhelm and Fanny (Lauser) Kellenbenz, was born at Württemberg, probably in Stuttgart. She married **Siegfried BOLLACHER**; born about 1904; died about 1984. Siegfried and Eugenia (Kellenbenz) Bollacher had the following children, born in Württemberg, probably in or near Stuttgart:

|    |      |                                                                                                                              |
|----|------|------------------------------------------------------------------------------------------------------------------------------|
| 27 | i.   | WOLFGANG, b. 1933; lawyer in Ludwigsburg, near Stuttgart, Baden-Wurttemberg; m. **Isle ____**; 3 ch.: i. Tilman, b. 1964. ii. Sebastian , b. 1966. iii. Christian, b. 1972. |
| 28 | ii.  | DIETRICH (Dieter), b. 1936; in Finance Ministry, Stuttgart; m. **Isolda _____**; 3 ch.: i. Florian, b. 1974. ii. Felix, b. 1976. iii. Philip, b. 1977. |
| 29 | iii. | MARTIN (1940-), b. 1940; Professor of German Literature, Bochum, Germany; m. **Yvonne _____**. 3 ch.: i. Oliver, b. 1969. ii. Maria, b. 1973. iii. Sophie. |

**23. FANNY KELLENBENZ,**[27] third daughter and third child of Karl Wilhelm and Fanny (Lauser) Kellenbenz, was born at Württemberg, probably in Stuttgart; died in 1968. She married **William KRÄMER**. William and Fanny (Kellenbenz) Kramer had one child:

|    |    |                                                                         |
|----|----|-------------------------------------------------------------------------|
|    | i. | HANS JOACHIM, born in 1929; was Prof. of Philosophy, Tübingen, Germany. |

**24. ANNA KELLENBENZ,** third daughter and sixth child of Henry and Mary Jane (Corr) Kellenbenz, was born 29 March 1917; died 25 April 1974. She married **John Henry HAYES** or **COATES**.
John Henry and Anna (Kellenbenz) Hayes had the following children, surname Hayes:

|    |      |                                              |
|----|------|----------------------------------------------|
|    | i.   | JANETTE BARBARA, b. 1939; d. 1995.          |
|    | ii.  | MARGARET MARY, b. 1942; d. 2005.            |

**25. _____ MITCHELL,** son of ___ and Anne (Kellenbenz) Mitchell, had a child, born in Philadelphia, surname Mitchell:

|    |    |                                                          |
|----|----|----------------------------------------------------------|
|    | i. | ANNE,[28] b. 1967; a paralegal, lives in Philadelphia, Pa. |

## Some Things about the Kellenbenz Family
### (*Etwas von der Sippe Kellenbenz*)

[illegible scanned German-text column image]

**Written by E.F. (name unknown), printed in Württemberg in about 1967**

- - - - - - - - - -

The family name of Kellenbenz is still known in Germany, although it is uncommon. Ancestry.com shows the Kellenbenz name in several German family trees, especially in Baden-Württemberg, and elsewhere in the Federal Republic.

## Hermann Kellenbenz[29]

The most notable person bearing the name Kellenbenz in recent years is Hermann Kellenbenz (1913-1990), who was a Professor of History, Economic and Social History (*Geschicte, Wirtschafts- und Sozialgeschicte*) at the University of Erlangen-Nürnberg at the time of his death.  Professor Kellenbenz was born 28 August 1913 in Süßen, District (*Kreis*) of Göppingen, Württemberg; died 26 November 1990 at Tannreid, Bavaria, Germany, at the age of 77.  His ancestry is unknown, but he was undoubtedly a member of the Kellenbenz family that had long resided in the area of Süßen, and before that in Eislingen.

**Map showing some locations in the life of Professor Hermann Kellenbenz**
Eislingen, where his family probably arose
Süßen, where he was born
Munich, where he worked at the end of World War II (note Dachau, nearby)
Tannreid, where he died
Tegernesse, where his funeral was held

Hermann Kellenbenz began his studies at the *Freihof-Gymnasium* in Göppingen, in the state of Württemberg. He then studied history and the history of art and literature at the Universities of Tübingen, Munich, Kiel, and Stockholm. In 1938, he received the *Dr. phil.* (Ph.D.) degree at the University of Kiel, with a dissertation on the Swedish *Domäne* of Holstein-Gottorf. In 1939, he entered military service. In August 1939, Germany invaded Poland, and World War II began. He was then twenty-six years old. The record does not elaborate on his service in the war, but he was soon, for some reason, declared a "war invalid" (*Kriegsinvalide*).

Kellenbenz became a worker (*Mitarbeiter*) at the Reich Institute for History of the New Germany (*Reichinstituts fur Geschicte des neuen Deutschlands*) in Berlin. The Institute had been founded in 1935; its director was Karl Alexander von Müller. Kellenbenz worked in the department of the Institute which studied "The Jewish Question" (*Forschungsabteilung Judenfrage*), a notorious anti-Semitic Nazi euphemism. He completed a manuscript on this subject in 1942. The head of the Institute, von Müller, was previously a professor at the University of Munich, where he was the doctoral advisor for Walter Frank (1905-1945).[30] Walter Frank, later known by the pseudonym Werner Fiedler, began his studies at Munich

University in 1923. He received his doctorate in 1927 with a dissertation about Adolf Stoecker (1835-1909), an anti-Semite and founder of the Christian Social Party. Walter Frank's advisor, von Müller, was also anti-Semitic, and he was active in the Nazi movement. Karl von Müller and Walter Frank worked together at the *Reichinstituts fur Geschicte des newuen Deuthchlands*. The *Reichinstitut* is said to have been sometimes called "Frank's Institute." Late in the war, Kellenbenz relocated to Munich, where in the spring of 1945, he is believed to have continued work on "The Jewish Question," although we are not told what that work might have been. The infamous concentration camp, Dachau, was near Munich. Patton's 3rd Army troops liberated the concentration camp of Flossenberg, near Nürnberg, on 23 April 1945. Dachau was liberated by the U.S. 7th Army on 29 April. On the next day, 30 April, a U.S. Army detachment accepted the surrender of German troops in Munich. On the same day, Hitler committed suicide in Berlin. Germany then surrendered, and V-E Day was celebrated by the Western Allies on 8 May 1945. The next day, 9 May, Walter Frank committed suicide at Brunsrode, near Braunschweig, about 240 km west of Berlin. How all of this affected Kellenbenz is unknown, but his life as a professor quietly resumed after the war. Nothing is mentioned in his curriculum vitae about his wartime service.

After the war, Kellenbenz produced a new version of his work, *The Hamburg Jewish Financiers and their Circle* (*Hamburger Finanzjudentum und seine Krise*). The re-titled version, *The Sephardim on the Lower Elbe* (*Sephardim an der unteren Elbe*), which eliminates the specific title reference to Jewish financiers, is now the standard work on the subject.

In 1948, he became a lecturer at the Regensburg *Hochschule*, and in 1950 he joined the faculty at the University of Würzburg as Privatdozent. In 1957, he was appointed Professor of Economic and Social History at the University of Nürnberg. From 1952 to 1953, he was also a Fellow of the Rockefeller Foundation in the U.S., at the Research Center for Entrepreneurial History at Harvard University, and also at the Johns Hopkins University. He was at the École Practique des Hautes Études from 1953 to 1954. In 1957, he became a professor of economic and social history at the *Hochschule* in Nürnberg, and in 1960, he was named director of the Rhine-Westfahlien Archive at the University of Cologne. He returned to the University of Nürnberg-Erlangen in 1970, and was professor of history there until he retired in 1983. He was then appointed scientific director of the Fugger archive.

Professor Kellenbenz has a long bibliography, having authored many books and papers, either alone or with others. His work on the Portuguese and Spanish banking activity of the Fuggers was published in 3 volumes in 1990 as *Die Fugger in Spanien und Portugal bis 1560*. He is also known for his publication, *The Rise of the European Economy: An Economic History of Continental Europe from the Fifteenth to the Eighteenth Century*, revised and edited by Gerhard Benecke (London: Weidenfeld and Nicholson, 1976), one volume in the series *World Economic History*, edited by Charles Wilson.

In addition to his work as a historian, Kellenbenz also showed considerable expertise as an artist. His pencil and red chalk drawings, made after World War II, were exhibited in the 1970s. They were published in a book, *Faces and Houses in Old Süße*n. At about the same time he showed, in his home county, an exhibit of his oil paintings, "Wandering in the Eifel" – a beautiful forest in the northern Rhine valley. His funeral was held at the Castle Chapel in Tegernsee in Bavaria, where the speakers included Count Albert Fugger Zu Glött and many of his former professional colleagues.

His honors included election to the Royal Danish Academy, Copenhagen; the Royal Flemish Academy, Brussels; the British Academy; the Royal Academy of History, Madrid; the

1982 Order of Merit from Bavaria (aka Bavarian Service Medal); and the Lappenberg Medal of the Hamburg Historical Association (*Vereins fur Hamburgische Geschichte*) for his work, *Verdienste um de Hamburgische Geschicte.* Kellenbenz was listed in *Wer is wer? Das deutsche Who's who* (1969/70). Although he is said to have remained fond of Süßen, the town where he was born, nothing is known of his immediate family, or whether he was married. He apparently left no direct descendants.

Photo from Biblioteca Nacional de Portugal

**Professor Hermann Kellenbenz, Dr. phil. (1913-1990)**

In addition to Hermann Kellenbenz, many others avoided mentioning their real roles in World War II. Two of the most famous were Gunter Grass and Kurt Waldstein.[31]

Gunter Grass (1927-2015), died at the age of 87, won the Nobel Prize for Literature in 1999, but hid the fact that he was a German soldier in the SS. He revealed this at age 79, only days before it was to be revealed in an unauthorized biography, *Peeling the Onion.* He then said it was with a great sense of shame that he had concealed it. But it appears that he did not disclose it at that time, except to pre-empt the author who was about to reveal it. Stephen Kinzler wrote in his obituary in *The New York Times* (13 April 2015), "Mr. Grass found defenders among his American friends, including the novelist John Irving, who assailed the dismantling of Mr. Grass's reputation 'from the cowardly standpoint of hindsight. You [Grass] remain a hero to me, both as a writer and a moral compass,' Mr. Irving wrote, adding that Mr. Grass's courage was heightened by the truth. Mr. Grass said he was 'not a pessimist, but a skeptic.' He rejected the view that artists should create rather than agitate. That, he said, leads to self-censorship that delights 'the powers of church and state.' "Yet [Grass] said he rued the years in which he did not speak the full truth about himself. 'The brief inscription meant for me reads: "I kept silent",' Mr. Grass wrote in his memoir. "Why was he attracted to the SS? 'It was the newsreels,' he concluded. 'I was a pushover for the prettified black-and-white "truth" they served up'."

It was revealed by Jacob Heilbrunn in *The New York Time*s (10 October 1993), that Kurt Waldheim (1918-2007), Secretary General of the United Nations (1972-1981) and President of Austria (1986-1972), hid the fact that he served in the Wehrmacht with the "Prince Eugen" division of the Waffen-SS, "perhaps the most notorious of all of Hitler's Waffen-SS units." Heilbrunn's article documents the long period, obscured carefully by Waldheim and his associates, of his highly decorated service in the Balkans. It was first revealed in 1982. "Waldheim himself apparently approved the transfer of a group of British commandos to a division of the SS for execution." The article was accompanied by a photo in which Waldheim appeared in a Wehrmacht newspaper (3 December 1944), when he was an intelligence officer with the High Command of Army Group E in the Balkans. His commander, Gen. Alexander Lohr is shown; Lohr was executed in 1947.

---

[1] The Kellenbenz family is said to have been in Württemberg since the 14th century. Many of them live in the Göppingen District. A genealogy of the Kellenbenz family has traced the family back to about the year 1200. A restaurant in Süssen, Germany, is said to have been in the Kellenbenz family since the 1300's. (letter of Anne Mitchell to GJH, 22 Feb 2009).

Ancestry.com adds very little to our knowledge about the Kellenbenz family. When accessed on 2/24/16, there were some 11,620 family trees that mentioned Kellenbenz, but most of them are duplicates. Two principal families are seen:

(1) Gottlieb Kellenbenz, son of Johann Georg and Anna Maria (Clement) Kellenbenz; b. 9 May 1839, Wurttemberg; d. 1 Nov 1907, Philadelphia; m. in Philadelphia (date varies) Katharine Frech (spelling varies). Their children are followed. Johan Georg and Anna Maria (Clement) Kellenbenz are shown in this chapter. Some of the Ancestry.com family trees show this Gottlief correctly as b. in Kleineislingen.

(2) Lorenz Kellenbenz, of unknown ancestry (1525-1595) m. Margareta Grupp (1530- ). They had 11 children, born in GrossSüssen, of whom only the 1st, Engla, has known descendants. This Lorenz Kellenbenz must surely be an ancestor or a collateral relative of our Kellenbenz family, but no connection is shown in Ancestry.com

Of the 11,600 Kellenbenz names in Ancestry.com family trees, there are 3,040 Kellenbenz entries with Kellenbenz b. in Germany, 958 b. in Württemberg, and 33 b. in GrossSüssen.

[2] George F. Jones, *German-American Names* (Baltimore: Genealogical Publishing Co., 1990), p. 178: Kell, etc., referencing the Introduction's paragraphs 80 (name-roots), 106 (wares), and 122 (city of origin); and *berg*, referencing paragraph 68; and p.77-8: Bentsen, etc., referencing the Introduction's paragraph 59 (patronymics).

See also: Karl R. Mesloh, New Bremen, Ohio, "German Surnames – Their Meaning & Origin," *The Towpath* (January 1993 - January 1994) at: http://newbremenhistory.org/GENEALOGY/German_Names.htm (accessed 1/15/16). Mesloh says there are seven broad categories of surname origins, and there are others that have no known origin. The known categories are: military, terrain, place, profession, religious, appearance, and miscellaneous. Other surnames have an origin that is unknown. Kellenbenz would be one of the unknowns. From Mesloh, I would surmise that "Kellenbenz" could be cognate with "Benz" (as in Mercedes-Benz, the marque of the automobile inventor, Karl Benz, but Mesloh does not give a meaning for either "Kellen" or "Benz." The inventor, Benz, was also from Swabia, so it may be a word that is peculiar to the Swabian dialect. More from Mesloh is quoted in smaller font, because many of Mesloh's expressions are given in quotation marks:

The earliest German names were just a single name. It was not a first name, or a last name, it was just a "name". This "name" was composed of two syllables with each syllable representing a "root", and each "root" having a specific meaning. This name was very important to the Germans, for it represented that whatever they were today, whatever they would be tomorrow, and whatever virtues they would pass along to their namesakes, all lay in that "name" and so the Germans chose their name very carefully.

Whenever the Germans wanted to emphasize some particular aspect of their "being", they used a tautological name; by tautological, it is meant that the name consisted of two different roots, but with each root having the same meaning. For example, an expert or adept swordsman might choose or be given the name "Schwerdecke" by his fellow warriors; "schwerd" meaning sword, and "ecke" meaning sword so the name meant, sword-sword. Another example would be the name "Richwald" as "rich" meant ruler and "wald" meant ruler and so the name meant, ruler-ruler (please note, the ancient root "wald" meant ruler but today "wald" means forest). There are at least three such tautological names in the local area: Mesloh meaning "swampy low forest" or simply "swampy forest", (the tautology being that a "low forest" grows in a swamp; Huckriede meaning "marsh-reed marsh"; Klipfels meaning "cliff-cliff" and so one would conclude that the Meslohs lived in or near a very swampy place, the Huckriedes in or near a very marshy place, and the Klipfels on a very high or steep or prominent (in some aspect) cliff.

There are various suffixes (or root endings) of interest, which earlier were of considerable importance:

1) "er" originally meant that the person whose name ended in "er" was an owner of a farm at the terrain feature indicated by the two "roots", for example, the name, "Rothenberger" would mean that a person by the name of Rothenberg owned a farm at "red mountain"; in time it also meant a dweller at, or near, or on red mountain. "Er" can also mean that the person "is a doer of something", for example, the name "Becker" can mean a "baker" (as well as a dweller, or farm owner on a stream). From these several examples it is seen that the specific geographical location is both necessary and important for an accurate interpretation of one's name. Incidentally, some names end in "ert" but the addition of the "t" neither adds nor subtracts anything from the meaning of the name; the "t" was added to help in pronunciation indicating that the "r" was not to be trilled.

2) The suffix "en" essentially meant "at" the terrain feature the "en" followed. An interesting name in which this suffix is highlighted is the name, "Ziegenbusch". The ancient root, "Ziege" means "goat" and although a literal translation of "Ziegenbusch" can be "goat bush" there is yet another, and even more interesting! In ancient days, whenever the wine of the new harvest was ready for drinking, the inn or tavern keepers would hang a

piece of greenery, such as a limb of a bush, on their doorframe to so indicate the new wine was ready. Thus, early on, all inn or tavern keepers were called Busch or Buschers or Buschman from this hanging out of a green bush. If an Englishman were asked as to where he was going, he would probably reply, "to the Red Lion" or "to the Silver Chalice", or to whatever the name of his favorite pub might be. A German so asked might reply, "Zum die Ziegen" or "at the Goat" and thus the name Ziegenbusch translates, "tavern or inn keeper at (or of) Goat Tavern". This practice of hanging out some "greenery" whenever the wine of the new harvest is ready to drink is still followed today in some parts of Germany and Austria; at least it was as late as July 1991, as this author can happily attest!

3) The suffix "ing" means "belonging to", e.g., the name "Kuenning" means "belonging to the Brave (family or clan or group of warriors, etc.)

4) The suffix "ingen" means the place where the "roots" people lived; for example, the village of Sulingen, in northern Germany, means "the place where Sul's people lived".

5) The suffix "sen" means "son of".

6) The suffix "ssen" originally meant "the first generation 'son of' to bear that particular name".

So much for "root" endings; let us look at the "roots" themselves. Essentially there are four major classifications of German name "roots":

1. Military

2. Terrain and Its Features

3. Professions

4. Miscellaneous, such as nicknames, personal characteristics, abnormalities etc. . . .

Names evolved through the centuries. As the population increased, the need to distinguish between persons having the same name living in the same general area arose. Say four Johanns were living close together. The one living among the oaks would be called Johann Eichner; the one living by the bridge would be Johann Bruecker; the one living near the church would be Johann Kirchner; the one at the ford would be Johann Furth and so began the use of a first and last name.

Christian names entered the scene in the mid 700s to 800 AD, the start of the Christian era, but progressed very slowly until the mid 1500s at which time the Roman Catholic Church required parents to give each newborn child the name of a saint as its first name. After having given the child a holy name, the parent could then add a secular middle name and so this was the start of having three names - a first, middle and last. The Protestants also followed this same procedure, except a different listing of saints was used. The passing of the surname from "father to son to son", while starting in the Christian era, most probably gathered its strength during this same general period of 1500-1600 AD.

[3] For the Kellenbenz name in the 1920 U.S. census, see www.ancestry.com/name-origin?surname=kellenbenz (accessed 2-15-16). The Kellenbenz name first appeared in the U.S. census of 1880, with three families: PA (1), CO (2) and 1 that is not shown on the Ancestry.com map. The 1890 census was destroyed by fire, and no calculation of the distribution of the family name was offered by Ancestry.com in the 1910, 1930 and 1940 censuses.

Ancestry.com has recorded the Kellenbenz name in 3,542 historical documents; 2,325 birth, marriage and deaths; 114 military records; 101 immigration records; 304 census and voter lists; and 698 member trees (accessed, as shown at the beginning of this note, 2/24/16).

[4] Martin Kellenbenz sent a copy of this article to Anne Mitchell, who kindly provided it to me. It is difficult to read, especially when reduced in the image inserted in this chapter. Anne Miller's translation (omitting her notes):

### The Kinship of Kellenbenz (translated by Anne Miller)

Almost 450 years before the first Reformation, the name Kellenbenz was in the area of Pfarrdorf Greater-Sussen. Today different branches of this kinship are in places still flourishing. For centuries long, some of these Kellenbenzs worked as restaurant operators and barkeepers. Some are still active today, like that in Ebersbach, Greater-Sussen, Klein-Eislingen, Stammheim, Waiblingen and Wiesensteig. In addition, female members of this kinship Kellenbenz were married to representatives of the restaurant operator/ barkeeper trade. Female members of this kinship often worked for their Fathers-In-Law in the guest economy.

The most prominent name of the kinship was Doctor Juris Bartholomaus Kellenbenz, active representative in Tubingen, who in September 1624 established a family scholarship of 4000 gold pieces from the Capitol for studying and hard work. This Bartholomaus Kellenbenz (born 31 August 1562) was the grandchild of Sussener Kellenbenz and was the fifth child (of seven sons and five daughters) of Lorenz Kellenbenz (born abt. 1530 died 1595), and was the host of "Alder" in Greater-Sussen. Alder is the oldest tavern that may be recognized in the realm city of Ulm and in the year 1592 was owned by Lorenz Kellenbenz (born 1572), who purchased it from the brother of the scholarship founder. This building was acquired later, in the year 1826, by the municipality in order to be converted into city hall.

Soon reputation, in addition to fortune, came to Dr. Jur. Bartholomaus Kellenbenz who married the already twice widowed Margarete (born Konigsbach) in his first marriage in Tubingen in the year 1588. Margarete's first husband was the rightist Professor Chilian Vogler (1516 to 1585). Her second husband was Johann Vischer, Professor of Medicine (1524 to 1587). In the year after the death of his first wife in 1618, Bartholomaus Kellenbenz married Catharina (Schorndort) in Tubingen, the widow of Andreas Walch.

The charter foundation for the Kellenbenz scholarship is on pages 100 ff. of the tenth booklet (of 1854) of the financial advice of Ferd. Fr. Faber published compilation Wtirttenburg. Family foundations, whose interest of about 300 gold pieces a year for distribution, became printed by the Academic Senate of the University of Tubingen around the year 1922/23 until the foundation capital, like in other similar cases, purged due to inflation and the Trustees had lost their basis.

       The uncle of the founder, Hans Kellenbenz, was already living in Klein-Eislingen around 1540/60. Then we know that a cousin of Bartholomaus Kellenbenz, the Lorenz Kellenbenz (died 1649) from Weinsteig made his home in the country of Hergerge in Ebersbach for a good twenty years. Then in the year 1664, a Nicholas Braun (born 1641) brought home and married Catharina Kellenbenz (born 1644).

       In the idyllic tenth decade in the 17th year of one hundred, George Kellenbenz, born as a Schultheiss in Klein-Eislingen in 1644, son of Johannes Kellenbenz the Eislinger. His oldest son Johannes Kellenbenz (born 1670) became a restaurant operator/barkeeper in Traube in Waiblingen, His brother Johann George Kellenbenz (1673 to 1703) dedicated himself and became a minister in Boll. The daughter of the aforementioned Schultheissen, Maria Margareta Kellenbenz (born 1681) married Andreas Hofelin the restaurant operator/barkeeper in Goppingen. -- The third oldest Schutheissen grandchild, a son of Sebastian Kellenbenz (born Klein-Eislingen 1677), the same Johann Jakob Kellenbenz (born 1702),was a Schultheiss who also spent a long time as the local chief in Klein-Eislingen .

       Then we find again in Wurttemberg, that in Waiblingen at the Trauben hotel, Johannes Kellenbenz ( 1722 to 1803) who was an official protestant pastor from 1745 to 1780 in the village of Rieth.

       Finally, I would like to mention the name Kellenbenz (Grandfather, Father and three Sons) are numerated and have learned the art of medicine and -- with the exception of Joh. Jakob Kellenbenz (the second), who was the oldest of the four sons, are all doctors practicing in Klein-Eislingen. Doctor Gottlieb Kellenbenz (the first) born in 1726 a surgeon in Klein-Eislingen, applied to work delivering babies. In the year 1779, Jakobine (born Schrag), had joined her relative, the latter son of Doctor Gottlieb Kellenbenz, II (born 1751) in his medical practice.

       Three generations in Klein-Eislingen have likewise learned to practice, with the exception of Gottlieb Kellenbenz, III (born 1784) and Johann Michael Kellenbenz (born in 1790) in Klein-Eislingen. The younger brother, Doctor Johann Leonhard Kellenbenz (born 1794) is the most envied person in Ansbach (Bayern). / E.F.

[5] Translation by GJH with the aid of "Babylon" software.

[6] The Reformation is typically stated to have begun with the posting of Luther's 95 theses in 1517. My estimate of the date of the article is derived from 1517 + 450 years.

[7] From: "Something about the Family of Kellenbenz: For almost 450 years, since the time of the Reformation [1517], was one of the name of Kellenbenz settled in Filstal, and also in at that time in the region of the free imperial city of Ulm, belonging to Gross-Süssen [Württemberg], a village with a church." (*Etwas von der Sippe Kellenbenz*: *Schon um die erste Zeit der Reformation also von beinahe 450 Jahren, war einer des Namens Kellenbenz im Filstal ansässig, und zwar in dem damals zum Gebiet der Reichstat Ulm gehörenden Pfarrdorf Gross-Süssen.*) The automatic translation with Babylon software is not very helpful, because it selects one translation for words, without considering the text: "Some of the Clan Trowel Benz (*Kellenbenz*): already at the first time of the reformation so of almost 450 years, was one of the name trowel Benz in filstal resident, and in the time to the territory of the Reich Stat Ulm's parish village large sweet (*Gross-Süssen*)." The family name Kellenbenz is considered to be a conjunction of the words for "trowel" + "benz" (the latter being untranslatable), and the names Filstal (untranslatable) and Gross- Süssen are not recognized as towns.

       Locations mentioned here, and in the full article, are: Filstal, Ulm, Gross-Süssen, Württemberg, Baden-Württemberg, Süssen, Swabia, Stuttgart, Ebersbach, Kleineislingen,Eislingen, Stammheim, Waiblingen, Wiesensteig, Tübingen, Löwen, Weinsteig, Hergerge County, Ebersbach, Traube., Boll, Göppingen, Ansbach, Bayern [Bavaria].

[8] Johannes Kellenbenz (?Johannes, Georg, Johannes), b. 1722; d. 1803, was in Wurttemberg, in Waiblingen at the Trauben Hotel, and was a Protestant pastor in village of Rieth, 1745-1780; his ancestry is uncertain, and he may be the son or grandson of Johannes Kellenbenz

[9] Schultheiss is the "head man" of the village. It is an old term, which was more or less equivalent to Burgomeister, or mayor in English. The town of Eislingen is adjacent to Süssen; Klein-Eislingen was "Small Eislingen," in contrast to what then may have been a larger town of Gross-Eislingen, or perhaps it was called "klein" to distinguish it from the larger town of Süssen. The name of the town of Eislingen, adjacent to Süssen, now stands unmodified by "small" or "large."

[10] "In the year 1779, Jakobine (born Schrag), joined her relative, the younger son of Doctor Gottlieb Kellenbenz II (born 1751), in his medical practice. Three generations of the Kellenbenz family in Klein-Eislingen have thus learned to practice medicine: Gottlieb Kellenbenz, III (born 1784) and Johann Michael Kellenbenz (born in 1790) in Klein-Eislingen, while the younger brother, Doctor Johann Leonhard Kellenbenz (born 1794), settled in Ansbach (Bayern)."

Children of Gottlieb II and Jakobine (Schrag) Kellenbenz:

      **9**      i.      Dr. GOTTLIEB III, b. 1784; perhaps had a son, Gottlieb, who has descendants in the United States. **11** i. ? GOTTLIEB IV

**11. Gottlieb IV KELLENBENZ,** perhaps the Gottlieb Kellenbenz who m. **Anna Maria STAUDENMAIER,** Kleineislingen; and had a son, Joseph (1836-80), who m. **Elisabethe Margarete KLEMENT** and had 8 ch., all b. in Kleineislingen, Donaukreis, Werttemberg. Gottlieb IV Kellenbenz and his wife, Anna Maria Staudenmaier, had one child, and perhaps more:

| | | |
|---|---|---|
| **15** | i. | Dr. JOSEPH (1836-1880) |
| | ii. | JOH. JAKOB II. |
| | iii. | Dr. JOHANN MICHAEL, b. 1790. |
| | iv. | Dr. JOHANN LEONHARD, b. 1794; physician in Ansbach (Bayern). |

[11] References for Johann Jakob Kellenbenz:

1. *Etwas von der Sippe Kellenbenz* (The Kinship of Kellenbenz), author E.T. (name unknown); written in Schwabische Deutch, but with late 20th century typescript, prob. 20th century, sent by Martin Kellenbenz (Germany) to Anne Mitchell, Jan 2998; translated by her.
2. "Keegan Family Tree" (Ancestry.com), accessed 1/12/2016, sassypa.
3. "Curry Family Tree" (Ancestry.com), accessed 1/12/2016, endcurry.
4. Anne Mitchell, "Johann Michael Kellenbenz + Clara Grozinger." Family Group Record (from Anne Mitchell collegebound67@yahoo.com, to GJH, 2/23/2009
5. "Kellenbenz Family," 22 Feb 2009ff, Mitchell, Anne - e-mails to George J. Hill.

-------------------

Nothing is given in Curry or Keegan FT about his parents, and no information in Mitchell abt his place of b,d,m.

[12] Württemberger Hof means "Württember Court," or "Württemberg Hotel" but in the 18th century, Württemberger Hof may have been the name of a town. No town by that name appears on a search of Google Maps in 2015. Google Maps shows many hotels and lodging houses in Baden-Württemberg with the name of Württemberg Hof. Schwabisch Hall, usually called just "Hall," is the name of a town in the district (*Kleis*) of Schwabish Hall, in the state (*Land*) of Baden-Württemberg. If Johann Jacob Kellenbenz and Christina Siller were married there, it would probably be because her family came from that town, or nearby. Jacob is also spelled Jakob (a more typical German spelling) and Siller is also spelled Sihler.

[13] The Curry and Keegan Family Trees on Ancestry.com give the name of his wife and a child, Johan Georg. Ann Mitchell says the son was called Georg.

[14] The Kellenbenz family has been in Württenberg since the 14th century. Many of them live in the Göppingen District. A genealogy of the Kellenbenz family has traced the family back to about the year 1200. A restaurant in Süssen, Germany, has been in the Kellenbenz family since the 1300's (letter of Anne Mitchell to GJH, 22 Feb 2009). Eva (Kellenbenz) Zimmermann was one of 16 children. Her father, Johannes Michael, was one of 13. (Ibid.) Gottlieb and Michael's parents were George Kellenbenz and Anna Maria Klement (Ibid.)

The Curry FT (Ancestry.com) says he was b., d., and was m. at Württenberger Hof [court], Schwabisch Hall [or just the city of Hall], Baden-Würtenberg, Germany. Anne Mitchell says these events occurred at Kleineislingen, Donaukreis, Württenberg, Germany. I will accept Mitchell's statement, because the family had long been in Eislingen, and I see no reason to believe they relocated to Württenberger Hof, in the district of Hall (aka Swabish Hall), about 20 miles to the N.

[15] Ancestry.com does not show any entry for Clara Grözinger, but there are 3 other women named Grözinger, born at about the same time, in Baden-Württemberg:

(1) Elizabeth Grözinger, daughter of Johannes Grözinger and Anna Maria Bauchle was b. 14 Nov 1826; m. Hehenstaufen, Württemberg.
(2) Dorthea Grözinger b. 1829 in Betzweiler, Baden-W.
(3) Ana Grözinger, b. Germany, 21 Aug 1832, dau of Jacob Grözinger and Ana Maria Fink; m. 2 Feb 1857, Württemberg.

[16] Their daughters, Eva and Clara came to America (letter of 22 Feb 2009 from Anne Mitchell to GJH), from Stuttgart, under the sponsorship of a German Lutheran pastor; they both worked as domestics in a Philadelphia home (from 20 Nov 2009, Jean Naples Hoxie to GJH).

[17] Anne Mitchell, his great-granddaughter, wrote to GJH 2/24/2009: "Most of the Kellenbenzs were weavers or dyers." Keegan FT says he lived in 1870 at Ward 19, District 57, Philadelphia. The Curry FT says he arrived in America in 1866, based on census record.

[18] In 1867 or 1868 when Gottlieb was 27, he married Katharine FRECH, in Philadelphia, Pa. (1868 fm Keegan FT). Born on 4 Jul 1847 in Germany (Curry FT says Württemberg Hof, Schwabisch Hall, Baden-W,. GE. Katharine died in Philadelphia, Pa. on 28 Sep 1924, she was 77.

----------

Ann Mitchell sent on 2/26/2009 a picture "Family.jpg 455KB" of a older woman in an oval frame, looking slightly to her right. Anne says, "I am pretty sure that this is Katharine because I have a picture of two of my aunts in the 1950's and a picture of this woman can be seen in the background. My aunt told me that the woman in the other picture was her Great-Grandmother Kellenbenz. Katherine Frech was born in Germany in 1847. She came to America in the 1860's. She married Gottlieb Kellenbenz in 1867 in Philadelphia. They had 13 children. All but 3 lived to adulthood. Katherine died in 1924. Gottlieb and Johann Michael Kellenbenz (Eva's father) were brothers."

------------

The U.S. census for 1880 shows in Philadelphia:
Kellenbenz Cath W F 33    M    Domestic "Insane" b. Germany both parents b. Germany
[She would be Katharine (nee Frech), b. 1847, d. 1924, wife of Gottlieb Kellenbenz; she had 6 or 7 more children after 1880, but I know nothing about the tick mark Insane.]

[19] Letter of 22 Feb 2009 from Anne Mitchell to GJH; and letter 20 Nov 2009, Jean Naples Hoxie to GJH. Their children from ref 292, Chart 6.

[20] letter from Anne Mitchell to GJH, 22 Feb 2009

[21] Barbara S. Zimmemann, *Mutterings* (Wynnewood, Pa.: Livingston Publishing Co., 1969), 134-5. Text is lightly edited here; the unedited text with notes is in the Appendix to this book.

[22] "Kellenbenz Family," 22 Feb 2009ff, Mitchell, Anne - e-mails to George J. Hill. Anne Mitchell, Johann Michael Kellenbenz + Clara Grozinger.
Family Group Record (from Anne Mitchell (collegebound67@yahoo.com) to GJH, 2/23/2009
"Pflug Family Tree, accessed 1/15/15," John Pflug.

[23] The only child who was not named in Keegan FT or Curry FT, but who was named by Anne Mitchell. "Kellenbenz Family," 22 Feb 2009ff, Mitchell, Anne - e-mails to George J. Hill. Anne Mitchell, Johann Michael Kellenbenz + Clara Grozinger. Family Group Record (from Anne Mitchell (collegebound67@yahoo.com)

[24] "Katherine Kellenbenz – Eva's aunt," 2/24-26/2009, e-mail from Anne Mitchell to GJH. 2/22-23/2009 Introductory letters from Anne Mitchell to GJH
2/24/09, Anne Mitchell sent information about the Fred Weigle family. He m. (1) Clara Kellenbenz, who d. bet 1920 and 1930; and (2) Laura ___.

[25] Frederick Weigle, a resident of Spring Hill, Fl., until his terminal illness; lived in Norristown, Pa.; veteran of the U.S. Army in WWII; relocated to Fl..; member of the Electric Railway Club, Suncoast Model Building Club, and East Pennsylvania Traction Club; d. in Brooksville, FL (obit *St. Petersburg Times* [15 Dec 2000]), at Hospice Care Unit on 13 Dec 2000, he was 76.; of Spring Hill, Fl., when he d.; b. Philadelphia, abt 1924; survived by his wife, two daughters, two sisters, five grandchildren, two great-grandchildren. Services at Brewer Memorial Funeral Home.

[26] Zimmermann and Kellenbenz Family Charts; copies made in November 1993 from originals or copies in the possession of Sue (Kelley) Carnwath. Transcriptions made by George J. Hill, M.D., 28 February 2003ff. Sue Carnwath's charts passed to her heirs after her death.

[27] Copies made in November 1993 from originals or copies in the possession of Sue (Kelley) Carnwath.

[28] "Kellenbenz Family," 22 Feb 2009ff, Mitchell, Anne - e-mails to George J. Hill.

[29] This biography of Hermann Kellenbenz is a composite, written by me. It is based on my translation of the entry for Hermann Kellenbenz in Wikipedia, principally "Wissenschaftlicher Mitarbeiter in der Forschungsabteilung Judenfrage." Wikipedia quotes "Creative Commons Attribution/Share Alike" and cites many primary sources:
1939 wurde Kellenbenz zum Wehr- und anschließendem Kriegsdienst eingezogen und kehrte als Kriegsinvalide zurück. Als Kriegsinvalide wurde Kellenbenz 1939 Mitarbeiter des von Walter Frank geleiteten „Reichsinstituts für Geschichte des neuen Deutschlands", Berlin, in der von Karl Alexander von Müller geleiteten „Forschungsabteilung Judenfrage". Dort erhielt er einen Forschungsauftrag über das Hamburger Finanzjudentum und seine Krise. Diese sephardischen Juden waren zu Beginn des 16. Jahrhunderts aus Spanien vertrieben worden und hatten in Hamburg Aufnahme gefunden. Kellenbenz hatte deren wirtschaftliche Bedeutung für Norddeutschland dargestellt. 1942 wurde Kellenbenz mit dem fertiggestellten Manuskript habilitiert. Im Frühjahr 1945 verbrannte Kellenbenz – vermutlich auf Befehl – in seiner Funktion als Forschungsbeauftragter tagelang sämtliche Aktenbestände der Münchner „Forschungsabteilung Judenfrage". 1958 veröffentlichte Kellenbenz eine veränderte Version seiner Habilitationsschrift „Hamburger Finanzjudentum und seine Krise" mit dem neuen Titel „Sephardim an der unteren Elbe". Diese gilt seitdem als Standardwerk.

I have also used the obituary with photo of Hermann Kellenbenz from Biblioteca Nacional de Portugal, in http://www.bnportugal.pt/index.php?option=com_content&view=article&id=899%3Amostra-conferencia-hermann-kellenbenz-1913-1990-ao-servico-da-historia-4-fev-18h00&catid=164%3A2014&Itemid=925&lang=en; and the obituary (below) which was sent to me by Anne Mitchell, translated by Richard Clark, from an unknown source:

### Prof. Dr. Kellenbenz

In Thannried in Upper Bavaria, Professor Doctor Hermann Kellenbenz died at the age of 77, who came from Süßen. The internationally known economic historian, who in 1913 was born in the then known Greater- Süßen, remained connected throughout his life with his home community. With his pencil and red chalk drawings created after the second World War, and his small volume "Faces and Houses in Old Süßen," published in conjunction with an exhibit in the seventies, he created long-lasting impressions. His oil painting exhibit "Wandering in the Eifel," shown a few years ago in the county savings and loan was well received beyond his former home and provided an impression of an artistic creativity of the many faceted scientist. At his funeral in Castle Chapel in Tegernsee, several of his professor and colleagues as well as Count Albert Fugger Zu Glött honored the life and work of Hermann Kellenbenz, who was offered a chair in1957 as Professor for Economics and Social History at the former University for Economic and Social Studies in Nurnberg, in 1960 he was appointed at the University of Cologne, where he was also the Director of Rhine-Westpahlien Economic Archives. From 1970 to 1983, he worked as a professor at the University of Erlangen-Nurnberg. In addition, he was the scientific director of the Fugger-Archives since 1970. The numerous books and more than a hundred articles in professional journals and collected works, which the deceased initiated or published, testified to his scientific research. His international reputation was expressed by his inclusion in the Royal Danish Academy Copenhagen, the Royal Flemish Academy Brussels, the British Academy and in the Royal Academy of History in Madrid. In recognition of his accomplishment in the field of international research, he received in 1982 the Bavarian Service Medal.

[Translation by Richard Clark – Great-Grandson of Anna Maria (Kellenbenz) Gehring]

[30] Martin Gilbert and Max Weinreich, *Hitler's Professors: The Part of Scholarship in Germany's Crimes Against the Jewish People* (Yale University Press, 1999), 45-50.

[31] Gunter Grass:  http://www.nytimes.com/2015/04/14/world/europe/gunter-grass-german-novelist-dies-at-87.html?_r=0 Grass also apparently volunteered for other services in the German military.

Kurt Waldstein:  Heilbrunn quotes from the book, *Betrayal*, by Eli M. Rosenblum.

http://www.nytimes.com/1993/10/10/books/waldheim-and-his-protectors.html?pagewanted=all

Others, such as rocket scientists, were protected by the U.S. in Operation Paper Clip.

# PART II

# JOHN ZIMMERMANN

## AND

# EVA KATHERINE KELLENBENZ

Rhoads, 1800 Frankford Ave., Philadelphia

**Wedding Photo, 1855**

**Their Final Home**
**1512 Allegheny Avenue**
**Philadelphia**

From e-bay 1_603bfa4c30cd4b65582faf

**Artloom Carpet**
**Made c. 1910.  It was 100 years old in 2010**

# 3

## John Zimmermann and Eva Katherine Kellenbenz

**1. JOHN[1] ZIMMERMANN,**[1] second son and second of the three children of Johann[A] and Anna Ursula (Yäger) Zimmermann, was born at Gussenstadt, Heidenheim district (*Kreis*), kingdom of Württemberg, now part of the state (*Land*) of Baden-Württemberg, Federal Republic of Germany), 18 November 1855.  He was baptized as a Lutheran at Gussenstadt, 30 November 1855.  He was baptized again at Camden, Camden Co., N.J., in the Reorganized Church of Latter Day Saints on 20 January 1884.  He died at Philadelphia, Pennsylvania, 23 May 1936, and was buried at Greenmount Cemetery, Philadelphia, near the south-east corner of North Front and West Cayuga Streets.

      Although John[1] Zimmermann's family name in Germany was for many generations spelled Zimmermann [two "n's"], between 1880 (six years after he arrived in America) and 1885 (when he was married), John[1] Zimmermann began, for no known reason, to spell his name as Zimmerman [one "n"].  His brother, two years older than John[1], consistently used the spelling as Zimmermann.  Zimmerman, with one "n" is the anglicized version of the German word, *Zimmermann* (carpenter), and perhaps this was his intention.  His children used the one "n" form at first, although all of them, and their children, later reverted to the two "nn" form of Zimmermann.  The change to one "n" by John[1] Zimmermann was probably never made official.  However, he used the one "n" form, Zimmerman, when he was married, and consistently thereafter until he died.  As a result of this informal but persistent change, his children were probably all registered as Zimmerman when they were born.  Some of them reverted as adults to the original spelling of Zimmermann.  However, the names of John[1] Zimmermann's children and grandchildren have often spelled or mis-spelled with one "n" in official records and newspaper articles.[2]  His obituary spells his name as John Zimmerman, with one "n."  I will often use the spelling of his name as Zimmerman after 1885, because that is the way he spelled his name in that year when he was married.  I apologize in advance to the reader for any inconsistencies in spelling of Zimmerman/Zimmermann that may appear in this chapter.

**Signature of John Zimmermann on his passport application, 1880**
**The signature shows a terminal "nn," and a double "mm" indicated by a superscript line, m̄**
**This is a rare instance in which the handwriting of John Zimmermann has been preserved**

At the time John[1] Zimmermann was born, his parents had another son, Johann Georg (George) Zimmermann, four years older than John[1].  In five years, they would have a third child, a daughter, Anna.  His grandfather Jacob[B] Zimmermann, age 50, was still alive, and he was probably living in the same house; Jacob[B] would die in 1864.  Also living in Gussenstadt, perhaps in the same house, or probably near by, was his father's younger brother, also named Johann Georg, who was twenty-one years younger than Johann[A].  The brother, who was John[1]

Zimmermann's uncle, was only thirteen years older than John[1]. He was probably like another older brother to both John[1] and George. This uncle, Johann Georg Zimmermann, was married in 1864, when John[1] was nine. The uncle and his bride, Margareta Bantzhaff, had six children in the next ten years, five of whom survived. Johann Georg and Margareta (Bantzhaff) Zimmermann moved to America in 1874. They settled in Elmira, Chemung Co., N.Y., near many other German immigrants, including members of their extended families. John[1] Zimmermann and his brother George would soon follow them to America.

Between 1855, when John[1] Zimmermann was born, and 1874, when his uncle Johann Georg emigrated to America with his wife and five children, the Zimmermann family in Gussenstadt was large and growing. They probably occupied two houses, both of which may still be extant, although their precise location is unknown. Johann[A] Zimmermann's house in Gussenstadt was last seen by John[1] Zimmermann's son Albert[2] in August 1937. Recent photos show that Gussenstadt still is small and very little appears to have changed in the last century. After Johann Georg Zimmermann emigrated to America with his wife and his children, followed by his nephews John[1] and George, the only Zimmermanns left in Gussenstadt were the parents of John[1]: Johann[A] and Anna (Yäger) Zimmermann, and their daughter Anna. The parents died in 1899 and 1901, respectively, and Anna moved closer to Stuttgart, leaving only the tombstones of Johann[A] and Anna as a reminder of the long tenure of the Zimmermann family in Gussenstadt and the surrounding area.

John[1] Zimmermann and his brother Johann Georg (aka George), were in the third generation of weavers in the Zimmermann family in Gussenstadt. The village of Gussenstadt was about 40 miles east of Stuttgart, the capital city of Württemberg. Stuttgart had long been the principal city of the ancient region known as Swabia. Swabia was the German-speaking part of central Europe that extended from the Palitanate on the west, beyond which French-speaking people lived; then east across the Rhine, into the valley of the Danube, and to the eastern border of Bavaria, where Slavic speakers were encountered; and south, to the height of the Alps, where Italian speakers lived – now Switzerland. To the north, the border of Swabia was less well defined; today it is the state of Hesse. At the time John[1] Zimmermann was born, Stuttgart was the hub of commerce and education in Württemberg, as it is to this day.

When John[1] Zimmermann was a boy, the public school system in Germany provided a system of compulsory free education for young men. The German school system was more advanced than was present in other countries of Europe or in many areas of the United States. Kindergarten was offered in most areas for children from age 2 to 6. *Grundschule* was compulsory from age 6 to 10. Several options were available after *Grundschule*, depending on the ability of the student and the time he had available for study. The result of the student's *Arbitur* examination was an important factor in determining his secondary school education. If he did well, *Gymnasium*, through grade 12, prepared students for *Hochschule*, and this would be the pathway to higher education. *Realschule*, through grade 10, provided education for students with lower grades and those who were planning to work in trade – either *Hauptshule*, for vocational training (which was the course that John[1] probably took), or *Realschulabschluss*, which was another opportunity to prepare for *Gymnasium*. John[1] clearly had a good primary and secondary school education, and he wrote with a good hand. However, it is unlikely that he was able to progress beyond *Realschule*, and there is nothing to indicate that he attended *Gymnasium*. Students only attended school in the morning; lunch was not provided, and they were free to do work in the afternoon.

It is likely that as a boy, John[1] helped in the family's weaving shop, with chores such as sweeping and winding yarn, and that he had also chores to do on the small family farm. If the family weaving business had work to do, he probably had little time to rest or play. His formal apprenticeship would have started when he reached the age of about 14. John[1] Zimmermann learned to weave in a one-room shop attached to the home in which his father, Johann[A] (aka Johannes) Zimmermann (1821-1899), and his father, Jacob[B] Zimmermann (1801-1864), had been weavers for more than half a century. It was a typical cottage industry. The skill and trade of weaving was then a possible path to success in that part of Germany, for it enabled a family to have a year-round occupation that would supplement the income that was derived from farming.

Later photographs of John[1] as an adult in Philadelphia show him as a man of rather small stature, when he is standing with other men. As a young man, he would probably not have had the large arms, shoulders, and legs that would make manual labor easy – either as a farm laborer, or as a weaver, operating a handloom. He would appreciate the development of machines that could be operated with much less physical effort. John[1] Zimmermann would later invent and patent some of those machines.

Weaving was an important occupation at that time in the area of the Swabian Alb (*Alb* = mountain, aka Alps). In 1855, the year of John[1] Zimmermann's birth, a weaving institute was established in the town of Reutlingen, 30 miles south of Stuttgart. The institute initially taught the skill of weaving, but it later also became a research institution. Reutlingen is now in the area of Greater Stuttgart, and the institute has evolved into the University of Reutlingen. Also, in Dekendorf, ITV Denkendorf, the Institute of Textile Technology and Process Engineering Denkendorf (*Deutsche Forschungsinstitut für Textilindustrie*), traces its origin to the institute that was established at Reutlingen in 1855.

**Reutlingen, Württemberg, Germany**
**Weaving Institute, founded 1855**

Weaving has long been a family occupation, providing work for the father, mother, and children. The act of weaving has usually been a man's occupation, for the work is best suited to those with physical strength and long limbs. Women have often prepared, by spinning and cutting, the materials that are in weaving – the warp and weft (also called woof). There are exceptions: in the Himalayas, men use an ancient tool known as a spindle to spin a fine yarn, while at the same time herding livestock (yaks and sheep); and my own grandmother used her own handloom to produce fine rugs. Children cleaned the floor under the loom and spinning wheel, when bits of yarn and clippings of fabric fell from the loom.

We have no records to show what type of loom or looms John Zimmermann and his brother George used for weaving. It is very likely that they would have used a simple handloom, also called a draw loom, operated by one person, in which the fabric is produced horizontally. For many decades, little has changed in the design or appearance of the handloom. There are three steps involved, and they are repeated continuously until the piece is finished. The weaver stands at one end of the loom, with single strands of thread ("warp") stretching out in front of him. The warp strands are attached at the far end to a warp beam, which unrolls the warp as the weaving progresses. The strands of warp are supported individually by "heddle needles." The threads of warp are kept apart by passing separately through a screen ("reed"). The weaver begins by pushing a lever ("batten") away from him to separate the strands of warp into two parts, one part being above the other. The alternating strands form a V-shaped "shed" into which one strand of yarn ("weft"), is pushed across ("picked in") between the strands of warp (the "shed"), which is pulled behind the shuttle. Each newly placed strand of weft is then bound tightly to the previous piece of weft as the weaver pulls the batten toward himself; this process is known as "beating in." The weaver then pushes back against the batten, which opens the shed; and the shuttle, with the weft of yarn still attached, is picked back through the shed. The steps of shedding, picking, and beating are repeated, again and again, to produce a "basic" weave.

The basic weave may be either a plain ("tabby") weave, in which the warp and weft alternate; or a "twill" or "satin" weave, in which the weft is passed over two or three warp yarns. Fabric produced on a handloom that is operated by one person is usually 2 to 3 feet in width. A so-called broadloom is wider, and it produces fabric 3 to 6 feet in width. A broadloom is operated by two weavers standing side-by-side, with one weaver passing the shuttle to the other, half way across the shed. Over a span of several decades, it appears that there were, in the Zimmermann house in Gussenstadt, at least two weavers, and sometime three, so they may have worked with a broadloom in addition to one-person handlooms.

## The Handloom

*Drawing of handloom, showing the uses of the various parts. Note how the shed is raised by the heddle to allow the shuttle to be passed between warp and weft.*

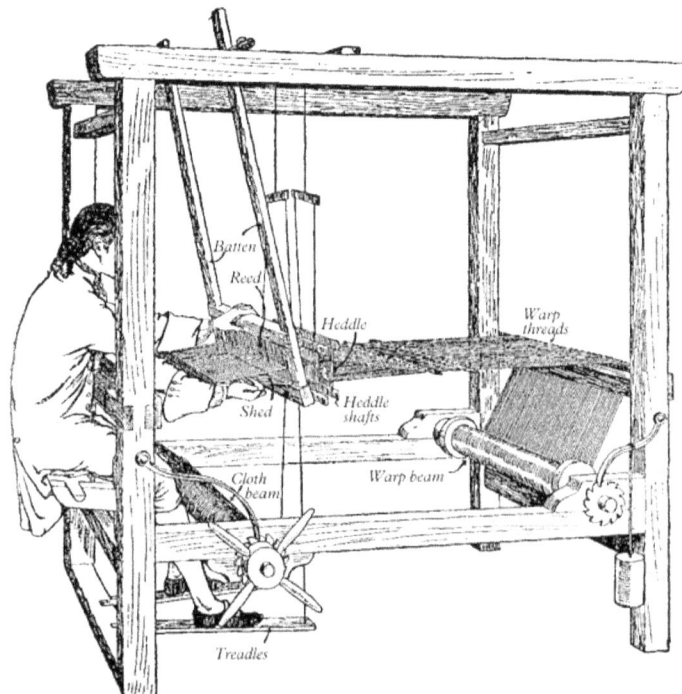

Enid Gauldie, *Spinning and Weaving: Scotland's Past in Action*
From jeandavidisabellaandjohn.wordpress.com (accessed 3-17-16)

The materials used in weaving in the nineteenth century, when John[1] learned to weave in Germany, and brought his skill to America, were natural fibers, of either animal (wool) or vegetable origin. Wool was usually sheared from sheep, although useful wool for the Zimmermanns could have been obtained from the coats of other animals such as goats or dogs. The fleece would be washed, combed, and spun. A few long hairs when twisted and spun together would make a fine warp; if more were added, the fibers would become ropes, and used as weft. Warp and weft could also be made from vegetable fibers, and both animal and vegetable fibers could be combined by the weaver. It is likely that flax was the principal vegetable fiber used by the Zimmermanns, because it was widely grown in Europe at that time. Imported cotton and silk would have been available to the Zimmermanns, but they were exotic and expensive. The production of useful fiber from flax is a labor-intensive operation, and probably the weavers bought finished flax fiber that had been prepared by the growers. The process involved many steps: threshing, retting, dressing, breaking, schutching, and heckling (combing). Heckled fibers of flax could be used as both warp and weft to weave a beautiful product, as in "flaxen" linen, with its natural color. Or it could be used as warp in combination with a heavy, twisted, wool weft, to become the cloth known for centuries as "linsey-woolsey." Another vegetable fiber that was available for use by the Zimmermann weavers was jute. For more than a century, jute had been imported into Hesse from the East Bengal area of the Indian sub-continent (now Bangladesh). Jute was exotic, but it was relatively inexpensive; and although it had a rough, humble brown appearance, the fibers were durable, and long – up to 13 feet in length. In its natural color, it is woven into burlap. Jute was also called "hessian," because it was woven into uniforms for Hessian soldiers. Hesse adjoined Württemberg, and supplies of jute/hessian were probably readily available for use by the Zimmermanns.

The color of fabrics, at the time the Zimmermanns were weaving in Gussenstadt, was either from their natural color, or from natural dyestuffs, which were obtained from plants or animals. Several synthetic dyestuffs were discovered in England at about that time, and they were soon utilized in various parts of Europe. However, synthetic dyestuffs would not have been available to the cottage industry of weavers in their own homes. Aniline dyes were developed as the result of an accidental discovery in England by William Perkin, who 1857 began to market "Tyrian Purple," later called "Mauve." In 1858, the azo dyes, which are now the principal synthetic dyestuffs, were discovered by a German worker, Johann Griess, in England. This discovery was not exploited until the 1870s, too late for John[1] Zimmermann to have used in Gussenstadt. In 1868, it was shown by German chemists that alizarin, an anthraquinone, is responsible for the color of the madder root. The synthetic dyes may have been studied at the new weaving institute in Reutlingen, but it is unlikely that this work had any immediate impact on local weavers, such as the Zimmermanns. All of these synthetic dyes would, however, be important in John[1] Zimmermann's factories in America. The natural dyes used by the Zimmermanns in Germany could produce colors of yellow, brown, blue, red, violet and black. Whether they prepared the dyestuffs, or purchased them, is unknown. Yellow and black were available from the bark of the oak; red was available from various animal products and madder root from Turkey; indigo, a favorite, was obtained from plants. Skill was necessary in order to obtain the correct color, hue, and fastness, and a mordant was often required – a chemical which would bond the dyestuff to the yarn.

Complex weave patterns can also be done on a horizontal hand loom. For example, tapestry weave: a "tabby," in which colored wefts are interlaced with warp to form patterns. Patterned fabric utilizes alternate warps of various colors. The French inventor Joseph-Marie

Jacquard (1752-1834) made a great improvement in the production of patterned fabric in 1801. In that year, he presented an improved drawloom, which was controlled by an operator using a foot treadle. It used punch cards to select the warp yarns automatically. Jacquard's invention was the forerunner of the IBM punch cards, which were used in the computers of the 1960s.

John[1] Zimmermann emigrated from Bremen or Hamburg, Germany, in September 1874 and he arrived in the U.S. in September or October. He probably came through New York City. John[1] went to Elmira, Chemung Co., N.Y., where he was welcomed by his relatives and others to whom he was related by marriage. They may have lived at first in "Germantown" in Elmira, near Madison Ave. and East Church Street, although they later became farmers.[3] The first members of this extended family in Elmira were Michael and Maria (Schwartz) Bantzhaff, and Maria's brother Jacob Schwartz. Jacob (b. Gussenstadt, 1854) was an 18-year old law student in Elmira in 1872. Michael Bantzhaff's sister, Margaretha (b. 1841), was married to Johann Georg Zimmermann (b. 1842), uncle of John[1] Zimmermann. Johann Georg and Margaretha (Bantzhaff) Zimmermann came to the U.S. from Germany in 1874. They lived in Elmira, where he became a farmer. With his wife, Margaretha, he had nine children – the last three born in Elmira.[4] John[1] probably came with his aunt and uncle to the U.S. in 1874, and then to Elmira, N.Y., where he filed his intention to become a naturalized citizen. At that time, an immigrant had to register an "intent" statement and then live in the U.S. for five years before becoming a citizen.

~~~IB~~~ R~~~AN~~~, John          329530

**The Naturalization Record of John Zimmermann in the Southern District of New York**
It is unknown if this is our John[1] Zimmermann. However, there are no others by the name of John Zimmermann (or John Zimmerman) in files of Ancestry.com of naturalized citizens in New York. His Nationalization Papers, dated 16 January 1880, are in Philadelphia Court of Common Pleas #2[5]

In 1876, "attracted to Philadelphia by the Centennial Exposition," John[1] Zimmermann moved to Philadelphia.[6] Soon after he arrived in Philadelphia, he contracted pneumonia, and was hospitalized at the German Hospital, where German was spoken.[7] While in the hospital he met weavers who worked in the Philadelphia textile industry, and he decided to remain in Philadelphia. Some of the weavers were members of the Reorganized Church of Latter Day Saints, and he thus began his affiliation with the RLDS. (For more on RLDS, see p.92)

"John Zimmermann" applied for a passport on 31 March 1880 in Philadelphia, signing his name with a firm hand in German script. The passport was granted on 7 April 1880. He stated on the application that he was a naturalized and loyal citizen of the United States, about to travel abroad; 24 years old. He was described as being 5 feet, 6½ inches in height; having a low forehead, brown eyes, a proportionate nose, healthy complexion, and oval face. He probably used this passport to return to Germany in 1880. However, he soon returned to Philadelphia, probably with his older brother, Johann Georg "George" Zimmermann. In 1881, Johann Georg Zimmermann, born in 1851, lived at 2259 Amber St., in the Kensington area of Philadelphia.[8] We can imagine John[1] back at his parents' home in Gussenstadt, telling his older brother about America, and about the American Dream he thought they could both achieve in Pennsylvania. George Zimmermann was married in Philadelphia 1882 to a Lutheran woman named Maria _____, born in 1856 in Pennsylvania. Her parents were born in Germany but they immigrated to America before she was born.[9]

In the early 1880s, John[1] Zimmermann was making rugs on a handloom, perhaps a 27-inch loom that he rented, and he was selling them successfully from a push cart on the streets of Philadelphia. He was baptized on 20 January 1884 in Camden, N.J., as a member of the RLDS Church, and later, on the same day, he was confirmed across the river in Philadelphia as a member of the Church. Both ceremonies – Baptism and Membership – were performed by Elder W. O. Owens.[10] The RLDS Church records show his name and the names of members of his family variously as either Zimmerman or Zimmermann, sometime within a single sentence. However, beginning in 1885, John[1] spelled it consistently with one "n," and that is how his name will usually appear hereafter in this chapter.[11]

In October 1885, one month before his thirtieth birthday, John Zimmerman was married to a woman who was born in Württemberg. She was two months younger than John. His bride, Eva Katharina Kellenbenz, a Lutheran, who came to America with her younger sister Clara, was working as a domestic servant. "Kellenbenz, Cath[ne]," 35 years old, born in Germany, from German parents, was recorded in the U.S. census of Philadelphia in 1880.

**Kellenbenz, Cath[ne]  35 W F Domestic   born in Germany  both parents born in Germany
U.S. Census – Philadelphia - 1880**

Family legend says that the Zimmermann and Kellenbenz families had been acquainted in Germany. Perhaps John met his wife when he returned to Germany for a short visit in 1880, although it seems more likely to me that they first met in America. Her name has been written many ways: Eva Katharina (in her birth and baptismal records), K. E. (in her marriage record), Katherine (in the 1900 census), Catherine (1880 and 1910 censuses), Evakaterina (in family notes), and Eva Katherine (on the death certificate). I will usually use Eva, or Eva Katherine, the anglicized version of the name on her birth and death certificates, except when quoting or paraphrasing from a document.

John and Eva Katherine would both have spoken the same, somewhat unusual, dialect of German, and they could thus have found each among those who spoke *Schwaben Deutch*. John and Eva worshiped at the RLDS church in Philadelphia, and John became a leader of the church, although Eva and her sister Clara continued to be Lutherans. Clara Kellenbenz was married in 1887, to Frederick Weigle, another man from Germany.[12]

John Zimmerman and Eva Kathcrine née Kellenbenz soon started their family. They had three children in their first five years of marriage: their first child, a daughter, Clara, was born in nine months, and their second, another daughter, Anna, was born seventeen months later. Their third child, also a daughter, Emily, was born in 1890. German was always spoken at home, although John also spoke English, with a heavy German accent. Eva never became fluent in English. In 1889, John and Eva lived at 2522 Fillmore, near John's brother George. In 1890, John Zimmerman lived in a newly-built house at 2812 North 5th St.[13]

The early records of the business operations of John[1] Zimmerman are incomplete, but it appears likely that John and his brother George cooperated in making and selling fabrics, probably rugs, that they made on handlooms. John was already thinking of how to produce rugs on a large scale, and he was experimenting with machinery to do this. After they were married in 1882, John's brother George and his wife Maria had two children, born in Philadelphia in 1882 and 1884. They then went back to Germany and had another child there in June 1888. By 1889, George and Maria Zimmermann and their children had returned to

Philadelphia, but by then, John[1] had gone into business with others in Philadelphia. The sequence of his business operations suggest that he may have had overlapping business activities, or some of the dates recorded may be incorrect. Or perhaps both of these are true.

| | |
|---|---|
| Name | John Zimmerman |
| Gender | Male |
| Spouse | K E Kellenbenz |
| Spouse Gender | Female |
| Marriage Place | Philadelphia, Pennsylvania, United States |
| Marriage Year | 1885 |
| Marriage License Number | 308 |
| Digital GSU Number | 4141945 |

**Passport application of John Zimmermann (L)**
**Philadelphia, 7 April 1880**
The signature shows a terminal "nn," and a double "mm"
indicated by a superscript line, $\overline{m}$

**Marriage record of John Zimmerman and K. E. Kellenbenz (R, above), Philadelphia, 1885**

Between 1884 and 1888, John[1] Zimmerman was engaged in a business arrangement of some kind with Bromley Brothers; he may have been an employee of the Bromleys. In about 1885, he also became a partner with Alexander Cameron, a member of the RLDS Church, in the firm known as Cameron and Zimmerman. The partnership produced Turkey red damask table covers and similar fabrics. The sole distributor for their products was Wasserman Bros. Co., at 240 Church St., in Central Philadelphia. Cameron died in 1891, and in 1892 the partnership of Cameron and Zimmerman was amalgamated with Wasserman Brothers & Co. to form a new corporation, Philadelphia Tapestry Mills. The new company was located in North Philadelphia, at Front & Allegheny Streets, in what would soon become the center of Philadelphia's textile industry.[14] John Zimmerman was later said to have been "a friend" of the Wassermans – Joseph, Benjamin, and Isaac. The Wassermans' parents were, like John's, from Württemberg.[15] By this time, John Zimmerman had developed marketable skills as a self-taught textile engineer, and he would soon become an inventor of important improvements in textile mills.[16]

The Wassermann brothers, Isaac (1856-1923), Joseph (1858-1937), and Benjamin (1867-1934), had a long history of working together. They were sons of Urias and Hannah (Fuchtler) Wasserman, both of whom were natives of Oberndorf, Württemberg, Germany. Oberndorf is about 80 km south of Stuttgart, and about 140 km south-west of Gussenstadt. Joseph Wasserman was educated at public schools in Philadelphia. When he was twenty, he went to New Mexico, then a "dangerous and barren territory." He returned to Philadelphia in 1882, where he was involved in textile importing with his brothers, Benjamin and Isaac.

Philadelphia was one of the great textile manufacturing centers of America at that time, and the Wassermans were attracted by the prospect of finding a good number of able and experienced workers. Although the Wassermans were Jewish, and Zimmerman came from a long line of Lutheran Protestants, they had much in common with Zimmerman. Joseph Wasserman was but three years younger than John Zimmerman, and, like Zimmerman, he must have been conversant in Swabian German. It was surely spoken by his parents at home. Both he and Zimmerman had been adventuresome in their youth – Joseph Wasserman had gone to New Mexico, and Zimmerman had left his family to come to America. In their work together, "The Wasserman brothers took charge of sales and finance; Zimmerman was a mechanical genius whose main interest lay in the development of machinery."[17]

Of the three brothers, Joseph Wasserman was said to have been the decision-maker. Joseph Wasserman and his wife, the former Edith Stix, had five children: Margaret, born in 1899; William Stix, born in (1901-1979); a son, born in 1903; Elizabeth Dinah, born in 1905; and Kathryn, born in 1907. Kathryn, who later married the financier Shelby Cullom Davis, died at the age of 106 in 2013. She left Philadelphia, and showed little interest in the Wasserman family business. William S. Wasserman, known as "Wild Bill," was reckless with his life and his investments. None of the children of "Wild Bill" Wasserman took a serious interest in the family textile business, although his cousin Howard Wasserman, a son of Benjamin, served on the board of the Arloom Corporation with William in 1947. The many differences between the children of the three Wasserman brothers and the children of John Zimmerman would play an important role in the joint venture of the Wassermans and the Zimmermanns – known as Artloom.[18]

John and Eva's fourth child, a son, was born on 6 June 1892. The son, John, Jr., would, like his father, become an inventor, and he would join his father and the Wassermans in the textile milling business. In the same year, the RLDS Church left Eureka Hall at 11th and Girard Avenue. Two years later, on 4 December 1894, John and Eva had a second son, William ("Bill") Zimmerman, who would also later join in his father's business. By 1895 the RLDS Church was meeting at 4th and Huntingdon, about one block south of John Zimmerman's residence. In 1895, Wasserman Brothers & Co., linens, was at that time located at 231 Church Street in Central Philadelphia, and John Zimmerman, upholsterer's materials, was in business as a mill at East Cambria and Ormes.[19] In the same year, John Zimmerman resided at 520 Somerset, about a half block south of his previous residence. In the Philadelphia Tapestry Mills, John Zimmerman was responsible for the development of machinery and ran the plant, while the Wassermans were in charge of sales and finance.[20]

A formal portrait photograph of John Zimmerman's family was taken in 1896. By 1897, the family had moved again, to 610 West Lehigh Avenue. They were living in the Lehigh Ave. house when their youngest daughter, Emily, died of diphtheria at age 6½. The family was devastated by the little girl's death. Another daughter, their sixth child, Lillian (known as a child as "Lily Mae"), was born 13 September 1897.[21]

In 1898, the Philadelphia Tapestry Mills and one other mill were the first in the United States to replicate "Gobelins" – the Artloom Couch Cover, with a Persian motif. The atlas of Philadelphia shows the Philadelphia Tapestry Mills at Allegheny and Howard in 1901. The mill would later double in size, and would cover two full blocks. However, a near-catastrophe then occurred, when the textile mill workers in the Kensington area went on strike.[22]

The Philadelphia "weaver's strike" on 1 December 1899 involved some 800 workers, who demanded a 55-hour work week and a ten-cent increase in hourly overtime. An additional

3,000 workers in 24 other mills went out on strike the following day. Five of the carpet manufacturers in the Kensington area were involved, the largest being the Philadelphia Tapestry Mills. Many members of the RLDS Church were involved, and because John Zimmerman was the Philadelphia Tapestry Mills' manager, he was caught between opposing sides in the struggle. Some of the striking weavers who were church members returned to work on 11 December, claiming to have "conscientious scruples against participating in a strike." They were led by a fellow weaver and church member named Hosea H. Bacon, who had previously been a spiritual leader over Zimmerman. As the mill's manager, Zimmerman was now a temporal leader over Bacon. Zimmerman brought in 31 non-union Church members from the RLDS Branch in Baldwin, Maryland, to bring the mill back into operation. On 22 December, Bacon persuaded them to join the strikers, and the strike continued. Zimmerman maintained his patience, in spite of picket lines, and he also did not let it be known publicly that he was a member of the LDS Church. The strike ended on 27 February 1900. The strikers gained the increase in overtime that they had demanded, at a collective cost of some $100,000 in wages.

Zimmerman was offered the Philadelphia Bishopric in the RLDS Church, but he declined at that time, and he waited five years before being ordained as bishop. The Church survived intact, and it benefited from the quietly effective compromise that was negotiated between the workers and the mill operators. The RLDS Church then moved ahead in 1901 with the construction of a new, permanent, house of worship. It was built at Howard and Ontario Streets, on a lot purchased by John Zimmerman, one block north of the Philadelphia Tapestry Mills. The new church building was in use by 1 December 1901, and his daughter, Clara, was baptized there at age 15 on 30 March 1902. A formal dedication of the new church building was held on 21 January 1907. It was the first building the RLDS Church had owned in Philadelphia. The RLDS district held a highly publicized conference in Baldwin, Maryland, in 1903, adopting resolutions which favored a Constitutional Amendment banning polygamy.[23]

In July 1899, John Zimmerman's father, Johann Zimmermann, died in Gussenstadt, Württemberg, at the age of 77. Eva and her daughters Clara (13) and "Lilly" (age 2) must have left immediately for Gussenstadt. They returned to New York on 24 August from Hamburg, via Southampton and Cherbourg, on the *Auguste Victoria*. His mother, Anna Ursula (Jäger) Zimmermann, died on 11 January 1901. The graves of John's parents are marked on a single stone in Gussenstadt.[24] On 11 June 1902, Albert Walter Zimmermann, the sixth and last child of John and Eva Zimmerman, was born at their home, 610 West Lehigh Ave. Their house on West Lehigh was across the avenue from a large Philadelphia Library Branch building; it is now gone, replaced with a small duplex. Within a year, the family would move again, to their final home, at 1512 Allegheny Ave. It was a grand house in a beautiful location.[25]

In 1904 John's brother, George, filed a patent for improvements for a "Loom for Weaving Double-Pile Fabric." The patent was for his own use as "George Zimmermann," at Fairhill & Rockland St., not for work with John at Philadelphia Tapestry Mills. George filed a patent application in the next year, for "Woven Pile Fabric," and he also received a patent for his 1904 filing for "Double-Pile Fabric" loom. George had already purchased two looms, to be operated with gas power.[26] The question of whether George and John had a falling out will probably never be answered. There must have been some awkwardness in their relationship, however. The four children of George (a daughter and three sons) and John (three daughters and three sons) would have been cousins, yet later records show few communications between them. And most of their children, who were second cousins, were unaware of the existence of both of the two Zimmermann brothers, John and George, who came to America.

In the meantime, starting in 1904, Philadelphia Tapestry Mills was promoting a major advertising campaign for "Artloom Tapestries." They were "considered 'pioneers' in mass advertising and they prospered mightily." Prominent in their line were the Moquette Couch Covers, made with a "rise-and-fall Jacquard machine" that Zimmerman developed. Arloom claimed that their "Curtains, Couch Covers and Table Covers" were woven by the "Largest Tapestry Mill in America." John Zimmerman filed applications for three patents on 18 January 1905; one was for "Pile Gage" and two were for "Woven Pile Fabric." The applications were approved and patents were granted for the three inventions on 20 February 1906.[27]

John Zimmerman was ordained as a bishop in the Reorganized Church of Jesus Christ of Latter Day Saints, for the District of New York and Philadelphia, on 15 April 1905, at the headquarters of the church in Lamoni, Iowa. The ordination was given "under the hands of Joseph Smith [III], W. H. Kelley, E. L. Kelley, and F. G. Pitt," and the Bishop's License for "John Zimmermann" was signed at Lamoni on 15 May 1905 by Joseph Smith [III], President of the Church, and R. G. Galyards, Secretary. President Joseph Smith [III] was a son of Joseph Smith, Jr., who founded the LDS Church. Ten years later, Richard Carlyle Kelley would marry John's daughter Anna; Wilfred Kelley and Edmund Levi Kelley were Richard's brothers. F. G. Pitt was pastor of the Pittsburgh branch. As John Zimmerman's partnership with the Wassermans prospered, so, too, did the RLDS Church in the Philadelphia-New York District. John Zimmerman was a generous benefactor of the church, and his children were also active members of the church.[28]

On 20 February 1906, John Zimmerman's three patent applications were granted and patents were issued. The applications are several pages long, with a wealth of details. He signed his application as John Zimerman, using a superscript over the m̄ and with a single terminal "n." In his summary of Patent #813,139 for Woven Pile Fabric, Zimmerman wrote:

> My invention relates to cut pile fabrics having outer and inner planes of wefts; and it consists in weaving a double cloth after the manner hereinafter described and illustrated in the accompanying drawings . . . The pile is cut in the usual manner during the process of weaving, so as to produce two distinct fabrics when finished, or this can be done after the cloth is off the loom by machine specially constructed for that purpose.[29]

The patents were originally intended for the manufacturing of fabrics, but they were "peculiarly adapted to the manufacture of rugs. And so in 1906, a rug manufacturing department was added to the Philadelphia Tapestry Mills under the trade name of Artloom Rug Mills."[30] These patents enabled the company (1) to weave rugs in nine-foot widths instead of the traditional 27-inch strips; (2) to produce patented weaves that speeded up the output of the looms; and (3) provided a method of weaving rugs face to face and then splitting them apart, "two rugs being produced by the same labor and machinery formerly required for one."

> Few carpet mills in America today can exist without the wide loom. But in 1906, John Zimmerman, one of the original founders of the Philadelphia Tapestry Mills, from which Artloom sprang, owned the exclusive patent-rights to the wide loom which he developed in nine-foot widths. Artloom's present battery of Wilton looms runs as wide as eighteen feet. The wide loom is one of the priceless assets which the new Artloom management planned for and installed as fast as the equipment arrived.[31]

In 1906, John had a formal portrait photograph taken of his family, which has since become the iconic image of the John Zimmerman(n) family. The children were well educated. The boys went to Philadelphia Central High School and then to the University of Pennsylvania, and the girls went to Girl's High School. Clara studied Domestic Science at Drexel and continued with private music studies. All of the girls played the piano, but Clara was the most professional. She played the organ at the formal designation of the Kensington area RLDS Church at Howard and Ontario on 21 January 1907. John's wife took Prophet Joseph Smith III (1832-1914) and his son Frederick on a tour of Philadelphia at that time. The Smith and Zimmerman families formed a close relationship that lasted for several decades.[32]

In 1907, John Zimmerman invented a "warp dyeing machine" that "made possible the production of patterned rugs with pre-dyed warp yarns." The "Artloom Rug Mills . . . department then became the major emphasis of the company, and it was a separate incorporated entity in 1919."[33] John and his brother George both received patents for weaving Pile Fabric in 1907, and George received another patent for Woven Pile Fabric in 1908. A contrast then became apparent between John Zimmerman and George Zimmermann. George's businesses gradually faded from sight, whereas John's business operations continued to grow. The Philadelphia Tapestry Mills succeeded as the result of John Zimmerman's inventions and his development of large, expensive, machines for weaving, combined with the Wassermans' creative marketing of carefully selected textile products, and their skillful financing of the entire operation.[34]

By 1908, the Artloom Rug Co. at Allegheny and Front St. was making seamless rugs, operating about 25 looms, and it was planning to expand. Front St. is about 100 yards east of Howard St. The Philadelphia Tapestry Mills announced a plan in March 1909, in which it proposed to build a 5-story addition, with a footprint of 58 feet by 86 feet, on the corner of Howard St. and Allegheny.[35]

John Zimmerman and his wife Eva Katherine had six children by 1910, and their family was continuing to prosper. After coming to Philadelphia in 1876, and returning briefly to Germany in 1880, John, now 55, had spent most of his time in Pennsylvania. On the other hand, his brother George came later to America. George worked in Philadelphia for a short time, but returned to Germany, then to Arkansas, and now was living in Philadelphia again. George's wife had died, and he was now a widower, living alone, with four children: Anna (27), John (26, a designer), George (23, foreman in a textile mill), and Walter (17, who later was a gardener for John[1]'s son, William[2]).[36] In 1910, the existence of another short-lived milling company bearing the family name was mentioned for the first time. Lion Hosiery Mill, operated by Zimmerman Brothers, proprietors, is "now located in more commodius and convenient quarters at the SW corner of Hancock and Turner Streets," and "new knitting machines have been installed." The spelling of the company name with one "n" and the apparent success of the operation suggests that this was a venture of John Zimmerman and his brother George, with John as the senior partner. John's sons were too young to be in business at this time, and there are no others who are known to be candidates for the partnership. Lion Hosiery Mill, at Mascher & Turner St., was mentioned again in the *American Textile Directory* in 1915. It apparently did not persist, and it was not mentioned again in the records of Philadelphia.[37]

In 1911, the Philadelphia Tapestry Mills added another department, the Philadelphia Pile Fabric Mills, which was designed to capture the market for velvet cloth. However, this venture was ultimately unsuccessful because plush imitations fell out of favor with American consumers after World War I. In the decade of the twenties, many Americans could afford silk shirts and fur coats, and they demanded better fabrics and draperies.[38]

The onset of war in August 1914 caught the Zimmerman family by surprise. John, Jr. and his brother Bill were on a vacation in Europe with Fletcher and Carl Schaum, two brothers who lived near by at 1508 Allegheny. They arrived back in New York on the *Lusitania*.[39] Seven months later the *Lusitania* was sunk by a German torpedo. Anti-German sentiment in the United States rose during the war, especially after the U.S. declared war on Germany in 1917. Several German words were anglicized; e.g., sauerkraut became "German cabbage," and the German Hospital of Philadelphia was renamed as the Lankenau Hospital.

Prophet Joseph Smith III died in December 1914 and was replaced by his son Frederick Smith. Bishop Zimmerman personally advanced $6,700 to pay part of the total cost of $12,000 for the new "Beacon Light" RLDS Church, at 3014 E Street. The crowded Kensington branch membership then exceeded 300, including John Sr.'s son William and his daughter Anna as new members.[40]

In 1915, the three companies that were controlled by the Wassermans and John Zimmerman occupied adjacent buildings in a massive complex that covered two city blocks, between Allegheny Avenue (S) and Westmoreland Street (N), Manchester St. (W) and Front St. (E): Philadelphia Tapestry Mills, Philadelphia Pile Fabrics Mills, and Artloom Rug Mills.[41] The mills were bisected by Howard Street, and the two sides were connected by a high bridge. John Zimmerman was shown as the vice president and superintendent of the Tapestry Mills, but he was surely the supervisor of all three mills. Zimmerman had long been responsible for the cost, volume, and quality of the final products; for the recruitment of hundreds of quality workers, and for their safety and morale; for choosing and overseeing the foremen who oversaw the teams of workers; and for the construction and maintenance of the enormous machines that produced the rugs, tapestry, and fabrics for the marketplace. It had been a busy, never-ending job, and now, at age 60, it was time for him give up working with the Wassermans. John Zimmerman's name did not appear again on the list of officers of the various businesses in which he had participated with the Wasserman brothers.

His son, John Zimmerman, Jr., filed a patent for a Warp-Printing Machine on 1 September 1915:

> The object of the invention is to provide a machine of the above character with devices whereby the warp threads as they pass continuously through the machine, may be supplied uniformly with coloring matter in accordance with a predetermined pattern.[42]

The patent was granted on 22 August 1916. "This machine, which made possible the production of patterned rugs with predyed warp yarns, led to the perfection of [the] fabulously successful Wilminster line" of Artloom rugs.[43] For reasons that are unknown, but which suggest tension in the relationship between the Wassermans and the Zimmermans, John, Jr. did not list Philadelphia Tapestry Mills or any other firm on the patent application, or thereafter. However, the son, John Zimmerman, Jr., was still active in the parent firm. In 1916, John Jr. became one of the five incorporators of a new but short-lived corporation, known as Philadelphia Silk Spinning Mills, with Joseph and Isaac Wasserman and two other men. John, Sr., was not listed in the new corporation, and his name did not appear thereafter on the roster of leaders of any of the Wasserman brothers' operations. By 1917, William ("Bill")

Zimmerman was working at the Philadelphia Tapestry Mills as a chemical engineer. John Zimmerman's employment of his sons in the mills was a sore point with the Wassermans, whose sons did not, or could not, do that sort of work.

One month after the U.S. declared war on Germany, Bill Zimmerman filed his Draft Registration Card. Bill served in the U.S. Army Infantry in the American Expeditionary Forces in Europe. When he returned from the war in 1918, John, Sr., and his sons formed the firm of John Zimmerman & Sons at Erie & Castor Avenues, manufacturing mohair furniture coverings. Bill became president of John Zimmerman & Sons, and Anna's husband, Richard Kelley, was a partner, serving as secretary of this family business. John Zimmerman, Jr., tried various business ventures in textiles. He worked for a time at John Zimmerman & Sons, but he later returned to Artloom. In 1919, the Artloom Rug Mills were incorporated, distinct from but side-by-side with the Philadelphia Tapestry Mills and the Philadelphia Pile Fabric Mils. The incorporators of the corporation were the three Wasserman brothers and two Zimmermans, John Sr., and John, Jr. In 1920, Artloom Rug Mills boasted that it was the "Largest Manufacturers of Seamless Jacquard Wilton Rugs in the World." In a touch of unintended irony, the Artloom ad appeared on a page above the ad for John Bromley & Sons, Inc. (est. 1845, inc. 1916), where John Zimmerman got his first job in Philadelphia.[44]

Eva Katherine (Kellenbenz) Zimmerman died on 12 October 1920, at age 65. She died of pernicious anemia, of one year's duration. Her daughters had gradually assumed the maternal role of their mother. She was buried next to her daughter Emily in Greenmount Cemetery.[45] After Eva Katherine's death, John Zimmerman, Sr., continued to devote his life to his family; to his partnership with his sons (where he was a dominant force); and to the Reformed Church of Latter Day Saints. In the last 16 years of his life, he would also remarry, travel abroad, and, perhaps, relax a bit. He was, however, always a serious man; and no photographs show him with even a trace of a smile.[46]

In February 1921, the old Beaumont Deer Park, near New Hope, Pennsylvania, was offered for sale. It was discovered by John, Sr., when he was driving in the country near Philadelphia in search of a place to hold summer reunions for the RLDS Church. He placed a $500 deposit to hold the property. It was purchased later that month for $5,000, with the Zimmerman family acting as agents. Five years later, the family deeded the property to the RLDS Church as a gift. Improvements were made at Deer Park, totaling nearly $19,000, including repairs to old buildings, a new choir platform for the Auditorium, and toilet facilities. A 75-foot concrete dam, two feet thick, was constructed, to form a swimming and fishing hole; and a 12-acre athletic field was created, with two baseball diamonds.[47]

The first reunion at Deer Park took place over a two-week period in July 1921, when a special train transported passengers on the Reading Railroad from New York City to a point just inside the southern edge of the park. Reunion-goers climbed down the embankment, crossed the creek, and climbed up the hill to the campgrounds. John Zimmerman, Sr., arranged for luggage to be transported by truck, and 100 tents were set up. The reunion was attended by the new RLDS president, Frederick M. Smith. On July 4, 5,000 people gathered, with 200 automobiles – both church members (called "saints") and local residents. Accompanied by the Lambertville Band (from across the river in New Jersey), the crowd sang both familiar and patriotic songs before evening fireworks. The Reunion Committee was responsible for a debt of $24,000, which the Church historian believes was mostly paid by John Zimmerman, Sr.[48]

Shortly after the reunion, in July 1921, John Sr.'s youngest child, Albert, sailed on a 3-month tour of Europe and northern Africa. He left on 23 July, for Algeria, France, Switzerland,

Holland, and Italy. Albert would later return to Europe with his wife in 1937, and to Algeria, as a U.S. Navy officer, in 1943. Foreign travel was one of many benefits that were offered to the children of John Zimmerman, Sr., and they, too, learned to be generous to others. On the other hand, John, Sr., expected his sons and sons-in-law to be prudent, and successful in business. In December, 1921, Clara's husband, Al Hoxie, wrote to his brother that he had a "poor business year." In 1922, he resigned as director of the choir at the Philadelphia RLDS church; and "in a strained departure," he also resigned from the Philadelphia Pile Fabric Mills.[49]

On 30 November 1922, John Zimmerman, Sr., married (2), as her 2nd husband, **Mrs. Anna (Anderson) DANCER,** age 58, in Lamoni, Iowa; daughter of Andrew K. Anderson and his wife Inger Ormsdotter. Anna Dancer was then vice president of the state savings bank of Lamoni. She was the widow of David Dancer, and mother of two of his sons. David Dancer previously married (1) Rosalia Harvey, by whom he had five children; of these, two sons survived. The ceremony was performed by Albert Carmichael, Bishop of the RLDS Church, witnessed by Anna's son, David A. Dancer, Jr., and John's daughter Clara (Zimmerman) Hoxie.[50] In addition to Anna's two sons with David Dancer – David A. Dancer, Jr., and Howard M. Dancer – she also brought into her second marriage two adult step-sons, Eugene and Walter Dancer, who were children of Dancer's first wife. The family of John Zimmerman, Sr., thus grew again, to include two step-sons, and their two half-brothers. John's children, however, did not accept their step-sons as brothers, nor did their children accept the children of the Dancer boys as cousins. No relationship has continued between the Zimmermann family and the Dancer family.[51]

In February 1923, John and Anna (Dancer) Zimmerman took a 3-month cruise to Europe and countries bordering the Mediterranean Sea, taking with them Lillian, who had recently graduated from the University of Pennsylvania. They went to Great Britain, France, Italy, Spain, Portugal, Holland, Switzerland, Egypt, Morocco, Algeria, Palestine, and Turkey. Lillian contracted "Palestine fever," and nearly died; she left the ship in England, and recovered in a nursing home in London. Anna's sister, also named Lillian, moved in with John, Sr., and Anna after they returned to Philadelphia. John's youngest son, Albert, graduated from the University of Pennsylvania in 1923, with a degree in electrical engineering. As an engineer, Al followed the same path as his father, who was a self-taught mechanical genius, and his brother, Bill, a chemical engineer. Albert then joined the family textile firm and soon showed his aptitude for business. John Zimmerman's youngest daughter, Lillian, was married in 1926, at his house, to James Fligg, an electrical engineer, who was the son of an RLDS Church missionary. The Fligg, Zimmerman, and Hoxie cabins were assembled at Deer Park in the summer of 1928 from prefabricated units, at a cost of $5,000 each.[52]

Jim Fligg then joined the family business, John Zimmerman & Sons, in 1926. He was 26 and his brother-in-law, Al, was 24. They were much younger than the others. John, Sr., 69, was the forceful leader of the firm, along with Anna's husband, Richard Kelley, 44. John Jr., 34; and Bill, 32, were a decade younger. John Jr. was a gifted inventor, and soon would have his own patents. John Jr. was president of Zimmerman & Sons, at Erie and Castor Streets, makers of mohair upholstery furniture coverings. He was perhaps also president of Zimmerman Mills, Inc., makers of furniture coverings, at 21st and Allegheny (2092 W. Allegheny Ave.), which was established in 1927. However, he also returned to work for Artloom. Bill remained with his father and brothers-in-law, but he was not happy. Tensions were high. The families socialized together on weekends and vacations, but the relationships between the branches of the family were "strangling."[53]

In 1924 the Artloom Corporation was formed from a merger of Artloom Rug Mills, Philadelphia Tapestry Mills, and Philadelphia Pile Fabric Mills. The business address was Howard and Allegheny. The decision to merge and use a simpler title was undoubtedly a wise business decision, and provided a better name for marketing the brand. The three units had shown, since 1919, "a brilliant record of success." However, within two years, by 1926, "the inevitable signs of age began to show," and "Artloom's 'hair was turning gray'."[54]

John Zimmerman, Jr., filed two patent applications in 1928 and another in 1929 for Double-Pile Fabric, not assigning them to any other party. He could thus use the inventions at either Artloom or his family's firms – John Zimmerman & Sons, and Zimmermann Mills. The patent applications were approved in 1931. In February 1929, he was elected to Sigma Xi, the national honorary scientific fraternity. In 1929, John, Jr., age 37, was back at Artloom as a vice president, and he was still president of Zimmermann Mills; Joseph Wasserman, now 71, was Artloom's president, and his brother Benjamin, 62, was another vice president of Artloom. Albert Zimmermann, age 27, the youngest brother of John, Jr., was secretary; he was five years out of college. Charles Wasserman, Isaac's son, age 33, was treasurer (Isaac had died in 1923). Artloom then began a decline. The management was dysfunctional – it was still controlled by the two surviving elder Wasserman brothers – and there was a huge age difference between the officers, ranging from 71 to 27. In such a Board, could there be any possibility of a collaborative decision? And then on 29 October, there was the stock market crash. In 1930, Artloom reported its first operating loss, followed by seven more years in which it lost nearly $1,000,000. Sales fell by 90% from $8,754,000 in 1925 to $875,000 in 1933. In 1931, the Federal Trade Commission forced Artloom to abandon its use of the term "Wilton" for its rugs, although it resumed advertising the sale of Wilton rugs before 1947.[55] Artloom later twice showed signs of improvement – in 1936, after it was purchased by a group of investors, headed by the chairman of Atlas Tack Corporation, and again in 1948 – but it never fully recovered. Artloom was, for a time, one of the largest carpet manufacturing companies in the United States, but it is no longer in existence.[56]

John Zimmerman's son William was married in 1929 to Margaret Peattie Lukens, whose parents, Edward Fell and Margaret (Patton) Lukens, were descended from early German Quaker and Mennonite settlers of Philadelphia. They were married in the RLDS Church. Also in 1929, John's daughter Lillian and her husband Jim Fligg began building a house in Elkins Park, adjacent to the house of her sister Anna and Richard Kelley.[57] John's daughter Clara and her husband Al Hoxie were renting a house at 3119 North 16th Street in 1930. Hoxie, now a "music director," was no longer connected to the Zimmermans' business operations. However, the Hoxies were still able to take a family trip to Europe, and to spend the rest of their summer at their place on Cape Cod. Clara Hoxie also advanced $540 to the RLDS Church to pay for outstanding obligations at Deer Park, after the bank which held the RLDS account collapsed.[58]

The three patent applications of John Zimmerman, Jr., for Double-Pile Fabric which were filed in 1929 were finally approved in March 1931. The application said that,

> The principal object of my present invention is to provide an improved double pile fabric which, when cut apart, will produce two rugs or carpets, each of the well known Wilton types . . . A further object of my invention is to provide a fabric of the type aforesaid, whereby seamless Wilton rugs of the larger or room size, may be more economically produced than heretofore.

John's patent described the face-to-face carpets, which Artloom later described as the third and last of its "three revolutionary advances": "(3) rugs could be woven face to face and then split apart, two rugs being produced by the same labor and machinery formerly required for one." The patent application by John Zimmerman, Jr., clearly shows that Artloom was referring to his invention. Whether or not others were involved in the invention of the "revolutionary" method of face-to-face weaving and cutting apart is unknown. However, there is no reason to believe the revisionist biography of the Wasserman brothers, published in 2001, which said, incorrectly, that Joseph Wasserman's "older brother Isaac found a way to slice a rug in half without damaging the weave – a technique that gave the Wassermans an obvious advantage: they could make two carpets from one loom." Indeed, none of the three Wasserman brothers is recorded as having any patent, much less one for this revolutionary invention.[59]

The question of whether or not the rugs produced by Artloom can be described as Wiltons became an issue in 1931, presumably because one of their competitors raised an objection to Artloom's use of the term "Wilton." The Federal Trade Commission ordered the Artloom Corporation to cease advertising their product as Wiltons, pending a judgment. In 1933, the Federal Trade Commission ruled that Artloom could not claim that their products were Wiltons, or to use that term in their advertising. Probably for this reason, Artloom began to refer to some of its products as Wilminster rugs: "The Wilminster is an exclusive Artloom development, a rug that combines the beauty of pattern and color of an Axminster with the strength and serviceability of a Wilton." By 1947, however, Artloom was again advertising several types of Wilton rugs, in both plain and oriental-type patterns.[60]

In 1932, John Zimmerman, Sr., retired from Artloom, where he was vice president and general manager. He probably continued with John Zimmerman & Sons, and perhaps also with Zimmerman Mills, although there is no record of this.[61] John and his second wife, Anna, and his son, John, Jr., took a cruise on the S.S. *Statendam*, from New York City, from 11-20 January 1934. The name of the ship suggests that the cruise may have been to Europe, although this was not specified. It was a very difficult time in Germany, which suffered inflation as a result of the Versailles Treaty obligations, and was in a political uproar. Helen Hayes, age 45, of 1512 Allegheny Ave., Philadelphia, accompanied them. Her relationship to the family is unknown. Bishop John Zimmerman must have been proud of his eldest son, John, Jr., who was high priest of the RLDS Church in Philadelphia. John and his son John, Jr., are seen in a group photograph taken in 1934 outside the Kensington branch, with Prophet Frederick Smith, grandson of the first prophet, Joseph Smith, Jr.; and John's son-in-law, Al Hoxie.

Two years later, on 23 May 1936, John Zimmerman, Sr., died at his home in Philadelphia, at the age of 80. His former partner, Joseph Wasserman, had resigned as president of Artloom in 1935, although he continued as chairman of the board of directors until 1936, when Arloom was sold to the Atlas Tack Corporation. Joseph Wasserman died in 1937. Funeral services for John Zimmerman were held at his home, and he was buried next to his wife and daughter Emily at Greenmount Cemetery.

Sometime in the next few weeks, in the summer of 1936, his widow, Anna, removed the contents of the house at 1512 W. Allegheny Ave., and returned to Lamoni with her sister Nellie. Anna and Nellie's departure and the clearing of the house was discovered after John's daughters, Clara Hoxie and Lillian Fligg, returned after vacationing with their families at Cape Cod. This must have been a shock. It did nothing to help a friendship develop between John Zimmerman's children and their step-siblings in Missouri. And no relationship has since developed between John and Catherine's grandchildren and their step-cousins in the Dancer family. Anna (Anderson) (Dancer) Zimmerman died at Lamoni, Iowa, on 7 July 1937, and was buried there.

----------------

John Zimmerman & Sons continued in existence for 26 years or more after John Zimmerman died. Zimmermann & Sons Plush & Pile Fabric, at Erie and Castor Ave., was seen on the Philadelphia Land Use Map (1942). The building is still there, mostly abandoned, but partly repurposed, on the SW corner of E Erie and Castor. The other firm founded by John Zimmerman, Zimmerman Mills, quietly went out of business at some point in time after John, Sr., died. The Zimmerman Mills building was standing but unoccupied in the 1950s on the SW corner of 21st and W Allegheny, 2092 W Allegheny, and it is still there, still abandoned.[62]

After John Zimmerman died, Artloom twice went through reorganization and attempted revitalizations, but in the end, it failed to persist as a corporate entity. The Philadelphia Land Use Map showed Artloom Corporation at Allegheny and Howard in 1942, and it was also there in 1962. Sometime after that, it disappeared from the record. After a fire destroyed part of the complex in 1976, the buildings were torn down, and not a trace remains to show that they ever existed.[63]

----------------

A brief summary of the history of the RLDS Church is given below, because of the crucial impact that service to the RLDS Church played in the life of John Zimmerman, and also because of his unique but largely forgotten role in the history of the RLDS Church, now known as the Community of Christ.

### Mormons, with a Special Focus on the Reorganized Church of Latter Day Saints[64]

The Church of Jesus Christ of Latter Day Saints (LDS), whose members are known as Mormons, is a religion founded by Joseph Smith, Jr. (1805-44) on 6 April 1830 in Fayette, N.Y. He proclaimed "a new dispensation, the restoration of the priesthood and rituals of the 'true church,' and the eligibility for the attainment of deity by all Mormons, the Latter-day Saints." His father, Joseph Smith, Sr., was "an impoverished New England farmer, living in that part of upstate New York now known, because of recurrent revivalistic enthusiasm as 'the burned-over district'." At about age 20, in 1825, Joseph Smith, Jr., went from his home in Palmyra, in upstate New York, to Harmony, Susquehanna Co., Pennsylvania, where worked with others who were looking for buried treasure. He boarded in Harmony with the family of Isaac and Elizabeth Hale, and he returned several times thereafter to court their daughter, Emma (1804-79). Her parents refused permission for her to marry Joseph, and the couple therefore eloped across the border to South Bainbridge, N.Y., where they were married on 17 January 1827. The newlyweds went north to his home in Palmyra. On 22 September 1827, Joseph and Emma went to a place now known as the "Hill Cumorah," where he "claimed to have received from an angel, Moroni, golden plates from which, with the use of special stones set in silver bows . . . he translated the *Book of Mormon*. Three associates solemnly testified that they, too, saw both the plates and the angel Moroni, and thereafter they and other converts frequently claimed visions and revelations." Joseph and Emma returned to Harmony in December 1827, where he continued work on the translation and editing of the *Book of Mormon*; it was published in

March 1830 in Fayette, N.Y. The LDS church that was established on 6 April 1830 in Fayette was originally called the Church of Christ.

In 1831, Joseph and Emma Smith moved with their family and other newly converted Mormons to Kirtland, Ohio, and then further west. The LDS established settlements in Missouri and in Illinois, where they founded the town of Nauvoo. Wherever Mormons went, violence soon followed. "Mormon self-assurance, commercial advantage, and political power provoked renewed hostility from the 'Gentiles,' while Smith's secret teaching and practice of plural marriage and his trade in land caused dissension among his ablest converts." An outbreak of disaffection that began in Nauvoo led to the arrest of the prophet, Joseph Smith, Jr., and his brother, Hyrum, and their incarceration in a jail in Carthage, Ill. A mob stormed the jail on 27 June 1844, and killed both men. The leadership of the LDS was then disputed between several men, including Brigham Young and the prophet's son, Joseph Smith III. Brigham Young, who was the president of the Quorum of the Twelve Apostles, was selected as the new prophet by the LDS congregation in Nauvoo. Relations between the LDS and their neighbors deteriorated, and in 1846, Brigham Young decided to lead the LDS to the Salt Lake Valley. An "important minority of Mormons rejected Young and remained in Iowa and Illinois, where they formed the Reorganized Church of Jesus Christ of Latter Day Saints (1852-60). . . . That branch of eventually set up its headquarters at Independence, Mo." The "New Organization" of the LDS was established at Amboy, Ill, on 6 April 1860. Emma (Hale) Smith and her son, Joseph Smith, III, remained in Nauvoo. The word "Reorganized" was added in 1872, and the Reorganized Church of Jesus Christ of Latter Day Saints was then known as RLDS. Joseph Smith III (1832-1914) was the prophet of the RLDS from 1860-1914. Joseph Smith III had three wives and many children. By his wife Bertha Madison, he had a son, Frederick Madison Smith, known as "Fred M." (1874-1946), who was prophet from 1915-1946. By another wife, Ada Clark, he had a son William Wallace (1900-1989), who was prophet from 1958-1978. Joseph Smith III and his son Fred M. Smith paid many visits to the new RLDS church building in Philadelphia, purchased with the help of John Zimmermann, at Ontario and Howard Streets. John Zimmermann was friends with the Smith family, and he and his wife hosted their visits to Philadelphia. The RLDS church building was one block north of the textile factory of Philadelphia Tapestry Mills, later Artloom, owned by John Zimmermann and the Wasserman brothers, at West Allegheny Ave. and Howard Street. The enormous mill complex was about ½ mile east of John Zimmermann's house at 1512 West Allegheny Ave. When he was bishop, John Zimmermann purchased and gave to the RLDS the retreat known as Deer Park, near New Hope, Pa.

The RLDS now "holds firmly to the *Book of Mormon* but rejects the evolutionary conceptions of deity and the theism implicit in it, the new covenant of celestial marriage, Baptism on behalf of the dead, plural marriage, and tithing. Secret ceremonies are not performed . . . and the Book of Abraham is not accepted as of divine origin. The church's presidents, descendants of the prophet, have been appointed by revelation. . . . The version of [the *Book of Mormon*] of the Reorganized Church includes fewer revelations from the last decade of Smith's life." The name of the RLDS Church was changed in 2001 to the Community of Christ. The retreat known as Deer Park, given to the church by John Zimmermann, is still in use, and it is the most visible public property of the Community of Christ in Pennsylvania. The Community of Christ and the LDS Church have recently cooperated in a study of a seminal Mormon manuscript entitled *Book of Commandments and Revelations*.

The early history of the LDS church has much to do with Pennsylvania. The first prophet, Joseph Smith, Jr., and his wife Emma worked in Harmony, Pa., to translate and edit the Book of Mormon. "On December 23, 1839 . . . Joseph Smith visited the city and officially established the Philadelphia Branch on the northeast corner of Seventh and Callowhill Streets" [Ellsworth]. Smith preached at the Universalist Church Hall in December 1839, at 412 Lombard St., corner of 4th and Lombard. After the prophet and his family went west, LDS missionaries remained in the east. The missionaries went to Pennsylvania from early LDS congregations in New Jersey, and from Pennsylvania to Europe. They arranged for Mormons who were converted in England and the European continent to travel to America. Although most of the European Mormons went through the port of New York City and on to Utah, some among them who were weavers came to Philadelphia and stayed in Pennsylvania and Maryland. The Philadelphia Branch recorded 344 members in 1844. Branch records were not preserved after 1859, but the Mormon Church persisted as the Philadelphia Branch of the RLDS. It was active and growing during the period of John Zimmermann's presence in Philadelphia, from about 1875 until his death in 1936. It persisted thereafter, although again with dwindling membership. The Philadelphia Branch of the RLDS is now part of the Community of Christ, headquartered in Independence, Mo.

The larger LDS Church, headquartered in Salt Lake City, considers that the LDS in Philadelphia was dormant from 1846 until 1960. The history of the RLDS in Philadelphia is completely elided from the LDS website. The Philadelphia LDS Temple website says, "The Church was first established in Pennsylvania in 1839 – growing to 450 members by October 1840. Membership fell following the migration of the Saints to Salt Lake but grew again as Mormon European emigrants arrived. Eventually the first stake was organized in 1960 with 1,100 members located in congregations in southeastern Pennsylvania, New Jersey, Delaware, and Maryland. Today there are nearly 48,000 members in Pennsylvania alone." The newly-constructed Philadelphia Temple is scheduled to be opened in September 2016.

-----------------

John Zimmerman's grandson, James Fligg, wrote this about him in 2003, spelling his name as Zimmerman, and noting that he "lived the American dream to the fullest"[65]:

The four patents that John Zimmerman took out in 1906 surely took advantage of the fact that steam power and perhaps some electric power was available. The wide looms that he developed were sensational at the time. Up to that time all the weaving was done at a 27 inch width. This was traditionally about the width that a normal person could throw a shuttle back and forth by hand. They would then sew these strips together to make wide rugs. He developed looms that would weave cloth 9 feet wide. This machinery as you can see by the pictures was gigantic for the time. Designing, develop, and making this machinery was no simple task! It was all done under the supervision of John Zimmerman. Most, if not all, of the machinery that is pictured in this book was designed and developed right there at Artloom under John Zimmerman's direction.

There were downsides as you can imagine. The noise of a textile factory with this type of equipment is unbelievable with the shuttles going back and forth at a terrific pace and the breast pars beating the yarn into the fabric with a resounding whack!, whack!, whack!. It's a wonder how any of the weavers could have survived even a day under those conditions of noise with those gigantic looms whacking away hour after hour. The pictures in the book of these looms speak for themselves. The factory took up more than two full city blocks.

You can also imagine the difference in appearance a 9 foot rug would make in a room instead of a rug with seams every 27 inches. The effect was sensational. Everyone had to have a seamless rug! He eventually pushed the loom with up to 12 feet. The rugs sold like wildfire. He then developed looms to weave cloth face to face and then cut them apart so there was a pile in-between. This doubled the production of each loom. I am not that familiar with his other patents but I assume they were equally revolutionary. This publication, dated about 1947, is obviously meant to promote a 'new' Artloom. [I have dated it 1948, because it includes data from the year 1947.] The depression and the war years were tough on Artloom. . . . However as I understand it all of the textile business started to move South where there was cheaper labor. Synthetic fibers came along and made a big difference in how weaving was done. New techniques of making rugs faster and cheaper were developed in the South such as hooking rugs on gigantic machines where a number of machines would hook the pile on at the same time. The rug would then be backed with rubber or a thin coating of plastic. . . .

In addition to the rugs I believe that they manufactured a lot of the plush draperies that were in vogue in most Victorian homes of that era. They apparently made miles of that fabric according to my father's recollections. / The book that I copied this from is actually larger than these sheets. It is 10.5" x 14.0" which is a very awkward size so I took the liberty of reducing it to a conventional paper size. I do hope you will enjoy looking at this book and letting your imagination go wild projecting yourself into those marvelous days with John Zimmerman as he gets off the boat from Germany, make a few friends in Philadelphia in the 'Reorganized Church of the Latter Day Saints . . . and proceeds to participate in a textile empire with the Wasserman brothers. They obviously had a great respect for him from the anecdotes in this book. They let him run the whole factory while they ran the business end of it. He recruited many of his weavers from the Reorganized LDS church and the German community . . .

One weaver he recruited was from Fall River Mass. John Zimmerman was there on business and attended church and met a weaver there who was having a tough time at work. He interviewed him on the spot and hired him to come work for him at Artloom. He arrived with his family which included a daughter, Evangeline, 'Vangie.' They would come and have dinner at the Zimmerman household on Sunday evenings. Vangie remembers that those dinners invariably consisted of oatmeal and bread despite John Zimmerman's affluence. John Zimmerman never gave up his simple ways of living. Vangie and my mother became fast friends. Vangie's engagement party was at our hose in Elkins Park. Her husband, Dr. Mays, was physician who later took care of my father at Jeane's Hospital when he had his first heart attack.

An anecdote that I remember my mother telling me is that the men that he had hired wanted a new church. They approached John Zimmerman and asked him to help them with a new church. He agreed that it was important that they have a new church and offered to finance the church. The Reorganized LDS church at Howard and Ontario was built with funds supplied by John Zimmerman for his men. He was Bishop in the Reorganized LDS church. This is more of an honor than an ecclesiastical position as I am led to believe.

Another story equally impressive is that John Zimmerman Jr., his son, approached him when he was very young and said that the men at the church (his friends) were in need of a weekend vacation place and that he had found just the place for that! Would you please consider helping out with this? John Zimmerman Sr. said he would look into it and later quietly purchased the 100 or so acres near New Hope that is now called Deer Park for the Reorganized LDS Church to use as a campground. It is there today as a retreat for the church, complete with an auditorium and a swimming pool.

If ever there was an immigrant who came with nothing and experience the thrill of fulfilling his hopes and expectations by coming to America it was John Zimmerman. With honesty, integrity, hard work and all the other values we hold dear he certainly lived the American dream to the fullest.

It is an honor to be one of his grandsons!

---------------

John Zimmerman married (1), at Philadelphia, 15 October 1885, **Eva Katherine KELLENBENZ**, daughter of Johann Michael and Clara (Gretzinger, aka Grözinger) Kellenbenz; born at (Klein) Eislingen, Donaukreis, Kingdom of Württemberg (now part of the state of Baden-Württemberg, Federal Republic of Germany), 18 September 1855; died at Philadelphia, 12 October 1920. (Part I, Chapter 2, Kellenbenz Family). John and Eva Katherine (Kellenbenz) Zimmermann had seven children (Part III, Chapters 4-10).[66]

After the death of Eva Katherine, John Zimmerman married (2), on 23 November 1922 in Decatur County, Iowa, as her second husband, **Mrs. Anna (Anderson) Dancer**, born at LaSalle, Ill., 30 September 1864; died at Lamoni, Iowa, 7 July 1937. She was the daughter of Andrew K. and Inger (Ormsdotter) Anderson. She had two children by her first marriage, as the wife of David A. Dancer, Sr., of Lamoni, Iowa, and two step-sons of David Dancer and his 1st wife. After John Zimmermann's death she returned to Lamoni, and she is buried there.[67]

# John Zimmerman's Obituaries

## Manufacturer Dies

**JOHN ZIMMERMAN**

*Retired textile manufacturer, of 1512 W. Allegheny ave., who died Saturday. He was a founder of the Zimmerman Mills and had been associated with several other firms. He will be buried today.*

## OBITUARY

### JOHN ZIMMERMAN

John Zimmerman, retired textile manufacturer, who died Saturday, will be buried this afternoon following services from his home, 1512 W. Allegheny ave. He was 81.

Born in Gussenstadt, Germany, Mr. Zimmerman came to Philadelphia in 1876, being attracted by the Centennial Exposition. A few years later he formed a partnership with his brother George, and both entered the textile manufacturing business.

In 1892 Mr. Zimmerman formed another partnership with Joseph, Isaac and Benjamin Wasserman under the name of Philadelphia Tapestry Mills. The four later founded the Philadelphia Pile Fabric Mills and the Artloom Rug Mills and united the three companies into the Artloom Corporation. In 1932 Mr. Zimmerman retired.

Prior to his retirement Mr. Zimmerman helped his sons in establishing the firm of John Zimmerman and Sons, Erie and Castor aves., manufacturers of upholstery fabrics.

He was also instrumental in founding the Zimmerman Mills, Inc., 21st st. and Allegheny ave. He is survived by his widow, Mrs. Anna Danner Zimmerman, three sons, three daughters and 21 grandchildren.

## Obituaries
### JOHN ZIMMERMAN

**Retired Textile Manufacturer Dies of Pneumonia at 80**

John Zimmerman, Sr., for years prominent in textile manufacturing circles in this city, died Saturday evening at his home, 1512 W. Allegheny av. from pneumonia.

Mr. Zimmerman, who was 80, retired from active business in 1932.

At the time of his retirement, he was vice president and general manager of the Artloom Corporation, at Front st. and Allegheny av. Born in Gussenstadt, Wuerttemburg, Germany, he came to this county in 1876. In his first business venture he formed a partnership with Archibald Cameron, the firm being Cameron and Zimmerman. At Mr. Cameron's death in 1892, the firm was amalgamated with Wasserman Brothers & Co. to form the Philadelphia Tapestry Mill, Front st. and Allegheny av.

In 1911 the firm became the Philadelphia Pile Fabric Mills, Inc., and in 1919, the Artloom Rug Mills, and finally the Artloom Corporation.

In 1919 Mr. Zimmerman, with his sons, formed the firm of John Zimmerman & Sons, Erie and Castor avs., manufacturers of mohair furniture coverings. In 1927 he also incorporated the Zimmerman Mills, 21st st. and Allegheny av., makers of furniture coverings.

He was a member of the Cedarbrook Country Club and was prominent in the reorganized Church of Jesus Christ, at Howard and Ontario sts. Surviving him is his widow, his sons, John, Jr., William and Albert, and his daughters, Mrs. Albert N. Hoxie, Mrs. R. C. Kelley and Mrs. James A. Flagg.

Philadelphia newspapers, unknown
Obituaries from Michael Bowman

**EVA KATHERINE KELLENBENZ**, third child and third of the sixteen children of Johann Michael and Clara (Grözinger) Kellenbenz, was born 28 September 1855 at Kleineislingen, in the Kingdom of Württemberg, now simply called Eislingen, in the present state of Baden-Württemberg, near Stuttgart, Germany; died at Philadelphia, Pennsylvania, 12 October 1920. She and a younger sister and a younger brother were the only survivors of the sixteen children of her parents who lived to become adults. The surviving sister also came to America; both women probably came with their uncle Gottlieb Zimmermann in about 1880. She married, at Philadelphia, 15 October 1885, **John ZIMMERMANN**, son of Johannes and Anna (Yäger) Zimmermann; born at Gussenstadt, Württemberg, 28 November 1855; died at Philadelphia, 23 May 1936. They had seven children, of whom six lived to adulthood. She was buried at the Greenmount Cemetery, on Front St., near Hunting Park Ave., in Philadelphia.

John and Eva Katherine (Kellenbenz) Zimmerman had the following children:

| | | |
|---|---|---|
| 2 | i. | CLARA (1886-1968) + |
| 3 | ii. | ANNA (1887-1974) + |
| 4 | iii. | EMILY "Emmely" (1890-1897)[68] |
| 5 | iv. | JOHN, Jr. (1892-1974) + |
| 6 | v. | WILLIAM "Bill" (1894-1978) + |
| 7 | vi. | LILLIAN "Lily Mae" (1897-1966) + |
| 8 | vii. | ALBERT WALTER "Al" (1902-1961) + |

## John and Eva Katherine Zimmerman and Their First Five Children

**c. 1896**
**John and Eva Katherine (Kellenbenz) Zimmermann, and their first five children Clara, Emily (d. 1897), John Jr., Billy, Anna. After Emily died, they had only four children Lillian and Albert Walter were born after this picture was taken**

# Eva Katherine Kellenbenz

**1900 U.S. Federal Census
Philadelphia**
John Zimmerman, with wife "Katherine" and children Clara, Annie, John, Willie Lillie, and servant Amelia Loffler

**1910 Census - Family of John Zimmerman, Sr., showing wife "Catherine" and children Clara, Anna, John, William, Lillian, and Albert**

**Death Certificate**
**"Eva Katherine Zimmermann" b. 29 Sep 1855; d. 12 Oct 1880 – pernicious anemia, 1 yr**

# John Zimmerman's Locations in Philadelphia

**German Hospital of Philadelphia**
SE corner of Girard & Corinthian Streets (between 20th & 21st Sts.)
Hospitalized there in about 1876

**2522 Fillmore (now "A" Street), between E. Huntington and E. Cumberland Sts.**
(one-half block S of the block occupied by Episcopal Hospital)
1889 – Earliest home address known for John Zimmerman
John and Eva Katherine and their daughters Clara and Anna lived here

**2812 North 5th St.**
1890 – Newly built house, between Cambria and Somerset,
Home for John and Eva Katherine, and Clara, Anna, and Emily
Cameron & Zimmerman's mill was at 2011 Ella St.

**520 Somerset Street**
1895 – One-half block SW of their previous residence
Home of John and Eva Katherine, and Clara, Anna, Emily, John, and William

**610 West Lehigh Ave.**
1897-1902 – On the S side of W Lehigh Ave., about one and a half block SW of their last residence.
Fairhill Reservoir is on the N side of the avenue.
Emily died here, 14 June 1897. Lillian is born here, 13 September 1897
Albert Walter was born here, 11 June 1902

**Reformed Church of Latter Day Saints (R.L.D.S. Church)**
SE corner, Howard and Ontario Streets
On a lot acquired for the church by John Zimmerman in 1900, construction started 1901

**1512 W. Allegheny Ave.**
SE corner of W. Allegheny Ave. and 16th St.
1903 – The house that the family lived in until John Zimmerman died in 1936
The house is adjacent to 3119 N. 16th St., which John gave to his daughter Clara

**Philadelphia Tapestry Mills, Philadelphia Pile Fabrics, and Artloom Tapestries**
Est. 1892 – W. Allegheny Ave. and N. Howard St. (NW corner)
These entities were merged into Artloom Corp., and covered two city blocks, bordered by:
Allegheny, Westmoreland, and Manchester, with Howard St. passing through

**John Zimmerman & Sons**
1919 – E Erie Ave. and Castor St.

**Zimmerman Mills**
1927 – 21st St. and W. Allegheny Ave., 2092 W. Allegheny Ave.

**Greenmount Cemetery, Philadelphia**
4301 North Front St.
The Zimmerman Monument is about 100 yds NW of the cemetery office

# Groups of Children of John and Eva Katherine Zimmerman

c. 1898
William (b. 1894), age 2-3, and Lillian (b. 1897), under age 1

Clara (3d fm L) Zimmermann (b. 1886),
Anna (b. 1887), Lillian (b. 1897) & friend,
at Clara's Wedding (10 Oct 1911)

Anna, Lillian (c. 6), and Albert (c. 1)
c. 1903

# Elmira, Chemung Co., N.Y.

## John Zimmerman's First Residence in the United States – 1874-1876

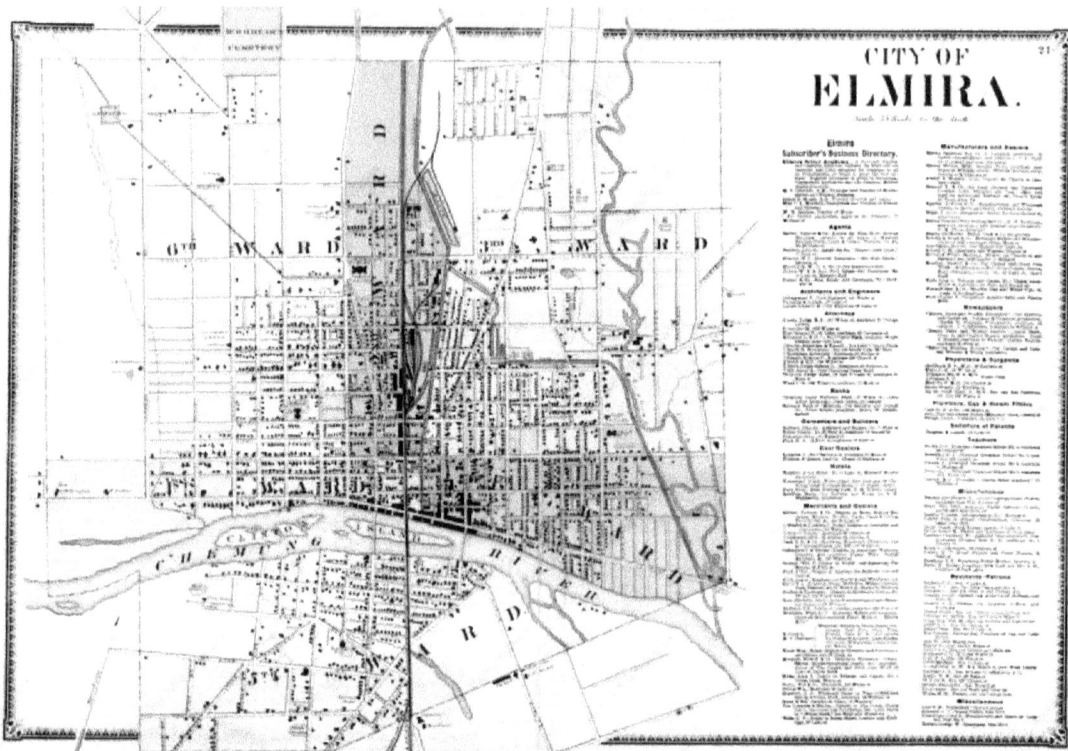

© Getty Images. Used with permission

## Elmira, N.Y., in 1869

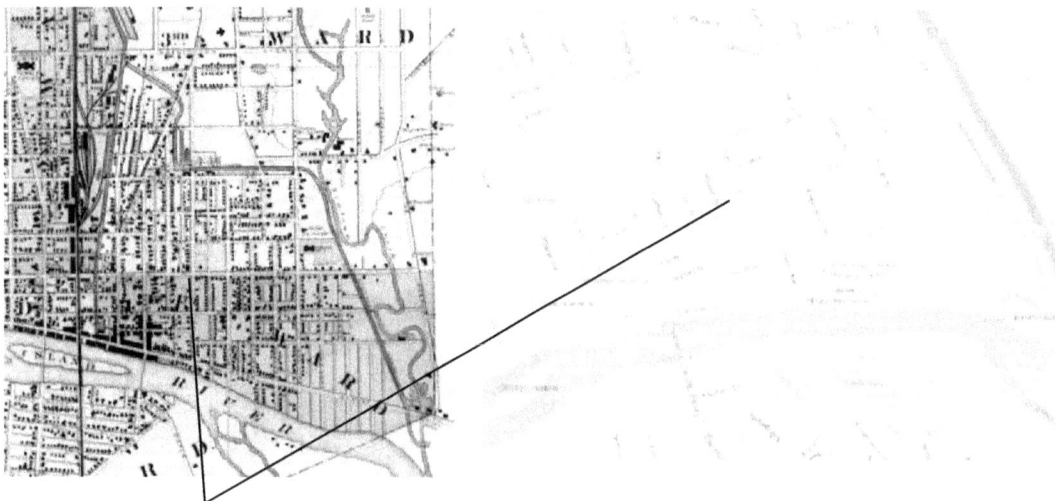

**"Germantown" was in the area of E. Church St. and Madison**

# John Zimmerman's Family Home
### His Last Residence, from 1904-1936
### 1512 Allegheny Ave., corner of 17th St.

Map and Photo from Jean Hoxie Naples

# The Zimmerman Boys and Their Cars

**1904 Winton, seats 4**
**"A four passenger Winton Automobile, practically new; a good hill climber. owner has ordered a**
**'1904 Winton.' Seen at S.E. Corner 16th and Allegheny Ave."**
[advertisement quoted by Michael Bowman, in JHN p. 11]

**1908 Winton, 6 passengers, with top down**
**Albert, John Jr., William - L to R. Lillian in back seat, center**
[from Katchie (Fligg) Lee, to JHN]

# John Zimmerman and the
# Reorganized Church of Jesus Christ of Latter Day Saints

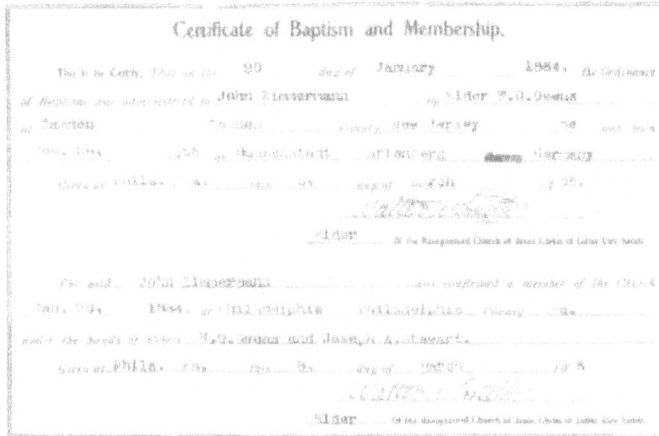

**John Zimmermann was baptized and confirmed on 20 January 1884**

**Bishop John Zimmermann, 1905**
From Michael Bacon

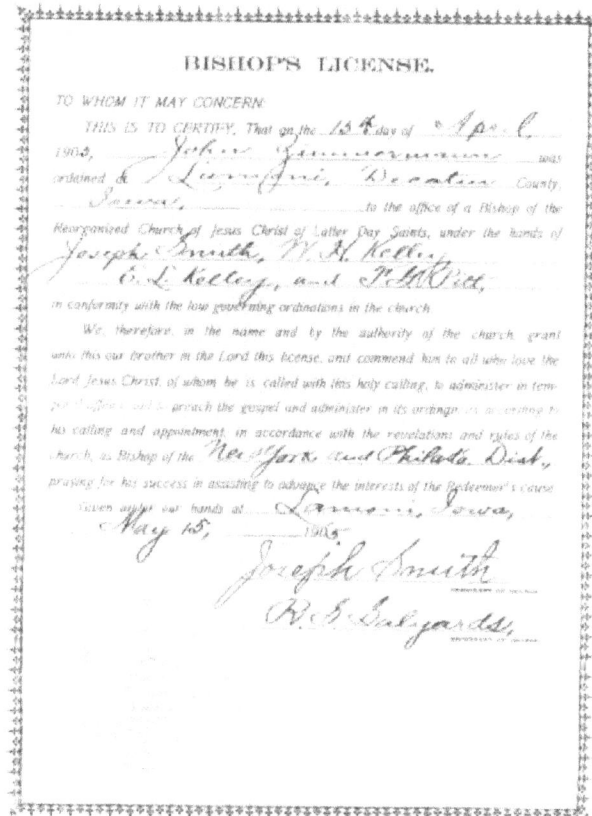

**John Zimmermann was made a Bishop on 15 April 1905**

## The New R.L.D.S. Church at Howard and Ontario

### Vacation Bible School

From Michael Bowman 8/27/2009

**1911**

**The new R.L.D.S. Church at Howard and Ontario is photographed here, shortly after the new addition was made.  Albert Zimmermann is at top L.**
**Pastor Walter W. Smith, great-grandson of Prophet Joseph Smith, Jr., front, 2d from L.**

## The Church Choir

**Front and center, L to R:  Prophet Fred Smith, Clara (Zimmerman) Hoxie, Al Hoxie
Albert W. Zimmerman is in rear row, nearly hidden, to R of lamp
Lillian is in 2d row, 5th from R.   Anna is in 1st row, 5th from R
Fred Smith is the grandson of the 1st President of the L.D.S. Church, Joseph Smith, Jr.**

**Congregation, in about 1914
Al Hoxie is in front row, directly in front of the church door, with hat in hand
His wife Clara is seated to his L.  Albert is the boy at far R.**

## The Philadelphia R.L.D.S. Church

**Prior to 1934**
Some of the men, with Prophet Fred Smith (front row, center, holding white hat)
Bishop John[1] Zimmerman, Sr., is 4 th from R
John Zimmerman, Jr., is in back row, to L of Prophet Smith
Albert N. Hoxie, Jr., son-in-law of John[1] Zimmerman, is to R of drain pipe, partially hidden

--------------------

## Deer Park
**Purchased by John Zimmerman for R.L.D.S. Church Members in 1921**
**Near New Hope, Pa.**

**Aquetong Spring**

# Deer Park

**Auditorium, built 1976**

About five thousand people visited the Deer Park Reunion on the Fourth of July, 1921.

**1921**

# Deer Park Today

## Deer Park Camp & Retreat Center
### 6290 Lower Mountain Road
### New Hope, PA 18938

**Entrance**

**The Auditorium**

**The website does not mention that it is supported by the Communion of Christ
However, the Communion of Christ website shows the connection:**
http://69.195.124.83/~cofchris/wp-content/uploads/2013/02/200CLRfigures.gif

# Notes

[1] Principal references:

Zimmermann and Kellenbenz Family Charts

Copies made in Nov 1993 from originals or copies in the possession of Sue (Kelley) Carnwath, made by George J. Hill, M.D., 28 Feb 2003ff. Sue Carnwath's charts passed to her heirs after her death.

---------

Jean Hoxie Naples, letters to GJH, 20 Nov and 15 Dec 2009 (hereafter JHN to GJH, 2009); Jean Naples / 115 Fir Ridge Lane / Beaufort, NC 29516. JHN died 4 March 2011. JHN's 28 page manuscript, "John Zimmermann (1855-1936)," includes a timeline, with each item given a citation by one of the following: JHN, AC (Aunt Cil Hoxie & Ben Fleet), MB (Mike Bowman, church historian), MaB (Mary Bacon, Deer Park, A History), BSZ (Barbara S. Zimmermann, wife of Albert Zimmermann), GH (George Hill, son-in-law of Al Zimmermann), AM (Anne Mitchell, Kellenbenz Family), KFL (Katchie Fligg Lee, daughter of Lillian Z), PS (Philip Scranton, *Figured Tapestry*), and obit (of which there are 2). JHN includes many graphics and photos with the JZ timeline, indicated in the text with red dots. I have included some of these in this book.

------------

James Fligg to George Hill (letter, 20 Feb 2003), quoted at the end of this biography. Fligg then lived at 60 Yacht Club Dr., #407), North Palm Beach, FL 33408. He died 16 March 2009. James Fligg sent copies of the pages of *Decade of Progress*, reduced to 8½ by 11in.

----------

Michael J. Bowman, "Reorganized Church of Latter Day Saints," thesis; 14pp. excerpt sent by Bowman to GJH, June 2009: "The Weaver's Strike," "A Place of Their Own," "New Missions," and "A 'Mormon Tent City'."

----------

Artloom Corporation, *A Decade of Progress, 1937-1947* (Philadelphia: Artloom Corporation, n.d. [1948]), pp. ii, 42. From a copy sent by James A. Fligg to George J. Hill, 20 Feb 2003 (emphasis added by Hill):

Excerpts: (text p. 1) "Sixty-three years ago in **1885**, Joseph, Benjamin, and Isaac Wasserman joined hands and fortunes with **John Zimmerman** and organized the Philadelphia Tapestry Mills for the purpose of manufacturing furniture upholstery fabrics. The Wasserman brothers took charge of sales and finance; **Zimmerman** was a mechanical genius whose main interest lay in the development of machinery.

"In February of **1906**, **Zimmerman** was granted three patents on machinery which he had designed and which were destined to play a major part in the history of Artloom. For these patented machines were peculiarly adapted to the manufacture of rugs. And so a rug manufacturing department was added to the Philadelphia Tapestry Mills under the trade name of Artloom Rug Mills.

"Artloom started operations with a triple advantage over competing rug mills because of its exclusive, patented machinery which made possible these revolutionary advances in rug manufacture: (1) rugs could be woven in nine-foot widths instead of the traditional twenty-seven-inch strips; (2) the patented weaves speeded up the output of each loom; (3) rugs could be woven face to face and then split apart, two rugs being produced by the same labor and machinery formerly required for one.

"In **1907**, **Zimmermann** conceived still another development which was to affect the fortunes of Artloom. . . the 'warp dyeing machine' which he patented. This machine, which made possible the production of patterned rugs with pre-dyed warp yarns, led to the perfection of today's fabulously successful Wilminster line!

"The inevitable result of this mechanical superiority was to shift the major emphasis of the Philadelphia Tapestry Mills to its Artloom Rug Mills department. Artloom's products were so far superior to their competition and were priced so much more attractively, that success was instant and spectacular.

"In **1911**, the company organized still another venture, the Philadelphia Pile Fabric Mills, for the manufacture of imitation seal plush fabrics. This turned out to be one of those anomalies which make business men old before their time. For as the nation entered the fabulous 'silk shirt' era after World War I, the American wage earners could afford genuine fur coats and disdained the plush imitation. Thus prosperity and inflationary boom conditions forced the conversion of the pile fabric mill to the manufacture of furniture upholstery fabrics and drapery materials.

"In **1919** the Artloom Rug Mills were incorporated as a separate and distinct entity. Side by side with the Philadelphia Tapestry Mills and the Philadelphia Pile Fabric Mills, Artloom grew, prospered, and reached maturity, backed by a brilliant record of success. On December 16, **1924** the three companies were merged into a single unit, the Artloom Corporation, which continued its amazing success until **1926**.

"And then the inevitable signs of age began to show. Artloom's 'hair was turning gray'."

The decline in Artloom's income and assets is described on the next text page (p.3), entitled "New Blood": In the fall of 1936 Herbert J. Adair, A. S. Mitchell, Jerry McCarthy, Godfrey Hammel, and John A. McNaughter, together with other associates, acquired a substantial holding of Artloom common stock. Three new directors were elected to the Board of Directors. / Failing to secure cooperation from the existing Artloom management in making the changes suggested by the new interests, Mr. A. S. Mitchell enlisted the assistance of Mr. Herbert J. Adair, one of the new directors, in the tremendous task of dusting off and overhauling Artloom.... On September 23, **1937**, the Board of Directors .. authorized the building of a twelve-foot printing machine, a twelve foot loom machine, and a twelve-foot Jacquarad... and the entire Artloom rug line was re-vamped . . . The new Wilminster lines of rugs and carpets, introduced at the July, 1938, markets, broke a five-year sales record. Net profits for the last six months of 1938 were the largest in five years.... The patented 'warp dyeing machine,' developed years before by Zimmerman, was improved to produce the brilliant Wilminster line we know today. Zimmerman's pioneering in broadloom, neglected for thirty-two years, finally bore fruit in **1938**, when Artloom built nine broadlooms to produce the types of carpets that were already accounting for 30% of the market's total volume. ... Artloom was on the way back!"

The following pages include photos of the corporate leaders, senior management, union leaders, and workers. The Board of Directors photo on p. 4 shows no Zimmermans but two Wassermans: Howard (2d on the L) and William S. (3d on the R). Also, interior and exterior views of the immense plant, the conveyor belts, the electrical power plant that consumed eighty tons of coal per day and generated enough power "to run a city the size of Providence, R.I." [17] "Wide looms, originated by Artloom in **1906**! Few carpet mills in America can exist without the wide loom. But in **1906**, **John Zimmerman**, one of the original founders of the Philadelphia Tapestry Mills, from which Artloom sprang, owned the exclusive patent-rights to the wide loom which he developed in nine-foot widths. Artloom's present battery of Wilton looms runs as wide as eighteen feet." The nine-foot and twelve-foot looms are shown. [21] "Producing the famous Wilminster. The Wilminster is an exclusive Artloom development, a rug that combines the beauty and color of an Axminster with the strength and serviceability of a Wilton. On the left we see the modern development of the 'warp dyeing machine' which **John Zimmerman** developed and patented. The warp yarn is dyed first and then is woven into the rug; the dyed yarn automatically forms the pattern of the rug as it is woven."

[26] "Not long after Pearl Harbor, Artloom converted its equipment to the manufacture of duck for military requirements. So successful was this conversion that over 25% of the duck used by the Navy in the Pacific was made by Artloom." [27] Net sales grew from $2,143,845 in 1937 to $10,859,709 in 1947, and net worth grew in the same period from $2,869,636 to $3,770, 938. [29] Average wages increased from $29.17 in 1938 to $67.94 in 1947. Pages 32-39 show illustrations of plain and patterned Artloom carpets installed in homes and restaurants, and Wanamaker's in Philadelphia: Duotuft (Wilton, plain), Kimberly (Wilminster, patterned), Roubaix (Wilton, oriental pattern), Deauville (Wilton, lightly patterned), Fantasy (plain, high pile), Allister (Axminster, dense pile, textured pattern). Artloom's addresses were: Allegheny & Howard, Philadelphia, Pa.; and the Textile Building, 295 Fifth Avenue, New York, N.Y. In **1947** it had 44 wholesale distributors in American cities from San Francisco to New Orleans, Chicago, New York, and Boston; the names and locations of the 40 whole-sale distributors are shown on a two-page map of the United States (pp. 40-41).

-----------

James Fligg to George Hill (letter, 20 Feb 2003). Excerpt from his 2p letter:
"Here is a copy of the book about Artloom that I told you about at Al Hoxie's funeral. I hope you find it interesting and useful for your purposes of documenting some of the things that John Zimmerman is in his life as well as dates when they were done. [Fligg spelled with Zimmerman one "n" throughout this letter]

---------

On weaving:
Wilton Weaving video – You Tube
Grosvenor Wilton Carpet in Production Part 1 – You Tube

--------

Two obituaries, summarizing his life, sent by Michael Bowman to GJH, 6 June 2009:
An obit with photo, paper unknown.
"Manufacturer Dies"
[photo of head and neck, in business suit]
JOHN ZIMMERMAN
*Retired textile manufacturer, of 1512 W. Allegheny ave., who died Saturday. He was a founder of the Zimmerman Mills and had been associated with several other firms. He will be buried today.*
"John Zimmerman, retired textile manufacturer, who died Saturday, will be buried this afternoon following services from his home, 1512 W. Allegheny ave. He was 81. / Born in Gussenstadt, Germany, Mr. Zimmerman

came to Philadelphia in 1876, being attracted by the Centennial Exposition. A few years later he formed a partnership with his brother George, and both entered the textile manufacturing business. / In 1892 Mr. Zimmerman formed another partnership with Joseph, Isaac and Benjamin Wasserman under the name of Philadelphia Tapestry Mills. The four later founded the Philadelphia Pile Fabric Mills and the Artloom Rug Mills and united the three companies into the Artloom Corporation. In 1932 Mr. Zimmerman retired. / Prior to his retirement Mr. Zimmerman helped his sons in establishing the firm of John Zimmerman and Sons, Erie and Castor aves., manufacturers of upholstery fabrics. / He was also instrumental in founding the Zimmerman Mills, Inc., 21st st. and Allegheny ave. He is survived by his widow, Mrs. Anna Dancer Zimmerman, three sons, three daughters and 21 grandchildren."

---------

Obit, paper unknown.
*Obituraries*
**JOHN ZIMMERMAN**
**Retired Textile Manufacturer Dies of Pneumonia at 80**
"John Zimmerman, Sr., for years prominent in textile manufacturing circles in this city, died Saturday evening at his home, 1512 W. Allegheny ave., from pneumonia. / Mr. Zimmerman, who was 80, retired from active business in 1932 / At the time of his retirement, he was vice president and general manager of the Artloom Corporation, at Front st. and Allegheny av. Born in Gussenstadt, Wuerttemburg, Germany, he came to this country in 1875. In his first business venture he formed a partnership with Archibald Cameron, the firm being Cameron and Zimmerman. At Mr. Cameron's death in 1892, the firm was amalgamated with Wasserman Brothers & Co., to form the Philadelphia Tapestry Mill, Front st. and Allegheny av. / In 1911 the firm became the Philadelphia Pile Fabric Mills, Inc., and in 1919, the Artloom Rug Mills, and finally the Artloom Corporation. / In 1919 Mr. Zimmerman, with his sons, formed the firm of John Zimmerman & Sons, Erie and Castor avs., manufacturers of mohair furniture coverings. In 1927 he also incorporated the Zimmerman Mills, 21st st. and Allegheny av., makers of furniture coverings. / He was a member of the Cedarbrook Country Club and was prominent in the reorganized Church of Jesus Christ, at Howard and Ontario sts. Surviving him is his widow, his sons, John, Jr., William and Albert, and his daughters, Mrs. Albert N. Hoxie, Mrs. R. C. Kelley and Mrs. James A. Fligg."

-------------

For reasons that are unknown, his death was apparently not recorded in Philadelphia vital records. A search for his death certificate failed to turn up anything. Also, a search of all records of deaths in Philadelphia on 23 May (45 records) and 24 May 1936 (48 records) did show any name that could have been misread from Zimmerman.
[2] John Zimmermann's mother's maiden name has long been said in one branch of the family to be Anna Ursula Yaeger, although this is difficult to confirm from the inscription on her tombstone. It appears to be confirmed by documents cited in Ancestry.com., although her ancestry is unknown.
[3] Diane Janowski, Elmira City Historian, "Elmira History: The Stories Behind Neighborhood Names" (*Star-Gazette* (15 Oct 2014): "'Germantown' existed around Madison Avenue and East Church Street" From http://www.stargazette.com/story/news/local/twin-tiers-roots/2014/10/11/elmira-history-place-names/16654275/ (accessed 3-28-16). The German community was marginalized. Very few German names appear as important people or sponsors of the map of Elmira in 1869.
[4] Jean Hoxie Naples, letter to GJH, 20 Nov 2009, enclosure "John Zimmermann (1855-1936)" timeline, p.2, that "Julian [Zimmermann] and Michael [Bantzhaff] live next door to each other in the township of Elmira and are listed as being farmers in the 1880 census." I have not been able to verify either of these names in the census records accessed on Ancestry.com, nor does a name search of the census records in 1880 or 1900 show any with the name of Zimmermann or Bantzhaff in Elmira. JHN is now deceased, and I don't know where she found this information.
[5] JHN, letter to GJH, "John Zimmermann" p.3: "1880 Jan 16 Court of Common Pleas #2 for the County of Philadelphia. Nationalization Papers" (copy not enclosed by JHN).
[6] "attracted to Philadelphia" from JZ's obituary. The Centennial International Exposition of 1876 was the first official world's fair in the United States. It was held in Philadelphia to celebrate the 100th anniversary of the signing of the Declaration of Independence. It was official called the "International Exhibition of Arts, Manufacturers and Products of the Soil and Mine." It was held in Fairmount Park, along the Schuylkill River. The Centennial was originally scheduled to begin in April 1876 but was delayed until May 10. The Main Building was

the largest building in the world, covering 21½ acres. It closed on November 10, with a daily average attendance of 115,000. A total of 10,164,489 visited the fair.

[7] The German Hospital was situated at the SE corner of Girard and Corinthian Sts., on the block bounded on the W by 21st St. and on the S by Poplar St. The hospital was relocated in 1917 and its name was changed to Lankenau Hospital. Also in this area, near Girard College, on Poplar St., were the German Reformed Church, the German Central Market, and the German Lutheran Church.

[8] The Philadelphia City Directory of 1881 shows a George Zimmerman at 2259 Amber St., and three other men named George Zimmerman (all with one n). The address of 2259 Amber St., is almost adjacent to the workshop of Archibald Cameron, at 2229 Amber St. JZ was later in partnership with Cameron. The John Bromley Mill, where JZ later worked is nearby (JHN's notes, p.4).

[9] Maria ___ m. George Zimmermann in 1882. In the 1900 census she is shown as having been b. 1856 in Pa., from parents who were b. in Germany.

[10] The Certificate of Baptism and Membership shows both Certificates on one page. The Certificate was issued on 8 March 1905 in Philadelphia, retroactively certifying the actions on 20 January 1884. The Certificates were signed by Elder Walter W. Smith, using a signature stamp. Walter W. Smith was for many years Historian of the RLDS Church; he is known to have held that position in 1906, and from 1919-23. His relationship to Joseph Smith, Jr., and his son, Joseph Smith III, is unknown, but it is likely that he was a descendant of the First Prophet.

[11] Bowman, Michael J., "History of the Reorganized Church of Latter Day Saints, draft, unpaginated, c.14 pp., quoting RLDS Philadelphia Branch Records, 1865-1919, Book B89: "John Zimmermann [sic] was a German immigrant who joined the branch in 1884."

[12] Family legends have said that Eva Catherine Kellenbenz came to America in 1881, but the census record shows that she was in Philadelphia in **1880**. Copy provided by Anne Mitchell (to GJH, 2009, op. cit.). Anne Mitchell also provided the name of Frederick Weigle, who m. Clara Kellenbenz.

The marriage index in Philadelphia (1860-1915) shows Kellenbenzs: Kellenbenz K. E. (Zimmerman [sic]) 1885 certificate number 308 / Eva's sister Clara was listed: Kellenbenz Clara (Weigle) 1887 certificate number 12495.

[13] John Zimmerman's residence in 1889 was 2522 Fillmore St. (a one-block long street, now "A" Street), about 5 blocks from 316 Huntington St., where George Zimmermann lived with his family. The Episcopal Hospital was just to the N of Fillmore St., between E Lehigh and E. Huntington Ave. Kensington Ave. ran diagonally across the short block of Fillmore.

----------

KHN, p.5, citing KFL (Katchie Fligg Lee): "Eva Cathryn is a German Lutheran and remained so all of her life. She performed her duties as the wife of an RLDS member on special occasions but was not active in that church. {She] never spoke fluent English. German was the language in the home. John spoke English but with a heavy German accent." KHN adds, "Their children spoke German as well."

[14] Wasserman Brothers was located at 240 Church St., Philadelphia (from JHN).

-------------

The corporate history of Artloom, *Decade of Progress*, p.1, says that Philadelphia Tapestry Mills was established in **1885** by the Wasserman brothers and John Zimmerman. This date conflicts with the history of Cameron and Zimmerman, which existed until Cameron died on 13 July **1891**. I believe the Artloom history is incorrect.

John Zimmerman's obituaries both state in 1892, after Cameron died, Cameron and Zimmerman amalgamated with Wasserman Brothers to form the Philadelphia Tapestry Mills, at Front & Allegheny Streets.

[15]

## WASSERMAN FAMILY

### First Generation

**1. ___ WASSERMAN,** had:

| | | |
|---|---|---|
| 2 | i. | Urias (1829-1907) + |
| 3 | ii. | David (1831-1905) |

### Second Generation

**2. Urias WASSERMAN.** Born 1 Jul 1829, Oberndorf, Hohenlohedreis, Württenberg; died in Philadelphia, PA, 19 May 1907, he was 77. He arrived in US in 1845; resided in Philadelphia Ward 3, 1860; resided Philadelphia Ward 4, District 14, 1870; Philadelphia, 1880; Philadelphia Ward 20, 1900. Probate 3 Jun 1907, Philadelphia. He married **Hannah Fox FUCHTLER**, daughter of Jacob Fox FUCHTLER, born 1 Mar 1832 in Bayern, Germany; died in Philadelphia, PA, 5 Jan 1909, she was 76.

They had the following children:

| | | |
|---|---|---|
| 4 | i. | Jacob (1854-1855) |

|     |       |                                                        |
|-----|-------|--------------------------------------------------------|
| **5**  | ii.   | Isaac (1856-1923) +                                    |
| **6**  | iii.  | Joseph (1858-1937) +                                   |
| **7**  | iv.   | Henrietta (1863-1940)                                  |
| **8**  | v.    | Theresa (~1865-1928)                                   |
| **9**  | vi.   | Benjamin J. (1867-1934) +                             |
| **10** | vii.  | Solomon (1871-1872)                                   |
| **11** | viii. | Celia (Cecile) (1876-1941)                            |

**3. David WASSERMAN**, b. 2 Oct 1831, Oberndorf, Württenberg; d. Altoona, Blair Co., Pa., 30 Mar 1905.

### Third Generation

**4. Jacob WASSERMAN.** Born 1854, Philadelphia, PA; died in 1855, he was 1.

**5. Isaac WASSERMAN.** Born 3 Apr 1856 in Princeton, Mercer, NJ; died in Philadelphia, PA, 30 Aug 1923, he was 67. He married **Flora KAHN**. Born 1866; died in 1940, she was 74.

They had the following children:

|     |      |                        |
|-----|------|------------------------|
| **12** | i.   | Herbert S. (1888-) +   |
| **13** | ii.  | Adele (1890-)          |
| **14** | iii. | Rita (1893-1987)       |
| **15** | iv.  | Charles Kahn (1896-1955) |

**6. Joseph WASSERMAN.** Born 26 Jul 1858 in Philadelphia, PA; died in Philadelphia, PA (bur. Mt. Sinai Cem). Ancestry.com says 28 Oct 1952; Rothchild, p36, says 1937) on 8 Sep 1937, he was 79; res 1860, Phila Ward 3 (age 2); Phila Ward 38, 1900 (age 38); Philadelphia Ward 21, 1920. On 22 Mar 1899 when Joseph was 40, he married **Edith STIX** in St. Louis, MO; born in 1874; died in 1974, she was 100.

They had the following children:

|     |      |                                                      |
|-----|------|------------------------------------------------------|
| **16** | i.   | Margaret (1899-)                                     |
| **17** | ii.  | William Stix (1901-1979) + (had children, not shown here) |
| **18** | iii. | [son] (1903-1903)                                   |
| **19** | iv.  | Elizabeth Dina (1905-)                              |
| **20** | v.   | Kathryn Edith (1907-2013) +                         |

**7. Henrietta WASSERMAN.** Born 1863, Philadelphia, PA; died in Philadelphia, PA, 25 Dec 1940, she was 77; m. **Herman KRAUS**, b. 1856.

They had the following children:

|     |      |                  |
|-----|------|------------------|
| **21** | i.   | Bernie (1882-) + |
| **22** | ii.  | Florence (1886-) + |
| **23** | iii. | Rena (1889-) +   |
| **24** | iv.  | Clara (1892-) +  |
| **25** | v.   | Gladys (1894-) + |
| **26** | vi.  | Beatrice (1896-) + |

**8. Theresa WASSERMAN.** Born abt 1865 in Philadelphia; died in 1928, she was 63; m. **Harry KOHN**, b. 1866.

**9. Benjamin J. WASSERMAN.** Born on 18 Nov 1867 in Pennsylvania. Benjamin J. died in 1934, he was 66; partner in Philadelphia Tapestry Mills with his brothers Joseph and Isaac; returned 18 September 1908 "from an extended trip abroad"; In 1898 at age 30, he married **Flora Emma DAHLMAN**, in Philadelphia, PA; died in 1955.

They had one child:

|     |      |                          |
|-----|------|--------------------------|
| **27** | i.   | Howard Dahlman (1900-1964) + |

**10. Solomon WASSERMAN.** Born in 1871 in Philadelphia, PA; died on 25 Aug 1872, he was 1.

**11. Celia (Cecile) WASSERMAN.** Born 11 Feb 1876 in Pennsylvania; died in Philadelphia, PA on 8 Sep 1941, she was 65; married **Samuel Clayton JEITLES**. Born in 1872; died in 1955, he was 83.

### Fourth Generation

**12. Herbert S. WASSERMAN.** Born in 1888.

**13. Adele WASSERMAN.** Born in 1890.

**14. Rita WASSERMAN.** Born in 1893. Rita died in 1987, she was 94.

**15. Charles Kahn WASSERMAN.** Born in 1896; died in 1955, he was 59; **Violet K ____**.

------------

**16. Margaret WASSERMAN.** Born on 13 Dec 1899.

**17. William Stix WASSERMAN.** Born on 24 Mar 1901 in Philadelphia, PA. William Stix died in 1979, he was 77.

**18. [son] WASSERMAN.** Born on 4 Jan 1903 in Philadelphia, PA. [son] died on 11 Jan 1903 in Philadelphia, PA.

**19. Elizabeth Dina WASSERMAN.** Born on 7 Oct 1905.

**20. Kathryn Edith WASSERMAN.** Born on 25 Feb 1907 in Philadelphia, PA; died in Hobe Sound, Florida on 23 Apr 2013, she was 106. On 4 Jul 1932, she married **Shelby Cullom DAVIS**, son of George Henry DAVIS & Julia Mabel CULLOM, in New York city hall; b. 1 Apr 1909 in Peoria, Ill.; d. in New York on 26 May 1994, he was 85. See Robin Finn, "A Feisty Philanthropist at 100, With a Five-Year Plan ," *New York Times* (c. 2007).

They had the following children:

| 28 | i. | Priscilla Alden (1942-1942) |
| 29 | ii. | [daughter] |
| 30 | iii. | [son] |

----------

**21. Bernie KRAUS.** Born in 1882.

**22. Florence KRAUS.** Born in 1886.

**23. Rena KRAUS.** Born in 1889.

**24. Clara KRAUS.** Born in 1892.

**25. Gladys KRAUS.** Born in 1894.

**26. Beatrice KRAUS.** Born in 1896.

------------

**27. Howard Dahlman WASSERMAN.** Born in 1900. Howard Dahlman died in 1964, he was 64. Princeton Class of 1922; Princeton Alumni Weekly 66 (1965):81, gave his obituary; says fm 1926-1934 he was a partner in Hanno Wasserman, and remained a director of Artloom; is in photo of Board meeting at Artloom in 1948; was v.p. of Artloom, working for his father. See Federal Communications Commissions Reports v.1-45 (1951), p. 198; married **Hortensia LUCAS**. Born in 1906.

They had the following children:

| 31 | i. | Howard Barton (1930-2004) + |
| 32 | ii. | [daughter] |

-------------

**28. Priscilla Alden DAVIS.** Born in 1942. Priscilla Alden died in 1942.

**29. [daughter] DAVIS.**

**30. [son] DAVIS**

### Fifth Generation

**31. Howard Barton WASSERMAN.** Born in 1930. Howard Barton died in 2004, he was 74.

**32. [daughter] WASSERMAN.**

## Notes

1. "Wasserman Family Tree, Ancestry.com," accessed 3-19-16ff, c/o John Simmons.

2. John Rothchild, *The Davis Dynasty: Fifty Years of Successful Investing on Wall Street* (New York: John Wiley & Sons, 2001); marriage date of Shelby Davis and Kathryn Wasserman is on p.26.

3. Robin Finn, "A Feisty Philanthropist at 100, With a Five-Year Plan," *New York Times* (c. 2007).

[16] Quote: "a friend," from *The Rohm and Haas Reporter* (Rohm & Haas Company, **1953**), vols. 11-53, snippet: "Artloom Carpet Company, Inc. . . . has long produced fine wool carpets – Wiltons, velvets, and Axminsters . . . [Artloom] Mills was formed as the joint enterprise of three brothers – Joseph, Benjamin and Isaac Wasserman – and **a friend, John Zimmerman**."

------------

"mechanical genius" from Artloom, *A Decade of Progress,* (text p. 1): "**Zimmerman** was a **mechanical genius** whose main interest lay in the development of machinery.

----------------

Cameron and Zimmerman's workshop was located at 2011 Ella St. (later called Arizona). Archibald Cameron d. 13 July 1891 (fm JHN). However, the partnership, "Cameron & Zimmerman; Philadelphia, tapestry manufacturers, enlarged facilities" (according to a newspaper item quoted by Michael Bowman, in JHN).

---------

John Zimmerman's obituaries show two business operations that preceded his joining the Wasserman brothers. One obituary states that a few years after he arrived in Philadelphia, he formed a partnership with his brother George in the textile manufacturing business. Another obituary says that in his first business venture he formed a partnership with Archibald Cameron, the firm being Cameron and Zimmerman. My text combines the events in these two obituaries.

Family legend says that he soon advanced to become manager of the Wassermans' company's works, as a result of his mechanical skills and his ability to attract new German immigrants to work for the company. This account of the evolution of the business from **1885** as Philadelphia Tapestry Mills to Artloom Corporation in **1924** is probably generally correct, but the corporate history is expanded differently in other accounts. The Philadelphia Tapestry Mills was probably established in **1892**, after the partnership of Cameron and Zimmerman was ended by the death of Archibald Cameron in **1891**.

-------------

Fourteen pages of a partial history of the Reorganized Church of Latter Day Saints [RLDS], written by Michael J. Bowman, sent to George J. Hill, 7 June 2009 (hereafter Bowman, RLDS History) include four sections, with 68 references: "The Weaver's Strike," "A Place of Their Own," "New Missions," and "A Mormon 'Tent City'." On pp. 1-2 (unnumbered):

"A textile strike involving an estimated 800 workers commended December 1, 1899. The demands included a fifty-five hour workweek and a ten-cent increase in hourly overtime. The next day, 24 Kensington mills were forced to shut down, affecting an additional 3000 supporting workers. By this time, many members of the Church were gainfully employed by at least five carpet manufacturers located in Kensington. The largest employer of them was the **Philadelphia Tapestry Mills**, managed by Church member John Zimmermann.

"John Zimmermann was a German immigrant who joined the [RLDS] branch in 1884. He had worked his way up through the ranks, initially with **Cameron**, then with the **Bromley Brothers**, where he came into contact with the **Wasserman** brothers, who employed him as vice president as well as production manager. Zimmermann was crucial to the success of the company, having 'invent[ed] a new lathe for hand looms which enabled them to weave nearly as much as on the power loom'."

[17] "The Wasserman brothers . . . mechanical genius" (quote from from Artloom . . .Early Days n.p., n.d.; unnumbered; copy from James Fligg, a grandson of John Zimmerman). John Zimmerman's early association with Bromley Brothers is mentioned briefly by Bowman, RLDS History (*supra*). Two men named Bromley are mentioned in *Transactions of the National Association of Cotton Manufacturers* (Issue 84, **1908**), *Cotton Manufacture*: 67: in Philadelphia. Edward Bromley, of John Bromley & Sons; and Joseph H. Bromley, Fourth and Lehigh Ave. On the same page is shown: "Philadelphia, Joseph Wasserman, Philadelphia Tapestry Mills."

---------------

*A Directory of the Textile Establishments in the United States and Canada* (Lord & Nagle Company, **1905**), 252-3: "PHILADELPHIA TAPESTRY MILLS; Allegheny Ave. and Front St; Map A; Sq. 70; Joseph Wasserman, pres; I. Wasserman, treas; B. Wazzerman [sic], sec; John Zimmerman, vice-pres. and supt.; Upholstery Fabrics; 210 looms; steam; sell direct; John Zimmerman, buyer"

-----------

John Zimmermann's obituaries show two business operations that preceded his joining the Wasserman brothers. One obituary states that a few years after he arrived in Philadelphia, he formed a partnership with his brother George in the textile manufacturing business. Another obituary says that in his first business venture he formed a partnership with Archibald Cameron, the firm being Cameron and Zimmerman. My text combines the events in these two obituaries.

Family legend says that he soon advanced to become manager of the Wassermans' company's works, as a result of his mechanical skills and his ability to attract new German immigrants to work for the company. This account of the evolution of the business from 1892 as Wasserman Brothers to Artloom Corporation in the 1920s is probably generally correct, but the corporate history is expanded differently in other accounts.

[18] James Terry White, *Cyclopedia of American Biography* (1967), 143: "WASSERMAN, Joseph, manufacturer, was born in Philadelphia, Pa., July 26, 1858, son of Urias and Hannah (Fuchtler) Wasserman, both natives of Oberndorf, Württemberg, Germany. He was educated at public schools in Philadelphia. At the age of twenty he went to New Mexico and became connected with a trading post at Albuquerque. While touring the then dangerous and barren territory looking for customers . . . Returning to Philadelphia in **1882**, he engaged in general textile importing with his brothers, Benjamin and Isaac Wasserman. Later the three brothers and John Zimmerman founded the Philadelphia Tapestry Mills and the Philadelphia Pile ..."

---------------

For additional details on the Wasserman family, although erroneous in several accounts, see: John Rothchild, *The Davis Dynasty: Fifty Years of Successful Investing on Wall Street* (New York: John Wiley & Sons). I have noted several obvious errors in the text by insertion with bracket, and there is nothing in the brief section on Notes in this book to show any source for the information or the quoted remarks about the Wasserman family.

On p 20: "the three Wasserman brothers, Joseph, Howard, and Isaac, opened the Philadelphia Carpet Mills in **1895** and the Philadelphia Pile Fabric Company shortly after. [n.b., the second brother was Benjamin, not Howard, who was Benjamin's son, and the Philadelphia Carpet Mills opened in 1892] The two entities were merged into Art Loom, a carpet company that occupied an entire city block on Lehigh Avenue. Art Loom went public in 1925. / Joseph Wasserman, the chief decision maker, had prior experience in retail sales in New Mexico. His older brother, Isaac, found a way to slice a rug in half without damaging the weave [this was the invention of John Zimmermann, not Isaac Wasserman] – a technique that gave the Wassermans an obvious competitive advantage: they could make two carpets from one [21] loom. The youngest brother, Howard [as above, Benjamin was the youngest brother, not Howard, who was a son of Benjamin], died of syphilis after refusing to take a Wasserman test (contributed to science by a distant relative in Germany) that would have detected the disease in its early stages [no reference is given for the diagnosis of syphilis; and the test was described by August von Wasserman (1866-1925), working in Berlin, who by his surname must have been an aristocrat and probably not a relative of the Wassermans, who were the sons of Urias Wasserman of Oberndorf, Württemberg (see genealogy, below, and White, *Cyclopedia of American Biography* (1967), 143] . . . . Joseph married Etith Stix, a fiery suffragette who showed her independence by siding with the workers in a strike against her husband's rug plant. When her husband warned, 'They get their way, and Art Loom is finished,' Edith ignored him – but not in bed. They produced two sons (one of whom died in infancy, and three daughters, Kathryn being the youngest. . . They traveled widely and filled their house at 600 Wissahickon Avenue, Philadelphia, with fine antiques and exotic souvenirs." [24] "The Wassermans were part of a canny minority who kept their money in government bonds and lost nothing in the Crash that cost four or five million American shareholders a combined $30 billion. 'The rug business is risky enough,' Joseph Wasserman told his children. 'I want to be conservative in savings.' He maintained an all-bond portfolio until his death in 1937." [25] Kathryn Wasserman married Shelby Cullom Davis on 4 July **1932**.

[35] "By **1936** . . . Art Loom was public already, but its overseers decided to sell more shares while the selling was good. Joseph Wasserman hired a Wall Street underwriter to lead this latest offering. His son, Wild Bill, who considered himself the guru on such matters, found a rival underwriter who agreed to sell the shares at a higher price than the one Joseph's underwriter had proposed. Faithful to his handshake, Joseph stuck with the deal, even though it cost him money. The sale took place in **1937** – an eventful year for the Wassermans, the Davises, and the world at large. . . . The Nazis were building a war machine. Cancer killed Joseph Wasserman. The bull market ended. Davis and Wild Bill were headed for professional breakup." [51] Davis invested the $30,000 that Kathryn's father had given her to buy a house at the time she was married. All of Joseph's children received the same amount. [100] Kathryn (Wasserman) Davis' nephew, Steve Davis (son of her brother Wild Bill), died in a mountaineering accident on Mt. Whitney in 1957, at age 15."

---------------

*Textile World Record* 33 (Lord & Nagle, **1907**), 179 "Recent Textile Patents" and 180: "PILE FABRIC. 855,153. John Zimmerman, Philadelphia, Pa., assignor to Philadelphia Tapestry Mills."

-------------------

*Textile World Journal* 51 (10 June **1916**): "New Addition Nearly Ready. The new addition to the plant of the Philadelphia Tapestry Mills, combined with the Philadelphia Pile Fabric Mills, on the Southeastern corner of Westmoreland and Howard Sts., Philadelphia, is now under roof. This building is immediately adjoining the rear of these plants, and is 60 x 250 feet, five stories and basement, of brick and concrete construction, of the highest type of modern mill construction. The floors are now being laid, and it is expected the building will be ready for occupancy by July 1 . . . The Philadelphia Tapestry Mills have recently consummated the purchase of a lot of land on the Southeast corner of Hancock and Westmoreland Sts. 210 x 236 feet. This is also in the immediate vicinity of their mill, and another addition is contemplated at a later date. The new addition, which is almost completed, has arrangements made for a roof garden, and rest rooms for their employees. Late reports state application has been made for a charter of incorporation under the laws of Pennsylvania as the Philadelphia Silk Spinning Mills, by Fred H. Stringer, Richard J. Steiner, Isaac Wasserman, Joseph Wasserman and John Zimmerman, Jr., the character and object of which is the manufacture and spinning of yarns. The company is a separate department of the Philadelphia Tapestry Mills and the Philadelphia Pile Fabric Mills, controlled by the same interest. The spinning machinery of the Charles Stringer plant at North Wales, Pa., has been bought and the company will spin its own tussah silk yarn. This equipment will be place in part of the new mill building soon to be completed."

-------------

John Zimmerman is mentioned in *American Dyestuff Reporter* 42 (**1953**), 450 (including *Proceedings of the American Association of Textile Chemists and Colorists*); citation not available to read on Google Books. A snippet shows "New members to the Board of Trustees of the Philadelphia Textile Institute Foundation include . . . William Zimmerman, President, John Zimmerman and Sons, Philadelphia."

-----------

The firm of "John Zimmerman and Sons" is mentioned in *PMA Monthly Bulletin* (Pennsylvania Manufacturers' Association, **1944**), 68: "Elected to Board of Textile Group. Election of seven new members to the Board of Trustees of The Philadelphia Textile Institute Foundation was announced recently . . . William Zimmerman, president, John Zimmerman and Sons, Philadelphia, pile."

-----------

*Technical Manual and Year Book of the American Association of Textile Chemists and Colorists* (American Association of Textile Chemists and Colorists, **1954**), book not available to read on Google Books; snippet shows "Supt. of Dyeing, John Zimmerman & Sons Co., Erie & Castor Aves., Philadelphia"

-----------

*American Carpet and Upholstery Journal* 25 (**1907**), 85: "Some Late Patents. . . . A double pile fabric, with outer and inner weft planes in each fabric, and a combined pile binding and figuring warp, engaging only the inner row of wefts in each fabric when making pile, is the latest invention of John Zimmerman, assignor to the Philadelphia Tapestry Mills."

-----------

*America's Textile Reporter: For the Combined Textile Industries* 27 (**1913**), 1386: "one of the busiest and most profitable textile organizations in the country is the Artloom Tapestry Mills and the Philadelphia Pile Fabric Company, of Philadelphia. These are separate concerns owned by the same people, namely, the Wasserman Brothers and John Zimmerman. The business end of both is largely handled by Joseph Wasserman. John Zimmerman is the practical man, and his inventions are the ones used. One specialty is a double pile fabric, a cloth with a pile on each side, largely used in the millenary trades."

-----------

*Textile World's Directory of the Mill Trade in the United States, 1897: Comprising Cotton Mills, Woolen Mills, Knitting Mills, Silk Mills, Flax, Jute and Linen Mills* (Guild and Lord, **1897**), 195: "PHILADELPHIA TAPESTRY MILL Co.; $250,000; Cambria and Ormes Sts; Map C; Sq. 70; J. Wasserman, pres; John Zimmerman, vice pres. and supt; B. Wasserman, gen. mgr.; Table Covers Upholstery Goods and Curtains; 82 looms; steam; sell direct; office, 229 and 231 Church St, Phila; John Zimmerman, buyer. *Plant to be enlarged this season.*" [ital in original; the buyer is probably John Jr.]

-------

*The Fitch Bond Book Describing the Most Important Bond Issues of the United States and Canada* (Fitch Publishing Co., **1929**), 54: "ARTLOOM CORPORATION. Office – Allegheny Ave. & Front St., Philadelphia, Pa. / Officers – Joseph Wasserman, Pres.; Benjamin Wasserman, John Zimmermann, V.P.s; Albert Zimmermann, Secy; Charles Wasserman"

----------------

*The Rohm and Haas Reporter* (Rohm & Haas Company, **1953**), vols. 11-53, snippet: "Artloom Carpet Company, Inc. . . . has long produced fine wool carpets – Wiltons, velvets, and Axminsters . . . [the] Mills was formed as the joint enterprise of three brothers – Joseph, Benjamin and Isaac Wasserman – and **a friend, John Zimmerman.**"

--------

[19] These business addresses suggest that the Wassermans and John Zimmerman had not yet completely amalgamated their operations into the Philadelphia Tapestry Mills, which together they are said to have formed in 1892. Or the founding year of Philadelphia Tapestry Mills as 1892 may have been given incorrectly in John Zimmerman's obituaries.

[20] JHN, p. 7-8; Artloom, *Decade of Progress*, 1; Bowman, "Weaver's Srike," 1.

[21] Bowman's note (in JHN). 1897 Jan 11, Emilie K Zimmerman d., was bur. In Greenmount Cem., 4301 N Front St., Phila; d. cert says family is living at 610 W Lehigh Ave.; 4301 N Front is near the SW corner of N. Front St. and W. Cayuga St.; it would later become the burial site for her parents.

-----------

JHN quotes KFL: "Legend has it that the two older sisters, 11 and 9, so disliked their German names that they persuaded the parents to let them name the new baby "Lily Mae." She was called Lillian and she didn't discover her real birth name until she had to apply for her birth certificate for a passport many years later." JHN adds that the passport application was in 1923.

[22] Philadelphia Tapestry Mills' Gobelins, quoted by JHN from Philip Scranton, *Figured Tapestry.*

[23] Bowman, "Weaver's Strike," R.L.D.S. History, p.1-4; and "A Place of Their Own," pp. 4-7, and quoted by JHN.

[24] JHN, "John Zimmermann," pp. 8-9. "polygamy" quotation from Bowman, p.5, citing *The Philadelphia Inquirer* (7 Sep 1903).

[25] JHN quotes JZ's granddaughter, Cil Hoxie Fleet (b. 1919), who lived next door, in answer to the question "What's at 1512): Pantry, as BIG as a kitchen; kitchen; laundry room; breakfast room for 12; dining room for 24 or more; piano room, where casket usually goes; long whatever room, overflow from the huge dining room; front door that none used; entrance at side of house; staircase, exhausted after climb up stairs; sewing room; living room with fireplace, windows looking at 3119 (Cil's parents' house); huge bath room with stained glass window, chamber pots for all the Z family kept under bed; master bedroom; 2 other bedrooms; another flight of stairs where Mom, Lil, Anna hung out; bath; 3 maids; big yard; garage for 3 cars; chauffer quarters; trolleys going by.

[26] JHN, p.11: George Zimmermann's patent application on 5 Nov 1904 was approved 5 Dec 1905 (#806,729). George's patent application for "Woven Pile Fabric" was filed on 14 Nov 1905.

[27] JHN, p. 11: "considered 'pioneers' in mass advertising" (quoting *American Carpet & Upholstery Journal* [cited in Scranton, *Figured Tapestry*]); "Moquette Couch Covers" (quoting JZ's obituary); "Largest Tapestry Mill" (from Artloom ad).

[28] JHN, "John Zimmermann," p. 11-12.

[29] US Patent 813,130, filed 18 Jan 1905; published 20 Feb **1906**, for "Inventors: John Zimmerman / Original Assignee Philadelphia Tapestry Mills / Woven pile fabric / Serial No. 241,538 / 1 image"; the quotation in this book is given in JHN, p.12.

[30] Artloom, *Decade of Progress*, 1: "these patented machines were peculiarly adapted."
*Davison's Textile "Blue Book": United States and Canada. Cotton, Woolen, Silk. With a full classified directory of cotton and woolen mills and textile supply directory* (Davison Publishing Co., **1922**), 474 (snippet): "Artloom Rug Mills. Allegheny Ave. and Front St. Est. **1907**. Inc. **1919**. Cap. $750,000. Jos. Wasserman, Pres; Isaac Wasserman, Treas. J. Zimmerman, Jr., Sec. and Buyer; J. Zimmerman, Sr. Supt. Seamless Wilton Velvet and Seamless Wilton Jacquard Rugs.

[31] "Artloom . . . Early Days" (op. cit.): The corporate history of Artloom summarizes the evolution of the company as follows: In **1911** company organized another venture, Philadelphia Pile Fabric Mills, Inc. In **1919**, the tapestry mill's Artloom Rug Mills Department was incorporated as a separate entity, Artloom Rug Mills. On 16 December **1924**, the three companies were merged into a single unit, the Artloom Corporation.

[32] Michael Bowman to KHN, personal communication, in KHN, p. 13.

[33] "Artloom . . .Early Days," op. cit.

[34] George Zimmerman's patent for Woven Pile Fabric (#849,877) was granted on 9 April **1907**; John Zimmerman's patent for Pile Fabric (#855,153) was granted on 28 May **1907**. George filed another patent for woven Pile Fabric on 8 March 1908; it was granted on 29 December **1908** (#908,371)

[35] JHN, p. 13-14: "25 looms" was mentioned in *Textile World Report* (Lord & Nagle Co., Apr.-Sept **1908**). The addition, to cost $30,000, was announced in *Textile World Record* (March 1924), 724 ("Mill News").
A rug made by Artloom, successor to the Philadelphia Pile Fabric Mills and Philadelphia Tapestry Mills, was offered for sale on e-Bay in 2010, described as follows:
ANTIQUE SILK RUG PHILADELPHIA TAPESTRY MILLS/ARTLOOM / ITEM CATEGORY: Textiles, Clothing & Accessories
SOURCE: eBay / SOLD DATE: Mar 30, 2010 / CHANNEL: Online Auction
A beautiful antique silk or possibly silk and wool blend woven pile rug, probably made about 1910-1920. It measures about 107" long and about 57" wide. The background is a golden yellow color and the bordered floral design is in dark brown, cream, light pink and olive green colors. I do not know if the design is Caucasian, Persian, Pakistani or just Floral. It has four patent numbers woven into the ends. Those patents date to 1906-1907 and were submitted by John Zimmermann and assigned to his company, the Philadelphia Tapestry Mills, which later became Artloom Rug Mills. It is in fairly good condition overall. It's been in storage for many years and has a slight musty odor. It is a bit dry, has a few dark stains and one red stain that I have tried to show in the photos, and a faded area visible in photo #9. However, the edges seem to be in good condition and I do not detect any holes or bare patches.
   I am listing items for a family who needs to close out a house this Spring, so anything that does not sell on Ebay will be returned to the family for an estate sale. I'm afraid I probably won't be able to relist items more than once.
Shipping cost includes Delivery Confirmation. Insurance at an additional $1.75 is recommended but not required. We are always happy to combine shipping. We estimate shipping on the high end. If the actual cost is lower, we will adjust the invoice. We appreciate payment within five days. / Please feel free to email us with any questions. Thanks for your interest! / RVS

[36] John[1] Zimmermann is seen in the U.S. census of **1910** for Philadelphia, showing the family of John Zimmermann, "Manufacturer of Rugs," his wife Catherine, and six children. The census states that John immigrated in 1874 and his wife immigrated in 1881. His wife's name is given as Catherine in the census.

[37] JHN, 15, quoting "Lion Hosiery Mill" from *The Textile American*, "Manufacturing in Philadelphia." And p.17, for note in **1915**.

[38] Artloom, *Decade of Progress*, 1. John Zimmerman's obituaries state that in **1911** the Philadelphia Tapestry Mills became Philadelphia Pile Fabric Mills. I think it is more likely that PPFM was a department of the parent company, PTM, but there seems to be no easy way to answer this question.

[39] JHN, p. 16. She speculates that it may have been a graduation gift for John, from college and Bill from high school. I doubt this, because although John would have been 22, and perhaps just graduated from college, Bill would have been 20 in 1914, and would probably have been a sophomore at Penn. The dates of their years in college are not immediately available.

[40] JHN, 16, quoting Michael Bowman.

[41] The complex was divided, with Howard St. running through the complex between Westmoreland and Allegheny. JHN, p.16, quotes *Official American Textile Directory* (World Record, 1915):
Philadelphia Tapestry Mills: Allegheny Ave. & Front St.: Joseph Wasserman, pres.; I. Wasserman, treas.; B. Wasserman, sec; John Zimmerman, v.p. and supt. . . . Joseph Wasserman, buyer. Phila Pile Fabrics Mills: Howard & Westmoreland St. . . . Richard J. Steiner, pres. and supt.; Isaac Wassserman, treas. . . . R. J. Steiner, buyer. . . Artloom Rug Mills: Allegheny & Front, seamless rugs; steam.

John Zimmerman's obituaries state, probably incorrectly, that the original company, Philadelphia Tapestry Mills (founded in **1892**) evolved by becoming Philadelphia Pile Fabric Mills in **1911**; that PPFM became Artloom Rug Mills in **1919**; and that Artloom Rug Mills became Artloom Corporation at some time thereafter. The obituaries were probably intentional simplifications of the true corporate history of the Zimmerman-Wasserman operations.

[42] From John Zimmerman's patent #1,195,322, application quoted by JHN, p.17

[43] Artloom, *Decade of Progress*, 1.

[44] William Zimmerman's war record (from JHN), and the formation of John Zimmerman & Sons, from JHN, 18, quoting the obit of John Sr. The obit of John Zimmerman, Sr., says that John Zimmerman & Sons was founded in **1919**. Artloom Rug Mills was in business in **1915**, as it appears on the city map of Philadelphia, but it was not incorporated as a separate entity until **1919**, as stated in *Decade of Progress*, 1; and in *The Upholsterer and Interior Decorator* 62, no. 1 (15 Jul **1919**), 64: "The Art Loom Rug Mills, Philadelphia, was listed among recent incorporations at Harrisburg, Pa., to manufacture and sell carpets, rugs and all kinds of textile fabrics. Capital, $750,000. The incorporators are Joseph Wasserman, Benjamin Wasserman, Isaac Wasserman and John Zimmerman, all of Philadelphia, and John Zimmerman, Jr., of Melrose, Pa." A terminal "n" was used for each of the names. "Largest Manufacturers of Seamless Jacquard Wilton Rugs in the World," from Arloom Rug Mills advertisement, *Price's Carpet & Rug News* 9, no. 1 (July **1920**), 15 (also seen on p.22).

[45] The spelling of her given name has been spelled many ways, as mentioned above. I have chosen to use the name Eva Katherine, as it appears on her death certificate. This is also the anglicized version of Eva Katharina Kellenbenz, which is seen on the transcript of her birth and baptismal record in Kleineislingen, Württemberg, on Ancestry.com. The only entry for her in Ancestry.com is the Kelley Family tree, in which it is spelled Eva Kellenbenz, without a source. The family plot in Greenwood Cemetery, Philadelphia, shows one tall monument for the family, marked ZIMMERMAN at the base. On the N side is MOTHER / E. KATHERINE and FATHER / JOHN, along with the dates of their births and deaths. Ancestry.com also shows no birth certificates for any of her seven children, which would presumably have shown her name.

Her physician recorded "pernicious anemia," duration 1 year, on her death certificate. JHN, p.19, says she died of "aplastic anemia," quoting KFL. Aplastic anemia in now known to be a blood cell disease of unknown origin, but with many causes, whereas pernicious anemia is due to deficiency in absorption of vitamin B-12. She gradually deteriorated, in spite of treatment, it is said, with raw liver. I am dubious about the "raw liver" story, because it was only in 1920 (the same year that Eva died) that George Whipple first described the discovery, by accident, that raw liver was useful in stimulating blood cell formation (so-called hematopoesis) in dogs that had been bled. It was unlikely that this unusual laboratory report would have reached the physicians who treated Catherine Zimmerman. However, liver may already have been used for some time in treatment of anemia; it was for that reason that liver was being used in Whipple's laboratory.

[46] John Zimmerman, Sr., may have worried about what has been called "the family disease." His sons and sons-in-law had episodes of depression, and for all we know, he (John [Sr.]) and his brother George may have suffered from depression, too. JHN wrote about this to GJH, 8 Oct 2009, "When I talked with Anne Mitchell . . . I mentioned the issue of the family disease. She said that she had discovered some cases in the Kellenbenz family. (I don't discuss things if they are stated as being private.) This is a note that my aunt (Lucile 'Cil' Hoxie Fleet) had written to me about the Zimmermann family in the 1990's when I first started the family genealogies: 'Depression: Sad part of it. There is help (thru medication and doctor's care) – Used to be hush-hush. Uncle John

Zimmerman [Jr.], mother's brother, had it, had to have shock treatments and in hospital for awhile. Same with her brother Bill Z., though not as bad. Runs in family – as my brother John grew older I felt he had it because aware of it. For I had it but got help right away. Cousin Dick Kelley still bad and in nursing home. Would never admit he was depressed and drank while taking medication, a real no-no. So be aware of signs, for it is in the family. Not my folks.' I asked my sisters (who made annual summer trips to see my parents on Cape Cod) if they ever saw any signs in my father in his latter years (died in 1984) and they said no. He too died of an aneurysm, at age 66."

[47] JHN, 19-20, quoting Mary C. Bacon, *Deer Park: A History* (Vestal, N.Y: Dataflow, Inc., 1996); and Michael Bowman, op. cit.

[48] JHN, 20, quoting Bacon, *Deer Park.*

[49] JHN, 21.

[50] JHN, 21, citing David Dancer's obit: "Anna's first husband, David Dancer, was a very successful business man in Lamoni, Iowa. He was also a devout member and generous contributor to the RLDS church located there. His first wife Rosalia died in Aug., 1893. On 20 Nov **1895**, David (age 68) married Anna (age 31). Two sons were produced by this second marriage with the last being born in 1893 in March. David dies seven months later, on 23 Oct. Anna at the time of his death was vice president of the state saving Bank of Lamoni and was recognized as a woman of marked business ability and unusual knowledge concerning financial affairs."

[51] JHN letter to GJH, 8 Oct 2009: Genealogy of David Dancer: David Dancer, son of William and Phoebe (Mix) Dancer, was b. 20 Feb 1827, Oneida Co., N.Y. He m. (1) 16 Mar 1851, Rosalia Harvey, b. 31 Jan 1833, Lower Canada, dau of Hiram and Nancy Harvey; 5 ch: Nancy (d. @ 22mos); Ella (d. @ 3 yrs); Albert (d. @ 22 yrs); Eugene, a resident of Canada, farming; Walter, farming at Myrtle Point, Oregon. Rosalia d. Aug 1893. He m. (2) 20 Nov 1895, Anna Anderson, b. 30 Sep 1864, LaSalle Ill., dau of Mr. and Mrs. Andrew K. Anderson; they moved to Lamoni, when she was young. David Dancer moved to Decatur Co. Iowa and operated a 1280 acre farm, and organized the State Saving Bank of Lamoni (of which he was pres); they had two ch.: David a. Dancer, Jr., b. 7 Oct 1896; and Howard M. Dancer (b. 30 Mar 1898); Dancer Sr. d. 23 Oct 1898, one of the wealthiest men in Decatur Co., Ia.. He was a devout member and generous financial supporter of the RLDS church. Anna Dancer m. John Zimmerman Sr. in 1922.

The census for **1920** shows two other children, who are not accounted for in the above genealogy. The widow, Anna Dancer, had living with her: David 23, Howard 21, and also Florence Dancer 23 and Elizabeth Dancer 22. I suppose David and Florence could have been twins, and Elizabeth was born between the twins and Howard.

[52] JHN, 21-2.

[53] JHN, 22., quoting KFL and AC (Aunt Cil Hoxie); and 24 (quoting KFL, who said, "The daily business relationships followed by weekend and vacation socializing was strangling."). John Zimmerman's obituaries give the founding years, business purposes, and addresses of John Zimmerman & Sons (1919) and Zimmerman Mills (1927).

[54] Artloom, *Decade of Progress*, 1: "In **1919** the Artloom Rug Mills were incorporated as a separate and distinct entity. Side by side with the Philadelphia Tapestry Mills and the Philadelphia Pile Fabric Mills, Artloom grew, prospered, and reach maturity, backed by a brilliant record of success. On December 16, **1924**, the three companies were merged into a single unit, the Artloom Corporation, which continued its amazing success until 1926. / And then the inevitable signs of age began to show. Artloom's 'hair was turning gray'."

[55] From https://casetext.com/case/artloom-corporation-v-national-bus-bureau : "On February 9, **1931**, the proceedings before the Federal Trade Commission culminated in an order that the plaintiff cease and desist from advertising its Bagdad rug as a Wilton rug. Two days later the plaintiff brought this suit, to enjoin the defendants from publishing or commenting upon this order to the plaintiff's customers, the trade and the public generally. A preliminary injunction is asked for." The request for an injunction was denied by Judge Patterson of the U.S. District Court (48 F.2d 897, S.D.N.Y. 1931). Judge Patterson added that "I am convinced that the plaintiff here has not even the shadow of a case."

[56] "Control of the Artloom Corporation . . . yesterday passed to new interests headed by Herbert J. Adair, chairman of the Atlas Tack Corporation. . . Joseph Wasserman, Artloom chairman, retired. . . Along with him went Charles Wasserman, a nephew . . . and Richard Kell[e]y. . . . The following directors were re-elected: . . . Albert Zimmermann . . . who has been secretary and assistant treasurer was elected to the newly created post as vice president, remaining as assistant treasurer." It was rumored that the purchase was organized by "Detroit automobile interests anxious to obtain control of an upholstery supply source." Richard Kelley was Albert Zimmermann's brother-in-law. (Source and date unknown, probably a Philadelphia newspaper; the year is **1936**, from the biography of Joseph Wasserman).

More on Atlas Tack Corporation, which appears to have gone out of business in the late 20th century: "Historic New England Town, Once Plagued by Tack Factory's Toxic Pollution, Enjoys Revitalized Coastal Marshes: UNE 12, 2013 -- For much of the 20th century, the Atlas Tack Corporation was the main employer in the historic coastal town of Fairhaven, Mass., a place settled in the 1650s by Plymouth colonists. But the presence of this tack factory, shuttered in 1985, left more than a history of paychecks for the area's residents. It also left saltwater marshes so stocked with cyanide and heavy metals that the U.S. Environmental Protection Agency (EPA) listed the location of the factory as a Superfund site in 1990 and slated it for three intensive rounds of cleanup . . . Henry H. Rogers, Standard Oil multimillionaire and friend of famed American author Mark Twain, formed the Atlas Tack Corporation after consolidating several tack manufacturing companies in 1895. The Fairhaven company became one of the nation's largest manufacturers of wire tacks, bolts, shoe eyelets, bottle caps, and other small hardware. However, decades of acids, metals, and other chemical wastes oozing through the factory floor boards and being dumped in building drains, the nearby Boys Creek marsh, and an unlined lagoon left the property contaminated with hazardous substances."

From http://response.restoration.noaa.gov/about/media/historic-new-england-town-once-plagued-tack-factorys-toxic-pollution-enjoys-revitalized- (accessed 3/29/16).

John Zimmerman, Jr.'s election to Sigma Xi was mentioned in *The Pennsylvania Gazette*, which said he was Consulting Engineer of Artloom Rug Mills (quoted by JHN, p.24).

At the time the company history was written in **1948**, it was said to be "on the way back," after some "hardening of the arteries." "Then some of the owners of the business, who had grown old with the years, died, and the others retired from active participation. And so the moving spirit behind the operations, development, and the continued expansion of Artloom passed on with them." Full recovery was not achieved. Artloom was later sold and its marque no longer exists.

[57] KFL, as told to JHN, p. 25. KHF was then 4, and her brother Jim (whose letter is quoted *infra*), was 1.

[58] JHN, 24-25, quoting Bacon (collapse of the U.S. Bank and Trust Co. of Phila, which was seized by the Sec of Banking of the Commonwealth of Pa. in **1929**); census of **1930**; cruise of the family, returning to NYC on the S.S. Bremen from Cherbourg, France; financial woes for Deer Park and $540 lent by Clara Zimmerman (from Bacon).

[59] John Rothchild, *The Davis Dynasty: Fifty Years of Successful Investing on Wall Street* (New York: John Wiley & Sons, 2001), 20-1. Other errors in the story of the Wassermans include the mis-naming in this book of one of the three brothers. The book says they were Joseph, Isaac, and Howard. The third brother was actually Benjamin. Howard, who is said (p.21) to have died of syphilis, was actually Benjamin's son. Howard Dahlman Wasserman (1900-1964), Class of Princeton, **1922**, son of Benjamin (1887-1934), served as a member of the Artloom Board in 1947. There is nothing to substantiate the story of his demise from syphilis in Rothchild's book. Indeed, there is nothing cited in Rothchild's Source Notes (pp. 296-7) as evidence regarding the Wasserman family, or of all of the quotations attributed to Wasserman members. Joseph Wasserman's daughter Kathryn (1907-2013) married Shelby Cullom Davis (1909-1994). The Source Notes refer to Shelby Davis's *America Faces the Forties* (Dorrance & Company, 1940), which may be the source of the errors about the Wassermans. It is unfortunate that Rothchild did not personally do more fact-checking.

[60] Artloom, *Decade of Progress*, 21. A photo appears on this page, with the legend: "This is one of the modern looms that weaves Wilminster in widths up to twelve feet." Wilton rugs are illustrated in *Decade of Progress*: "Duotuft" (plain, in six colors), p.33; "Roubaix" (bordered, oriental-type), p.34; "Duotuft"(floral design, high loop construction, in four colors), p.35; and "Deauville" (plume figure, textured ground, in four colors), p.36. All of these specifically state that they are "Wilton" rugs.

[61] His obituaries simply state that he "retired in 1932."

[62] John Zimmerman's granddaughter, Helene (Zimmermann) Hill, recalls seeing the water tower on the top of the building as she passed by on the Pennsylvania Railroad train in the 1940s. The name on the water tower had been changed to ZIMMERMANN. The present deteriorated water tower is nameless.

[63] The later history of Artloom is taken from *Decade of Progress* and JHN, p.28. Images of the company's operations and products are seen in *Decade of Progress*, in archival photos, and in family photos. See: http://digital.library.temple.edu/cdm/search/searchterm/Business%20and%20Industry%20%20(Name)--Art%20Loom%20Rug%20Mill/mode/exact /

Temple University Special Collections / Thumbnail Title Date Description Collection / Weaving looms at Art Loom rug mill / 1950-12-14 / Employees weave looms at the Art Loom rug mill. / George D. McDowell Philadelphia Evening Bulletin Photographs

----------------

Abandoned Art Loom rug mill factory / **1976**-03-01 / Exterior of abandoned Art Loom rug mill factory on Mascher Street and Allegheny Avenue. / George D. McDowell Philadelphia Evening Bulletin Photographs

----------

Demolition of the abandoned and fire-gutted Art Loom rug mill at Mascher Street and Kensington Avenue began yesterday in line with its promise that City Managing Director Hillel S. Levinson made to Kensington residents on Friday. / George D. McDowell Philadelphia Evening Bulletin Photographs

------------

Smoothing rugs at Art Loom rug mill / **1948**-12-20 / This operation is known as "smoothing" and is one of the preliminary steps in the large-scale manufacture of rugs. It is being performed here by Alvin Casey, Huntington Valley, at the plant of the Artloom Carpet Co. / George D. McDowell Philadelphia Evening Bulletin Photographs / Smoothing rugs at Art Loom rug mill / **1948**-12-20 / George D. McDowell Philadelphia Evening Bulletin Photographs

[64] Notes for Mormons and the RLDS:

1. *The New Encyclopaedia Brittanica*, 15th ed. (Chicago: Encyclopaedia Brittanica), 8:328-9: "Mormon" (for all quotations mentioned above except those otherwise specified).

2. **13 Articles of Faith:** 1. We believe in God, the Eternal Father, and in His Son, Jesus Christ, and in the Holy Ghost. 2. We believe that men will be punished for their own sins, and not for Adam's transgression. 3. We believe that through the Atonement of Christ, all mankind may be saved, by obedience to the laws and ordinances of the Gospel. 4. We believe that the first principles and ordinances of the Gospel are: first, Faith in the Lord Jesus Christ; second, Repentance; third, Baptism by immersion for the remission of sins; fourth, Laying on of hands for the gift of the Holy Ghost. 5. We believe that a man must be called of God, by prophecy, and by the laying on of hands by those who are in authority, to preach the Gospel and administer in the ordinances thereof. 6. We believe in the same organization that existed in the Primitive Church, namely, apostles, prophets, pastors, teachers, evangelists, and so forth. 7. We believe in the gift of tongues, prophecy, revelation, visions, healing, interpretation of tongues, and so forth. 8. We believe the Bible to be the word of God as far as it is translated correctly; we also believe the Book of Mormon to be the word of God. 9. We believe all that God has revealed, all that He does now reveal, and we believe that He will yet reveal many great and important things pertaining to the Kingdom of God. 10. We believe in the literal gathering of Israel and in the restoration of the Ten Tribes; that Zion (the New Jerusalem) will be built upon the American continent; that Christ will reign personally upon the earth; and, that the earth will be renewed and receive its paradisiacal glory. 11. We claim the privilege of worshiping Almighty God according to the dictates of our own conscience, and allow all men the same privilege, let them worship how, where, or what they may. 12. We believe in being subject to kings, presidents, rulers, and magistrates, in obeying, honoring, and sustaining the law. 13. We believe in being honest, true, chaste, benevolent, virtuous, and in doing good to all men; indeed, we may say that we follow the admonition of Paul-We believe all things, we hope all things, we have endured many things, and hope to be able to endure all things. If there is anything virtuous, lovely, or of good report or praiseworthy, we seek after these things."

from https://www.mormon.org/beliefs/articles-of-faith (accessed 6/21/16).

3. Brant W. Ellsworth, "Mormons (the Church of Jesus Christ of Latter-day Saints)":

"Within a few weeks of establishing the LDS Church, Smith began sending missionaries into surrounding regions to share the gospel message and sell copies of the *Book of Mormon*. The first missionaries to Pennsylvania arrived as early as 1833, though their efforts were not especially fruitful. In August 1839, Benjamin F. Winchester (1817–1901), a twenty-two-year old native of Lindy's Lane, Erie County, Pennsylvania, became the first LDS missionary assigned to preach in the Philadelphia area. Winchester had previously experienced remarkable success preaching in New York, Delaware, Maryland, and especially near Toms River, New Jersey, where he established a small congregation of believers. On December 23, 1839, just a few months after Winchester's arrival in Philadelphia, Joseph Smith visited the city and officially established the Philadelphia Branch on the **northeast corner of Seventh and Callowhill Streets.**

(from http://philadelphiaencyclopedia.org/*Philadelphia Encyclopedia* and http://philadelphiaencyclopedia.org/archive/mormons-the-church-of-jesus-christ-of-latter-day-saints/ (accessed 6/21/16).

4. The Community of Christ Church (formerly RLDS) recognizes that "perception of truth is always qualified by human nature and experience" and the Community of Christ offers a number of the commonly held beliefs of its members and leaders as the "generally accepted beliefs of the church." The Community of Christ generally accepts the doctrine of the Trinity and other commonly held Christian beliefs. The concept of Zion as both a present reality of Christian living and as a hoped for community of the future is a rather strongly held belief in the Community of Christ and it ties closely to the peace and justice emphasis of the denomination. The movement also differs from most other Christian faiths in its belief in prophetic leadership, in the Book of Mormon, and in an open canon of scripture recorded in its regularly appended version of the Doctrine and Covenants. (See: http://www.cofchrist.org/, accessed 6/22/16).

5. David J. Whittaker, "The Philadelphia Pennsylvania Branch: Its Early History and Records" *Mormon Historic Studies* (Spring 2005), 53-66 (accessed 6/20/16):

55- "by September 1844, 334 members (the highest number) were recorded" in Philadelphia. 56- the record of "this Church units held in the archives of the Community of Christ Church (formerly RLDS) in Independence, Missouri." The record contains the minutes of the meetings of the Philadelphia Branch "from 23 December 1839 to the last entry, 16 April 1854." 57- William Smith was "in conflict" with others in the period from 1839-1854. He was a member of the Quorum of the Twelve Apostles, but was later "cut off." 58- "Walter W. Smith, 1 April 1906 [was] then the historian of the Reorganized Church of Jesus Christ of Latter Day Saints." "The records suggest that over 40 percent of the branch members were excommunicated after August 1844." The Prophet, Joseph Smith, Jr., founded the Philadelphia Branch on his 34th birthday, 23 December 1839. He preached at the Universalist Church Hall in December 1839, at 412 Lombard St., corner of 4th and Lombard.

6. For LDS Philadelphia Temple, see: http://www.ldschurchtemples.com/philadelphia/ (accessed 6/21/16). 7. Douglas D. Alder, "Die Auswanderung," *Utah Historical Quarterly* 52 (no. 4, Fall 1984), 370-88:

"The most numerous and long-lived group settlements in the West were clearly those of the Mormons in the Great Basin where thousands of Latter-day Saints gathered from Europe and North America. Those emigrants who came from German-speaking lands in Europe to the Great Basin are examples of both the individual and the group undertaking. For example, the Mormon-sponsored emigrants from Germany,

Switzerland, and Austria who came prior to World War I were generally transported in groups. Most often they traveled directly from Central Europe to Utah with the guidance of church emigration agents all the way to the Great Basin. German-speaking people of other religious persuasions came to Utah also, but generally they came individually and indirectly, often living several years in other parts of the United States prior to their move to Utah. . . . The German-speaking Mormon emigration began in 1853, a decade after British and Scandinavian emigrants had begun the trek. The organization, financing, routing, and destinations had become much more definite by 1853, and the Germans benefited by it. As soon as the missions gained a solid footing in Germany, the Liverpool shipping office was ready to handle their emigration business." [also see Gilbert Scharff, *Mormonism in Germany* (Salt Lake City: Deseret Book Co., 1970)].

8. Ronald E. Romig, "Response to the Book of Commandments and Revelations Presentations":

"The publication of the Book of Commandments and Revelations manuscript is extraordinary. It is a foundational document of the entire Restoration movement. The papers presented by Joseph Smith Papers editors Robert Woodford, Robin Jensen, Steven Harper, and Grant Underwood during the 2009 Mormon History Association conference afford important insights about the history, provenance, and early uses of the BCR manuscript. As current MHA president and as the former Archivist for the Community of Christ, I am pleased to respond to these papers. . . . How many BCR manuscript pages did the RLDS Church obtain? Walter W. Smith, who was RLDS Church Historian from 1919 to 1923, initially suggested there were eleven pages. However, rather detailed descriptions from the mid-1920s by subsequent RLDS Church Historian Samuel Burgess indicate there were eight pages, meaning four leaves: pages 111–12, 117– 20, and 139–40. All of these pages, except 111, contain content not published in the Book of Commandments. . . . Community of Christ President Stephen M. Veazey [affirmed] that 'seeing both the faithfulness and human flaws in our history makes it more believable and realistic, not less.' . . . The Community of Christ Archives is allied with the LDS Archives to ensure that scholars have access to all known BCR content. We are highly pleased that the Community of Christ's eight pages of manuscript material are included in the first volume of the Revelations and Translations series of The Joseph Smith Papers. As an extension of this collaboration in the Papers project, the LDS Archives offered to help." file:///C:/Documents%20and%20Settings/George/My%20Documents/Downloads/48.3RomigResponse-d41f995d-23a4-474e-84c2-bc0d28de123a.pdf (accessed 6/22/16).

9. There has long been dissent between the Saints of the LDS, who believe in the *Book of Mormon,* and others. Although it is unlikely that he read it, or that he would have been moved by it, a scathing, sarcastic discussion on this subject was published when John Zimmerman was 75 years old. It was by a Pulitzer Prize winning author, as the lead article in one of the major literary journals of that time: Bernard DeVoto, "The Centennial of Mormonism," *The American Mercury* 19 (No. 71, Jan **1930**), 1-14. It begins, "Tuesday, April 6, 1830, was computed to be exactly eighteen hundred years after the Resurrection. Therefore, in Heaven, Jehovah moved to fulfill the prophesies He had set down in Holy Writ by restoring His True Church . . . For the scene of this final Restoration, Jehovah selected a mangy village named Fayette [and] he chose a frontiersman named Joseph Smith [who] had long been in communication with Jehovah."

[65] James Fligg to George Hill (letter, 20 Feb 2003): "Here is a copy of the book about Artloom that I told you about at Al Hoxie's funeral. I hope you find it interesting and useful for your purposes of documenting some of the things that John Zimmerman is in his life as well as dates when they were done. [Hoxie spelled with Zimmerman one "n" throughout this letter]. The letter continues in the text, with a few redundancies omitted. It was concluded, "It is an honor to be one of his grandsons! / Enjoy! / Jim Fligg" [unsigned]

[66] Catherine (Kellenbenz) Zimmerman was also known as Katherine, Eva, Evakaterina, Eva Kathryn, or Eva Catherine. Many records show the name of the town of her birth as Kleinfislinger, but this spelling probably results from an error in transmission of the town named Kleineislingen. The prefix, *klein*, no longer is used for the village of Eislingen, adjacent to a larger town, formerly known as Gross Süssen, now simply called Süssen.

Anne Mitchell to GJH, 23 Feb 2009 (e-mail): *Philadelphia Inquirer* (14 Oct **1920**), 20. "Oct. 13, Eva K., wife of John Zimmerman [sic, one "n"]. Funeral services Fri., 2:30 P.M. at her late residence, 1512 W. Allegheny Ave. Int. Greenmount Cem. Remains may be viewed Thurs. eve."

"On May 23 [**1936**]. JOHN husband of Anna Dancer Zimmermann. Relatives and friends are invited to the services Tuesday, 2:30 P.M. at his late residence 1512 W. Allegheny Ave. Interment private. Friends may call Monday eve." *Philadelphia Inquirer* (25 May 1936), 31.

[67] The Dancer-Anderson genealogy is summarized from a one-page attachment "David Dancer," enclosed with JHN's letter to GJH, 8 Oct 2009. I believe JHN used Ancestry.com as her main source for this information.

[68] Emily was born 10 July **1890**; died 14 June **1897**. She was buried two days later in Greenmount Cemetery in Philadelphia. She appeared in a formal portrait of the family taken before she died. Her death greatly affected her brothers and sisters, and it was rarely mentioned. Emily Zimmerman's death certificate was found by Anne Mitchell and forwarded to George J. Hill on 1 March 2009. This shows that she d. of diphtheria on 14 June 1897 at the age of six and was buried two days later in Greenmount Cemetery, Philadelphia. Her name was spelled Emmely Zimmerman in the d.c. and her parents' names were spelled John Zimmerman (one n) and Eva K.

# John Zimmerman's Businesses
## Philadelphia Tapestry Mills
## West Allegheny Ave. at Howard St.

Photograph courtesy of Michael Bowman
## c. 1912

John Zimmerman and three Wasserman Brothers formed Philadelphia Tapestry Mills in 1892. The firm added Philadelphia Pile Fabrics and Art Loom Fabrics.

The companies consolidated and became Artloom Corporation in 1924

The original mill was expanded to cover two square blocks along Allegheny Ave., from Mascher St. to Front St., with Howard St. passing through the property.

The small red square at the top of the map is the location of the RLDS church at Howard and Ontario

Map and annotation by Jean Hoxie Naples
## Philadelphia Land Use Map 1910

## John Zimmerman worked for Bromley Brothers from 1884-1888

PRICE'S CARPET AND RUG NEWS

# ARTLOOM RUG MILLS

Largest Manufacturers of Seamless Jacquard Wilton Rugs in the World

## Almeda Jacquard SEAMLESS Wilton Rugs
## Turkestan SEAMLESS Rugs

WE SPECIALIZE IN SEAMLESS RUGS ONLY

ONE THING—WE DO IT THOROUGHLY

NEW YORK SALESROOM, 141-147 FIFTH AVENUE, ELEVENTH FLOOR

Also Showrooms at { Boston, Mass. 16 Boylston St.  San Francisco, Cal. 833 Market St.

Mills, Allegheny Avenue and Front Street, Philadelphia       MICHAEL J. PHELAN, Selling Agent

Cable Address, "Connisseur," New York.   Marconi International Code

# JOHN BROMLEY & SONS, Inc.

ESTABLISHED IN 1845. INCORPORATED 1916.

Lehigh Avenue, below Front Street, Philadelphia

### SOUNDNESS AND SOLIDITY

SIMPLE WORDS—but they stand for the most important qua...
These qualities are needed today as they never were before. Th...
anchor his business to them as to a rock. He will therefore be irre...
to the **Bromley Line of Dependable Floor-Coverings.**

Axminster Rugs          Seamless Chenille Rugs          Bath and Rag Rugs

*Price's Carpet & rug News* 9 (no. 1, July 1920), 22

John Bromley & Sons—Carpets and Axminster Rugs

John J. MacFarlane, *Manufacturing in Philadelphia, 1683-1912*, 21
### 201-203 E. Lehigh Ave., destroyed by fire in 1972

**Artloom's Major Advertising Campaign in 1904 – 1906**

This Artloom Couch Cover $5.00

Here is something new —the first time a Gobelin

pattern has been reproduced in this country in a tapestry that is perfectly reversible.

Philadelphia Tapestry Mills, Philadelphia

Advertisement courtesy of Jean Hoxie Naples

Advertisements courtesy of Jean Hoxie Naples

## Artloom in 1936

**LPHIA**

### ARTLOOM REINS PASS TO CHIEF OF ATLAS TACK

H. J. Adair Takes Control as Wasserman Family Sells Holdings.

**ELECTS 5 TO BOARD**

Rumor of Stock Buying by Detroit Interests Partly Denied.

Control of the Artloom Corporation, rug, carpet and upholstery manufacturing concern, yesterday passed to new interests headed by Herbert J. Adair, chairman of the board of Atlas Tack Corporation.

At the annual meeting of the stockholders, Joseph Wasserman, Artloom chairman, retired from the board of directors. Along with him went Charles Wasserman, a nephew; Lionel Levy, a son-in-law; Yale L. Schekter, understood to be counsel for the family, and Richard Kelly.

Elected in their stead were Adair, John A. McNaughton, a director of Atlas Tack and partner in Beekman, Bogue & Clark; J. A. M. Adair, vice-president of Atlas Tack and president of the First National Bank of Portland, Ind.; Graham Blaine and Herbert E. Metcalss.

**Secrecy Maintained.**

No one would say at the meeting whether the new directors were acting for themselves, or, as rumored, for Detroit automobile interests anxious to obtain control of an upholstery supply source. Later Herbert J. Adair said he was acting purely in his own interests.

He refused to say how much stock he or his associates control, or how many buyers were represented in the acquisition of a large block of the Wasserman holdings. The company has outstanding 200,000 common shares and a small issue of preferred.

The Adair group quickly took control by electing five of the 10 directors and also made Herbert J. Adair chairman and McNaughton secretary.

**Five Directors Re-elected.**

Stockholders cast a total of 138,671 votes for all directors. In addition to the election of the Adair group, the following directors were re-elected:

C. S. Newton, Albert Zimmermann, Howard Wasserman, Roland Palmedo, John T. McDade.

The directors re-elected Newton as president and general manager, McDade as treasurer and made William H. Alden, Jr., assistant treasurer. Zimmermann, who has been secretary and assistant treasurer, was elected to the newly created post as vice president, remaining as assistant treasurer.

**Board Issues Statement.**

The board issued a statement which said in part:

"In order that our stockholders, customers and friends may know of the developments in the Artloom Corporation, we desire to inform you that the interests owned by the various members of the Wasserman family have recently been purchased by a group of practical and exceedingly well-connected business men.

"It is the desire of this group to further the interests of the Artloom Corporation through the benefit of not only their experience, but their contacts with the business world."

Artloom Corporation's control passed to "now interests headed by Herbert J. Adair, chairman of the board of Atlas Tack Corporation." Co-founder and Artloom chairman Joseph Wasserman retired, along with two members of his family. His nephew, Howard Wasserman, remained as a director. Albert Zimmermann, son of co-founder and former manager of the works, John Zimmerman (d. 1936), was elected vice president and continued as assistant treasurer.

# Artloom in 1947

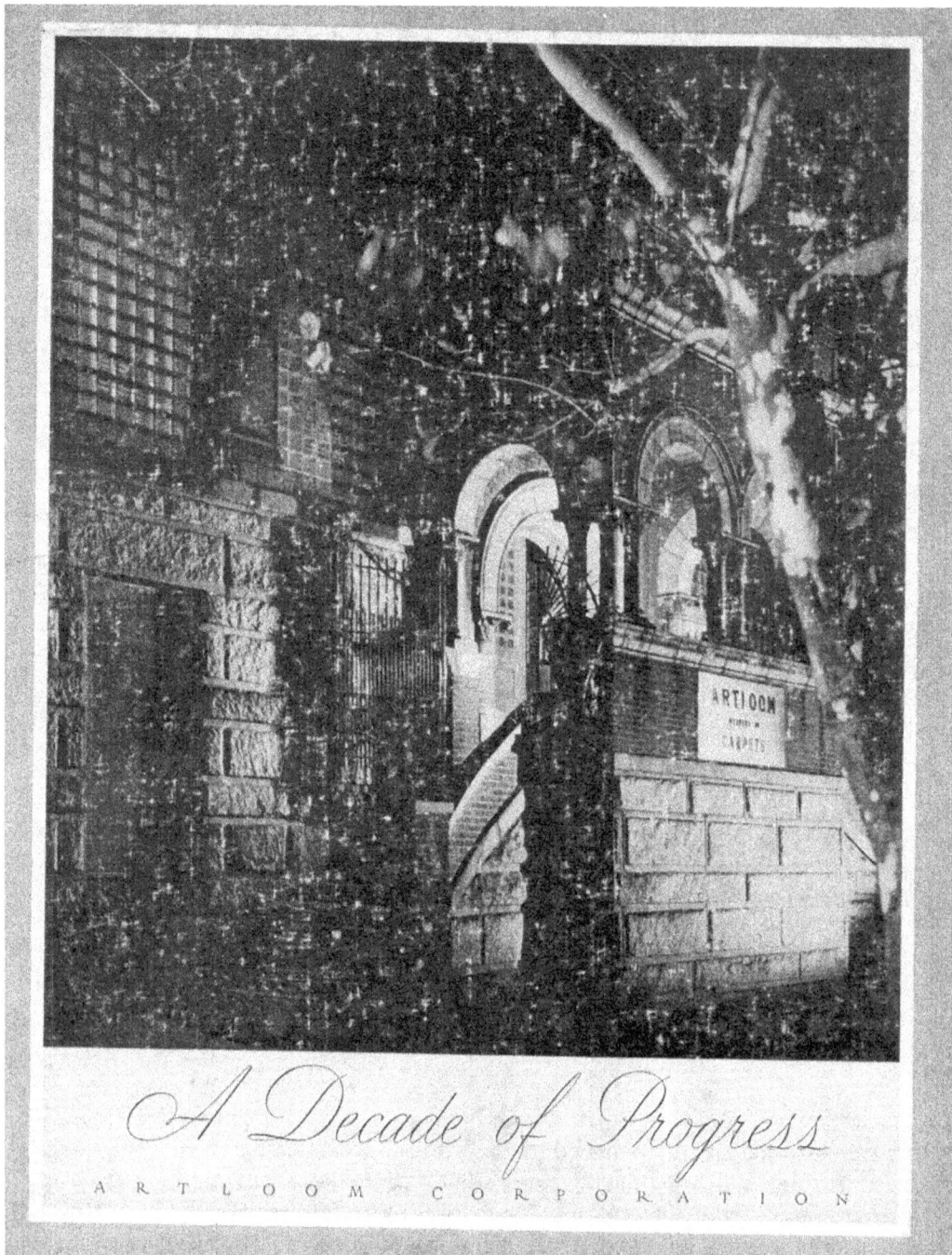

*A Decade of Progress*

ARTLOOM CORPORATION

*A Decade of Progress*

1937 – 1947

A R T L O O M

C O R P O R A T I O N

Allegheny and Howard                    Philadelphia, Pa

**Drawing of Artloom from Allegheny Ave., looking N, with a bridge over Howard St.
The original building is on the R, extending to Front St.
(See photo with tower in 1912, p. 127, showing the corner of Allegheny & Howard)**

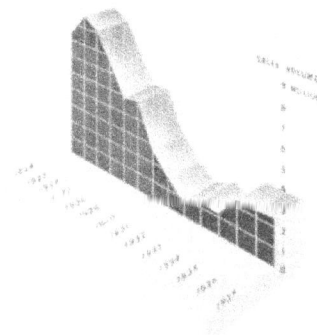

**Howard Wasserman is in tan suit at L.
William "Wild Bill" Wasserman is leaning forward on R**

# Later Development of John Zimmerman's Machines
## From *A Decade of Progress, 1937-1947*

The "warp dyeing machine, developed by Zimmerman, was improved to produce the brilliant Wilminster line we know today. Zimmerman's pioneering in broadloom finally bore fruit in 1938, when Artloom built nine broadlooms" (p.3)

"Few carpet mills in America today can exist without the wide loom. But in 1906, John Zimmerman, one of the original founders of the Philadelphia Tapestry mills, owned the exclusive patent-rights to the wide loom which he developed in nine-foot widths. The wide loom is one of the priceless assets" of the company (p.17)

**Wide Loom**

"On the left we see the modern development of the 'warp dyeing machine' which John Zimmerman developed and patented. The warp yarn is dyed first and then is woven into the rug; the dyed yarn automatically forms the pattern of the rug as it is woven." (p.21)

**Warp Dyeing Machine**

# Artloom from the 1940s until the 1970s

## Artloom Rugs

Smoothing Rugs 1948

Weaving Looms 1950

## Destruction of the Fire-Gutted Artloom Factory

From Temple University Libraries, Urban Archives, photo by Craig, *Philadelphia Evening Bulletin*

**Before the fire, view along Allegheny Ave, probably looking W at Front St. intersection
After the fire, on 1 March 1976, view at Mascher St. & Kensington Ave.**

# John Zimmerman's Patents

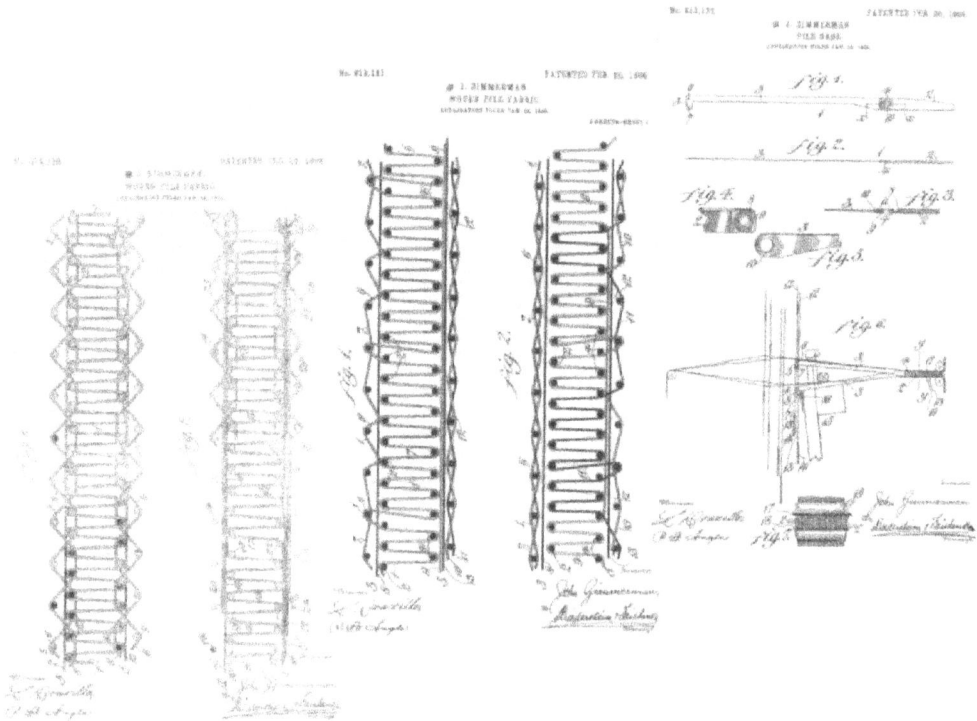

**1906**
**John Zimmerman**
**Three Patents**
**Two for "Woven Pile Fabrics" and one for "Pile Gage"**

No. 855,153.

J. ZIMMERMAN.
PILE FABRIC.
APPLICATION FILED MAY 5, 1906.

PATENTED MAY 28, 1907.

2 SHEETS—SHEET 1.

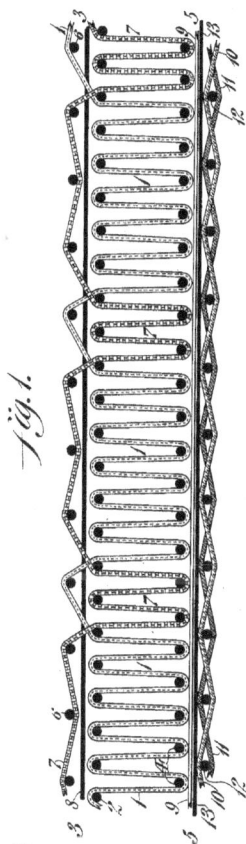

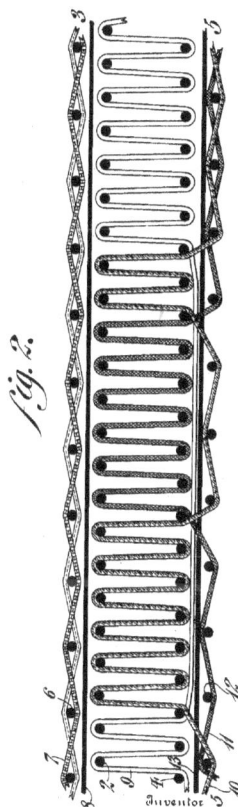

Witnesses

Inventor

**1907**
**John Zimmerman**
**"Pile Fabric"**

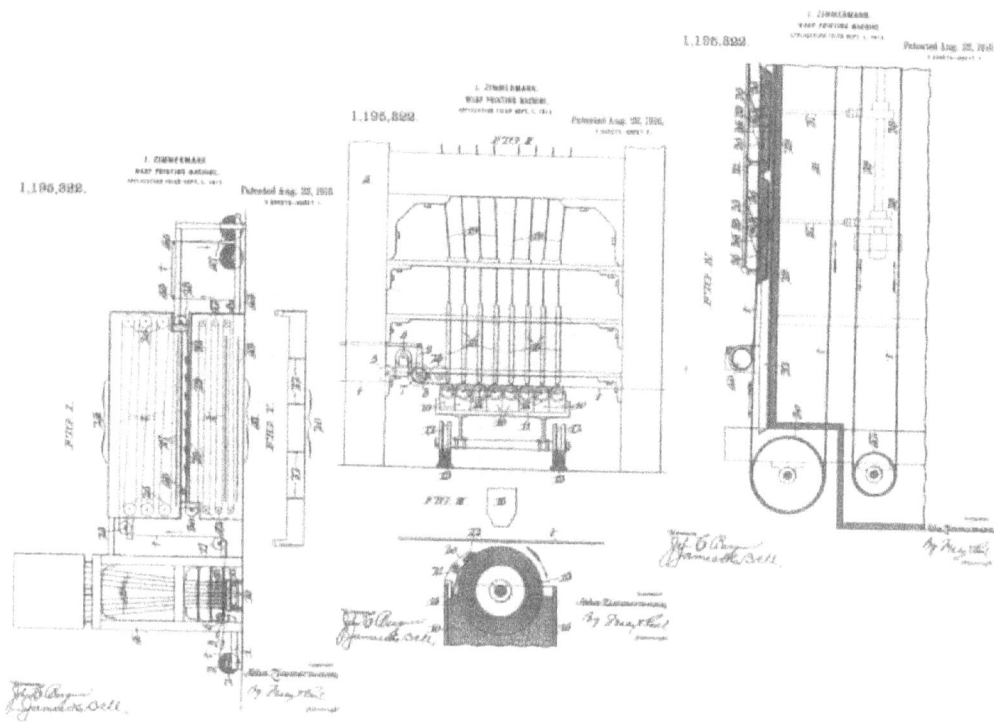

**1916**
**John Zimmerman**
**"Warp Printing Machine"**

# Former Site of Artloom Mill
### North side of Allegheny Avenue at Howard, extending W to Mascher St. and E to Front St.
### Abandoned, destroyed by fire, and removed in 1976

**View from Allegheny Ave. to N on Howard St.**
**The RLDS Church at Howard and Ontario was 1 block to the N**
**A bridge between the two parts of the Artloom factory crossed Howard St.**

photographs by George J. Hill

**Allegheny and Howard.  L:  View to NW.  R:  View to NE**

# John Zimmerman & Sons
## Plush & Pile Fabrics
## Est. 1918
## East Erie & Castor Avenues

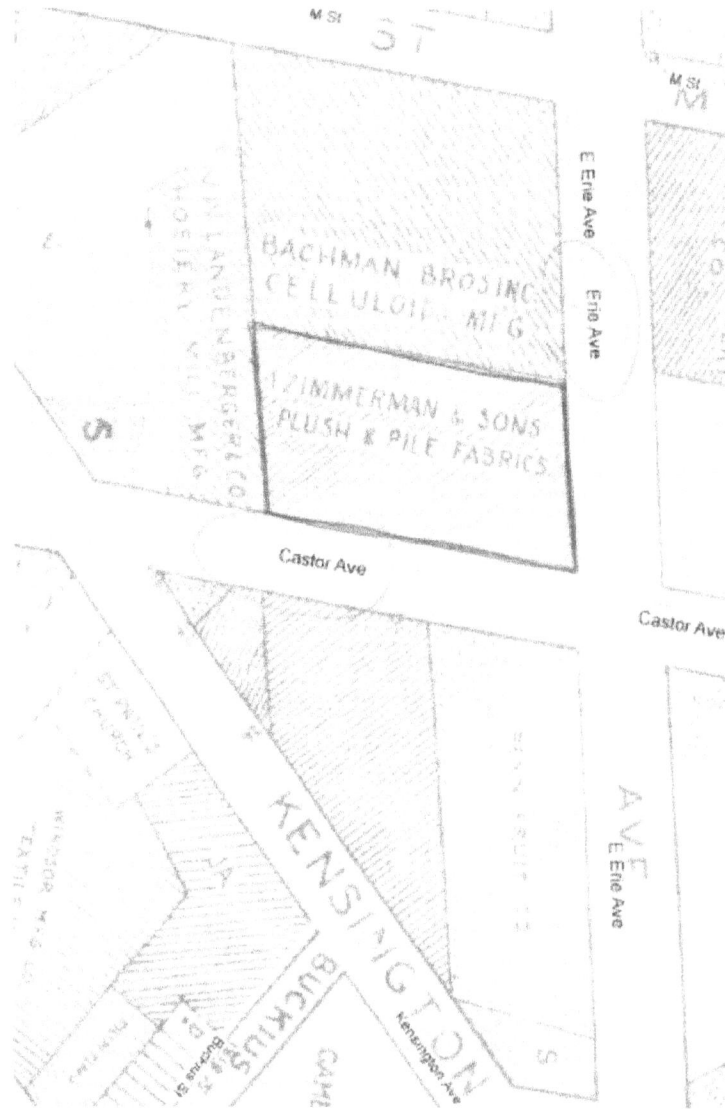

Map found and marked by Jean Hoxie Naples

## Land Use Map of Philadelphia 1962

# John Zimmerman & Sons

**Mostly abandoned, partially reused**
**The water tower now black, was once was painted with "Zimmermann"**

# Zimmerman Mills
### Est. 1927
### 21st and Allegheny – 2092 W. Allegheny Ave.

Image from Jean Hoxie Naples

**The Zimmerman Mills building was probably abandoned by the time this image was made in 1950**

05/01/2016

**The building was totally abandoned by 2016**

# Advertisements for Zimmerman – Zimmermann Mills

## BACK AGAIN! FAMOUS 'ZIMMERMAN' KID MOHAIR SOFAS & CHAIRS

**"Simmons"** innerspring mattresses with 210 coil springs

**26.75**

*The finest fabric made by this fine Philadelphia maker!*

**$233** **$118**

FINE FURNITURE

## WHAT IT MEANS WHEN THE SALESMAN SAYS:
### *"It is a Zimmermann Fabric!"*

## JOHN ZIMMERMANN AND SONS
*Manufacturers of Fine Upholstery Fabrics*

Images from Joseph Carnwath, Ph.D.

143

# Weaving

## Examples of Woven Objects, from Many Materials

**Navaho rug, 64in. x 44in., from animal fibers**

**Navaho weaving from vegetable fibers**
**Basket, 7in. diam. x  3in. height.**          **Tray, 14in. x  8in.**

# Handicrafts from Asia

**Woven Cap, sheep wool, Uzbekistan**
**8in. diameter x 2.5in. high**

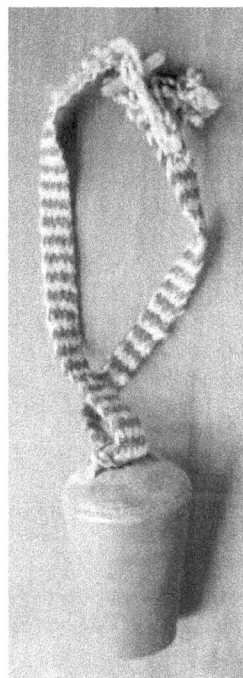

**Saddle blanket, yak wool (L above), 17in. x 17in.**
**Yoke for bell, yak wool (R above), 14in. x 1in.**

# Handicrafts from the U.S.

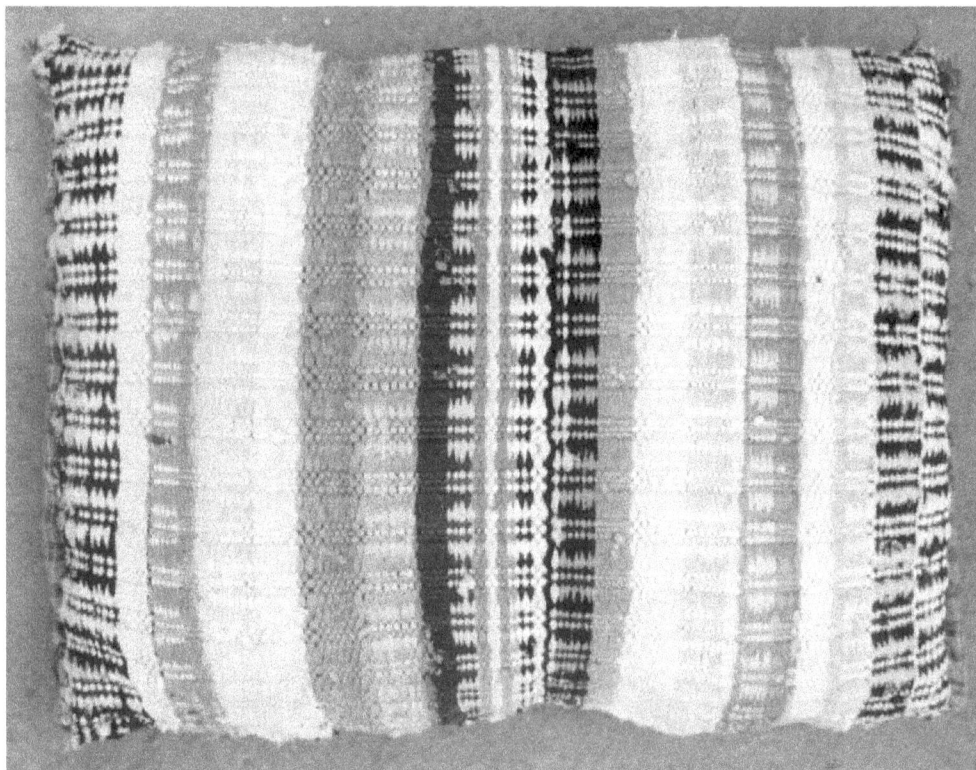

**Rag rug, remade into a pillow cover, of mixed cotton and wool, 13in. x 10in.
Made on broad hand loom by Sarah D. (Rundall) Thompson**

**Decorative embroidery – smocking (L, above)
12in. x 7in.
Potholder, cotton – made on small hand loom (R)
6in. x  6in.**

**Made by Helene (Zimmermann) Hill, 2014-2016**

# Some of
# John[1] Zimmermann's Locations in Philadelphia

**2092 W Allegheny Ave. – Zimmermann Mills**
**Unlabelled dot to the E is 1512 Allegheny Ave – the family home from 1903-1936**
**W Allegheny Ave & No Howard St – Philadelphia Tapestry Mills & Artloom**
**W Ontario St & N Howard Ave – RLDS church**
**Castor Ave & E Erie Ave – John Zimmermann & Sons**
**4301 N Front St. – Greenmount Cemetery, where John and Eva are buried**

# Zimmermann Gravestone
## Greenmount Cemetery
## Philadelphia, Pennsylvania

**The north side of the monument shows:**

**MOTHER**

**E. KATHRINE**

**BORN SEPT 29 1855     DIED OCT 12 1920**

**FATHER**

**JOHN**

**BORN NOV 28 1855     DIED MAY 23 1936**

**ZIMMERMAN**

# PART III

## Descendants of
## John[1] and Eva Katherine (Kellenbenz) Zimmermann

### Their Children

| | | | Chapter |
|---|---|---|---|
| **1** | i. | CLARA (1886-1968) + | 4 |
| **2** | ii. | ANNA (1887-1974) + | 5 |
| **3** | iii. | EMILY (1890-1897) | 6 |
| **4** | iv. | JOHN, Jr. (1892-1974) + | 7 |
| **5** | v. | WILLIAM "Bill" (1894-1978) + | 8 |
| **6** | vi. | LILLIAN "Lily Mae" (1897-1966) + | 9 |
| **7** | vii. | ALBERT WALTER "Al" (1902-1961) + | 10 |

**Part III includes 172 known descendants of
John[1] and Eva Katherine Zimmermann**

7 Children – Second Generation – Brothers and Sisters
23 Grandchildren – Third Generation – First Cousins
72 Great-grandchildren – Fourth Generation – Second Cousins
60 Great-great-grandchildren – Fifth Generation – Third Cousins
10 Great-great-great-grandchildren – Sixth Generation – Fourth Cousins

**The Patriarch**

**John[1] Zimmermann (1855-1936)**

**Portrait photo – 1936**

"He was very frugal raising his kids – girls were limited to two new dresses a year"

But

Each of John's children got a million dollars when they were married."[1]

# Stories about John Zimmermann and His Family

## Grandfather Z.[1]

As young children we saw quite a bit of Grandfather Zimmermann. He loved to go for rides and Sam, then later Malcolm (or vice versa) would bring him by the several houses to see his grandchildren. Although I was happy enough to see him I always dreaded the kissing hello. He had a very moist, not to say spitty kiss which I was too polite to wipe off. His visits were always short. Just checking to see if were being raised properly, I guess.

Every year during the Thanksgiving weekend the whole family celebrated his birthday with a big family, catered dinner at the big house in North Philadelphia. I have always wondered if it was really as big (the house not the dinner) as I remember it. There was the huge ball-room type room on the first floor across from the library and large dining room, a breakfast room where casual family meals were served when we visited, usually on a Sunday night and, of course, the kitchen. At the top of the stairs there was a very large sitting room where everyone gathered before and after the dinner, then a short flight of stairs to reach two large bedrooms, a bathroom and Grandfather's and Grandmother's very large bedroom

I always looked forward to the celebration because the cousins had a great time together. The house was perfect for hide and seek. Mother and Uncle Al Hoxie always told us to accept offers of demitasse coffee from the waiters so they could get enough coffee to drink. That's the only part of the menu I remember. It probably wasn't really memorable

For the most part our greater family life was somewhat centered around Grandfather. I realize now, looking back on it, that he was gradually deteriorating even to the point of speaking mostly in German, the country of his birth. Whether he had Alzheimer's or another form of dementia who can say so many years later, but I do know that the family, especially his own children who were devoted to him grew more and more concerned.

I remember in May, probably around 1936 or so, my father took me out to dinner for my birthday. Grandfather was dying and there was a veritable death watch at his bedside that Friday night and all day Saturday. Exactly when he died I can't say, but I know I went with my mother and father to Grandfather's house on Sunday. I stayed in the car and listened to a Yankees game with the old murders row in full bloom! Later on I went inside and up to his room where a lot of family were still gathered. Aunt Lil asked me if I would like to see him, (which I wouldn't, my very first dead person) and pulled back the sheet that covered him. What a memory!

He was buried from his house, having been "laid out" in the big room downstairs. I was put in one of the limousines with my mother and father and for the only time in my life I saw my father cry. Funny the things that stick in your mind.

---

[1] Mary Jane (Zimmermannn) Clark, "Mom's Stories."

## You Asked for It

Grandfather and Grandmother John Zimmermann Sr. had a large house in north Philadelphia. Right next door to them lived Aunt Clara, married to Albert Hoxie. There were three Hoxie children: Albert, John and Lucile.

Aunt Anna came next. She was married to Richard Kelley. They had seven children: Joan, Dick, Sue, Marian, Anita, Don and Nancy. (Their means of contraception was to sleep in different bedrooms.) They lived across the footbridge from our house on Prospect Avenue and later built a much larger house about a mile away on Cedar Road, a gorgeous home on a gorgeous piece of property. (Aunt Anna and Uncle Richard had separate bedrooms here, too.) Nancy, a sweet, sweet child died when she was maybe ten, a terrible blow to our whole family.

My father, John Jr., was next in line. In a very German family he was the favored son of a doting mother. He married Ethel Grace Kinnaman and they had four remarkable children: Betty, Mary Jane, Johnny and Carlie (two miscarriages between Betty and Mary Jane).

William was next in line. He married Margaret Lukens, Peg, and they had three children: Bill Jr., Peggy, and Bobby. They set up housekeeping in the suburban Chestnut Hill area and then built a beautiful home in Wyncote, not far from the rest of us, on a wonderful piece of property that allowed Uncle Bill to indulge in his gardening hobby. Later on Aunt Anna and Uncle Richard built a smaller house next door. The two families were conveniently near The Oaks, the nursing home where my father spent the last six years of his life, and they were very good about visiting and taking him for rides.

Lillian was the youngest daughter, preceded by Emily who died when she was a young girl. Lil married Jim Fligg and they had two children: Kathryn Lucile and Jim Jr. They lived across the footbridge near the Kelleys and built a handsome Georgian home next to the Kelleys on Cedar Road which worked out well for family parties. Nancy Kelley's death was a terrible blow as she and "Katchie" had been very close. Uncle Jim had a serious heart attack at this time and the claim was that it was a true broken heart.

Last came Albert, who married the very socially conscious, anti-Semitic (ask my sister) Barbara Shoemaker. They had four children: Babs, Helena, Warren and Albert. They built another Zimmermann type home (big and beautiful) out along the Main Line in Haverford. We didn't see much of them - they were too busy being social, although they did come to the family New Years Day party/dinner at Kelley-Fliggs.

I never knew my Grandmother Z. She died before I was born, but I know my mother was very fond of her. The second Mrs. Z. Sr. was the grandmother I knew, a matriarch from Iowa, whose family hurried East when Grandfather died to swoop up as many of the spoils as possible, including possessions of the natural children. (Now I'm telling tales out of school!)

## New Year's

On New Years Day we always had a big family party after the Kelleys and the Fliggs got settled in their new homes. Dinner was served at the Kelleys' their dining room and breakfast room being more adaptable. Aunt Anna (or her cook) would do one turkey and Aunt Lil another, with oyster stuffing. Good stuff. My mother always brought her special sweet potatoes done up with cinnamon apples and marshmallows on the top. Aunt Clara brought rolls and I'll guess that Aunt Peg and Aunt Barbara brought potatoes and a vegetable, except one year Aunt Barbara didn't because she was busy having a New Years baby, my cousin Albert. There were undoubtedly other odd orts. I can't imagine a big gathering without candy and nuts.

Tomato juice probably, but nothing stronger.

After dinner we kids were herded over to the Fligg basement to be entertained. For a while it was rented movies, but in a few years the creative juices got flowing and puppet shows were born. First there was a small stage and equally small puppets, but then Aunts Lil and Anna and my mother really got going. Aunt Lil had a stage (about the size of this computer table) built complete with curtain. There were two productions: The Three Wishes, wherein a poor couple was granted three wishes of their own choosing by a good fairy. After debating what they should wish for, the husband forgot himself and wished, idly, that they had some sausage. His furious wife when the sausage sure-enough appeared, wished that it was hanging from his nose. And there it was (a date seed pulled by a string through a hole in the table). Two wishes down! He couldn't spend the rest of his life with sausage hanging from his nose so they agreed to wish only to be as they were before. My Aunts were the puppeteers, my mother did all the sound effects and Sue and I did the voices, and the moral:

> So all three wishes came to naught,
> You know I rather thought they would,
> For idle longing never brings
> To wise or foolish any good.
> The wise folk when they want a thing,
> Don't need the fairies' help a bit.
> They just make sure they want it first
> Then go ahead and work for it.

We were all extremely committed to our assignments.

Another show had a clown dance as the opener. The back stage show was much better than the audience's view. Aunt Anna really getting into it as she maneuvered that clown around the stage was a sight to behold!

The triumph came with The Frog Prince wherein the beautiful princess sitting on the edge of a pond kisses (ugh) the frog and he turns into a properly attired prince. Those puppets were works of art. They outdid themselves on the beautiful princess and the handsome prince who had been a frog. My mother was masterful with her sound effects: thunder, lightning, music all on queue (sp.?) And of course, Sue and I prided ourselves on the voice-work. All in all we worked up pretty good shows and had calls for same at several different venues

And it was a good way to spend time after dinner while the adults relaxed next door at the Kelleys'.

## A Bit of This, a Bit of That

My parents and their parents were members of the Reorganized Church of Latter Day Saints, emphasis on the Reorganized, although they did have copies of the Book of Mormon in their homes. We were taken to the R.C.L.D.S. Church in the Kensington district of Philadelphia, one of the city's poorer neighborhoods. But the Kelleys were there, the Hoxies were there, Aunt Lil Fligg was in charge of the children's program, so the family was very much involved. The only recollections I really have about "worshipping" there was that we had a fake birthday cake, pink wood (!) which was hauled out every time there was a birthday to celebrate also as we closed for the morning we always asked the Lord "Through the weepy witthus" and I never could find out what a weepy withus was.

What was REALLY impressive was that upstairs, near the pulpit, there was a covered body of water which looked like a small swimming pool and was uncovered and used to dunk FULLY CLOTHED individuals in the manner of John the Baptist. I always dreaded the thought of being dunked, especially in front of a lot of people I didn't know, but I never was. (It was when I was finally preparing to be an Episcopalian that I was finally baptized, but that was only a little sprinkle on the head not even enough to spoil my hairdo.)

After a few years the Kelleys took off and started attending the Presbyterian Church in Jenkintown, but not before one Sunday morning when we were driving home from R.C.L.D.S. and for some reason stopped by a nice field probably to pick flowers. I had on my brand new shoes, brown ones with a wide strap and gold buckle and evidently the field had recently been visited by cows, because I stepped in some cow flop or plop, but I never wore those beautiful shoes again. I just stuffed them in the back of my closet. If my mother or anyone else noticed, nothing was ever said. Shortly thereafter I went with them, I'm back to the Kelleys. They called for me every Sunday morning, a very convenient arrangement (and a boon to my parents) especially since they sometimes invited me to Sunday dinner. (Having any of them might not have been much of a boon. They had leg of lamb while we always had a standing beef rib roast - it made for variety. Sue and I were in the same Sunday school class with Miss Gilchrist, a maiden lady who lived next door to her sister, Mrs. Fought and Mrs. Fought's husband and daughter, Amy Lou. The sisters had gone to the church since the year one and were pillars. They entertained their Sunday school classes in their homes and their Women's Guild had us bring our puppet-marionette show to one of their meetings which we did and received many accolades for our talented troupe. I don't know what got into me, but I tore the leaves of one of those spiny long-leaf plants right down the middle where there was an inviting crease, in a fit of great temptation. They probably wondered how on earth it happened, but you're the only one I've ever told. The meeting was held at Mrs. Muysken's. She was the wife of the minister which made it doubly naughty. (Remember, I had that streak in me that caused me to be spanked on my birthday.)

Miss Gilchrist had us memorize Bible verses and after each successful attempt Miss Gilchrist would give us a sticker of Jesus' head which I put in my Bible. I ran across the very same when we were emptying out 2045 Mallard Drive and felt a little abashed to see that I only had three. Maybe I lost some. The hardest one was John 1,1-15: "In the beginning was the Word, and the Word was with God, and the Word was God. He was in the beginning with God, all things were made through him, and without him was not anything made that was made. Etc.,etc.,etc." We were never told that this was John's version of the birth of Christ, just to memorize it. It certainly was not like the Luke version that's so popular and it wasn't until many years later that I found the explanation. Also lacking was any clue at all about who or what the Holy Ghost was. I'd never even heard of the Holy Spirit or Pentecost. I wonder if Presbyterians still conjure up visions of Halloween figures dressed in their mothers' sheets with holes cut out for their eyes in their Sunday school classes.

In time various members of the Kelley family joined the Presbyterian Church and of course I thought it would be a good idea to do the same. They were becoming active and respected members of the congregation. But when I said something to my father about this latest wrinkle he did not particularly give the idea his blessing, but instead asked me to go to church, the R.C.L.D.S, with him on Sundays. In truth he was something of an on again off again member and at that particular time he was on. I don't remember that anyone else in our family was really any kind of a church-goer at the time, although Carl may have given it a try.

All of this lasted long enough for me to know it was not for me. My father drifted into one of his off again periods so the whole idea was dropped. Strangely, he had some high designation in the Church, even giving sermons on occasion. Aunt Clara remained a faithful member, and built a cottage at Deer Park as did Aunt Lil and my grandparents. (Uncle Jim Fligg's father was very big in the Church (R.C.L..D.S.) My cousin, Lucile Hoxie, she of the Kennedy-like compound on Cape Cod, married Ben Fleet, who is now a Bishop in their Church. I imagine most of their family are members too. Ben came down from the Cape to officiate at my father's funeral. Did a good job, too. I don't remember who did my mother's service. I just remember David Z. at the organ playing the theme music from Star Trek and Mary Ann with her sweet, sweet voice singing a lullaby, surprising us all, and almost breaking up the show. Both my father's and my mother's funerals were in the new R.C.L.D.S. church, a very nice venue.

In college I gave the Presbyterians another go. It seemed a good and appropriate thing to do on Sundays and besides one of my good friends usually went. That, too, petered out.

# 4

## Clara[2] Zimmermann and Her Descendants

**1. CLARA[2] ZIMMERMANN,**[2] eldest daughter and first child of John and Eva Katherine (Kellenbenz) Zimmermann, was born at Philadelphia, Pa., 20 July 1886. She was baptized at the Reorganized Church of Latter Day Saints (RLDS Church) in Philadelphia on 30 March 1902. She died at Philadelphia, 19 October 1968, and was buried at Greenmount Cemetery on North Front Street in Philadelphia, adjacent to the graves of her sister Emily and her parents.[3]

Clara went to Girl's High School in Philadelphia and she then studied Domestic Science at Drexel. All of John and Eva Zimmermann's daughters became piano players, but Clara was the "most professional." Clara had a private teacher for music studies and was a gifted keyboard artist on both the organ and piano. She studied at the Julliard School of Music in New York City, and she played the organ for the formal dedication of the new RLDS Church at Ontario and Howard Streets. On the weekend of the dedication, Joseph Smith III, son of Joseph Smith, Jr., First Prophet of the LDS Church, and Joseph III's son Frederick were given a tour of Philadelphia by Clara's mother. Clara was John Zimmermann's favorite child. When she was married, he purchased for her the north half of a duplex at 3119 N. 16th St., adjacent to his home at 1512 Allegheny Ave.[4] The house was unusual in that its main entrance was located on the long northern side of the house and not on the street front. Clara's father's house thus could easily be accessed by her. "He adored her and he in turn remained perhaps the most important man in her life."[5]

Clara's journal shows that in 1910 (from 2 June to 10 September) she went on a three month cruise, visiting the Azores, Gibraltar, Italy, Switzerland, Germany, France and England. She arrived back in Philadelphia aboard the *Friesland* and was greeted by "Momma, Poppa, sister [Anna], brother, John Jr., and 'Mae'."[6] In 1930, she traveled to Europe with her husband, Albert N. Hoxie, Jr., and their children, Clara, John, and Lucille. They returned on 14 July on the S.S. *Bremen* from Cherbourg, France. They then continued to Boston for a visit at Cape Cod.[7] Hoxie, now a "music director," was no longer connected to the Zimmermann family's business operations. However, as a result of John Zimmermann's gifts to Clara, the Hoxies were able to take a family trip to Europe, and to spend the rest of their summer at their place on Cape Cod. Clara Hoxie later advanced $540 to the RLDS Church to pay for outstanding obligations at Deer Park, after the Philadelphia bank which held the RLDS account collapsed.[8]

She married, at the home of her father, 1512 West Allegheny Ave., Philadelphia, on 10 October 1911, **Albert Nickerson HOXIE, Jr.**, son of Albert Nickerson and Aravilla (Follet) Hoxie; born at Boston, Mass., 3 September 1884; died at East Sandwich, Mass., 20 August 1942.[9] He was a descendant in the 9th generation from an early settler of Sandwich, Mass., whose surname was Hoxie. The ancestral Hoxie home in Sandwich, which dates to about 1630, is preserved as the "Sandwich Hoxie House."

Hoxie was initially a sales representative for the Philadelphia Tapestry Mills, and the other textile mills that were owned and operated by John Zimmermann and the Wasserman brothers. However, his skill and interests were greater as a musician and music director, and he soon drifted away from the family business to make a career in music. He was supported by Clara's money, until it ran out. He formed the "Hoxie Messiah Choir" which performed in 1916, and thereafter, at the RLDS Church. He led many public "Community Sings" in Philadelphia. A photograph taken on 1 July 1917 shows him leading thousands in song, soon after the U.S. entered the Great War.  He led a "Liberty Sing" at the Philadelphia Navy Yard in the winter of 1917-1918.  His choir was photographed again in 1922.  In the 1920s, he formed the Philadelphia Harmonica Band, with 60 boys in military-style uniforms, who traveled widely across America.  The Harmonica Band played for Presidents Coolidge and Hoover, and at one time its guest conductor was John Phillips Sousa.  Hoxie is said to have been responsible for harmonica's popularity at that time, and for the inadvertent success of the Hohner Co., which was the leading harmonica maker of Germany (and later the Third Reich).  In 1938, Hoxie formed his own company to manufacture harmonicas.  The life of Albert N. Hoxie, Jr., has recently been profiled in three YouTube videos.  These videos include photographs of John Zimmermann and his other children, as well as many of the Hoxie family.[10]

Albert and Clara (Zimmermann) Hoxie had the following children:

| | | |
|---|---|---|
| **1.1** | i. | ALBERT NICKERSON[3], III, "Albo" (1914-2003) + |
| **1.2** | ii. | JOHN ZIMMERMANN (1917-1984) + |
| **1.3** | iii. | EDITH LUCILLE "Cil" (1919-2007) + |

# Clara[2] (Zimmermann) Hoxie and Her Descendants

## Albert Nickerson[3] Hoxie, III, and His Descendants

**1.1 ALBERT NICKERSON[3] "Albo" HOXIE, III,** elder son and first child of Albert Nickerson [Jr.] and Clara (Zimmermann) Hoxie, was born 31 August 1914; died in Philadelphia, Pa., 24 January 2003; buried 1 February 2003, Willow Grove, Pa.  He was the eldest of John and Eva Zimmermann's 23 grandchildren.  At his funeral on 1 February 2003 at Bryer's Funeral Home, Willow Grove, Pa., he was described as a "Teacher, student, scholar, musician, photographer, pilot, athlete, technophile, and so much more."  His principal athletic interests were golf and tennis.  He played many musical instruments, and a recording of him performing his composition, "Nikki," was played at the end of the service.  The service was organized by his only child, James Hoxie, M.D.  It was coordinated by Bishop Edward Lee, husband of Albo's cousin, Kathryn "Katchie" (Fligg) Lee.  Reflections were provided by friends and family members, including his son and daughter-in-law, Jim and Dory Hoxie, and their three children, Brooke, Christopher, and Julie.

He married **Geraldine "Jean" WENNER**, who died in about Jan 2000.  They were divorced after the birth of their child.

Albert N. and Geraldine (Wenner) Hoxie had one child, surname Hoxie:

| | | |
|---|---|---|
| **1.1.1** | i. | Dr. JAMES[4] "Jim" + |

**1.1.1 JAMES[4] "Jim" HOXIE, M.D.,**[11] married **Doris Ann "Dee" "Dory" D'ORAZIO**, born in 1948.  Physician; chief of AIDS research at the U. of Penna. School of Medicine in 2003.  They had the following children, surname Hoxie:

| | | |
|---|---|---|
| **1.1.1.1** | i. | BROOKE[5], b. 1979; in 2003 she was a graduate of James Madison University and was teaching elementary school in eastern Pennsylvania; developed a genealogical chart showing that she is in the 12th generation of a Hoxie emigrant who was one of the first English settlers on Cape Cod; original Hoxie house in Sandwich, Mass., is still standing; Hoxie Pond in Sandwich, Mass., is named for the emigrant ancestor. |
| **1.1.1.2** | ii. | CHRISTOPHER JAMES, b. 1982. |
| **1.1.1.3** | iii. | JULIA "Julie", b. 1986. |

## John Zimmermann[3] Hoxie and His Descendants

**1.2 JOHN ZIMMERMANN[3] HOXIE**, second son and second child of Albert Nickerson [Jr.] and Clara (Zimmermann) Hoxie, was born in 1917; died in 1984. He married **Mary Joyce LEWIS**, born in 1922; died in 1996.

John and Mary Joyce (Lewis) Hoxie had the following children, surname Hoxie:

| | | |
|---|---|---|
| **1.2.1** | i. | MARY JANE[4] (1944- ) + |
| **1.2.2** | ii. | JEANETTE (1947-<2015) + |
| **1.2.3** | iii. | JEAN (1947-2011) + |
| **1.2.4** | iv. | JOANN (1950- ) + |

**1.2.1 MARY JANE[4] HOXIE,** born 1944; married **Eugene L. CRUMP, Jr.**, born 1941; child, surname Crump:

> **1.2.1.1**      i.      LINDSAY JOANN[5], b. 1969; m. **Damoe PORZIO**; child, surname Porzio:
> **1.2.1.1.1**   i.   SARA[6], b. 1995.

**1.2.2 JEANETTE[4] HOXIE,** born 1947, probably a twin of Jean; died before 2015; married **Roger Creighton FIELD**, born 1946; one child, surname Field:

> **1.2.2.1**      i.      HEATHER[5], b. 1968; m. (1) **Brendon Joseph CARLIN**; m. (2) **Doug CARLTON**; 2 ch., surname Carlin:
> **1.2.2.1.1**   i.   TAYLOR ANNE[6], b. 1992.
> **1.2.2.1.2**   ii.   MADISON FIELD, b. 1995

**1.2.3 JEAN[4] HOXIE,** born 25 October 1947; died 4 March 2011, Carteret, N.C. She compiled much of the information recorded in this book about the Zimmermann Family in America. Jean (Hoxie) Naples's contributions also included assembling the charts for the Zimmermann Family in Württemberg. She also obtained from Kathy Brandt Bonnell the names of many of the descendants in six generations from Johann Michael[F] Zimmermann (b.c. 1682) to Johann Georg[C] Zimmermann (1768-1835), great-grandfather of John[1] Zimmermann, the emigrant.[12] Jean (Hoxie) Naples developed a 28-page typescript that included the time line for John[1] Zimmermann and his family from 28 November 1855 – December 1963, and she collected information from many others. Her legacy includes the 28-page typescript and a 1-inch thick file of photos and maps, annotated in her careful handwriting. I am grateful to her for her work and her file, which she thoughtfully sent to me about two years before she died. She married (1) **Barry Ward WILLIS**, born 1941; two children; after he died, she married (2) **John R. NAPLES,** born 1936.

Barry and Jean (Hoxie) Willis had the following children, surname Willis:

> **1.2.3.1**      i.      ZACK DRIVER[5], b. 1973.
> **1.2.3.2**      ii.      POPPY ANN, b. and d., 1975.

**1.2.4 JOANN[4] HOXIE,** born 1950; married (1) **Paul Kevin MAGUIRE**; three children; married (2) **Pat DEVLIN**.

Paul and Joann (Hoxie) Maguire had the following children, surname Maguire:

> **1.2.4.1**      i.      BRIAN McLAUGHLIN[5], b. 1978.
> **1.2.4.2**      ii.      GREGORY LEWIS, b. 1982.
> **1.2.4.3**      iii.      EMILY JANE, b. 1984

## Edith Lucille[3] Hoxie and Her Descendants

**1.3  EDITH LUCILLE[3] "Cil" HOXIE,** daughter and third child of Albert Nickerson [Jr.] and Clara (Zimmermann) Hoxie, was born in 1919; died in 2007.  Her grandfather, John Zimmermann, Sr., was photographed in 1923, holding "Cil."  Her mother often brought her to Cape Cod in the summer to escape from the heat of the city.[13]  She married **Benjamin D. FLEET**, born in 1920.

Benjamin and Edith Lucille "Cil" (Hoxie) Fleet had the following children, surname Fleet:

| | | |
|---|---|---|
| **1.3.1** | i. | DONALD JAMES[4] (1944-) + |
| **1.3.2** | ii. | JOHN WILLIAM (1947-) + |
| **1.3.3** | iii. | SUZANNE KATHRYN (1952-) + |
| **1.3.4** | iv. | KENNETH BENJAMIN (1954-1965) |
| **1.3.5** | v. | RICHARD NELSON (1955-) |

**1.3.1  DONALD JAMES[4] FLEET,** born 1944, married **Nancy Ann SCHAEGEL**, born 1946. Donald and Nancy (Schaegel) Fleet had the following children, surname Fleet:

| | | |
|---|---|---|
| **1.3.1.1** | i. | WENDY ALYSON[5] (1971-) |
| **1.3.1.2** | ii. | ALISSA ANN (1973-) |
| **1.3.1.3** | iii. | BENJAMIN DAVID (1975-) |

**1.3.2  JOHN WILLIAM[4] FLEET,** born in 1947, married **Donna WOOD**, born in 1948. John and Donna (Wood) Fleet had the following children, surname Fleet:

| | | |
|---|---|---|
| **1.3.2.1** | i. | TRACEY[5] (1969-) |
| **1.3.2.2** | ii. | CAROLYN (1973-) |

**1.3.3  SUZANNE KATHRYN[4] FLEET,** born in 1952, married **Daniel Lynn McMILLAN,** born in 1955. They were divorced.  Daniel and Suzanne (Fleet) McMillan had the following children, surname McMillan:

| | | |
|---|---|---|
| **1.3.3.1** | i. | BETH LAUREN[5] (1980-) |
| **1.3.3.2** | ii. | SCOTT DAVID (1983-<2009) |
| **1.3.3.3** | iii. | KATHRYN ANNE (1986-) |

**1.3.4  KENNETH BENJAMIN[4] FLEET,** born in 1954; died in 1965.

**1.3.5  RICHARD NELSON[4] FLEET,** born in 1955, married **Candice DAVIS**, born in 1953.

# 5

## Anna[2] Zimmermann and Her Descendants

**2. ANNA[2] ZIMMERMANN,**[14] second daughter and second of the seven children of John and Eva Katherine (Kellenbenz) Zimmermann, was born at Philadelphia, Pa., 25 December 1887; died at Abington Memorial Hospital, Abington, Pa., 7 August 1974.

Anna Zimmermann was educated at the Philadelphia Normal School and at the University of Pennsylvania, where she was a member of the Kappa Kappa Gamma sorority. She took additional courses at the Philadelphia Academy of the Fine Arts. She was a teacher in the Philadelphia elementary schools and was editor of Sunday School quarterlies of the Reorganized Church of Latter Day Saints (RLDS Church). Her interests included flower gardening, the Philadelphia Orchestra, and knitting. She enjoyed painting oils of still life and landscapes, and she was president of the Cheltenham Township School District PTA. She was later a Sunday School teacher and member of the Women's Association of the Grace Presbyterian Church. Her funeral services were conducted there prior to burial at the Lawnview Cemetery, Rockledge, Pennsylvania. She married, at her parents' home, 1512 Allegheny Ave., Philadelphia, 10 August 1915, **Richard Carlyle KELLEY**, son of Edmund Levi and Catherine (Bishop) Kelley; born at Coldwater, Mich., 30 September 1882; died at Abington, Pa., 7 April 1976, and was buried at Lawnview Cemetery, Rockledge, Pa.

**RICHARD CARLYLE KELLEY,**[15] third son and third child of Edmund Levi and Catherine (Bishop) Kelley, of Lamoni, Iowa, was born at Coldwater, Michigan, 30 September 1882; died at Abington, Pennsylvania, 7 April 1976. His father was an educator, lawyer and bishop of the Reorganized Church of Latter Day Saints. As an RLDS bishop, Edmund L. Kelley was one of the men who laid hands on John[1] Zimmermann when John became a bishop. Edmund and Catherine Kelley moved several times during their lives. After their marriage in Malvern, Iowa, they lived in Glenwood, Iowa; Kirtland, Ohio; and Lamoni, Iowa. They lived in Independence, Missouri, for many years, and it was there that they died.

Richard Kelley was educated at Graceland College for two years and then attended the University of Iowa, from which he received the B.S. degree in 1903. He did graduate work in the College of Education at the University of Chicago, and he received the M.A. from the Teachers College at Columbia University in 1918. He was a teacher from 1903 until 1917. For two years, from 1903-1905, he organized and was a principal of trade schools in the Philippine Islands. He later installed the manual training departments in the Ottumwa and Sioux City, Iowa, high schools. He met Anna Zimmermann when she came with her parents to a meeting of the RLDS church in Iowa. When he and Anna were married, he was superintendent of manual training in the Iowa City high school and instructor of manual training at the University of Iowa. In 1917, he and Anna returned to Pennsylvania. In 1919 he became a partner with his brother-in-law, William Zimmermann, in the development of a family upholstery manufacturing company, John Zimmermann & Sons. The business prospered and provided well for the family. It was sold in December 1963. Mr. Kelley was a member of the Cheltenham Township School Board from 1928-1952 and of the Cheltenham Township School Authority from 1952-1966. He was a volunteer in United Way campaigns, and he enjoyed golf, gardening, and the Shakespeare Club. Although he had been active as a leader in the Philadelphia Branch of the RLDS, in later life, he and his wife were members of the Grace Presbyterian Church in Abington, Pa.

Richard and Anna (Zimmermann) Kelley had seven children. Their eldest child was born at Iowa City, Ia., and the third at Melrose Park, Pa.; the rest were born at Philadelphia. All lived to maturity except Nancy, who died of aplastic anemia.

Richard and Anna[2] (Zimmermann) Kelley had the following children:

| | | |
|---|---|---|
| **2.1** | i. | JOAN CATHERINE[3] (1916-2011) + |
| **2.2** | ii. | RICHARD CARLYLE (1919-2000) + |
| **2.3** | iii. | SUSAN DOROTHEA (1920-2002) + |
| **2.4** | iv. | MARIAN (1921-) + |
| **2.5** | v. | ANITA (1923-) + |
| **2.6** | vi. | DONALD EDMUND (1925-2014) + |
| **2.7** | vii. | JANET NANCY (1927-1938) |

# Anna[2] (Zimmermann) Kelley and Her Descendants

## Joan Catherine[3] Kelley and Her Descendants

**2.1 JOAN CATHERINE[3] KELLEY,**[16] eldest child of Richard Carlyle and Anna (Zimmermann) Kelley, was born at Iowa City, Iowa, 11 May 1916; died 19 September 2011 in West Chester, Pa. She was the first granddaughter of John and Eva Katherine (Kellenbenz) Zimmermann. She attended Cheltenham, Pa., high school from 1929-1933, and after graduation there, she attended Swarthmore College from 1933-1937. She was awarded the B.A. from Swarthmore, and then did a year of graduate study at the Cooperative School for Teachers in New York City. She taught third grade in private schools in Akron, Ohio, and Greenwich, Conn. She was married in 1940 to a physician, Dr. Ward Fowler, and had two children. They lived in Rochester, Minn., where he was on the staff of the Mayo Clinic. After her younger son reached high school, she joined the Rochester Reading Center to tutor dyslexic children in reading and spelling. She taught classes of elementary and junior high school students in the Rochester Public Schools at the Quarry Hill Nature Center, and she was a board member of the center. She was also active in the startup of a birding group in Rochester, which later became affiliated with the Minnesota Ornithologists Union and the National Audubon Society. In September 2000, she moved to Kendal at Longwood, in Kennett Square, Pa. A celebration of her life was held there on 1 October 2011.

She married, at Elkins Park, Pa., 3 September 1940, **Ward Scott FOWLER, M.D.,** son of John Joseph and Leila (Moore) Fowler; born at Summerfield, Kansas, 23 October 1915; died at Rochester, Minnesota, 23 February 1982. Ward and Joan (Kelley) Fowler had two children: Robert Scott (b. 1947); and Thomas Richard (b. 1953).

**WARD SCOTT FOWLER, M.D.,**[17] was educated at Swarthmore College, where he was a classmate of Joan Catherine Kelley. He received the B.S. in 1937, and he then attend the Harvard Medical School and received the M.D. in 1941. He was a captain in the U.S. Air Force medical corps from 1941-1945. He then studied lung function at the Pennsylvania Graduate School of Medicine with Dr. Julius Comroe. In 1952, he joined the Mayo Clinic as a pulmonologist and continued his research on pulmonary function. He was associate dean for academic affairs at the Mayo Medical School from 1969-1976.

Ward and Joan (Kelley) Fowler had the following children, surname Fowler:

**2.1.1**   i.   ROBERT SCOTT[4] (1947- )
**2.1.2**   ii.   THOMAS RICHARD (1953- )

**2.1.1 ROBERT SCOTT[4] FOWLER**,[18] born 20 March 1947, Abington, Pa..; married **Ellen T.**

**2.1.2 THOMAS RICHARD[4] FOWLER**,[19] born 12 April 1953, Rochester Minn.

### Richard Carlyle[3] Kelley and His Descendants

**2.2 RICHARD CARLYLE[3] KELLEY, Jr.**,[20] eldest son and second child of Richard Carlyle and Anna (Zimmermann) Kelley, was born at Philadelphia, Pa., 17 March 1919; died in Pennsylvania, 14 September 2000. He attended the B. R. Myers School and in 1936 he graduated from Cheltenham High School, where he was a member of the wrestling team. He became an Eagle Scout while he was in high school, and he then attended Lehigh University for four years and received the B.S. in chemical engineering in 1940. He belonged to Delta Upsilon and the ROTC while in college, and he was named in *Who's Who in Colleges of America* in 1940. He worked for DuPont Chemical before being called into active duty as an Army Ordnance Supply Officer attached to the Air Force. He served in India and Burma for three years and was honorably discharged with the rank of captain in 1944.[21] From 1944 to 1963 Mr. Kelley was employed in the sales department of John Zimmermann & Sons of Philadelphia, an upholstery and carpet manufacturing company founded by his grandfather, his father and three of his uncles. As the Midwest sales representative for John Zimmermann & Sons for nineteen years, he was probably the only grandchild of John Zimmermann, and the only one of the 23 Zimmermann cousins, to be active in the family textile businesses. In July-August 1965 he took the Registered Representative securities course at Paine Webber in New York City. From 1965-1984 he was a Registered Representative in securities in Philadelphia. He enjoyed bee keeping and fishing and he was a volunteer with the Wyncote Civic Association. He was also active with the Wyncote Men's Club, the Lehigh Alumni Association, the Morris Arboretum, Grace Presbyterian Church, and the Pennsylvania Beekeepers Association. He held a small-aircraft license and had a great love for flying. He died at the age of eighty-one. Services were held at Grace Presbyterian Church, Old York and Visla Road, Jenkintown, Pennsylvania, on 22 September 2000.

He married (1), at Westfield, New Jersey, 9 September 1944, **Jeanne Hope ADAMS**,[22] daughter of James Earl and Florence (Smith) Adams; born 30 September 1920; died in 1987, after a stroke. After she died, he married (2), at Wyncote, Pennsylvania, 16 April 1988, as her second husband, **Mrs. Janet (BEST) CREIGHTON**, daughter of Arthur Conrad and Emily (Knodel) Best; born at Brooklyn, New York, 10 March 1919.

Richard [Jr.] and Jeanne (Adams) Kelley had the following children; 1st born Memphis, Tenn.; 2-5 born Abington, Pa.; surname Kelley:

**2.2.1**   i.   Dr. NANCY HOPE[4] (1945- ) ?+
**2.2.2**   ii.   LINDSAY ANN (1946- ) ?+
**2.2.3**   iii.   WENDY ADAMS (1950- ) ?+
**2.2.4**   iv.   LAURA EILEEN (1951- )
**2.2.5**   v.   STACY VALENTINE "Giza" (1953- )

Richard (Jr.) and Jeanne (Adams) Kelley had nine grandchildren (**2.2.?.1 – 2.2.?.9**).[23]

**2.2.1** **NANCY HOPE**[4] **KELLEY, M.D.**, born 15 October 1945; lived in Warren, Seattle, Wash.; married (1) **Jay V. WHITE**; she married (2) **Warren WATSON**.[24]

**2.2.2** **LINDSAY ANN**[4] **KELLEY**, born 7 December 1946; lived in Rochester, N.Y.; married **Robert S. HOLMES**.

**2.2.3** **WENDY ADAMS**[4] **KELLEY**, born 9 March 1950; lived in Seattle, Wash.; married **Richard W. BORTON**.

**2.2.4** **LAURA EILEEN**[4] **KELLEY**, born 28 February 1951; lived in Rochester, N.Y.; married **Gary HAAG**; they were divorced and she resumed her maiden name.[25]

**2.2.5** **STACY VALENTINE**[4] **"Giza" KELLEY,** born 30 Apr 1953; lived in Whitefish, Mont.

### Susan Dorothea[3] Kelley and Her Descendants

**2.3 SUSAN DORTHEA**[3] **KELLEY,**[26] second daughter and third child of Richard Carlyle and Anna (Zimmermann) Kelley, was born at Melrose Park, Pa., 2 October 1920; died at Kendal at Longwood, near Philadelphia, Pa., 21 October 2002. Her cousin Mary Jane (Zimmermann) Clark later recalled her childhood, when five young girl cousins played together:

#### Early Friendships[1]
Over the years I've had some very good friends. Certain cousins could always be so designated from day one: Marian, Anita and especially **Sue Kelley** and Lucile Hoxie. I spent a lot of time with them. I know Sue and Marian were at the famous birthday party when my mother took me upstairs and spanked me - right in the bathroom over my guests - I'm sure I was doing something insufferable or completely thoughtless of my guests, but did she have to entertain them in this way? It probably didn't do much good, either.

Susan Dorothea Kelley was educated at the B. R. Myers Grammar School and graduated from Cheltenham, Pa., High School in 1938. She attended Oberlin College and the Oberlin Conservatory of Music from 1938-1942. After marriage in November 1942, she and her husband lived in Washington, D.C., while he served with the War Shipping Administration. After the war ended, they lived in Summit, N.J., for several years, at which time he worked as Director of Planning for the United States Lines Shipping Co. in New York City. After he joined his brother in the family packaging business, they returned to the Philadelphia suburbs.

They later moved to Braebourne Farms, Piperville, in a rural area of Bucks Co., Pa., near the Delaware River. Their old fieldstone farmhouse was artfully restored and expanded for modern living, and the rolling grassy hills of the farm provided a beautiful pastoral view in every

---

[1] Mary Jane (Zimmermannn) Clark, "Mom's Stories" (Ibid.) Emphasis added.

season. She enjoyed gardening, tennis, playing the piano, and reading. She was active in hospital volunteer work, and was a leader of the junior choir and Sunday School teacher in her church. She continued to travel, and took a vacation trip to Antarctica in 1993.

She married, at Jenkintown, Pa., at Grace Presbyterian Church, 14 November 1942, **Joseph Wallace CARNWATH**, son of Robert and Margaret (Wallace) Carnwath; born at Jenkintown, 21 May 1913; died in Pennsylvania, 25 June 1983. He was an admiralty lawyer who later became the chief executive officer of the family firm, which he had developed into the Pennsylvania Pacific Corporation. Joseph and Susan (Kelley) Carnwath had two sons, born at Abington, Pennsylvania: Joseph Wallace, Jr. (b. 1944); and Richard Kelley (b. 1948). At the time that Susan (Carnwath) Kelley died, they also had five grandchildren and one great-grandchild.

**JOSEPH WALLACE CARNWATH**, son of Robert and Margaret (Wallace) Carnwath, was born at Jenkintown, Pa., 21 May 1913; died 25 June 1983. He attended the William Penn Charter School and then the Wharton School of the University of Pennsylvania, from which he graduated in 1935. He then attended law school at the University of Pennsylvania and received the LL.B. there in 1938. He was an admiralty lawyer who later became the CEO of the Pennsylvania Pacific Corporation, a packaging company.

Joe Carnwath joined the Pennsylvania National Guard in 1941. He was mobilized into the U.S. Army after the outbreak of World War II, and rose to the rank of captain. He served with the War Shipping Administration until he was released from active duty in 1945. He was active in church and civic affairs, serving as an elder in the Presbyterian Church, and as chairman of the Zoning Hearing Board of Tinicum Township, Bucks Co. Pa. He enjoyed overseeing work on his farm, reading, and playing the piano. Perhaps his most noteworthy attribute was the courageous demeanor with which he accepted the devastating diagnosis of multiple sclerosis while he was in his late forties. He wore leg braces to keep his feet from dragging, walked with two canes, and operated his automobile with hand controls. In spite of his disability, he led an active and satisfying life.

Joseph and Susan (Kelley) Carnwath had the following children, born at Abington Memorial Hospital, Abington, Pa., surname Carnwath:

|  |  |  |
|---|---|---|
| **2.3.1** | i. | Dr. JOSEPH WALLACE[4], Jr. (1944- ) + |
| **2.3.2** | ii. | RICHARD KELLEY (1948- ) + |

**2.3.1  JOSEPH WALLACE[4] CARNWATH, Jr., Ph.D.,**[27] born 13 January 1944; received his Bachelor's degree from Yale in 1966, M.S. from Lehigh in 1976, and Ph.D., Cambridge University (England), 1983. He was a volunteer in the Peace Corps in the Western Caroline Islands, 1966-1969; production manager of the Pennsylvania Pacific Corporation, Warminster, Pa., 1970-72; and research assistant, department of biology, Lehigh University, 1975-6. He went to England in 1967 to study at Cambridge University, where he enjoyed rowing as well as studying. After he received his Ph.D. in 1983, he was a scientist in the department of zoology at Oxford University from 1983-7. He was then a career scientist with the German Department of Agriculture (*Bundesministerium für Ernährung und Landwirtschaft*) at the Fraunhofer Institute, Hannover, Germany, from 1987 until he retired in 2009.
He recalled in 2016 that,

> Our most interesting project at the Institute was genetically altering pigs to provide spare parts for humans. We were the first to perform a double knockout (homozygous) transgenic pig for that

purpose - removing the Alpha 1, 3-galactosyltransferase gene which causes a strong rejection reaction in humans. Looking back, I see that I moved from electron microscopic analysis of single cells, to light microscopic studies of mice and eventually to genetic manipulation of large farm animals.

He married, 16 May 1970, **Susan Smiley CASPARI,** born 17 February 1947; they were divorced in 1995. Soon after they were married, she left college to become a ballet dancer in New York, and she ran her own ballet school while they were living in Pennsylvania. After they were divorced, she finished her undergraduate degree and then moved to Cambridge, England.

From 1997-2012, Joseph W. Carnwath, Jr., lived in Hannover, Germany, with his *Lebensabschnittsgefährte,*[28] **Sigrun Kalk KLOEPFER.** She died in 2012 of pancreatic cancer. Sigrun's two children from previous marriages, Niklas – a banker in New York – and Anna – a physician in Switzerland – have children of their own, and Joseph Carnwath is "considered to be grandfather by their children."

Joseph and Susan (Caspari) Carnwath had three children, surname Carnwath:

2.3.1.1    i.    JOSEPH "Joey" CASPARI[5], b. 1972; a professional musician, living in Sweden; plays guitar in Rock 'n' Roll music with his brother as "The Rockhouse Brothers" in Germany; m. **Sara HEDEN**; 3 ch., surname Carnwath[29]:

> 2.3.1.1.1   i. KATE SARA[6] (2007-).
> 2.3.1.1.2   ii. SILVIA GABRIELLE (2010- ).
> 2.3.1.1.3   iii. CHRISTOPHER JOSEPH (2014- ).

2.3.1.2    ii.    JAMES WALLACE[5], b. 1976; a professional musician in Germany, playing contrabass with his brother in "The Rockhouse Brothers"; unm.; one son:

> 2.3.1.2.1   i. BO JAMES[6] von MINDEN (1998- ).[30]

2.3.1.3    iii.    Dr. JOHN DOUGLAS[5], b. 1980; undergraduate and master's degrees at U Cal. Santa Barbara; Ph.D., Northwestern U.; doctoral dissertation on funding of theatre and the arts in Germany during the 18th and 19th centuries; works in San Francisco with a firm that advises charities, and theaters and museums looking for funding; will go with his family to Palau in summer of 2016 to help some of his father's former Peace Corps students to obtain crown funding in order to document canoe-building technology before the skills are lost; m. **Julie SCANLIN**; 2 ch., surname Carnwath[31]:

> 2.3.1.3.1.   i. BARNABY BEMAR[6] (2013- ).
> 2.3.1.3.2   ii. HENRY THEODORE (2016- ).

**2.3.2   RICHARD KELLEY[4] CARNWATH,** born 13 July 1971; married **Roberta Anne CARLSON,** born 2 October 1945; they are divorced; two children, surname Carnwath:

2.3.2.1    i.    KELLEY MacDONALD[5], b. 1976; B.A. 1998, Trinity Coll., Hartford, Conn., International Studies; M.P.H., Univ. Alabama at Birmingham, 2004, in International Health; graduate of National Outdoor Leadership School (NOLS); she is active in crew and community service; in 2016 was at Qualis Health, Seattle, Wa.; unm.[32]

2.3.2.2    ii.    Dr. GUNNAR CARLSON[5], b. 1978; Ph.D. in forestry, Univ. Montana; works for U.S. Forest Service; will move from Baker City, Ore., to Bozeman, Mont., in 2016; m. **Brooke HEWES**; 2 ch., surname Carnwath[33]:

> 2.3.2.2.1   i. GRACE KELLEY[6] (2013-).
> 2.3.2.2.2   ii. CEDAR ROSE (2015- ).

## Marian[3] Kelley and Her Descendants

**2.4 MARIAN[3] KELLEY,**[34] third daughter and fourth child of Richard Carlyle and Anna (Zimmermann) Kelley, was born at Philadelphia, Pa., 29 October 1921. She was educated at the B. R. Myers grammar school and Cheltenham, Pa., High School. She graduated from Oberlin College in 1943 with the B.A. degree. In 1994 she was living in Carrboro, N.C., where she enjoyed reading, swimming, movies, and psychology. She married, at Elkins Park, Pa., 8 September 1943, **William H. POTEAT**, son of Edwin McNeill and Wilda (Hardman) Poteat, Jr.; born at Keifeng, China, 19 April 1919; died at Durham, N.C., 17 May 2000. William and Marian (Kelley) Poteat had three children. They later separated and were divorced, and he married (2) Patricia Lewis, in 1980.

**Professor WILLIAM HARDMAN "Bill" POTEAT**, Ph.D.[35] philosopher and scholar, was the son of Edwin McNeill and Wilda (Hardman) Poteat, Jr. His parents were Baptist missionaries, and his father later was president of Colgate-Rochester Divinity School. His grandfather, Edwin MacNeill Poteat, Sr., was president of Furman University, and his great uncle, Dr. William Louis Poteat, was president of what is now Wake Forest University. William H. Poteat attended Oberlin College, from which he received the B.A. in 1941 (Phi Beta Kappa) and Yale Divinity School, which awarded him the B.D. in 1944. He did graduate work at Duke University, where he received the Ph.D. in 1950. He was a professor of philosophy, religion, and culture at the University of North Carolina at Chapel Hill from 1947, and was a professor of religion and philosophy at Duke University from 1960 until his retirement in 1987. He was a charismatic and very popular instructor, using the Socratic method of teaching. Bill Poteat received many honors, including Outstanding Teacher at the University of North Carolina in 1955, and election to the National Faculty of the Humanities in 1969. His work was instrumental in the intellectual culture of post-modernism in America, which he called "Post-Critical." His papers are archived at the Yale Divinity School Library. His funeral was held at the chapel at Duke University in May 2000, and he was honored by a festschrift, the William H. Poteat Conference, at Yale on 23 November 2014. At that time, the keynote address was given by Bruce Lawrence. The symposium was recorded on YouTube, entitled "Who Was William H. Poteat."

William and Marian (Kelley) Poteat had children, born at Durham, N.C., surname Poteat:

| | | |
|---|---|---|
| **2.4.1** | i. | ANNE CARLYLE[4] (1946- ) |
| **2.4.2** | ii. | SUSAN COLQUITT (1947- ) |
| **2.4.3** | iii. | EDWIN McNEILL, III (1950- ) |

**2.4.1 ANNE CARLYLE[4] POTEAT**, born in 1946 at Durham, N.C.; married, 1 April 1978, Chapel Hill, N.C., **Verne DREGALLA;** divorced 24 August 1987, Durham, N.C.

**2.4.2 SUSAN COLQUITT[4] POTEAT**, born 9 December 1947; married 20 December 1969, Chapel Hill, N.C., **John C. UHLER.**

**2.4.3 EDWIN McNEILL[4] POTEAT, III,** born 13 September 1950; married 21 December 1974, Chapel Hill, N.C., **Martha L. KIRBY**

## Anita[3] Kelley and Her Descendants

**2.5 ANITA[3] KELLEY,**[36] fourth daughter and fifth child of Richard Carlyle and Anna (Zimmermann) Kelley, was born at Philadelphia, Penna., 15 March 1923. She attended the Benjamin R. Myers Grammar School in Philadelphia and graduated from Cheltenham, Pa., High School. She then attended Swarthmore College, from which she received the B.A. degree in 1944. She took postgraduate courses at Radcliffe College in the spring of 1946 and 1947. Following her marriage she moved to California, where her husband was on the faculty of the University of California at Berkeley, and where they raised their family. She was a research associate in biology at the university in the field of comparative endocrinology, specializing in the development and morphology of the pituitary glands of cold-blooded vertebrates. She also did field work in mammalogy with her husband in South America. She was a community service volunteer and she enjoyed playing the piano, tennis and reading.

She married, 4 November 1944, in Elkins Park, Montgomery Co., Pa., **Dr. Oliver Payne PEARSON**, son of Forrest Garfield and Olive Payne (Corning) Pearson; born at Germantown, Philadelphia, Pa., 21 October 1915; died at Walnut Creek, Calif., 4 March 2003.

**OLIVER PAYNE "Paynie" PEARSON, Ph.D.,**[37] was an eminent mammalogist and professor of zoology. Oliver P. Pearson graduated from the Chestnut Hill Academy in Philadelphia, and received his B.A. from Swarthmore College in 1937. He was a conscientious objector during World War II. He received the A.M. from Harvard University in 1940 and the Ph.D. in 1947. In his career as a zoologist he was an authority on the mammals of South America, particularly the southern Andes. He and his wife, **Anita KELLY,** a biologist who was also his professional colleague, conducted field studies near Lake Titicaca in Peru and they spent many seasons in Argentina. Dr. "Paynie" Pearson was professor of zoology and director of the Museum of Vertebrate Zoology at the University of California at Berkeley. He served on the board of directors and as trustee of the American Society of Mammalogy for many years. He was active in community service and his hobbies include chopping vegetation and reading. He received many honors, including the Hartley H. T. Jackson Award in 1984, and a *Doctor Honoris Causa* from the University of La Plata, in Argentina. He was an honorary member of the American Society of Mammalogists and of the Cooper Ornithological Society. After he died, the American Society of Mammologists established the Oliver Pearson Award in his honor. Two rodent species are named for him, *Ctenomys pearsoni* and *Andalgalomys pearsoni*; and also a genus, *Pearsonomys* Patterson. When he received the honorary doctorate in Argentina, he said, *"Yo soy un simple atrapator de ratones, y nada hubiese side possible sin Anita"* ("I am a simple mouse-trapper, and nothing would have been possible without Anita").

Oliver Payne and Anita (Kelley) Pearson had the following children, surname Pearson:

| | | |
|---|---|---|
| **2.5.1** | i. | CAROL ANN[4] (1947- ) + |
| **2.5.2** | ii. | PETER KELLEY (1949- ) + |
| **2.5.3** | iii. | MICHAEL CORNING (1955-1956) |
| **2.5.4** | iv. | SANDIA CORNING "Sandy" (1956- ) |
| **2.5.5** | v. | ALISON PAYNE (1958- ) |

**2.5.1 CAROL ANN[4] PEARSON**, born 6 August 1947, Berkeley, Alameda Co., Calif.; married 3 June 1973, Orinda, Ca., **Clement John RALPH**, son of Clement Leo and Margaret MacDonald (Lochhead) Ralph; born 3 Sep 1940, Oakland, Alameda Co., Calif.; 2 children, surname Ralph:[38]

| | | |
|---|---|---|
| **2.5.1.1** | i. | PETER LOCHEAD[5] (1978- ) |
| **2.5.1.2** | ii. | DUNCAN KELLEY (1981- ) |

**2.5.2 PETER KELLEY[4] PEARSON**, born 3 March 1949, Berkeley, Calif.; scientist; computer specialist; theoretical chemist; married 9 February 1975, Berkeley, **Karen Beth WRIGHT**, daughter of Victor Louis and Evelyn Alice (Hansen) Wright (changed from Wojtkowski), born 11 August 1952, West Palm Beach, Florida; 3 children, surname Pearson:[39]

| | | |
|---|---|---|
| **2.5.2.1** | i. | JUSTIN PAYNE[5] (1983-) |
| **2.5.2.2** | ii. | STEPHANIE KELLEY (1985-) |
| **2.5.2.3** | iii. | SPENCER ROSS (1992-) |

**2.5.3 MICHAEL CORNING[4] PEARSON**, born 5 January 1955, Walnut Creek, Contra Costa Co., Calif.; d. 9 July 1956, of necrosis of the cerebellum.

**2.5.4 SANDIA CORNING[4] PEARSON**, born 20 October 1956; writer, musician; married 6 January 1979, in Reno, Nev., **Douglas Kent IVEY**, son of Donald Allen and Louise Marie (Albertazzi) Ivey; born 4 May 1954, Napa, Napa Co., Ca.[40]

**2.5.5 ALISON PAYNE[4] PEARSON,** born 23 January 1958, Walnut Creek, Ca..; artist; married 27 July 1991, Maui, H.I., **David Cole PHILLIPS**, son of William Clayton and Elizabeth (Zellom) Phillips; born 14 November 1954, New Haven, Ct.[41]

### Donald Edmund[3] Kelley and His Descendants

**2.6 DONALD EDMUND[3] KELLEY,**[42] second son and sixth child of Richard Carlyle and Anna (Zimmermann) Kelley, was born at Philadelphia, Pa., 6 February 1925; died at Plymouth Meeting, Montgomery Co., Pa., 27 March 2014. He was educated at the Benjamin Myers School and Cheltenham, Pennsylvania, High School. He received the B.S. in mechanical engineering from Swarthmore College. He later attended graduate classes at the Business School of the Drexel Institute of Technology. During World War II he was enrolled in the U.S. Navy V-12 and V-5 aviation cadet programs. After the war he became a mechanical engineer and was employed in that profession with the Philadelphia branch of Philco Corporation. He lived in the Philadelphia suburb of Glenside, where he enjoyed camping and tennis. He was a Scoutmaster and a member of the vestry of his Episcopal parish.

He married, at Westfield, N.J., at St. Paul's Episcopal Church, 31 August 1946, **Phyllis Helen KINKEAD**, daughter of Herbert Edward and Viola Eva (Wick) Kinkead; born at Philadelphia, 18 January 1926; baptized 28 March 1926, St. Mark's Episcopal Church, Philadelphia. She was also a graduate of Swarthmore and was later a teacher.

**PHYLLIS HELEN KINKEAD**, daughter of Herbert Edward and Viola Eva (Wick) Kinkead, graduated from high school in Westfield, N.J. She attended Swarthmore College, from which she received the B.A. degree in mathematics. She has raised six children and has been a teacher at the Abington Friend's School. She was active in her church, and is a volunteer with Meals on Wheels and the American Red Cross. In her spare time she enjoys sewing, tennis and reading.

Donald and Phyllis (Kinkead) Kelley had the following children, born in Abington, Montgomery Co., Pa., surname Kelley[43]:

| | | |
|---|---|---|
| **2.6.1** | i. | DONALD EDMUND[4], Jr., Esq. (1948- ) + |
| **2.6.2** | ii. | DAVID EMLIN (1950- ) |
| **2.6.3** | iii. | CAROL PHYLLIS (1954- ) |
| **2.6.4** | iv. | PETER EDWARD (1956- ) |
| **2.6.5** | v. | SUSAN PATRICIA (1958- ) |
| **2.6.6** | vi. | PAMELA ANN (1958- ), twin |

**2.6.1 DONALD EDMUND[4] KELLEY, Jr., Esq.,** born 2 December 1948; Yale, B.A., 1970 (Phi Beta Kappa, *summa cum laude*); law degree from Stanford U. Law School, 1973 (Order of the Coif); clerked for Associate Justice William O. Douglas; a partner in Folger & Levin, LLP, San Francisco; 30 years of experience as a business attorney; married 13 September 1988, **Susan GETMAN**, Palo Alto, Ca.; 2 children, surname Kelley.[44]

| | | |
|---|---|---|
| **2.6.1.1** | i. | JORDAN[5] (son). |
| **2.6.1.2** | ii. | DEVAN (daughter). |

**2.6.2 DAVID EMLIN[4] KELLEY,** born 12 August 1950; married 10 July 1976, **Rita BINGHAM**, in Ann Arbor, Mich.

**2.6.3 CAROL PHYLLIS[4] KELLEY,** born 24 December 1954; married 24 May 1975, **David J. NEWELL**, Glenside, Pa.

**2.6.4 PETER EDWARD[4] KELLEY,** born 6 September 1956; married 18 March 1989, **Elizabeth EATON**, Alexandria, Va.

**2.6.5 SUSAN PATRICIA[4] KELLEY,** born 14 August 1958; married 30 December 1988 **Charles CARABBA**, Glenside, Pa.

**2.6.6 PAMELA ANN[4] KELLEY,** born 14 August 1958; married 25 July 1981 **Michael PIOTROWICZ**, Glenside, Pa.

# Janet Nancy[3] Kelley

**2.7 JANET NANCY[3] KELLEY**, fifth daughter and seventh child of Richard and Anna (Zimmermann) Kelley, was born at Philadelphia, Pa., 5 June 1927; died at Elkins Park, Pa., 10 October 1938, of aplastic anemia, at age 11. Janet Kelley was the playmate and best friend of her cousin, Kathryn (Kathchie) Fligg. On the morning of her death, Katchie's father, Jim Fligg, heartbroken at the news, and suffering from tensions within the family business, had a heart attack and never returned to the Zimmermann Mills.[45]

# 6

## Emily² Zimmermann

**3. EMILY² ZIMMERMANN,**[46] third daughter and third child of John and Eva Katherine (Kellenbenz) Zimmermann, was born 10 July 1890 and died 14 June 1897, of diphtheria. She was buried two days later in Greenmount Cemetery in Philadelphia. She appeared in a formal portrait of the family taken before she died. Her death greatly affected her brothers and sisters, and it was rarely spoken of. Her sisters were then 12, 11 and 1 year old, and two brothers were 4 and 6; the youngest brother was not yet born.

| | |
|---|---|
| Name: | Emily Zimmerman |
| Birth Date: | abt 1891 |
| Birth Place: | Philadelphia, Pennsylvania, USA |
| Death Date: | 14 Jan 1897 |
| Death Place: | Philadelphia, Philadelphia, Pennsylvania |
| Age at Death: | 6 |
| Burial Date: | 16 Jan 1897 |
| Burial Place: | Philadelphia, Pennsylvania |
| Gender: | Female |
| Race: | White |
| Street address: | 610 West Lehigh Avenue |
| Residence: | Philadelphia, Pennsylvania |
| Cemetery: | Greenmount |
| Marital Status: | Single |
| Father: | John Zimmerman |
| Mother: | Eva H Zimmerman |
| FHL Film Number: | 1011826 |

# 7

## John² Zimmermann, Jr.[47]

**4. JOHN² ZIMMERMANN, Jr.,**[48] eldest son and fourth child of John and Eva Katherine (Kellenbenz) Zimmermann, was born at Philadelphia, 6 June 1892; died there, 15 October 1974.

He went to Philadelphia Central High School and in 1908, at age 16, he became a leader of the Philadelphia Reorganized Church of Latter Day Saints (RLDS) Church group at summer camp in Onset, Mass. At age 23, in 1914, he graduated from the University of Pennsylvania. That summer, he went to Europe with his brother William (age 19) and two other boys, Fletcher and Carl Schaum, who lived near them at 1508 Allegheny. It was the summer that World War I broke out in Europe. They arrived back on 18 September 1914 on the *Lusitania*, which was sunk by a German torpedo 7 months later. He then returned to the University of Pennsylvania and in 1916 he was studying mathematics and economics as a first year student in graduate school. He soon joined with his brothers and his brother-in-law in the firm John Zimmermann & Sons, which manufactured mohair furniture coverings.[49] Founded in 1919, their factory was at E. Erie Ave. at Castor Ave.[50] He later became president of another family company, Zimmermann Mills., Inc., maker of furniture coverings, with a factory at 21st and West Allegheny Ave.[51] He filed 3 patent applications in 1928 and 1929, and was elected as a member of Sigma Xi[52]; the patents were granted on 3 March 1931. These were the last patents for textiles that were obtained by one of John[1] Zimmermann's descendants, although 20 years later, his brother-in-law, James Fligg, obtained a patent for "Woven Fabric." He took a cruise to Europe from 11-20 January 1934 on S.S. *Statendam* out of New York City, with his father and step-mother. At that time, he lived at 2 Surrey Road, Oak Lane, Philadelphia. Later that year he was photographed outside the Kensington RLDS church, where he was said to be a "high priest," with Prophet Fred Smith, grandson of Joseph Smith, Jr., Founder of the LDS Church, and his father Bishop John Zimmermann, Sr.[53]

John Zimmermann, Jr., married, at Kansas City, Jackson Co., Mo., 17 April 1916, **Ethel Grace "Nonnie" KINNAMAN**; a vocalist; born 11 June 1892; died 13 August 1979; daughter of Don Carlos and Elizabeth (Lewis) Kinnaman. After she was married she often appeared as a contralto in performances in Pennsylvania and elsewhere in the eastern United States.[54]

The following narrative about Kinnaman Family and other stories about the family of John Zimmermann, Jr., were told in "Mom's Stories," written by John Zimmermann, Jr.'s younger daughter, Mary Jane (Zimmermann) Clark, shortly before she died.[55]

### The Other Side

Let's not forget the Kinnamans. Our genes are more Z than K, but they're still there. Grandfather and Grandmother Kinnaman lived on S. 17th Street in St. Joseph, Missouri, better known in the family as St. Joe. Their oldest, a daughter, was Mary Lenore, later to be called "My," who married J. William Sauer, "Uncle Billy." They were childless, but spent a great deal of time with us. They lived in various places in the Philadelphia area and, for a while in Ventnor, New Jersey, and various and sundry other places in the east. Don't try to understand. It gets complicated.

Second, another daughter was **Ethel Grace who married John Zimmermann, Jr**. You may remember that they had the four remarkable children: Betty, Mary Jane, Johnny and Carlie.

They lived for a long time in Melrose Park, Pennsylvania, moving to Leopard Road in Abington, Pennsylvania, after the remarkable children were married and had flown the coop.

Now the male Kinnamans:  It was almost as if Grandfather and Grandmother had two families, as they were quite a bit younger.  Don Carlos, Jr. married Dorothy Twohill (sp.?) and they had two children:  Mary Lenore and Don Carlos, III, Don.  They, too, lived in various places, always in the greater Philadelphia area, finally settling in Oreland.

Jack came next and he married Margaret Frans.  They had three daughters: Joan Kay, Ethel Lenore, and Peggy. They lived for quite some time in various cold spots in the mid-west before moving to Bergenfield, New Jersey.

Last, but certainly not least, came Norman Potter Kinnaman.  He married Elizabeth Adams, a southern belle, before going off to war and after having worked in the textile trade, as had his brothers, in Philadelphia.  After his return from the South Pacific, they lived in and around the Philadelphia area, finally moving to High Point, North Carolina, where he plied his trade.  They remained childless, to their great disappointment, and finally adopted Anne: Andy.

## God Bless New Hampshire

New Hampshire was probably my father's favorite state in the union and he was very fond of quoting Whittier:

> God bless New Hampshire,
> From her granite peaks
> Once more the voice of _____ and _____
> (Fill in the blanks) speaks.

He had gone to camp there as a boy and it was only natural, I guess, that he wanted to introduce his family to the state.  He knew all sorts of trivia which never ceased to amaze me, so we felt as if we knew something about the state before we even set our feet on the soil.

Somehow or other he was able to rent a wonderful cottage on Lake Winnipesaukee out Meredith Neck and it didn't take long for us to become converts.  The cottage belonged to two sisters and their husbands who had been coming from Boston for years, but were taking the summer off so the cottage was available.  We got to know several of the neighbors: a family right across on Pine Island with two attractive boys who thought my sister [Bette] was pretty special (the feeling was mutual; they didn't know her the way I did).  And a great family from Ohio who had a big house two doors away where we often went swimming.  A favorite sport was to dive off the end of their dock into schools of little fish.  The fish weren't very intelligent - they kept coming back so we could do it again and again.  Neighbors didn't take up all of our time as my sister regimented us.  For various activities, on, in and off the water, I wasn't permitted to forget that I was an ONEKA girl first and foremost.  Somehow or other those awful brown serge bloomers had found their way to New Hampshire and became uniform of the day as she chose.

My father saw to it that we could become acquainted with many of the state's wonders:  we drove up several times into the White Mountains, saw the Old Man of the Mountain, drove over to Center Harbor, where we could see Becky's Garden, the smallest of the dozens of Winnipesaukee islands where someone had put a doll's house, into Laconia, the largest "city" around where we could get my favorite ginger ice cream for a special treat, perhaps stopping by The Weirs if we were making a day of it, around the lake in the mail boat which delivered mail to some of the larger islands of which there were dozens, around the lake in a big side wheeler, I guess you'd call it, the *Mount Washington*, Lost River, the Flume, out to Cow Island to visit my father's boyhood camp: Idlewild.  The only way to get there was on the mail boat or to charter a boat.  My brothers would attend Idlewild with equal relish a few years later.  Believe or not, my father convinced the camp director quite a few years later that he should be sort of a counselor, teaching the campers to make hammocks, which were his specialty.

But to get back to the subject at hand, it was indeed a wonderful summer: both cars, the two German girls, maybe it was just Lena, her sister Elizabeth may have been married by that time. Come on, I can't remember everything, I only know that my mother was afforded a great summer, too, as she didn't have household chores to attend to for the most part and she loved to go in to Meredith where she soon made friends with the butcher at the bottom of the hill, the owner of the A&P at the top of the hill, the druggist and other assorted shopkeepers. (It was fun to go with her and see Missouri in action with those New Englanders.)

Yes, God Bless New Hampshire! Where else do you think I dragged your father on our honeymoon? And ask your sister [Bette] what her favorite town is. Yes, it has a quilt shop today. She manages to work it in when she's in the state.

Sorry if I got carried away!!! I'll quick push send.

### Up Red Hill

Needless to say I have many special memories of the several years the family went up to New Hampshire. One that stands out particularly is the total eclipse in the early thirties. We climbed up Red Hill, or was it Pinnacle Point Hill, anyway it was the best vantage point for viewing this unusual event. I recall that we had had creamed dry beef for lunch, an especially salty dish, and my father spent most of the afternoon going up and down to get us water.

A telescope had been set up in such a way that it caught the progress on a white sheet. We knew we shouldn't look at the sun directly. When the time came for totality we saw the corona and then it was like dusk. We were told that all the animals and birds had settled in for the night thinking it was time. And then it was over and the sun started to appear again. I'll never forget that strange light and it seemed so very quiet. We found out that a group of Boston scientists who had come up to observe went farther north as the eclipse was due to last a few seconds longer at their planned destination. And it rained there, while we had perfect viewing weather!
Quite an experience...

### Subsequent New Hampshire Summers

We didn't get back to New Hampshire for at least a couple of years. It was the heart of the depression and people were reining in their lives. We did spend some time at [the RLDS] Deer Park and at some point we were up on Cape Cod with various aunts, uncles and cousins. The Hoxies had a veritable compound in East Sandwich, on the order of the Kennedys'. In fact they're there today. Anyway, they expanded to include us.

When we got back to New Hampshire (I'm a little uncertain of the chronology) we rented a cottage right next to the one we had before. Not nearly as nice, but the Fields and Camerons were wonderful neighbors each with a daughter the age of my sister and me: Helen Field and Margie Cameron. Helen liked to play with paper dolls as I did and Margie was ever so pleased to be part of the action, or at least observe the action with the Pine Island boys my sister attracted. I'll keep you in suspense by continuing this part of the saga another day. Remember, I'm endeavoring to be less wordy.

### More New Hampshire

The first summer we were at the second cottage, hereinafter known as the Collins Camp, the young men from Pine Island became more and more omnipresent. Heretofore we had known only the Wardens, Bob and Buddy, but this year a relative by the name of Mervyn Knight appeared on the scene and he was completely smitten with my sister. One day he had come over to the mainland to wash his uncle's car and he left the door open and sloshed a whole bucket of water inside as she made her appearance.

Another time, on taking leave of my sister, he pushed off his canoe with a good shove but forgot to get in it. He waded out after it, took off his very wet shoes and dumped the water from them into the canoe. He was the kind of individual who kept you wondering what he might do next but at the same time you felt kind of sorry for him.

As I recall we heard that all of these guys were war casualties, either killed or seriously wounded. But these weren't the only flames. There was Bob Thompson who lived further around Pine Island and Joe Carson, the one my sister really fell for. One time she had borrowed a very dainty platinum bracelet that my mother had brought to me from Missouri. She went out for a walk with Joe, wearing the bracelet, but when they returned the bracelet was gone and I never did know what happened to it. She claimed that she didn't know either, but I've always wondered!

Joe stayed in the picture for a while. As I recall he came from Bloomfield, New Jersey, so she had a chance of seeing him after the summer was over. However, she moved on to greener pastures [m. Edward James]. Looking back on all of the above I can see that she would have been entitled to write again:

> I have a little sister,
> Her name is Mary Jane.
> Though people call her darling,
> I cannot think the same.

I sure nosed into her affairs and tried to make it my business to see that I didn't miss a thing. It's remarkable that we're such good friends today!

John Zimmermann, Jr., and Ethel Kinnaman had the following children:

| | | |
|---|---|---|
| **4.1** | i. | BETTE³ (1918-~2015) + |
| **4.2** | ii. | MARY JANE (1921-2008) + |
| **4.3** | iii. | JOHN, III (1923-1998) + |
| **4.4** | iv. | CARL (1924-1984) + |

# John² Zimmermann, Jr. and His Descendants

## Bette³ Zimmermann and Her Descendants

**4.1 BETTE³ ZIMMERMANN,**[56] elder daughter and first child of John and Ethyl (Kinnaman) Zimmermann, was born in 1918; died about 2015. She married **Edward JAMES**. They lived in Nutley, N.J. Some of her children moved to Grand Rapids, Mich.

Many years later, her sister Mary Jane (Zimmermann) Clark recalled their childhood together in her unpublished memoir, entitled "Mom's Stories":

### Learning to Drive

My parents had gotten a Ford convertible in hopes of enticing my sister [**Bette**] to learn to drive. She was rather gun-shy after driving the Pierce Arrow into a telephone pole instead of turning into the driveway. My mother was her instructor and that's probably why I was handed over to my father. The Pierce Arrow had headlights on the fenders and looked very broad nor was it a pretty sight after the telephone pole incident. Needless to say, the convertible became my car of choice even though there was a Cadillac and a Lincoln Zephyr in the mix. Most of my good friends had their licenses by the time I got mine and sometimes we all managed to get to drive to school on the same day. I lost the Ford when Ed James, later to become my sister's husband and father of Jim, Mary and Greg, came into the picture. He had been my father's nurse when my father had been a patient at Pennsylvania Institute and came home with him. They did a lot of riding in the Ford and were involved in an accident so the Ford became history. But by this time I was going off to college and we were facing gas rationing with things heating up in Europe. End of story. I had the skill but no opportunity to use it for some long time. I did have a lot of fun for the short time I got to drive the Ford, though, and it made the other kids quite envious when a convertible pulled up, but I think I was driving the Cadillac or as my mother called it the Caddy when my picture was taken grinning out the window.

Edward and Bette (Zimmermann) James had the following children, surname James:

| | | |
|---|---|---|
| **4.1.1** | i. | EDWARD[4], Jr. |
| **4.1.2** | ii. | MARY, m. ____ **LEWIS**.[57] |
| **4.1.3** | iii. | GREG. |

**4.1.1**   **EDWARD[4] JAMES, Jr.**, lives in Grand Rapids, Mich.[58]

**4.1.2**   **M ARY[4] JAMES,** lives in Grand Rapids, Mich.; married ____ **LEWIS**.

**4.1.3**   **GREG[4] JAMES.**[59]

## Mary Jane[3] Zimmermann and Her Descendants

**4.2 MARY JANE[3] ZIMMERMANN**, second daughter and second child of John and Ethyl (Kinnaman) Zimmermann, was born in 1921 and grew up in Nutley, N.J. She married **Gerald CLARK.** She wrote "Mom's Notes" shortly before she died (c. 2008).[60] They were written for her son, Peter, who died of bone cancer soon thereafter:

### Kindergarten Tragedy

When I was in kindergarten at a very tender age I wet my pants one morning. Kind Mrs. Armstrong rinsed them out and put them on the hall radiator to dry. A little while later Miss McSparren, the much feared principal (she was rumored to keep a rubber hose in the bottom drawer of her desk for use on children who were sent to her office) happened in and for some reason knew immediately that the cotton panties were Mary Jane's and proceeded to trumpet the fact for the whole class to hear. I couldn't hold my head up for days. However, I never did find out whether the rubber hose story was truth or rumor. I didn't weep when she left Myers school. Her successor, Miss Coburn, was a joy and she and Nonnie [her mother, Ethyl] had a great time running the school.

### Rice Pudding

Come to think about it, this is about the time that I was being regaled with a bit of A. A. Milne:

> What is the matter with Mary Jane?
> She isn't sick and she hasn't a pain,
> And it's lovely rice pudding for dinner again.
> What IS the matter with Mary Jane?

This, and additional verses, was accompanied by an illustration showing a naughty little girl kicking up her heels in protest in her high chair, obviously very upset. It seemed to me that all the grownups had read this particular poem and thought they should see to it that I heard it too. I didn't ever think it was particularly funny. Besides, I liked rice pudding. So much for Mr. Milne!

**Family Weddings**

When I was about three, my Aunt Lil (later to be Katchie's mother) and Uncle Jim [Fligg] were married in the Zimmermann "ball room" in Philadelphia. Aunt Lil wanted me to be her trainbearer, but my mother said she couldn't live through that ordeal and placated me, along with my cousin Sue [who later married Joseph Carnwath], by telling us we could be ONLOOKERS! We took up our positions in front of the fireplace and as Aunt Lil swept by with her long train my mother was horrified to hear me say "Let's step on it!" and grabbed us, feet raised, in the nick of time.

Sue and I were old hands at this wedding business by the time our Uncle Al and Aunt Barbara [née Shoemaker] were married in a very posh society wedding. Eight o'clock at night was a little late for two five year olds to be up after rehearsing the night before. We had to precede the bride with our flower baskets and scatter rose petals for her to walk on. Small wonder that the wedding pictures showed us glaring at each other, held down by the nearest male attendant. We were not invited to be in Uncle Bill Z's and Aunt Peg's wedding [William Zimmermann married Margaret Lukens].

Gerald and Mary Jane (Zimmermann) Clark had the following children, surname Clark:

| | | |
|---|---|---|
| **4.2.1** | i. | GERALD[4], Jr. (1951- ) |
| **4.2.2** | ii. | MARY. |
| **4.2.3** | iii. | PETER (1955?-2013?)[61] |

**4.2.1  GERALD[4] CLARK, Jr.,** was born in 1951; lives in Nutley, N.J.[62]

**4.2.2  MARY[4] CLARK** was director, Import/Export Operations for Asia Pacific at the Asia Pacific Trading Center. She was married to _____ **SCHEIBNER.**[63]

**4.2.3  PETER[4] CLARK,** born about 1955; died about 2013, of "bone cancer."

## John[3] Zimmermann, III, and His Descendants

**4.3  JOHN[3] ZIMMERMANN, III,** elder son and third child of John Zimmermann, Jr., and Ethyl née Kinnaman, was born in 1923. All of his children live in New Jersey.[64]

He had the following children, surname Zimmermann:

| | | |
|---|---|---|
| **4.3.1** | i. | JOHN[4], IV (1951- ). |
| **4.3.2** | ii. | RICHARD "Rick" ( 1954- ) |
| **4.3.3** | iii. | NANCY. |
| **4.3.4** | iv. | BARBARA (~1964- ). |

**4.3.1  JOHN[4] ZIMMERMANN, IV,** was born in 1951.

**4.3.2  RICHARD[4] "Rick" ZIMMERMANN** was born in about 1954; married **Janie _____**.[65]

**4.3.3  NANCY[4] ZIMMERMANN.**

**4.3.4  BARBARA[4] ZIMMERMANN** was born about 1964.

## Carl[3] Zimmermann and His Descendants

**4.4  CARL[3] ZIMMERMANN**, younger son and fourth child of John and Ethyl (Kinnaman) Zimmermann, was born 25 November 1924; died 20 July 1984.  He lived at 17 Surrey Park, Melrose, Pa., in a house that was still standing in 2016.  He married **Mary Ann HOWER**, born about 1925.[66]

His sister, Mary Jane (Zimmermann) Clark wrote:

### My Victims[1]

My sister [Bette] may have had me under her thumb, but I had two brothers [John III and **Carl**] under mine.  And they gave me plenty of ammunition.  I remember their lopping the heads off all of the Gerstleys' beautiful tulips between their house and ours.  And I remember spotting **Carl**, clad only in his undershirt out on the sun porch roof.  He had climbed out the window of their bedroom when he was supposed to be taking a nap.  And mother's makeup.  But the be all and end all was when they played garage man, filling the gas tank of her new Cadillac which she planned to show off at a luncheon.  The car had to be towed, of course, and Mother was livid.  Small wonder that I was quoted as saying "Mother, come see what the boys are doing NOW!"  I didn't feel that I was a tattletale.  I felt she ought to know.

Carl and Mary Ann (Hower) Zimmermann had the following children, surname Zimmermann:

| | | |
|---|---|---|
| **4.4.1** | i. | ELIZABETH ANN[4] (1948-) |
| **4.4.2** | ii. | CARL KINNAMAN, Jr. (1950-) |
| **4.4.3** | iii. | JOHN HOWER (1951-) |
| **4.4.4** | iv. | THOMAS DAVID (1952-) |
| **4.4.5** | v. | WILLIAM JOSEPH (1954-) |
| **4.4.6** | vi. | SUSAN (1956-) |
| **4.4.7** | vii. | PETER CLAIR (1957-) |
| **4.4.8** | viii. | PAUL (1964-) |

**4.4.1  ELIZABETH ANN[4] ZIMMERMANN,** born 5 June 1948; married ___ **MATTHEWS.**

**4.4.2  CARL KINNAMAN[4] ZIMMERMANN, Jr.,** born 10 January 1950; married **Margaret H. _____.**

**4.4.3  JOHN HOWER[4] ZIMMERMANN,** born 31 May 1951, Bryn Mawr, Pa.  He recalls his home in Melrose Park, Pa., and spending time as a child at Deer Park, the RLDS camp in New Hope, Pa.  He attended grammar school at Myers Public Melrose Park, Pa.; St. James R.C. School, Elkins Park, Pa.; St. Joseph R.C. School, Cheltenham, Pa.; Mary E. Roberts Public School, Moorestown, N.J.; and Our Lady of Good Counsel R.C. School, Moorestown, N.J.  He attended high School at Moorestown H.S., Moorestown N.J.; and Nutley H.S., from which he graduated in 1969.  He attended Rutgers University, New Brunswick, N.J., and received the B.A. degree in 1973.  He is a purchasing agent in Kearny, N.J.  He and his wife enjoy music, travel, history, literature, and physical fitness.
He married, at Nutley, N.J., 10 November 1973, at Vincent Methodist Church, **Sandra Gayle GALASSO**, daughter of David Peter and (Francis) Lorraine (Davis) Galasso.

---

[1] From Mary Jane (Zimmermannn) Clark, "Mom's Stories" (Ibid.)

John Hower and Sandra (Galasso) Zimmermann have one son, surname Zimmermann:

**4.4.3.1** i. JAMES DAVID[5], b. 9 Jun 1982, Somerville, N.J.; principal clarinet, Nashville (Tenn.) Symphony since 2008; B.M., Univ. So. Cal. Thornton School of Music ; M.M., Univ. Minn.; studied under Yehuda Gilad and Burt Hara; won the Gino B. Cioffi Prize for Outstanding Woodwind Performance at Tanglewood Music Center; previously was a member of Pacific Symphony; is a music teacher, active in recording projects; works out at YMCAs before rehearsals; m. (1) 27 Aug 2005, Lyon House, Salt Lake City, Utah, **Candice LEE**, b. 23 Jun 1976; d. 16 May 2015, Nashville, suddenly, of a cerebral hemorrhage; a direct descendant of **Brigham Young**; she was a talented actress and vocalist; 2 children; he m. (2) 2016, **Kristie KLEIN**; they are expecting a child in 2016.

Children of James and Candice (Lee) Zimmermann, surname Zimmermann:

| | | |
|---|---|---|
| **4.4.3.1.1** | i. | CAROLINE[6], b. abt 2010. |
| **4.4.3.1.2** | ii. | MOLLY, b. abt 2013. |

**4.4.4 THOMAS DAVID[4] ZIMMERMANN**, born 22 August 1952.

**4.4.5 WILLIAM JOSEPH[4] ZIMMERMANN**, born 30 April 1954.

**4.4.6 SUSAN[4] ZIMMERMANN**, born 10 August 1956; married _____ **NILSEN.**

**4.4.7 PETER CLAIR[4] ZIMMERMANN**, born 28 December 1957.

**4.4.8 PAUL[4] ZIMMERMANN**, born 1 February 1964.

# 8

## William[2] "Bill" Zimmermann

**5. WILLIAM[2] "Bill" ZIMMERMANN,**[67] second son and fifth child of John and Eva Katharine (Kellenbenz) Zimmermann, was born at Philadelphia, Pa., 4 December 1894; died at Abington, Pa., 14 March 1978. Bill Zimmermann graduated from Philadelphia Central High School in 1914. On 18 September 1914, shortly after war broke out in Europe, Bill, then 19 years old, his brother John, and two other young men who lived near them in Philadelphia – Fletcher and Carl Schaum – arrived in New York City from a cruise on the *Lusitania*. Seven months later, the ship was sunk by a German torpedo. Bill and his sister Anna became members of the Reorganized Church of Latter Day Saints (RLDS) on 30 September 1914. He filed a Draft Registration Card on 5 June 1917, at age 23, when he was a student at the University of Pennsylvania. He graduated with a B.S. in chemical engineering in 1918. During World War I, William Zimmermann served in the U. S. Army infantry in the American Expeditionary Force, with duty in Belgium or France.

After graduating from college, he became a chemical engineer with the Philadelphia Tapestry Mills, which was owned by his father and three Wasserman brothers. The employment of John, Jr., and Bill Zimmermann in this partnership was the source of considerable ill feeling, which led to the formation of a separate corporation by the Zimmermanns after the war. When he returned from service in the war, he entered the carpet manufacturing business with his father, his brother John, and their brother-in-law, Richard Kelley; they were later joined by their younger brother, Albert. Their company, John Zimmermann & Sons, founded in 1919, manufactured mohair furniture coverings at Erie and Castor Avenues in Philadelphia. It achieved considerable success, and was still in operation in the early 1960s, although it is no longer is in existence. In 1927, the Zimmermanns formed another company to manufacture furniture coverings. This company, Zimmermann Mills, Inc., was located in a large factory building at 21st and Allegheny. This company, too, no longer exists.

William Zimmermann's professional activities included membership on the Philadelphia Textile Institute Board. He was also a member of the board of the Frankford Hospital, and he was a member of the Wyncote Bird Club and the Wissahickon Ski Club. He was active in Civil Defense during World War II. He often traveled to New Hampshire with his brother John, and their children became close friends. He enjoyed gardening, golf, skiing, and birding. He died of liver cancer at the age of 83 and was buried in the Lawnview Cemetery.

He married, in Philadelphia, at the RLDS Church, on his 35th birthday, 4 December 1929, **Margaret Peattie LUKENS**, daughter of Edward Fell and Margaret (Patton) Lukens; born at Philadelphia, 8 June 1897; died 15 August 1981. Margaret Lukens was a distant cousin of Bill's sister-in-law, Barbara (née Shoemaker), who three years earlier had married his brother Albert. Both Margaret and Barbara were descendants of early Quaker settlers in Philadelphia.[68]

**MARGARET PEATTIE "Peg" LUKENS**, daughter of Edward Fell and Margaret (Patton) Lukens, was born at Philadelphia, Pennsylvania, 8 June 1897; died 15 August 1981. Margaret Lukens was educated at the Germantown Friends School of Philadelphia and at Goucher

College, from which she received the B.A. degree. After her marriage, at the age of 32, she was active as a Visiting Nurse, with the Society of Germantown Board, the Florence Crittenden Home Board, and the Jenkintown Day Nursery Board. She was Treasurer of the Women's Board of the Germantown Hospital and Treasurer of the Jenkintown Red Cross. Peg Lukens was President of the Parents Auxiliary of the Germantown Friends School and she was an Alumnae Trustee of Goucher College. She enjoyed knitting and playing the piano, and was rightly proud of the accomplishments of her three children. She died at age 84, of heart failure, and was buried beside her husband.

William and Margaret (Lukens) Zimmermann had three children, born at Philadelphia, surname Zimmermann:

|  |  |  |
|---|---|---|
| **5.1** | i. | Dr. WILLIAM³ "Bill", Jr. (1930- ). + |
| **5.2** | ii. | MARGARET ANN "Peggy" (1932- ) + |
| **5.3** | iii. | Dr. ROBERT ALAN "Bob" (1937- ) + |

# Descendants of William² "Bill" Zimmermann

## William³ "Bill" Zimmermann, Jr., and His Descendants

**5.1 WILLIAM³ "Bill" ZIMMERMANN, Jr., Ph.D.,**[69] elder son and first child of William and Margaret (Lukens) Zimmermann, was born at Philadelphia, Pa., 28 October 1930. He graduated from Amherst College in 1952 with an A.B. in physics, and he received the Ph.D. in physics from California Institute of Technology in 1958. In 1959, he became a member of the Department of Physics at the University of Minnesota. He rose to the rank of professor and was made an emeritus professor upon his retirement. His work focused on the "experimental study of superfluidity in liquid 4He and 3He/4He mixtures." That is to say, he studies superfluidity in liquid helium mixtures. He selected the following publication as an example of his work: W. Zimmermann, Jr., "The Classical Electromagnetic Modes of a Rectangular Resonant Cavity with particular reference to the text Quantum Physics by R. Eisberg and R. Resnick," *arXiv*: 1207.0792 (2012). The paper is summarized in the following abstract: "Three approaches to the derivation of the classical electromagnetic modes of a rectangular cavity are described. In so doing, some apparent errors in a widely used physics text are pointed out."

Bill was co-chairman of the International Symposium on Quantum Fluids and Solids QFS 2000 at the University of Minnesota in June 2000. The symposium drew about 210 participants from all over the world, including two Nobel laureates. Bill Zimmermann was admired as a teacher and mentor, and he has been recognized by many of his former students in their publications. He married, on 8 September 1962, **Elizabeth Wilke "Betsy" STROUT,** a horticulturalist; born 3 May 1941, Washington, D.C. She is a graduate of Carleton College, B.A., 1962. Bill, on the flute, and Elizabeth, on the violin, are members of the Amity ensemble of musicians in Minneapolis, playing music from the Baroque period. Elizabeth says that, "after an abundance of education, and years of having to be up, and out, and functioning at 8 a.m.," she "is now retired and playing a lot of fine music. Her other pleasures are English country dance and aerobics class, working crosswords, various arts and crafts, and stopping to pet a puppy when she gets the chance."

William and Elizabeth (Strout) Zimmermann have three children, surname Zimmermann:

| 5.1.1 | i. | MICHAEL STROUT[4] (1965- ) |
| 5.1.2 | ii. | SARAH LUKENS (1967- ) |
| 5.1.3 | iii. | CHRISTOPHER LEE (1972- ) |

**5.1.1 MICHAEL STROUT[4] ZIMMERMANN**, born 31 July 1965, Minneapolis, Minn.

**5.1.2 SARAH LUKENS[4] ZIMMERMANN**, born 26 November 1967, Helsinki, Finland.

**5.1.3 CHRISTOPHER LEE[4] ZIMMERMANN**, born 10 September 1972, Minneapolis.

### Margaret Ann[3] Zimmermann and Her Descendants

**5.2 MARGARET ANN[3] "Peggy" ZIMMERMANN,** daughter and second child of William and Margaret (Lukens) Zimmermann, was born at Philadelphia, 5 May 1932. She became an occupational therapist and began working with children who had cerebral palsy at the Children's Rehabilitation Institute in Baltimore. She married, 6 June 1959, at Philadelphia, **Eric W. FONKALSRUD, M.D.,** who was then a surgical intern at Johns Hopkins. They met on a blind date, which was arranged by his roommate.

**ERIC WALTER FONKALSRUD, M.D.,**[70] son and only child of George and Ella F. Fonkalsrud, was born at Baltimore, Maryland, 31 August 1932. George Fonkalsrud was born on a farm near Oslo, Norway, where the family name had been known for more than 250 years. He received his engineering degree in Germany, where he met his wife, Ella. She was a native of Darmstadt, in the state of Hesse, Germany. George and Ella Fonkalsrud came to America through Ellis Island in the late 1920s. His father's first job was as a structural engineer for the Holland Tunnel in New York City. They then moved to Baltimore, where Eric was born at the Johns Hopkins Hospital. In 1934, the family moved to Tennessee, where his father worked on the Tennessee Valley Authority (T.V.A.) project as a civil engineer. His father then was recruited to design bridges across the Columbia River, and the family moved to Seattle in 1942. Eric became a Cub Scout in Tennessee and then a Boy Scout in Seattle. He earned the Eagle Scout award with three palms. His father had been a skier and a ski jumper, and his son, Eric, began skiing in 1943. He became the cross-country and jumping champion for two years in high school, and was captain of the ski team. He graduated from Queen Anne High School in 1949.

Eric Fonkalsrud attended college at the University of Washington, Seattle, where he was a member of the National Championship Rowing Crew. He graduated with the degree of B.A. in 1953, and he received the degree of M.D. from Johns Hopkins University in 1957. He interned in surgery at the Johns Hopkins Hospital in 1957-58 and was assistant resident there in 1958-59. He then transferred to the University of California Medical Center, Los Angeles, where he completed his residency in general surgery at U.C.L.A. in 1963. He was resident in pediatric surgery at Ohio State University in 1963-65.

Dr. Fonkalsrud then began an illustrious career as one of the leaders in the field of surgery in the latter part of the 20th century. He joined the faculty in the department of surgery at U.C.L.A. in 1965 as assistant professor and chief of pediatric surgery. He was promoted to associate professor in 1968 and to full professor in 1971. He retired as professor emeritus in 2001. He was one of the earliest to specialize in pediatric surgery, and was a pioneer in that field. In his career, he performed more than 14,000 operations. He has been recognized by both his peers and by his students, and he has been honored in many ways – as a teacher, scholar, scientist, editor, and leader of surgical societies.

Dr. Fonkalsrud is the author or co-author of 455 scientific publications, 123 book chapters, and seven books. He has served on the editorial boards of 15 major surgical journals, and he has been president of nine surgical societies, including the American Pediatric Surgical Association, the Society of University Surgeons, the Association for Academic Surgery, and the Pacific Coast Surgical Association. He has also been an adult leader in the Methodist Church of Westwood, and in the Boy Scouts. He was active in the YMCA Indian Guides program with his children, and his three sons became Eagle Scouts. His many awards, honors, offices, and books are listed in *Who's Who in America*.

After retiring from surgery, he has continued to be active in swimming, cycling and running, and he has participated in more than 30 triathlons. Having planted thousands of seedlings on land purchased in the 1940s by his father, he was named Tree Farmer of the Year in Western Washington in 1998. In 2009, he and his wife established the Margaret Z. and Eric W. Folkalsrud Endowed Scholarship at the University of Washington School of Medicine.

Eric and Margaret (Zimmermann) Fonkalsrud have the following children, surname Fonkalsrud:

| | | |
|---|---|---|
| **5.2.1** | i. | ERIC[4], Jr. (1961- ) |
| **5.2.2** | ii. | MARGARET LYNN (1962- ) |
| **5.2.3** | iii. | DAVID LOREN (1965- ) |
| **5.2.4** | iv. | ROBERT WARREN (1967- ) |

**5.2.1 ERIC WALTER[4] FONKALSRUD, Jr.,** born 1961, Los Angeles; Eagle Scout.

**5.2.2 MARGARET LYNN[4] FONKALSRUD,** born 1926, Los Angeles.

**5.2.3 DAVID LOREN[4] FONKALSRUD,** born 1965, Los Angeles; Eagle Scout.

**5.2.4 ROBERT WARREN[4] FONKALSRUD,** born 1967, while his parents were living in Santa Monica, Calif.; Eagle Scout.

Eric and Margaret (Zimmermann) Fonkalsrud also have six grandchildren, who will be assigned numbers **5.2.?.1 – 5.2.?.6** in the index of this book.

### Robert Alan[3] Zimmermann and His Descendants

**5.3 ROBERT ALAN[3] "Bob" ZIMMERMANN, Ph.D.,**[71] younger son and third child of William and Margaret (Lukens) Zimmermann, was born at Philadelphia, Pa., in July 1937. He is the youngest of the 23 grandchildren of John and Eva Katherine (Kellenbenz) Zimmermann.

Robert A. Zimmermann received his Ph.D. from the Massachusetts Institute of Technology and he had postdoctoral training at the Harvard Medical School and the University of Geneva. He is now retired from his position as professor of biology at the University of Massachusetts at Amherst. One of his students wrote that, "Dr. Zimmermann was my advisor and mentor from 1978 to 1980. A fantastic human being and lucid, brilliant scientist. I will never forget him and his lab group."

Bob Zimmermann's seminal publications on ribosomal proteins include 8 published in the premier journal, *Proceedings of the National Academy of Sciences*, from 1971-1997, including three as first author in the early years, and eight as team leader in the later years. He has also published in *Science* and *Nature*, the top two journals in the field of science. As a sole author, he also published several review articles on ribosomal proteins and RNA, including a summary of his personal research in 2015. One of his last papers was "The Double Life of Ribosomal Proteins," *Cell* 115 (2003): 130-132. His honors include the Helen Hay Whitney Foundation Fellowship; National Institutes of Health Research Career Development Award; University Faculty Fellowship; and the Distinguished Faculty Leadership Award.

He married (1) **Linda SAPUTELLI.** They were divorced, and he married (2), as her second husband, **Athlene ELLINGTON**, a teacher of French literature. By her previous marriage, she had a child, Laura, who was running a language school, "Interculturu," in 1994-5 in Costa Rica.

Robert and Athlene (Ellington) Zimmermann have the following children:

    **5..3.1**   i.     LAURA[4], a step-daughter of Robert Zimmermann.
    **5.3.2**   ii.    HANNAH (~1985- )

**5.3.1 LAURA[4] ELLINGTON,** daughter of Athlene (Ellington) Zimmermann by her previous marriage.

**5.3.2 HANNAH[4] ZIMMERMANN**, born about 1985, was in third grade in 1994-5.

# 9

## Lillian[2] "Lily Mae" Zimmermann

**6. LILLIAN[2] "Lily Mae" ZIMMERMANN**,[72] fourth daughter and sixth child of John and Eva Kathrine (Kellenbenz) Zimmermann, was born at Philadelphia, Pa., 18 September 1897; died there, 12 September 1966. During much of her childhood, her mother was severely fatigued from anemia,[73] and Lillian and her younger brother, Albert, were largely raised by their older sisters, who were "surrogate mothers" to the younger children. She attended public schools in Philadelphia and she then received a B.A. degree as a member of the Class of 1921 at the University of Pennsylvania. She was a member of the Kappa Kappa Gamma sorority in 1920, following her older sister, Anna, who was also a "Kappa." In February 1923, John and Anna (Dancer) Zimmermann took a 3-month cruise to Europe and countries bordering the Mediterranean Sea, taking John's daughter Lillian with them as a graduation present from college. They went to Great Britain, France, Italy, Spain, Portugal, Holland, Switzerland, Egypt, Morocco, Algeria, Palestine, and Turkey. While on the trip, Lillian contracted "Palestine fever," and nearly died; she left the ship in England, and recovered in a nursing home in London.[74]

Lillian Zimmermann often visited her elder sister Clara (Zimmermann) Hoxie at Cape Cod and loved to fish and enjoy clambakes there. She married, 24 December 1924, **James Alma FLIGG**, son of William Irving and Matilda Maud (Quick) Fligg; born 21 June 1900, London City, Ontario, Canada; died in 1975, Dallas, Texas.

**JAMES ALMA FLIGG**[75] was the eldest child of an RLDS missionary, William Irving Fligg, and his wife Matilda Maud Quick. He left school in the eighth grade to help support his five younger brothers and sisters. In 1923 he entered the University of Kansas to study electrical engineering, where he met his future wife, Lillian Zimmermann, who was an assistant to the dean. In 1927, "after graduating as an electrical engineer, he joined John Zimmermann's sons in business." He had a heart attack on the same morning that Janet Nancy[3] Kelley (Clara[2] [Zimmermann] and Richard Kelley's daughter) died in 1938, and "never returned to the mill." Nancy Kelley died of aplastic anemia; she was "very close" to her cousin, Kathryn "Katchie" Fligg, daughter of James and Lillian (Zimmermann) Fligg. Jim Fligg did, however, continue to work in the textile industry. He filed an application for a patent on 26 October 1948 as the inventor of a process entitled "Woven Fabric." The patent application, #2,541,231, was approved on 13 February 1951. This was the last patent that was granted to a member of the Zimmermann family in methods of weaving.

Some recollections of the Fligg family, by Kathryn Fligg's cousin, Mary Jane Zimmermann[1]:

### A Bit of This, a Bit of That[76]

My parents and their parents were members of the Reorganized Church of Latter Day Saints, emphasis on the Reorganized, although they did have copies of the Book of Mormon in their homes. We were taken to the R.C.L.D.S. Church in the Kensington district of Philadelphia, one of the city's poorer neighborhoods. But the Kelleys were there, the Hoxies were there, Aunt **Lil Fligg** was in charge of the children's' program, so the family was very much involved. . . . Aunt Clara remained a faithful member, and built a cottage at Deer Park as did Aunt Lil and my grandparents. (Uncle Jim **Fligg's** father was very big in the Church (R.C.L.D.S.)

---

[1] Mary Jane[3] Zimmermannn (John[1-2] Zimmermannn).

### New Year's

On New Years Day we always had a big family party after the Kelleys and the **Fliggs** got settled in their new homes. Dinner was served at the Kelleys', their dining room and breakfast room being more adaptable. Aunt Anna (or her cook) would do one turkey and **Aunt Lil** another, with oyster stuffing. Good stuff. My mother [Ethel (née Kinnaman)] always brought her special sweet potatoes done up with cinnamon apples and marshmallows on the top. Aunt Clara brought rolls and I'll guess that Aunt Peg [née Lukens]and Aunt Barbara [née Shoemaker] brought potatoes and a vegetable, except one year [1937] Aunt Barbara didn't because she was busy having a New Years baby, my cousin Albert [Zimmermann, Jr.]. There were undoubtedly other odd sorts. I can't imagine a big gathering without candy and nuts. Tomato juice probably, but nothing stronger.

After dinner we kids were herded over to the **Fligg** basement to be entertained. For a while it was rented movies, but in a few years the creative juices got flowing and puppet shows were born. First there was a small stage and equally small puppets, but then Aunts Lil and Anna and my mother really got going. **Aunt Lil** had a stage (about the size of this computer table) built complete with curtain. There were two productions: The Three Wishes, wherein a poor couple was granted three wishes of their own choosing by a good fairy. After debating what they should wish for, the husband forgot himself and wished, idly, that they had some sausage. His furious wife when the sausage sure-enough appeared, wished that it was hanging from his nose. And there it was (a date seed pulled by a string through a hole in the table). Two wishes down! He couldn't spend the rest of his life with sausage hanging from his nose so they agreed to wish only to be as they were before. My Aunts were the puppeteers, my mother did all the sound effects and Sue and I did the voices, and the moral:

> So all three wishes came to naught,
> You know I rather thought they would,
> For idle longing never brings,
> To wise or foolish any good.
> The wise folk when they want a thing,
> Don't need the fairies' help a bit.

### Further Persecution

We (my sister and I) used to take piano lessons at the Kelleys' house. It was a short walk across the footbridge over the Reading Railroad tracks, then a couple of blocks more on Prospect Avenue. (They moved from there later on when they and the **Fliggs** then living nearby on Mountain Avenue built their big houses a mile away on Cedar Road - maybe more on that later.

One evening at dusk we were crossing the footbridge after our lessons and I made a wish on the evening star. My sister told me that I had said the Star Bright routine improperly and only she could rescue me from the dire consequences that would thereafter ensue. The solution? I must thereafter do everything she told me to do to protect myself. It wasn't until I had worked a similar con on our brothers that I felt I had worked my way out of that one.
 We sure were a gullible bunch!

### A Banner Year

Meantime my father went to Europe and my mother and our brothers went to Cape Cod with Hoxies and **Fliggs** and had a great time. Mother [Ethyl (Kinnaman) Zimmermann] cooked lobster and **Aunt Lil** made excuses for my brothers when they got into trouble.

### Ohhhhhh 'Neka
[Camp Oneka]

'Neka 'Neka Rah rah
'Neka 'Neka Rah rah
Hurrah, Hurrah
Neka 'Neka Rah rah
Ohhhhhhhhhhh'Neka!

... I was a lofty Senior as were Sue, Marian and Anita. Nancy was a Junior and lived in a cabin with **Katchie Fligg.** [In this sentence, Mary Jane Zimmermann (1921-2008) mentions her cousins: Susan Kelley (1920-2002), Marian Kelley (1921->2011), Anita Kelley (1923- ); Janet Nancy Kelley (1927-1938); and Katchie Fligg]

James and Lillian (Zimmermann) Fligg had the following children, surname Fligg:

   **6.1**    i.     KATHRYN LUCILLE[3] "Katchie" (1925- ).
   **6.2**    ii.    JAMES ALMA, Jr. (1928-2009).

## Descendants of Lillian[2] "Lily Mae" (Zimmermann) Fligg

### Descendants of Kathryn Lucille[3] "Katchie" Fligg

**6.1 KATHRYN LUCILLE[3] "Katchie" FLIGG,**[77] an artist, daughter and elder child of James and Lillian (Zimmermann) Fligg, was born at Independence, Missouri, 9 October 1925. She received a Bachelor of Fine Arts degree from the University of Pennsylvania in 1951, and after graduating from Penn, she trained in illustration at the Pennsylvania Academy of Fine Arts. She then studied abroad on two travelling fellowships from the Academy. After finishing a large bank mural in Philadelphia, she went abroad again to Florence to study Italian. Her first job was illustrating books in 1954-55 for a Florentine publisher, Adriano Alani. After returning to the U.S., she illustrated books for various publishers, including Doubleday, D. C. Heath, Houghton Mifflin, and several magazines. She also did historic murals for architectural firms. Her work included commissions for the Budd Company's long distance trains. She did wildflower paintings for the covers of the menus and in the rooms of the Denver Zephyr, and she did murals in the Twin Zephyr and California Zephyr dome-coaches. She also had mural commissions from the First Federal Savings and Loan Association Bank of Upper Darby, and an apartment house by Central Park in New York City. From 1959-1963 she was head of the illustration department at Moore College of Art. She is now a member of the Muse Gallery in Philadelphia. She was married in 1961. She wrote that,

> [My] early professional career was in book and magazine illustration and mural painting. In mid-career I moved to Florence Italy for my husband's work with our young daughter and we lived there for ten years. Such a rich and powerful experience changed me. These collages that I now create echo the bas-reliefs that are seen throughout Tuscany. In lifting shapes up off the picture plane and by folding, scoring, curling and using painted papers I obtain an interplay of light and shadow that is the essence of bas-relief. Taking a classic form and rendering it anew with 20th century materials is fascinating to me. . . . My color choices come from Johannes Itten of the Bauhaus. His theory deals with color from an artist's point of view, and in its brilliant geometric simplicity it provides me with a whole new control of color.

One of her early publications was for the book, Donald Barrie, *Phoebe and the MacFairlie Mystery*, illustrated by Kathryn Fligg (New York: Lothrop, Lee & Shepard Co., 1963).[78] Her work was summarized for an exhibit of paintings in February and March 2009: "Collages: Flat and Floating / Trained in illustration at the Pennsylvania Academy of Fine Arts and the University of Pennsylvania, Kathryn has turned her focus with these deep set and recessed collages into a celebration of color and spirit." On 9 December 2011, her work was on exhibit at Cathedral Village and in the anniversary show at MUSE Gallery.

She married, 17 June 1961, **Rev. Edward L. LEE, Jr**., now the Rt. Rev. Edward Lee; born at Philadelphia, Pa., in 1934; son of Edward L. Lee, Sr. (~1903- ) and Adlyn C. "Addie" Frings (1904-1981).

**Rt. Rev. EDWARD L. LEE, Jr., D.D.,**[79] was born in Philadelphia in 1934 and baptized in 1935. He was raised in Fort Washington, Pa., and he was confirmed in 1946. He graduated from Springfield Township (Pa.) High School in 1952. He received the B.A. degree from Brown University in 1956 and the degree of Bachelor of Sacred Theology from the General Theological Seminary in 1959. He was awarded the D.D. (*hon.*) in 1990. He was ordained to the diaconate by Bishop Hart in May 1959 at St. Thomas Church, Whitemarsh, Pa., and to the priesthood by Bishop Armstrong in December 1959. His first parish was at Holy Trinity Church, Philadelphia, where he was curate from 1959 to 1964. He was Episcopal advisor, University Christian Movement, at Temple University, 1964-73; rector, St. James Church, Florence, Italy, 1973-82; rector, St. John's Church, Georgetown, Washington, D.C., 1982-1989; and 7th bishop of the Diocese of Western Michigan, 1989-2002, at which time he and his family resided in Kalamazoo, Michigan. He retired in 2002 and returned to the Philadelphia area, where he has since served as a part-time assisting bishop in the Diocese of Pennsylvania. Edward and Kathryn (Fligg) Lee now live in Merion, Pa.

Edward and Kathryn (Fligg) have one child, surname Lee:
    **6.1.1**        i.        KATHRYN[4].

**6.1.1 KATHRYN[4] LEE**, married **Mark _____**. They have two children:
    **6.1.1.1**      i.        LUKE[5], who has the artistic skills of his grandmother Fligg.
    **6.1.1.2**      ii.      NIKKO.

# James Alma[3] Fligg

**6.2 JAMES ALMA[3] FLIGG, Jr.,**[80] an aeronautical engineer, only son and younger child of James and Lucille (Zimmermann) Fligg, was born 31 August 1928; died 16 March 2009 at North Palm Beach, Fla. In 1946, at the age of 17, he graduated from Cheltenham High School in Cheltenham, Montgomery Co., Pa.

He spent his entire professional career as an engineer with United Aircraft Corp. and its subsidiary, Pratt & Whitney. He began his work at the U.A. plant in Hartford, Conn. In April 1965, he filed for a patent as an inventor, on behalf of the United Aircraft Corp., entitled "Splitter Vane Construction for Turbofan Engine." The patent was awarded on Nov. 8, 1966. This patent, #3,283,995, has been cited many times in the literature and it is a seminal work on the subject. At about the same time, he presented a paper at the 2nd Propulsion Joint Specialist Conference in Colorado Springs, Colo., entitled "Tests of a Low Speed Three-stage Axial Flow Compressor at Aspect Ratios of One, Two, and Four." This paper, too, is an important work, and it, too, has been cited many times in the literature. The annual conference on Joint Propulsion still continues, although the conference name has changed several times.

By 1972, he had become a member of the group at Pratt & Whitney Aircraft's Florida Research & Development Center, West Palm Beach, Fl., which contributed to several reports published by the National Aviation and Space Administration (NASA). An example of the sophistication of this work was the document published in September 1972 by A. L. Morris, et al, "High-Loading, 1800 Ft/Sec Tip Speed Transonic Compressor Fan Stage I. Aerodynamic and Mechanicac Design," in which J. A. Fligg and other members of his team appear in the credits. The abstract shows:

> A single stage fan with a tip speed of 1800 ft/sec (548.6 mlsec) and hub/tip ratio of 0.5 was designed to produce a pressure ratio of 2.285: 1 with an adiabatic efficiency of 84.Wo. The design flow per inlet annulus area is 38.7 Ibm/ft2-sec (188.9 kg/m2-sec). Rotor blades have modified multiple-circular-arc and precompression airfoil sections. The stator vanes have multiplecircular-arc airfoil sections.

-------------------------

Jim Fligg was a gentle, thoughtful man, who never married. His written recollections and appreciation of his grandfather John Zimmermann are an important contribution to the history of the Zimmermann family. He spoke of his grandfather Zimmermann's achievement of the American Dream, which is incorporated into the title of this book.

# 10
## Albert Walter[2] "Al" Zimmermann

**7. ALBERT WALTER[2] "Al" ZIMMERMANN,**[81] third son and youngest child of John and Eva Katharine (Kellenbenz) Zimmermann, was born at Philadelphia, Philadelphia Co., Pa., 11 June 1902; died at Haverford, Montgomery Co., Pa., 24 July 1961. The source of his first name is unknown, but it is likely that he was given his middle name in honor of Walter W. Smith, who was pastor of the RLDS Church in Philadelphia and RLDS Church historian when Albert was born – a man who was a close friend of his father, Bishop John Zimmermann.

Al Zimmermann attended public schools in Philadelphia and then the University of Pennsylvania, from which he graduated in 1923 with a degree in mechanical engineering, with a specialty in electrical engineering. He was a member of Sigma Tau, the honorary engineering fraternity; and the Sphinx Senior Society. He was also president of the Glee Club. Three years after he graduated from college, he was married to the daughter of a prominent Philadelphia ophthalmologist in what was said to be the society wedding of the season. Soon after graduating from college, he joined his father, his two brothers, and two brothers-in-law in the Zimmermann family textile businesses. He was also involved in his father's original enterprises with three Wasserman brothers in a group of companies that were eventually merged into one corporation – Artloom. At that time, Artloom was one of the largest rug manufacturers in America. He was a partner in two family textile businesses in Philadelphia – Zimmermann Mills, and John Zimmermann & Sons – which manufactured upholstery products and other fabrics. In the late 1930s, he rose to become a junior officer in these companies; and as a vice president and assistant treasurer, he was the last of his family to be involved with Artloom. He also was in partnership with a fellow Orpheus Club member, John Ott, in a successful wool brokerage firm known as Ott and Zimmermann. The firm imported and sold fine wool from all over the world. Although Ott was shown as the first name on the title, Zimmermann was president of the firm.

Al and his wife, Barbara (née Shoemaker), took an extended honeymoon after they were married. They lived for a short time in an apartment in Bryn Mawr. They then moved into a newly built, architect-designed, cut-stone house nearby, in the Philadelphia suburb of Haverford. Their home, an ivy-covered mansion called "Cotswold Corners," is said to have been modeled on houses in Cornwall, in the southeast of England. Haverford was a town on the upscale "Main Line" of the Pennsylvania Railroad – the commuter line that went west from Philadelphia to Paoli. Al and Barbara joined the usual country clubs – Philadelphia Country Club, Merion Cricket Club, and the Gulf Mills Golf Club. Al was also a member of the exclusive Fourth Street Club, and he was a soloist in the Orpheus Club. His wife Barbara became a member of the Acorn Club. As a member of The Savoy Company of Philadelphia, Al sang the role of the Lord Chancellor in *Iolanthe* in the same performance in which Nelson Eddy played the Arcadian shepherd, Strephon. His children recall, perhaps with some revisionist memory, that the reviewers were more favorably impressed with the amateur, Albert Zimmermann, than the professional, Nelson Eddy. After the war, Al and Barbara became members of the Maidstone Club, in East Hampton, New York, where they had a large summer home known as "Full House," near the beach. Their cabaña at the Maidstone Club had previously been owned by John "Black Jack" Bouvier, father of Jacqueline Bouvier. She later became the wife of Senator John Fitzgerald Kennedy, known to the world as "Jackie" Kennedy, First Lady of the United States, and later as Jacqueline Kennedy Onassis.

In December 1941, soon after World War II broke out, Al Zimmermann began to look for a way to serve in the armed forces. He was then 39 years old, and color blind, so his options were limited. However, he had the social and educational connections that were important at that time for men who were selected to work in Navy intelligence. He was also independently wealthy, as were many of the other men in Navy intelligence, and later those who were in the O.S.S. (nicknamed "Oh so social"). Zimmermann had already demonstrated his skills in intelligence work, having photographed for the F.B.I. a wedding in Philadelphia in which some of the participants, in the German Bund, wore uniforms with swastikas on their arm bands. He also had taken surreptitious movies of Nazi soldiers marching in Stuttgart, Germany, in 1937. Al Zimmermann was a friend of Commander Jack Kane, deputy chief of Navy intelligence in Philadelphia, and of Captain Tom Thornton, also an intelligence officer in the Third Naval District, who was later deputy chief of the Joint Intelligence Collection Agency (JICA) in Cairo, Egypt. Zimmermann also had several social connections with Commander Vincent Astor, USNR, who was appointed by his friend and neighbor, President Franklin Delano Roosevelt, to be the coordinator of Navy intelligence in the New York-Philadelphia region. With all of this background, it is hardly a surprise that Zimmermann was accepted by the Office of Naval Intelligence. On 21 September 1942, he took the oath of office as a lieutenant, USNR. He received basic training as a Navy officer in Washington from October to November 1942; intelligence indoctrination at Dartmouth College from November 1942 to January 1943; French language school in D.C. until April 1943; and advanced intelligence school in New York City, which he completed in May 1943. He was then sent to India by a series of airplanes, from NYC to Botwood, Newfoundland; Limerick, Ireland; Port Lyautey and Casablanca, Morocco; Oran and Algiers, Algeria; Constantine and Sousse, Tunisia; Tripoli and Benghasi, Lybia; Cairo, Egypt; Habanniah, Iraq; and finally to Karachi, India.

Lieutenant Al Zimmermann became Executive Officer of the Naval Liaison Office in Karachi, India (now Pakistan) when he arrived on 19 July 1943, and he was appointed Commanding Officer of the NLO in March 1944. In November 1943, he was sent on a secret mission with two other intelligence officers, Major Gordon Enders of the U.S. Army and Major Sir Benjamin Bromhead of the Indian Army, along the border of India (now Pakistan) and Afghanistan. The story of the Anglo-American officers' 34-day trip along the border from Peshawar, gateway to the Khyber Pass, to the remote principality of Chitral in the north, and then to Quetta in the south, are told in a book by his son-in-law, *Proceed to Peshawar* (2013). This book also tells of Zimmermann's flights by seaplane to Allied military headquarters in Ceylon before and after his trip to Peshawar. On these trips, he traveled to the regional headquarters of the U.S. Navy and the OSS, and to the South-East Asia Command (SEAC) headquarters of the regional Commander-in-Chief, Admiral Lord Mountbatten.

As Commanding Officer of the NLO Karachi, Zimmermann was responsible for Navy intelligence in the four provinces that now constitute the entire country of Pakistan, including the North-West Frontier Province (NWFP, now Khyber Pakhtunkhwa Province). Zimmermann's command included responsibility for the Navy enlisted personnel that manned the Navy communications center and supply depot in Peshawar. He was probably one of the first fifteen Americans ever to cross the summit of the Khyber Pass. Zimmermann is the first known American official to travel to all four of the provinces of what is now Pakistan, including Sind (where Karachi is located), Punjab, the NWFP, and Baluchistan. Zimmermann's position as the senior U.S. Naval officer in Pakistan is now usually held by a flag officer – a Rear Admiral.

Zimmermann was relieved of duty in Karachi and returned to the U.S. in May 1945, suffering from a duodenal ulcer. After hospitalization at St. Albans Navy Hospital on Long Island and convalescent leave at home, he was released from active duty on 30 December 1945. He returned to his work as a civilian, but he continued as a Navy reserve officer for another two years. He was promoted to lieutenant commander before he resigned his commission.

Al Zimmermann returned to Africa, India, and Pakistan in 1950 with his wife and his elder daughter. He renewed friendships that he had made in Karachi during the war and did some business with wool brokers in that area. His photographs and movies taken on that trip complement the many photos and movies that he took in 1943-1945. In later years, he was a generous contributor to his friends who were in need, and to various charities, including Episcopal churches in Pennsylvania and Long Island, the University of Pennsylvania, and the Southern Home for Children, on whose board he served for many years.

As a young man, Al Zimmermann was raised in the Reorganized Church of Latter Day Saints (RLDS), and his wife was raised in the Swedenborgian Church, also known as the Church of the New Jerusalem. After their marriage, they became affiliated with the Episcopal Church. He died suddenly at the age of 59 of a ruptured cerebral aneurysm, following a golf match on one of the hottest days in summer. He is buried beside his wife in the churchyard of the Church of the Redeemer, Bryn Mawr, Pa.

Al Zimmermann was a man with many abilities. He was a handsome man, a fine golfer and tennis player, an excellent bridge player, a disarming conversationalist, a notable amateur singer, a skillful photographer, an amateur silversmith, a shrewd investor, and a generous person. He was also a consummate intelligence officer. He listened and analyzed thoughtfully, took careful photographs and movies, wrote well, and kept quiet. The book about his work in India and along the border of Afghanistan in World War II is the only story of a U.S. Navy intelligence officer in that war that has yet been told, and that probably ever will be told. His jeep was the first motor vehicle to cross the Lowari Pass into the remote region of Chitral, situated at the point where Pakistan's border meets with the borders of China, Afghanistan, and India. He and the Army intelligence officer who drove the jeep along the Afghan border in November 1943 were probably the first Americans to meet a *mehtar* (hereditary ruler) of Chitral, a *wali* of Swat, and a *nawab* of Dir. Zimmermann observed drily that only one other American had been in Chitral before him, and he was the first Navy man to be there. His movies taken in Chitral of Tirich Mir – the highest peak in the Hindu Kush range, unclimbed until 1950 – were probably the first ever taken of that mountain. The book, *Proceed to Peshawar,* is based on his letters, journals, photographs, and scrapbooks. His papers were arranged by his wife and they were preserved by his elder daughter. The wartime papers of Albert W. Zimmermann are now in the Special Collections of the U.S. Naval Institute at Annapolis.

**BARBARA SHOEMAKER,**[82] daughter of Dr. William Toy and Mabel (Warren) Shoemaker, was born at Philadelphia, Pa., 13 February 1902; died at Haverford, Pa., 24 July 1985. She came from a long line of Quakers in Philadelphia, but her parents and paternal grandparents had left the Friends to become Swedenborgians – members of the Swedenborg Church. She was active throughout her life as a leader in Philadelphia society. She belonged to the Acorn Club and the National Society of Colonial Dames of America, and she was a member of the Church of the Redeemer, Bryn Mawr, Pa. Barbara Shoemaker grew up in the city of Philadelphia near Rittenhouse Square, where her father, an ophthalmologist, had his office. He also was the senior ophthalmologist at the Lankenau Hospital, which until 1917 was known as the German Hospital of Philadelphia. Barbara's older sister, Dorothy, recalled that although the family was prominent in society, they were not wealthy, and they never had their own horse and carriage. Barbara Shoemaker was educated at private schools and did not attend college – a college education then was rarely undertaken by young women in her social group. An attractive woman with blond hair and fair skin, she had many suitors and was very popular at the parties and balls where young people of her age gathered. Her hand was won by Albert Walter Zimmermann, a bright and handsome young graduate of the University of Pennsylvania, and she married him. Their wedding and their honeymoon cruise to the Caribbean was recorded on the first of more than 50 10-inch reels of 16 mm film that her husband took over the next three and a half decades. Their new house was constructed at 400 North Rose Lane in Haverford, Pa., in the style of an English manor house, with ivy covered walls and flower and vegetable gardens, above a stream on a steep wooded hillside. After spending summer vacations in Chatham, Mass., and elsewhere in New England, they purchased a large summer home in East Hampton, on Long Island, N.Y. While in East Hampton they were members of the Maidstone Club.

In Philadelphia, Barbara (Shoemaker) Zimmermann was active in support of many charitable organizations, most notably the Church Farm School in Exton, Pa., and the Graduate Hospital Board. She represented the Board Volunteers' organization, which she had founded. She traveled widely with her husband, and after his sudden and unexpected death in 1961, with her friend Mrs. Amelie Kane, widow of Commander Jack Kane, USNR. Her last long trip was to Australia and the islands of the Pacific in 1975. Her health was then beginning to fail, and she spent most of the rest of her life at her home in Haverford, eventually being largely confined to bed, where she was attended by nurses around the clock for several years. Late in life Barbara was often unaware of much that went on around her, and she was bitterly disappointed by the loss of an eye following cataract surgery. She passed away quietly on the exact anniversary of her husband's death, 24 years previously. It seemed to her children that she was in fact aware of that date, and that she allowed her life to slip away then. Barbara was buried beside her husband in the churchyard of the Church of the Redeemer in Bryn Mawr. The two graves were framed by azalea bushes that she had selected. The azaleas overgrew the markers, and were replaced by a flowering dogwood tree, which now shades the gravestones. Barbara (Shoemaker) Zimmermann was an incisive and determined person with a forceful personality and a wry sense of humor. Her autobiography, *Mutterings*, was printed and published privately. It offers insight into the mid-20th Century world of society and privilege. She will be remembered vividly by all who knew her, and the stories of "Baba" – as she was known by her grandchildren – will be passed down for generations to come.

Albert Walter Zimmermann married, at Philadelphia, 29 January 1926, in a ceremony conducted by a minister of the Swedenborgian Church, **Barbara SHOEMAKER**, daughter of Dr. William Toy and Mabel (Warren) Shoemaker of Philadelphia, Pa.; born at Philadelphia, 13 February 1902; died at Haverford, Pa., 24 July 1985. Albert and Barbara (Shoemaker) Zimmermann had four children. All four children married, and twelve grandchildren and three great-grandchildren have been born as of July 2016.

Children of Albert and Barbara (Shoemaker) Zimmermann, born at Philadelphia, surname Zimmermann:

| | | | |
|---|---|---|---|
| **7.1** | i. | BARBARA WARREN[3] "Babs" (1927-2011) + |
| **7.2** | ii. | Dr. HELENE "Lanie" (1929-) + |
| **7.3** | iii. | Amb. WARREN "Zimmer" (1934-2004) + |
| **7.4** | iv. | Dr. ALBERT WALTER "Al," Jr. (1937-) + |

# Descendants of Albert Walter[2] Zimmermann

## Barbara Warren[3] Zimmermann and Her Descendants

**7.1 BARBARA WARREN[3] "Babs" ZIMMERMANN,**[83] elder daughter and first child of Albert and Barbara (Shoemaker) Zimmermann, was born at Philadelphia, Pa., 26 July 1927; died there, 30 November 2011. She grew up at "Cotswold Corners," her family's home, at 400 North Rose Lane, Haverford, Pa. She first attended the Baldwin School in nearby Bryn Mawr, Pa., and she spent her last two years of secondary school at Chatham Hall School, Chatham, Va., from which she graduated in 1944. Her father was then a Navy officer, stationed in Karachi, India, now Pakistan, and she was – along with the rest of her generation in America – profoundly affected by World War II. Rationing of sugar, butter, heating fuel, gasoline and many other commodities affected all of life. Her father was in Navy intelligence, and he was said to have been in the first jeep ever to cross one of the high passes along the border with Afghanistan.

She attended Smith College, from which she graduated in 1948, and she then began to work for the Central Intelligence Agency. Although at the time, it was not to be spoken of, her family knew that her work as a secretary in various U.S. embassies in the Middle East was simply her "cover" job – she was really working for the CIA. It was at the height of the cold war, and many other Ivy League graduates were also working in similar, mysterious jobs. Those who could read between the lines knew they, like Barbara, were in some sort of intelligence work. When she was in Amman, Jordan, she met "H.M." (His Majesty, King Hussein) many times at social and professional functions. In Lebanon, she traveled widely in the field. Her travels included a trip to the then rarely visited ruins at Petra.

While in the Middle East, Barbara met **Melvin T. JOHNSON**, who had worked for the U.S. Agency for International Development for many years. In addition to its stated government work, the USAID was also used as a "cover" for many intelligence workers. Barbara and Mel were married in 1963 in the Lutheran Church of Devon, Pa., on the same weekend that her younger brother, Al, was married. Babs and Mel continued in government service for a tour of duty in Yemen, and then retired to the suburbs of Philadelphia, where Mel purchased the region's best known candy manufacturing company, the Maron Company. They made their home in Radnor, where they were members of St. Martin's Episcopal Church. Babs and Mel have two daughters, Barbara and Alice. The older, her namesake, graduated from Smith College exactly 40 years after her mother. Babs and Mel were members of the Gulph Mills Golf Club.

Barbara (Zimmermann) Johnson was active in volunteer work as an officer of the Philadelphia chapter of the League of Women Voters, and for her church. She was also an officer of the Smith College Alumni Association and a docent of the Philadelphia Zoo, teaching inner city school children about animals, and traveling abroad on behalf of the zoo. She was known for her poise, for her sense of humor and compassion, and for her skills as a mother, a cook, and a public speaker. She developed an unusual form of lung cancer called alveolar cell cancer, not believed to be related to tobacco. It was inoperable when it was diagnosed, and slowly progressive in spite of chemotherapy. She had periods of hospitalization but mainly lived in her retirement apartment at Fox Hill, Whitemarsh Township, near Flourtown, Pa. After spending Thanksgiving with her children in Maryland, she was admitted to Chestnut Hill Hospital in Philadelphia, and died two days later, on 30 November 2011. After a memorial service, her cremains were interred at St. Martin's Church, Radnor, on 10 December 2011.

**MELVIN THORNTON "Mel" JOHNSON,**[84] son and second child of Thomas Edward and Maria (Thorson, aka Thornton) Johnson, was born at Newton, Mass., 10 June 1913; died at Devon, Pa., 30 March 2002. He graduated from Newton High School, and was employed by the U.S. Agency for International Development until he retired from government service and became the owner of the Maron Candy Company in Philadelphia.

In 1949 the Greek government awarded him the Royal Order of the Golden Cross of the Phoenix, in Athens, for his work with CARE after World War II. In his late sixties, he began to suffer from angina pectoris. It was relieved by coronary artery by-pass surgery and he resumed normal activities including golf. In September 2000 he suffered a stroke that left him unable to ambulate. He began to fail and his family gathered at his bedside at the Bryn Mawr Care Center, Devon, Pa., where he died. His funeral was held at St. Martin's Episcopal Church, Radnor, Pa., on 6 April 2002, and his ashes were interred in the Memorial Garden there.

He married (1) Elizabeth McGill, by whom he had one son, Robert Johnson. He divorced her and married (2) at Devon, Pa., 21 June 1963, **Barbara Warren ZIMMERMANN**, daughter of Albert Walter and Barbara (Shoemaker) Zimmermann.

Barbara Warren Zimmermann married, 21 June 1963, at Devon, Pa., as his second wife, **Melvin Thornton "Mel" JOHNSON,**[85] son of Thomas Edward and Maria (Thorson, aka Thornton) Johnson; born at Newton, Mass., 10 June 1913; died at Devon, Pa., 30 March 2002.

Melvin and Barbara (Shoemaker) Johnson had the following children, surname Johnson:
- **7.1.1**    i.      BARBARA WARREN[4] (1966- ) +
- **7.1.2**    ii.     ALICE THORNTON (1970- ) +

**7.1.1 BARBARA WARREN**[4] **JOHNSON** was born 20 April 1966 at Wynnewood, Pa. She graduated from Agnes Irwin School in 1984, and Smith College, B.A., in 1988. She was a top advertising salesperson for *The Washington Times* from 1991-1994. In 1995 she resigned to take a new position with *The Hill* newspaper in Washington, D.C. Like her grandfather Albert Zimmermann, she is an excellent photographer. She married, at Radnor, Chester Co., Pa., in 1993, **Thomas A. RILEY III, J.D.**[86]

**THOMAS A. RILEY, III, Esq.,** graduated from the Episcopal Academy, Merion, Pa., in 1983, and from Georgetown University, Washington, D.C., in 1987 with a B.A. in History and English; Distinction was awarded in History. He then attended Villanova Law School, where he concentrated in international law and U.S. constitutional law. He was president of the International Law Society and was a staff writer for the *Villanova Docket*. He received the J.D. from Villanova in 1990. After further study at Georgetown University, in 1993 he received the degrees of M.S. in Foreign Service and M.A. in History, with concentration in national security and U.S. and European history and diplomacy. He was director of advertising services for Acme Newspapers in 1988 and was a reporter for the *Main Line Times*, Ardmore, Pa., 1988-90. He was a legal intern at the United Nations in 1989 and was a research assistant for the Republican Study Group, U.S. House of Representatives, in 1992. He was a research assistant for the American Enterprise Institute in 1992-93. In 1994 he was appointed senior political analyst for The Center for Media and Public Affairs, Washington, D.C. Mr. Riley is a member of the Pennsylvanian Bar Association and has been trustee and counsel for the Connelly Foundation since February 1993. During the administration of President George W. Bush, from 2001-09, he was associate director of National Drug Control Policy at the White House.

Thomas and Barbara (Johnson) Riley have the following children, surname Riley:

| | | |
|---|---|---|
| **7.1.1.1** | i. | FIONA JUDITH[5] (~1997-) |
| **7.1.1.2** | ii. | PENELOPE QUINN "Nell" (2000-) |
| **7.1.1.3** | iii. | JOHN WARREN (2001-) |
| **7.1.1.4** | iv. | THOMAS VINCENT (2004-) |
| **7.1.1.5** | v. | RICHARD XAVIER "Rex" (2010-) |

**7.1.2 ALICE THORNTON[4] JOHNSON,** younger daughter and second child of Melvin and Barbara (Zimmermann) Johnson, was born at Wynnewood, Pa., 22 August 1970. After graduating from the Agnes Irwin School and Colby College, she was a development officer for the National League of Women Voters, Washington, D.C. She resigned in January 1995 to travel in Asia for six months.

She married, at St. Martin's Episcopal Church, Radnor, Pa., 10 June 2000, **Brian Keith HANDWERK**, son of Keith and Marilee Handwerk of Jersey Shore, Pa. Brian and Alice (Johnson) Handwerk lived in Washington, D.C., after they were married, where he was employed by the National Geographic Society. They now live in Amherst, N.H., where he is a free-lance writer and she is associate director of advancement at the Derryfield School, Manchester, N.H.

Brian and Alice (Johnson) Handwerk had the following children, surname Handwerk:

| | | |
|---|---|---|
| **7.1.2.1** | i. | LILIAN THORNTON[5] (2005-) |
| **7.1.2.2** | ii. | PHOEBE WATERS (2008-) |

## Helene[3] Zimmermann and Her Descendants

**7.2  HELENE[3] ZIMMERMANN,**[87] second daughter and second child of Albert Walter and Barbara (Shoemaker) Zimmermann; was born at Philadelphia, Pa., 10 April 1929.  She is the youngest granddaughter of John and Eva Katherine (Kellenbenz) Zimmermann.  She was born at the Lankenau Hospital, where her grandfather, Dr. Warren T. Shoemaker, was the chief of the department of ophthalmology.  The Lankenau Hospital, now the Lankenau Medical Center and relocated to Lower Merion Township, was founded as the German Hospital of Philadelphia.  It was renamed as the Lankenau in 1917.  The German Hospital was in a smaller building in 1876 when John Zimmermann, Helene's grandfather, was a patient there with pneumonia.

Helene, known as "Nanie" as a child, and later as "Lanie," attended the Baldwin School, Bryn Mawr, Pa., through the tenth grade, and then the Chatham Hall School, Chatham, Va., from which she graduated in 1946.  She studied at Smith College from 1946-50, majoring in premedical studies and French, and took her junior year abroad in Paris.  She graduated with the B.A. degree in 1950.  She took graduate courses at M.I.T. and worked as a laboratory technician at Memorial Sloan Kettering Cancer Center in New York City until 1952.  She resumed her graduate studies at Brandeis University, Waltham, Mass., in 1957, and received the Ph.D. in biology in 1964.  She was a postdoctoral fellow at the Harvard Medical School from 1964-66, and at University of Colorado Medical Center from 1966-67.  She was appointed assistant professor of biophysics at the University of Colorado in 1967, and associate professor of radiology at Washington University, St. Louis, Missouri, in 1973.  She was associate professor (1976-80) and professor (1980-81) of biochemistry at Marshall University, Huntington, W.Va.  She was appointed professor of radiology at the UMDNJ (now Rutgers)-New Jersey Medical School, Newark, N.J., in 1981, and was additionally appointed professor of microbiology and molecular genetics, and professor of biochemistry and molecular biology.

Her honors include the Smith College Medal; the Lifetime Achievement Award from the Baldwin School; Visiting Scientist at the Jagiellonian University, Krakow, Poland; Honorary Member of the Bolivian Society of Surgery; and president of the Washington University Chapter of Sigma Xi-The Scientific Research Society.  She has published more than 60 scientific papers, abstracts and book chapters.  Her research has been supported by national peer-reviewed grants from the American Cancer Society and the National Institutes of Health.  From 1994-98 she was a member of the Council of the American Society of Photobiology, and served two terms as secretary of that organization; and in 1996 she was president of the New Jersey Academy of Science.  Dr. Hill has been a member of the Alumni Council of Chatham Hall School and of the Alumni Advisory Council of the Baldwin School.  She was a sustaining member of the Junior League, and she is a member of the Garden Club of the Oranges  She has been a member of the Board of Directors of the South Mountain YMCA and of the Board of the Smith Club of the Oranges, in Essex Co., N.J.  She is a member of the Appalachian Mountain Club and of its "4,000 Footer Club," having climbed all of the mountains 4,000 feet or higher in New Hampshire.  She is a member of the Board of Directors of the National Society Colonial Dames of America in the State of New Jersey (President, 2012-3), and by right of descent, she is also a member of the Order of the Crown of Charlemagne, Order of the Norman Conquest, Welcome Society, and Military Order of the World Wars.  Her hobbies include hiking, ballroom dancing, and the family tree farm in Eaton, N.H.

Helene Zimmermann married (1), at Bryn Mawr, Penn., 3 May 1952, **James Hedgcock GROVER, Esq.**, son of Charles and Mary (Hedgcock) Grover; born at Boston, Mass, in 1917; died in New Hampshire, 1 May 2010. He was a graduate of Harvard College (S.B. '40) and Boston University Law School; he was an attorney in Boston and later in Sharon, Mass. They were divorced at Montgomery, Alabama, in May 1960 and he married (2), Carol McKinnon; died 1995; they had a daughter, Robin Lee Grover.

Helene Zimmermann married (2), at Amagansett, Suffolk Co., N.Y., 16 July 1960, **George James HILL, M.D., D.Litt.,** son of Gerald Leslie and Essie Mae (Thompson) Hill, born at Cedar Rapids, Linn Co., Ia., 7 October 1932.[88]

**GEORGE J. HILL** entered first grade at Lisbon, Ia., in 1938 and graduated from Sac City, Ia., High School in 1949. He entered Yale University in 1949 on a scholarship and received the A.B. degree with High Orations in 1953. He received the M.D. from the Harvard Medical School in 1957. He was an intern-in-surgery at The New York Hospital-Cornell Medical Center, 1957-58. He was a research fellow and surgical resident at Harvard Medical School and Peter Bent Brigham (now Brigham and Women's) Hospital, in 1958-61 and 1963-66. He was on active duty as a physician in U.S. Public Health Service at the National Institutes of Health, Bethesda, Md., 1961-63. Dr. Hill was appointed chief resident and instructor in surgery at the University of Colorado Medical Center, Denver, in 1966. He was promoted to assistant professor in 1967, and to associate professor in 1972. He moved to Washington University, St. Louis, Mo., in 1973, as professor of surgery and lived in University City, Mo. In 1976 he accepted a position as professor and founding chairman of the Department of Surgery at Marshall University School of Medicine, Huntington, W.Va. He relocated to New Jersey in 1981 as professor of surgery and chief of surgical oncology at the University of Medicine and Dentistry of N.J.-New Jersey Medical School, in Newark. He became emeritus professor of surgery in 1999. The institution became Rutgers-New Jersey Medical School in 2013.

Dr. Hill was a member of the Platoon Leaders Class in the U.S. Marine Corps Reserve while a student at Yale, 1950-52; he rose to the rank of sergeant, and received an honorable discharge to continue his education as a premedical student. He was in the U.S. Public Health Service Reserve from 1960-68 as a senior assistant surgeon (equivalent to lieutenant, USN). He was on active duty from 1961-1963 at the National Institutes of Health, Bethesda, Md., during the Cuban Missile Crisis. He transferred to the U.S. Navy Reserve in 1968 as a lieutenant commander; he was promoted to commander in 1972 and to captain in 1976. He retired after a ceremony at the National Naval Medical Center on 7 October 1992. His awards include the U.S. Meritorious Service Medal, Navy Unit Commendation Ribbon, Meritorious Unit Commendation Ribbon with bronze star attachment, Vietnam Service Medal with one campaign star, National Defense Service Medal with two bronze star attachments, Armed Forces Reserve Medal with silver hourglass and mobilization "M" attachments, Navy Rifle Expert medal, Navy Pistol Expert medal, Republic of Vietnam Unit Citations (Gallantry Cross Color and First Class Color with palm and frame), Navy and Marine Corps Parachute Badge, USMC Rifle Expert with bar for second award, Outstanding Service Medal of the Uniformed Services University of the Health Sciences, New Jersey Distinguished Service Medal, and New Jersey Vietnam Service Medal.

George James and Helene (Zimmermann) Hill have two daughters. In 1964 he legally adopted his wife's two sons by her first marriage.

George and Helene (Zimmermann) Hill had the following children, surname Hill:

**7.2.1**     i.     JAMES WARREN[4], J.D. "Jim" (1954-) (adopted 1964).

**7.2.2**     ii.     DAVID HEDGCOCK "Dave" (1955-2004) (adopted 1964) +

**7.2.3**     iii.     SARAH, Ph.D. (1962-) +

**7.2.4**     iv.     HELENA RUNDALL "Lana" (1964-)

## James Warren[4] Hill

**7.2.1 JAMES WARREN[4] "Jim" HILL, J.D.,**[89] elder son and eldest child of George James and Helene (Zimmermann) Hill, was born at Boston, Suffolk Co., Mass., in 1954; christened at St. Peter's Episcopal Church, Weston, Mass., in 1954. He is the son of Helene Zimmermann by her first marriage to James Hedgcock Grover. He was adopted by George J. Hill in 1964, at which time his surname was changed from Grover to Hill, and his birth certificate was thus changed by Massachusetts law to show George Hill as his father. James W. Hill was educated at the Park School in Brookline, Mass., and at public schools in Bethesda, Md., and Denver, Colo. He completed his secondary education at The Gunnery School in Washington, Conn. After working in various building trades in Minnesota and West Virginia for ten years, he entered Rutgers University in New Brunswick, where he majored in philosophy and graduated B.A. (with honors) in 1985. He continued his education with studies of philosophy and law at Rutgers. He graduated with the J.D. degree in 1993, and became a member of the Bar of New York and New Jersey. He began his career as a public defender in Orange County, N.Y., and he continued this work in Dutchess County, N.Y. He has resided in the town of Poughkeepsie since 1994.

Mr. Hill enjoys hiking in the Appalachian Mountains and kayaking on rivers and lakes in New York state and New Hampshire. He is also co-owner and non-resident manager of his family's property, known as Hilltree Farm, in Eaton, N.H., which is certified by the National Tree Farm Association. In July 2011, he completed a 45-mile bicycle ride round trip from the east base to the summit of the Kancamangus Pass. In the summer of 2012, he completed the 105-mile Gran Fondo bike race from Manhattan to Bear Mountain to Weehauken, N.J.

He and his companion **Uma NARAYAN, Ph.D.**, live in Poughkeepsie, N.Y. Dr. Narayan is the Mellon professor of philosophy at Vassar College.

## David Hedgcock[4] Hill and His Descendants

**7.2.2 DAVID HEDGCOCK[4] "Dave" HILL,**[90] second son and second child of George J. and Helene (Zimmermann) Hill, was born at Boston, Mass., 29 August 1955; christened in 1955 in St. Peter's Episcopal Church, Weston, Mass.; died at Glen Ridge, N.J., 4 January 2004. He was the son of James Hedgcock Grover, Esq., and Helene Zimmermann; they were divorced in 1960. In 1964 he was adopted by his stepfather, George J. Hill. His surname was changed to Hill, and the name of his father on his birth certificate was also changed by law to be George J. Hill.

Mr. Hill studied at the Dearborn School, Cambridge, Mass., and at private and public schools in Bethesda, Md.; in Denver, Co.; and in the suburbs of St. Louis, Mo. As a boy he was a Cub Scout and a First Class Boy Scout, and he was an acolyte in the Episcopal Church. He graduated from University City, Missouri, High School in 1975.  He then attended Fontbonne College in Clayton, Mo., and later was a student at Glenville, West Virginia, State College.  He also attended Union County, N.J., State College.  In 1994 he graduated from the Empire Technical School, East Orange, .N.J, as a certified medical secretary.  He enjoyed composing music and writing essays and poetry.  Some of his works were published during his lifetime and some were edited and published posthumously.

Mr. Hill was employed for several years as a nursing assistant at St. Barnabas Medical Center, Livingston, N.J., and in 1994 he was a salesman for Sears, Roebuck, and Co. at Livingston, N.J.  He enjoyed walking and long distance bicycle riding, working with computers and crossword puzzles, and he was a member of the choir and a lay reader at the Church of the Holy Innocents, West Orange, N.J.  He was completely disabled on 20 September 1994 as the result of a severe stroke caused by an occlusion of the right internal carotid artery.  He probably bruised his carotid artery in a fall at work, but the origin of the occlusion could never be determined.  In 2001 he was living near his parents in Essex County, N.J., and writing poetry and composing music for the piano and organ.  As he became increasingly disabled, he was hospitalized at the Essex County Hospital, Cedar Grove, N.J., and it was there that he had a fatal episode of cerebral ischemia on 25 November 2003, probably due to aspiration of food at breakfast.  After resuscitation, he was taken to Mountainside Hospital in Glen Ridge, N.J.  It became apparent that he had no hope for recovery; he was taken off of life support on 30 December and he died on 4 January 2004.  A memorial service was held at the Church of the Holy Innocents in West Orange on 10 January 2004.  His cremains were divided; some were interred in the Bethel Cemetery, Parkersburg, W.V., near the grave of his former wife, Sheri (Wilson) (Hill) Graham.  Other ashes were scattered in the Memorial Garden at the Church of the Holy Innocents, and others in the Hill plot at the Snowville cemetery, Eaton, N.H.

He married, at Washington Bottom, W.Va., 18 April 1981, when he was 25, **Sheri Lynn WILSON**, daughter of George S. and Regina L. (Marion) Wilson; born at Parkersburg, W.Va., 4 October 1958; died of an acute asthmatic attack at Parkersburg, 11 February 2003, age 44.  She was David Hill's classmate at Glenville State College, and she later became a public school teacher.  She received the B.S. from Glenville (W.Va.) State College in 1978, and later the degree of M.Ed.  She was employed in the Calhoun County school system for many years and was principal at Arnoldsburg Elementary School before becoming assistant principal at Jackson Junior High School in Parkersburg.  She attended Mineral Wells Baptist Church.  Services were held on February 15, 2003, at Sunset Memorial Funeral Home, Parkersburg (Minister Robert Summers, officiating), followed by burial in Bethel Cemetery, beside Bethel Baptist Church.  David and Sheri Lynn (Wilson) Hill were divorced on 29 July 1983.  They had one child:

**7.2.2.1**    i.    HEATHER DAWN[5] HILL, b. 1982; was a student at Rumsey School and Greer School; graduated from Parkersburg South H.S., Parkersburg, W.Va.; attended classes at W.V.U.-Parkersburg; aquatics administration at Camden Clark Medical Center, receptionist at Parkersburg YMCA and lifeguard at Parkersburg YMCA; m. Wood Co., W.Va., 12 Sep 2002, **Jason Frederick HAUGHT**, son of Frederick John Haught and his second wife, Marcina Ann (née Plant).  Jason and Heather Haught were later divorced and he remarried.

Children of Jason and Heather (Hill) Haught, surname Haught:
    **7.2.2.1.1**    i.    MARCINA LYNN[6] (b. 2005).
    **7.2.2.1.2**    ii.    LANDON JASON (b. 2007).
    **7.2.2.1.3**    iii.    CHRISTIAN DEAN (b. 2009).

## Sarah[4] Hill and Her Children

**7.2.3  SARAH[4] HILL, M.A., Ph.D.,**[91] elder daughter and third child of George J. and Helene (Zimmermann) Hill, was born at Bethesda, Maryland, 5 January 1962.  She was baptized later that year at St. Mary Anne's (Episcopal) Church, North East, Md., where her father's maternal ancestors had been vestrymen before and during the Revolutionary War.  She attended public and private schools in Denver, Colorado; in the suburbs of St. Louis, Missouri; and in Huntington, West Virginia.  She was a student at Mary Institute, Ladue, Mo.; and she graduated in 1980 from Chatham Hall, Chatham, Va., where she was a member of the Chatham Athletic Council and the Student Council.  She then attended Kenyon College in Gambier, Ohio, where she majored in English and received the B.A., cum laude, in 1985.  While at Kenyon she played field hockey and lacrosse.  She received seven varsity letters and as a senior she was co-captain of the field hockey team which competed in the national NCAA meet.

Sarah Hill spent the summer after her junior year in high school in Nice, France, as a student with the Experiment in International Living.  She took a semester off after her third year at Kenyon and worked as a marine biology technician on a Smithsonian Institution research vessel.  She spent her last semester in college as an exchange student in Vienna, Austria, studying German and teaching English as a foreign language to Viennese high school students.  After graduation from college she worked in finance for Lebenthal & Co., in New York; and she was a development officer for Very Special Arts, Inc., in Washington, D.C.  She then studied Spanish in Antigua, Guatemala, and was a writer for InforPress, Guatemala City.  Ms. Hill also travelled extensively in Europe and Central America.  She is fluent in French, German and Spanish.  She enjoys photography and is an avid reader, hiker, and runner, and she climbed Mt. Kenya in Africa and several volcanoes in Guatemala.

In 1990 she entered graduate school in the Department of Anthropology at Johns Hopkins University, Baltimore, Md.  She completed her course work for the Ph.D. in 1994 and was awarded the M.A. degree; she then began her field work in El Paso, Texas, and Ciudad Juarez, Mexico, on a Fulbright Scholarship. From 1995-98 she lived in El Paso.  In 1999 she returned to Baltimore to complete her dissertation, and she received her Ph.D. at Johns Hopkins University in May 2001.  She was an assistant professor of anthropology at Temple University in 2001-2, and she then moved to the University of Western Michigan as an assistant professor in the Departments of Anthropology and Environmental Studies.  She was promoted to associate professor with tenure in 2008, and she is now only in the Department of Environmental Studies.  Her 2010 *Boston Review* article on the war for drugs in Juarez, Mexico, won fourth place in international recognition that year by longform.org, ranking higher than all but three others, including an article in *The New Yorker* by Atul Gyande.  Dr. Hill is a member of the Society of Mayflower Descendants and of the Descendants of Early American Witches.

Sarah Hill married, at the Sherman Lake YMCA Camp, Augusta, Mich., on 31 October 2015, **Megan REYNOLDS, Esq.,** daughter of the Hon. Judge Michael Reynolds and his wife Alice, of Wilmington, Del.  Megan Reynolds was a midwife and then a staff member of the Casey Foundation before moving to Michigan.  She graduated from high school in North East, Md., near the church where Sarah was baptized in 1962.  She graduated from Antioch College and in 2008, from Michigan State University Law School.  Since 2009, she has provided legal aid for non-citizen farm workers.  Megan and Sarah are members of the People's Church in Kalamazoo.  They have daughters by the same anonymous sperm donor.  Sarah had Georgia Clare Hill and Megan had Rosalie Mairead Hill, who are thus half-sisters.

Sarah Hill and Megan Reynolds have two children, born at Kalamazoo, surname Hill:

**7.2.3.1**        i.        GEORGIA CLARE[5] HILL, b. 2004; was a student in a bi-lingual (Spanish and English) public school in Kalamazoo; plays the violin and string bass; enjoys running; Life Member of the Mayflower Society.

**7.2.3.2**        ii.      ROSALIE MAIRED HILL, b. 2008; started 1st grade in 2014.

## Helena Rundall[4] "Lana" Hill

**7.2.4 HELENA RUNDALL[4] "Lana" HILL**, younger daughter and fourth child of George J. and Helene (Zimmermann) Hill, was born at Boston, Mass., 1 May 1964, shortly before her mother received her Ph.D. degree. She was christened in 1964 at St. Paul's Episcopal Church, Brookline, Mass. She was educated in public and private schools in Denver, Colorado; the suburbs of St. Louis, Missouri; and Huntington, West Virginia. She attended Mary Institute, Ladue, Mo., and she graduated in 1982 from Chatham Hall, Chatham, Va., where she was a member of the Student Council and president of the Chatham Athletic Council. Ms. Hill spent a summer in Norway with the Experiment in International Living. In 1982-3, she studied environmental engineering at the University of Colorado, where she was a member of Rocky Mountain Rescue. In 1985 she completed the Rural Resource Management Program and was awarded the A.A. degree from Sterling College, Craftsbury Common, Vermont.

Lana Hill has been employed in various outdoor activities, including tree surgeon's assistant, Tamworth, N.H.; and professional ski patroller and ski instructor at Sunday River, Bethel, Maine. From 1987 until 2007 she was employed by Outward Bound, beginning at the Hurricane Island, Maine, Outward Bound School, as a rock climbing instructor and outdoor educator. From 1992-93 she was base site manager for Outward Bound in Baltimore, and she later was assistant director of Outward Bound for alumni relations. She has been a certified Wilderness First Responder and a Licensed Maine Guide. Lana Hill is an avid lover of the outdoors, having walked from northern Vermont to the Atlantic Ocean and canoed from southern Canada to Hudson's Bay. She has climbed Mt. Kenya in Africa and volcanoes in Ecuador, and she has climbed many technical "walls" and towers in Utah, West Virginia, and New York State. She has rafted the Bio-Bio River in Chile, and she enjoyed sea kayaking and "pullboat" sailing off the coast of Maine. She also enjoys working with wood and fabrics. She has run many road races, including the Marine Corps, Chicago, San Diego, and New York Marathons.

From 2000-2003, she was a member of the faculty and director of the Hardie Center at the Gilman School in Baltimore, Md. In October 2004, she was appointed program director for Outward Bound's Urban Centers in the Mid-Atlantic Region (Philadelphia and Baltimore). From 2007-2010 she was employed by Cradlerock, Inc., a management consulting firm in Stamford, Connecticut, and travelled widely for Cradlerock from her home in Baltimore, Maryland. In 2010 she became a member of the leadership development team of the British Embassy in Washington, D.C., with duties that ranged over all of the Western Hemisphere. In September 2014, she began work as senior lead client engagement – enterprise learning, for T. Rowe Price, Inc., of Baltimore. She has been a member of the American Alpine Club, and she is a member of the National Society Colonial Dames of America in the State of New Jersey; the New Jersey Society of Mayflower Descendants; and the Associated Descendants of Early American Witches. She lives by the goals of an Outward Bound Professional: team-building, creative problem-solving, communication, risk-taking, leadership skills, and trust.

## Warren[3] Zimmermann and His Descendants

**7.3 Ambassador WARREN[3] "Zimmer" ZIMMERMANN,**[92] elder son and third child of Albert Walter and Barbara (Shoemaker) Zimmermann, was born in Philadelphia, Pa., 16 November 1934; died at Great Falls, Va., 3 February 2004. He was baptized at home in Haverford, Pa., in a Swedenborgian ceremony in about 1935. He grew up at his family's home in Haverford, Pa., and he graduated from the Deerfield School in Deerfield, Mass., in 1952. He then attended Yale College, where he was an editor of the *Yale Daily News*, a member of Scroll and Key, and the Elizabethan Club. He was one of Yale's best squash players at that time. He graduated in 1956. After a year of teaching at Yale, he studied at Cambridge University, where he received the M.A. degree in 1958. He then worked for two years as a reporter in Washington, DC, and he entered the U.S. Foreign Service in 1961.

Warren Zimmermann was consular and political officer in Caracas, Venezuela, 1962-64; student of Serbo-Croatian languages at the Foreign Service Institute, 1964-65; political officer in Belgrade, 1965-68; Soviet policy analyst in the State Department Bureau of Intelligence and Research, 1968-70; speechwriter to the Secretary of State, 1970-73; student of Russian Language, Foreign Service Institute, 1973; deputy counselor of political affairs, U.S. Embassy Moscow, 1973-75; special assistant for policy planning, 1975-77; counselor for political affairs, U.S. embassy Paris, 1977-80; deputy chairman, U.S. delegation, Conference on Security and Cooperation in Europe, Madrid, 1980-81; deputy chief of mission, U.S. embassy Moscow, 1981-84; visiting fellow, Council on Foreign Relations, 1984-85; deputy to head U.S. delegation to Nuclear and Space Arms negotiations with USSR with rank of ambassador, Geneva, 1985-86; chief U.S. delegation to CSCE, Vienna, 1986-89; and ambassador to Yugoslavia, 1989-91.[93]

He was then director, Department of State Refugees Bureau, until January 1994, at which time he resigned in protest over U.S. policy regarding the former Yugoslavia and retired from the Foreign Service. He then became a teacher and senior consultant with the RAND think tank. He was frequently quoted in 1995 as an advocate of force, particularly air strikes by the U.S. and NATO, to bring an end to the conflict in Bosnia.

Warren Zimmermann married **Corinne "Teenie" [IV] CHUBB**, daughter of Percy [II] and Corinne [III] (Alsop) Chubb. Percy Chubb, II, was then head of the Chubb Insurance Company, which was founded by his father, Hendon Chubb, and his uncle, Percy Chubb. Corinne [III] Alsop was the granddaughter of Corinne [I] Roosevelt, sister of President Theodore Roosevelt. Corinne [I] Roosevelt married Douglas Robinson, and their daughter Corinne [II] married an Alsop. The children of this marriage included the newspaper columnists and writers, Joseph and Stuart Alsop, in addition to Corinne [III], who married Percy Chubb II, and was Teenie's mother. Warren and Teenie Zimmermann traveled widely during Warren's career in the Foreign Service. Their permanent home was in Great Falls, Va., and they had country homes in the Republic of Ireland and in Puerto Rico.

The first of the three children of Warren and Teenie Zimmermann was named Corinne [V] for her four ancestors who bore this name. Being the fifth in this line, she was called "Quinnie." She is an art historian and museum curator. The other two children attended Yale, as did their father. Warren, Jr., known as "Tim," studied for the Ph.D. in London and in 1994 was an editor of *U.S. News and World Report* in Washington, DC. He produced the acclaimed documentary *Blackfish* in 2013, exposing the mistreatment of the orcas, known as "killer whales," by Sea World. Their youngest child, Elizabeth "Lily" Zimmermann was married to one of her fellow students at Yale – Charles Metcalfe, a London businessman who is a great-grandson of Lord Curzon. She and Charles had a son, Louis Warren Metcalfe, born in November 1993; Lily later died of leukemia.

Warren Zimmermann developed pancreatic cancer in 2003. Treatment was unsuccessful and he died at his home in Great Falls, Va., on 3 February 2004.

He married, in April 1959, **Corinne "Teeny" [IV] CHUBB**, daughter of Percy [II] and Corinne [III] Roosevelt (Alsop) Chubb.

**CORINNE "Teeny" [IV] CHUBB**[94] was the fourth in her family to bear the name Corinne. Her mother, Corinne [III] Alsop, was the daughter of Joseph and Corinne [II] (Robinson) Alsop, whose sons Joseph and Stewart Alsop were noted political columnists. Her grandmother, Corinne "Corinney" [II] Robinson (1886-1971), was the daughter of Douglas (1855-1918) and Corinne "Conie" [I] (Roosevelt) Robinson, II. Douglas Robinson II was the son of Douglas Robinson, Sr.; and his mother Fanny Monroe was related to President James Monroe.

The other children of Corinne Chubb's great-grandparents, Douglas and Corinne Robinson, included Theodore Robinson (1883-1934), who married Helen Roosevelt, daughter of Franklin Delano Roosevelt's half-brother, James "Rosy" Roosevelt. Corinne [I] "Conie" Roosevelt (1861-1933) was the daughter of Theodore Roosevelt, Sr. (1831-1878) and Martha Bulloch (1835-1884). Their other children included President Theodore Roosevelt (1858-1919) and Elliott (1860-1894). Elliott Roosevelt married Anna Hall (1863-1892); their children included Eleanor Roosevelt (1884-1962), who married Franklin Delano Roosevelt (1882-1945), later President of the United States. Franklin was a great-great grandson of Nicholas Roosevelt (1658-1742). First Lady Eleanor (Roosevelt) Roosevelt was a great-great-great-granddaughter of the same Nicholas Roosevelt, so she and her husband were third cousins, once removed. Franklin and Theodore Roosevelt were third cousins. Corinne "Teeny" [IV] (Chubb) Zimmermann is thus a first cousin, twice removed, of Eleanor Roosevelt, and a great-great niece of President Theodore Roosevelt.

Warren and Corinne (Chubb) Zimmermann had the following children, surname Zimmermann:

| | | |
|---|---|---|
| **7.3.1** | i. | CORINNE ALSOP[4] "Quinnie" + |
| **7.3.2** | ii. | WARREN "Tim" + |
| **7.3.3** | iii. | ELIZABETH B. "Lily" (1964-2005) + |

**7.3.1 Corinne Alsop[4] [V] "Quinnie" ZIMMERMANN** graduated from Duke University. She is an art historian and museum curator in the Boston area. She married **Paul WORTHINGTON.**

Paul and Corinne (Zimmermann) Worthington have two children, surname Worthington:

| | | |
|---|---|---|
| **7.3.1.1** | i. | CORINNE[5], "the sixth", named for her lineal ancestor, Corinne [I] Roosevelt. |
| **7.3.1.2** | ii. | ARTHUR. |

**7.3.2 Warren[4] "Tim" ZIMMERMANN Jr.**[95], graduated from Yale University, B.A., 1983; was a Ph.D. student, and then senior editor and diplomatic correspondent for *U.S. News and World Report.* He is now a correspondent for *Outside* magazine. He was associate producer and co-writer of the documentary *Blackfish.* He is the author of *The Race: The First Nonstop, Round-the-World, No-Holds-Barred Sailing Competition* (2002). He married, in Annapolis, Md., on 14 September 2001, **Ilana FOGELMAN, Ph.D.**, daughter of Mirian Fogelman; born in Brazil. Tim and Ilana (Fogelman) Zimmermann have one child, surname Zimmermann:

| | | |
|---|---|---|
| **7.3.2.1** | i. | JAMIE WARREN[5] (2004-) |

**7.3.3  Elizabeth B.**[4] **"Lily" ZIMMERMANN,**[96] younger daughter and third child of Warren and Corinne (Chubb) Zimmermann, was born 13 April 1964; died of leukemia at London, England, 16 July 2005.  She attended Yale College, from which she graduated B.A., 1985.  She married a fellow Yale student, Charles M. Metcalfe (Class of 1986), with whom she had two children.  A memorial service for Lily was held on 30 September 2005 at the Church of St. John the Evangelist, Notting Hill, London; Rev. William Taylor, Vicar.  Speakers and readers included her brother, Tim Zimmermann, and Starr Osbourne, Nancy Weltchek, Stephen Dunbar Johnson, and Sarah Lyall.  Following the service, a reception was held at 20th Century Theatre, 291 Westbourne Grove, Notting Hill.  Her family plans to create a rose garden in her memory adjacent to the church.  A memorial scholarship at Yale has also been created in her honor.

She married, as his first wife, **Charles Michael METCALFE,**[97] son of David P. and Alexa Metcalfe; born in England.  He is a great-grandson of Lord Curzon, who was Viceroy of India, by his daughter Alexandra "Baba" (b. 1904).  Alexandra Curzon married Edward "Fruity" Metcalfe and had a son, David P. Metcalfe, who was the father of Charles Michael Metcalfe.  Charles Metcalfe remarried after the death of his first wife, Elizabeth "Lily" Zimmermann.  Charles and Elizabeth (Zimmermann) Metcalfe had the following children, surname Metcalfe:

| | | |
|---|---|---|
| **7.3.3.1** | i. | LOUIS WARREN[5] "Louie" (~1993-) |
| **7.3.3.2** | ii. | PERCY ROGER HUMPHREY. |

## Albert Walter[3] Zimmermann, Jr., and His Descendants

**7.4 ALBERT WALTER[3] "Al" ZIMMERMANN, Jr., M.D.,**[98] second son and youngest child of Albert and Barbara (Shoemaker) Zimmermann, was born at Philadelphia, 1 January 1937, and was christened in 1937 at the Church of the Redeemer, Bryn Mawr, Pa. His cousin, Bob Zimmermann, was born in July 1937; he and Bob are the last two of the 23 grandchildren of John and Eva Katherine (Kellenbenz) Zimmermann.

Al Zimmermann was raised at his family's home in Haverford, Pa. He graduated from the Deerfield School, Deerfield, Mass., in 1954, and from Harvard College, *cum laude*, in 1958. Having made a late decision to enter the medical profession, it was a happy coincidence that the dean of the School of Medicine at the University of Pennsylvania had been his pediatrician. He completed medical school four years later with the M.D. degree. He followed his grandfather into a career in ophthalmology. He received his training in Philadelphia, and entered practice in the suburb of Chestnut Hill, later moving his office to Plymouth Meeting, also in the northern suburbs of Philadelphia.

Albert W. Zimmermann, Jr., married **Lenore LISBINSKI** on 22 June 1963, one day after his older sister, Barbara, was married to Melvin Johnson. Al and Lenore have lived for most of their married life in Flourtown, near Plymouth Meeting, in a fieldstone house with apple trees, a swimming pool and a tennis court. The architect for the colonial-revival house, Brognard Okie, was a distant in-law. He was the great-uncle of Al's aunt Nancy Okie, who married his uncle Robert "Bob" Shoemaker. It is there that their three daughters grew up, and where Lenore has developed her outstanding horticultural activities – outdoors, and indoors, using the hydroponic technique. Al followed his father into membership in the Philadelphia choral society, the Orpheus Club. Al and Lenore are members of the Philadelphia Cricket Club, where they are known and feared on the courts as outstanding doubles tennis players.

He married, at St. John Vianney's Roman Catholic Church, Gladwyn, Pa., 22 June 1963, **Lenore Marie LISBINSKI**, daughter of Anthony and Anna (Vajda) Lisbinsky; born at Hazelton, Pa., 23 November 1937; christened there in 1937.

Albert and Lenore (Lisbinski) Zimmermann had the following children, surname Zimmermann:

| | | |
|---|---|---|
| **7.4.1** | i. | ANNE CATHERINE[4] (1964-) + |
| **7.4.2** | ii. | Dr. SUSAN MARIE "Susie" (1966-) + |
| **7.4.3** | iii. | AMANDA THERESA (1969-) + |

**7.4.1 ANNE CATHERINE[4] ZIMMERMANN** was born at Philadelphia, 26 March 1964; christened there in 1964 in the Roman Catholic Church, Westmont, Pa. She graduated from Colgate University (B.A., 1964), and was then a paralegal until she married and began to raise her children. She married, at Flourtown, Pa., **Joseph Patrick CRIMMINS, Esq.**, son of Mathew and Joyce Crimmins; born at Lexington, Mass., in 1964. They were married at St. Genevieve's R.C. Church in Flourtown, and they now live in Swampscott, Mass.

Joseph and Anne (Zimmermann) Crimmins had the following children, surname Crimmins:

| | | |
|---|---|---|
| **7.4.1.1** | i. | SAMUEL ALBERT[5] "Sam" (1994-) |
| **7.4.1.2** | ii. | IAN. |

**7.4.2 SUSAN MARIE[4] "Susie" ZIMMERMANN, Ph.D.**, a sociologist, was born at Philadelphia, 7 September 1966. She was born at the Lankenau Hospital, where her grandfather,

Dr. William T. Shoemaker, M.D., had been head of ophthalmology, and her great-grandfather, John Zimmermann, had been hospitalized for pneumonia (when it was called the German Hospital) in 1876.

She was christened in 1966 at the Holy Cross R.C. Church, West Mt. Airy, Pa. After receiving the B.A. degree for Colby College in 1988, she received her M.A. (1993) and Ph.D. from Brown University. She married **Michael "Mike" LAIDLAW, M.D., Ph.D.**, a pulmonologist, in Concord, N.H.

Michael and Susan (Zimmermann) had the following children, surname Laidlaw:

| | | |
|---|---|---|
| **7.4.2.1** | i. | OLIVER[15] (2001-) |
| **7.4.2.2** | ii. | SIMON (2004-) |

**7.4.3 AMANDA THERESA[4] ZIMMERMANN** was born at Philadelphia, 30 June 1969, at the Lankenau Hospital (see the entry for her sister Susan, above, for more about the Lankenau Hospital, now called Lankenau Medical Center). She was christened at St. Genevieve's R.C. Church in Flourtown, Pa. in 1969. She received a B.A. (1991) from Bowdoin College and an M.S.Ed. (1992) from the University of Pennsylvania. She was an elementary school teacher in New York City before she was married and began to raise her family.

She married, at Flourtown, in 1994, **Ray DIFFLEY**. He is admissions director for the Choate School, and they live in Wallingford, Conn.

Ray and Amanda (Zimmermann) Diffley had the following children, surname Diffley:

| | | |
|---|---|---|
| **7.4.3.1** | i. | ANNA[5] |
| **7.4.3.2** | ii. | ELIZABETH LOUISE "Lisa" (2000-) |
| **7.4.3.3** | iii. | RYAN ANTHONY (2005-) |

--------------------------

For a thousand years in thy sight are but as yesterday when it is past, and as a watch in the night. Thou carriest them away as with a flood. *Psalm* 90:4-5.

# Reorganized Church of Jesus Christ of Latter Day Saints (RLDS)
### The first church building owned by the RLDS in Philadelphia

Photo by George J. Hill, 5/1/2016

## RLDS Church at Howard and Ontario, 1 block north of Artloom factory
### Built on land purchased by John Zimmerman and given to the RLDS
### First in use in 1901, dedicated 1907

**Howard Avenue façade, scene of many photos of RLDS church members**

## Notes

[1] Jean Hoxie Naples (JHN), letter to GJH, 23 Sep 2009.

> Throughout Part III, I will usually spell the name of the emigrant as John Zimmermann, although in his lifetime, sometime between 1880 and 1885, he changed the spelling to Zimmerman, and he used the one "n" spelling consistently thereafter until he died. His name is spelled with one "n" in his obituaries. I thus used the one "n" spelling throughout his lifetime, in Part II. His children spelled the name with one "n" for many years, but they gradually changed the spelling to the two "nn" spelling that is now used by all of his descendants. The name has often been accidentally misspelled by others, often on the same page, within the same document. My use of one "n" is thus variable, and I apologize for the apparent inconsistency.

[2] Kathryn "Katchie" Fligg Lee (KFL) to JHN, quoted in letter to GJH, 8 Oct 2009, enclosure, p.13.

[3] Greenmount Cemetery is located in north Philadelphia, on the E side of N Front St. The cemetery formerly was on both sides of N Front St., but the W side is now Hunting Park, and there are no graves there. The entrance is at 4301 N Front St., near what was formerly the E extension of Cayuga St. The 160 sq ft Zimmermann(n) plot is about 50 yds NW of the cemetery office. It is marked by a grey granite monument, about 8 feet high, adjacent to a tall pine tree, with names carved on three sides, and a corner marked "Z" at one edge of the lot. The name "ZIMMERMAN" is shown at the base of the monument. The plot is suitable for 6 graves, in addition to those whose ashes could be interred there. The file card in the cemetery office shows: "FV 83 JOHN ZIMMERMANN" with a diagram showing 5 people who are buried in that plot and their locations around the N side of the monument, ranging from E to NE to NW to W, as follows: Jan. 1897 Emily Zimmermann / Oct. 1920 . . . Eva K. Zimmermann / May 1936 . . . John Zimmermann / Oct 1968 . . Clara Z. Hoxie / 10/18/74 . . . John Zimmermann, Jr. / 8/16/79 . . . Ethyl K. Zimmermann (#2755), ashes at head.

> The reverse side of the card shows the following names, some of which have been overwritten and others crossed out: "Mrs. Anna Z. Kelley – dau./ 323 Rice's Mill Road/ Wyncote, Pa.; Mr. John Zimmermann – son / 925 Leopard Road / Jenkintown, Pa.; Mr. Wm. Zimmermann – son / Rice's Mill & Deaver Rd. / Wyncote, Pa. / Mrs. Ethyl Zimmermann – wife of John, Jr. / Benson Manor Apts. #628 / Jenkintown, Pa. 19046 / died; John Hoxie – grandson, died / 777 Old Eagle Sch. Rd. / Wayne, Pa. / 223 Westown Drive #61 / Avon Lake, OH 44012; John Zimmermann / 187 Pearlcroft Road / Cherry Hill, NJ 08034 / 207 E Pease [& more words, illegible]."

[4] The U.S. census for 1930 shows that Clara and her husband Al Hoxie were renting a house at 3119 North 16th Street in 1930. Why they are shown as renting instead of owning the house is somewhat of a mystery.

[5] KFL to JHN, letter to GJH, 8 Oct 2009, p.15. It was said by many of the grandchildren of John Zimmermann that he gave a million dollars to each of his children when they were married, and he was generous in helping them later.

[6] Ibid.

[7] KFL to JHN, letter, p.25.

[8] From KFL to JHN, 24-25; Mary Bacon, *Deer Park: A History*; and Bowman, "History of the R.L.D.S. Church in Philadelphia": collapse of the U.S. Bank and Trust Co. of Phila, which was seized by the Sec of Banking of the Commonwealth of Pa. in 1929; census of 1930; cruise of the family, returning to NYC on the S.S. *Bremen* from Cherbourg, France; financial woes for Deer Park and $540 lent by Clara Zimmermann.

[9] Michael Bowman, e-mail to John Zimmermann III, 13 July 2009 (copy to GJH): "By 1940, Hoxie moved to Cape Cod, Mass. Stricken with what witnesses describe as the 'Yellow Jaundice,' Hoxie quietly entered one of his Seaside cabins and took his own life with a 'self-inflicted wound' in August 1942." The cause of death was never openly mentioned, and I have not seen the death certificate.

> Hoxie is mentioned in *The Music Trade Review* (9 May 1925), 39, "Thousands of Participants Take Part in Philadelphia's Harmonica Contest." Excerpt: "Much credit for the success of the whole affair must be given to Albert N. Hoxie, Jr., who gave unsparingly of his time and energy to make the contest a successful one. The contest and concerts on Thursday evening were under his direction."

> His obituary was in *The Billboard* (5 Sep 1942), 25, "The Final Curtain": "HOXIE – Albert N., Jr., 57, harmonica player and former leader of the Philadelphia Harmonica Band, August 20 in East Sandwich, Mass. A harmonica teacher, Hoxie had instructed over 100,000 boys during his career. He leaves his wife, two sons and daughter."

[10] Bowman, letter to John Zimmermann III, 13 July 2009, continues:

> "Despite all his success, Hoxie was a troubled soul. As legend has it, John Z. Sr. gave each of his children on their respective wedding days a million dollars. Whatever Clara received, she attempted to invest wisely. They lived off the interest and not the principal. To finance the travel of 60 boys of the Philadelphia Harmonica Band in

the 1920's, however, Hoxie blew through enormous amounts of money, eventually eating up the principal. The stock market crash hurt Clara's investment further, and her husband had to shut down the band in 1936.

"Furthermore Albert and Clara separated for various reasons. For one, she didn't like all the fanfare of the harmonica band and got tired of playing second fiddle to his interest. Second, several old timers in the Church confirmed an affair Albert had with his secretary while he kept office at the Widener Building in Philadelphia during the 1930's. It is even rumored that she moved up to Cape Cod with him, though I can't verify that.

"Albert saw his body of work (harmonica band) turned into vaudevillian slapstick by his closest rival, Borrah Minevitch, leader of the more famous 'Harmonica Rascals.' Additionally, Albert must have watched (in horror) as the Hohner Co., Germany's leading harmonica manufacturer funneled millions of dollars into the Third Reich. In the teens, Hohner sold 7 million harmonicas annually in the U.S. Thanks to Hoxie's success, that number soared to 25 million by the 1930's. They began stamping swastikas on the harmonicas themselves and then marketed them to German youth. I can only imagine how Albert must have felt watching those news reels in the movie theatres watching Hitler Youth parade around in uniforms, compared to his own youth parading around in uniforms holding German-made harmonicas. This may be one of the impetuses that encouraged Hoxie to manufacture his own beginning in 1938."

----------

Albert N. Hoxie, Jr., is profiled in three YouTube videos, made by Michael Bowman for "A Rutgers University Student Project":
"The Life of Albert N. Hoxie, Jr." (3 Mar 2010), Uploaded by OrliviaTheCat; 8:06.
(www.youtube.com/watch?v=XS_GcgNwmTo) "This short narrative describes the contributions of Mr. Hoxie to the musical world, including his Community."

--------

"The Life of Albert N. Hoxie, Jr." (24 Jan 2012), Uploaded by Harmonicando; 8:06
(www.youtube.com/watch?v=dnLovSDMv1Y). The video shows images of John Zimmermann, Sr., and his family, and of Albert Hoxie, Jr., and his wife Clara and their family. Brief images of Artloom Mills factory, and one of Albert Hoxie, III, "Albo" as a child. It is probably the same as the 3 Mar 2010 version.

---------

Continued on "Albert Hoxie and his Philadelphia Harmonica Band" on YouTube
(www.youtube.com/watch?v=SDkmXR_dNrI), Uploaded by Harmonicando; 3:10.

------------

[11] James Hoxie, M.D., lived in January 2003 at 560 Winston Way, Berwyn PA  610-644-1190.

[12] Kathy Brandt Bonnell was at kbonnell@byu.net (14 Nov 2009).

[13] JHN, op. cit., p. 22, quoting Cil.

[14] 1. Photographs of Anna, her siblings and her parents, were inscribed by her daughter, Susan (Kelley) Carnwath, with her date of birth (25 Dec 1887) and the year of her death (1974). Copies were given to her niece, Helene (Zimmermann) Hill in 1993.
2. Biographical Information provided by her daughter, Anita (Kelley) Pearson, on Family Group Record dated 25 July 1994; reviewed and edited by her, October 1994. Additional biographical information was provided by her daughter, Susan (Kelley) Carnwath, 16 Nov 1994. Anna Zimmermann died at Abington (PA) Memorial Hospital.
3. Her great-grandson, Joseph W. Carnwath, Jr., sent to GJH (email, 6 Apr 2016) the following recollections and a copy (from Google search) of the announcement of her marriage:
My Aunt Anita (who is alive and well and living near Oakland California) says that it was her understanding that John Zimmermann was a member of the Church of the Latter Day Saints, perhaps even before coming to Philadelphia. That was why Anna Zimmermann and her family happened to meet Richard C. Kelley (my grandfather) and his family in Iowa. It was a meeting of members of the Church of the Latter Day Saints. The Zimmermanns were apparently on a tour out west which was a big deal in those days. The first Model T Ford was produced in 1908 and the meeting took place just before my Grandfather left for a couple of years teaching in the Philippines in 1911. He must have maintained contact with Anna during that period because they were married shortly after he returned.
*The Iowa Alumnus* v. 13 (1915), 30 (accessed on Google Books):
ZIMMERMANN-KELLEY Richard C. Kelley and Miss Anna Zimmermann were married on August 10, 1915, at the home of the bride's parents, Philadelphia. The bride is a former student of the University of Pennsylvania, and a member of the Kappa Kappa Gamma sorority.
Mr. Kelley was graduated from the College of Liberal Arts in 1903. For two years he was an organizer of and principal of trade schools in the Philippine Islands. He has also installed the manual training departments in the Ottumwa and Sioux City, Iowa, high schools. He is now superintendent of manual training in the Iowa City high school and instructor of manual training in the University of Iowa.
Mr. and Mrs. Kelley are at home in Iowa City at 821 North Gilbert Street.

[15] 1. Edmund Levi Kelley (b. 17 Nov 1844, Vienna, IL; d.10 May 1930, Independence, MO) was the son of Richard Yancey Kelley (b. 1814; d. 10 Jun 1861, Mills Co., IA; m. 31 May 1837 Sarah E. F. Ballowe, who was b. in

Virginia, 3 Jul 1814; d. in Iowa, 18 Nov 1873). Edmund Kelley m., at Malvern, IA, 21 Dec 1876, Catherine Bishop (b. 9 Nov 1853 near Albia, IA; d. 21 Nov 1944, Independence, MO); she was the dau. of John and Mary Jane (Humston) Bishop.

2. Information was provided by his daughter, Anita (Kelley) Pearson and text was reviewed by her in October 1994. A Family Group Record and a Biographical Information sheet were prepared by his daughters Susan (Kelley) Carnwath and Joan (Kelley) Fowler and forwarded to George J. Hill, 16 Nov 1994. Five of the children were born at the Germantown Hospital, Philadelphia, PA.

3. JHN, p.17: 10 Aug 1915, John's 2nd eldest daughter Anna Zimmermann marries Richard Carlyle Kelley of Lamoni, Iowa. He is the son of Edmund Levi Kelley and Catherine Bishop. His father is prominent in the RLDS church in Lamoni and had signed John's Bishop's Certificate.

[16] Biographical Information form prepared by Joan (Kelley) Fowler, 7 July 1994; forwarded to George J. Hill, 16 Nov 1994. Her birth is noted by JHN, p.17.

Her obituary was published in *The Daily Local* (26 Sep 2011):

Joan Kelley Fowler of Kennett Square. Joan Kelley Fowler, 95, of Kennett Square, died Monday, September 19, 2011 at the Chester County Hospital in West Chester Pennsylvania. Born in Iowa City, Iowa, she was the first child of Richard C. Kelley and Anna Zimmermann Kelley. Joan graduated from Swarthmore College and did a year of graduate study at the Cooperative School for Teachers, 69 Bank Street, New York City. She taught 3rd grade in private schools in Akron, Ohio and Greenwich, Connecticut. In 1940 she married Ward Scott Fowler, a graduate of Swarthmore College and Harvard Medical School. Ward enlisted in the Air Force Medical Corps in 1942. After the war he began studying lung function at Pennsylvania Graduate School of Medicine in Dr. Julius Comroe's research laboratory. In 1952 Dr. Fowler joined the Mayo Clinic, Rochester, Minnesota, where he continued research and publication of his studies on pulmonary function. When the Mayo Medical School opened in 1972 he was appointed Associate Dean of Academic Affairs. He retired at the end of 1976 and died in 1982. The Fowlers had two sons, Robert Scott Fowler of Ithaca, New York and Thomas Richard Fowler of Palo Alto, California. After Tom reached high school, Mrs. Fowler joined the Rochester Reading Center to tutor dyslexic children in reading and spelling. The opening of Quarry Hill Nature Center offered her an opportunity to expand a life-long interest in plants and animals by assisting with classes of elementary and junior high school students from Rochester Public Schools. She also was active in getting a birding group started in Rochester which later became affiliated with the Minnesota Ornithologists Union and National Audubon Society. In September 2000, Mrs. Fowler moved to Kendal at Longwood, located in Kennett Square, Pennsylvania. In addition to her sons, Mrs. Fowler is survived by two sisters; Anita K. Pearson of Orinda, California, and Marian Kelley Poteat of York; and a brother, Donald E. Kelley of Glenside. A public celebration of Joan's life will be held 2 p.m. Saturday, October 1, with a reception to follow at the Auditorium of Kendal at Longwood, Kennett Square, PA 19348. Arrangements are being handled by the Foulk & Grieco Funeral Home Inc. (610-869-2685) of West Grove.

See more at: http://www.legacy.com/obituaries/dailylocal/obituary.aspx?pid=153835766#sthash.yxp3HKq4.dpuf

[17] The dates of his birth and death were confirmed by his sister-in-law, Susan (Kelley) Carnwath; to G. J. Hill, 16 Mar 1995. The names of his children were from Susan Carnwath, and their recent/current addresses were found by searches for their names and towns, shown in their mother's obiturary.

[18] Robert Scott Fowler lived in 2016 at 404 Savage Farm Dr., Ithaca, N.Y. 14850. From From:http://www.familytreenow.com/records/people/fowler/ellen/rbj7xphfyl5hw6tdfmdm2q (accessed 1 Apr 2016)

[19] Thomas Richard Fowler probably is an electrical engineer; he lived in 2016 at 832 Richardson Ct., Palo Alto CA 94303 (telephone 415-858-0841). He was shown in his mother's obituary. His b.d. is from Susan (Kelley) Carnwath.

[20] Richard and Jeanne (Adams) Kelley had five daughters: Nancy Hope (b. 1945); Lindsay Ann (b. 1946); Wendy Adams (b. 1950); Laura Eileen (b. 1951); and Stacy Valentine (b. 1953). The eldest was born at Memphis, Tennessee, and the others were born at Abington, Pennsylvania. Richard Kelley was born at the Germantown Hospital, Philadelphia, PA. He completed a Biographical Information form on 9 Sep 1994. Information on his status in March 1995 came from his sister, Sue (Kelley) Carnwath, to G. J. Hill, 16 Mar 1995. His obituary was published in the *Times Chronicle-Glenside News* [Glenside, Pa.] (20 Sep 2000). He was survived by his five daughters, his second wife, nine grandchildren, four step-children, and nine step-grandchildren.

[21] Capt. Dick Kelley, Jr., passed twice through Karachi, India (now Pakistan), where he stayed with his uncle, Albert W. Zimmermann, who was then a Lieutenant, USNR. Zimmermann was Executive Officer of the Naval Liaison Office, Karachi, on Kelley's first visit in September 1943, and he was the Commanding Officer of the NLO when Kelley returned on 31 July 1944. Kelley had then been overseas for 2 ½ years, and was then on his way back to the U.S. He had malaria upon arrival in Karachi and was hospitalized for treatment, and he then showed gastro-intestinal symptoms ("ptomaine poisoning") and remained in hospital for two weeks. Zimmermann looked forward to seeing his nephew, but by the time he left, he had soured a bit on the younger man. He wrote to his wife that

"Dick Kelley is still here. He got out of the hospital on Tuesday. His treatment for malaria was finished on Saturday but unfortunately he ate something that didn't agree with him so he had to stay several more days. He's sort of a moody guy, quite independent and a bit stubborn. I would say that he has broadened quite a bit – is not adverse to drinking scotch etc and smokes as much as I do. I would think he would be rather difficult to live with but I guess I'm feeling my generation." Tensions were high during WW II, and opinions like that were not uncommon in Zimmermann's letters. He and his nephew were reconciled after the war. (Letters to Barbara Zimmermann in Papers of Albert W. Zimmermann, Special Collections, U.S. Naval Institute, Annapolis, Md.)

[22] Information on her status in March 1995 came from her sister-in-law, Sue (Kelley) Carnwath, to G. J. Hill, 16 Mar 1995.

[23] The obituary of Richard C. Kelley, Jr., says he had 9 grandchildren. Their names and the names of their parents were not mentioned. Therefore, they are assigned the following numbers: **2.2.?.1 – 2.2.?..9**.

[24] Her name was Nancy Hope White Watson on 20 September 2000, and she lived at Seattle. Her father's obit says that she was m. to Warren Watson, and lived in Seattle; it does not mention a marriage to White.

[25] Laura Eileen Kelley is shown in Intelius as living with Linda Utter. In September 2000 she lived in Rochester, N.Y. Her father's obituary shows her as married to Linda Utter, in Rochester

[26] Susan (Kelley) Carnwath completed her Biographical Information form on 7 Jul 1994, and revised the text of these Notes on 16 Mar 1995.

Her obituary was published in Philly.com on Oct. 21, 2002:

SUSAN KELLEY CARNWATH died October 17, 2002 in the company of her family in Kendal at Longwood. The third of seven children of Richard C. and Anna Zimmermann Kelley, she grew up in Elkins Park, graduated from Cheltenham High School, Class of 1938 and attended Oberlin College where she studied music. She met Joseph Wallace Carnwath at Grace Presbyterian Church in Jenkintown where they were eventually married in 1942 and where they subsequently taught Sunday School for many years. During that period she also did volunteer work at Abington Hospital. Mrs. Carnwath maintained a life long interest in music and tennis. She played the piano in Sunday School and was a member of the tennis team at the Germantown Cricket Club and the Buckingham Racket Club. She was an avid reader who loved astronomy, book club, the theater and travel. She enjoyed the serene beauty of rural life - spring flowers, hay in the field, fall foliage - at the family farm in Bucks County, which she managed after the death of her husband in 1983. She is survived by her two sons, Joseph W. Carnwath, Jr. and Richard K. Carnwath, five grandchildren, one great grandchild and by her sisters Joan Fowler, Marion Kelley, Anita Pearson and her brother Donald Kelley. A memorial service will be held at the Tinicum United Church of Christ at 1:00 P.M. Saturday, October 26 at 310 Dark Hollow Road, Pipersville. In lieu of flowers, the family suggests that memorial gifts can be made to: The Village Improvement Association, Doylestown Hospital, 595 West State Street, Doylestown, PA 18901.

Published on Philly.com on Oct. 21, 2002 - See more at:

http://www.legacy.com/obituaries/philly/obituary.aspx?page=lifestory&pid=550918#sthash.g2LAOOTq.dpuf

[27] From prabook.org (accessed 4-6-16):

Joseph Wallace Carnwath / molecular geneticist, researcher / Carnwath, Joseph Wallace was born on January 13, 1944 in Abingdon, Pennsylvania. Son of Joseph Wallace and Susan (Kelley) Carnwath. / Education / Bachelor, Yale University, 1966; Master of Science, Lehigh University, 1976; Doctor of Philosophy, Cambridge (England) University, 1983. / Career / Volunteer Peace Corps, Western Caroline Islands, 1966-1969. Production manager Pennsylvania Pacific Corporation, Warminster, 1970-1972. Research assistant department biology Lehigh University, Bethlehem, Pennsylvania, 1975-1976. / Scientist department zoology University Oxford, England, 1983-1987. Scientist Fraunhofer Institute, Hannover, Germany, 1987-1991, Department of Agriculture, Hannover, Germany, since 1991. / Interests: Rowing.

--------------------

Co-author of (found on websearch for his name):

Arpad Baji Gal, Joseph Wallace Carnwath, Andras Dinnyes, Doris Herrmann, Heiner Niemann and Christine Wrenzycki, "Comparison of real-time polymerase chain reaction and end-point polymerase chain reaction for the analysis of gene expression in preimplantation embryos" *Reproduction, Fertility and Development* 18 (no.3, 2006): 365-71; and H. Niemann, C. Wrenzycki, A. Lucas-Hahn, T. Brambrink, W.A. Kues, and J.W. Carnwath "Gene Expression Patterns in Bovine In vitro-Produced and Nuclear Transfer-Derived Embryos and Their Implications for Early Development" *Cloning and Stem Cells* 4 (no.1, July 2004): 29-38.

He has many other publications, which can be seen on PubMed.

-----------

He worked with Wolfgang Deppert of the Pette Institute in Hamburg, "our local expert on p53." His job "was analysis of carcinogenesis. After making several additions of transgenic mice, I moved . . . to start a molecular genetics lab and make transgenic farm animals."

----------

 e-mail to GJH 4-6-16:

Joseph Carnwath <carnwath@me.com>

Hi George, . . .

 My Aunt Anita (who is alive and well and living near Oakland California) says that it was her understanding that John Zimmermann was a member of the Church of the Latter Day Saints, perhaps even before coming to Philadelphia. That was why Anna Zimmermann and her family happened to meet Richard C. Kelley (my grandfather) and his family in Iowa. It was a meeting of members of the Church of the Latter Day Saints. The Zimmermanns were apparently on a tour out west which was a big deal in those days. The first Model T Ford was produced in 1908 and the meeting took place just before my Grandfather left for a couple of years teaching in the Philippines in 1911. He must have maintained contact with Anna during that period because they were married shortly after he returned.

 *The Iowa Alumnus* - Volume 13 - Page 30 - Google Books Result

ZIMMERMANN-KELLEY Richard C. Kelley and Miss Anna Zimmermann were married on August 10, 1915, at the home of the bride's parents, Philadelphia. The bride is a former student of the University of Pennsylvania, and a member of the Kappa Kappa Gamma sorority. Mr. Kelley was graduated from the College of Liberal Arts in 1903. For two years he was an organizer of and principal of trade schools in the Philippine Islands. He has also installed the manual training departments in the Ottumwa and Sioux City, Iowa, high schools. He is now superintendent of manual training in the Iowa City high school and instructor of manual training in the University of Iowa. Mr. and Mrs. Kelley are at home in Iowa City at 821 North Gilbert Street.

Here is an old advertisements on the internet thanks to some scanning work by Google.

This is a clipping from the web archive which was a link to The Sunday Morning Star, Wilmington, Delaware, September 7, 1947. I liked the ad for real Zimmermann Mohair. Note that they spelled Zimmermann wrong. As The family spelled their name with two final nn's like good Germans.

Zimmermann:

By the way, if you want to read the original patents awarded to Great Grandfather Zimmermann, they have been scanned in (not very good quality) by Google.

Patent US813131 - Woven pile fabric. - Google Patents
www.google.com/patents/US813131
Inventors, John Zimmermann. Original Assignee, Philadelphia Tapestry Mills.

Patent US813132 - Pile-gage. - Google Patents
www.google.com/patents/US813132
Inventors, John Zimmermann. Original Assignee, Philadelphia Tapestry Mills.

Patent US855153 - Pile fabric. - Google Patents
www.google.com/patents/US855153
Inventors, John Zimmermann. Original Assignee, Philadelphia Tapestry Mills.

Searching further with Google, I found an advertisement in the *Spokane Daily Chronicle* dated February, 1936, for a sofa with Zimmermann mohair. Click on the following URL and look at the details of the Palace February Furniture Sale. The sofa in our living room is one of those. I am living in the family museum.

http://news.google.com/newspapers?nid=1338&dat=19360213&id=z9pYAAAAIBAJ&sjid=BfUDAAAAIBAJ&pg=4635,3456150

[28] Typically, this would mean simply an unmarried partner. Joe Carnwath translates it beautifully as "people traveling together for a portion of their lives," based on the actual meaning of the 3 portions of the complex word.

[29] The three children of Joseph Caspari Carnwath were named by his father, Joseph Wallace Carnwath, in e-mail to GJH, 4/15/16.

Joseph Caspari Carnwath is profiled in German at www.rockhousebrothers.de: Joey. Spielt Gitarre.

Er begann seine Karriere als Straßenmusiker in London. Während der ersten sieben sonnigen Tage wurden Bill Wyman, der Bassist der Rolling Stones, und Bono von U2 auf ihn aufmerksam - der nicht nur 200 Pfund in den Gitarrenkoffer warf, sondern sich auch noch inspiriert fühlte, das Mikrofon zu nehmen und mitzusingen! Die nächsten anderthalb Jahre verliefen mit gelegentlichen Regenschauern und ohne Interesse weiterer Berühmtheiten. Einige Leute (Joey selbst) denken, er sei das Mastermind hinter den Rockhouse Brothers und hielte alle Fäden in der Hand. Joey wäre fast gestorben als er die Ziellinie des Stockholm-Marathons überquerte und fragt sich immer noch, wie er Wolfmans Vorschlag, einen Band-Marathon zu laufen, jemals zustimmen konnte. Wenn er nicht auf der Bühne steht, kocht Joey Kaffee bei Wolfman Records und CCR Booking.

[30] James Wallace Carnwath is profiled in German at www.rockhousebrothers.de: Jamie. Spielt Kontrabass. Er nahm die Herausforderung, das Instrument in nur acht Wochen zu lernen, an, nachdem er 1996 einen verzweifelten Telefonanruf von Joey erhalten hatte, der einen Ersatzbassisten für eine große Schwedentour benötigte. Einige Leute (Bob Moore, der Bassist von Elvis Presley) sagen, dass er die schnellste Rechte-Hand-Technik hat, die sie jemals gesehen haben! Andere Leute (Joey) fragen sich, was das wohl bedeutet. Jamie war Finalist des Hannoveraner Klimmzugcontest 2001, einer Sportveranstaltung, die gewaltige Körperkraft mit der Fähigkeit Unmengen von Bier zu trinken kombiniert. Wenn er nicht auf der Bühne steht, leitet Jamie die Booking-Agentur CCR Booking und ist deshalb verantwortlich dafür, ungefähr 200 Auftritte im Jahr für die Band zu organisieren.

[31] The two sons of John Douglas Carnwath were named by his father, Joseph Wallace Carnwath, in e-mail to GJH, 4/9/16. They are assigned numbers in this genealogy, and can be found in the Index in the Descendants of Anna Zimmermann: **1.3.1.3.1** Barnaby Bemar Carnwath; and **1.3.1.3.2** Henry Theodore Carnwath.

[32] Kelley McDonald Carnwath's office address was found via info@QualisHealth; her personal address is kcarnwath@yahoo.com. Her uncle Joseph W. Carnwath, Jr., is at carnwath@me.com, and her father, Richard Carnwath, is at carnwathd@gmail.com, and LinkedIn (https://www.linkedin.com/in/kelleycarnwath).

[33] The two daughters of Gunnar Carlson and Brook (Hewes) Carnwath were named by his uncle, Joseph Wallace Carnwath, in e-mail to GJH, 4/15/16.

[34] Marian Kelley was born at the Germantown Hospital, Philadelphia, PA. She completed a Biographical Information form on 15 Aug 1994. The obituary of William Poteat says that her middle initial was K., but I cannot confirm this.

[35] A festschrift for William H. Poteat can be seen on YouTube, "Who Was William H. Poteat" (23 Nov 2014), the William H. Poteat Conference, at Yale University, with Bruce Lawrence, et al. Poteat was a philosopher noted for

his work on the mind-body duality. His biography, conference papers, and YouTube presentation can be seen at www.whpoteat.org.

Biography on William H. Poteat website:

William Hardman Poteat was born in Kaifeng, Honan, China, on April 19, 1919, to Baptist missionary parents, Edwin MacNeill Poteat Jr. and Wilda Hardman Poteat. / His father later served as president of Colgate-Rochester Divinity School and twice as minister of Pullen Memorial Baptist Church in Raleigh, NC. His grandfather, Edwin MacNeill Poteat, Sr., was president of Furman University and his great-uncle, Dr. William Louis (Billy) Poteat, was a legendary president of what is now Wake Forest University in the 1920s. His great-aunt, Ida Poteat, was head of the Art Department at Meredith College. / Poteat spent the first ten years of his life in China, where his two younger siblings Elisabeth and Haley were also born. He completed his high school education in Raleigh, NC, in 1937. He pursued undergraduate study at Oberlin College where he earned a BA degree with Phi Beta Kappa honors in 1941. From there he went to Yale Divinity School, receiving a BD (equivalent to today's MDiv) in 1944. His primary mentor at Yale was the Christian theologian H. Richard Niebuhr. / In 1943 he married Marian K. Kelley, also a student from Oberlin two years behind him. Poteat and his wife moved to Chapel Hill, NC, in the summer of 1944, where William had been hired as General Secretary of the YMCA, a capacity in which he served for three years. At the time the Chapel Hill YMCA was a center for Christian fellowship and a hub of political and intellectual activity for UNC students. While there, he was asked to teach a couple of courses in the Philosophy Department at UNC, which soon became quite popular—so much so that Poteat was hired to teach philosophy as a full-time Instructor in 1947. / In 1955, having risen to the rank of Associate Professor, he received an Outstanding Teacher award. He was for several years one of UNC's most popular philosophy teachers until he left in 1957. In 1956-57, Carolina students launched a campaign (unsuccessful) to make him UNC Chancellor. / When Poteat was at Yale Divinity School he took some graduate courses in the Philosophy Department and there became a good friend of Robert Cushman, an aspiring Plato scholar. Cushman was later hired by Duke University in Durham, NC, in close proximity to UNC at Chapel Hill, to build at Duke an academic PhD program in Religion. / Initially Poteat had intended to return to Yale to pursue a doctorate in philosophy, but several factors led him to remain in North Carolina. He and Marian had two children close together at this time and Cushman's launching of the PhD program at Duke made it attractive. / While teaching philosophy full-time in mornings at UNC, Poteat took afternoon graduate coursework at Duke in 1947. As a graduate student, he was appointed a Gurney Harris Kearns Fellow and a Kent Fellow in 1949. / Poteat completed his Duke PhD in 1951, with a dissertation entitled Pascal and Modern Sensibility, which he claimed to have written in 90 days during the Summer of 1950. His oral defense of the dissertation took place on November 15, 1950. / He later was to claim of his dissertation that he "was thus well begun by this early essay in becoming a post-critical thinker." It was here that his lifelong intellectual agenda was set: Though the dissertation was ostensibly about Pascal, it was really about what Pascal sought to be about—namely, identifying, combating, and overcoming the self-abstracting, self-alienating, person-occluding tendencies inherent in modern modes of reflection from the Renaissance forward but particularly of the sort epitomized in Descartes. / In the early 1950s he joined the Episcopal Church, in which he remained a member in good standing for the remainder of his life. In 1955 Poteat traveled to England to speak and participate in a Student Christian Conference at Oxford, and again in 1957. This provided him with the opportunity to travel to Manchester University for his first meeting (in 1955) with scientist-philosopher Michael Polanyi, beginning a life-long personal and professional relationship cherished by both men. This relationship was to shape much of the course of Poteat's subsequent thinking and research. / From Polanyi he received and immediately began reading a typescript of Polanyi's Gifford Lectures (1951-52), that was to be revised and later published as Personal Knowledge: Toward a Post-Critical Philosophy (1958). He had earlier first encountered Polanyi's writing in 1952—specifically, "The Stability of Beliefs," in the British Journal for the Philosophy of Science, which essay was incorporated in Personal Knowledge. Poteat later speaks of this initial encounter with Polanyi's work as having "accredited and greatly enriched the context within which initially to obey my own intimations." / Between 1957 and 1960, Poteat taught for three years at the Episcopal Theological Seminary of the Southwest at Austin, TX. Having been professor of Philosophy at the University of North Carolina, he was asked to develop courses in Christianity and Culture for the seminary, specifically courses in Philosophical Theology and Christian Criticism. / In 1960, Poteat joined the faculty of Duke University Divinity School as Associate Professor of Christianity and Culture. / As did several other members of Duke's Divinity School faculty, he regularly taught academic graduate courses in Duke's Department of Religion, including regular seminars in Polanyi's Personal Knowledge. During these years he arranged for Polanyi to give the Duke Lectures ('64-'65), entitled "Man in Thought." Poteat was also a participant in the Study Group on Foundations of Cultural Unity in August 1965 and August 1966 held at Bowdoin College, MA, organized by Edward Pols, Michael Polanyi, and Marjorie Grene. (Participants included Elizabeth Sewell, John Silber, Iris Murdoch, Charles Taylor, and of course Polanyi, Grene, and Pols). / In the Summer of 1968, he and his colleague, Thomas A. Langford, completed their editorial work on Intellect and Hope: Essays in the Thought of Michael Polanyi, published that year by Duke University Press for the Lilly Endowment Research Program in Christianity and Politics. This book, a festschrift, was the first book-length, serious, interdisciplinary discussion of Polanyi's philosophical work by major scholars in the US and Europe. In 1962, Poteat went to Oxford University again, this time for a semester as Senior Fellow at Merton College. / In 1968, Poteat transferred from the Divinity School to teach full time in Duke's Department of Religion as Professor of Religion and Comparative Studies. This enabled him to concentrate more on teaching graduate seminars and directing doctoral theses. It also enabled him to teach a course to undergraduates each semester until his retirement in 1987. / In 1969 he was named a member of the National Humanities Faculty. He served as head of the Department of Religion from 1972 to 1978. / After a separation and divorce from his first wife, he **married Patricia Lewis in 1980**. During Fall Semester 1968, Poteat went to Greece (principally Athens) for a sabbatical. / Soon after his arrival in Athens, he happened to encounter the art and subsequently the person of Greek sculptor Evangelos Moustakas, which occasioned a profound reformation of his thinking about a great many things and completely disrupted his sabbatical plans. This was not a result of Poteat stepping outside his specialty into a new discipline and medium, as he had long been pursuing serious study of visual art, drama, and literature, and regularly incorporating it into his teaching. / He later characterized this encounter as "an Orphic dismemberment. The intellectual categories upon which I had relied no longer fit. My whole being—my mindbodily being—was riven."

-------------

William H. Poteat's bibliography:

- Adams, E. M. 'Poteat on Modern Culture and Critical Philosophy.' Tradition and Discovery, 21: 1 (1994-95): 45-50.
- Berkman, John. 'Poteat Changed My Life.' Tradition and Discovery, 36: 2 (2009-10): 64-65.
- Breytspraak, Gus. 'Polanyi's Role in Poteat's Teaching Cultural Conceptual Analysis: 1967-1976.' Tradition and Discovery, 35: 2 (2008-2009): 14-19.
- Cashell, K. 'Making Tacit Knowing Explcit: William H. Poteat's Adaptation of Polanyi's Post-Critical Method.' Tradition and Discovery, 35: 2 (2008-09): 48-59.

- Cannon, Dale. 'Haven't You Noticed that Modernity is Bankrupt? Ruminations on the Teaching Career of William H. Poteat.' Tradition and Discovery, 21: 1 (1994-95): 20-32.
- 'Polanyi's Influence on Poteat's Conceptualization of Modernity's "Insanity" and Its Cure.' Tradition and Discovery, 35: 2 (2008-09): 23-31.
- Haddox, Bruce. 'Meditations on the Shared Life.' Tradition and Discovery, 21: 1 (1994-95): 12-19.
- Hall, Ronald L. 'Poteat's Voice: The Impact of Polanyi and Wittgenstein.' Tradition and Discovery, 35: 2 (2008-09): 19-23.
- Jardine, Murray (2009-10). 'Bill Poteat's Post-Critical Logic and the Origins of Modernity.' Tradition and Discovery, 36: 2 (2009-10): 54-58.
- Ladner, Benjamin. 'Why Said What.' Tradition and Discovery, 21: 1 (1994-95): 7-10.
- Mead, Walter B. 'A Symposium Encounter: The Philosophies of William Poteat and Michael Polanyi.' Tradition and Discovery, 35: 2 (2008-09): 6-13.
- --'William Poteat's Anthropology: "Mindbody in the World."' Tradition and Discovery, 21: 1 (1994-95): 33-37.
- Melvin Keiser, R. 'But Bill: Poteatian Meditations.' Tradition and Discovery, 36: 2 (2009-10): 43-50.
- Mullins, Phil. 'W. H. Poteat: An Oblique Introduction.' Tradition and Discovery, 36: 2 (2009-10): 40-43.
- Newman, Elizabeth. 'W. H. Poteat and the Convertibility of Logic and Love.' Tradition and Discovery, 36: 2 (2009-10): 50-53.
- Osborne, Robert T. 'Bill Poteat: Colleague?' Tradition and Discovery, 35: 2 (2008-09): 44-48.
- Rutledge, David. 'William Poteat: The Primacy of the Person.' Tradition and Discovery, 40: 2, 36-45.
- Scott, R. Taylor. 'William H. Poteat: A Laudatio.' Tradition and Discovery, 20: 1 (1994-95): 6-12.
- Stines, J. W. 'William H. Poteat: Liberating Theologian For Polanyi?' Tradition and Discovery, 35: 2 (2008-09): 39-44.
- Stone Johnston, Araminta (2009-10). 'Thanks for Everything Poteat!': An Intellectual (but Personal) Autobiography.' Tradition and Discovery, 36: 2 (2009-10): 59-63.
- Yeager, D. M. 'Salto Mortale: Poteat and the Righting of Philosophy.' Tradition and Discovery, 35: 2 (2008-09): 31-38.
- All articles in Tradition and Discovery: The Polanyi Society Periodical are available on the Polanyi Society Website: www.missouriwestern.edu/orgs/polanyi

[36] 1. Biographical Information form completed for G. J. Hill, 13 July 1994.

2. Family Group Record completed by Anita (Kelley) Pearson, 25 July 1994. Additional information from her sister, Susan (Kelley) Carnwath, 16 Nov 1994. She was born at the Germantown Hospital, Philadelphia, PA.

[37] 1. Biographical Information from Anita (Kelley) Pearson, 13 July 1994.

2. *Harvard Alumni Directory*, 1990.

3. Family Group Record completed by Anita Pearson, 25 July 1994.

[38] Information on Family Group Record completed 25 July 1994 by Carol Ann (Pearson) Ralph.

[39] Information on Family Group Record, completed 25 July 1994 by Anita (Kelley) Pearson.

[40] Information from Anita (Kelley) Pearson, on Family Group Record, 25 July 1994.

[41] Information from Anita (Kelley) Pearson, on Family Group Record, 25 July 1994.

[42] Donald Kelley was born at the Germantown Hospital, Philadelphia, PA. He prepared his Biographical Information form on 8 Sep 1994.

[43] Information provided by Susan (Kelley) Carnwath; to G. J. Hill, 16 Mar 1995.

[44] Donald E. Kelly, Jr., Esq., of Folger & Levin, LLC, San Francisco / Folger Levin LLP 199 Fremont St Fl 20. San Francisco, CA 94105. The website of the company shows:

-----------

Don Kelley is a partner in our Corporate & Real Estate Practice Group. With more than 30 years experience as a business attorney, Don has handled a broad range of complex transactional and business counseling matters. He assists clients in such diverse areas as commercial real estate acquisition, development, leasing and land use; formation of business entities and joint ventures; corporate counseling and governance; business acquisitions, dispositions, reorganizations and restructurings; financing and securities transactions, including venture capital investments; commercial transactions; and estate planning and wealth transfer issues, in conjunction with the firm's Estate Planning Group.

Don received his law degree from Stanford University Law School (Order of the Coif) in 1973. He received his undergraduate degree in Philosophy (summa cum laude, Phi Beta Kappa) from Yale University in 1970. / Following law school, Don served as a law clerk for Justice William O. Douglas of the United States Supreme Court and for Judge Robert F. Peckham of the United States District Court for the Northern District of California. He also taught a Business Planning class for many years as a lecturer at the University of California, Berkeley School of Law (Boalt Hall), and for a number of years chaired the Human Subjects Review Committee for the Northern California Cancer Program. Don is a member of the California Bar.

[45] JHN, quoting KFL, p.28. She was born at the Germantown Hospital in Philadelphia

[46] The years of Emily's birth and death were provided by her niece, Sue (Kelley) Carnwath, 16 Nov 1994, who said she was b. in 1891 and d. in 1898. However, her d.c. was found by Anne Mitchell and forwarded to George J. Hill on 1 March 2009. This shows that she d. of diphtheria on 14 June 1897 at the age of six and was buried two days later in Greenmount Cemetery, Philadelphia. Her name was spelled Emmely Zimmermann in the d.c. and her parents' names were spelled John Zimmermann (one n) and Eva K.

[47] John Hower Zimmermann, sent the following message to GJH 4-5-16:

Thank you . . . A couple of years ago, the first of John Zimmermann Jr's grandchildren (my first cousins) passed away. The remaining (17) are alive and well. He was Peter Clark, youngest of Mary Jane Zimmermann Clark's (3) children. He succumbed to bone cancer and of course it was horrible. But shortly before he died, he shared with me some memoirs his mother had written (don't know when) and passed down to him. She died in 2008 I think, and had typed these onto her computer during her last days. . . she was our next door neighbor in Nutley NJ for a while during my high school years. . . . When I was 5 years old (1956) my grandparents (John Jr. and Ethel Z) decided to downsize from their big house at 2 Surrey Road Melrose Park. PA

https://www.google.com/maps/place/2+Surrey+Rd,+Melrose+Park,+PA+19027/@40.0644558,-

75.125383,3a,75y,157h,90t/data=!3m7!1e1!3m5!1s0wVSVqDPsXF4cXGeH1eJEw!2e0!6s%2F%2Fgeo0.ggpht.com%2Fcbk%3Fpanoid%3D0w

VSVqDPsXF4cXGeH1eJEw%26output%3Dthumbnail%26cb_client%3Dsearch.TACTILE.gps%26thumb%3D2%26w%3D392%26h%3D106%

26yaw%3D157.15685%26pitch%3D0!7i13312!8i6656!4m2!3m1!1s0x89c6b73a025e4b8f:0x98f21c2b14acc3f8!6m1!1e1

--------

They had the house built around 1900 and their children were literally born and raised in this house. When they decided to sell the house, they sold it to their youngest son Carl (my dad) who by then had 6 children. There were 2 more to come. So you see, I grew up in that house also - a house full of secret passageways, WWI weapons and other memorabilia my grandfather had left behind. My Aunt Mary Jane's ramblings tell me a little bit about what went on there a generation before me, like a window to another time, and I love that sort of thing. At age 5, I took one of the "maid's rooms" on the 3rd floor with a dormer overlooking 5-way intersection out front. (We all migrated to southern NJ in the 1960's Moorestown/Cherry Hill area and most of us worked our way north.) / Terminology: "Nonnie" refers to Ethel, so called by her children and grandchildren. "Myers" is the elementary school across street where 2 generations of Zimmermann children attended classes and went sleigh riding. Folklore has it that Nonnie ran that school, with some help from a succession of various principals. "Kinnaman" is Ethel's family name, another remarkable family like the Zimmermanns with many accomplished people and STRONG educated women! Finally, I misspoke in a previous email, when I said my father was named after other "Carl's" and "Don Carlos's" of his Zimmermann ancestors. I forgot for a moment that his name comes from the Kinnaman side.

-------------

The Howers were from Bloomsburg PA, schoolteachers and musicians. On that side, we can trace our ancestry back to a Peter Andreas of English/Irish decent, who came over on the Mayflower and was a founder of Yale University. Since my father married an Irish Catholic, there wasn't much RLDS in our house. That was "Nonnie and Boppy's" church.

[48] John Zimmermann, Jr., p. 13, in "John Zimmermann (1855-1936)," 20 Nov 2009 and 15 Dec 2009, Jean Hoxie Naples (sent to GJH, 16 Dec 2009); hereafter JHN.

"Richard Kelley evidently very domineering and 10 years older than John Jr. There were a lot of conflicts of personalities which produced a lot of tension" (JHN 20 Nov 2009). The names and b. dates of John Zimmermann, Jr., 4 ch. were given by JHN on a FT "The Zimmermann Line" (Nov 2009). John Zimmermann, Jr., is in several Ancestry.com family tree

------------

*University of Pennsylvania Bulletin* (1916), 179: John Zimmermann [sic: one "n"], Jr., 1512 W Allegheny Ave (B.S. Pennsylvania 1914) / 1st year graduate student in Mathematics, Economics.

[49] The brother-in-law, Richard Kelley, was the dominant voice in this generation, according to Jean Hoxie Naples (sent to GJH, 16 Dec 2009); hereafter JHN: "Richard Kelley evidently very domineering and 10 years older than John Jr. There were a lot of conflicts of personalities which produced a lot of tension" (JHN 20 Nov 2009).

[50] JHN p.18, quoting KFL (Kathryn Fligg Lee). A large, abandoned factory building still exists on the SW corner of E. Erie Ave. and Castor Ave., at 1474-1498 E. Erie Ave., with a water tower on top. Helene (Zimmermann) Hill recalls that as she passed by on the railroad just north of the North Philadelphia station, a water tower on the top of her father's factory, painted with the name John Zimmermann (2 "n") & Sons. The water tower no longer has a name on it.

[51] Obit of JZ for activities of the company, from JHN, p.23.

[52] JHN, p.24

[53] JHN, p.26.

[54] Ethyl Kinnaman's references: JHN, p. 17. John Hower Zimmermann, her grandson, said he bragged about her as a musician, and quoted her obituary in the *Saints Herald* to Michael Bowman on Michael Bowman on 6/12/09. JHN spelled her name as Ethyl Kinnaman, but my wife, Helene (Zimmermann) Hill, recalls seeing her when she was a child, and has no doubt that the entry is correctly spelled "Ethel" as in Ancestry.com. The Kinnaman line is traced back from Ethel to her ancestors, based on several family trees in Ancestry.com, seen on 4/19/16. All give census records for the last three generations before Ethel, and refer to the book: Lester B. Kinnamon, *The Kinnamon Family in America: Its European Origin, Early Colonial History and Lines of Descent in America* (1979?), Chapter 9 "John Thomas Kinnaman of Stokes County, N.C." [accessed on Ancestry.com, filmstrip] This book is shown elsewhere on OCLC WorldCat as published by L. B. Kinnamon, Easton, Md., in 1982.

Ethel Kinnaman is the daughter of Don Carlos Kinnaman (1861-1932), who m. Elizabeth Lewis (~1869). Don Carlos is the son of John Thomas Kinnaman (1829-1899), who m. Mary Bell Bear (1833-1909). John Thomas

is the son of Richard Kinnaman (1784-1850), who m. Lydia Davis (1796- ), Preble, O., 28 Oct 1819.
Richard is the son of John Thomas Kinnamon [sic] (1747-1831, Winston Salem, Stokes Co., N.C), who m. Eleanor Thompson (1759-1843). The unusual given name of "Don Carlos" also appears in the family of the Founding Prophet of the LDS Church, Joseph Smith, Jr., and his wife Emma (Hale) Smith. Don Carlos Smith (1840-1841) was the 7th of their 9 children. He was a short-lived younger brother of Joseph Smith III, who became prophet of the RLDS Church.

[55] As noted previously, Mary Jane Zimmermann was a daughter of John Zimmermann, Jr. "Mom's Stores" were written for her children and were forwarded to her nephew, John H. Zimmermann; and from him to George J. Hill, on 5 April 2016. See Appendix for the rest of "Mom's Stories." Emphasis added.

[56] Information about Bette's marriage and her children is from John H. Zimmermann, son of her brother, Carl, to GJH, April 2016 (e-mails).

[57] She is in Grand Rapids, Mich.

[58] Edward James, Jr., was in 2016 at 2936 Cascade Rd., SE, Grand Rapids, MI 49506 Jimjamesrealtor@aol.com

[59] Greg James' e-mail address has been jamesassoc@aol.com

[60] "Mom's Notes" were passed to his first cousin, John H. Zimmermann, who sent them to GJH, 4-5-16.

[61] Peter Clark died of "bone cancer," according to his cousin, John H. Zimmermann. His mother wrote the collection of stories entitled "Mom's Notes," that is quoted here.

[62] Gerald Clark, Jr., was in 2016 at 173 High Street, Nutley, NJ 07110 gjclark2@aol.com

[63] Information from John Hower Zimmermann, April 2016.

[64] John Zimmermann, IV, was mentioned in e-mail 1 Apr 2016 from his cousin, John H. Zimmermann, son of Carl. He and his 3 siblings "all remain in southern NJ near where they grew up."

[65] John Hower Zimmermann provided his address: 908 W Front St., Glendora, NJ 08029 856-939-9882.

[66] Mary Ann (Hower) Zimmermann was alive, "going strong at 89½," when her son, John H. Zimmermann, wrote to GJH in April 2016.

[67] The Family Group record and Biographical Information form for the William and Margaret Zimmermann family were completed by William Zimmermann, Jr., 1 August 1994. References for William Zimmermann: obituaries of John Zimmermann, Sr., and JHN, p.18.

[68] Margaret[7] Lukens (Edward[6], Ezra[5], George[4], John[3], Abraham[2], Johan[1] [Jan], Wilhelm[A] Lukens, Hermann[B] Op den Graeff) was a 5th cousin, once removed, of Barbara[8] Shoemaker (William[7], Julian[6], Charles[5] Shoemaker, Hannah[4]Lukens [m. Jonathan Shoemaker], Joseph[3], Peter[2], Johan[1] [Jan], Wilhelm[A] Lukens, Hermann[B] Op den Graeff). Both Margaret and Barbara were descendants of Jan Lukens, a founder of Germantown, Philadelphia, and were thus related to all of the 13 founding families of Germantown, and from Hermann Op den Graeff ["of the Graf"]. He is believed to be the morganatic son (i.e., born to a wife who is a commoner) of a noble, Johann Wilhelm de la Marck, Graff (Duke) of Jülich-Cleves-Berg and Anna Van Aldekerk

[69] References for William Zimmermann, Jr.:
From https://www.physics.umn.edu/people/Zimmermann.html:
SHEPLAB 149 (office), 624-4387 / PAN 376 (lab), 624-0262 / zimme004 @ umn.edu _
http://www.physics.umn.edu/research/cm/ _ curriculum vitae :
Summary of Interests
Experimental study of superfluidity in liquid 4He and 3He/4He mixtures.
About My Work / In pure liquid 4He, my work has included the study of persistent superfluid flow, the quantization of superfluid circulation, the trapping of ions by superfluid vortices, the superfluid critical velocity and the alteration of the superfluid density in fine pores near the lambda transition, and superfluid vortex generation in flow through orifices of submicron size. My work has also included the study of some of these same effects in superfluid 3He/4He mixtures, measurements of the heat capacity and concentration susceptibility of these mixtures near the tricritical point, and studies of the thin superfluid film that forms on the walls of a vessel containing the normal phase of the mixtures near the tricritical point. Currently, I am investigating the effect of applying large electric fields to superfluid 4He near the lambda transition. Such fields are being applied to the helium in the pores of membranes that are being used to generate and detect second sound in the liquid. The fields are observed to affect the efficiency with which the membranes generate and respond to second sound at temperatures of a few tenths of a millikelvin below the lambda temperature.
------------

He was co-chairman of the symposium in 2000 mentioned in the text. The full report is at:
http://archive.iupap.org/commissions/c5/reports/qfs-00.html
----------

Jackie Renzetti , [Minneapolis] *Minnesota Daily* (June 24, 2015):
http://www.mndaily.com/news/campus/2015/06/24/tate-lab-undergo-two-year-renovation

"Since his arrival to Tate Laboratory of Physics in 1959, physics professor William Zimmermann said the building has seen periodic updates to its labs. Now, it's in for a total makeover."

-----------------------------------------------------------------------------------------------------------------

From http://www.amity-baroquemusic.com/ (accessed 5/3/16)

Amity / Based in Minneapolis, Amity plays popular music from the Baroque period - the 1600's and early 1700's, including composed music and popular tunes for dancing. . . . Flute / William Zimmermann . . . Violin / Elizabeth Zimmermann . . . Cello / Anne Anderson . . . Piano / Carol Lilygren . . . Venue: Underground Music Cafe, Falcon Heights (photo courtesy of Arlys Arnold)

------------

William Zimmermann - flute . . . William is retired as a faculty member of the University of Minnesota. His hobbies include physics, gardening, bee-keeping, and playing the flute.

----

Elizabeth Zimmermann - violin . . . After an abundance of education, and years of having to be up, and out, and functioning at 8 a.m., Elizabeth is now retired and playing a lot of fine music. Her other pleasures are English country dance and aerobics class, working crosswords, various arts and crafts, and stopping to pet a puppy when she gets the chance.

[70] An interview with Dr. Fonkalsrud at the American Surgical Association is given in: https://www.aap.org/en-us/about-the-aap/Pediatric-History-Center/Documents/Fonkalsrud.pdf. From this, we learn that the family name is believed to derive from "fornkarl," which is a type of Norwegian troll, and "rud," which is a small community.

--------------

His faculty profile at UCLA / David Gefflen School of Medicine / Professor Emeritus of Surgery / Chief, Emeritus, Pediatric Surgery http://people.healthsciences.ucla.edu/institution/personnel?personnel_id=7817 (accessed 4/19/16):

Dr. Eric Fonkalsrud grew up in Seattle, where he graduated from the University of Washington and was a member of the National Championship Rowing Crew. He attended the Johns Hopkins University School of Medicine and completed a General Surgery internship and a year of residency at Johns Hopkins Hospital. He completed his residency in General and Thoracic Surgery at the UCLA School of Medicine. Following a two-year fellowship in Pediatric Surgery at the Columbus Children's Hospital, he joined the full-time faculty in the Department of Surgery at the UCLA Medical Center and was appointed Chief of Pediatric Surgery in 1965. During his 36 year tenure as Chief of Pediatric Surgery at the UCLA School of Medicine, Dr. Fonkalsrud has developed an active clinical and research program in the management of Inflammatory Bowel Disease in children and adults. He was among the pioneers who developed the ileoanal pouch procedure for patients with severe ulcerative colitis and began studies of the physiological implications of this extensive operation. His group has performed colectomy and ileoanal pouch procedures on more than 150 children and 600 adults, which represents one of the country's largest clinical experiences with this operation. Dr. Fonkalsrud initiated liver transplantation at the UCLA Medical Center in the 1960's and is a world authority on the management of congenital chest wall malformations, gastroesophageal reflux disease in children, and neonatal surgery. He has performed more than 14,000 operations. Dr. Fonkalsrud is also a volunteer surgeon at the Venice Family Clinic. Fourteen of his residents and research fellows have gone on to train in Pediatric Surgery Fellowship programs. Dr. Fonkalsrud has authored 448 publications in scientific journals, 120 book chapters, and 5 books. He has served on the editorial boards of 15 major surgical journals, and as President of 9 Regional, National, and International Surgical Societies, including the American Pediatric Surgical Association, the Society of University Surgeons, the Association for Academic Surgery, and the Pacific Coast Surgical Association. He has received the Mead Johnson Scholarship Award in Academic Medicine, and the Markle Scholar Award in Academic Medicine. He was a consultant to the NIH for four years and a James IV Traveling Surgical Scholar to the United Kingdom in 1971. Dr. Fonkalsrud is an Honorary Fellow of the German, Japanese, and Polish Surgical Societies. He was awarded the Herbert Coe Medal for lifetime contributions to the field of Pediatric Surgery from the Pacific Associations of Pediatric Surgeons. Listed in the "Best Doctors in America," "Who's Who in America," and "Who's Who in the World," Dr. Fonkalsrud was honored as "Man of the Year" by the Crohn's and Colitis Foundation of Southern California in 1999. He was elected to the Johns Hopkins University Society of Scholars in 2003, and received the UCLA Medical Alumni Professional Achievement Award in 2003.

-------------

http://depts.washington.edu/givemed/scholarships/margaret-and-eric-fonkalsrud/Margaret Z. and Eric W. Fonkalsrud, M.D. Endowed Scholarship / EST. 2009:

Dr. Eric W. Fonkalsrud, professor and emeritus chief of pediatric surgery at UCLA Medical Center, was born shortly after his parents emigrated to the U.S. from Norway. His father, a civil engineer, was recruited to design bridges across the Columbia River, and the family moved to Seattle in 1942. / Dr. Fonkalsrud graduated from Queen Anne High School, and received a B.S. in zoology from the University of Washington in 1953. He was a member of the national championship crew in 1950 and 1952. He retains a strong affection for the University, although he earned his medical degree at the Johns Hopkins School of Medicine in 1957. Dr. Fonkalsrud completed a residency in general and thoracic surgery at Johns Hopkins and the UCLA School of Medicine, and a fellowship in pediatric surgery at the Columbus Children's Hospital. He was appointed chief of pediatric surgery at the UCLA Medical Center in 1965.

A prolific author, Dr. Fonkalsrud's clinical and research programs included pioneering investigation in the surgical treatment of ulcerative colitis with restorative proctocolectomy, liver transplantation, congenital chest wall malformations, gastroesophageal reflux disease, and neonatal surgery. He was honored as "Man of the Year' by the Crohn's and Colitis Foundation of California in 1999, elected to the Johns Hopkins University Society of Scholars in 2003, and received the UCLA Medical Alumni Professional Achievement Award in 2003. He is a recipient of the Golden Apple award at UCLA, and other awards from national and international surgical societies for lifelong contributions to children's surgery and student mentorship.

[71] References for Robert A. Zimmermann: http://www.biochem.umass.edu/emeritus-faculty/robert-Zimmermann gives his professional address as: LGRT 1021J / Zimmermann@biochem.umass.edu (413) 545-0936. Also: https://www.bio.umass.edu/mcb/faculty/Zimmermann.html and http://www.ratemyprofessors.com/ShowRatings.jsp?tid=82516 and https://www.researchgate.net/profile/Robert_Zimmermann2

[72] The story of her childhood and the surrogate mothers is from JHN to GJH, 20 Nov 2009. Lillian Zimmermann's class at the Univ. Pa., is from JHN, 16 Dec 2009, p. 20; her cruise to Europe, Africa, and Asia is from JHN, 22, quoting KFL; and her visits to Cape Cod is from JHN, p.22, quoting her niece Cil. Her m. date is from a photo sent to GJH from JHN. His b. is said by JHN to be at Toronto, Canada.

------------

*Women's Undergraduate Record, University of Pennsylvania* (1920), shows two entries for Lillian Z.:
[page 28/64] "Class of 1921 ... LILLIAN ZIMMERMANN, 1512 W. Allegheny Ave."
[page 60/64] "Kappa Kappa Gamma . . LILLIAN ZIMMERMANN, 21'."

------------

Note that her name is spelled with one "n" in the class list but with "nn" in the sorority list.

[73] Eva Kathrine (Kellenbenz) Zimmermann died in 1920 of what has been called "aplastic anemia," although her death certificate says she died of pernicious anemia – which is a different disease.

[74] "Palestine fever" is still unidentified, but it has been referred to since at least 1895 and as recently as the early 21st century. "Palestine fever" is still unidentified as a specific disease, but it has been referred to since at least 1895 and as recently as the early 21st century. Its symptoms include high fever, swollen and aching joints, swollen lymph nodes, and a rash. It may be an unusual presentation of rubella (German measles), occurring with another infectious disease. See: *National Druggist* 25 (no. 2, Feb. 1895); and Archie Bell, *The Spell of the Holy Land* (1915), viii; and https://www.reddit.com/r/AskReddit/comments/dqx1a/palestine_fever_has_this_unknown_disease_since/

[75] References for James A. Fligg: JHN, 20 Nov 2009 and 16 Dec 2009, p. 28.
Patent US2541231 - Woven fabric - Google Patents https://www.google.com/patents/US2541231
J. A. FLIGG WOVEN FABRIC Feb. 13, 1951 Filed Oct. 26, 1948 Patented Feb. 13, 1951 UNITED STATES PATENT OFFICE WOVEN FABRIC / James A. Fligg, Elkins Park, Pa. / Application October 26, 1948, Serial No. 56,479. The patent is #2,541,231.

[76] Recollections about the Fligg family by Mary Jane (Zimmermann) Clark in "Mom's Stories." Emphasis added to show the Fligg family.

[77] References for Kathryn (Fligg) Lee:
http://www.kathrynflee.com/resume.html; bpedwardlee@yahoo.com; http://www.kathrynflee.com/; http://www.saintasaphs.org/Arts%20&%20Music.html (all accessed 4-22-16); http://kathrynfligglee.blogspot.com/; http://kathrynfligglee.blogspot.com/2011/11/kathryn-fligg-lee-is-noted-collage.html [Posted 21st November 2011] (accessed 4-22-16): "Kathryn Fligg Lee is a noted collage artist in the Philadelphia area. She has worked extensively in the medium of paper and has shown her work over the past few decades at a number of fine art galleries. Her work can be found at MUSE galleries."
http://streamlinermemories.info/?p=1758 (accessed 4-22-16): Dining on the Denver Zephyr (Posted on January 12, 2013 by Train Lover).

[78] © Lothrop, Lee & Shepard Co., Inc.; 16Dec63; A663777.

[79] References for Edward L. Lee, Jr.: http://www.livingchurch.org/sidelined-cathedral; http://myemail.constantcontact.com/Friday-Report-from-St--Thomas--Church--Whitemarsh.html?soid=1102727622835&aid=h6MAzqlcekc (accessed 4-22-16); *Ludwington Daily News* (27 Sep 1990); and Episcopal Press and News (1962-2006), The Archives of the Episcopal Church June 22, 1989 "Western Michigan Elects Lee."

[80] Several internet sources show a James A. Fligg living in North Palm Beach, Fl., at the age of about 88 in 2016 (i.e., born 1928). This may be an error, or an incredible coincidence. Our James A. Fligg, Jr., died in March 2009. References for James A. Fligg, Jr.: http://cheltenhamalumni.org/thank-you.htm: The Cheltenham High School Alumni Association / "James A. Fligg, '46 donated $100 to our scholarship fund."

James A. Fligg, Jr., "Tests of a Low Speed Three-stage Axial Flow Compressor at Aspect Ratios of One, Two, and Four," Abstract and paper for 2nd Propulsion Joint Specialist Conference, 1966, Colorado Springs, CO. From http://dx.doi.org/10.2514/6.1966-613 (accessed 4-25-16).

Patent US3283995 - Splitter vane construction for turbofan ... https://www.google.com/patents/US3283995 United States Patent Ofiice 3,233,995 SPLITTER VANE CONSTRUCTION FOR TURBOFAN ENGINE James A. Fligg, Jr., East Hartford, Conn, assignor to United Aircraft Corp. / Publication number US 3283995 A Publication type Grant / Publication date Nov 8, 1966 / Filing date Apr 28, 1965 / Priority date Apr 28, 1965 Inventor Fligg Jr James A / Original Assignee United Aircraft Corp / Export Citation BiBTeX, EndNote, RefMan

From: http://ntrs.nasa.gov/archive/nasa/casi.ntrs.nasa.gov/19720023124.pdf --- J. A. Fligg appears in the list of contributors to: Florida Research & Development Center / P. 0. Box 2691 / West Palm Beach, Florida 33402, which produced the report in September 1972 entitled HIGH-LOADING, 1800 FT/SEC TIP SPEED TRANSONIC

COMPRESSOR FAN STAGE I. AERODYNAMIC AND MECHANICAC DESIGN, by A.L. Morris, J.E. Halle, and E. Kennedy, PRATT & WHITNEY AIRCRAFT DIVISION / UNITED AIRCRAFT CORPORATION. This was prepared for NATIONAL AERONAUTICS AND SPACE ADMINISTRATION / NASA Lewis Research Center / Contract NAS 3- 13493 / W. L. Beede, Project Manager / Fluid System Components Division / Abstract: "A single stage fan with a tip speed of 1800 ft/sec (548.6 mlsec) and hub/tip ratio of 0.5 was designed to produce a pressure ratio of 2.285: 1 with an adiabatic efficiency of 84.Wo. The design flow per inlet annulus area is 38.7 Ibm/ft2-sec (188.9 kg/m2-sec). Rotor blades have modified multiple-circular-arc and precompression airfoil sections. The stator vanes have multiplecircular-arc airfoil sections."

[81] His life is summarized in the book by George J. Hill, *Proceed to Peshawar* (Annapolis, Md.: Naval Institute Press, 2013). This book won a Finalist Medal from the Independent Book Publishers at the Indie Book Festival in 2015. Also see: George J. Hill, *Quakers and Pilgrims: The Shoemaker, Warren and Allied Families. Ancestors and Descendants of William Toy Shoemaker and Mabel Warren, Who Were Married in Philadelphia in 1895* (Westminster, Md.: Heritage Books, 2015).

His birth certificate was requested from the Philadelphia Archives on 14 Jan 2001. On 19 Jan 2001 the Archives sent a copy of the Return of Births in Philadelphia for the month of June 1902 showing seven births: The fifth birth for the month, on 11 June 1902, was Albert Walter Zimmermann [sic], a white male, was born at 610 W. Lehigh Ave., 9th Ward. His parents were John & Cathrina Zimmermann [sic]. His father's occupation was: Manufacturer. [The terminal "n" was missing from the family name in this record.]

His service record was obtained by his daughter, Helene (Zimmermann) Hill on 28 January 2004 from the National Personnel Records Center, 9700 Page Ave., St. Louis, MO 63132-5100. It shows that his service number was 205 065. He was "Lt.S(I), USNR" and his birth date was 6/11/02 (Philadelphia, Pa.). He was said to be a Wool Dealer with 8 years of grammar school, 4 years of H.S., 4 yrs of college; BS in EE Mechanical Eng. His fingerprint and full signature are on the Notice of Separation.

He was commissioned 8/1/42. He entered active service 10/18/42 at Intell. Office Washington D.C. He was a white male, married U.S. Citizen who resided at 400 Rose Lane North, Haverford, Montgomery Co., Pa. He attended Basic ONI, Advanced ONI, and Port Director Schools and was qualified as "Liaison Officer - Foreign Service." He served at Liaison Office, Iarachi [sic], India. He was released from active duty on 12/30/45 and had 52 days of terminal leave. Net service was 3 yrs, 3 mos, 15 days. He had "No citations / Not eligible for promotion under A1 Nav -- 317 / Asiatic Area Ribbon / World War II Victory Medal."

[82] The biography of Barbara (Shoemaker) Zimmermann is abbreviated from a longer version in Hill, *Quakers and Puritans* (op. cit., *supra*).

It has been said that the presses were stopped to hold a line for her in the *Genealogy of the Shoemaker Family of Cheltenham, Pennsylvania*, which was compiled by Benjamin R. Shoemaker, and printed for private circulation by J. B. Lippincott Co., Philadelphia, in 1903. Her entry (#5024), p. 400, is one of the last in chronological order, and neither of her younger brothers (b. 8-20-1903 and 12-16-1904) are included in this book. In fact, her entry is also one of the last in the genealogy of her mother's family, *The Warren, Jackson, and Allied Families*, by Betsy Warren Davis, which was also printed for private circulation by the J. B. Lippincott Co. in 1903. In this book, she appears as person #120 in the Warren family, on p. 37.

Barbara Shoemaker Zimmermann died 24 July 1985 at 400 N. Rose Lane, Haverford, Lower Merion Twp., Montgomery Co., Pennsylvania (which was also her residence). She "never worked." She was a white female widow, SSN 160-24-2765; she was 83 years old when she died at 12:45 p.m. of respiratory failure due to pneumonia of 6 days duration; no autopsy was performed. She was the daughter of William Toy Shoemaker and (maiden name) Mabel Warren. Her attending physician was James Hykas, M.D.; the informant was Barbara Johnson of 520 Montgomery Lane, Radnor, Pa. She was cremated at West Laurel Hill Cemetery, Bala-Cynwyd on 24 July 1985, attended by Stuard Funeral Directors, Inc., 104 Cricket Ave., Ardmore, Pa.

Letter sent on 20 August 2000 to Montgomery County Records Dept., 1880 Markley Street (basement), Norristown, PA 19401 (610-278-3441), for her will. Reply 8/28/00, from Carole Faust, Records Supervisor: "I have one of the Estates mentioned in your letter of August 20, 2000. . . . The Estate that I can locate is: Barbara S. Zimmermann (died 24 July 1985; Lower Merion Twp.) / RW# 46-85-1905 = contains 52 pages of copy. / OC# 87-480 = contains 67 pages of copy. / The documents can be copied at fifty cents per page, plus a one-dollar mailing fee. The staff would be able "to choose six or more pages from either file containing the most genealogical value." We have postponed doing that, pending determination of a need for the information that may be in this will.

For the record of her parentage and birth, see B. H. Shoemaker, *Shoemaker Family*, p. 400; and B. W. Davis, *Warren Family*, p. 37. Her birth certificate was requested from the Philadelphia Archives on 14 Jan 2001. On 19 Jan 2001 the Archives sent a copy of the Return of Births in Philadelphia for the month of February 1902 showing one birth: 13 February 1902, Barbara Shoemaker, white female, b. at 2038 Arch St. Her parents were

William T. and Mabel Shoemaker. Her father's occupation was: Physician.

Albert W. Zimmermann's birth certificate was requested from the Philadelphia Archives on 14 Jan 2001. On 19 Jan 2001 the Archives sent a copy of the Return of Births in Philadelphia for the month of June 1902 showing seven births. The fifth birth for the month, on 11 June 1902, was Albert Walter Zimmerman [sic], a white male, born at 610 W. Lehigh Ave., 9th Ward. His parents were John & Cathrina Zimmerman [sic]. His father's occupation was: Manufacturer. [The terminal "n" was missing from the family name in this record.]

Ltr to Phila Marriage License Bureau for marriage record, 1/14/01. 2nd Ltr for m.r., sent to Phila Marriage License Bureau (Orphans' Court), 1/20/01. This letter and check were returned on 1/30/01 (recd 1/31/01) with the statement that "A search . . . fails to reveal an application for a marriage license in the name(s) of Barbara Shoemaker and Walter Zimmermann from the years 1917 to 1938 in Philadelphia County." 3rd Ltr for m.r. sent to Phila Marriage License Bureau 2/2/01, asking for a search for Barbara Shoemaker and Albert Zimmermann in January 1926. No such record could be found in the Philadelphia Marriage License Bureau.

e-mail to Rev. Susannah Currie, Swedenborgian Church, Temenos Retreat Center, 1564 Telegraph Rd., West Chester, PA 19382 610-696-8145, asking for help in locating the m.r. Downloaded Swedenborgian church homepage information from www.swedenborg.org. Her reply of 2-05-01 by e-mail: Her church "IS the Philadelphia church," and she will ask her archives committee to research the marriage when it meets on 2-18-01. Acknowledged with thanks by e-mail on 2-06-01. (Bounced back once, and resent.) e-mail sent to Rev. Susannah Currie on 2/10/01 requesting any information regarding the marriage or membership in the church of Julien and Hannah (Hester) Shoemaker.

On 21 April 2001, 33 pages of photocopied records of typed pages, representing all that could be found regarding the Shoemaker and Zimmermann families, were mailed by the Temenos Retreat Center, West Chester, Penna. These records included one page that showed the family of William Toy Shoemaker and his wife Mabel Warren Shoemaker, on which was stated that their fourth child and second daughter was Barbara (Mrs. Albert W. Zimmermann) Born 1-13-02, Baptized 6-5-02, Confirmed 4-4-20, and Elect. Mem. 4-26-20. On three other pages the records of three of the children of Albert W. Zimmermann and Barbara (Shoemaker) Zimmermann were listed (Barbara, born July 26th, 1927, Haverford, Penna.; baptized May 5th, 1935 at Cotswold Corner, Rose Lane, Haverford, Penna., by Rev. Chas. W. Harvey; Helene, born April 10th, 1929, at Haverford, Penna., baptized May 5th, 1935 at Cotswold Corner, Rose Lane, Haverford, Penna., by Rev. Chas. W. Harvey; and Warren, born Nov. 16th, 1934, at Haverford, Penna., baptized May 5th, 1935 at Cotswold Corner, Rose Lane, Haverford, Penna., by Rev. Chas. W. Harvey.

Letter to Pennyslvania Vital Records for death certificates for both, 12 Jan 2001. On 5 Feb 2001 the death certificates were mailed and were received on 6 Feb 2001. They showed:

Albert Zimmermann died 24 July 1961 at 400 N. Rose Lane, Haverford, Montgomery County, Pa. (which was also his residence). He was a white male, married, a wool merchant, in the textile business. He was born 11 June 1902 at Philadelphia, son of John Zimmermann and Eva Katherine Kellenberg [sic]; he died at the age of 59 years. He died of acute myocardial infarction; no autopsy. The informant was Warren Zimmermann of Haverford, Pa. His physician (name illegible) stated that he died at 10:30 a.m. He was cremated on 27 July 1961 at West Laurel Hill Crematory, Bala-Cynwyd, Pa. The death certificate was No. 066598.

[83] Her obituary in the *Social Register* (2012), [with her photo, head and shoulders, white dress, facing partly left, black head band] http://www.socialregisteronline.com/#!barbara-Zimmermann-johnson/cv45

Barbara Zimmermann Johnson / Mrs. Melvin T. Johnson (Barbara "Babs" Zimmermann) of Lafayette Hill, PA, died on November 30, 2011, at Chestnut Hill Hospital in Philadelphia.

Born in Haverford, PA, on July 26, 1927, to Albert W. Zimmermann, president of the wool-brokering firm Ott and Zimmermann, and the former Barbara Shoemaker, she was educated at The Baldwin School, Chatham Hall, and Smith College. She enjoyed summers at the Maidstone Club in East Hampton, and made her debut in Philadelphia in 1944. After graduation she taught at the Episcopal Academy before embarking on a somewhat more adventurous phase of life as an officer with the Central Intelligence Agency. / Perhaps the most consequential of her various postings in the Middle East during the 1950s was her assignment to the embassy in Amman, Jordan, where she met her future husband. Mr. Johnson, a Harvard alumnus who worked in numerous capacities for the U.S. government and international relief organizations in the Middle East during the Second World War and in post-war Europe, later became the owner and president of the venerable Philadelphia confectionery Maron Famous Candies. His two animating passions were golf and peace in the Middle East, an unusual combination that may have best found expression in his winning the Tripoli Golf Championship in 1955. Mr. Johnson died in Bryn Mawr in March 2002.

As newlyweds the Johnsons lived in Georgetown and then in Yemen before ultimately settling in Radnor, PA, where they raised their two daughters. Babs never lost her dutiful sense of civic-mindedness. She was an active member of the vestry and choir of Saint Martin's Church, a longtime docent at the Philadelphia Zoo, a diligent subscriber to the Philadelphia Orchestra and Opera, and a volunteer with Philadelphia area chapters of the League of Women Voters. She always retained her enthusiasm for international travel, studying French, Arabic, and German. An avid bridge and tennis player, she was a member of Gulph Mills Golf Club, and made a point of completing the Sunday New York Times crossword puzzle every week.

Mrs. Johnson is survived by her daughters, Mrs. Thomas A. Riley III (Barbara W. Johnson) of Radnor, and Mrs. Brian Handwerk (Alice J. Johnson) of Amherst, NH; a brother, Dr. Albert W. Zimmermann Jr. of Flourtown, PA; a sister, Mrs. (Dr.) George J. Hill (Helene Zimmermann) of West Orange, NJ; and seven grandchildren, Fiona, Penelope, John, Vincent and Richard Riley, and Lillian and Phoebe Handwerk.

----------------------

*Smith Alumnae Quarterly* (Spring 2013),77 [obituary by her daughter, Barbara]:

"BARBARA (BABS) ZIMMERMANN JOHNSON '48, Nov. 30, '11, in Philadelphia. After receiving a degree in history, Babs had a career in the CIA, with overseas posts in Jordan and Yemen. She and her husband returned to Philadelphia, where they raised two daughters. Babs was an active docent at the Philadelphia Zoo, and she played tennis and golf. She loved playing bridge and knitting, both of which she had learned while at Smith, living in Hopkins Hous. She is survived by her sister, HENENE ZIMMERMANN HILL '50, two daughters, two sons-in-law and seven grandchildren. -- Barbara Johnson Riley '88, her daughter. [I would add that she also was survived by her brother, Albert W. Zimmermann, Jr.]

[84] The Royal Order of the Golden Cross of the Phoenix consists of a white enamel cross superimposed on a golden cross, suspended from a gold ribbon edged in black. A large bird, representing the phoenix, facing its right wing, is in the center of the cross, and the cross is joined to the ribbon by a crown. The recipient is entitled to wear a miniature rosette of gold and black ribbon cloth. / A short narrative of his childhood, "Growing Up," was privately printed in a collection of stories by Mel and his fellow students in a writing class in the 1990s. This narrative and his poem, "Youth," were on pp. 85-91 of this book, a photocopy of which was available for guests at the reception at his home following the service at St. Martin's Church Memorial Garden on 6 April 2002.

The question of whether his work for USAID was a cover for intelligence operations cannot be answered, and he never discussed it. USAID is said to have been a cover for CIA operatives and probably other intelligence organizations as well. Some examples on the www are:

http://voices.washingtonpost.com/spy-talk/2010/04/cia_chief_promises_spies_new_a.html / Posted at 4:47 PM ET, 04/26/2010 / Washington Post Jeff Stein, "CIA chief promises spies 'new cover' for secret ops" . . . "Other U.S. government agencies provide cover as well. In South Vietnam, the U.S. Agency for International Development (USAID) provided cover for CIA operatives so widely that the two became almost synonymous."

-----------

http://www.intrepidreport.com/archives/12659 (accessed 4/28/16)

*Intrepid Report* (on line)

Wayne Madsen, "USAID: A history of front companies acting on behalf of the CIA" (posted 8 Apr 2014)

"(WMR)-The recent disclosure by the Associated Press that the U.S. Agency for International Development (USAID), a notorious nexus for contract fraud within the State Department, contracted out a project to develop a rival to Twitter in order to foment rebellion in Cuba has refocused attention on USAID's long history of acting as a contract vehicle for various CIA covert activities."

Also see: http://www.intrepidreport.com/archives/12659#sthash.KWv8EUcX.dpuf

[85] Melvin T. Johnson told GJH that his parents' names were Thomas Edward Johnson and Maria Thornton. His son-in-law, Thomas Riley, discovered that his parents were Swedish, and that his mother's name was Thorson.

[86] From Episcopal Academy Upper School e-newsletter, 23 November 2008: Thomas A. Riley, III graduated from EA in 1983. He went on to graduate from Georgetown University, from which he also has masters degrees in foreign policy and history. Mr. Riley also holds a law degree from Villanova. After working on public policy statistics and media at a number of think tanks in Washington during the 1990's, Mr. Riley was named Associate Director of National Drug Control Policy at the White House in 2001. Since then, Mr. Riley has served as the Administration's spokesman on all aspects of drug policy, from treatment, to prevention, to international interdiction and law enforcement. He also oversees the National Youth Antidrug Media Campaign, the government's largest social marketing campaign, with over $1 billion of advertising since 2001. Mr. Riley led the development of the award-winning "Above the Influence" brand of prevention advertising. Mr. Riley lives in Bethesda, MD with his wife Barbara (whom he met while she was at Agnes Irwin), their four children, and 10 pets.

[87] Her biography appears in *Who's Who in the East, American Men and Women in Science, Who's Who of American Women, Who's Who Directory of Professionals and Resources in Cancer, Who's Who in Science and Engineering, and Who's Who in America*. Her most frequently cited paper is Hill, HZ: "The function of melanin or six blind people examine an elephant." *BioEssays* 14:49-56, 1992. She is the author of more than 50 scientific articles,

several book chapters, and more than 75 abstracts of papers presented at national and international meetings (see Science Citation Index). She has been a speaker at many scientific meetings in the United States, and in Banff and Edmonton, Canada; Cambridge and London, England; Krakow, Poland; Vienna, Austria; Barcelona, Spain; Cairo, Egypt; and LaPaz and Santa Cruz, Bolivia.

[88] George J. Hill's other honors include: Damon Runyon Fellow; American Cancer Society Professor of Clinical Oncology; The Gorgas Medal of the Association of Military Surgeons of the U.S.; the Margaret Hay Edwards Achievement Medal of the American Association for Cancer Education; and the Silver Beaver and Silver Antelope awards from the Boy Scouts of America. He also received the National Divisional Award (St. George Medal) of the American Cancer Society, the Outstanding Service Medal of the Uniformed Services University of the Health Sciences, and the National William Spurgeon III Award of the Boy Scouts of America. He was elected Fellow of the Royal Society of Medicine and Fellow of the Explorers Club, New York City. He is a member of the American Alpine Club and a Life Member of the Harvard Mountaineering Club. He was President of several organizations, including the American Association for Cancer Education, Academy of Medicine of New Jersey, Essex County (N.J.) Medical Society, and the American Cancer Society, New Jersey Division, Inc. He has published more than 200 scientific papers, letters and book chapters, and has written or co-authored more than a dozen books, some of which have been translated into Spanish and have also been reprinted in additional printings and editions. His biography appears in several editions of *Who's Who in the United States* and in other publications of Marquis *Who's Who*. He is a member of about 40 hereditary and lineage societies. His offices include Governor General, Descendants of the Founders of New Jersey; Governor General, Order of the First Families of New Hampshire; Deputy Governor General of the Society of Mayflower Descendants; Deputy Governor General and Surgeon General of the Society of Colonial Wars; Historian General of Order of the Founders and Patriots of America; Vice President General, Sons of the American Revolution; Vice President of the Order of the Blue and Gray; Surgeon General of the Order of the Merovingian Dynasty; Elder General of the National Society, Sons and Daughters of the Pilgrims; Chancellor General, Order of the Descendants of Colonial Physicians and Chirurgiens; Chancellor General of the Winthrop Society; Marshal of the Order of the Justiciars; and Marshal of the Society of Descendants of Lady Godiva . He has been state society president of several of these organizations, and of the N.J. Society, Sons of the Revolution. He is also a member of the National Gavel Society, New Jersey Society of the Cincinnati, Jamestowne Society, Order of Indian Wars, Order of the Loyalists and Patriots of the American Revolution, Welcome Society, Colonial Society of Pennsylvania, Huguenot Society, St. Nicholas Society of NYC, St. Andrews Society of NYC, Friendly Sons of St. Patrick of Pennsylvania, Order of the Three Crusades, Americans of Royal Descent; and Order of the Norman Conquest.

[89] He was featured in *New York* magazine, regarding his client, Gary McGivern, 6 Mar 1995, p. 14.

[90] 1. David Hill, "The Statue and the Strands," in Deborah Case and Sharon Derderian (Editors), *Passages: An Anthology of Contemporary Literature* (Troy, Mich.: Iliad Press/Cader Publishing Co., 1992) [ISBN 0-8187-0164-1], p. 80.

2. David H. Hill, "The Hunchback Inside of Me," which received the "Editors Choice Award" from the National Library of Poetry in 1997. In Diana Ziegler (Editor), *Endless Skies of Blue: The National Library of Poetry 1997* (Owings Mills, Md.: Watermark Press, 1997) [ISBN 1-57553-611-0], p. 205.

3. David H. Hill, "Untitled," in Howard Ely (Editor), *Best Poems of 1998: The National Library of Poetry* (Owings Mills, Md.: Watermark Press, 1998) [ISBN 1-57553-954-3], p. 256.

4. David Hedgcock Hill (edited by George J. Hill, M.D.), *A Lesson in Reality: Poems and Essays, 1991-2000* (West Orange, N.J.: Hilltree Farm Press, 2007, 67 pp.).

[91] Her birth is recorded in *The Manly Genealogy*, 45. Sarah Hill, Untitled. Her black and white photograph of a children's swing was published facing the back cover in the Kenyon College literary magazine, *Hika*, v. 44, no. 2, 1984. G. J. Hill and S. Hill, "Lead Poisoning due to Hai Ge Fen," Letter to the Editor of the *Journal of the American Medical Association*, 1994.

[92] Warren Zimmermann's resignation from the Foreign Service was widely reported in the news media. From the many newspaper articles, three are quoted below:

"There then followed an astonishing exodus of the elite from the State Department. Just this month, Warren Zimmermann, a senior diplomat who was our last ambassador to Yugoslavia and a onetime defender of our policy in that region, gave Secretary Christopher his letter of resignation." (*Inquirer – The Philadelphia Inquirer Magazine,* 30 Jan 1994).

"The prolonged tragedy of Bosnia was further cemented in both symbols and substance last week. Two symbols – of dissent over the

West's response to the conflict in the former Yugoslavia – were the announced departures of the commander of United Nations peacekeeping forces and a State Department expert on the Balkans. The substance was Serbian artillery, lots of it, raining down with renewed fury on Sarajevo and killing dozens. The resignations-in-protest, hardly the first of the conflict, were tendered by Lieut. Gen. Francis Briquemont of Belgium, the United Nations commander, and Warren Zimmermann[n], the head of the State Department's refugee programs and a former Ambassador to Yugoslavia. Though General Briquemont called his reasons personal, he had criticized the United Nations just days before for failing to back up its resolutions with troops and and action to insure deliveries. Mr. Zimmermann[n] had faulted American policy along similar lines, though he also was miffed (as were colleagues of his) at his not being elevated to a new, higher-profile refugee post that the Clinton Administration wants to give to a woman or nonwhite male" (*New York Times* "Week in Review", 10 Jan 1994).

"One State Department official who had a part in the Bush policy on Yugoslavia has had the courage to recognize the disaster. That is Warren Zimmermann, a Foreign Service officer for 33 years, who was the U.S. minister in Moscow and Ambassador to Yugoslavia. Mr. Zimmermann, like his chiefs in the Bush Administration, thought it was best to try to hold Yugoslavia together. But by late 1991 he saw that the policy had encouraged the worst in Mr. Milosevic and was bankrupt. Last week Warren Zimmermann resigned, in part in disgust at this country's failure to act against the slaughter in Bosnia. He was the fifth and by far the highest-ranking Foreign Service officer to quit on that issue." (Anthony Lewis: "Abroad at Home – What Might Have Been", *N.Y. Times*, 10 Jan 1994).

Zimmermann, Warren: "Many people in the Balkans may be weak or even bigoted, but it is their leaders – Milosevic, Karadzic, and Tudjman – who are criminal." In "The Captive Mind," (p. 6) in *The New York Review*, Feb. 2, 1995, pp. 3-6. [a Review of Thompson, Mark: FORGING WAR: THE MEDIA IN SERBIA, CROATIA AND BOSNIA-HERCEGOVINA. Article 19, Washington, DC: International Centre Against Censorship, 275 pp., 1994]

Zimmermann wrote in *Foreign Affairs* magazine that Slobodan Milosevic was a man of extraordinary coldness... and mendacity" with a personality trait that "made it possible for Milosevic to condone, encourage and even organize the unspeakable atrocities committed by Serbian citizens in the Bosnian war." Milosevic, he says, was driven "by power rather than nationalism. He has made a Faustian pact with nationalism as a way to gain and hold power." Of Radovan Karadzic, leader of the Bosnian Serbs, Zimmermann wrote: "He was the architect of massacres in the Muslim villages... [who] "invites comparison with a monster from another generation, Heinrich Himmler." (Zimmermann, W.: "The Last Ambassador," in *Foreign Affairs*, latest issue, quoted appreciatively by Anthony Lewis in "Fanatical and Ruthless," *The New York Times*, Op-Ed, p. A29, 10 Mar 1995). Lewis also quoted Zimmermann in his Op-Ed column, Ibid., 31 Mar 1995, in defense of a reporter who sued *Time* magazine for libel. Mr. Zimmermann recalled the reporter's veracity from his days as Minister to the Soviet Union.

Zimmermann, "A Cry for Action: A vehement critic of U.S. Bosnia policy says Clinton should get tougher with the Serbs. . . . Former Ambassador to Yugoslavia Warren Zimmermann (at home in Virginia) [photo shown] believes that acts like the taking of U.N. hostages (French peacekeepers, [photo] left) make the use of force imperative. 'Air power,' he says, 'could do the job.' ... 'I'm afraid the only language the Bosnian Serbs understand is force.'" *People* magazine (6/19/95), pp. 97-98.

Zimmermann, Warren: "Bombs, Not Words, in Bosnia: Only NATO air power can end the conflict." "...The West will have to use force if it wants to influence the outcome ... There are no flawless alternatives to avert disaster. But paradoxically, the least risky course in the long run would be for NATO, led by the United States, to use its air power to force a compromise with which all of the combatants can live." From "*The New York Times*" Op-Ed, Friday, June 23, 1995.

John Farmer, syndicated columnist, wrote on 3 May 1999: "Isn't it time, as the Rev. Jesse Jackson said yesterday, to negotiate with Milosovec? Not according to Warren Zimmermann [sic], former ambassador to Yugoslavia. Not so long as Milosevic has reason to believe he can retain power in Belgrade . . . Only when it's clear he's at risk of losing control in Belgrade or Kosovo or both will negotiations be productive, as Zimmermann see it." From Newark *Star-Ledger* (3 May 1999), p.4.

Warren Zimmermann's obituary by Christopher Marquis in the *New York Times* (Thursday, 5 February 2004), B9: "Warren Zimmermann, the last American ambassador to Yugoslavia, who held senior diplomatic posts in several other countries, died Tuesday at his home in Great Falls, Va. He was 69. The cause was pancreatic cancer, said his son, Tim. Mr. Zimmermann served in a united Yugoslavia beginning in 1989 and was recalled by the elder Bush's administration in 1992 to protest the increasing violence of the civil war there. Seeing the country's breakup and the further increase in violence along nationalist lines, he urged the Clinton administration to take military action. When that administration at first demurred at the use of force, Mr. Zimmermann resigned in protest from his next job, as director of refugee affairs, in 1994. . . . He was a student of history and wrote three books.  His first, *Origins of a Catastrophe: Yugoslavia and Its Destroyers*, won the American Academy of Diplomacy book award for 1997. . . .  His last book, *First Great Triumph: How Five Americans Made Their Country a World Power, also won the book award from the American Academy of Diplomacy. . . .*  [The obituary said in error that a "second book, released in 2002, is about the rise of America as a world power after the Spanish-American War."]

"Ex-Envoy to Balkans Dies.  Warren Zimmermann, the last American ambassador to Yugoslavia, who quit the Foreign Service in 1994 to emphasize the need for intervention in Bosnia, was 69."  His photo c. 2002 accompanies the obituary.  On 1 February, the *New York Times Book Review* section on New & Noteworthy Paperbacks said of *First Great Triumph*, "In 2002 our reviewer, David Nasaw, called this a 'brilliantly readable book'."

His obituary by Bart Barnes in the *Washington Post* (5 February 2004), B05, spells his name incorrectly in both the title ("Warren Zimmermann Dies; Last U.S. Envoy to Yugoslavia") and throughout the text.  However, the obituary is longer and more complete than the obit in the *Times*.  "Warren Zimmermann, 69, the last U.S. ambassador to Yugoslavia who was recalled from Belgrade in 1992 to protest Serbian intervention? in the former Yugoslav republic of Bosnia-Herzegovina, died of pancreatic cancer Feb. 3 at his home in Great Falls.  Mr. Zimmermann was a 33-year Foreign Service officer, an author and a professor.  In his diplomatic career, he had also served in Paris, Moscow and Caracas.  Before his appointment as ambassador to Yugoslavia, he was ambassador to the Conference on Security and Cooperation in Europe in Vienna, which produced human rights advances in Eastern Europe and the Soviet Union.  In 1994, Mr. Zimmermann resigned from the Foreign Service.  His family said he was 'frustrated over the Clinton administration's reluctance to intervene forcefully in the Bosnian war'. . . .  Mr. Zimmermann, an advocate of human rights throughout his Foreign Service career, received the Scharansky Award from the Union of Councils for Soviet Jews for his work in Jewish emigration from the Soviet Union."

Quotations from Colin Powell and former Ambassador Arthur Hartman are included in the obituary.  He is said to have been the No. 1 player on the varsity squash team at Yale and that he graduated *magna cum laude*.  He was a Fulbright scholar at Cambridge University, where he earned a master's degree in history.

Summary from State Department website:  Military service: US Army (1959) / Wife: Corinne (three children) / Daughter: Corinne / Daughter: Lily / Son: Tim / High School: Deerfield Academy, Deerfield, MA / University: BA, Yale University (1956) / University: MA, Cambridge University (1958) / Scholar: Distinguished Fellow, New School for Social Research (1994-97) / Teacher: School of Advanced International Studies / Teacher: Columbia University/ Author of books: *First Great Triumph: How Five Americans Made Their Country a World Power* (2002, history); *Origins of a Catastrophe: Yugoslavia and Its Destroyers: America's Last Ambassador Tells What Happened and Why* (1996, history).

[93] *Who's Who in America*, 47th Ed., 1992-93, p. 3680.

[94] Corinne (Chubb) Zimmermann's Roosevelt ancestors are outlined in Peter Collier and David Horowith, *The Roosevelts: An American Saga* (New York: Simon & Schuster, 1994); family tree, unnumbered pp. 10-11. Additional comments and quotations of her great-grandmother, Corinne (Roosevelt) Robinson, appear in Nathan Miller, *Theodore Roosevelt: A Life* (New York: Quill/Morrow, 1992).

The first Corinne, Corinne (Roosevelt) Robinson, was a well-known poet in her day, and was active in politics as well.  Her poem, "To General Leonard Wood," dated 11 November 1918, from her book *Service and Sacrifice: Poems*, served as the introduction to a popular biography of General Wood by Joseph Hamblen Sears, *The Career Of Leonard Wood* (NY: Appleton, 1919), at the time Wood was a leading candidate for the Republican presidential nomination.  Wood, then a colonel, and Theodore Roosevelt, then a lieutenant colonel, had commanded the "Rough Riders," a regiment of volunteers that fought in the Spanish-American War, and they had been friends ever after.  Although Wood came to the convention in 1920 with the largest number of delegates, he eventually lost to Warren Harding, who went on to become President.  The period 1918-1919 was particularly sad for Corinne.  Her youngest brother, Quentin Roosevelt, a fighter pilot, was shot down and killed in Europe near the end of World War I; her husband, Douglas Robinson II, also died in 1918; and her brother, the former President, died in January 1919.  Her photograph appears on the fourth photo page following p. 94 of Edwin M. Yoder, Jr., *Joe Alsop's Cold War: A Study of Journalistic Influence and Intrigue* (Chapel Hill: University of North Carolina Press, 1995).

The second Corinne, Corinne (Robinson) "Ma" Alsop, was a strong-willed woman, a politician (one of the first women elected to the Connecticut senate), who "had the same instinct for seizing events by the throat that had made her eminent uncle a fabled maelstrom of energy and drive."  Corinne Alsop seconded Alf Landon's nomination on the Republican ticket, in opposition to her distant cousin, Franklin Roosevelt. (Yoder, 36-37) Her photograph appears on the second photo page following p. 94. Corinne Robinson married Joseph Wright Alsop IV and had four children, Joseph V "Joe," Stewart, John, and Corinne, who married Percy Chubb.

The third Corinne was "Teenie" (Chubb) Zimmermann's mother, Corinne (Alsop) Chubb, who appears in the *Social Register*, 1993. She, too, appears in Yoder's book about Joseph Alsop, her brother (p. 37). Their youngest brother, John, was said to have coined the term, "egghead," that became the signature description of the bald intellectuals who surrounded Adlai Stevenson when he was campaigning for the Presidency against Dwight Eisenhower in 1952 (p. 93).

The fourth Corinne, "Teeny" (Chubb) Zimmermann, was the first person thanked by Yoder, p. xi. Her husband, Warren, and her son Timothy [sic] were also thanked by Yoder, on pp. xi and xii. Joseph Wright Alsop V was her uncle, a brother of her mother.

[95] From Tim Zimmermann's website, his publications and resumé:
From https://timZimmermann.com/ (accessed 5-3-16):
*Outside*
September 2012, Talk To Me
July 2011, Blood In The Water
February 2011, The Long Way Back
July 2010, The Killer in the Pool
February 2008, Hell in High Water
July 2006, It's Hard Out Here for A Shrimp
June 2006, On Top of the World
August 2005, Raising the Dead (Finalist, National Magazine Award for Feature Writing)
June 2005, Break on Through
April 2005, Miles to Go Before I Sleep
July 2004, Rough Beast
July 2003, Record Collector
January 2002, Knives in the Water
----------

*Sports Illustrated*
November 29, 1999, Around the World in 70 Days?
------------

*US News & World Report*
November 1996, All Propaganda, All the Time
October 1995, If World War III Comes, Blame Fish
October 1995, The Russian Connection (Winner, Investigative Reporters & Editors "Thomas Renner Award" for best reporting on organized crime)
-----------

Books
*The Race: The First Nonstop, Round-the-World, No-Holds-Barred Sailing Competition* (Houghton Mifflin, 2002)
*The Best American Sports Writing 2006*, Contributor; Michael Lewis, editor (Houghton Mifflin, 2006)
*The Best American Science and Nature Writing 2011*, Contributor; Mary Roach, editor (Houghton Mifflin)
[96] Donations were requested in Lily's name for Leukaemia Research, 48 Great Ormond Street, London WC1N 3JJ, to be referenced "Lily Metcalfe W10 5UN."
[97] Miranda Carter, Review of Ann de Courcy, *The Viceroy's Daughters: The Lives of the Curzon Sisters* (New York: William Morrow, 2002), in *New York Times Book Review* (2 June 2002), 19. Carter says that Curzon had three children (the daughters who were the subject of this book). Irene did not marry, and Cimmie (who married Oswald Mosely) died at 34 after an operation for appendicitis. Baba married Edward Dudley Metcalfe and was the mistress of Oswald Mosely. Photographs in the book show Baba Curzon and Edward Dudley Metcalfe, and their son David, father of Charles Michael Metcalfe.
[98] DIRECTORY OF MEDICAL SPECIALISTS, 1987-88: "… intern (Pa Hosp) 62-63 Res Oph (Hosp of Penn) 63-66 Retinal Fell 66-67 now Ass Surg Retina Ser (both at Wills Eye Hosp) Att Surg (Chestnut Hill Hosp) (all Phila) (Montgomery Hosp Norristown Pa). Member American Medical Association, American Academy of Ophthalmology and Otolaryngology."

# PART III – Photo Album

## Descendants of John[1] and Eva Kathryn (Kellenbenz) Zimmermann

------------

### Chapter 4

### Clara[2] (Zimmermann) Hoxie (1886-1968)
### Her Family and Her Descendants

**Clara[2] Zimmermann married Albert N. Hoxie, Jr. (1884-1942) on 10 October 1911**

**Clara² (Zimmermann) and Al Hoxie in the 1920s**

**With their children**
**John³ (1917-1984), Albert III³ "Albo" (1914-2003), Lucille³ "Cil" (1919-2007)**

**Clara's Inscription on the Zimmermann Family Monument, Greenmount Cemetery, 4301 N Front St., Philadelphia**

**Albert N. Hoxie, Jr., Directing**

**The Messiah Choir, 1916**

**McPherson's Square, Philadelphia, 1 July 1917**

**Philadelphia Navy Yard, winter of 1917-1918**

**1926**

From philadelphiaencyclopedia.org
**At the Philadelphia Sesquicentennial**

**1929**
**The White House**

**The Philadelphia Harmonica Band**
**With President Herbert Hoover and Director Albert Hoxie**

From Median (http://de.playhohner.com/medien/?mode=select&media=7261#image_7261)

**1936**
**The Philadelphia Harmonica Band**

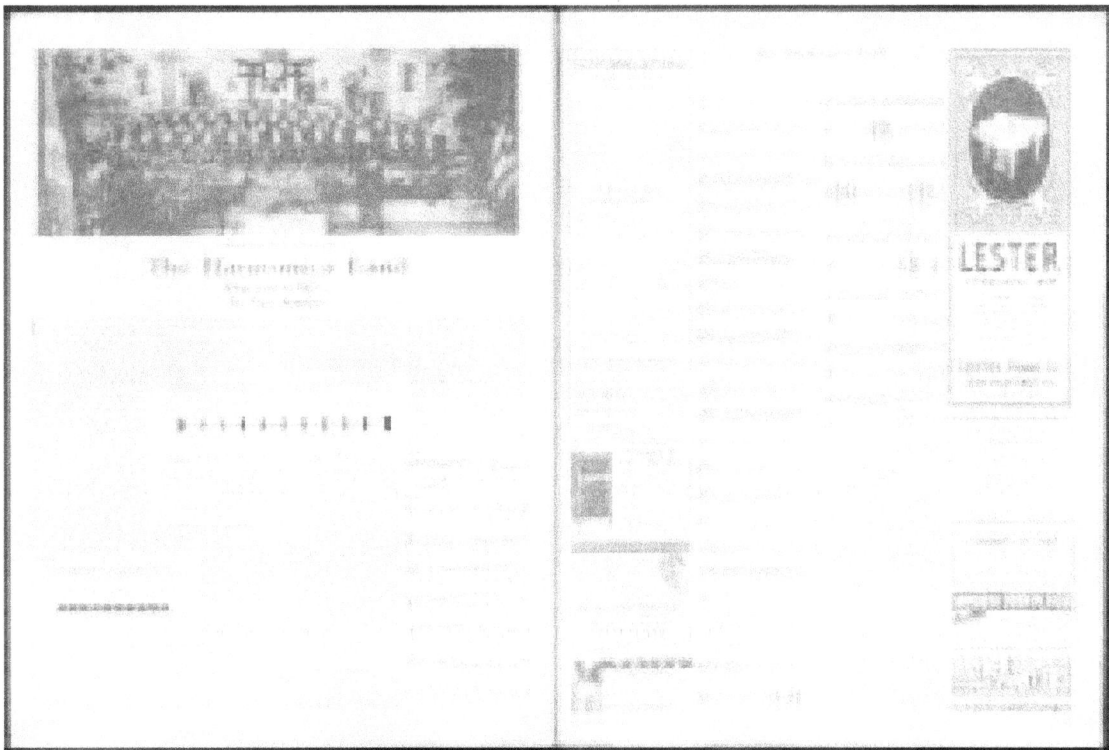

From Janela aberta – Blogue de harmonica riskas513.blogspot.com

229

# Clara[2] (Zimmermann) Hoxie's descendants

A Tribute to the Life of Albert N. Hoxie III
*August 31, 1914 – January 24, 2003*

Funeral card for Albert N. Hoxie, III

https://www.pennmedicine.org/providers/profile/james-hoxie

**His only son, James[4] Hoxie, M.D.**

**Her oldest child, the eldest of John[1] and Eva Katherine Zimmermann's
23 grandchildren, Albert Nickerson[3] "Albo" Hoxie, III**

# Chapter 5

# Anna[2] (Zimmermann) Kelley's Family and Descendants

Photo from Jean Hoxie Naples, labeled by her

**Anna[2] Zimmermann (1887-1974)**
**and her husband, Richard Carlyle Kelley (1882-1976)**
**with one of their 7 children**

231

# Sons-in-law of Anna[2] (Zimmermann) and Richard C. Kelley

## Their fourth child, Marian[3] Kelley (b. 1921), married William H. Poteat

From websites for William Poteat
**Professor William Poteat, B.D., Ph.D. (1919-2000)**

---------------------------

## Their fifth child, Anita[3] Kelley (b. 1921), married Oliver Pearson, Ph.D.

Photographs from Google images

**Professor Oliver Payne "Paynie" Pearson, Ph.D., Dr. (*hon. caus.*) (1915-2003)**

# Later Generations in the Line of
# Anna[2] (Zimmermann) and Richard C. Kelley

Website for Donald E. Kelley

https://ballotpedia.org/John_C._Uhler

**Donald Edmund[4] Kelley, Jr., Esq. (1948- ), son of Donald[3], their 6th child (L)**
**Hon. John C. Uhler, husband of Susan Colquitt[4] Poteat, daughter of Marian[3] (R)**

Photo on LinkedIn

**Kelley MacDonald[5] Carnwath,**
**daughter of Richard Kelley[4] Carnwath, and**
**granddaughter of their 3d child, Susan[3] (Kelley)**
**Carnwath**

Photo from Rockhouse Brothers website

**Joseph Caspari[5] Carnwath, son of Joseph**
**Wallace[4] Carnwath, Jr., Ph.D., and grandson**
**of their 3d child, Susan[3] (Kelley) Carnwath**

233

# Chapter 5

## Emilie K.[2] Zimmermann (1890-1897)

**The first member of the Zimmermann family to be buried at Greenmount,
Emilie died when she was six and a half years old.
The dates of her birth and death are shown here as 10 July 1890 – 14 January 1897**

**Greenmount Cemetery, the Zimmermann Family plot
Cemetery office is in the background, on the left at
4301 North Front St., Philadelphia**

# Chapter 7

# John[2] Zimmerman, Jr. (1892-1974)
# His Family and His Descendants

**John Zimmermann, Jr. (1892-1974) in New Hampshire
Called "Boppy" by his grandchildren**

**John Zimmermann, Jr., with his son, Carl, and two grandsons**
**After climbing Mount Chocura, up Weetamoo Trail and down Piper Trail**

Front row:  John[2] Zimmermann, Jr. "Boppy" beside Carl K.[4] Zimmermann, Jr. (b. 1950)
Back row: William "Bill" [2] Zimmermann (L) and Carl[3] Zimmermann
Photo by John Hower[4] Zimmermann (b. 1951), age 9 – c. 1960

Google Street View

www.musiciansofthenashvillesymphony.org

Home of John[2] Zimmermann, Jr., and his children, 2 Surrey Road, Melrose Park, Pa. (L)
On R:  James[5] Zimmermann (John Hower[4], Carl[3], John[2] Jr, John[1]) (b. 1982)
and his wife Candice Lee (1976-2015)

John[2] Jr., and wife Ethyl
Zimmermann Gravestone
Greenmount Cemetery, Philadelphia

# Chapter 8

# Descendants of William[2] Zimmerman and his wife, Margaret Lukens
## (1894-1978)

Amity website
**William[3] Zimmermann, Jr., and his wife Elizabeth (L), with the Amity quartet**

Photos from professional websites of Robert Zimmermann and Eric Fonkalsrud

**Robert[3] Zimmermann, Ph.D. (L)**
**Eric Fonkalsrud, M.D. (R), husband of Margaret "Peggy"[3] Zimmermann**

# Chapter 9

# Lillian[2] Zimmermann (1897-1966), Her Family and Her Descendants

**Lillian, about age 1.  Wedding to James A. Fligg (1900-1975), 27 December 1924**
**Attendants:  Albert[2] Zimmermann and Clara[2] (Zimmermann) Hoxie**
Flower girls: Edith Lucille[3] Hoxie (1919-2007), Bette[3] Zimmerman (1918-~2015), Mary
Jane[3] Zimmermann (1921-2008)

**Images for Lillian[2] (Zimmermann) Fligg's daughter, Kathryn[3] "Katchie" (Fligg) Lee:**
**Her husband, Bishop Edward Lee; her daughter, Kathryn[4] and husband Mark;**
**her grandchildren, Luke[5] and Nikko[5]; and a work of her abstract art**

# Patents of James A. Fligg and His Son, James A.[3] Fligg, Jr.

Feb. 13, 1951      J. A. FLIGG      2,541,231

WOVEN FABRIC

Filed Oct. 26, 1948

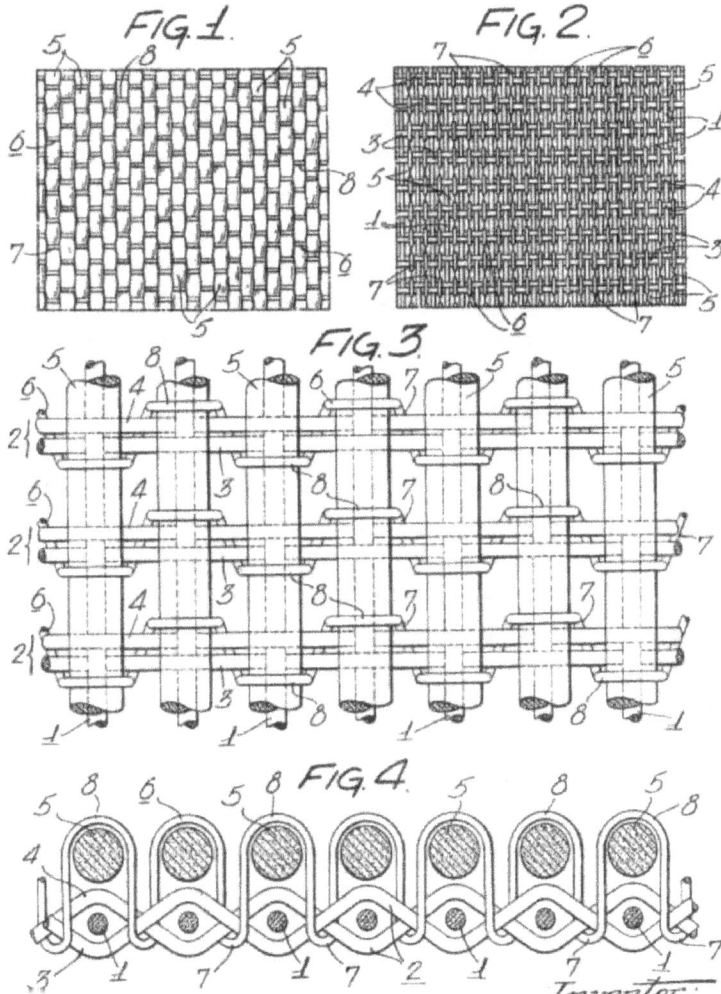

FIG. 1

FIG. 2

FIG. 3

FIG. 4

Inventor:
James A. Fligg
by his Attorneys
Howson & Howson

**James A. Fligg, application filed 26 October 1948**
**"Woven Fabric"**

Nov. 8, 1966  J. A. FLIGG, JR  3,283,995

SPLITTER VANE CONSTRUCTION FOR TURBOFAN ENGINE

Filed April 28, 1965  2 Sheets-Sheet 1

FIG. 1

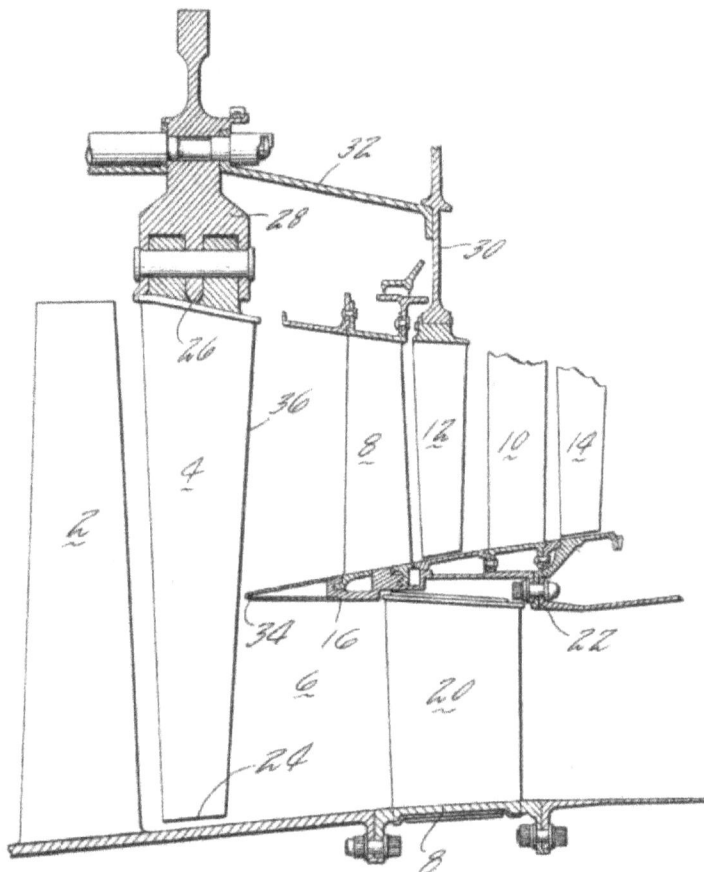

INVENTOR
JAMES A. FLIGG, JR.

BY  Charles A. Warren

ATTORNEY

**James A. Fligg, Jr.**
**Application filed 28 April 1965**
**"Splitter Vane Construction for Turbofan Engine"**

# Chapter 10

# Albert Walter[2] Zimmermann and His Descendants

**Albert Zimmermann as a boy**

**His birthplace at 610 W Lehigh Ave., Philadelphia, has been replaced**

**Barbara Shoemaker, who married Albert Zimmermann on 29 January 1926**

**Their home, "Cotwold Corners"**
**400 North Rose Lane, Haverford, Pa.**

**Their graves at Church of the Redeemer, Bryn Mawr, Pa.**

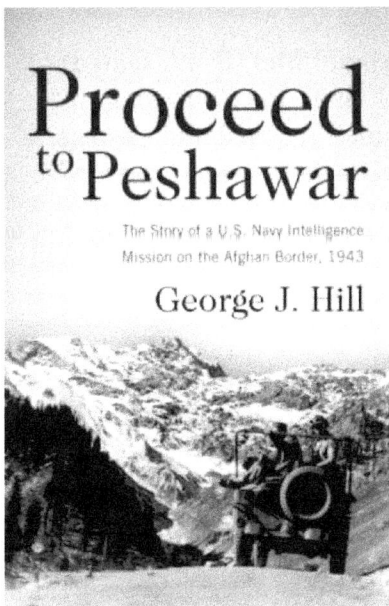

# Proceed to Peshawar

The Story of a U.S. Navy Intelligence Mission on the Afghan Border, 1943

### George J. Hill

The story of LT Albert Zimmermann, USNR, and his secret mission along the Afghan border in 1943 is told in this book.

Zimmermann is at the right rear seat of the jeep

Three intelligence officers are crossing the Lowari Pass, north of the Khyber Pass. It is the first time a motor vehicle has ever crossed this pass. The road is usually closed by this time, at the end of November.

# The Children and Some of the Grandchildren of
# Albert W.[2] Zimmermann and His Wife, Barbara née Shoemaker

**Formal Photograph in 1993**
**Wedding of Barbara Warren[4] Johnson and Thomas A. Riley, III**

Barbara[3] (Zimmermann) Johnson and her husband Mel (front, seated)
Albert W.[3] Zimmermann, Jr., and his wife Lenore (left, standing)
Helene[3] (Zimmermann) Hill (pink dress, rear) and her husband George
Warren[3] Zimmermann (bow tie, R rear) and his wife Corinne "Teenie"

This was the last time that the four children and their spouses of Albert and
Barbara (Shoemaker) Zimmermann were together

# More Photos of Albert[2] Zimmermann and His Family

## Wedding of Albert W. Zimmermann and Barbara Shoemaker

From Barbara Zimmermann, labeled by her, copy in Zimmermann Files

**Swedenborgian Church of the New Jerusalem, Philadelphia, 29 January 1926**

Top Row:  Robert Shoemaker – younger brother of the bride
       Schuyler Dillon – husband of bride's favorite cousin, Connie Warren
       William Steeble – family lawyer
       Sam Huhn – don't know anything about him
       William Zimmermann – older brother of the groom
       Ted Shoemaker – older brother of the bride
2d Row:  Mary Louise Shoemakder – wife of Ted and sister of Bix Beiderbecke
       Orus J. Matthews – friend from Penn (?)
       Dorothy S. Boericke – older sister of the bride, Matron of Honor
       Albert Zimmermann – groom
       Barbar Shoemaker – bride
       Walter Johnson – Best Man, artist and musician
       Betty Beard – lifelong friend
       Amelie Seixas, soon to be Kane – lifelong friend
       Stan Welsh –family broker
3d Row:  Connie Young – lifelong friend
       Mary Jane Zimmermann – niece of groom
       Sue Kelley – niece of groom
       Louise Parsons – soon to be Ott – lifelong friend
       Kay Welsh – wife of Stan

Photos in Zimmermann Files, from Babara (Zimmermann) Johnson, original source unknown

**Al and Barbara, photos c. 1924**

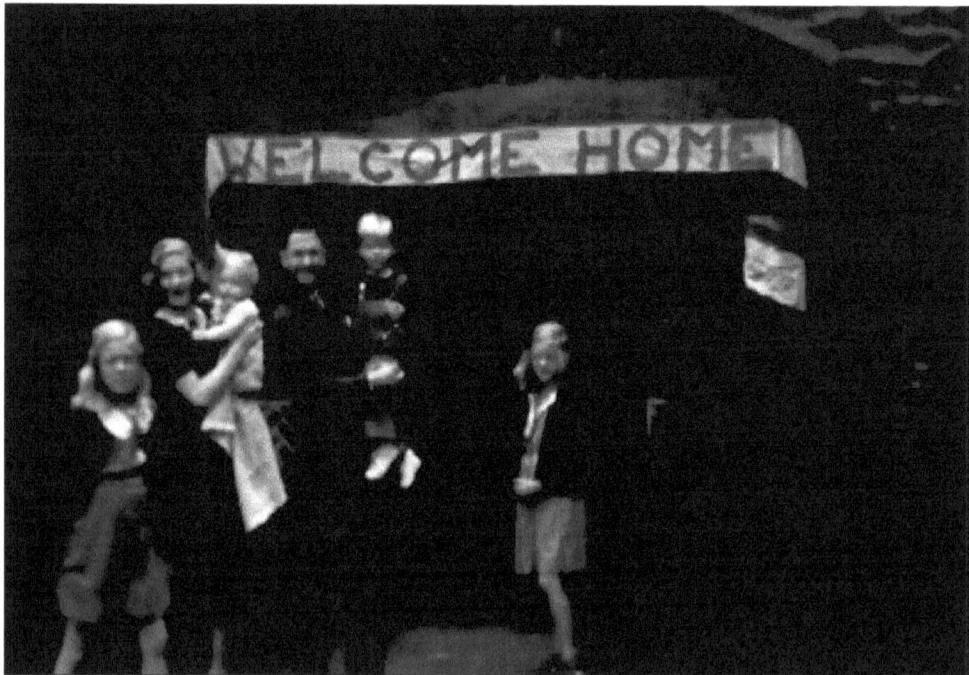

Photo still from 16mm movie, Albert Zimmermann Collection

**Albert and Barbara return from their trip to Europe,**
**"Welcome Home" from their children at Haverford, Pa., August 1937**
**At the front door of "Cotswold Corners", L to R**
**Barbara (1927-2011), Helene (b.1929), Albert Jr. (b.1937), Warren (1934-2004)**

# Bibliography

## Books and Chapters

Adams, James Truslow. *Epic of America*. Boston: Little, Brown and Co., 1931.

Bacon, Mary C. *Deer Park: A History*. Wendy J. Bacon: ePub, 1996.

Bacque, James. *Crimes and Mercies: The Fate of German Civilians Under Allied Occupation, 1944-1950*. Boston: Little, Brown, 1997.

Barrie, Donald. *Phoebe and the MacFairlie Mystery*. Illustrated by Kathryn Fligg. New York: Lothrop, Lee & Shepard Co., 1963.

Bell, Archie. *The Spell of the Holy Land*. Boston: The Page Company, 1915.

Bogen, F. W. *The German in America*. Boston: B. H. Greene, 1851.

Bruford, W. H. *Germany in the Eighteenth Century: The Social Background of the Literary Revival*. Cambridge: The University Press, 1971.

Collier, Peter, and David Horowith. *The Roosevelts: An American Saga*. New York: Simon & Schuster, 1994.

Davis, Betsey Warren. *The Warren, Jackson, and Allied Families*. Philadelphia, Pa.: J. B. Lippincott Co., 1903.

de Courcy, Ann. *The Viceroy's Daughters: The Lives of the Curzon Sisters*. New York: William Morrow, 2002.

Fisher, David Hackett. *Albion's Seed: Four British Folkways in America*. New York: Oxford University Press, 1989.

Galton, Francis. *Hereditary Genius: An Inquiry into its Laws and Consequences*. London: Macmillan and Co., 1869.

Gilbert, Martin, and Max Weinreich. *Hitler's Professors: The Part of Scholarship in Germany's Crimes Against the Jewish People*. New Haven: Yale University Press, 1999.

*Harvard Alumni Directory*. Boston: Harvard University Press, 1990.

High, Grace Mildred Ridings. *The Manly Family: A Record of the Descendants of William Manly and Rachel Jackson Manly, His Wife, of Cecil County, Maryland*. Claflin, Kansas: Claflin Clarion, 1962.

Hill, David H. "The Statue and the Strands." In *Passages: An Anthology of Contemporary Literature*. Edited by Deborah Case and Sharon Derderian. Troy, Mich.: Iliad Press/Cader Publishing Co., 1992.

_____. "The Hunchback Inside of Me." In *Endless Skies of Blue: The National Library of Poetry 1997*. Edited by Diana Ziegler. Owings Mills, Md.: Watermark Press, 1997.

_____. "Untitled." In *Best Poems of 1998: The National Library of Poetry*. Edited by Howard Ely. Owings Mills, Md.: Watermark Press, 1998.

_____. *A Lesson in Reality: Poems and Essays, 1991-2000*. Edited by George J. Hill. West Orange, N.J.: Hilltree Farm Press, 2007.

Hill, George J. *Proceed to Peshawar: The Story of a U.S. Navy Intelligence Mission on the Afghan Border, 1943*. Annapolis, Md.: Naval Institute Press, 2013.

_____. *Hill: The Ferry Keeper's Family; Luke Hill and Mary Hout, Who Were Married in Windsor, Connecticut, in 1651, and Fourteen Generations of Their Known and Possible Descendants*. Westminster, Md.: Heritage Books, 2011.

_____. *Western Pilgrims: The Hill, Stockwell and Allied Families; Ancestors and Descendants of George J. Hill and Jessie Fidelia Stockwell, Who Were Married in Wright County, Iowa, in 1882*. Berwyn Heights, Md.: Heritage Books, 2014.

_____. *Quakers and Pilgrims: The Shoemaker, Warren and Allied Families; Ancestors and Descendants of William Toy Shoemaker and Mabel Warren, Who Were Married in Philadelphia in 1895*. Berwyn Heights, Md.: Heritage Books, 2015.

_____. *Fundy to Chesapeake: The Thompson, Rundall and Allied Families; Ancestors and Descendants of William Henry Thompson and Sarah D. Rundall, Who Were Married in Linn County, Iowa, in 1889*. Berwyn Heights, Md.: Heritage Books, 2016.

_____. *American Dreams*. 4 bks., 7 vols. Berwyn Heights, Md.: Heritage Books, 2014-16.

Holborn, Hajo. *A History of Modern Germany*. Vol. 1, *The Reformation*. Princeton: Princeton University Press, 1959. Vol. 2, *A History of Modern Germany, 1648-1840*. Vol. 3. *A History of Modern Germany, 1840-1945*. Princeton: Princeton University Press, [1964] 1982.

*The Holy Bible. Authorized King James Version*. New York: Oxford University Press, n.d. [1942].

Jones, George F. *German-American Names*. Baltimore: Genealogical Publishing Co., 1990.

Keeling, Ralph Franklin. *Gruesome Harvest: The Costly Attempt to Exterminate the People of Germany*, Chicago: Institute of American Economics, 1947

Kellenbenz, Hermann. *The Rise of the European Economy: An Economic History of Continental Europe from the Fifteenth to the Eighteenth Century*. Revised and edited by Gerhard Benecke. In *World Economic History*. Edited by Charles Wilson. London: Weidenfeld and Nicolson, 1976.

_____. *Deutsche Wirtschaftsgeschichte*. Band I. *Von den Anfängen bis zum Ende des 18. Jahrhunderts*. München: Verlag C. H. Beck, 1977.

[Kelley-Zimmermann] *The Iowa Alumnus*. Iowa City, Ia.: University of Iowa, 1915. Vol.13.

Kinnamon, Lester B. *The Kinnamon Family in America: Its European Origin, Early Colonial History and Lines of Descent in America*. L. B. Kinnamon, Easton, Md., 1982.

Lehmann, Chris *The Money Cult: Capitalism, Christianity, and the Unmaking of the American Dream*. New York: Melville House, 2016.

*Harvard Alumni Directory*. Boston: Harvard University Press, 1990.

Herman Melville, *The Confidence-Man: His Masquerade*. [1857] New York: Oxford University Press, 1999.

MacDonogh, Giles. *After the Reich: The Brutal History of the Allied Occupation.* New York: Basic Books, 2007.

MacFarlane, John J. *Manufacturing in Philadelphia, 1683-1912.* Philadelphia: Philadelphia Commercial Museum, 1912.

Miller, Nathan. *Theodore Roosevelt: A Life.* New York: Quill/Morrow, 1992.

*The Book of Mormon: Another Testament of Jesus Christ.* [Palmyra, N.Y, 1830] Salt Lake City, Utah: The Church of Jesus Christ of Latter-day Saints, 2013.

Ozment, Stephen. *A Mighty Fortress: A New History of the German People.* New York: HarperCollins, 2004.

Robinson, Corinne Roosevelt. *Service and Sacrifice: Poems.* New York: Charles Scribner's Sons, 1919.

Rosenbaum, Eli M. *Betrayal: The Untold Story of the Kurt Waldheim Investigation and Cover-up.* New York: St. Martin's Press, 1993.

Sears, Joseph Hamblen. *The Career of Leonard Wood.* New York: Appleton, 1919.

Shoemaker, Benjamin R. *Genealogy of the Shoemaker Family of Cheltenham, Pennsylvania.* Philadelphia, Pa.: J. B. Lippincott Co., 1903.

Shorto, Russell. *The Island at the Center of the World: The Epic Story of Dutch Manhattan and the Forgotten Colony That Shaped America.* New York: Vintage Books/Random House, [2004] 2005.

*Social Register.* New York: Social Register Association, 2012. http://www.socialregisteronline.com/#!barbara-Zimmermann-johnson/cv45

*University of Pennsylvania Bulletin.* Philadelphia: University of Pennsylvania, 1916.

Weber, Max. *The Protestant Ethic and the Spirit of Capitalism.* [1905] Boston: Unwin Hyman, 1930.

*Women's Undergraduate Record, University of Pennsylvania.* 1920.

Yoder, Edwin M., Jr. *Joe Alsop's Cold War: A Study of Journalistic Influence and Intrigue.* Chapel Hill: University of North Carolina Press, 1995.

Zimmermann, Barbara Shoemaker. *Mutterings.* Wynnewood, Pa.: Livingston Publishing Co., 1969.

Zimmermann, Tim. *The Race: The First Nonstop, Round-the-World, No-Holds-Barred Sailing Competition.* New York: Houghton Mifflin, 2002.

_____. Contributor to *The Best American Sports Writing 2006.* Edited by Michael Lewis. New York: Houghton Mifflin, 2006.

_____. Contributor to *The Best American Science and Nature Writing 2011.* Edited by Mary Roach. New York: Houghton Mifflin, 2012.

Zimmermann, Warren. *Origins of a Catastrophe: Yugoslavia and Its Destroyers; America's Last Ambassador Tells What Happened and Why.* New York: Hill & Wang/Farrar, Straus and Giroux/Macmillan, 1996.

_____. *First Great Triumph: How Five Americans Made Their Country a World Power.* New York: Farrar, Straus and Giroux/Macmillan, 2002.

**Periodicals**

Anon. *Etwas von der Sippe Kellenbenz.* Source unknown, probably from a newspaper in Stuttgart, Baden-Württemberg, Germany, c. 1967.

[Carnwath] Baji Gal, Arpad, Joseph Wallace Carnwath, Andras Dinnyes, Doris Herrmann, Heiner Niemann and Christine Wrenzycki, "Comparison of real-time polymerase chain reaction and end-point polymerase chain reaction for the analysis of gene expression in preimplantation embryos," *Reproduction, Fertility and Development* 18 (no.3, 2006): 365-71.

[Carnwath] Niemann, H. ,C. Wrenzycki, A. Lucas-Hahn, T. Brambrink, W.A. Kues, and J.W. Carnwath "Gene Expression Patterns in Bovine In vitro-Produced and Nuclear Transfer-Derived Embryos and Their Implications for Early Development," *Cloning and Stem Cells* 4 (no.1, July 2004): 29-38.

DeVoto, Bernard. "The Centennial of Mormonism." *The American Mercury*, no. 73 (January 1930), 1-13.

Robin Finn, "A Feisty Philanthropist at 100, With a Five-Year Plan," *New York Times* (c. 2007). [Re: Kathryn Edith Wasserman, wife of Shelby Cullom Davis]

Hill, G.J., and S. Hill, "Lead Poisoning due to Hai Ge Fen." Letter to the Editor, *Journal of the American Medical Association* (1994).

Hill, HZ. "The function of melanin or six blind people examine an elephant." *BioEssays* 14:49-56, 1992.

[Hoxie] *The Billboard* (5 Sep 1942).

[Hoxie] *The Music Trade Review* (9 May 1925).

*Inquirer – The Philadelphia Inquirer Magazine* (30 Jan 1994).

[Kelley, Richard Carlyle, Jr.] *Times Chronicle-Glenside News* [Glenside, Pa.] (20 Sep 2000).

Livingston, James. "The Gospel of Wealth," *New York Times Book Review* (19 June 2016), 19. Review of Chris Lehman,*The Money Cult: Capitalism, Christianity, and the Unmaking of the American Dream.*

*Ludwington Daily News* (27 Sep 1990).

Mesloh, Karl R. "German Surnames – Their Meaning & Origin," *The Towpath* (Jan 1993-Jan 1994) at: http://newbremenhistory.org/GENEALOGY/German_Names.htm

[Minneapolis] *Minnesota Daily* (24 June 2015).

*National Druggist* 25 (no. 2, Feb. 1895).

Newark [N.J.] *Star-Ledger* (3 May 1999).

*New York* [magazine] (6 Mar 1995).

*The New York Review* (2 Feb 1995).

*New York Times* "Week in Review" (10 Jan 1994).

Rich, Motoko, Amanda Cox, and Matthew Bloch. "Money, Race and Success: How Your School District Compares" *New York Times* (29 April 2016).

*Saints Herald.* LDS Church.

*Smith Alumnae Quarterly* (Spring 2013).

*Spokane Daily Chronicle* (February 1936). http://news.google.com/newspapers?nid=1338&dat=19360213&id=z9pYAAAAIBAJ&sjid=BfUDAAAAI BAJ&pg=4635,3456150

*Washington Post* (5 February 2004).

Zimmermann, Warren: "The Last Ambassador." *Foreign Affairs* (1995).

_____. *People* [magazine] (6/19/95).

**Standard References**

*American Men and Women in Science.*

*Directory of Medical Specialists.*

*Encyclopaedia Brittanica.* 15th ed. Chicago: Encyclopaedia Brittanica, 1989.

Babylon. Software for translations.

Pennsylvania, State. Vital Records.

U.S. Census records.

*Who's Who in America.*

*Who's Who Directory of Professionals and Resources in Cancer.*

*Who's Who in the East.*

*Who's Who in Science and Engineering.*

**Miscellaneous – Videos, Movie, and Theses**

Bowman, Michael. "History of the R.L.D.S. Church in Philadelphia." Thesis, Rutgers University, n.d., c. 1999.

_____. "The Life of Albert N. Hoxie, Jr." (3 Mar 2010), Uploaded by OliviaTheCat; 8:06. (www.youtube.com/watch?v=XS_GcgNwmTo). "
_____. "The Life of Albert N. Hoxie, Jr." (24 Jan 2012), Uploaded by Harmonicando; 8:06 (www.youtube.com/watch?v=dnLovSDMv1Y).
_____. "Albert Hoxie and his Philadelphia Harmonica Band" on YouTube (www.youtube.com/watch?v=SDkmXR_dNrI), Uploaded by Harmonicando; 3:10.

Robbins, Charles. "The Origin of the Book of Mormon." Thesis submitted to History Department, Yale University, 1942/3; MS typed, 94pp. Robbins was at Yale College, Class of 1944. A copy of this thesis was kindly provided to me by his associate, Samson Wang, Class of 1967, of Morristown, N.J.

Zimmerman, Albert W., Sr. Home movies, 16mm, taken in Europe in 1937. With the Albert and Barbara

(Shoemaker) Zimmermann Files, to place into a Special Collection.

Zimmermann, Tim. Co-producer, *Blackfish*. IMDb movie, 2013.

## Personal Communications

Bowman, Michael. Letters to GJH, 13 July 2009, *et seq*.

Currie, Rev. Susannah. Swedenborgian Church, Temenos Retreat Center, 1564 Telegraph Rd., West Chester, PA 19382.

Lee, Kathryn "Katchie" Fligg, abbreviated KFL in text.

Mitchell, Anne. "Prof. Dr. Kellenbenz." Obituary, translated by Richard Clark, from an unknown source.

Naples, Jean Hoxie (JHN), letter to GJH, 23 September 2009, *et seq*., and a narrative, "John Zimmermann" which provided the timeline for his life and much information about his children.

## Internet Sources

Biblioteca Nacional de Portugal, in
http://www.bnportugal.pt/index.php?option=com_content&view=article&id=899%3Amostra-conferencia-hermann-kellenbenz-1913-1990-ao-servico-da-historia-4-fev-18h00&catid=164%3A2014&Itemid=925&lang=en

Bonnell, Kathy Brant. "Zimmermann Genealogy." Rootsweb.

[Carnwath, Susan Kelley]
www.legacy.com/obituaries/philly/obituary.aspx?page=lifestory&pid=550918#sthash.g2LAOOTq.dpuf

Caspari brothers. www.rockhousebrothers.de.

Fligg, James A. [Sr.] Patent US2541231 - https://www.google.com/patents/US2541231
J. A. FLIGG WOVEN FABRIC Feb. 13, 1951 Filed Oct. 26, 1948 Patented Feb. 13, 1951.

Fligg, James A., Jr. "Tests of a Low Speed Three-stage Axial Flow Compressor at Aspect Ratios of One, Two, and Four." Abstract and paper for 2nd Propulsion Joint Specialist Conference, 1966, Colorado Springs, CO. From http://dx.doi.org/10.2514/6.1966-613 (accessed 4-25-16).
_____. http://cheltenhamalumni.org/thank-you.htm [James A. Fligg].
_____.Patent US3283995 - Splitter vane construction for turbofan ...
https://www.google.com/patents/US3283995 / United States Patent Ofiice 3,233,995 SPLITTER VANE CONSTRUCTION FOR TURBOFAN ENGINE [James A. Fligg, Jr.]
_____. http://ntrs.nasa.gov/archive/nasa/casi.ntrs.nasa.gov/19720023124.pdf. [James A. Fligg, Jr.]

Fligg, Kathryn. (all accessed 4-22-16):
http://www.kathrynflee.com/resume.html; bpedwardlee@yahoo.com; http://www.kathrynflee.com/;
http://www.saintasaphs.org/Arts%20&%20Music.html http://kathrynfligglee.blogspot.com/;
http://kathrynfligglee.blogspot.com/2011/11/kathryn-fligg-lee-is-noted-collage.html
http://streamlinermemories.info/?p=1758

Fonkalsrud, Eric. https://www.aap.org/en-us/about-the-aap/Pediatric-History-Center/Documents/Fonkalsrud.pdf.
_____. http://people.healthsciences.ucla.edu/institution/personnel?personnel_id=7817 (accessed 4/19/16):

_____. http://depts.washington.edu/givemed/scholarships/margaret-and-eric-fonkalsrud/Margaret Z. and Eric W. Fonkalsrud, M.D. Endowed Scholarship / EST. 2009:

[Fowler, Joan Kelley]
http://www.legacy.com/obituaries/dailylocal/obituary.aspx?pid=153835766#sthash.yxp3HKq4.dpuf

[Fowler, Robert Scott] www.familytreenow.com/records/people/fowler/ellen/rbj7xphfyl5hw6tdfmdm2q (accessed 1 Apr 2016).

Grafeneck, Germany.
https://www.google.com/search?newwindow=1&espv=2&rlz=1C1ARAB_enUS454US552&q=grafeneck+killing+center&oq=Grafeneck+c&gs_l=serp.1.2.0j0i22i30l9.19392.21227.0.26111.5.5.0.0.0.0.128.483.3j2.5.0....0...1c.1.64.serp..0.5.481.P4L6WAvUs9M (accessed 2/1/16).

Grass, Gunter:  http://www.nytimes.com/2015/04/14/world/europe/gunter-grass-german-novelist-dies-at-87.html?_r=0

Gussenstadt, Baden-Württemberg.  http://www.hirsch-gussenstadt.de/index_en.html (accessed 1/27/16).

Jews, Baden-Württemberg.  http://www.jta.org/1960/05/18/archive/8500-jews-of-baden-wurttemberg-annihilated-by-nazis-survey-shows (accessed 2/1/16).

Jewish / Holocaust. https://www.jewishvirtuallibrary.org/jsource/Holocaust/cclist.html (accessed 2/11/16).

Johnson, Barbara. http://www.socialregisteronline.com/#!barbara-Zimmermann-johnson/cv45

Kellenbenz. www.ancestry.com/name-origin?surname=kellenbenz

Kellenbenz, Hermann. Wikipedia in German, principally *"Wissenschaftlicher Mitarbeiter in der Forschungsabteilung Judenfrage."* Wikipedia quotes "Creative Commons Attribution/Share Alike"

Kellenbenz, Hermann [obituary] Biblioteca Nacional de Portugal, in http://www.bnportugal.pt/index.php?option=com_content&view=article&id=899%3Amostra-conferencia-hermann-kellenbenz-1913-1990-ao-servico-da-historia-4-fev-18h00&catid=164%3A2014&Itemid=925&lang=en

Lee, Edward. http://www.livingchurch.org/sidelined-cathedral; http://myemail.constantcontact.com/Friday-Rcport-from St--Thomas--Church--Whitemarsh.html?soid=1102727622835&aid=h6MAzqlcekc (accessed 4-22-16).

Lee, Kathryn (Fligg).  See Fligg, Kathryn. [KFL]

Mesloh, Karl R. New Bremen, Ohio, "German Surnames – Their Meaning & Origin," *The Towpath* (January 1993 - January 1994) at: http://newbremenhistory.org/GENEALOGY/German_Names.htm (accessed 1/15/16).

Mormon. Articles of Faith. https://www.mormon.org/beliefs/articles-of-faith) (accessed 6/21/16).

Nazi Death Camps. http://www.tracesofevil.com/ [anonymous] and go to:
 http://www.tracesofevil.com/2007/04/various-sites-in-germany-contd.html (accessed 2/1/16).

Palestine Fever.
https://www.reddit.com/r/AskReddit/comments/dqx1a/palestine_fever_has_this_unknown_disease_since/

Poteat, William. www.whpoteat.org.

_____. YouTube, "Who Was William H. Poteat" (23 Nov 2014).

[Rockhouse Brothers] www.rockhousebrothers.de

Swedenborgian Church. www.swedenborg.org.

USAID. http://voices.washingtonpost.com/spy-talk/2010/04/cia_chief_promises_spies_new_a.html / Posted at 4:47 PM ET, 04/26/2010.
www.intrepidreport.com/archives/12659#sthash.KWv8EUcX.dpuf / *Intrepid Repor*t. (accessed 4/28/16)

Waldheim, Kurt: http://www.nytimes.com/1993/10/10/books/waldheim-and-his-protectors.html?pagewanted=all

Walter, Anna. http://awtc.ancestry.com/cgi-bin/igm.cgi?op=GET&db=*v05t1769&id=I316 (accessed 1/24/16).

Wikipedia, "Creative Commons Attribution/Share Alike"

Zimmermann, Barbara. See: Johnson, Barbara.

Zimmermann, John - Patents
www.google.com/patents/US813131 - Patent US813131 - Woven pile fabric. - Google Patents
Inventors, John Zimmermann. Original Assignee, Philadelphia Tapestry Mills.
www.google.com/patents/US813132 - Patent US813132 - Pile-gage. - Google Patents
Inventors, John Zimmermann. Original Assignee, Philadelphia Tapestry Mills.
www.google.com/patents/US855153 -  Patent US855153 - Pile fabric. - Google Patents
Inventors, John Zimmermann. Original Assignee, Philadelphia Tapestry Mills.

Zimmerman, John, and Ethyl – house at 2 Surrey Road Melrose Park. PA
https://www.google.com/maps/place/2+Surrey+Rd,+Melrose+Park,+PA+19027/@40.0644558,-75.125383,3a,75y,157h,90t/data=!3m7!1e1!3m5!1s0wVSVqDPsXF4cXGeH1eJEw!2e0!6s%2F%2Fgeo0.ggpht.com%2Fcbk%3Fpanoid%3D0wVSVqDPsXF4cXGeH1eJEw%26output%3Dthumbnail%26cb_client%3Dsearch.TACTILE.gps%26thumb%3D2%26w%3D392%26h%3D106%26yaw%3D157.15685%26pitch%3D0!7i13312!8i6656!4m2!3m1!1s0x89c6b73a025e4b8f:0x98f21c2b14acc3f8!6m1!1e1.

Zimmermann, Robert. http://www.biochem.umass.edu/emeritus-faculty/robert-Zimmermann
Zimmermann@biochem.umass.edu
https://www.bio.umass.edu/mcb/faculty/Zimmermann.html
http://www.ratemyprofessors.com/ShowRatings.jsp?tid=82516
https://www.researchgate.net/profile/Robert_Zimmermann2

Zimmermann, William, Jr.  https://www.physics.umn.edu/people/Zimmermann.html:
SHEPLAB 149 (office), 624-4387 / PAN 376 (lab), 624-0262 / zimme004 @ umn.edu _
_____. http://www.physics.umn.edu/research/cm/ _ curriculum vitae :
_____. Baroque Music. _____. http://www.amity-baroquemusic.com/ (accessed 5/3/16).
_____. http://archive.iupap.org/commissions/c5/reports/qfs-00.html
_____. Renzetti, Jackie. [Minneapolis] *Minnesota Daily* (June 24, 2015):
http://www.mndaily.com/news/campus/2015/06/24/tate-lab-undergo-two-year-renovation

# Index
## Parts I and II
## Kellenbenz and Zimmermann Families in Germany

**?**

| | |
|---|---|
| ? | Zimmermannn spouse of 1 |
| ? | Zimmermannn spouse of 22 |
| Apollonia | Zimmermannn spouse of 3 |
| Betty | Kellenbenz spouse of 26 |
| Maria | Zimmermannn spouse of 27 |

**AMGINTER**

| | |
|---|---|
| Jamessa [11111212] | Zimmermannn child of 21 |
| Johannes Georg [11111211] | Zimmermannn child of 21 |
| Johnann G. | Zimmermannn spouse of 21 |

**ANDERSON DANCER**

| | |
|---|---|
| Anna, Mrs. | Zimmermannn spouse of 28 |

**BANTZHAFF**

| | |
|---|---|
| Margareta | Zimmermannn spouse of 25 |

**BARTH**

| | |
|---|---|
| Maria | Zimmermannn spouse of 5 |

**BOLLACHER**

| | |
|---|---|
| Christian (1.3.3.1.3) | Kellenbenz child of 27 |
| Dietrich (Dieter) (1.3.3.2) | Kellenbenz 28 |
| Felix (1.3.3.2.2) | Kellenbenz child of 28 |
| Florian (1.3.3.2.1) | Kellenbenz child of 28 |
| Isle (?) | Kellenbenz spouse of 27 |
| Isolda (?) | Kellenbenz spouse of 28 |
| Maria (1.3.3.3.2) | Kellenbenz child of 29 |
| Martin (1.3.3.3) | Kellenbenz 29 |
| Olivier (1.3.3.3.1) | Kellenbenz child of 29 |
| Philip (1.3.3.2.3) | Kellenbenz child of 28 |
| Sebastian (1.3.3.1.2) | Kellenbenz child of 27 |
| Siegfried | Kellenbenz spouse of 22 |
| Sophie | Kellenbenz child of 29 |
| Tilman (1.3.3.1.1) | Kellenbenz child of 27 |
| Wolfgang (1.3.1) | Kellenbenz 27 |
| Yvonne (?) | Kellenbenz spouse of 29 |

**BOLLINGER**

| | |
|---|---|
| Catharina | Zimmermannn spouse of 2 |

**BÜHNER**

| | |
|---|---|
| Apollonia | Zimmermannn spouse of 11 |

**CLEMENT or KLEMENT**

| | |
|---|---|
| Anna Maria | Kellenbenz spouse of 10 |

**CORR**

| | |
|---|---|
| Mary Jane | Kellenbenz spouse of 19 |

**FRASCH**

| | |
|---|---|
| Anna Maria | Zimmermannn spouse of 20 |
| Maria Catharina | Zimmermannn spouse of 19 |

**FRECH**

| | |
|---|---|
| Katharine | Kellenbenz spouse of 14 |

**GIEGNER**

| | |
|---|---|
| Anna Regina | Zimmermannn child of 9 |
| Johann Michael | Zimmermannn spouse of 9 |

**GOTT**

| | |
|---|---|
| Maria Katherine | Zimmermannn spouse of 18 |

**GRöZINGER or GRETZINGER**

| | |
|---|---|
| Clara | Kellenbenz spouse of 12 |

**HAYES COATES**

| | |
|---|---|
| Janette Barbara | Kellenbenz child of 24 |
| John Henry | Kellenbenz spouse of 24 |
| Margaret Mary | Kellenbenz child of 24 |

**HOLDER**

| | |
|---|---|
| Anna Catharina | Zimmermannn spouse of 19 |

**HUMMEL**

| | |
|---|---|
| ? | Zimmermannn child of 23 |
| Albert Friedrich Christian | Zimmermannn child of 26 |
| Anna Maria | Zimmermannn 26 |
| Anna Maria | Zimmermannn child of 23 |
| Anna Maria | Zimmermannn child of 23 |
| Catharina | Zimmermannn child of 23 |
| Christian Friedrich | Zimmermannn child of 23 |
| Johann Michael | Zimmermannn spouse of 23 |
| Karl Friedrich Otto | Zimmermannn child of 26 |
| Karl Friedrich | Zimmermannn child of 23 |
| Karl Friedrich | Zimmermannn child of 23 |
| Karl | Zimmermannn child of 23 |

**JÄGER**

| | |
|---|---|
| Anna Ursula | Zimmermannn spouse of 24 |

**KELLENBENZ**

| | |
|---|---|
| _____ (son) | Kellenbenz child of 12 |
| 11 more children | Kellenbenz 13 |
| Albert | Kellenbenz child of 14 |
| Andrew | Kellenbenz child of 14 |
| Anna Maria | Kellenbenz child of 12 |
| Anna Maria | Kellenbenz child of 12 |
| Anna Maria | Kellenbenz child of 15 |
| Anna Maria | Kellenbenz child of 15 |
| Anna | Kellenbenz 24 |
| Anne | Kellenbenz 20 |
| August | Kellenbenz child of 12 |
| Catherine | Kellenbenz child of 19 |
| Charles Joseph | Kellenbenz child of 19 |
| Charles | Kellenbenz child of 14 |
| Christina | Kellenbenz child of 12 |
| Christina | Kellenbenz child of 12 |
| Clara Katharina Rosina (1.1) | Kellenbenz 17 |
| David | Kellenbenz child of 14 |
| Elizabeth Margarete | Kellenbenz child of 15 |
| Ellen F. | Kellenbenz child of 19 |
| Eugenia (1.3.2) | Kellenbenz 22 |
| Eva Katharina | Kellenbenz child of 12 |
| **Eva Kathryn (1.2)** | **Kellenbenz 16** |
| Eva Kathryn (1.2) | Zimmermannn spouse of 28 |
| Fanny (1.3.1) | Kellenbenz 23 |
| Fred | Kellenbenz child of 14 |
| George | Kellenbenz 2 |
| George | Kellenbenz child of 13 |

| | |
|---|---|
| George | Kellenbenz child of 14 |
| Dr. Gottlieb I surgeon, obstetrician | Kellenbenz 6 |
| Dr. Gottlieb II | Kellenbenz 7 |
| Dr. Gottlieb III | Kellenbenz 9 |
| Gottlieb IV | Kellenbenz 11 |
| Gottlieb | Kellenbenz 14 |
| Gottlieb | Kellenbenz child of 12 |
| Gottlieb | Kellenbenz child of 15 |
| Gottlieb David | Kellenbenz child of 14 |
| Gustav | Kellenbenz child of 14 |
| Harry | Kellenbenz child of 19 |
| Henry | Kellenbenz 19 |
| Joh. Jakob II | Kellenbenz child of 7 |
| Johann Christian | Kellenbenz child of 15 |
| Johann Georg (known as Georg) | Kellenbenz 10 |
| Johann George | Kellenbenz child of 2 |
| Johann Gottlieb [Gottlob] | Kellenbenz child of 15 |
| Johann Gottlieb | Kellenbenz child of 12 |
| Johann Jacob [Jakob] | Kellenbenz 8 |
| Johann Jakob, Schultheiss | Kellenbenz 5 |
| Dr. Johann Leonhard | Kellenbenz child of 7 |
| Dr. Johann Michael | Kellenbenz child of 7 |
| Johann Michael | Kellenbenz 12 |
| Johannes "the Eislinger" | Kellenbenz 1 |
| Johannes | child of 3 |
| Johannes | Kellenbenz 3 |
| John J. | Kellenbenz child of 19 |
| John | Kellenbenz child of 14 |
| Joseph | Kellenbenz 15 |
| Karl | Kellenbenz child of 12 |
| Karl Wilhelm (1.3) | Kellenbenz 18 |
| Katherina Barbara | Kellenbenz child of 15 |
| Katie | Kellenbenz child of 14 |
| Leonard | Kellenbenz child of 19 |
| Louis | Kellenbenz child of 15 |
| Maria Friederike | Kellenbenz child of 12 |
| Maria Margareta | Kellenbenz child of 2 |
| Rosina Friederike | Kellenbenz child of 12 |
| Rudolf | Kellenbenz child of 12 |
| Sebastian | Kellenbenz 4 |
| William | Kellenbenz child of 14 |
| **KLEMENT** | |
| Elisabeth Margarete | Kellenbenz spouse of 15 |
| **KöPF** | |
| Anna Ursula | Zimmermannn spouse of 10 |
| **KRÄMER** | |
| Hans Joachim (1.3.1.1) | Kellenbenz child of 23 |
| William | Kellenbenz spouse of 23 |
| **KRÖNER** | |
| Joseph | Zimmermannn spouse of 9 |
| **L.** | |
| Anna | Kellenbenz spouse of 21 |
| **LAUSER** | |
| Fanny | Kellenbenz spouse of 18 |

**MERZ**
   ?                             Zimmermannn child of 20
   Anna Catharina          Zimmermannn child of 20
   Anna Mararethe        Zimmermannn child of 20
   Anna Maria              Zimmermannn 23
   Dorothea               Zimmermannn child of 19
   Elisabetha             Zimmermannn child of 13
   Georg Adam           Zimmermannn child of 20
   Gottfried              Zimmermannn child of 19
   Jakob Johann         Zimmermannn child of 19
   Jakob                  Zimmermannn child of 13
   Johann Friedrich      Zimmermannn 20
   Johann Friedrich      Zimmermannn child of 19
   Johann Friedrich      Zimmermannn child of 20
   Johann Georg         Zimmermannn child of 13
   Johann Heinrich      Zimmermannn child of 20
   Johann Jakob         Zimmermannn 19
   Johann Jakob         Zimmermannn child of 20
   Johann Jakob         Zimmermannn spouse of 13
   Margarethe           Zimmermannn child of 13
   Sophia Margarethe    Zimmermannn child of 20
   Wilhelm               Zimmermannn child of 19
**MITCHELL**
   ————                  Kellenbenz spouse of 20
   ————                  Kellenbenz 25
   Anne                   Kellenbenz child of 25
**REHM**
   Barbara               Zimmermannn spouse of 11
**SATTLER**
   Margareta (Margarethe)   Zimmermannn spouse of 7
**SCHRAG**
   Dr. Jakobine         Kellenbenz spouse of 7
**SEIBOLD**
   Anna Catherine      Zimmermannn spouse of 11
**SILLER or SIHLER**
   Christina              Kellenbenz spouse of 8
**STAUDENMAIER**
   Anna Ursula         Zimmermannn spouse of 14
**STAUDENMAIER**
   Anna Maria          Kellenbenz spouse of 11
**STÖCKLE**
   Marx                   Zimmermannn spouse of 9
**STRÖSSNER**
   Anna Barbara        Zimmermannn spouse of 8
**WALTER**
   Anna (2)               Zimmermannn spouse of 4
**WEIGLE**
   Debra                 Kellenbenz child of 26
   Frederick             Kellenbenz spouse of 17
   Frederick             Kellenbenz child of 17
   Frederick             Kellenbenz 26
   Linda                 Kellenbenz child of 26
   Louise               Kellenbenz child of 21
   Ruth                  Kellenbenz child of 21

| | |
|---|---|
| William | Kellenbenz 21 |
| William | Kellenbenz child of 21 |
| **WIDRUSSEN** | |
| Anna Maria (4) | Zimmermannn spouse of 6 |
| **WILHELM** | |
| Anna | Kellenbenz child of 18 |
| **YOUSERT** | |
| Katarine Margarete | Zimmermannn spouse of 12 |
| **ZIMMERMANN** | |
| Emily | Kellenbenz child of 16 |
| John (Johannes) [111121112] Sr. | Kellenbenz spouse of 16 |
| Adam | Zimmermannn 2 |
| Adam | Zimmermannn child of 2 |
| Agnes | Zimmermannn child of 4 |
| Andrass (23) | Zimmermannn child of 8 |
| Anna | Zimmermannn child of 27 |
| Anna [1111121] | Zimmermannn 21 |
| Anna [111121113] | Zimmermannn child of 24 |
| Anna [111121121] | Zimmermannn child of 25 |
| Anna Barbara (6) | Zimmermannn child of 6 |
| Anna Catharina | Zimmermannn child of 2 |
| Anna Catharina | Zimmermannn child of 3 |
| Anna Katarina (5) | Zimmermannn child of 6 |
| Anna Margarethe | Zimmermannn child of 11 |
| Anna Maria | Zimmermannn child of 11 |
| Anna Maria | Zimmermannn 9 |
| Anna Maria | Zimmermannn child of 3 |
| Anna Regina | Zimmermannn child of 11 |
| Anna Ursula (33) | Zimmermannn child of 18 |
| Arlena | Zimmermannn child of 25 |
| Augusta Maria (10) | Zimmermannn child of 6 |
| Augusta Maria (11) | Zimmermannn child of 6 |
| Barbara (20) | Zimmermannn child of 8 |
| Catharina | Zimmermannn child of 10 |
| Christoph | Zimmermannn child of 7 |
| Christoph | Zimmermannn child of 10 |
| Christoph [111122] | Zimmermannn child of 11 |
| Elisabeta (34) | Zimmermannn child of 18 |
| Elisabetha Margarethe | Zimmermannn child of 11 |
| Elizabeta Magdalena (15) | Zimmermannn child of 6 |
| Emily | Zimmermannn child of 28 |
| F_____ Maria [1111141] | Zimmermannn child of 15 |
| Friederike Dorothea | Zimmermannn 13 |
| Frikopf [111115] | Zimmermannn 16 |
| Frikopf F. | Zimmermannn child of 16 |
| Georg [or F__] Christoph [1111] | Zimmermannn 7 |
| Georg Malifion (25) | Zimmermannn child of 8 |
| George | Zimmermannn child of 27 |
| Hans Jacob | Zimmermannn child of 3 |
| Ingrifon [111111] | Zimmermannn child of 10 |
| Jacob [1111211] | Zimmermannn 22 |
| Jakob | Zimmermannn child of 11 |
| Herr Jakob [1] | Zimmermannn 3 |
| Jakob [111121122] | Zimmermannn child of 25 |

| | |
|---|---|
| Johann (32) | Zimmermannn child of 18 |
| Johann Friedrich [111114] | Zimmermannn 15 |
| Johann Georg | Zimmermannn child of 10 |
| Johann Georg | Zimmermannn child of 4 |
| Johann Georg [11111] | Zimmermannn 10 |
| Johann Georg [111112] | Zimmermannn 14 |
| Johann Georg [111121] | Zimmermannn 17 |
| Johann Georg [111121111] | Zimmermannn 27 |
| Johann Georg [11112112] | Zimmermannn 25 |
| Johann Georg [111121124] | Zimmermannn child of 25 |
| Johann Georg (18) | Zimmermannn 8 |
| Johann Georg (24) | Zimmermannn child of 8 |
| Johann Georg (8) | Zimmermannn child of 6 |
| Johann Jacob [112] (3) | Zimmermannn 6 |
| Johann Jakob (17) | Zimmermannn child of 6 |
| Johann Jakob (27) | Zimmermannn 12 |
| Johann Malifion (22) | Zimmermannn child of 8 |
| Johann Michael [111] | Zimmermannn 5 |
| Johann [Albert] Jakob [11] (1) | Zimmermannn 4 |
| Johannes [111121126] | Zimmermannn child of 25 |
| John | Zimmermannn child of 27 |
| John (Johannes) [11112111] | Zimmermannn 24 |
| **John[1] (Johannes) [111121112] Sr.** | **Zimmermannn 28** |
| Jos. (30) | Zimmermannn child of 18 |
| Jos. Andras (36) | Zimmermannn child of 18 |
| Jos. Gottlieb (35) | Zimmermannn child of 18 |
| Josaumt (29) | Zimmermannn child of 18 |
| Josef Andrass (28) | Zimmermannn 18 |
| Katharina (16) | Zimmermannn child of 6 |
| Katharina (7) | Zimmermannn child of 6 |
| Katherine [111121123] | Zimmermannn child of 25 |
| Katherine Margarete (31) | Zimmermannn child of 18 |
| Ludwig | Zimmermannn child of 11 |
| Ludwig | Zimmermannn child of 11 |
| Margarete [111121125] | Zimmermannn child of 25 |
| Margarethe [111113] | Zimmermannn child of 10 |
| Margarethe (14) | Zimmermannn child of 6 |
| Maria (12) | Zimmermannn child of 6 |
| Maria (13) | Zimmermannn child of 6 |
| Maria Augusta (9) | Zimmermannn child of 6 |
| Maria Barbara | Zimmermannn child of 4 |
| Maria Katharina (26) | Zimmermannn child of 8 |
| Martha | Zimmermannn child of 2 |
| Martha | Zimmermannn child of 2 |
| Martin Albert | Zimmermannn child of 25 |
| Mary | Zimmermannn child of 25 |
| Matthaeus | Zimmermannn child of 2 |
| Mattis | Zimmermannn 1 |
| Melchior | Zimmermannn child of 11 |
| Pfilippina (21) | Zimmermannn child of 8 |
| Sara | Zimmermannn child of 2 |
| Sigmund Christoph [Friedrich] [11112] | Zimmermannn 11 |
| Sigmund Friedrich | Zimmermannn child of 11 |
| Walburga | Zimmermannn child of 3 |

| | |
|---|---|
| Walburga | Zimmermannn child of 3 |
| Walburga | Zimmermannn child of 2 |
| Walter | Zimmermannn child of 27 |
| Wolfgang Ulrich (19) | Zimmermannn child of 6 |
| John (1.2.1) Jr. | Kellenbenz child of 16 |
| John (1.2.1) Jr. | Zimmermannn child of 28 |
| Lillian (1.2.2) "Lily Mae" | Kellenbenz child of 16 |
| Lillian (1.2.2) "Lily Mae" | Zimmermannn child of 28 |
| Clara (1.2.3) | Kellenbenz child of 16 |
| Clara (1.2.3) | Zimmermannn child of 28 |
| William (1.2.4) | Kellenbenz child of 16 |
| William (1.2.4) | Zimmermannn child of 28 |
| Anna (1.2.5) | Kellenbenz child of 16 |
| Anna (1.2.5) | Zimmermannn child of 28 |
| Albert Walter "Al" (1.2.6) Sr. | Kellenbenz child of 16 |
| Albert Walter "Al" (1.2.6) Sr. | Zimmermannn child of 28 |

## Part III
### Descendants of John[1] and Eva Kathryn Zimmermann
### Their children, in the order shown below, were:

| | |
|---|---|
| Clara | 1 |
| Anna | 2 |
| Emily | 3 |
| John, Jr. | 4 |
| William | 5 |
| Lillian | 6 |
| Albert Walter | 7 |

------------------------------

**?**

| | |
|---|---|
| Ellen T. | spouse of 2.1.1 |
| Utter, Linda | spouse of 2.2.4 |
| [grandchild 1 of Eric Fonkalsrud] | 5.2.?.1 |
| [grandchild 2 of Eric Fonkalsrud] | 5.2.?.2 |
| [grandchild 3 of Eric Fonkalsrud] | 5.2.?.3 |
| [grandchild 5 of Eric Fonkalsrud] | 5.2.?.4 |
| [grandchild 5 of Eric Fonkalsrud] | 5.2.?.5 |
| [grandchild 6 of Eric Fonkalsrud] | 5.2.?.6 |
| [grandchild 1 of R.C.Kelley, Jr.] | 2.2.?.1 |
| [grandchild 2 of R.C.Kelley, Jr.] | 2.2.?.2 |
| [grandchild 3 of R.C.Kelley, Jr.] | 2.2.?.3 |
| [grandchild 4 of R.C.Kelley, Jr.] | 2.2.?.4 |
| [grandchild 5 of R.C.Kelley, Jr.] | 2.2.?.5 |
| [grandchild 6 of R.C.Kelley, Jr.] | 2.2.?.6 |
| [grandchild 7 of R.C.Kelley, Jr.] | 2.2.?.7 |
| [grandchild 8 of R.C.Kelley, Jr.] | 2.2.?.8 |
| [grandchild 9 of R.C.Kelley, Jr.] | 2.2.?.9 |
| Janie | spouse of 4.3.2 |
| Luke | 6.1.1.1 |
| Margaret H. | spouse of 4.4.2 |
| Mark | spouse of 6.1.1 |
| Nikko | 6.1.1.2 |

**ADAMS**

| | |
|---|---|
| Jeanne Hope | spouse (1) of 2.2 |

**BEST**

261

| | |
|---|---|
| Janet (Creighton) | spouse (2) of 2.2 |
| **BINGHAM** | |
| Rita | spouse of 2.6.2 |
| **BORTON** | |
| Richard W. | spouse of 2.2.3 |
| **CARABBA** | |
| Charles | spouse of 2.6.5 |
| **CARLIN** | |
| Brendon Joseph | spouse (1) of 1.2.2.1 |
| Madison Field | child of 1.2.2.1 |
| Taylor Anne | child of 1.2.2.1 |
| **CARLSON** | |
| Roberta Anne "Bobbie" | spouse of 2.3.2 |
| **CARLTON** | |
| Doug | spouse (2) of 1.2.2.1 |
| **CARNWATH** | |
| Barnaby Bemar | 2.3.1.3.1 |
| Bo James von MINDEN | 2.3.1.2.1 |
| Cedar Rose | 2.3.2.2.2 |
| Christopher Joseph | 2.3.1.1.3 |
| Grace Kelley | 2.3.2.2.1 |
| Gunnar Carlson | 2.3.2.2 |
| Henry Theodore | 2.3.1.3.2 |
| James Wallace | 2.3.1.2 |
| John Douglas | 2.3.1.3 |
| Joseph Caspari | 2.3.1.1 |
| Joseph Wallace | spouse of 2.3 |
| Joseph Wallace Jr. | 2.3.1 |
| Kate Sara | 2.3.1.1.1 |
| Kelley MacDonald | 2.3.2.1 |
| Richard Kelley | 2.3.2 |
| Sylvia Gabrielle | 2.3.1.1.2 |
| **CASPARI** | |
| Susan Smiley | spouse of 2.3.1 |
| **CHUBB** | |
| Corinne "Teeny" | spouse of 7.3 |
| **CLARK** | |
| Gerald | spouse of 4.2 |
| Gerald | 4.2.1 |
| Mary | 4.2.2 |
| Peter | 4.2.3 |
| **CREIGHTON** | |
| Janet (née Best) Mrs. | spouse (2) of 2.2 |
| **CRIMMINS** | |
| Ian | 7.4.1.2 |
| Joseph Patrick Esq. | spouse of 7.4,1 |
| Samuel Albert | 7.4.1.1 |
| **CRUMP** | |
| Eugene L. Jr. | spouse of 1.2.1 |
| Lindsay Joann | 1.2.1.1 |
| **DAVIS** | |
| Candice | spouse of 1.3.5 |
| **DEVLIN** | |
| Pat | spouse (2) of 1.2.4 |

**DIFFLEY**
    Anna      7.4.3.1
    Elizabeth Louise "Lisa"      7.4.3.2
    Ray      spouse of 7.4.3
    Ryan Anthony      7.4.3.3

**D'ORAZIO**
    Doris Anne "Dee" "Dory"      spouse of 1.1.1

**DREGALLA**
    Verne      (div) spouse of 2.4.1

**EATON**
    Elizabeth      spouse of 2.6.4

**ELLINGTON**
    Athlene      spouse (2) of 5.3
    Laura (see Robert Zimmermann 5.3)      5.3.1

**FIELD**
    Heather      1.2.2.1
    Roger Creighton      spouse of 1.2.2

**FLEET**
    Alissa Ann      1.3.1.2
    Benjamin D.      spouse of 1.3
    Benjamin David      1.3.1.3
    Carolyn      1.3.2.2
    Donald James      1.3.1
    John William      1.3.2
    Kenneth Benjamin      1.3.4
    Richard Nelson      1.3.5
    Suzanne Kathryn      1.3.3
    Tracey      1.3.2.1
    Wendy Alyson      1.3.1.1

**FLIGG**
    James Alma Jr.      6.2
    James Alma      spouse of 6
    Kathryn Lucille "Katchie"      6.1

**FOGELMAN**
    Ilana Ph.D.      spouse of 1.3.2

**FONKALSRUD**
    David Loren (1.2.4.2.3)      5.2.3
    Eric Walter, Jr. (1.2.4.2.1)      5.2.1
    Eric Walter M.D.      spouse of 5.2
    Margaret Lynn (1.2.4.2.1)      5.2.2
    Robert Warren (1.2.4.2.4)      5.2.4

**FOWLER**
    Ellen T.      spouse of 2.1.1
    Robert Scott      2.1.1
    Thomas Richard      2.1.2
    Ward Scott M.D.      spouse of 2.1

**GALASSO**
    Sandra Gayle      spouse of 4.4.3

**GETMAN**
    Susan      spouse of 2.6.1

**GROVER**
    James Hedgcock J.D.      (div) spouse of 7.2

**HAAG**
    Gary      (div) spouse of 2.2.4

**HANDWERK**
| | |
|---|---|
| Brian Keith | spouse of 7.1.2 |
| Lilian Thornton | 7.1.2.1 |
| Phoebe Waters | 7.1.2.2 |

**HAUGHT**
| | |
|---|---|
| Christian Dean | 7.2.2.1.3 |
| Jason Frederick | (div) spouse of 7.2.2.1 |
| Landon Jason | 7.2.2.1.2 |
| Marcina Lynn | 7.2.2.1.1 |

**HEDEN**
| | |
|---|---|
| Sara | spouse of 2.3.1.1 |

**HEWES**
| | |
|---|---|
| Brooke | spouse of 2.3.2.2 |

**HILL**
| | |
|---|---|
| David Hedgcock "Dave" | 7.2.2 |
| Father of Georgia and Rosalie | see 7.2.3.1 & 7.2.3.2 |
| George James M.D., D.Litt. | spouse of 7.2 |
| Georgia Clare | 7.2.3.1 |
| Heather Dawn | 7.2.2.1 |
| Helena Rundall "Lana" | 7.2.4 |
| James Warren "Jim" J.D. | 7.2.1 |
| Rosalie Mairead | 7.2.3.2 |
| Sarah M.A., Ph.D. | 7.2.3 |

**HOLMES**
| | |
|---|---|
| Robert S. | spouse of 2.2.2 |

**HOWER**
| | |
|---|---|
| Mary Ann | spouse of 4.4 |

**HOXIE**
| | |
|---|---|
| Albert Nickerson Jr. | spouse of 1 |
| Albert Nickerson "Albo" III | 1.1 |
| Brooke | 1.1.1.1 |
| Christopher James | 1.1.1.2 |
| Edith Lucille "Cil" | 1.3 |
| James "Jim" M.D. | 1.1.1 |
| Jean | 1.2.3 |
| Jeanette | 1.2.2 |
| Joann | 1.2.4 |
| John Zimmermann | 1.2 |
| Julia "Julie" | 1.1.1.3 |
| Mary Jane | 1.2.1 |

**IVEY**
| | |
|---|---|
| Douglas Kent | spouse of 2.5.4 |

**JAMES**
| | |
|---|---|
| Edward | spouse of 4.1 |
| Edward Jr. | 4.1.1 |
| Greg | 4.1.3 |
| Mary | 4.1.2 |

**JOHNSON**
| | |
|---|---|
| Alice Thornton | 7.1.2 |
| Barbara Warren | 7.1.1 |
| Melvin Thornton "Mel" | spouse of 7.1 |

**KELLEY**
| | |
|---|---|
| Anita | 2.5 |
| Carol Phyllis | 2.6.3 |

| | |
|---|---|
| David Emlin | 2.6.2 |
| Devan [daughter] | 2.6.1.2 |
| Donald Edmund | 2.6 |
| Donald Edmund Jr., Esq. | 2.6.1 |
| Janet Nancy | 2.7 |
| Joan Catherine | 2.1 |
| Jordan [son] | 2.6.1.1 |
| Laura Eileen | 2.2.4 |
| Lindsay Ann | 2.2.2 |
| Marian | 2.4 |
| Nancy Hope M.D. | 2.2.1 |
| Pamela Ann | 2.6.6 |
| Peter Edward | 2.6.4 |
| Richard Carlyle | spouse of 2 |
| Richard Carlyle Jr. | 2.2 |
| Stacy Valentine "Giza" | 2.2.5 |
| Susan Dorothea | 2.3 |
| Susan Patricia | 2.6.5 |
| Wendy Adams | 2.2.3 |

**KINKEAD**

| | |
|---|---|
| Phyllis Helen | spouse of 2.6 |

**KINNAMAN**

| | |
|---|---|
| Ethyl | spouse of 4 |

**KIRBY**

| | |
|---|---|
| Martha L. | spouse of 2.4.3 |

**KLEIN**

| | |
|---|---|
| Kristie | spouse (2) of 4.4.3.1 |

**KLOEPFER**

| | |
|---|---|
| Sigrun Kalk | *Lebensabschnittsgefährte* of 2.3.1 |
| Niklas | child of Sigrun |
| Anna | child of Sigrun |

**LAIDLAW**

| | |
|---|---|
| Michael "Mike" M.D., Ph.D. | spouse of 7.4.2 |
| Oliver | 7.4.2.1 |
| Simon | 7.4.2.2 |

**LEE**

| | |
|---|---|
| Candice | spouse (1) of 4.4.3.1 |
| Edward L. Jr., Rt. Rev. | spouse of 6.1 |
| Kathryn | 6.1.1 |

**LEWIS**

| | |
|---|---|
| ? | spouse of 4.1.2 |
| Mary Joyce | spouse of 1.2 |

**LISBINSKI**

| | |
|---|---|
| Lenore Marie | spouse of 7.4 |

**LUKENS**

| | |
|---|---|
| Margaret Peattie | spouse of 5 |

**MAGUIRE**

| | |
|---|---|
| Brian McLaughlin | 1.2.4.1 |
| Emily Jane | 1.2.4.3 |
| Gregory Lewis | 1.2.4.2 |
| Paul Kevin | spouse (1) of 1.2.4 |

**MATTHEWS**

| | |
|---|---|
| ? | spouse of 4.4.1 |

**McMILLAN**

| | |
|---|---|
| Beth Lauren | 1.3.3.1 |
| Daniel Lynn | (div) spouse of 1.3.3 |
| Kathryn Anne | 1.3.3.3 |
| Scott David | 1.3.3.2 |
| **METCALFE** | |
| Charles Michael | spouse of 7.3.3 |
| Louis Warren "Louie" | 7.3.3.1 |
| Percy Roger Humphrey | 7.3.3.2 |
| **MINDEN, von** | |
| Bo James | 2.3.1.2.1 |
| **NAPLES** | |
| John R. | spouse (2) of 1.2.3 |
| **NARAYAN** | |
| Uma, Ph.D | companion of 7.2.1 |
| **NEWELL** | |
| David J. | spouse of 2.6.3 |
| **NILSEN** | |
| ? | spouse of 4.4.6 |
| **PEARSON** | |
| Alison Payne | 2.5.5 |
| Carol Ann | 2.5.1 |
| Justin Payne | 2.5.2.1 |
| Michael Corning | 2.5.3 |
| Oliver Payne Ph.D. | spouse of 2.5 |
| Peter Kelley | 2.5.2 |
| Sandia Corning "Sandy" | 2.5.4 |
| Spencer Ross | 2.5.2.3 |
| Stephanie Kelley | 2.5.2.2 |
| **PHILLIPS** | |
| David Cole | spouse of 2.5.5 |
| **PIOTROWICZ** | |
| Michael | spouse of 2.6.6 |
| **PORZIO** | |
| Damoe | spouse of 1.2.1.1 |
| Sara | child of 1.2.1.1 |
| **POTEAT** | |
| Anne Carlyle | 2.4.1 |
| Edwin McNeill III | 2.4.3 |
| Susan Colquitt | 2.4.2 |
| William Hardman Ph.D. | (div) spouse of 2.4 |
| **RALPH** | |
| Clement John | spouse of 2.5.1 |
| Duncan Kelley | 2.5.1.2 |
| Peter Lochhead | 2.5.1.1 |
| **REYNOLDS** | |
| Megan Esq. | spouse of 7.2.3 |
| **RILEY** | |
| Fiona Judith | 7.1.1.1 |
| John Warren | 7.1.1.3 |
| Penelope Quinn "Nell" | 7.1.1.2 |
| Richard Xavier "Rex" | 7.1.1.5 |
| Thomas A. III, J.D. | spouse of 7.1.1 |
| Thomas Vincent | 7.1.1.4 |
| **SAPUTELLI** | |

| | |
|---|---|
| Linda | spouse (1) of 5.3 |
| **SCHAEGEL** | |
| Nancy Ann | spouse of 1.3.1 |
| **SCANLIN** | |
| Julie | spouse of 2.3.1.3 |
| **SCHEIBNER** | |
| ? | spouse of 4.2.2 |
| **SHOEMAKER** | |
| Barbara [5024] [140] | spouse of 7 |
| **STROUT** | |
| Elizabeth Wilke "Betsy" | spouse of 5.1 |
| **UHLER** | |
| John C. | spouse of 2.4.2 |
| **von MINDEN – see MINDEN, von** | 2.1.1.2.1 |
| **WATSON** | |
| Warren (2) | spouse of 2.2.1 |
| **WENNER** | |
| Geraldine "Jean" | spouse of 1.1 |
| **WHITE** | |
| Jay V. | spouse (1) of 2.2.1 |
| **WILLIS** | |
| Barry Ward | spouse (1) of 1.2.3 |
| Poppy Ann | 1.2.3.2 |
| Zack Diver | 1.2.3.1 |
| **WILSON** | |
| Sheri Lynn | spouse of 7.2.2 |
| **WOOD** | |
| Donna | spouse of 1.3.2 |
| **WORTHINGTON** | |
| Arthur | 7.3.1.2 |
| Corinne | 7.3.1.1 |
| Paul | spouse of 7.3.1 |
| **WRIGHT (originally WOJKOWSKI)** | |
| Karen Beth | spouse of 2.5.2 |
| **ZIMMERMANN** | |
| Albert Walter "Al" (1.2.6) Sr. | 7 |
| Albert Walter "Al" Jr., M.D. | 7.4 |
| Amanda Theresa | 7.4.3 |
| Anna (1.2.5) | 2 |
| Anne Catherine | 7.4.1 |
| Barbara | 4.3.4 |
| Barbara Warren "Babs" | 7.1 |
| Bette | 4.1 |
| Carl | 4.4 |
| Carl Kinnaman Jr. | 4.4.2 |
| Caroline | 4.4.3.1.1 |
| Christopher Lee (1.2.4.1.3) | 5.1.3 |
| Clara (1.2.3) | 1 |
| Corinne Alsop "Quinnie" | 7.3.1 |
| Elizabeth Ann | 4.4.1 |
| Elizabeth B. "Lily" | 7.3.3 |
| Emily | 3 |
| Hannah (1.2.4.3.1) | 5.3.2 |
| Helene "Lanie" Ph.D. | 7.2 |

| | |
|---|---|
| James David | 4.4.3.1 |
| Jamie Warren | 7.3.2.1 |
| John (1.2.1) Jr. | 4 |
| John Hower | 4.4.3 |
| John III | 4.3 |
| John IV | 4.3.1 |
| Laura (see Ellington, Laura) | 5.3.2 |
| Lillian (1.2.2) "Lily Mae" | 6 |
| Margaret Ann "Peggy" (1.2.4.2) | 5.2 |
| Mary Jane | 4.2 |
| Michael Strout (1.2.4.1.1) | 5.1.1 |
| Molly | 4.3.1.2 |
| Nancy | 4.3.3 |
| Paul | 4.4.8 |
| Peter Clair | 4.4.7 |
| Richard "Rick" | 4.3.2 |
| Robert Alan "Bob" (1.2.4.3) Ph.D. | 5.3 |
| Sarah Lukens (1.2.4.1.2) | 5.1.2 |
| Susan | 4.4.6 |
| Susan Marie "Susie" Ph.D. | 7.4.2 |
| Thomas David | 4.4.4 |
| Warren "Tim" Jr. | 7.3.2 |
| Warren "Zimmer" Ambassador | 7.3 |
| William (1.2.4) | 5 |
| William "Bill" (1.2.4.1) Jr., Ph.D. | 5.1 |
| William Joseph | 4.4.5 |

## Other Family Names and Notable Individuals[*]

| | ancestors of |
|---|---|
| Adams | spouse of 7.2 |
| Allyn | spouse of 7.2 |
| Alsop | spouse of 7.3 |
| Archibald | spouse of 7.2 |
| Atherton | spouses of 7. & 7.2 |
| Avery | spouse of 7.2 |
| Bishop | spouse of 7.2 |
| Boulter | spouse of 7.2 |
| Bourne | spouse of 7.2 |
| Brown | spouse of 7.2 |
| Budd | spouse of 7.2 |
| Cadwalader | spouse of 7. |
| Carnwath | spouse of 2.3 |
| Carpenter | spouse of 7.2 |
| Chapin | spouse of 7.2 |
| Chichester | spouse of 7.2 |
| Chubb | spouse of 7.3 |

---

[*] Ancestors of spouses of 7. and 7.2 are in the indices of books by George J. Hill, *Hill: The Ferry Keeper's Family*; *Western Pilgrims*; *Quakers and Puritans*; and *Fundy to Chesapeake*. (Full titles in Bibliography)

| | |
|---|---|
| Clapp | spouse of 7.2 |
| Comly | spouse of 7. |
| Corning | spouse of 7.2 |
| Derehaugh | spouse of 7.2 |
| Dickinson | spouse of 7.2 |
| Eager | spouse of 7.2 |
| Eyre | spouse of 7.2 |
| Feake | spouse of 7.2 |
| Fletcher | spouse of 7. |
| Fligg | spouse of 6. |
| Fogelman | spouse of 7.3.2 |
| Fowler | spouse of 2.1 |
| Fuller | spouse of 7.2 |
| Giddings | spouse of 7.2 |
| Gillett | spouse of 7.2 |
| Hale | spouse of 7.2 |
| Halsey | spouse of 7.2 |
| Herrick | spouse of 7.2 |
| Hill | spouse of 7.2 |
| Halsey | spouse of 7.2 |
| Hobby | spouse of 7.2 |
| Holbrook | spouse of 7.2 |
| Holmes | spouse of 7.2 |
| Howell | spouse of 7.2 |
| Hout | spouse of 7.2 |
| Hoyt | spouse of 7.2 |
| Hoxie | spouse of 1. |
| Hyde | spouse of 7. & 7.2 |
| Iredell | spouse of 7.2 |
| Jackson | spouses of 7. & 7.2 |
| Jeanes | spouse of 5. |
| Johnson | spouse of 7.1 |
| Jones | spouse of 7. |
| Kelley | spouse of 2. |
| Kingman | spouse of 7.2 |
| Kinkead | spouse of 2.6 |
| Kinnaman | spouse of 4. |
| Knapp | spouse of 7.2 |
| Lee | spouse of 7.2 |
| Leech | spouse of 7. |
| Lloyd | spouse of 7. |
| Long | spouse of 7.2 |
| Lukens | spouses of 5. & 7. |
| Lum | spouse of 7.2 |
| Lyon | spouse of 7.2 |
| Manly | spouse of 7.2 |
| McVaugh | spouse of 7. |
| Morton | spouse of 7.2 |
| Moors | spouse of 7. |
| Munroe | spouse of 7. |
| Nurse | spouse of 7.2 |
| Ober | spouse of 7. |
| Ogden | spouse of 7.2 |
| Op den Graeff | spouses of 5. & 7. |
| Palgrave | spouse of 7. |
| Palmer | spouse of 7.2 |

| | |
|---|---|
| Parker | spouse of 7. |
| Pearson | spouse of 2.5 |
| Pellet | spouse of 7.2 |
| Pennington | spouse of 7.2 |
| Penrose | spouse of 7. |
| Phelps | spouse of 7.2 |
| Phippen | spouse of 7.2 |
| Pierce/Pearce/Peirce | spouses of 7. & 7.2 |
| Potter | spouse of 7.2 |
| Prince | spouse of 7.2 |
| Poteat | spouse of 2.4 |
| Potts | spouse of 7. |
| Prescott | spouse of 7.2 |
| Putnam | spouse of 7.2 |
| Richardson | spouse of 7. |
| Robinson | spouse of 5. |
| Rundall/Rundle | spouse of 7.2 |
| Sanghurst | spouse of 7.2 |
| Saxe | spouse of 7.2 |
| Sharpless | spouse of 7.2 |
| Shoemaker | spouse of 7. |
| Singletary | spouse of 7.2 |
| Smith | spouses of 7. & 7.2 |
| Spalding | spouse of 7. |
| Stewart | spouse of 7. |
| Stockwell | spouse of 7.2 |
| Stratton | spouse of 7. |
| Swaine | spouse of 7.2 |
| Thompson | spouse of 7.2 |
| Thorndike | spouse of 7. |
| Tillinghast | spouse of 7.2 |
| Tompkins | spouse of 7.2 |
| Townsend | spouse of 7.2 |
| Trowbridge | spouses of 7.& 7.2 |
| Tyson | spouses of 5.& 7. |
| Underwood | spouse of 7. |
| Wall | spouse of 7. |
| Walter | spouse of 7.2 |
| Ward | spouses of 7.& 7.2 |
| Warren | spouse of 7. |
| Weaver | spouse of 7.2 |
| Wheeler | spouse of 7.2 |
| Willard | spouses of 7. & 7.2 |
| Young, Brigham | spouse of 4.4.3.1 |

and also

| | |
|---|---|
| Charlemagne | spouses of 7.& 7.2 |
| de Clare, Richard "Strongbow" | spouses of 7.& 7.2 |
| Conant , Governor Roger | spouse of 7. |
| Curzon, Lord George Nathiel ,1st Marquess of Kedleston | spouse of 7.3.3 |
| Fuller, Edward, of the *Mayflower* | spouse of 7.2 |
| Godiva, Lady | spouses of 7.& 7.2 |
| John "Lackland," King of England | spouses of 7.& 7.2 |
| Malcolm Canmore III, King of Scotland | spouses of 7.& 7.2 |
| Margaret, Saint, Queen of Scotland | spouses of 7.& 7.2 |

Magna Carta Sureties        spouses of 7.& 7.2
Munro, George, 10th Baron Fowlis        spouse of 7.
Nurse, Rebecca "Goody" (Towne), hanged as a witch        spouse of 7.2
Roosevelt, Sr., Theodore        spouse of 7.3
William I, "the Conqueror," King of England        spouses of 7.& 7.2
de Warrenne, William, 1st Earl of Surrey        spouse of 7.& 7.2

# Zimmermann Line
## Charts Prepared by Jean Hoxie Naples – 2009

### August 2009 Chart

Updated / revised Aug. 2009
Jean Hoxie Naples

The  Zimmermann  line

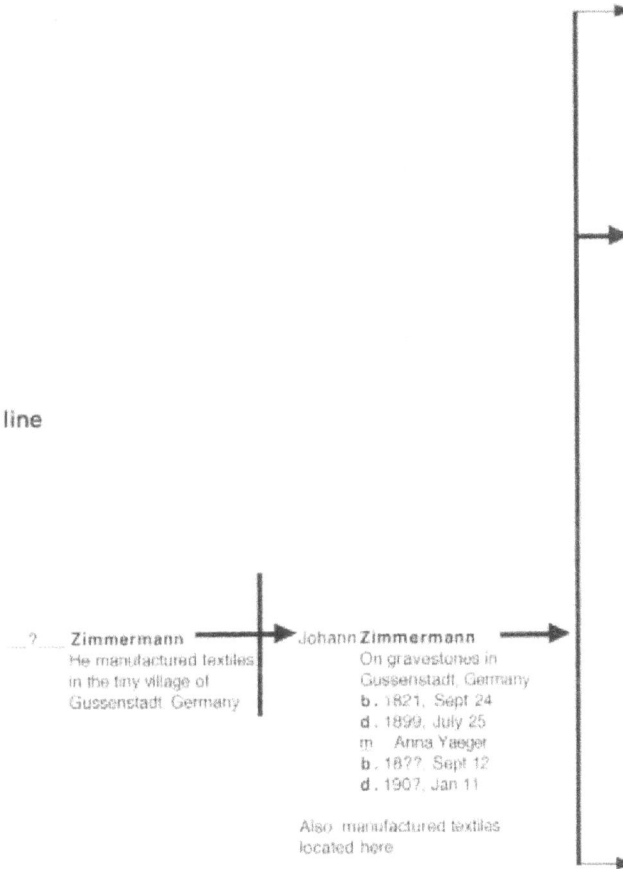

?    **Zimmermann**
He manufactured textiles
in the tiny village of
Gussenstadt, Germany

Johann **Zimmermann**
On gravestones in
Gussenstadt, Germany
**b .** 1821, Sept 24
**d .** 1899, July 25
**m** Anna Yaeger
**b .** 18??, Sept 12
**d .** 1907, Jan 11

Also  manufactured textiles
located here

**August 2009, p.1**

Johann Georg Zimmermann →
  b . June 5, 1851
  Gussenstadt, Kingdom of
  Winttenberg (Germany)
  m Maria ? in 1882 Phila, Pa
  b . Pennsylvania
  Her parents were born in
  Germany
  George came to US in 1881

Johann (John) Zimmermann
  b . Nov. 28,1855
  Gussenstadt, Germany
  d . May 23,1936 Phila.,PA

m (1) Evakaterina →
  (Eva Kathryn) Kellenbenz
  on Oct 15, 1885, Phila
  dau of Clara Gretzinger
  and husband Kellenbenz
  of Germany
  b . Sept 18, 1855
  Kleinfislinger, Germany
  d . Oct 12 , 1920 Phila.,PA

m (2) Mrs. Anna Anderson
  Dancer
  on Nov 23, 1922
  in Decatur Co., Iowa
  b . Sept 30, 1864
  La Salle, Illinois
  d . July 7, 1937 Lamoni,
  Iowa
  dau of Mr & Mrs Andrew
  Anderson of Lamoni, IA
  no issue with JZ. After
  John's death she returns
  to Lamoni, Iowa where her
  son is living

Anna Zimmermann
  b . c1856, Germany
  still living there in 1937

  b . 1964

Anna Zimmermann, **b** . Oct 1884, Phila
John Zimmermann, **b** . Dec 1885 Phila
George Zimmermann, **b** . June 1888, Germany
Walter Zimmermann, **b** . Aug 1893, Arkansas

Clara Zimmermann
  b . July 20, 1886 in Phila
  d . Oct 19, 1968
  m Albert Nickerson **Hoxie**, II
  on Oct. 10, 1911, Phila
  1884-1942

Anna Zimmermann
  b . Dec. 1887 in Phila., PA
  d . 1974
  m Richard Carlyle **Kelley**
  on Aug 10, 1915
  b . Sept 30, 1882
  d . 1976
  son of Edmond Levi Kelley &
  Cassie Bishop of Lamoni, IA

Emile K Zimmermann
  b . July 10, 1890
  d . Jan 14, 1897

John **Zimmermann**, Jr. →
  b . June 6, 1892
  d . Oct 15, 1974
  m Ethel Kinnaman
  in 1916 in Kansas City, MO
  b . June11, 1892
  d . Aug 13, 1979

William "Bill" **Zimmermann** →
  b . Dec 4, 1894
  d . 1978
  m Peggy Lukens in 1929
  b . ?
  d . ?

Lillian Zimmermann
  b . Sept 13, 1897
  d . 1966
  m James Alma **Fligg**
  on Dec 27, 1924
  b . ca 1899, Canada
  d . ?

Albert "Al" Walter **Zimmermann** →
  b . June 11, 1902
  d . 1961
  m Barbara Shoemaker
  in 1926
  b . 1902
  d . 1985

Albert Nickerson **Hoxie** III      1.
  1914 - 2003
  m Geraldine (Jean) Wenner
John Zimmermann **Hoxie**            2.
  1917 - 1984
  m Mary Joyce Lewis 1922 - 1996
Edith Lucile Hoxie                  3.
  1919 - 2007
  m Benjamin D. **Fleet** 1920 -

Joan Catherine Kelley 1916-          4.
  m Ward Scott **Fowler** 1915-1982
Richard Carlyle **Kelley**, Jr. 1919-  5.
  m Jeanne Hope Adams
  1920-1987
Susan Dorothea Kelley 1920-          6.
  m Joseph Wallace **Carnwath**
  1913-1983
Marian Kelley 1921-                  7.
  m William K **Poteat** 1919-
Anita Kelley 1923-
  **Pearson**
Donald Edmund **Kelley** 1924-        8.
  m Phyllis Helen Kinkead 1926-
Janet Nancy **Kelley** 1927-1938

Bettye **Zimmermann**
Mary Jane Zimmermann
  m Gerald **Clark**
Carl **Zimmermann**
John **Zimmermann**

William **Zimmermann** (PhD) 1930-
Margaret Ann "Peggy" Zimmermann 1932
  m Stanley **Leonard**
Robert Alan **Zimmermann** (PhD) 1937-

Kathryn Fligg                        9.
  b . Oct 9, 1925
  m Edward **Lee** (1928- )
James Alma **Fligg**, Jr
  b . Aug 31, 1928
  d . March 16, 2009

Warren **Zimmermann** 1934 - Feb 10 2004
  Ambassador to Yugoslavia
  m Corinne
Barbara "Babs" **Zimmermann**
  m Johnson
Helen "Lanie" Zimmermann
  m George J. **Hill**
Dr Albert "Albie" **Zimmermann**

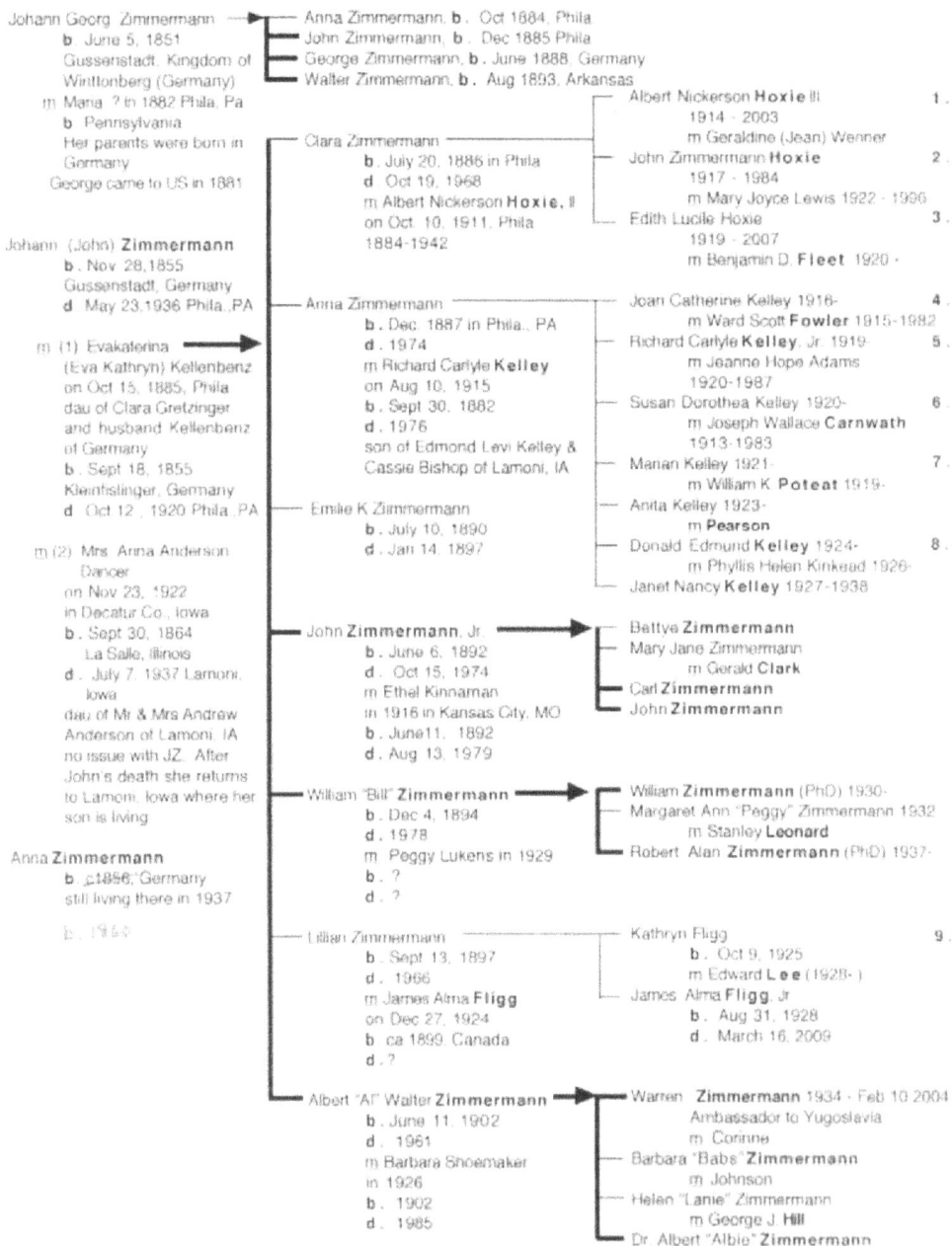

**August 2009, p.2**

1.
- James **Hoxie**, 1950-
  - m Doris (Dee) Anne D'Orazio, 1948-
    - Brooke **Hoxie**, 1979-
    - Christopher James **Hoxie**, 1982-
    - Julia **Hoxie**, 1986-

2.
- Mary Jane Hoxie, 1944-
  Div. m Eugene L. **Crump**, Jr. 1941-
  - Lindsay Joann Crump, 1969-, m Daniel **Porzio**, 1962 — Sara **Porzio** 1995-
  - Josh Lewis **Crump**, 1971-
- Jeanette Hoxie, 1947-
  Div. m Roger Creighton **Field**, 1946-
  - Heather Field, 1968-, m Brendan Joseph Carlin — Taylor Anne **Carlin** 1992-
    m DOUG CARLTON
    - Madison Field **Carlin** 1995-
- Jean Hoxie, 1947-
  m (1) Barry Ward **Willis**, 1941-
  m (2) John Robert **Naples**, 1936-
  - Zack Diver **Willis**, 1973
  - Poppy Ann **Willis**, 1975-1975
- Joann Hoxie, 1950-
  Div. m Paul Kevin **Maguire**
  m PAT DEVLIN
  - Brian McLaughlin **Maguire**, 1978-
  - Gregory Lewis **Maguire**, 1982-
  - Emily Jane **Maguire**, 1984-

3.
- Donald James **Fleet**, 1944-
  m Nancy Ann Schaegel, 1946-
  - Wendy Alyson **Fleet**, 1971-
  - Alissa Ann **Fleet**, 1973-
  - Benjamin David **Fleet**, 1975-
- John William **Fleet**, 1947-
  Div. m Donna Wood, 1948- DIED
  - Tracey **Fleet**, 1969-
  - Carolyn **Fleet**, 1973-
- Suzanne Kathryn Fleet, 1952-
  Div. m Daniel Lynn **McMillan**, 1955-
  - Beth Lauren **McMillan**, 1980-
  - Scott David **McMillan**, 1983- DIED
  - Kathryn Anne **McMillan**, 1986-
- Kenneth Benjamin **Fleet**, 1954-1955
- Richard Nelson **Fleet**, 1955-
  m Candice Davis, 1953-

4.
- Robert Scott **Fowler**, 1947-
- Thomas Richard **Fowler**, 1953-

5.
- Nancy Hope Kelley, 1945-
  m Jay V. **White**
- Lindsay Ann Kelley, 1946-
  m Robert S. **Holmes**
- Wendy Adams Kelley, 1950-
  m Richard W. **Barton**
- Laura Eileen Kelley, 1951-
  m Gary **Haag**
- Stacy Valentine **Kelley**, 1953-

6.
- Joseph Wallace **Carnwath**, 1944-
- Richard Kelly **Carnwath**, 1948-

7.
- Anne Carlyle Poteat, 1946-
  m Verne **Dregalla**
- Susan Colquitt Poteat, 1947-
  m John C. **Uhler**
- E. McNeill **Poteat**, 1950-
  m Martha Kirby

8.
- Donald Edmund **Kelley**, Jr. 1948-
  m Susan Getman
- David Emlin **Kelley**, 1950-
  m Rita Bingham
- Carol Phyllis Kelley, 1954-
  m David J. **Newell**
- Peter Edward **Kelley**, 1956-
  m Elizabeth Eaton
- Susan Patricia Kelly, 1958-
  m Charles **Carabba**
- Pamela Ann Kelly, 1958-
  m Michael **Piotrowicz**

9.
- Kathryn **Lee**

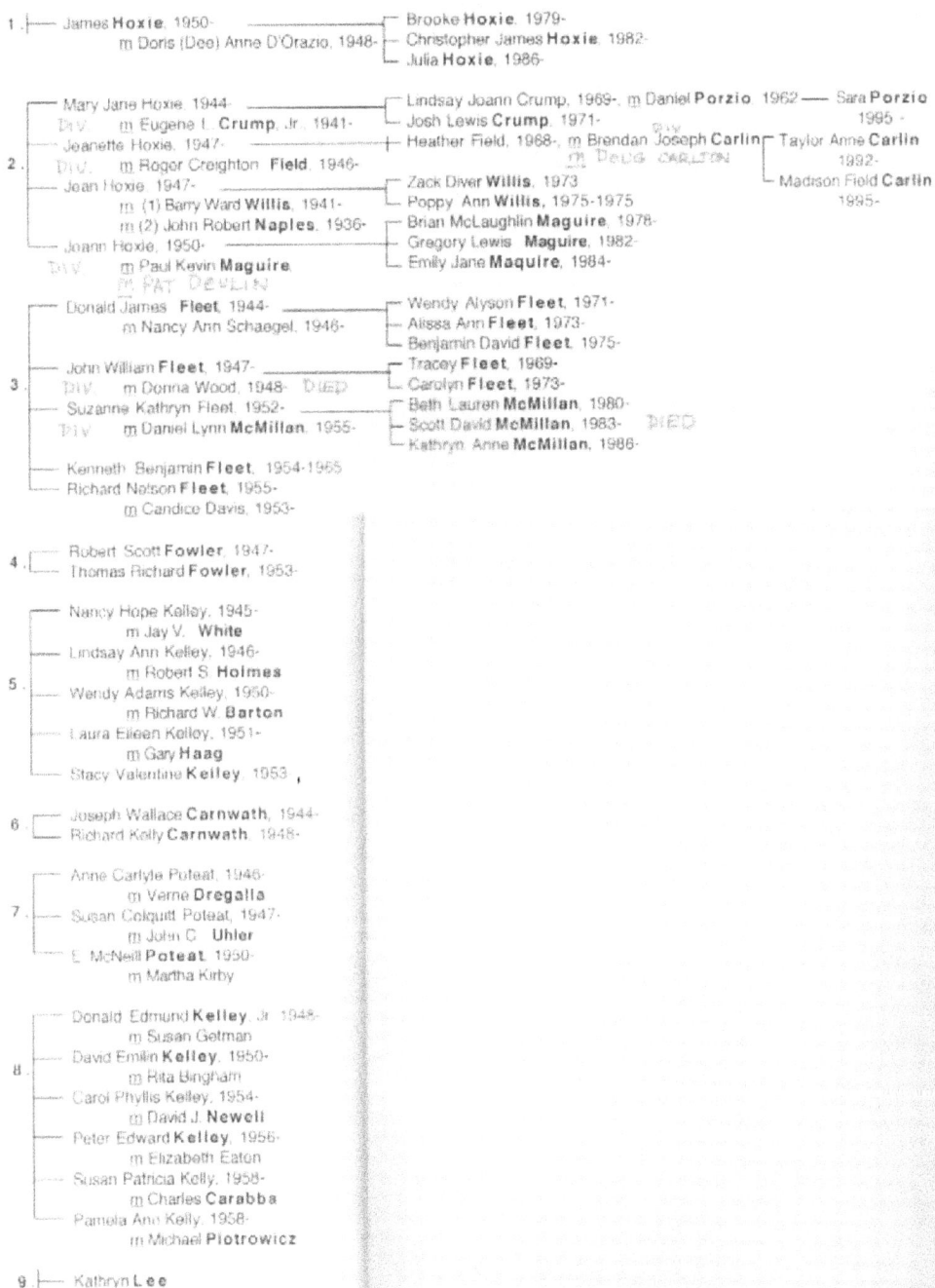

**August 2009, p.3**
**Showing More of Hoxie Family**

275

## November 2009 – Jean Hoxie Naples' Final Charts
## Chart 1

The Zimmermann line

Updated / revised Nov 2009
Jean Hoxie Naples

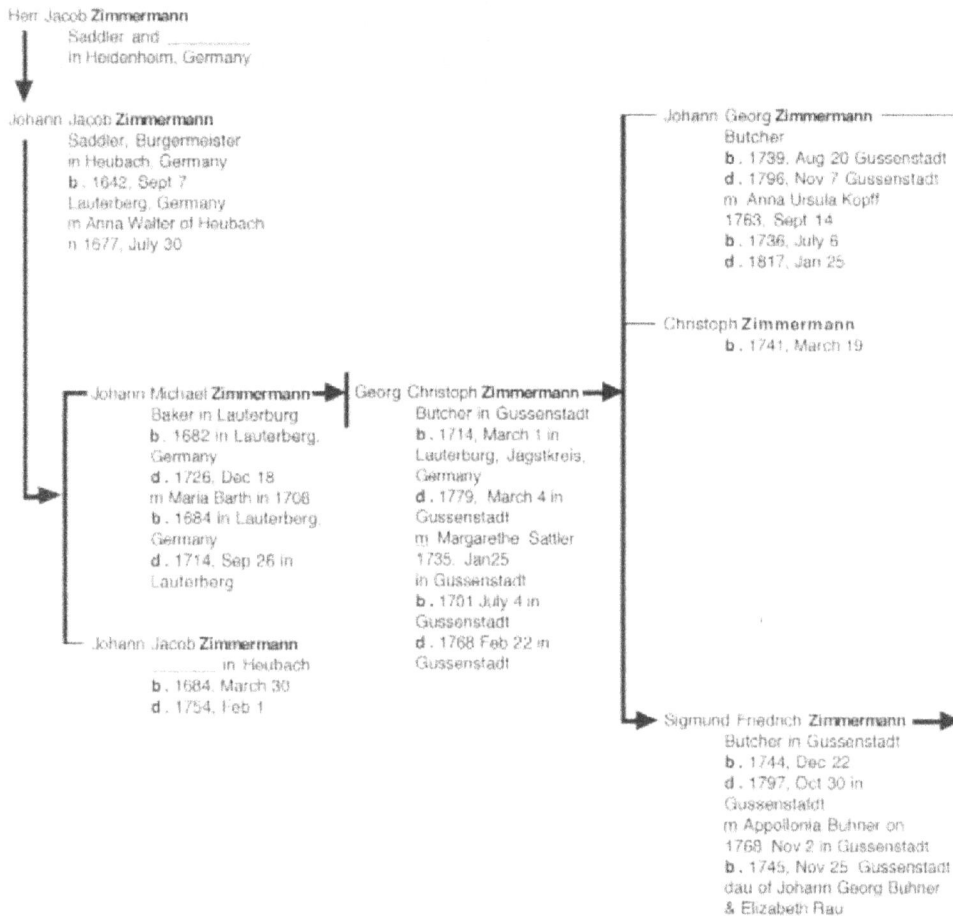

Herr Jacob **Zimmermann**
    Saddler and _____
    in Heidenheim, Germany

Johann Jacob **Zimmermann**
    Saddler, Burgermeister
    in Heubach, Germany
    **b** . 1642, Sept 7
    Lauterberg, Germany
    m Anna Walter of Heubach
    n 1677, July 30

Johann Michael **Zimmermann**
    Baker in Lauterburg
    **b** . 1682 in Lauterberg,
    Germany
    **d** . 1726, Dec 18
    m Maria Barth in 1708
    **b** . 1684 in Lauterberg,
    Germany
    **d** . 1714, Sep 26 in
    Lauterberg

Johann Jacob **Zimmermann**
    _____ in Heubach
    **b** . 1684, March 30
    **d** . 1754, Feb 1

Georg Christoph **Zimmermann**
    Butcher in Gussenstadt
    **b** . 1714, March 1 in
    Lauterburg, Jagstkreis,
    Germany
    **d** . 1779, March 4 in
    Gussenstadt
    m Margarethe Sattler
    1735, Jan25
    in Gussenstadt
    **b** . 1701 July 4 in
    Gussenstadt
    **d** . 1768 Feb 22 in
    Gussenstadt

Johann Georg **Zimmermann**
    Butcher
    **b** . 1739, Aug 20 Gussenstadt
    **d** . 1796, Nov 7 Gussenstadt
    m Anna Ursula Kopff
    1763, Sept 14
    **b** . 1736, July 6
    **d** . 1817, Jan 25

Christoph **Zimmermann**
    **b** . 1741, March 19

Sigmund Friedrich **Zimmermann**
    Butcher in Gussenstadt
    **b** . 1744, Dec 22
    **d** . 1797, Oct 30 in
    Gussenstaldt
    m Appollonia Buhner on
    1768, Nov 2 in Gussenstadt
    **b** . 1745, Nov 25 Gussenstadt
    dau of Johann Georg Buhner
    & Elizabeth Rau

**Chart 1, p.1**

Updated / revised Nov 2009
Jean Hoxie Naples

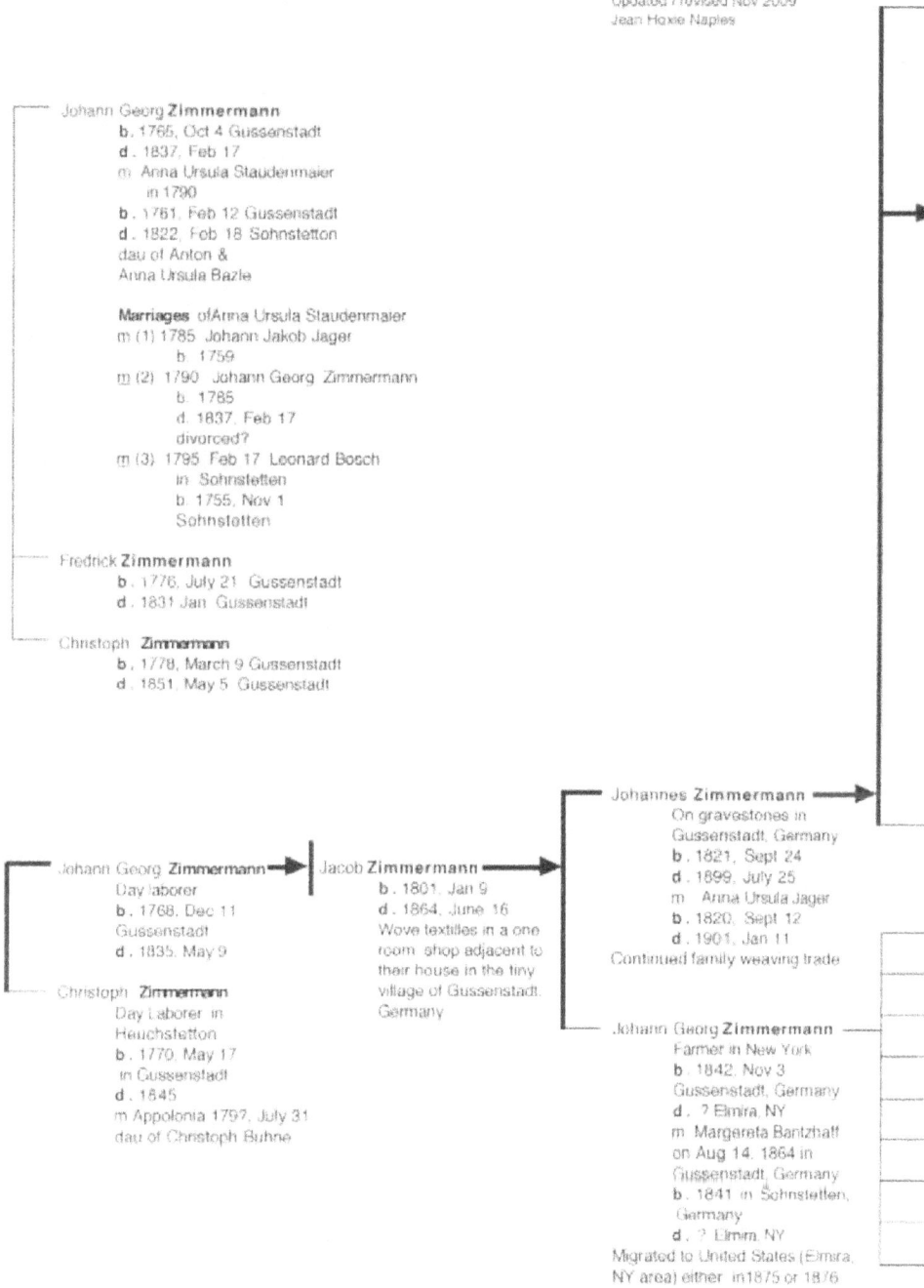

Johann Georg **Zimmermann**
    **b** . 1765, Oct 4 Gussenstadt
    **d** . 1837, Feb 17
    m  Anna Ursula Staudenmaier
        in 1790
    **b** . 1761, Feb 12 Gussenstadt
    **d** . 1822, Feb 18 Sohnstetton
    dau of Anton &
    Anna Ursula Bazle

    **Marriages** of Anna Ursula Staudenmaier
    m (1) 1785  Johann Jakob Jager
            b . 1759
    m (2) 1790  Johann Georg Zimmermann
            b . 1785
            d . 1837, Feb 17
            divorced?
    m (3) 1795 Feb 17 Leonard Bosch
            in  Sohnstetten
            b . 1755, Nov 1
            Sohnstetten

Fredrick **Zimmermann**
    **b** . 1776, July 21  Gussenstadt
    **d** . 1831 Jan  Gussenstadt

Christoph  **Zimmermann**
    **b** . 1778, March 9 Gussenstadt
    **d** . 1851, May 5  Gussenstadt

Johann Georg **Zimmermann**
    Day laborer
    **b** . 1768, Dec 11
    Gussenstadt
    **d** . 1835, May 9

Christoph  **Zimmermann**
    Day Laborer  in
    Heuchstetten
    **b** . 1770, May 17
    in Gussenstadt
    **d** . 1845
    m Appolonia 1797, July 31
    dau of Christoph Buhne

Jacob **Zimmermann**
    **b** . 1801, Jan 9
    **d** . 1864, June 16
    Wove textiles in a one
    room  shop adjacent to
    their house in the tiny
    village of Gussenstadt,
    Germany

Johannes **Zimmermann**
    On gravestones in
    Gussenstadt, Germany
    **b** . 1821, Sept 24
    **d** . 1899, July 25
    m  Anna Ursula Jager
    **b** . 1820, Sept 12
    **d** . 1901, Jan 11
    Continued family weaving trade

Johann Georg **Zimmermann**
    Farmer in New York
    **b** . 1842, Nov 3
    Gussenstadt, Germany
    **d** . ? Elmira, NY
    m  Margereta Bantzhaff
    on Aug 14, 1864 in
    Gussenstadt, Germany
    **b** . 1841 in Sohnstetten,
    Germany
    **d** . ? Elmira, NY
    Migrated to United States (Elmira,
    NY area) either in 1875 or 1876

**Chart 1, p.2**

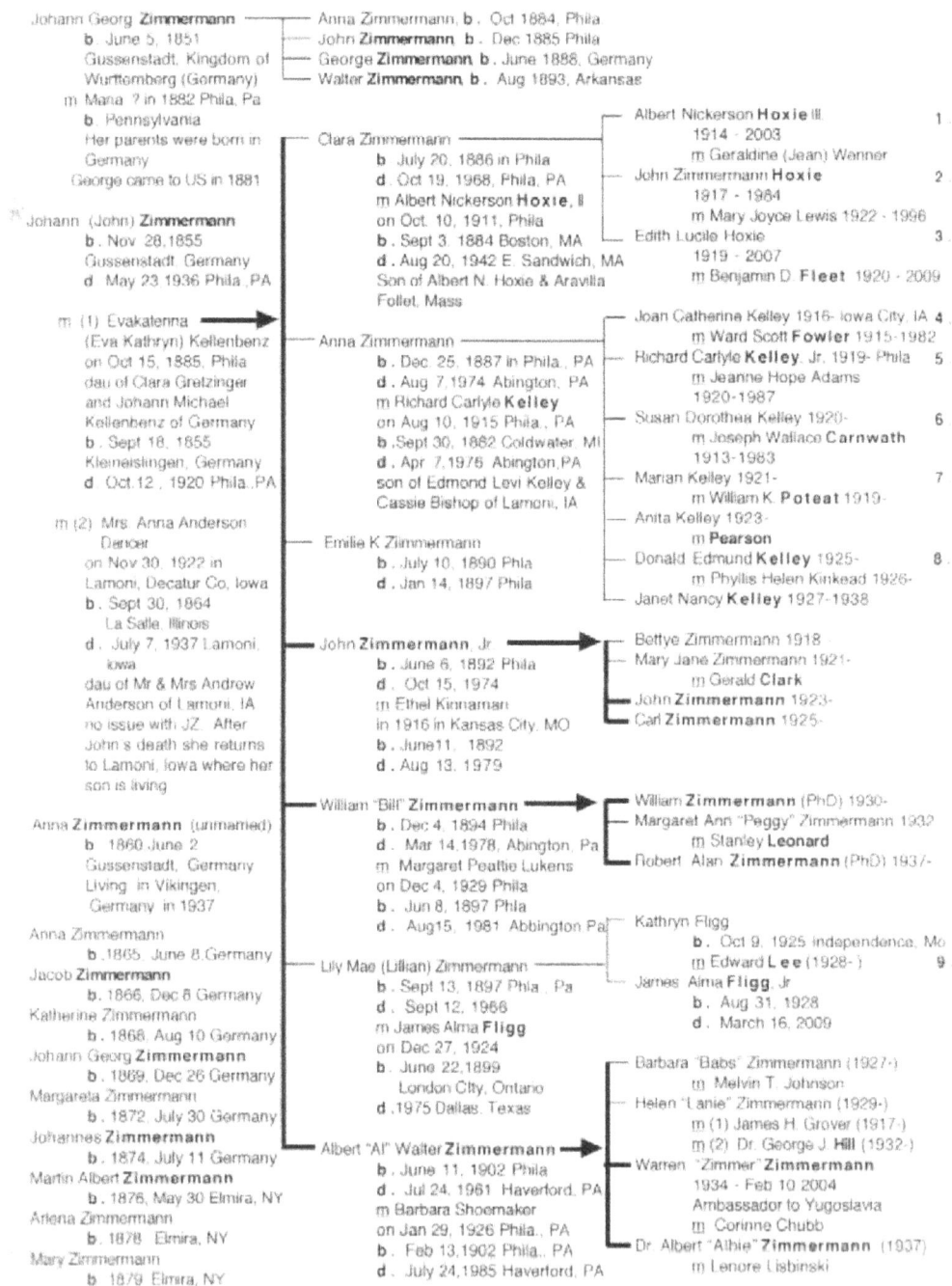

**Chart 1, p.3**

## November 2009 – Jean Hoxie Naples' Final Charts
## Chart 2

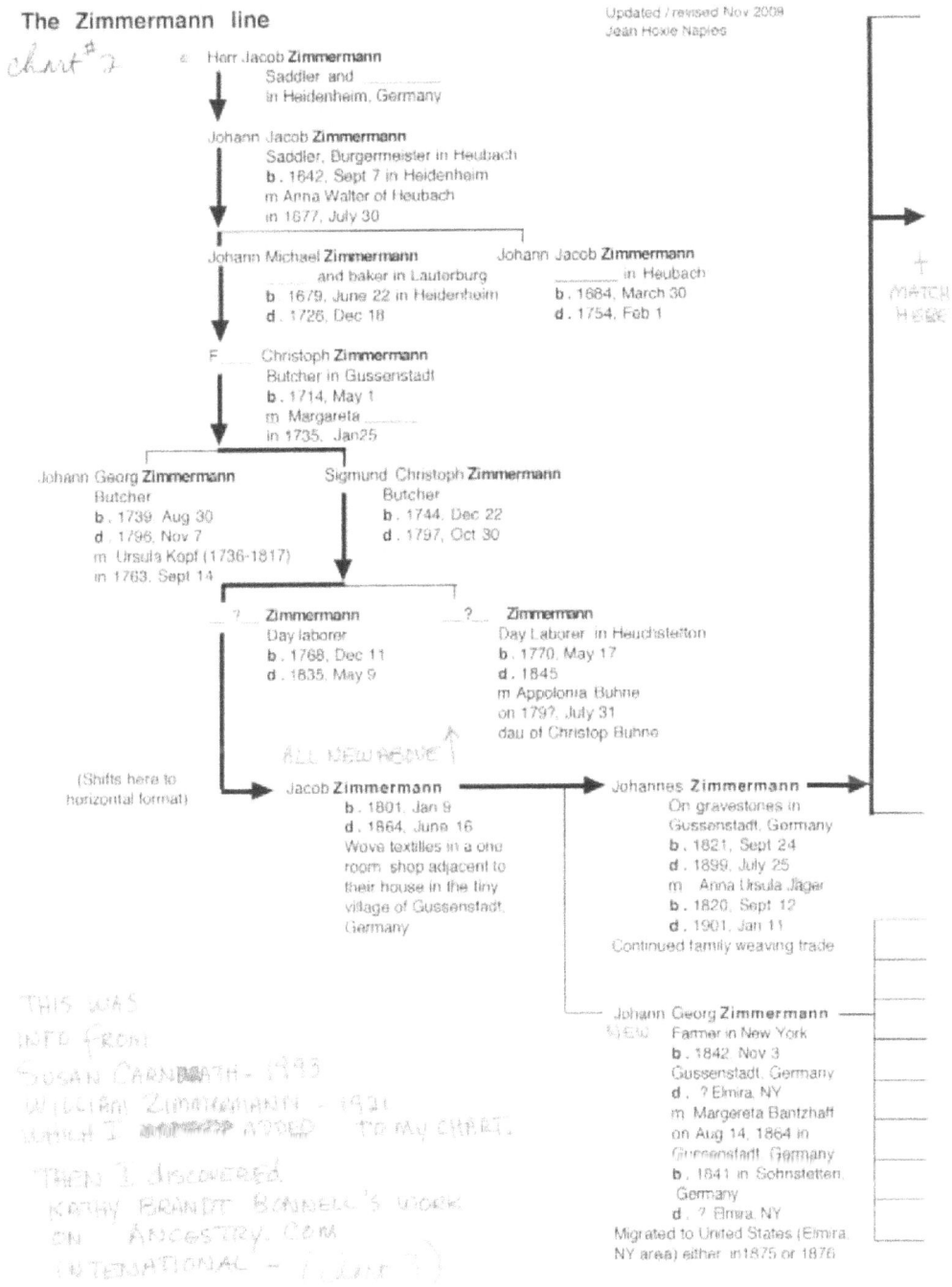

The Zimmermann line

*chart #2*

Updated / revised Nov 2009
Jean Hoxie Naples

Herr Jacob **Zimmermann**
Saddler and
in Heidenheim, Germany

Johann Jacob **Zimmermann**
Saddler, Burgermeister in Heubach
b . 1642, Sept 7 in Heidenheim
m Anna Walter of Heubach
in 1677, July 30

Johann Michael **Zimmermann**
and baker in Lauterburg
b . 1679, June 22 in Heidenheim
d . 1726, Dec 18

Johann Jacob **Zimmermann**
_____ in Heubach
b . 1684, March 30
d . 1754, Feb 1

F____ Christoph **Zimmermann**
Butcher in Gussenstadt
b . 1714, May 1
m Margareta _____
in 1735, Jan 25

Johann Georg **Zimmermann**
Butcher
b . 1739, Aug 30
d . 1796, Nov 7
m Ursula Kopf (1736-1817)
in 1763, Sept 14

Sigmund Christoph **Zimmermann**
Butcher
b . 1744, Dec 22
d . 1797, Oct 30

? **Zimmermann**
Day laborer
b . 1768, Dec 11
d . 1835, May 9

?__ **Zimmermann**
Day Laborer in Heuchstetton
b . 1770, May 17
d . 1845
m Appolonia Buhne
on 1792, July 31
dau of Christop Buhne

ALL NEW ABOVE ?

(Shifts here to
horizontal format)

Jacob **Zimmermann**
b . 1801, Jan 9
d . 1864, June 16
Wove textiles in a one
room shop adjacent to
their house in the tiny
village of Gussenstadt,
Germany

Johannes **Zimmermann**
On gravestones in
Gussenstadt, Germany
b . 1821, Sept 24
d . 1899, July 25
m Anna Ursula Jäger
b . 1820, Sept 12
d . 1901, Jan 11
Continued family weaving trade

Johann Georg **Zimmermann**
NEW    Farmer in New York
b . 1842, Nov 3
Gussenstadt, Germany
d . ? Elmira, NY
m Margereta Bantzhaff
on Aug 14, 1864 in
Gussenstadt, Germany
b . 1841 in Sohnstetten,
Germany
d . ? Elmira, NY
Migrated to United States (Elmira,
NY area) either in 1875 or 1876

+
MATCH
HERE

THIS WAS
INFO FROM
SUSAN CARNBRATH - 1993
WILLIAM ZIMMERMANN - 1921
WHICH I _____ ADDED   TO MY CHART.

THEN I discovered
KATHY BRANDT BONNELL'S WORK
ON  ANCESTRY.COM
INTERNATIONAL - (____?)

**Chart 2, p.1**

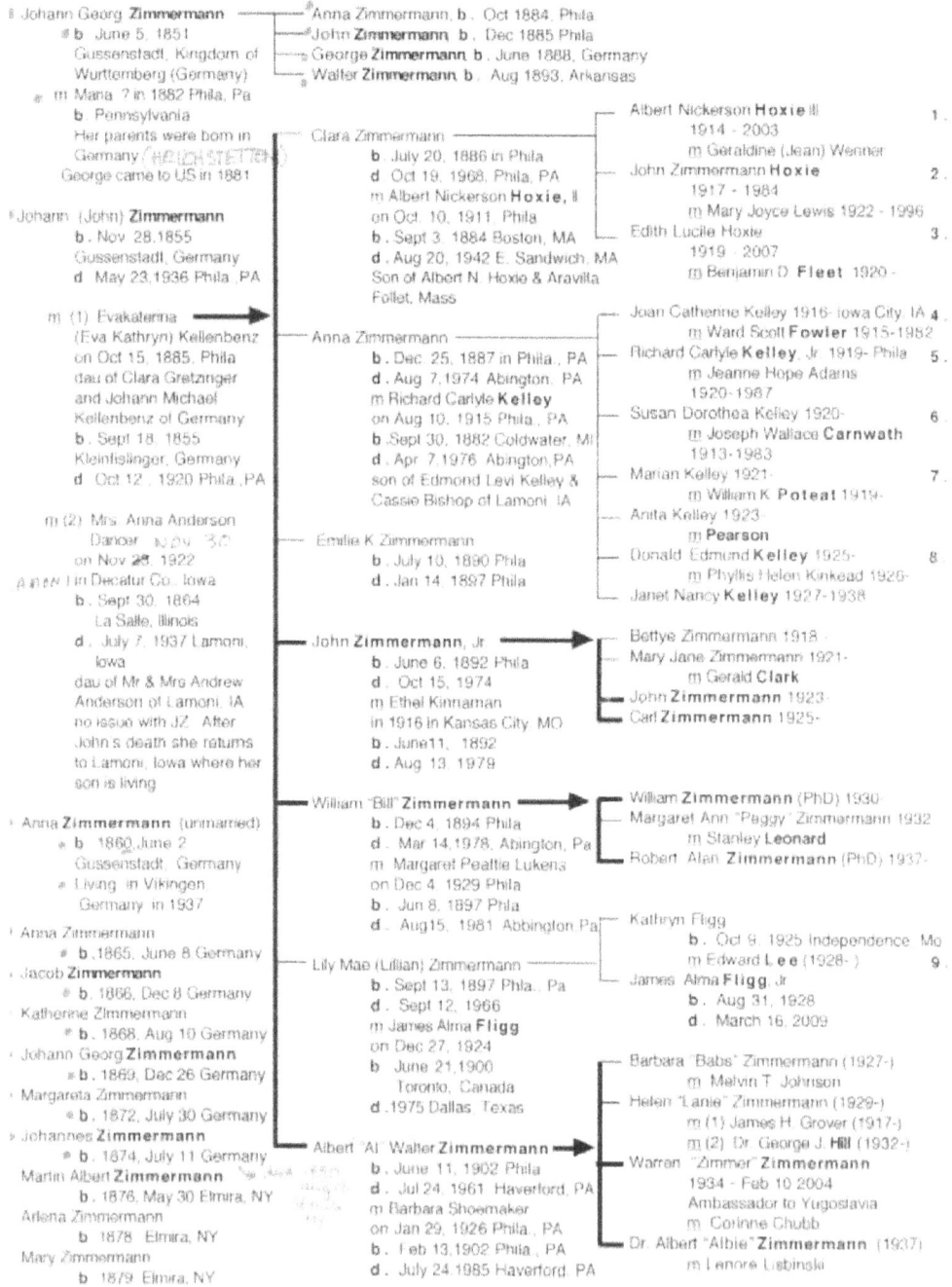

**Chart 2, p.2**

**November 2009 – Jean Hoxie Naples' Final Charts**
**Chart 3**

The Zimmermann line

*Chart # 3*

Updated / revised Nov 2009
Jean Hoxie Naples

Herr Jacob **Zimmermann**
    Saddler and _____
    In Heidenheim, Germany

Johann Jacob **Zimmermann**
    Saddler, Burgermeister
    in Heubach, Germany
    b . 1642, Sept 7 *IN HEIDEN HEIM*
    Lauterberg, Germany
    m Anna Walter of Heubach
    n 1677, July 30

Johann Michael **Zimmermann**
    Baker in Lauterburg
    *1679* b . 1682 in Lauterberg,
    *Heubach* Germany
    d . 1726, Dec 18
    m Maria Barth in 1708
    b . 1684 in Lauterberg,
    Germany
    d . 1714, Sep 26 in
    Lauterberg

Johann Jacob **Zimmermann**
    _____ in Heubach
    b . 1684, March 30
    d . 1754, Feb 1

*E*
Georg Christoph **Zimmermann**
    Butcher in Gussenstadt
    b . 1714, March 1 in
    Lauterburg, Jagstkreis,
    Germany
    d . 1779, March 4 in
    Gussenstadt
    m Margarethe Sattler
    1735, Jan25
    in Gussenstadt
    b . 1701 July 4 in
    Gussenstadt
    d . 1768 Feb 22 in
    Gussenstadt

Johann Georg **Zimmermann**
    Butcher
    b . 1739, Aug 20 Gussenstadt
    d . 1796, Nov 7 Gussenstadt
    m Anna Ursula Kopff
    1763, Sept 14
    b . 1736, July 6
    d . 1817, Jan 25

Christoph **Zimmermann**
    b . 1741, March 19

*CHRISTOPH*
Sigmund Friedrich **Zimmermann**
    Butcher in Gussenstadt
    b . 1744, Dec 22
    d . 1797, Oct 30 in
    Gussenstadt
    m Appollonia Buhner on
    1768, Nov 2 in Gussenstadt
    b . 1745, Nov 25 Gussenstadt
    dau of Johann Georg Buhner
    & Elizabeth Rau

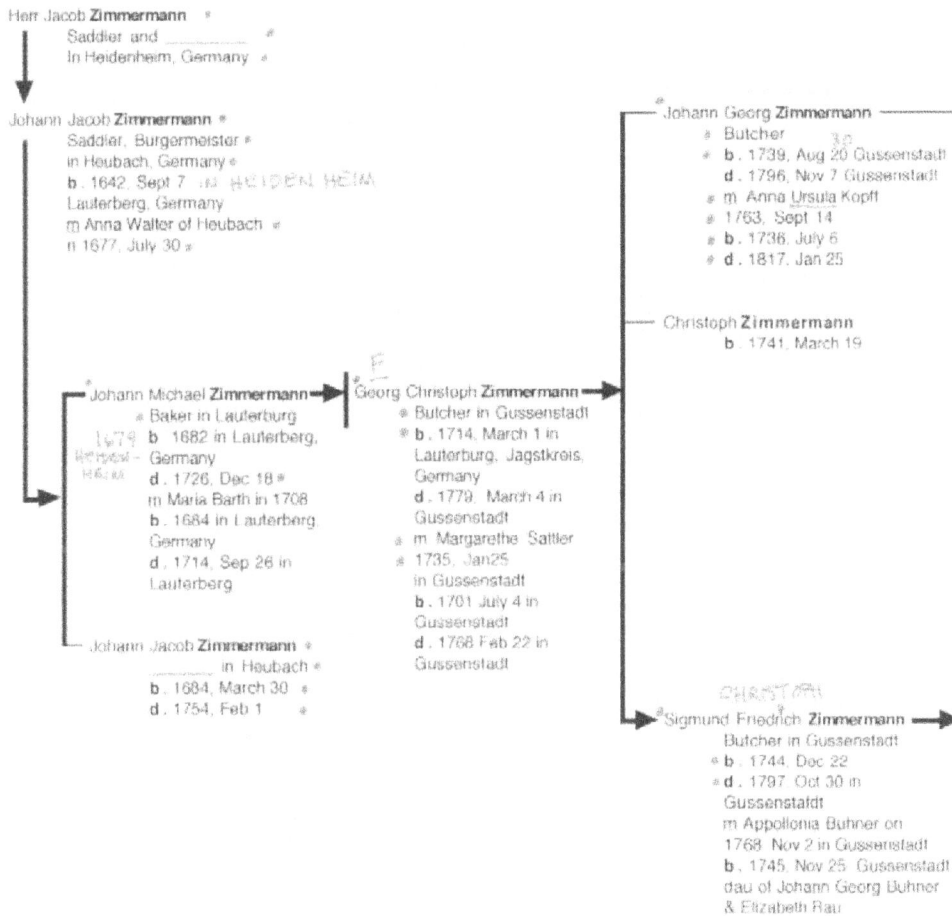

*KATHY BRANDT BONNELL*
*SUSAN CARNWATH 1995*
*WILLIAM ZIMMERMANN 1921*

**Chart 3, p.1**

Updated / revised Nov 2009
Jean Hoxie Naples

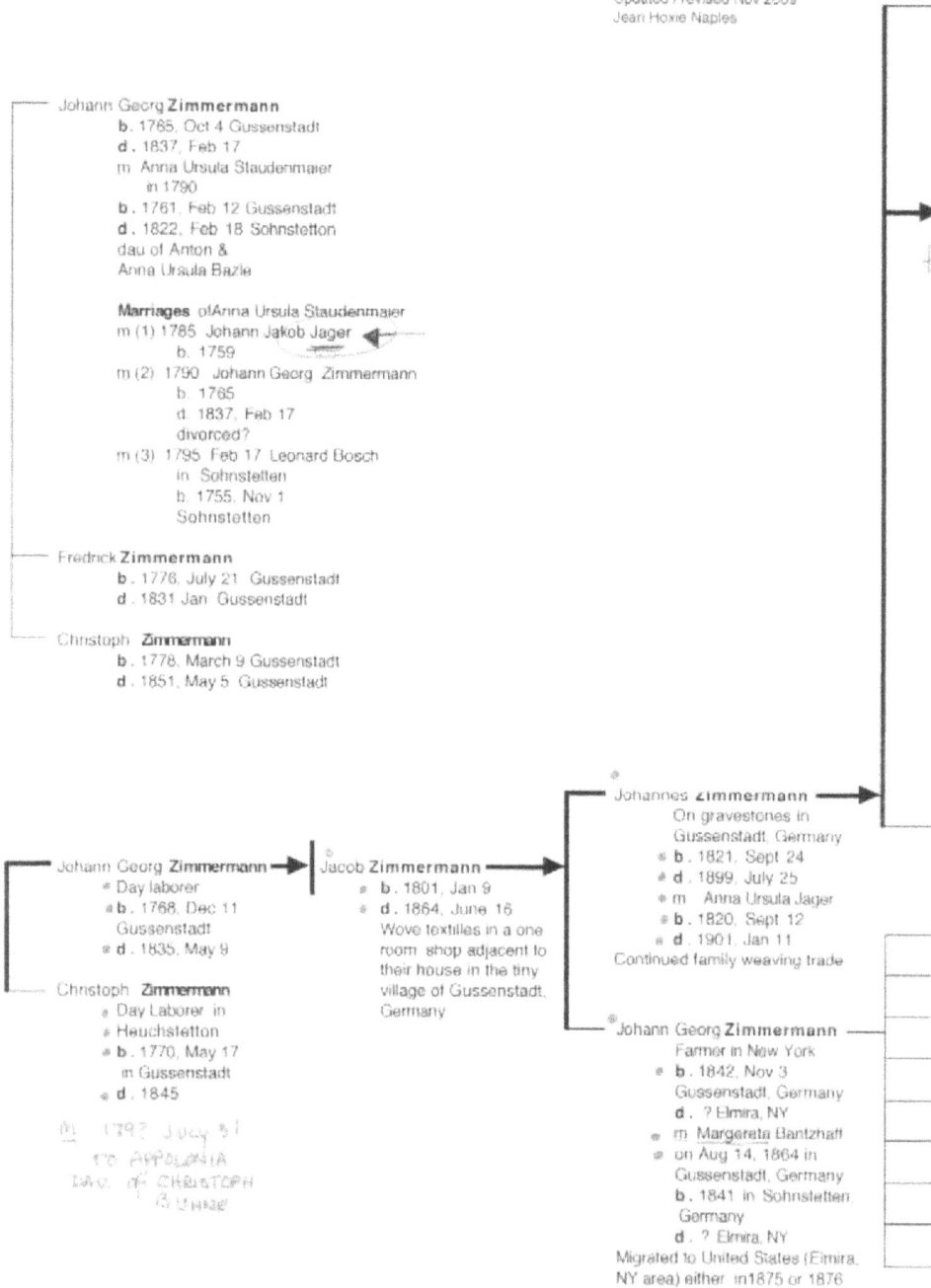

Johann Georg **Zimmermann**
  **b** . 1765, Oct 4 Gussenstadt
  **d** . 1837, Feb 17
  m  Anna Ursula Staudenmaier
    in 1790
  **b** . 1761, Feb 12 Gussenstadt
  **d** . 1822, Feb 18 Sohnstetton
  dau of Anton &
  Anna Ursula Bazle

  **Marriages** of Anna Ursula Staudenmaier
  m (1) 1785  Johann Jakob Jager
      b . 1759
  m (2)  1790  Johann Georg  Zimmermann
      b . 1765
      d . 1837, Feb 17
      divorced?
  m (3)  1795  Feb 17  Leonard Bosch
      in  Sohnstetten
      b . 1755, Nov 1
      Sohnstetten

Fredrick **Zimmermann**
  **b** . 1776, July 21  Gussenstadt
  **d** . 1831 Jan  Gussenstadt

Christoph  **Zimmermann**
  **b** . 1778, March 9 Gussenstadt
  **d** . 1851, May 5  Gussenstadt

Johann Georg **Zimmermann**
  Day laborer
  **b** . 1768, Dec 11
  Gussenstadt
  **d** . 1835, May 9

Christoph  **Zimmermann**
  Day Laborer  in
  Heuchstetton
  **b** . 1770, May 17
  in Gussenstadt
  **d** . 1845

M  1792 July 5?
TO  APPOLONIA
DAU. of CHRISTOPH
    BUHME

Jacob **Zimmermann**
  **b** . 1801, Jan 9
  **d** . 1864, June 16
  Wove textiles in a one
  room  shop adjacent to
  their house in the tiny
  village of Gussenstadt,
  Germany

Johannes **Zimmermann**
  On gravestones in
  Gussenstadt, Germany
  **b** . 1821, Sept 24
  **d** . 1899, July 25
  m   Anna Ursula Jager
  **b** . 1820, Sept 12
  **d** . 1901, Jan 11
Continued family weaving trade

Johann Georg **Zimmermann**
  Farmer in New York
  **b** . 1842, Nov 3
  Gussenstadt, Germany
  **d** . ? Elmira, NY
  m  Margereta Bantzhaff
  on Aug 14, 1864 in
  Gussenstadt, Germany
  **b** . 1841 in Sohnstetten
  Germany
  **d** . ? Elmira, NY
Migrated to United States (Elmira,
NY area) either in 1875 or 1876

**Chart 3, p.2**

282

# Appendix B
# John Zimmermann's Family Timeline
### Prepared by
### Jean Hoxie Naples
### December 15, 2009

*Dec 15, 2009*
*Jean Hoxie Naples*

JHN-    Jean Hoxie Naples
AC-    Aunt Cil Hoxie & Ben Fleet
MB-    Mike Bowman- church historian
MaB-    Mary Bacon (Deer Park, A History)
BSZ-    Barbara S. Zimmermann, wife of Al Z
GH-    George Hill, son-in-law of Al Zimmermann
AM-    Anne Mitchell (Kellenbenz family)
KFL-    Katchie Rigg Lee, daughter of Lillian Z
PS-    Philip Scranton's Figured Tapestry
obit-    obituary, of which there are three

### John   Zimmermann (1855-1936)
*"Zimmermann means carpenter in German"*

1855 Nov 28

John Zimmermann is born in the tiny village of **Gussenstadt**, (east, southeast of Stuttgart), Wurttemberg, Germany     -JHN
He is the second child and second son of Johann and Anna Ursula Yaeger Zimmermann.    -GH
He will represent the third generation in his family to manufacture textiles. The family "factory" is a tiny house with one factory room attached.
He attends a technical school (engineering school)   - BSZ

"Barbara and Albert Zimmermann in 1937 went to see that house in the Swabian Alb. One took a train from Stuttgart to a small town, then changed to a cable car, and finally did the last part on foot up steep mountain paths, crossed by geese. They found the small house with the weavers shack in the back where he learned the trade from his father. Apparently his father was harsh and brutal. He never spoke of him or his mother."    -KFL

1870-71    Franco-Prussian (Germany) War

1872    Elmira, NY - City Directory
Jacob **Schwartz** is listed as living in Elmira, NY. He is 18 years old, one year older than our John Z (1855) and he is a law student in Elmira. Jacob was born in Gussenstadt, Germany and has a sister Maria Schwartz (1852) who is married to Michael **Bantzhaff** (born 1845 in Sohstetten, Germany which is 2 1/4 miles north of Gussenstadt). Michael has a sister Margaretha Bantzhaff (born 1841) who is married to Johann George Zimmermann (born 1842 in Gussenstadt). Johann George Zimmermann is our John's uncle. -JHN

1874 Sep    John Zimmermann (almost 19) immigrates to US from the port of Hamburg, or Bremen, Germany. He stays in Elmira (Chemung County),

*\* = graphic/photo to follow*

**1855-1874**

## 1874-1876

NY before going to Phila. Elmira is a town which has numerous German immigrants. His arrival to the US (port unknown) is confirmed by his statement in the 1900 Census.    -JHN

1875     On the heels of John's immigration to Elmira is Maria & Michael Bantzhaff whose first child George E. Bantzhaff is born in Elmira Sept 9 1875 Possibly journeying with this couple is John's uncle Johann Georg Zimmermann and his family. Johann Georg's sixth child Martin Albert Z is born in Elmira May 30 1876. Johann and Michael live next door to each other in the township of Elmira and are listed as being farmers in the 1880 census.    -JHN

An immigrant initially had to register an "**Intent**" **statement** and then live in the US five years before they could get their nationalization papers and become a citizen.    -JHN

1876

May 10  - Nov 10

"Being attracted to Philadelphia by the **Centennial   Exposition** in 1876, John (now 21) recognized in the exhibits of American textile mills that there was a good opening in this field for a man of his training and experience."   -obit

"Soon after his arrival in Philadelphia, John Zimmermann contracts pneumonia and becomes very ill. He is hospitalized at the **German Hospital of Philadelphia** which was then located at Girard and Corinthian St (20th & 21st)." It provided the German-speaking emigres with a medical facility in which their mother tongue was spoken. Later, in 1917 this hospital moved and was renamed Lankenau Hospital.  -JHN

While in the hospital he meets some weavers who work in Philadelphia's textile industry and John decides to remain in Philadelphia. -KFL

"Some of the weavers are members of the Reorganized Church of Jesus Christ of Latter Day Saints (RLDS)  and later John becomes a devout member."   -GH

On a 1875 map of Phila a German Ref. Church, a German Central Market and a German Lutheran Church are located within blocks of this hospital. This little German section of Phila is just across the Schuylkill River from the 1876 Centennial fairgrounds. Many German textile workers are living here.  -JHN

"John was a gifted weaver, and he initially supported himself by selling his own woven rugs from a pushcart in downtown Phila."    -GH

# 1876-1881

**Note:** During this time it was a common practice for men to rent a hand loom (27" wide), buy the necessary weaving materials, and then work out of their own homes. Selling their products was not easy.    -JHN

1880   Jan 16
            Court of Common Pleas #2 for the County of Phildelphia.
                Naturalization  papers
        Mar 31
            John applies for a passport
                " I am a naturalized and loyal citizen of the United States, and
            about to travel abroard.." (presumably Germany)
            His description on the application: 24 years old,  stature- 5'61/2",
            forehead- low; eyes- brown; nose- proportionate; mouth- proportionate;
            chin- round; hair- brown; complexion- healthy,  face- oval.
                Included in this application by the official submitter    " Enclosed,
            please find Certificate of Naturalization, of John Zimmermann for whom
            you will be kind enought to transmit a passport to"

            **Note:** On this early document we have John's actual signature as  "John
            Zimermann".  Above the first "m" is a dash which at first appeared to be a
            smear from doting the "i".  Discovered on an 1874 Hamburg emmi-
            gration list of various "zimmermanns" was the name  "zimerman" with
            dashes above the first "m" and the last "n".  I believe this was an old world
            method used for abbreviating the full name  This is maybe why in
            America many "undashed" and various spellings appear .
                Also true, as shown on census documents, passenger lists, etc .
            names were often orally given but spelled incorrectly by the person who
            recorded the information -JHN

        Apr 7  John is issued a **Passport**    -JHN

    1881        Evakaterina (Eva **Kathryn**) Kellenbenz (on 1900 census) arrives in US
            She is John's future wife.     -JHN
            Eva Kathryn and her sister Clara immigrated to the US from Stuttgart,
            Germany. They came under the sponsorship of a German Lutheran
            pastor who arranged for young Germans who wanted to immigrate to find
            work in Phila. The two sisters worked as domestics in a Philadelphia
            home. -KFL

            Johann **Georg** Zimmermann (on 1910 census), age 30 arrives in US
            He is John's older brother,  born June 5, 1851 in Germany     -JHN

    1881        **Gopsill's** Directory (Philadelphia)    -JHN
            Georg Zimmermann, designer,  (is living at)
                *       2259 Amber St

                        page 3

## 1881-1885

Archibald Cameron, carpets,
* 2229 Amber St, workshop
* 362 Stella Ave, home

**no** John Z listed
**no** K Kellenbenz listed

Georg's location, called the "**Kensington**" area in Phila, may have influenced John to leap from the Girard Ave German area to here. Possibly this is how John came to know Archibald Cameron who had his workshop on the same block where George is living. -JHN
Nearby is a John Bromley Mill where for several years John worked -obit

There are also three other Zimmermann families living in this same area. They are not part of our family line but it is interesting that Josep Zimmermann (54), baker; wife Josephine (48), children John (26), Lizzie (22), Emma (20), Mary (18) and Catharine (10) are listed as living at 2242 Amber St.

1882     **Georg** Zimmermann marries Maria, last name unknown - On the 1900 census she states she was born June 1856 in Pennsylvania. Both her parents were born in Germany, immigrated to US before her birth. -JHN

1882     Chart for manufacturers of cotton goods and carpets in Philadelphia

| | # of establishments | men workers | women | youths | total | product value |
|---|---|---|---|---|---|---|
| carpets | 237 | 6402 | 3622 | 1019 | 11043 | $20,300,445 |
| cotton goods | 81 | 3332 | 5019 | 1172 | 9523 | $13,110,033 |

1884 Jan 20   John Zimmermann is baptised into the Reorganized Church of Jesus Christ of Later Day Saints (**RLDS**) in the Phila branch -AC

1885     John goes into partnership with **Archibald Cameron** who is also a member of the RLDS church in Phila. -obit, -MB
The company becomes **Cameron and Zimmermann** and is listed in Gopsill's Directory of 1890 as being located at 2011 Ella St (later called Arizona) -JHN
Their products (Turkey red damask table covers and similar fabrics) become popular -Obit
The **Wasserman** Brothers Company (Joseph, Isaac, Benjamin and Howard) are the sole distributors for the products produced by the Cameron and Zimmermann Mill. -obit
**Note:** Wassermann Bros. Co is located at 240 Church St ( 1/2 block north of Market ) as indicated in Gopsill's Phila City Directory of **1890**
They were initially importers of fine linens and other textiles before representing Cameron & Zimmermann. Their homes are located at 1338

page 4

## 1885-1889

& 1406 Franklin (between 7th & 8th streets), just a few blocks north of Girard Ave.

Members of a Phila **RLDS** branch are meeting at **Eureka Hall**, 11th and Girard Ave possibly to accomondate the branch's German textile workers.     - MB

Oct 15   Thurdsay
John Zimmermann (age 30) marries Evakaterina (Eva **Kathryn**) Kellenbenz (age 30) in Phila. She is the third child of sixteen children born to **Clara** (Gretzinger) and Johann **Michael** Kellenbenz. She and two younger sisters are the only ones to survive to adulthood. She was born on Sept 18, 1855 in the tiny village of Kleineislingen, Donaukreis, Wurttemberg, Germany.    -AM, -JHN
Note: Klein eislingen is slightly east of Stuttgard.      -JHN

Eva Kathryn is a German Lutheran and remained so all of her life. She performed her duties as the wife of a RLDS member on special occasions but was not active in that church.     - KFL

Where the couple lives after they are married is **unknown**. A German speaking neighborhood would have been ideal.
"Eva Kathryn never spoke fluent English, German was the language in the home. John spoke English but with a heavy German accent. " -KFL
Their children spoke German as well.    -JHN

1886 Jul 20   **Clara** Zimmermann is born to John and Eva Kathryn Zimmermann.
address **unknown**
1887 Dec 25 **Anna** Zimmermann is born to John and Eva Kathryn Zimmermann
address **unknown**

1888  Jun   **Georg** (age 36), John's older brother is now back in Germany where his third child is born. His family now consists of wife Maria (35), daughter Anna (3), son John (2) and new born son George

1889   In **Gopsill's** Phila City Directory  -JHN

John ZImmermann (Cameron & Zimmerman) is listed as living at
*    2522 Fillmore, which is 1/2 block south of the **Episcopal Hospital** at Front and Lehigh Ave. This is the Kensington area where George first was living. Cameron & Zimmermann's factory is 3 blocks southwest of here. This is the earliest address we have for John & his family.

Georg Zimmermann, designer, is living at
*    316 Huntingdon Ave

page 5

## 1890-1895

1890

Census  Most of the 1890 Federal Census Records for the whole country were destroyed by fire.

Gopsill's Phila City Directory of 1890    -JHN

John ZImmermann (Cameron & Zimmerman) is listed as living at
*        2812 N 5th St. (newly built)
Georg Zimmermann, designer, is living at
*        316 Huntingdon Ave
Archibald Cameron, (Cameron & Zimmermann), cotton goods,
*        2011 Ella St., mill
*        2054 E. Cumberland Ave, home

Jul 10  Emily K Zimmermann is born to John and Eva Kathryn Zimmermann -MB
She may have been the first to be born in their new house   -JHN

?       Membership in the church at the Eureka Hall drops to 44 members  -MB

1891 Jul 13  Archibald  Cameron John's partner, dies      -MB

1892 Jun 6  John Zimmermann Jr is born to John and Eva Kathryn Zimmermann  -MB

Aug 26 Newspaper item. "Cameron &  Zimmerman, Philadelphia, tapestry manufacturers, enlarged facilities."     -MB

Nov     The church branch leaves Eureka Hall at 11th and Girard Ave   -MB

1893     The World's Columbian Exposition in Chicago presents to the American public the Turkish theme- Ottamans, divans, turkish carpets, and other exotic items of decor. The impact takes off like wildfire  -JHN

Aug     Georg, brother of John, is now in Arkansas where his last child Walter is born.

1894     Graceland  College in Lamoni, Iowa is founded

Dec 4 William "Bill" Zimmermann is born to John and Eva Kathryn ZImmermann  -JHN

1895 Jul  The church has been meeting regularly at 5th and Huntingdon. -MB
Note: This is one block south of where John is now living.   -JHN

1895     In Gopsill's Phila, Pa Directory  -JHN

# 1895-1897

Wassermann Brothers & CO., **linens**, (importing)
*       231 Church St.
John Zimmerman, **upholsterer's mtls** (materials)
*       E. Cambria & Ormes, mill  (This is shown on the city atlas map as a mill but not named)
*       520 Somerset, home. This is just 1/2 block south from where he was living before.

Not listed:     **Georg** Zimmermann (may still be in Arkansas)
                Cameron & ZImmermann (John evidently is no longer
                working as Cameron & Zimmermann)
                Phila Tapestry Mill.
**City Atlas** of 1895
                A carpet mill is shown at the **old** Cameron & Zimmermann
                site at 2011 Ella St. but is not named.
                Allegheny & Howard (future site of Phila Tapestry Mills) has
                not been developed  (no buildings).

At some point John Zimmermann goes into partnership with the Wasserman brothers who were the sole distributors for Cameron & Zimmermann products. The new company is called **Phila Tapestry Mill**. The Wassermann brothers Joseph, Isaac and Benjamin handle the sales and finance while John with his technical & mechanical inventiveness runs the mill.
    He attracts fellow German workers to come and work for them. The new company makes rapid progress and soon gains a leading position in the industry.  -obit

1896    John has a formal portrait taken of his family    -GH

1897 Jan 14 **Emilie K** Zimmermann age 6 1/2 **dies** in a diphtheria epidemic. She was the third daughter, third child to be born to John and Eva Kathryn Zimmermann. Burial is in Greenmount Cemetery- 4301 N Front St. in Phila. -MB
    NOTE:  On her death certificate it states the family is living at
            610 W. **Lehigh** Ave.

Sep 13 **Lily Mae (Lillian)** Zimmermann is born to John and Eva ZImmermann
            "Legend has it that the two older sisters 11 and 9 so disliked their German names that they persuaded the parents to let them name the new baby "Lily Mae". She was called Lillian and she didn't discover her real birth name until she had to apply for her birth certificate for a passport many years later "      -KFL
            Note: 1897 is the year she gave for her birth year when she applied for a

## 1897-1900

passport in 1923 - JHN

1898     **Philadelphia Tapestry Mill** and one other mill are the first in the United States to replicate 'Gobelins'- (Artloom's Couch Cover, persian motif)
       "Gobelins were considered to represent European finery. It gave them a huge competitve edge over other mills."      -PS
Note: It appears that the mill may have moved into their new building at Allegheny and Howard (near Front). The first time the mill is shown on an atlas of the City of Phila is in 1901    -JHN

1899 Mar     Joseph **Wasserman** marries Edith Stix in St. Louis, Missouri

Jul 25     John Z's father, Johann Zimmermann, **dies** in Gussenstadt, Germany, age 77      -JHN

Aug 24     "Eva" (age 44), Clara (13) and "Lilly" (2) Zimmermann depart from Hamburg, Germany on board the ship "Auguste Victoria". They sail to the ports of Southampton, England and Cherbourg, France before arriving in NY. Her husband John is not listed as being with them. This visit may have been to help John's mother after the funeral   -JHN

      "For the most part, passports were not required of US citizens for foreign travel until WWI. An Executive Order was given in 1915, and then later an act of Congress given in 1918, established the passport requirement for citizens traveling abroad. This law lapsed with the formal termination of WWI through treaties with Germany, Austria, and Hungary in 1921. In 1941, with the onset of WWII, the Congressional act of 1918 was reinstated. U.S. citizens have been required to carry a passport for foreign travel ever since." -JHN

### Phila Mills strike  -MB

1899 Dec 1     800 textile workers go on strike demanding 55 hour work week and 10 cent increase in hourly overtime.

Dec 2     24 Kensington mills are forced to shut down, affecting 3000 supporting workers. Many members of the church are employed by at least 5 carpet manufactures in **Kensington**. The largest is the Philadelphia Tapestry Mills, owned by church member John ZImmermann and the Wasserman brothers.

Dec 11     Some weavers, who are church members, return to work.

Dec ?     John Zimmermann brings in 31 non-union Church members from the Baldwin, MD branch to resume work at the looms.

Dec 22     Fellow weaver and church member **Hosea H. Bacon** (wife is Dora) convinces his fellow Saints to join the strike

1900 Feb 1     13 weavers (unknown church affiliation) return to Zimmermann's mills

page 8

290

## 1900-1902

Feb 27  Strike called off

John Zimmermann is offered the Phila Bishopric through the General Church, but declines at this time  -MB

1900      **Census**  June 6

John Zimmermann (44), manufacturer of **upholstery** goods, is living at
*        610 Lehigh Ave. across the street from Fairhill Reservoir.
Wife: Kathryn (44), Clara (13), Annie (12), John (7), Willie (5), Lillie (2), Amelia Leffler (20)- maid.   John owns house

Georg Zimmerman (48), designer, is renting a house at
*        2817 Lawrence St. (two blocks east of where John used to live).
Wife: Maria (47), Anna (15)- milliner, John (14), George (11) and Walter (6)

Walter H Geissinger (41) is living at
*        1512 Allegheny Ave- John's future home.  Walter bought this house in 1900.
Wife: Mary A. (40), Walter (12), Margaret S Coon (71) mother-in-law, and Eugene Peterson (25).

Aug 30  John Zimmermann buys from John B Mayer a lot which he hopes will represent the first permanent location of a **RLDS** church in Phila. This is located on Ontario St  between Howard and Hope in Phila.  -MB, -JHN
This lot is located one block north of where John Z's company Phila Tapestry Mill is now located.
Across the street from the new church site is a public bath house  The church hopes to attract new members at this location.

1901
Jan 11 John's mother, **Anna  Ursula** Jager Zimmermann, **dies** in Gussenstadt, Germany and is buried next to her husband.  -GH

May    Construction begins on the new **RLDS** Church in Phila
Dec 1  First services held. The congregation finally has a permanent place of worship after a wandering career since 1868.  -MB

1902
Mar 30  **Clara** Zimmermann (age 15 1/2) is baptized    -MB

Apr 19  John Zimmermann buys from Wm. Henkel a lot at
*        **Luray** St. E. 5th St. - MB
Between 1903 and by 1910 Roosevelt Boulevard is built just 1/2 block

## 1902-1903

north of here.
Other interesting observations about this area   -JHN
        John B. Mayer has several large unbuilt properties just a block
south of here. He's the one that John bought the church property from.
        James E. Cooper & **M. Ehret , Jr** own a huge undeveloped city
block just a block northeast of here.  Coincidently, M. Ehret Jr is shown
on a 1901 atlas as living at 1510 Allegheny Ave, next door to
Geissenger.

Jun 11

**Albert** Walter Zimmermann is born at home (610 W. Lehigh Ave) to John
& Eva Kathryn Zimmermann. He is the last of their children.  -GH

1903          "About 1903, they (John Zimmermann & family) moved to a house at
              **1512   Allegheny** in the developing north of the city. The street was famous
              for the large homes and beautiful gardens. They had a large domestic
              staff, colored maids, chauffeur- many girls brought over from Germany
              and trained to do domestic work in America."   -KFL

              John is the 3rd owner of this house since it  first appeared on the City
              Atlas Map of Philadelphia in **1875**    -JHN

              John Z **Sr's** house on 1512 Allegheny Ave as described by his grand-
              daughter Cil Hoxie Fleet who lived next door (born 1919)
                      What's at 1512?
              Pantry (as BIG as a kitchen)
              Kitchen
              Laundry room
              Breakfast Room for 12
              Dining Room for 24 or more!
              Piano Room (where casket usually goes)
              Long whatever room! Overflow from the huge dining room
              Front door that none used-
              entrance at side of house
              Staircase (exhausted after climb up stairs)
              Sewing  Room
              Living Room with fireplace, windows looking at 3119 (Cil's parents
              house)
              Huge Bath room with stained glass window- many chamber pots for all
              the Z family, kept under bed
              Master bedroom- 2 other bedrooms
              another flight of stairs where Mom, Lil, Anna hung at ; Bath
              3 maids
              House on busy Allegheny Ave, Trolleys going by
              Big yard and Big Garage for 3 cars and chauffer quarters

                              page 10

                                292

## 1903-1905

Apr 3    Ad for "Man and Wife"- Respectable young colored couple, man to wait
         and be generally useful, wife to cook; reference required. Southeast
         corner 16th and Allegheny ave."    -MB

Apr 26   Ad for " Special built four passenger Winton Automobile. with full top  in
         perfect order. Southeast corner 16th and Allegheny avenue"   -MB

Oct 3    Ad for  " A four passenger Winton Automobile, practically new; a good hill
         climber, owner has ordered a "1904 Winton." Seen at S. E. corner 16th
         and Allegheny ave. "    -MB

1904 Nov 5   **George** Zimmermann, of Philadelphia, Pennsylvania,  (brother of John
             Zimmermann) files a patent (has invented certain improvements) for a
             **Loom** for **Weaving   Double-Pile   Fabric** -JHN

1904-6   Phila Tapestry Mills promotes a major ad campaign for "**Artloom
         Tapestries**" a division of **Phila  Tapestry  Mills** -JHN
         Their ads started showing up in the fall of 1904.
                  "They were considered 'pioneers' in mass advertizing and they
         prospered mightily" - American Carpet & Upholstery Journal     -PS
                  "Prominent in their line are the Moquette Couch Covers and some
         unique tapestries made with a rise-and-fall Jacquard machine which Mr.
         Zimmermann  has developed." -obit
                  "Curtains, Couch Covers and Table Covers   woven by the
         Largest Tapestry Mill in America" - Artloom ad

1905 Jan 18

         John Zimmermann, of Philadelphia, Pennsylvania. Assignor to
         Philadelphia Tapestry Mills files for 3 patents:
                  **Pile   Gage** and 2 **Woven  Pile  Fabric**      -JHN

Apr 15   John Zimmermann becomes a **RLDS   Bishop** for the New York and Phila
         districts in a ceremony held at the RLDS headquarters in Lamoni, Iowa

?        **George** Zimmermann begins manufacturing   -JHN
                  "George Zimmermann, Fairhill & Rockland St. (5th-6Th W.
         Rockland) is about to go into the manufacture of **upholstery** goods at this
         address. He has already purchased 2 looms which he will operate by
         gas power." (This is 3 blocks north of John 's lot at Luray & 5th -JHN)
                  - 1905 Textile World Record,  pub. Lord & Nagle Co Phila., PA

Nov 14   **George** Zimmermann, of Philadelphia, Pennsylvania, files a patent for a
                  **Woven  Pile  Fabric** -JHN

Dec 5    **George** is granted his patent for:
                  **Loom** for **Weaving  Double-Pile  Fabrics** (#806,729)
         This loom produces 2 independent fabrics, each with a cut pile       -JHN

page 11

# 1906

John's 1905 patents for **Pile Gage** (#813,132) and **Woven Pile Fabric** (#813,130 and #813,131) are granted and issued -JHN

"My invention relates to cut pile fabrics having outer and inner planes of wefts; and it consists in weaving a double cloth after the manner hereinafter described and illustrated in the accompanying drawings...... The pile is cut in the usual manner during the process of weaving, so as to produce **two distinct fabrics** when finished, or this can be done after the **cloth** is off the loom by machine specially constructed for that purpose. " - Patent description

It was supposedly these three patents which were responsible for a new rug manufacturing department to be added to the Philadelphia Tapestry Mills according to a company publication: **Artloom Corporation, A Decade of Progress 1937-1947**, c1948  The patents were originally for the manufacturing of fabrics but " these patented machines were peculiarlly adapted to the manufacture of rugs".  The new department was called **Artloom Rug Co.**  -JHN

" Artloom started operations with a triple advantage over competing rug mills because of its exclusive, patented machinery which made possible these revolutionary advances in rug manufacture:
(1) rugs could be woven in nine-foot widths instead of the traditional twenty-seven inch strips;
(2) the patented weaves speeded up the output of each loom;
(3) rugs could be woven face to face and then split apart, two rugs being produced by the same labor and machinery formerly required for one"

NOTE  The first patent to mention the third feature (specifically for rugs) was invented by John Zimmermann **Jr** in March of 1931 which is listed in this work -JHN

"The inevitable result of this mechanical superiority was to shift the major emphasis of the Philadelphia Tapestry Mills to its Artloom Rug Mills department  Artloom's products were so far superior to their competition and were priced so much more attractively, that success was instant and spectacular." -Artloom Corporation, A Decade of Progress 1937-47 c1948  - GH

?     John Z. is listed as living at 1512 Allegheny Ave. in the RLDS church directory  -MB
Note  This is the first official document  we have with this address  -JHN

May 5    John Zimmermann, of Philadelphia, Pennsylvania, Assignor to Philadelphia Tapestry Mills files a patent for a **Pile fabric**  -JHN

# 1906-1908

? John has **formal family portrait** made    -KFL
"All the children were well educated. The boys went to Phila
Central High School and then to University of Pennsylvania. The girls
went to Girl's High. Clara went to Domestic Science at Drexel, and
continued with music study privately. All the girls played the piano but
Clara was the most professional, she continued to play all her life." -KFL

? The annual church conference which had been held in Lamoni, Iowa is
now moved  to the church's new headquarters in Independence, Mo -MB
1907 Jan The Herald (church newspaper) located in Lamoni burns down. Many
records are destroyed in this fire.       -MB
Jan 21 Formal dedication of the new RLDS "**Kensington   area**" church  at Ontario
and Howard (PA).
**Clara** Zimmermann (20) is the organist at this special event.
Prophet **Joseph   Smith** III (1832- 1914) and his son Frederick are given a
tour of Phila by  Mrs. John Zimmermann (**Eva   Kathryn**) and a Mrs.
Robinson. The Smith's and the Zimmermann families form a close bond
that lasts for decades.    -MB
Membership of the church is 167. The church is free of debt       -MB

1907  Apr 9 **George** Zimmermann is granted his patent for **Woven  Pile  Fabric**
(#849,877)   -JHN

May 28 John's patent for **Pile  Fabric** is granted (#855,153)     -JHN

1908  Mar 8 **George** Zimmermann, of Philadelphia, Pennsylvania,  files another
patent for **Woven  Pile  Fabric**    -JHN

* Apr-Sep Issue of Textile World Record:
"Artloom **Rug** Co operating about 25 looms on **seamless  rugs**,
report that the plant will be greatly increased within a short time. The
production is sold through W.G. Hockridge & Co, New York
The mill is located at Allegheny & Front "
**Note**: this is the earliest documented acknowledgement of Artloom Rug
Co    -JHN

? The Mass. District **RLDS** church  purchases land in **Onset**, Mass so they
can have summer reunions.    -JHN
Jul? The RLDS conducts a camp meeting at Onset, pitching white tents
throughout the treed acreage.  Prophet Joseph Smith comments on
Albert Hoxie's (Al-2)  ability to stir up members to sing as he leads them
with his violin; and that John Zimmermann Jr, as a leader of the Phila
group, is also there.      -MB

page 13

## 1908-1910

❀ Dec 29 **George** Zimmermann is granted his patent for **Woven Pile Fabric** (#908,371)  -JHN

1909  "Of the $33,000,000 worth of cotton goods made in Pennsylvania
 $7,238,999 was the value of the lace,
 $4,163,683, the value of tapestries;
 $1,072,348 of all other upholstery goods, or a total of
 $12,473,000 for **upholstery** goods."
- Manufacturing in Philadephia 1638 - 1912 by John J. MacFarlane, A.M.

* Mar Issue of Textile World Record, Lord & Nagle Co. under "mill news"- page 724
 "Pennsylvania, Philadelphia- an **addition** 58' x 86', to cost in the neighborhood of $30,000, will be built to the plant of the **Phila Tapestry Mills.**, N.E. corner of Howard St and Allegheny. The addition will be 5 stories high."

❀ ? At some point late in life **Eva Kathryn** Zimmermann developes **aplastic anemia.** "Anna and Clara became surrogate mothers for the younger kids. Eva Kathryn was often fatigued and the remedy at that time was to eat liver once or even twice a day according to what Lillian related to Katchie."  -KFL

1910 **Census** April
Georg Zimmermann (59), designer, **textile work**, living at
* 529 Rockland St.  He owns this house.
Georg is listed as a **Widower** (when Maria died is unknown), children Anna (27); John (26) -designer- **textile** work; George (23) - foreman- textile mill; and Walter (17). In this census he states that he and his parents were born in Germany. And that he came to this country in 1881.

John Zimmerman Sr, manufacturer of **rugs** living at
* 1512 Allegheny Ave.
Wife: Catherine (sp)(55), Clara (23), Anna (21), John (17), William (15), Lillian (12), and Albert (7)

Johnson (Silvenon) Diamond (48), manufacturer of Ladies ? is living at
* **3119 N. 16th St** - This abuts John's backyard (south)-
Wife- Bertha (34), Paecli (6), Wilhemina (5), Zelman (3), brothers: Ralph (22) and Elisa (19). The Diamonds came to US in 1880 from Germany.
Note: This north section of the house (duplex) becomes Albert and

page 14

## 1910-1912

Clara Z Hoxie's home sometime after their marriage in 1911.

June 2- Sep 10
**Clara** Zimmermann goes on a three month cruise visiting the Azores, Gibraltar, Italy, Switzerland, Germany, France and England. Arriving back in the port of Phila aboard the ship "Friesland" she is greeted by "Momma, Poppa, sister and brother John Jr. and "Mae" according to her journal.

Dec
"**Lion Hosiery Mill, Zimmerman Bros**, proprietors, is **now** located in more commodius and convenient quarters at the SW corner of Hancock and Turner Streets. New knitting machines have been installed."
'The Textile American', - Manufacturing in Phila      -JHN
Note This is the first time that this mill and owners have been mentioned. Unknown as to who the "Zimmermann Bros" are.

1910-11
The RLDS Kensington Church in Phila adds onto its east side, and includes a fully equipped gym below   -MB

1911
In addition to Phila Tapestry Mills another mill is established **Phila Pile Fabric Mills**. It makes imitation "seal" plush fabrics for the coat and suit trade.        This may be located in the new building.

Oct 10 Tuesday
John's eldest daughter **Clara Zimmermann** marries **Albert Nickerson Hoxie II** at John's home at 1512 W. Allegheny Ave. Albert is the son of Albert Nickerson Hoxie and Aravilla Follet of Boston, Mass.
Clara and Al-2 at some point make their home at 3119 N. 16th St which is just behind her father's house. Both this house and her father's are indicated on the **1875** Atlas of Phila. Clara's house is a duplex with an adjoining large side lot. It was a wedding present from her father. The house was unusual in that its' main entrance was located on the long northern side of the house and not on the street front   -JHN
"Clara's father's house could be easily accessed by her. He adored her and he in turn remained perhaps the most important man in her life."      - KFL

According to family rumor, each one of John's children received a million dollars when they got married
"It seems that John Zimmermann was very, very wealthy, and a million was well within his means as a wedding gift to each child "- GH

1912
**Bromley's Tower** description of how industrialized Phila has become.
"From the tower of the Bromley Mill at Fourth and Lehigh Avenue there is within the range of vision more textile mills than can be found in

page 15

297

## 1912-1915

any other city in the world. For miles in every direction is seen the smoke of thousands of mills and factories. To the Northeast one continuous line of factories extends through Frankford to Tacony, six miles away. To the Northwest through the smoke rising from the Midvale works at Nicetown the mills of Germantown are seen. To the west another line of mills stretches to the Falls of Schuylkill and Manayunk. To the southwest is Baldwin's and other foundries and mills of that section. To the south are the hat and leather factories and to the southeast is Cramp's Shipyard and the numberless industries clustered along the river. Beyond all these are the mills and factories of South and West Philadelphia, some of them eight miles away."
- Manufacturing in Philadephia 1638 - 1912 by John J. MacFarlane, A.M

1914

Sept 18 **John Jr.** (22) , his brother **William** Zimmermann (19), along with Fletcher and Carl Schaum, two brothers who live at 1508 Allegheny, arrive in NY from a cruise on the Lusitania. 7 months later this boat is sunk by a German torpedo    -JHN
This cruise may have been a graduation gift for John Sr's sons- one graduating from college, the other from high school. -JHN

After his sons graduated from college John Z would get them jobs at the mill. This created much ill feeling with the Wassermann brothers. -KFL

Sep 30 The Phila RLDS church establishes a 2nd church, **Beacon Light Church** at 3014 E Street , north of Indiana.
After overextending their budget Bishop Zimmermann personnally advances nearly $6700 to pay down the $12,000 total cost of the effort. He often underwrote the church's efforts. This church has only 36 chartered members, while the crowded Kensington branch has exceeded 300. Included in the new members are both John Z Sr's son **William** and daughter **Anna**      -MB

Dec 10 Prophet Joseph Smith III **dies**. He is replaced by his son Frederick Smith

1915

In the 1915 Official American Textile Directory, compiled by the World Record, the following Phila., Pa mills are described:
**Phila Tapestry Mills** : Allegheny Ave & Front St; Joseph Wasserman- pres; I. (Isaac) Wasserman, tres; B (Benjamin) Wasserman, sec; John ZImmermann, vice-president and supt; Upholstery Fabrics 250 looms, steam, sell direct, Joseph Wasserman buyer
**Phila Pile Fabrics Mills:** Howard & Westmoreland St (north side of Phila Tapestry Mill complex) $100,000; Richard J Steiner, pres and supt, Isaac Wasserman, tres; Seal Plushes & Velvets; 100 broad looms, steam and electric, dye & finish, Rusch & Co, NY's agts' R.J. Steiner, buyer, buy

## 1915-1916

cotton, and silk yarns.
    **Artloom Rug Mills** : Allegheny & Front; Seamless Rugs; steam;
W.G. Hockridge & Co, 126 Fifth Ave, NY agents

    **Lion Hoisery Mill** : Mascher & Turner St. Ladies' & Misses' Ribbed
and Infants and Children's Hosiery, 240 needle, 110 latch needle knitting
machines, 50 ribbers, 10 loopers; finish; steam; sell direct, buy 18s to 50s
combed Peeler on cones. -JHN

Albert **Hoxie** (Al-2) is listed as a salesman for the Phila Pile Fabric Mill -
in his obit

Aug 10  Tuesday
John's 2nd eldest daughter **Anna  Zimmermann** marries **Richard  Carlyle
Kelley** of Lamoni, Iowa. He is the son of Edmund Levi Kelley and
Catherine Bishop. His father is prominent in the RLDS church in Lamoni
and had signed John's Bishop certificate    -JHN
    "Anna went to the University of Penna. She took additional
courses at the Philadephia Academy of Fine Arts and became a teacher
in Philadelphia Elementary Schools." -GH

Sep 1  John Zimmermann, of Philadelphia, Pennsylvania files a patent for a
        **Warp-Printing  Machine.**
    **Note:** John does not list himself as an assignor to the Philadelphia
Tapestry Mills on this patent or on any hereafter !!    -JHN

1916  Apr  Prophet Frederick **Smith** visits churches in Phila.
    Prophet Fred Smith, Clara and Al 2 in choir photo    -MB
    Choir leader Albert Hoxie II gains approval for a modern Estey Reed
organ -MB
    Note: Clara did not play the organ.    -AC

?  John's eldest son **John Jr** marries **Ethel  Kinnaman** in Kansas City, MO

Joan Catherine Kelley is born to Richard and Anna Z Kelley in Iowa
City, IA They eventually move to Elkins Park, PA and have a total of
seven children.    -AC

Aug 22  John's patent for a **Warp-Printing  Machine** is granted (#1,195,322). -JHN
    "The object of the invention is to provide a **machine** of the above
character with devices whereby the warp threads as they pass
continuously through the machine, may be supplied uniformly with
coloring matter in accordance with a predetermined pattern " - patent
description
    "This machine, which made possible the production of patterned
        page 17

# 1916-1920

-

rugs with predyed warp yarns, led to the perfection of today's fabulously successful Wilminister line!" - notes of Artloom Corp., ca 1948

1917 Apr    US declares war against Germany

It appears that this is when **Sam** is engaged as the family's chauffer, and lives in the apartment above the 3-car garage. - A. W. Z.'s passport of 1921. -JHN

Jun 5    **William** ZImmermann (age 23) files a WWI Draft Registration Card. He is a chemical engineer working for the Philadelphia Tapestry Mill. -JHN
        During WWI he serves in the U.S. Army infantry in the American Expeditionary Force with duty in Belgium or France. -GH

1918 Nov    **WWI ends**
After WWI- imitation "seal" plush fabric for coats and suits soon becomes outdated. The **Phila Pile Fabric Mill** is forced to switch to the manufacturing of furniture upholstery fabrics, drapery material (velvet) of which they produced miles of it, and plushes for the automobile trade.

1919    **Artloom Rug Mill** becomes incorporated as a separate and distinct entity

1919    John with his sons form the firm of **John Zimmermann & Sons**, Erie & Castor Aves., which manufactures mohair furniture coverings. -obit

Richard **Kelley**, now living in the Philadelphia area with his wife Anna, daugher Joan and son Richard, becomes a partner with his brother-in-law, **William** ZImmermann, in the development of a family upholstery manufacturing company, John Zimmermann & Sons. The business prospered and provided well for the family.    - GH
        Bill Zimmermann (25)- president,
            B.S. in Chemical Engineering from U. of Penna..
        Richard Kelley (37)- secretary
            Latin Teacher

It is unknown whether **John** ZImmermann **Jr** (27) was part of this company in the beginning. -JHN
        "He tried several business ventures in textiles which were unsuccessful and eventually returned to work at JZInc." -KFL

1920    **Census** Jan 13 -JHN
For some strange reason 10 dwellings were not recorded for people living in ward 38, district 1346 on Allegheny Ave. from 16th to Broad St.
        Albert & Clara Hoxie's house (last on 16th St) was next to be visited but fails to appear on the following page along with all the

## 1920-1921

dwellings on Allegheny Ave including John Z's !
Dwelling sequence went from 59 on the botttom of page 3 to 69 on the
top of page 4. -JHN

Oct 12  **Evakaterina** (Eva Kathryn) ZImmermann, age 65, wife of John
Zimmermann **dies** in Phila. She is buried nex to their daughter Emily K in
Greenmount Cemetery in Phila.  -MB
Surviving her:
    Husband    John Zimmermann, age 64
    Her daughters
        Clara Zimmermann Hoxie, age 34
          children: Al (6), John (3) Cil (1)
        Anna Zimmermann Kelley, age 33
          children: Joan (4), Richard (1), Susan (-1)
        Lilian Zimmermann, age 23
    Her sons:
        John Zimmermann, Jr., age 28
          children: Bettye(2),
        William Zimmermann, age 25
        Albert Zimmerman, age 18

### Deer Park

1921 Feb    The old Beaumont Deer Park (est. 1870s), located outside New Hope,
PA goes up for sale. This 76-acre tract is discovered by John Z, Jr while
he is riding around looking for a place to hold summer reunions for the
church (RLDS). -MaB
John Zimmermann Jr places a deposit of $500 on the Deer Park property
to hold it.    -MaB

Feb    The property is purchased for $5000 and improvements worth $18,746
began in Feb - repairs were made to the old park buildings; a kerosene
engine and generator were installed to provide electricity and to pump
water from the spring. The Commissary was reshingled and a kitchen
was added on the back, a new choir platform graced the Auditorium (built
1876); sanitary facilities were renovated. A concrete dam, seventy-five
long and two feet thick with a floodgate, stemmed a stream to form a
swimming and fishing hole. Nearby, a 12 acre athletic field was cleared
by dynamiting stumps and roots to make way for two baseball diamonds
-MaB

Mar 1    The Zimmermann family with John Zimmermann Jr (and wife Ethel)
acting as agents take title to the 76 acre **Deer** **Park** in New Hope, PA
(This remains in the Zimmermann family until it was deeded over to the
RLDS church in 1966).    MB, MaB

page 19

# 1921

First RLDS Deer Park Reunion

Jul 2    A special **reunion** **train** ran from Wayne Junction in Phila; specific cars on the regular trains from New York City and other points were connected to the train, transporting passengers to Deer Park. The Reading Railroad ran just inside the southern edge of the park, so a request from passengers halted the train short of the scheduled Reeder Station stop. Reunion-goers then climbed down the embankment, crossed the creek and climbed up the hill to the campgrounds. Luggage was shipped by train to New Hope, while John Zimmermann, Sr. arranged for trunks and camping gear to be transported to the park by truck. 100 tents had been erected. Cots, chairs and other necessities had been constructed or purchased. The park's infamous green benches were assembled by a work crew that included then President of the Reorganized Church Frederick Madison Smith. This reunion lasted two weeks.        -MaB, MB

Jul 4    Deer Park Camp celebration, locals & RLDS members attend, over 5000, including John Zimmermann Sr., owner of Phila Pile Fabric Mills (?), office located at 345 Fourth Avenue, **NYC**. (JZ Sr. is also listed as the only Gentile director of the National Farm School.)

"The first Deer Park Reunion celebrated quite a Fourth of July. A long morning of swimming postponed lunch until two o'clock. Baseball games, one with New Hope and one with Lambertville, took up the afternoon. At six-thirty the Lambertville Band began to play, 1200 people, both saints and local residents, gathered on the Athletic Field to sing familiar and patriotic songs. By the time the fireworks were ready to be displayed the crowd had swelled to approximately 3,000 with a lane of almost 200 automobiles encircling the Athletic Field. It was estimated that there were over 5000 persons roaming the grounds during the day." -MaB

The 1919-1921 Reunion Committee bore the responsibility of clearing the $24,000 debt, including the costs of land, equipment, labor, reunion expenses and $133.75 rent due the Library Company of Philadelphia under the 1861 agreement. It is probably safe to say that John Zimmermann, Sr. met most of that first reunion's cost; how much was repaid to him is unknown, and the support of the Zimmermann family was continuous.        - MaB

1921    **Lillian** M Zimmermann, daughter of John Z, is an undergraduate student at the University of Pennsylvania (class of 1921)    -JHN

Jun 20
         **Albert** Walter Zimmermann, John's youngest son applies for a passport.
                                    page 20

302

## 1921-1923

Sam, the family chauffer, acts as his witness.
Desription of Applicant:
Age 19; Stature 5' 8 1'/2"; Forehead - Medium, Eyes; Blue; Nose-Straight; Mouth - Medium; Chin- regular; Hair - Light Brown; Complexion-Fair, Face- Oval.

Jul 23 He sails on a 3 month tour which includes: Algeria, France,Switzerland, Holland & Italy. England, Scotland & Germany have been crossed out on his application. -JHN

Dec Albert **Hoxie** (Al 2) writes to his brother stating that they had had a poor business year. He encloses a statement showing what it would cost to "save" their little shore place at Cape Cod. The return address on the envelope:
**Philadephia Pile Fabric Mills** ,345 Fourth Ave., **New York** -JHN

1922 Al-2 resigns as choir director      -MB
Al-2 resigns from the Phila Pile Fabric Mills.
"It was a strained departure." -KFL

Nov 30 Thursday, Lamoni, Iowa
John Zimmermann Sr (age 66) marries **Mrs. Anna Anderson Dancer** (age 58) of 408 South State Street, Lamoni, Fayette Township, Iowa according to the Decatur County records.
She is the daughter of Andrew K. Anderson and wife Inger Ormsdotter of Lamoni, Iowa. -JHN
The marriage occurs on a Thursday. Albert Carmichael, Bishop (RLDS) performs the marriage. Witnesses are David A. Dancer of Lamoni (Anna's son) and Clara Hoxie of Phila.

Anna's first husband, David Dancer was a very successful business man in Lamoni, Iowa. He was also a devout member and generous contributor to the RLDS church located there. His first wife Rosalia died in Aug. 1893. In Nov 20, 1895 David (age 68) married Anna (age 31)   Two sons were produced by this second marriage with the last being born in 1898 in March. David dies seven months later on Oct 23   Anna at the time of his death was vice president of the state savings Bank of Lamoni and was recognized as a woman of marked business ability and unusual knowledge concerning financial affairs. (David Dancer's obit)

1923 Jan 5 **Lillian M.** Zimmermann, John's daughter, applies for a passport
Description of Applicant:
Age 25; Stature 5' 4"; Forehead- Medium, Eyes - blue, Nose-Straight; Mouth- Regular. Chin - Round, Hair - Brown, Complexion - fair; Face   Round.      -JHN

# 1923-1925

Feb 1   Thursday edition of the Lamoni Chronicle
"Mr & Mrs John Zimmermann expect to sail for a trip abroad Feb7. They will be gone about two months most of which time will be spent in cruising the Mediterranean and visiting those countries which border on the sea. They will be accompanied by Miss Lillian Zimmermann."  -JHN

Their cruise includes: Great Britain, France, Italy, Spain, Portugal, Holland, Switzerland, Egypt, Morocco, Algeria and Turkey  -JHN

"They took **Lillian**, newly graduated from the Univ of Penna with them on a 3 month cruise to the Holy Land. Lillian contracted Palestine fever while there, nearly died and the three had to leave the ship in England while she recovered in a nursing home in London."  -KFL

After their "honeymoon" Anna's sister **Nellie** moves in with them (Phila)  - AC

?   **Albert** Walter Zimmermann graduates from the University of Penna with a BS degree in Electrical Engineering, Mechanical engineering. He joins the family textile business. Later he becomes a world wide wool dealer with John Ott after serving in WWII from 10/18/42- 12/30/45. He becomes highly successful.  -GH

Jun?   John Z Sr. holding Cil Hoxie (?) at Cape Cod.  Clara would often spend part of the summer there with her children to escape the city's heat Lillian  frequently visited her and loved to fish and have clambakes  -AC

Dec   The second Phila Church (located at 3014 E St.) closes its doors after having been opened for 10 years  -MB

1924 Dec 16  All three business (Phila Tapestry Mill, Phila Pile Fabric Mill and Art Loom Rug Mill) merge into one **The Artloom Corporation** - They are still located at Howard & Allegheny.

Dec 27 Monday
John's youngest daughter **Lillian M. Zimmermann** marries **James Alma Fligg** at John's home.
    James Alma Fligg is the oldest child of a RLDS missionary, born 1899 in London City, Ontario, Canada. His parents are William Irving Fligg and Matilda Maud Quick. Jim left school in 8th grade to help support his 5 younger brothers and sisters. In 1923 he entered the University of Kansas to study electrical engineering. There he met Lillian who was an assistant to the dean.  -KFL

1925

## 1925-1927

Jan 24 **Albert W. Z.**, age 22, now 5' 10", occupation - manufacturing, is going off on a 2nd tour. He leaves NY and travels for 3 months visiting Brazil, Argentina, Peru, Chile, Bolivia, Equador, Paraguay, Uruguay, and Columbia.   -JHN

Feb 2- Mar 25
    **Cruise**  John Z Sr and Anna arrive in NY on the S.S. Reliance

?     **Graceland  College**, located in Lamoni, Iowa was established in 1894. John Zimmermann Sr. at some point has donated funds to the school and **Zimmermann  Hall** opens in 1925.   -AC
John Zimmermann's daughter Anna had married Richard C Kelley in 1915. Her father-in-law Edmund Levi Kelley was one of the projectors and promoters of Graceland College.   -JHN

1926
    Jan 29 Sunday
        John's youngest son **Albert  Walter  Zimmermann** marries **Barbara Shoemaker** in Phila. She is the daughter of Dr. William Toy Shoemaker and Mabel Warren of Philadelphia.

    June     Title to **Deer  Park** is transferred from John Zimmermann, Jr. and Ethel Zimmermann (wife) to Presiding Bishop Albert Carmichael, Trustee for the RLDS.   -MB, -MaB

    Jul 1     **Anna  Zimmermann** (42), daughter of Georg Zimmermann arrives back to NY on the S.S. Columbus from Bremen, Germany. She is listed as living at 529 Rockland St. in Phila. Unknown if Georg is still alive.   -JHN

    Aug 9     **Cruise**  John Z Sr and his wife Anna arrives in NY on the S.S. Deutschland from Hamburg, Germany.

1927
    Feb22-Mar19
        **Cruise**  John Sr. & Anna sail on SS Columbus out of NY.   JHN

    ?     Decline in the Artloom Corporation's income and assets. -PS

    ?     John is instrumental in founding the **Zimmermann  Mills,  Inc,** 21st and Allegheny, makers of furniture coverings   -Obit
        Note: His son **John Z Jr.** is president.

    Apr 3     Returning to NY on board the S.S. Avon from **Bermuda** is Clara Z. Hoxie (40), her children Al (12), John (9) and Lucile (7). Accompanying them is Clara's brother William Zimmermann (age 30) who is still living at his

## 1927-1929

parents house, 1512 Alleghney Ave.      -JHN

Jim **Fligg**, after graduating as an electrical engineer from the University of Kansas joins the family's business John Zimmermann & Son in Phila.

"The business proved to be a clash of unlike personalities. The Zimmermann boys were overpowered by a strong father and Richard Kelley (10 years older than John Jr.) who set the tone of the place.
The tension was high, all 3 sons had a series of "nervous breakdowns" (the social term sometimes used for bi-polar). In fact a wing in the Institute of the Pennsylvania Hospital was donated by them... The daily business relationships followed by weekend and vacation socializing was strangling." -KFL

1928 Mar 27 **John Z, Jr** files a patent application for **Double-Pile   Fabric**
He is listed as living - Oak Lane, Phila

1928 Apr 13 **John Z, Jr** files a patent application for **Double-Pile   Fabric**   -JHN

1928      **Deer   ParK**
The Fligg, Zimmermann, Hoxie and Wilson Cabins are erected. Prefabricated units from the Brooks Skinner Company of Quincy, Mass are assembled (leaving footprints on the Wilson Cabin ceiling) and are placed on prepared foundations, the cost for each cottage totals $5000. The Caretaker's Cottage also goes up this year.
The new tile lined swimming pool, 60' by 100' is ready for use and the new porcelain drinking fountains are installed through-out the grounds. -MaB

1929 Feb   "**John   Zimmermann,   Jr.**, Consulting Engineer of Artloom Rug Mills and President of **Zimmerman   Mills,   Inc** was recently elected a member of Sigma Xi, a national honorary scientific fraternity."      -The Pennsylvania Gazette.

Mar 23 **Cruise**  John Z Sr and Anna

Oct 29 **Stock   market   crash**

Nov 12 **John Z, Jr** files a patent application for **Double-Pile   Fabric**   -JHN

?        "Realization of the Saint's dreams stopped short with the Great Depression. The United States Bank and Trust Company of Philadephia, which held the reunion (RLDS Deer Park) account, was seized by the Secretary of Banking of the Commonwealth of Pennsylvania at the close of 1929." -MaB

page 24

306

## 1929-1931

Dec 4    Friday
John's son **William** "Bill" Zimmermann marries **Margaret Peattie Lukens** in RLDS church (Phila). She is the daughter of Edward Fell Lukens and Margaret (Patton).

?    Jim and Lillian **Fligg** start building their house on Cedar Road in Elkins Park, Pa. This is next door to the Kelley's who had already built theirs. It originally was a large farm, and the Kelleys had the woods. -KFL (Katchie is 4, Jim 1)

1930    The **Great Depression** begins

    **Census** March 31
Albert Hoxie (44), music director, is listed as living at
*    3119 North 16th St. He is **renting** this house.
Clara (42); Albert Jr (15), John (12), and Lucile (10)
John Zimmermann Sr's house at 1512 Allegheny Ave is not listed.

Jul 14    **Cruise**
Returning to NY on the S.S. Bremen from Cherbourg, France is Albert (Sr), Clara, Al (Jr), John and Lucile Hoxie. Once in NY they switch boats and continue to Boston for a summer visit at Cape Cod. -JHN

1930 Jul    Financial woes for Deer Park. **Clara** Zimmermann Hoxie loans the park $540 to pay down other obligations.    -MaB

1930    **Art Loom Corp** The original team retained a controlling interest when common and preferred shares were sold to raise added capital but the Depression triggered re-adjustments. -PS

    Common shares fell from $42 in 1928 to $2.50 in 1933 and $3.75 in 1935. -PS

1931 Mar 3    **John Z, Jr.** is granted his three patents for **Double-Pile Fabric**
    (#1,795,156, #1,795,157, #1,795,158)    -JHN
    "The principal object of my present invention is to provide an improved double pile fabric which, when cut apart, **will produce two rugs or carpets**, each of the well known **Wilton** types....
    A further object of my invention is to provide a fabric of the type aforesaid, whereby seamless **Wilton rugs of the larger or room size**, may be more economically produced than heretofore. " - patent description -JHN

    Church Reunions at Deer Park are cancelled
    page 25

# 1931-1936

Church member Ethan Wilson loses his textile mill trying to help his fellow impoverished Saints. Some are living at Deer Park as opposed to being homeless- MB

Annual Report of the Federal Trade Commission
Artloom Rug Mills, under Artloom Corporation, is charged with falsely advertizing their product as being Wiltons, told to cease until the Commission makes a judgement    -JHN

1932 Jan    Investors in the stock market become truly devastated when stocks hit bottom, far worse than the 1929 crash ("Great Oops") where stocks made a snappy comeback

1932    John Zimmermann Sr. **retires** from the textile manufacturing business. He was the vice president and general manager of the Art Loom Corp.  -obit

1933
    Apr 5  Albert Zimmermann and wife Barbara return from a vacation in Bermuda on the S.S. Monarch of Bermuda.    -JHN

    May    The Federal Trade Commission decides that Artloom cannot claim their products to be Wiltons nor use it in their advertizing.   -JHN

1934
    Jan 11-20
        **Cruise**- S.S. Statendam out of NY
        John Z. (78), Anna (69), and John Z., **Jr.** (42)
        Jr's address -  2 Surrey Road, Oak Lane, P.O. Phila., PA
        Also listed is Helen Hayes (age 45) who is living at 1512 Allegheny Ave.
        -JHN

        **photo** Men outside Kensington Church- Prophet Fred Smith, AL 2, "High Priest" John Zimmermann, Jr., and John Zimmermann Sr. -MB

1834    **Art Loom Corp's** losses are mounting to above $200,000 annually. -PS

1935    Joseph Wassermann resigns as President of the Artloom Corporation to become chairman of the board of directors.

1936 May 23 John Zimmermann Sr. **dies** of pneumonia on a Saturday evening at his home 1512 W Allegheny Ave. He was 80 years old. Following services at his home he is buried next to first wife Evakaterina and their daughter Emily K. Zimmermann in the family plot at Greenmount Cemetery in Phila. -obit

page 26

# 1936

Surviving family members are:
> His 2nd wife, Anna (age 71)
> His daughters:
>> Clara Z. Hoxie, age 49 of Phila.
>>> Her children, Albert III (22), John Z. (18), Lucile (16)
>> Anna Z. Kelley, age 48 of Elkins Park, PA
>>> Her children, Joan Catherine (20), Richard Carlyle (17), Susan Dorothea (16), Marian (15), Anita (13), Donald (12), Janet Nancy (9).
>> Lilian Z. Fligg, age 38, of Elkins Park
>>> Her children: Kathryn (10), James (7).
> His sons:
>> John Zimmermann, Jr., age 43 of Phila.
>>> His children: Bettye(18), Mary Jane (15), Carl (13), John (11).
>> William Zimmermann, age 42
>>> His children: William (6), Peggy (4),
>> Albert Zimmerman, age 34 of Haverford (?) , PA
>>> His children if born: Barbara (9), Helen (7), Warren (2)

> His sister Anna, age 78, living in Germany -BZ
> His brother Georg is not mentioned (deceased?)

"The line was 2 blocks long that came to G'Pa Z wake. Amazing, all the mill people he was so good to. Mother wanted to be buried next to him if she died in Phila. A bench there, and I'd sit on the bench and cry. Sam the chauffer, cried so when G'Pa Z died. He wasn't much comfort then." -AC

At some time after John Zimmermann's death his widow Anna removes the contents of the house at 1512 W. Allegheny Ave. and she and her sister Nellie go back to Lamoni to live with Anna's son. This occured without notice while John's daughters Clara Hoxie and Lillian Fligg were vacationing with their families at Cape Cod in the summer -AC

1936    In 1936 a Detroit based group (Chrysler) offered to buy 80,000 shares at $14 each from the Artloom Corp; a deal was quickly struck. After a spurt to $22, common stock slumped below $5 in the 1937 recession. Mounting losses brought dismissal of the company president, a holdover from the old regime but this purge did little good. -PS

1936    Joseph Wassermann sells his holdings, retires entirely from business.

1937 Jul 7    Anna Anderson Dancer Zimmermann dies in Lamoni, Iowa

page 27

# 1936-1978

Name on her tombstone: Anna Zimmermann Dancer

Sep 8   Joseph Wassermann dies in Boson, MA   -JHN
"With the post 1929 deaths of several founders (Artloom Corp);
their holdings, which had depreciated greatly in value, were divided
among heirs."   -PS

1938   Elkins Park, PA
Janet Nancy Kelley, age 10, daughter of Anna & Richard Kelley dies.
She had aplastic anemia. This is the same blood disease that her
grandmother Eva Kathryn Zimmermann had. Nancy was Katchie Fligg's
(12) main playmate and lived next door. On the morning of Nancy's
death, Jim Fligg, Katchie's father, heartbroken at the news and strained
from the various tensions occuring within the family business suffers a
heart attack and never returns to the Zimmermann Mill. -KFL

1942   1942 Phila Land Use Map
John Zimmermann's house at 1512 Alleheny is still standing
Artloom Corporation at Allegheny and Howard is still active
Zimmermann & Sons at Erie and Castor Ave is still active, shown as
Zimmerman & Sons Plush & Pile Fabric
No name shown at 22nd & Allegheny- (Zimmermann Mills)

1952   John Zimmermann (our JR) of Phila, Pa, Harold Wolf, Clifton, NJ. and
Louis Weiner, Phila, Pa file a patent for "Shrinkage Resistance
Treatment of woolen goods "

?   What happened to the ownership of John Z Sr's house (ca1875) is
unknown. It was still standing in the late 1940s. During the early 50s it
was bulldozed down, and apartment buildings replaced it by early1960s

1962   Artloom Corporation at Allegheny and Howard is shown on the 1962
Land Use Map of Phila
Zimmermann & Sons at Erie and Castor Ave is still indicated.

1963. Dec   John Zimmermann & Sons is sold   -GH

| | |
|---|---|
| 1961, July 24 | Albert Walter Zimmermann dies (age 59) |
| 1966, Sept 12 | Lillian Zimmermann Fligg dies (age 69) |
| 1968, Oct 19 | Clara Zimmermann Hoxie dies (age 82) |
| 1974, Aug 7 | Anna Zimmermann Kelley dies (age 87) |
| 1974, Oct 15 | John Zimmermann Jr dies (age 82) |
| 1978, March 14 | William Zimmermann dies (age 84) |

page 28

# Appendix C

Barbara S. Zimmermann, *Mutterings* (Wynnewood, Pa.: Livingston Publishing Co., 1969), vi, 148 pp.

[106]
## INTRODUCTION TO "MY FIRST TRIP TO EUROPE, 1937"

Perhaps this diary should not be included, but the year of my first trip to Europe was 1937, a rather uncomfortable one. We were watched with great care in Germany. An exact count was kept of the marks we spent. After two weeks in Germany I was called to the bank in Nurnberg. Of course, Daddy [Albert Walter Zimmermann, AWZ] went with me. I had spent too many marks. Fortunately, this was easily explained as I had been supporting Daddy but when my marks were gone he, in turn, would support me. But how did they do this.

Also my negative reaction to Vienna is explained by the fact that the writing was on the wall – Hitler moved in six months later. . . .

[130]
After arriving back at the Carlton [hotel, probably in Volendam, the Netherlands] we had dinner and embarked on the sleeper for Berlin. Quite the most comfortable one I've ever been on. We spent a pretty fair night and arrived at 6 A.M. which was too early.

Tuesday, Aug. 3 [1937]

Boy, what a city! It is certainly on an heroic scale. Magnificent wide streets, tremendous buildings, heavily and substantially built and beautiful. London has such charm it makes us feel at home, but it is not lovely as Berlin. We drove about this morning and gasped at the spaciousness of it all. . . .

[132]
Thursday . . . We went to the tea dance at the Eden, where we saw the only truly "smart " people we saw in all of Germany. The entire population (that is the ambulant populous) seems made up of a peasant type. In and about Berlin there is a very noticeable undercurrent of a people oppressed. No one dares say anything but it was hinted to us, in a whisper, that they have not truly forgotten the many atrocities, that they would welcome the return of a Hohenzollern, that they would like to call their souls their own. This from a veteran of the World War, who came out with one too few lungs. Hitler is much feared and is a little afraid himself! They say that in spite of four or five different Berlin newspapers none of them dare print anything but what is prescribed. . . .

[133]
Friday – left Berlin for Nurnberg, arriving in the late afternoon. This was really quite disappointing but with interesting features. It is a very large (400,000) and an industrial city. Nothing quaint about it in general but of course certain places in particular have the old world air of the picture postals. We drove Saturday to Rothenberg (50 miles) which is what we've been looking for – a town dating as early as 900 but for the most part sort of new, 1200, with its original walls in entirety, its original buildings

inside and nothing new or modern to spoil it all. It has had a population of 9000 people for about 500 years. There are no trolleys or buses or new stores. It is all we've cried for in quaintness and interest and is overlooking a most lovely valley. The country we passed thru on our drive was all farming country as is all of Germany apparently. Every inch of ground is used and worked, if necessary by soldiers. The farmers for the most part are very poor and harness their cows, not being able to afford horses. Of course this cuts down on the milk supply. All the women and children work in the fields also. Here in the south the feeling for Hitler seems stronger. Perhaps it is a more ignorant or, I should say, a more poorly informed class, but it is certainly in the majority. There is bitterness for certain of his policies and great admiration for others, in which we must admit we can join [sic: she doesn't say which of Hitler's policies they admire], but on the whole there seems to be more loyalty. There are no longer Boy Scouts in Germany; that is in the international sense. They are Hitler Boys in black and khaki and of course were not represented [134] at the Jamboree in Holland. (44 other countries were! Italy and Spain were among those missing).

## HEIDELBERG

Sunday – left Nuremburg for Heidelberg and by the way we are having some bad heat, or first so we cannot complain, a little hard on tired feet however. Heidelberg is a perfect city, built along the banks of the Necktar, with mountains as a background and the beautiful castle partly in ruins, set halfway up the mountains.[1] . . .

Monday – Stuttgart – On arriving we immediately set out to see Annie, Bab's and Nanie's[2] nurse for six years. We found her in a suburb, nicely settled in a flat on the river, with the opposite bank covered with vineyards – very pretty. She was glad to see us and vice versa. We had dinner with Al's cousin[3] who speaks very little English. I have accused Al, who claims to speak [135] German, of talking baby talk as he learned it as a baby. No one seemed to understand him at first but he's improving and even I can understand a good deal, a relic of the Illg regime in our household. This cousin is very much opposed to Hitler although she wouldn't talk until we took her up to our room and then in decided undertones.

Tuesday we hired a car and with Annie's brother Ludwig as an interpreter started out for the birthplaces of Al's parents. We found the town but not the house. It was a sweet little town.[4] From there we went up into the Swabian Alps, very beautiful country and after going up for miles we found ourselves on a broad plateau, above all the surrounding mountains, so that not even a peak was visible, a very odd sensation after driving up steep mountains for two or three hours. Here is Gussenstaat[5] where Mr.

---

[1] BSZ does not mention it, but her Shoemaker ancestors came to Pennsylvania in the 17th century from Cresheim, in the Palitanate, on the west side of the Rhine, near Heidelberg.

[2] AWZ & BSZ's daughters, Barbara (1927-2011) and Helene (b. 1929).

[3] She is probably Eugenia (Kellenbenz) Bollacher: "Two of Eva's nieces (Anna and Eugenie, both born in Stuttgart), came to the U.S. in 1922 for a visit and stayed with the Zimmermanns" (letter from Anne Mitchell to GJH, 22 Feb 2009). Eugenia Kellenbenz m. Siegfried Bollacher (c.1904-c.1984), a lawyer in Ludwigsburg, Germany, a town 12 miles from the center of Stuttgart. There are no close Zimmermann relatives known to be living in Germany in 1937.

[4] Gussenstadt.

[5] Should be spelled Gussenstadt

Zimmermann[6] was born eighty years before and where he started a factory, more than sixty years ago. The original factory is still there and being used, a tiny house with one large factory room attached. This little town has not changed, I'm sure in those sixty years. It cannot be reached by train and has very little connection or communication with the rest of the world. It is very picturesque, and so sweet and peaceful, I wondered how Mr. Z. had the breadth of vision to leave it, altho' in technical schools (our engineering school) I guess he heard that there were other places. We were a curiosity as a great many people remembered the family even tho' there are none there now. We visited the little cemetery and saw the graves of Al's grandparents[7], date 1820 and 1821! We did stop on the way back to see an aunt, Mr. Z's sister, a nice little old lady (nearly eighty) who lives very happily with a companion maid of many years, in quite a cunning little cottage. Aunt Anna[8] is a great Hitlerite, having lost everything during inflation, and now sitting pretty due to the Nazi regime.
[136]

We went back to Annie's for dinner with Paul and Berta's sister. We had a nice meal, everything Annie remembered Al liked and enjoyed it all immensely. They are very happy and comfortable and are strongly in favor of "our Leader." Paul is a fine looking young chap. He paints questionable landscapes in oil, plays the zither and is a very good amateur photographer as well as being director of swimming in some athletic club. His real job is in an aeroplane factory and he is most enthusiastic, as are so many people in Germany, in high powered automobiles and auto racing.

The travel marks in Germany made us a bit weary. Very troublesome to get money albeit your own. The bankers look like day laborers, no collars, ties etc. and no manners! In fact we were pretty glad to get out of Germany, altho' it is a very beautiful country and interesting. The hotels were all excellent, beautifully equipped and so clean. The same with railroad trains, but the feeling of restraint among all the people with whom we came in contact made us uncomfortable and a little mad, when we considered that we were Americans and should not need to be affected by the regime of another country.

Wednesday, Zurich

Having crossed the border into Switzerland the first thing we did was to buy a pack of Chesterfields. In Holland we were able to buy them for just what we pay here and why we didn't stock up I will never know, just optimistic I guess. We found ourselves in Germany with none and all the time we were there were unable to buy anything but a German made cigarette at any price! . . . Here we are much happier as our conscience is clear. Even doing nothing wrong in Germany (except smuggling a camera [137] out) we had a depressing feeling of guilt.

---

[6] Her father-in-law, John Zimmermann, born 1855

[7] AWZ's paternal grandparents were John[A] (Johannes) Zimmermann (1821-1899) and Anna Ursula Jäger (1820-1901).

[8] Anna Zimmermann (b. 2 June 1860, Gussenstadt) was the third and youngest child of John[A] and Anna (Jäger) Zimmermann; she was the sister of AWZ's father, John[1] Zimmermann (b. 1855).

## Other Books by the Author

*Leprosy in Five Young Men*

*Outpatient Surgery*

*Clinical Oncology*

*Edison's Environment:*
*Invention and Pollution in the Career of Thomas Edison*

*Intimate Relationships: Church and State in the U.S. and Liberia*
*Race, Religion, Rubber, and Politics in the Liberia Education Project,*
*1917-1947*

*Proceed to Peshawar:*
*The Story of a U.S. Navy Intelligence Mission on the Afghan Border, 1943*

## Projected

*Rolling with Patton: A Red Cross Man in Europe, 1945*
*From the Letters and Photos of Jerry Hill, Field Director, American Red Cross*
*With the 97th Division, to VE Day at Marienbad, Czechoslovakia*

*The Letters and Photos of Lieutenant Albert Zimmermann, USNR*
*U.S. Naval Intelligence Officer, Karachi, India, 1943-1945*
*Edited by George J. Hill*

*©JanPressPhotomedia*

## ABOUT THE AUTHOR

**GEORGE J. HILL, M.D., M.A., D.Litt.,** is Professor of Surgery Emeritus at the New Jersey Medical School, Rutgers University. He has been a Fellow in Molecular Biology at Princeton University and he was an Adjunct Professor of History at Kean University, Union, New Jersey. A native of Iowa, Dr. Hill received his B.A. degree with honors from Yale University and the M.D. from Harvard. After retiring from the practice of surgery, he earned an M.A. in history at Rutgers-Newark and the D.Litt. in history from Drew University. Dr. Hill has written more than a dozen books on a wide range of topics, including prize-winning books on surgery, oncology, and leprosy. His master's thesis became a book on the environmental impact of Thomas Edison, and his doctoral thesis on church and state in the U.S. and Liberia was also published as a book. He received the 2012 David A. Cowen Award from the Medical History Society of New Jersey. Dr. Hill was a non-commissioned officer in the U.S. Marine Corps Reserve during the Korean War, and he was on active duty with the U.S. Public Health Service during the Cuban Missile Crisis. As a U.S. Navy Medical Officer, he served in Vietnam and he was recalled for duty as a surgeon during the First Gulf War. In 2013 the Naval Institute Press published his book, *Proceed to Peshawar*, about a secret and long forgotten mission taken by his father-in-law as a Naval Intelligence Officer in World War II. He received the U.S. Meritorious Service Medal when he retired as a Captain in 1992. Dr. Hill is also an alpinist and an explorer, having hiked and climbed on all seven continents.

As a student of genealogy, Dr. Hill has proved his descent from many early Americans. He is a member of more than forty lineage societies. His ancestors include James Feake, Sr., a goldsmith of London in 1615; Edward Fuller, who came on the *Mayflower* in 1620; Luke Hill and Mary Hout, who were married in Windsor, Connecticut, in 1651; Jonathan Gillett, who died there in 1677; Henry Herrick, who became a freeman of Salem, Mass., in 1630; Rebecca (Towne) Nurse, who was hanged there in 1692; Edward Howell, a Lord of the Manor in England who came to New England in 1638 and was a founder of the Hamptons on Long Island; Thomas Trowbridge, who was in New Haven, Conn., in 1638, and who had Royal ancestors; Robert Long, a member of the Ancient and Honorable Artillery Company in 1639; Jesse Irish, descendant of early settlers of Rhode Island and a Loyalist in the American Revolution; James Prescott, of Hampton, New Hampshire, in 1665; William Rundle, a freeholder of Greenwich, Conn., in 1667; John Sharples, who came to Pennsylvania in 1682 with William Penn; John Manley, of Cecil County, Maryland, in 1712; and John Archibald, who died in Derry, New Hampshire, in 1651, and whose descendants were pioneer settlers of Truro, Nova Scotia.

Of making many books there is no end
*Ecclesiastes* 12:12

www.ingramcontent.com/pod-product-compliance
Lightning Source LLC
Chambersburg PA
CBHW080412270326
41929CB00018B/2990